1,000,000 Books

are available to read at

www.ForgottenBooks.com

Read online
Download PDF
Purchase in print

ISBN 978-1-333-46894-1
PIBN 10508304

This book is a reproduction of an important historical work. Forgotten Books uses
state-of-the-art technology to digitally reconstruct the work, preserving the original format
whilst repairing imperfections present in the aged copy. In rare cases, an imperfection in
the original, such as a blemish or missing page, may be replicated in our edition. We do,
however, repair the vast majority of imperfections successfully; any imperfections that
remain are intentionally left to preserve the state of such historical works.

Forgotten Books is a registered trademark of FB &c Ltd.
Copyright © 2018 FB &c Ltd.
FB &c Ltd, Dalton House, 60 Windsor Avenue, London, SW19 2RR.
Company number 08720141. Registered in England and Wales.

For support please visit www.forgottenbooks.com

1 MONTH OF
FREE
READING

at

www.ForgottenBooks.com

By purchasing this book you are eligible for one month membership to ForgottenBooks.com, giving you unlimited access to our entire collection of over 1,000,000 titles via our web site and mobile apps.

To claim your free month visit: www.forgottenbooks.com/free508304

* Offer is valid for 45 days from date of purchase. Terms and conditions apply.

English
Français
Deutsche
Italiano
Español
Português

www.forgottenbooks.com

Mythology Photography **Fiction**
Fishing Christianity **Art** Cooking
Essays Buddhism Freemasonry
Medicine **Biology** Music **Ancient
Egypt** Evolution Carpentry Physics
Dance Geology **Mathematics** Fitness
Shakespeare **Folklore** Yoga Marketing
Confidence Immortality Biographies
Poetry **Psychology** Witchcraft
Electronics Chemistry History **Law**
Accounting **Philosophy** Anthropology
Alchemy Drama Quantum Mechanics
Atheism Sexual Health **Ancient History**
Entrepreneurship Languages Sport
Paleontology Needlework Islam
Metaphysics Investment Archaeology
Parenting Statistics Criminology
Motivational

A

HISTORY AND GENEALOGY

OF THE

CONANT FAMILY

IN

ENGLAND AND AMERICA,

THIRTEEN GENERATIONS, 1520-1887;

CONTAINING ALSO SOME
GENEALOGICAL NOTES ON THE

CONNET, CONNETT AND CONNIT FAMILIES.

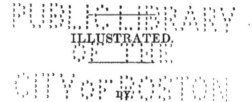

ILLUSTRATED.

BY

FREDERICK ODELL CONANT, M. A.,

OF

PORTLAND, MAINE, U. S. A.

PRIVATELY PRINTED.
PORTLAND:
1887.

*C311
.C743
1887

350 COPIES, OCTAVO.
10 COPIES, QUARTO.

No. *49*

PUBLIC LIBRARY
OF THE
CITY OF BOSTON

PRESS OF HARRIS & WILLIAMS, PORTLAND, ME.

" I have taken this pains not for the present age but a future; many things which were known to our grandsires are lost to us, and our grandchildren will search in vain for many facts which are most familiar to us."

DEDICATED TO HIS DAUGHTERS,

Elizabeth Merrill and Persis Loring,

WITH THE HOPE THAT THEY MAY SOME DAY ENJOY

READING THIS BOOK AS MUCH AS THEIR

FATHER HAS ENJOYED ITS

COMPILATION.

CONANTI · DABITUR

ARMS OF SIR NATHANIEL CONANT, KNIGHT.

1 and 4. Conant; 2 and 3. Wake; inescutcheon, Whiston.

PREFACE.

The time has passed when it was thought necessary to apologize for presenting a family history to the public, and the usefulness of such works is now so generally admitted that any *raison d' être* for this work may be omitted. I will only state that my own interest in the subject was awakened at an early age—before I could have been influenced by such a feeling as family pride—for before I was old enough to write I remember getting my aunt to copy a brief pedigree of the family I found in possession of my grandfather, giving his ancestry back to Roger Conant, which pedigree I have carefully preserved to this day. How my attention was called to the subject I cannot say. About 1879 a desire to know more of the family history and what manner of people my ancestors were led me to take up the subject again, and I then began the collection and arrangement of materials for the present Genealogy. The only important record of the family then in print was a condensed account of descendants of Nathaniel Conant, contained in Mitchell's *History of Bridgewater, Mass.* I was fortunate in finding in the library of the Essex Institute, at Salem, a quite complete manuscript record of the earlier generations of the family, prepared several years ago by the late Dr. J. F. Worcester, of Salem, to which I am indebted for many pedigrees that it would have been difficult, perhaps impossible, to construct correctly at the present time. I desire also to acknowledge my deep obligation, and at the same time my gratitude, to the late Hon. Charles Francis Conant, of Cambridge, Mass., for his many kind words of encouragement, advice and assistance in procuring town, probate and other records; to Miss Frances Batchelder James, of Cambridge, Mass., for her aid in procuring copies of English records, and to Hon. John A. Conant, of Willimantic, Conn., for information about the Connecticut branch of the family. Many other correspond-ents, both in England and the United States, have rendered substantial aid, and to them I return thanks. For those members of the family who have failed to answer my repeated letters of inquiry I have no words of reproach, but hope they may see the error of their way and send the desired information even now, so that a corrected copy of this book may be deposited in some public library.

In 1884 I published a "Pedigree of the Conant Family," embracing eight generations and giving the names of about six hundred descendants of Roger Conant. While the tabular form has its advantages, the impossibility of attaining completeness by its use decided me in undertaking the present Genealogy.

The plan adopted is substantially that of the New England Historic Genealogical Society. Only those names are numbered which are subsequently taken up as the head of a family, and as the names are treated consecutively no difficulty will be experienced in tracing any particular line of ancestors or descendants. For example, to find the account of the father of **135. Zenas**[6] (on p. 251), turn back until the name and number 135. Zenas is found in small type (on p. 200), and it will be found that he was son of (63) Thomas[5]; to find the account of 283. Oliver, son of **135. Zenas**[6], turn ahead until that name and number is found in heavy type (p. 319). The small index number above and after a name indicates the generation from Roger Conant, and the names in italics enclosed in parenthesis after the name of a person give the male line of ancestry of that person back to Roger Conant. When a woman's name occurs enclosed in parenthesis, it is to be understood that the enclosed name was her maiden name, or name before marriage. A few abbreviations, which will be readily understood, are used, such as *b.* born, *bapt.* baptized, *m.* married, *unm.* unmarried, *d.* died, *d. y.* died young, *ch.* children, *dr.* daughter, *g. s.* grand-son or grave-stone, *grad.* graduated, etc. Down to September 2, 1752, dates are given in the "old style" and may be made to correspond with the new or Gregorian calendar by adding ten days to dates between A. D. 1582 and 1701, and eleven days between A. D.

1700 and September 2, 1752. Before 1752 the *legal* year began on Lady Day, or March 25th, and March was called the first month, April the second, and so on. The *historical* year began on January 1st, and hence arose the custom prevalent in England and its colonies of using double dates between January 1st and March 25th; thus, 20: 11: 1677-8, would be Jan. 20th, 1678, as we reckon now, or adding ten days for the difference in time, Jan. 30th, 1678.

The materials for the work have been collected with care, and at considerable expense, from printed works, from the Massachusetts Archives, from town and church records, from the records in the offices of the Registers of Deeds and Probate of Plymouth, Essex, Middlesex and Barnstable counties in Massachusetts, Cheshire and Rockingham counties in New Hampshire, York and Cumberland counties in Maine, and from an extensive correspondence with members of the family. Besides the above, which was conducted personally, I have caused an extensive search to be made in the Probate Offices at Somerset House, London, and Palace Gate, Exeter, the Public Record Office, College of Arms and Marriage Licenses of the Archbishop of Canterbury, in London, the Marriage Licenses of the Bishop of Exeter and the Parochial Registers of more than twenty parishes, and among other public and private records.

In a work of this class it is well nigh impossible to insure absolute correctness. Doubtless some, perhaps many, mistakes may be found, and I beg that any one noticing such, either of dates, names or facts, will kindly report the same to me. I shall be happy to receive additional family records, and dates of births, marriages or deaths, from members of the family, and should a sufficient number be obtained a supplement may be issued embodying these, together with any corrections. The list of additions and corrections beginning on page 572 is important, and all having occasion to use this book should consult it to see that statements made in the text are not thereby modified.

The book contains the names of some 4300 Conants, about 1700 other *surnames* and about 1000 names of places, and is, I

think, so far as relates to Conants, as complete as any work
its kind, a fact largely due to the care with which family recor
have been preserved in the various branches of the fami
The descendants of Roger Conant, *by name Conant*, me
tioned in the book, number 3457.   .

Attention is called to the large number of the name wl
served in the Revolutionary army. The names of sevent
three have been preserved. It is doubtful if any family
corresponding numbers furnished so many.

FREDERICK ODELL CONANT.

139 PARK STREET,

      PORTLAND, Dec. 20, 1887.

GENERAL INDEX.

LIST OF ILLUSTRATIONS.

INTRODUCTION.

INTRODUCTION.

The Conant family appears to be, primarily, of Celtic descent, for the name Conan or Conon, from which the name is derived, is found at a very early period among various races of Celtic origin, including the Britons, Welsh, Irish, Gaels and Bretons. Nobody knows when the Celts first settled in Britain, for at the beginning of authentic history the island was inhabited by them. When Britain was invaded by the Anglo-Saxons, these Celtic inhabitants retreated before them into Cornwall and Wales, where they retained their language and customs for a long time. Some crossed the English Channel southward and joined their kinsmen in Armoric Brittany.

Though Anglo-Saxon influence predominates, the English character of to-day is in no small degree an inheritance from Celtic ancestors. This influence is fully realized by Emerson, who says: "The sources from which tradition derives their stock are three. And first they are of the oldest blood of the world—the Celtic. Some peoples are deciduous or transitory. Where are the Greeks? Where the Etrurians? Where the Romans? But the Celts or Sidonides are an old family, of whose beginning there is no memory, and their end is likely to be still more remote in the future; for they have endurance and productiveness."

Whether the family was of the Breton or the Cornish branch of the Celtic race, it is impossible to say. As the name is somewhat Gallic in form, it is possible the family is descended from some Breton follower of William the Conqueror. At all events, they were settled in Devonshire as early as the beginning of the fourteenth century. Three hundred years later, in the very vanguard of English emigration to America, two brothers of the name left Devonshire for the New World, from the younger of whom nearly all the Conants in America are descended. The Conants have almost invariably married

(1)

into families of English descent, and moreover, into families long settled here, so that the branch of the family on this side of the ocean may be regarded as typically American.

Records remain to show that the name Conant, in very nearly its present form, has existed in England for over six hundred years, and a more extended search would doubtless reveal its earlier existence. This is, however, a very respectable antiquity for the name, when the difficulty of tracing any particular name, and the fact that surnames have been in general use for only eight hundred years, is considered. The orthography has varied considerably, the variation being principally due to the ignorance of clerks. In England thirty-two ways of writing the name have been found, as follows: Couenaunt, Conaunt, Cownat, Conat, Conant, Connant, Conante, Conannt, Conannte, Connante, Connannt, Conenant, Conenaunt, Counant, Connat, Connatt, Cornet, Conet, Conett, Connet, Connett, Counett, Conott, Connot, Connott, Coonet, Coonnet, Cunnet, Cunnant, Cunnatt, Cunnante, Conennte; and in America eighteen ways (nine of which are included among the foregoing), as follows: Conant, Connant, Cannant, Connont, Connontt, Connott, Connanght, Connunght, Connaught, Conet, Connet, Connett, Conat, Cunnet, Cunnant, Conit, Connit, Connitt; making forty-one variations in all.

In Devonshire, the old home of the family, though the name is written Conant, the common pronunciation is Connet or Cunnet. All descendants of Richard Conant, of East Budleigh, however, both in England and the United States, have so far as known adhered to the form *Conant*, generally pronounced Cō-nant, with the accent on the first syllable; a few families in the United States accent the last syllable.

The earliest example of the name with the final "t" yet found, occurs in the Patent Rolls* of England, in the year 1277, when Solomon de Rochester and Thomas de Sodington were appointed to take the assize of novel disseizin arraigned by Robert Couenaunt against Filota, late wife of Richard Couenaunt, touching a tenement in Alton (or Alveton), Staffordshire. Four years later, a Robert Conet was a tenant of the

* Patent Rolls, 5 Edward I, m. 9, dors. 72.

manor of Horncastle, Lincolnshire. In the year 1327 Alexander Conaunt* was living in the Hundred of Exminster, Devonshire; five years later, Alan Conaunt† was living in the Hundred of Axminster; and in 1379 Hugh Conaunt‡ was living near Exeter. The three last named were probably of our family, as they lived within twenty-five miles of the home of John Conant, with whom we begin the Genealogy.

The name is derived from the Celtic Conan,§ formerly of Wales and Cornwall, and subsequently of Brittany. After the Conquest this name became common in England, and is frequently found in the Public Records, almost always in some family of Breton origin. Among the Breton followers of William who settled in Devon, was Judhæl of Totnes, a relative of the Duke of Britanny. The King granted him 107 manors in Devonshire, and he also held houses in Exeter. Count Brian, of Brittany, was sent by King William to the relief of Exeter, then besieged by the English, in the year 1069. He defeated Harold's sons in battle and was granted large estates. In the time of William Rufus, Cono, a monk of Battle Abbey (whose name indicates that he was a Breton), was sent to Exeter to look after the property of that house, and under his care the settlement there grew into a separate priory.‖

The surname of the descendants of Geoffrey de Dinan, a Breton who settled in the north-western part of Devonshire, became, in course of time, Dinant, a change analagous to that from Conan to Conant. These facts indicate the probability of a Breton origin of the name, a supposition rendered more likely by the fact that the name went through a somewhat similar change in Brittany.

Arthur, in his "Etymological Dictionary of Family and

* Exchequer Lay Subsidies, Devon, Roll $\frac{95}{6}$

† Ibid., Roll $\frac{95}{7}$

‡ Muniments of Exeter, Doc. 950.

§ As the Celts were descended from the same stock as the ancient Greeks, perhaps the name is from the same root as that of the Grecian Conon, (an Athenian general, contemporary of Xenophon,) who rebuilt the walls of Athens, B. C. 393, and that of the mathematician, Conon of Samos, who flourished about 200 years later.

‖ Historic Towns: Exeter.

Christian Names," says: "CONANT, (Welsh and Gaelic). Conan, a river, Counant, a cataract in North Wales, from *cau*, a
chasm, a deep hollow, shut up, and *nant*, a rivulet." As this
derivation did not seem entirely satisfactory, efforts were made
to obtain the true etymology, and the opinion of several eminent philologists was sought, with the following results:

W. M. Hennessy, Esq., of Her Majesty's Public Record
Office, Dublin, writes: "Conan is not a very general name in
the Calendar of Saints, only seven of the name (besides two
Connans) being mentioned in the Martyrology of Donegal,
which gives a very full list. *Conan* (which means 'little
hound,' from *con*, the genitive form of *cu*, *an*, a diminutive
particle) is, under the corrupt form *Cynan*, a very general
name in Welsh Chronicles."

In this connection, the secondary meaning of the word
(champion, great warrior, *vide seq.*) as suggested by Prof.
Rhys, is worthy of note. In Irish Mythology, Conn (valor),
son of Diancécht (god of the powers of healing), figures
largely; and in the "Chronicles of the Four Masters" is represented as a descendant of Heremon, son of Milesius, and the
110th King of Ireland. He is known as Conn Ceadcatha, or
Conn of the Hundred Battles, and was Monarch of Ireland in
the second century. His posterity possessed the kingdom of
Connaught, the name of which is derived from his name coup-
led with "iacht" or "iocht," signifying children or posterity.
Hence Connaught, or Coniacht as it was anciently written,
means the territory possessed by the descendants of Conn.

W. F. Skene, LL. D., Historiographer Royal of Scotland, writes: "Conan is a personal name belonging to names
of Irish or Gaelic origin, and existed, both in Ireland and
Scotland, at an early period. It appears in the Irish Calendar
as St. Conan, (d. about A. D. 648) Bishop of Sodor and Man,
and in Scotland several parishes were dedicated to him, as, for
instance, Kilchonan, in the district of Atholl. It appears also
at an early period as a Christian name in various Scottish
families."

But more satisfactory and definite are the two letters following: M. E. de Kerlinou, of Vannes, in the department of

Morbihan, France, writes: "The name Conan is well known in Brittany; many of our sovereign dukes have borne it, and it is still frequently used as a baptismal name, or borne by a great number of families *which came originally from Great Britain*. Only one noble family of Brittany has borne the name Conan or Conen; it is still in existence; its arms are, 'Or and argent, a lion counterchanged, armed, crowned and tongued gules.' In regard to the etymology of the word Conan, I must first state that the name of Conan Meriadec,* accounted first King of the Armoric Bretons, is written by ancient authors, Conus, Cono (Canao), Conn, Cann or Can, which is, according to one of our historians, only an abridgment or slight alteration of the name Conan. We find, also, Caton, Coton and Cathon, which are the same but more altered than Canao, Conn and Conan. This King died about A. D. 421.

"The radical *con* is not employed in modern Breton, but it is found in many names of ancient places, where it signifies *angle*

---

* In the year 388 the Roman general, Maximus, having deposed the Emperor Valentinian II, led an army into Gaul and Italy, against the Emperor Theodosius. He was accompanied in the expedition by Conan (or Kynan) Meriadec, one of the princes of Powys, and cousin to Helen, wife of Maximus, at the head of 6000 Britons. They were defeated at the battle of Aquiliea; those that escaped made their way across France as far as Armorica, and settling there got possession of that country, which took the name of Brittany from this fact. Maximus had conferred the sovereignty of Brittany upon Conan, a gift confirmed by Theodosius. From him descended the Breton dukes, terminating in the fifteenth century in Anne, daughter of Francis II, successively the wife of Charles VIII and Louis XII, Kings of France. In the third generation from Conan was Constantin, King of the Britons, whose son, Uter Pendragon, was the father of King Arthur. The stories of Arthur's deeds lingered in Brittany long after they were effaced in England by the Anglo-Saxon conquest. Arthur was succeeded by his nephews, Constantine, Aurelius Conanus and Malgo Canones, from whom descended the kings of Wales.

From Aldroen, brother of Constantin, was continued the line of the dukes of Brittany. They maintained a semi-independent state, at times free and at others subject to the French Crown. Under Charlemagne the power of France over Brittany increased, but its rulers, availing themselves of the weakness of his successors, regained their independence, and their duke was acknowledged king by Charles the Bald. At the beginning of the tenth century, the country was troubled by internal dissensions among its princes; finally Juhel Berenger, Count of Rennes, and Alan Barbe-torte, Count of Nantes, united their forces against the Normans, and a measure of tranquility was restored. The trouble with the Normans was settled by a double marriage, Geoffrey, son of Conan le Tort, and grandson of Juhel Berenger, married Hadwisa, daughter of Richard the Fearless, Duke of Normandy: and Judith, sister of Geoffrey, by marrying Richard the Good, became the grandmother of William the Conqueror.

Under Alan V, son of Geoffrey, Brittany enjoyed peace many years, and on the death of Robert le Diable he was appointed guardian of William, then a minor. Alan died A. D. 1039 and was succeeded by his son, Conan the Fat, who rose against William of Normandy, and, it is said, though upon doubtful authority, was poisoned by him at the siege of Chateau Gontier, A. D. 1066. The next duke after Conan was Hoel, son of Alan Cognant, Count of Cornouaille, who was descended from Budic, brother of Juhel Berenger. He married Hadwisa, sister

in the special sense of an angle formed by the meeting of two
rivers, in French *confluent*, e. g., Mençon, Conlo, Condé, etc.
In a figurative sense, *con* signifies a reunion, an assemblage,
and our ancient traditions inform us that Conan Meriadec came
from Great Britain and reunited under his sceptre, to his ancient subjects, who emigrated with him, the Celts and Cymri
who inhabited Armorica. They took the name Bretons and
the country of Arvor (my country) that of Little Britain. In
a precise sense, *Con* or *Conan* (*an* is a simple plural) is more
a title than a name. Many of our historians in speaking of
him, say, 'the Conan Meriadec,' 'the Chief Meriadec,' following the meaning. *Con* in the Welsh and Cymric languages
seems to have the meaning of *Brenn* (*chief*) in Celtic.

"At times he is called *Can*, or *Cau*, signifying *combat*,
Canao (another plural), *the combats*. He is then the victor,
the conqueror, the chief, the imperator of the Romans.

"Finally, at the Court of Assizes of Morbihan, an interpreter

---

of Conan, and was the father of Alan Fergand, who became Count of Brittany in 1083. Alan
made war on William, whom he defeated at the siege of Dol (1086), soon after which he married Constance, daughter of William. Constance died childless and he married Hermengarde,
daughter of Fulk, Count of Anjon, by whom he had a son, Conan, who married Matilda,
natural daughter of King Henry I. On the death of Conan, the succession was disputed between his son, Hoel, who was disowned by his father, and Eudes or Odo, Count of Porhoet,
who had married Bertha, daughter of Conan, as her second husband. At length Conan le
Petit, son of Bertha by her first husband, Alan the Black, Earl of Richmond, took Eudes
prisoner and united all parts of the country under his control, calling it the County of Brittany.
His daughter and heiress married Geoffrey, third son of King Henry II; their son Arthur, on
the death of King Richard, was the heir to the throne of England, but was assassinated by
King John, 1203. The duchy then passed to Alix, daughter of Constance by her third husband, Guy of Thuars, who married Pierre de Dreux. Their son, John, became head of the
ducal family, which reigned till the beginning of the sixteenth century. Another branch of
the family rendered substantial aid to William in his conquest of England. Odo, Count
Penthievence, brother of Alan V, married Agnes, daughter of Alan Cognant, and had several
children. Alan Fergant, one of the number, led the Bretons in the battle of Senlac, and was
granted all the lands which had belonged to Earl Eadwin, amounting to 442 manors. He
built the Castle of Richmond, and was succeeded as Lord of Richmond by his brothers, Alan
the Black, and Stephen, Count Penthievence. Stephen was succeeded by his son, Alan, who
married Bertha, daughter of Conan the Little, thus uniting the English earldom and the Breton
duchy. Ribaldus, another of Odo's sons, Lord of Middleham, Yorkshire, is the ancestor of
the Neville and Tailbois families. Another, Brian, is the ancestor and founder of the Chateau
Briant family in France; he also took part in the Conquest, and defeated Harold's sons in battle in Devonshire. Beside Conan, Duke of Brittany, Alan and Bertha had several other
children, among whom were Brian, father of Alan, Lord Bedale, Guy, ancestor of the Barons
Strange, and Reginald, who went to Scotland.

The arms of the Dukes of Brittany were "Ermine," said to have been adopted by the first
Conan from the fact that an ermine took refuge under his shield and was spared by him, its
skin thereafter forming the arms of Brittany (Miss Yonge's *Christian Names*), with the
motto " Malo mori quam foedari."

of Finisterre, in translating a deposition, did not hesitate to employ the equivalent *Count* for the proper name *Conan*. Conan Meriadec, then, signifies the Chief Meriadec, or the Chief of many Chiefs, the Count. It is, perhaps, from this fact that French historians have taken the title Count of Brittany for our sovereigns who called themselves kings or dukes.

"As to the frequence of the name Conan among the families of the people, it is due to two causes: first, from its use as a Christian name among various patronymics; second, as a family name borne by all a clan, the same in Brittany as in Scotland."

Prof. Loth, who is professor of Celtic at the Faculty of Sciences at Rennes, in the department of Ille et Vilaine, says: "Conant, in the 14th century, of the county of Devon, is an Armoric Breton or Cornish name, but surely it is not Welsh. It is almost certainly an Armoric name. The ordinary form in Armorica to-day is Conan; in the 9th century it was Cunan. It is the same name as the Welsh Cynan. We find in Wales, in an inscription of the 6th century, a genitive form, *Cunegni*,* which presupposes for the same time a nominative form, *Cunagno-s*. The root is the same as in the name of the British King, *Cuno-belinos*, of the British king in· Gildas, *Maglocunos* (later Maelgwn), and probably as in the Welsh verb *cynu*, to raise, to exalt."

The statement of Prof. Loth is very interesting, as Cunobe-

---

* "Cunegni, (Traws Mawr near Carmarthen). This name is singular in its being *Cunegni* and not *Cunagni*, which is the form analogy suggests: but it should perhaps be regarded as an early instance of *a* modulated into *e* by the influence of *i* in the following syllable, a change well known later in Welsh. In that case *Cunegni* would be a variation of Cunagni, which is to be regarded as the early form of the name which appears subsequently as *Conan*, *Cinan*, and *Cynan*." (Rhys' *Lectures on Welsh Philology*, p. 400.)

The same author (*see Celtic Britain, p. 286*), writing about the name Cuneglassos, says: "This is given by Gildas in the vocative as Cuneglase, which he asserts to have meant in Latin, *lanio fulva*, the tawny butcher. But this is difficult to accept, for though *glas* may have meant any colour that might be described as blue, green or gray, there is no indication that the word ever denoted any colour inclining to red or yellow. The other element, *Cune*, is more usually met with as *Cuno* or *Cuna*, as in Cunobelinos and Cunalipi. The reason for the variation is that the formative vowel was already but slightly pronounced; later it disappeared altogether, leaving these names in the forms *Conglas* and *Conbelin*, whence later *Cynlas* and *Cynfelyn*. The meaning and origin of Cuno are obscure; but Gildas may have had in his mind the Welsh word for dog, which was *ci*, plural *cwn*, though in his time it was probably *cū*, genitive *cūno(s)*, and what he renders lanio may well have meant, considering the mood he was in, a champion or great warrior. The corresponding Teutonic vocable was *hun*, the meaning of which is also obscure, though that of giant has been suggested."

lin, who was King of Britain at the beginning of the Christian era, was the original of Shakespeare's Cymbeline, and Maglocunos was the fourth king after the renowned Arthur.

The conclusion, then, seems to be that Conan, the early form of Conant, is the equivalent of the Welsh *cân*, (a chief); Irish *cean*; Saxon *cyning*, (a leader, a king); German *könig;* Dutch *koning;* Swedish *konung;* and also of the Oriental *khan;* all meaning *head, chief, leader* or *king.*

GENEALOGICAL NOTES.

PAROCHIAL REGISTERS OF GITTISHAM, CO. DEVON.

BURIALS—(Records begin 1559.)

1559 John Conant, 4 of September.

1570 Harrye Conennte, xxiiij. Januarye.

1572 Agnyse Conante, ye first of Februarye.

1576 Elizabeth Connant, wydoe, ye vii. of September.

1597 Elizabeth Conannte, ye xx^{th} of Apryell.

Eu/   1605 Henrias Conante, ye xxviii. August.

1628 Henry, ye sonne of Henry Conet, was bur^d 24 Junii.

1638 Elizabeth, the daughter of Henry Conant, ffeb. 18.

1643 Christopher, the sonne of Henry Conant, July 2.

1643 Mary, the daughter of Henry Conant, July 14.

1643 Richard, the sonne of Henry Conant, Aug. 15.

1665 Mary, the wife of Henery Connet, february the 23th.

1684 Grace, ye daughter of Tho: Conet, Senr, was buried on tuesday, ye 27th day of January. Affidavit was made by Joane Wyat, certified by Sir Tho. Putt, Bart., Jan. 30th. Witnesses, Charles Churchill & John Michell.

1691 Margaret, wife of Thomas Connet, Senr, June 15. Affidavit made by Mary Hodge, widow, certified by Henry Fry, Esq., June 18. Witnesses, William Husey, Daniel Pring.

1694 Sarah, wife of Salter Conet, October 26. Affidavit made by Jane, wife of James Lugg, certified by Henry ffry, Esq., Octob^r 30. Witnesses, George Passener, Daniel Pring.

1705 Salter Conant, yeoman, May 30. Affidavit made by Grace Hawkins, certified by Sr Tho: Putt, Bart., June 6. Witnesses, Eliz. Crossing, Reginaldo Putt.

MARRIAGES—(Records begin 1571.)

1608   Johes Connant, uxorem duxit Marriam Eveleighe, quorto die Julii, An° 1608.

1613   Christopher Mathew, of Oterye St. Marye, was married unto Elizabeth Cornet, ye daught^r of Henry Connet, deseased, of Gittisham, in Devon, 9: of June.

1613   (Goyn?) Thorne, of Cotley, was married to Al'ce Connat, of Gitsam, alis Giddisham, (ye daughter of Henry Connat, disseased,) the 16: day of August.

1647   Salter Conant to Sarah Corkeram, July 25.

1655   Thomas Connet, ye sonne of Henery Connet, of Gittisham, was lawfully married ye thirten day of June, 1655, unto Margaret Knook, ye dafter of Richard Knook, of Salcom, before Robert Duke, Esqr, on of ye Justisses of Peace of ye county.

1663   William Michell to Johan Connet, August 27.

1682   John Stockdale and Elizabeth Conant, of Buckerill, Novemb. 30th.

1697   Thomas Capron, widower, and Mary Conet, ye daughter of Salter Conet, Novemb. 15.

1698   John Conant & Mary Kingman, ffebra 2^d.

1702   Jonathan Conant & Mary, daughter of William Wood, both of Branscomb, were married July 27.

CHRISTENINGS—(Records begin 1559.)

1574   Nycholas Conannt, ye vi. of Julye.

1578   Jone Conannte, ye xxv. day of Aprrell.

1580   Bettey Connant, a man child baptised ye xxiii. of June, named John.

1586   Elizabeth Conannte, ye viii. of Julye.

1612   Elizabeth, ye daught^r of Henry Conat, was baptised ye 27: day of September.

1614   Christofer, ye sone of Henry Conet, was baptised ye 1: day of Januarie.

1616   Joane, ye daughter of Henry Conet, nata 13°, Baptisata 15° Februarii.

1619   Salter, ye sonne of Henry Cunnet, 14 Decembris.

1621 Mary, ye daughter of Henry Conett, was borne ye 21 and Baptised ye 24th day of Februarii.

1625 Catharin, ye daughter Henry Conet, was baptised ye tenth day of April.

1627 Henry, ye sonne of Henry Conet, was Bap: 16° February.

1630 Thomas, ye sonne, of Henry Conet, was Bap: 5° Septemb.

1650 Thomas, ye sonne of Salter Conant, May 19.

1654 Mary, ye daughter of Salter Conant, Septemb. 6.

1659 Mathew, ye sonne of Salter Conant, Febr. 24.

1662 Benjamin, ye soon of Salter Connet, January the 20.

1663 Josup, the soone of Thomas Counnet, Aprill the i.

1665 Margaret, ye daughter of Thom: Conant, Febr. 23.

1666 James, ye sonne of Salter Conant, Oct: 18.

1671 Sarah, ye daughter of Thom. Conant, Aug. 31.

1700 Elizabeth, daughter of John and Mary Conant, August 19.

BIRTHS.

1654 Mary Connet, ye dafter of Salter Connet, was borne ye six day of September.

1656 Henery, ye soon of Salter Coonet, was borne ye 8th of March.

1659 Mary Coonnet, ye dafter of Thomas Connet, was borne ye 19th day of February. Mathae Coonet, the soone of Salter Coonnet, was borne ye 24th of Feberary.

(On a fly leaf apart from the other entries:)

Salter Conant was baptised Decm. 14, A. D. for yt he died aged 85 yeares old & 5 months & 22 days.

The Rector of Gittisham, Rev. F. T. Salmon, states that he has given every entry relating to the name Conant down to the year 1702; and also that there are still persons in his parish bearing the name Connet, who are in humble circumstances.

PAROCHIAL REGISTERS OF COLYTON, CO. DEVON.

CHRISTENINGS—(Records begin 1538.)

1539 Oct. 16, Thomas Clarke, the son of Richard Clarke.

1539 Nov. 27, Walter Clarke, the son of John Clarke.

1541 June 30, Maryen Clarke, the dafter of John Clarke, of Coliton.

1548 May 16, Annes Clarke, dafter of John Clarke, of Coliton.

1582 Oct. 26, John Clarke, son of John Clarke, the younger, of Coliton.

1589 Mch. 8, Annys Clarke, dafter of Edward Clarke, of Coliton.

1589 Sep. 28, William Clarke, son of John Clarke, the elder, of Coliford.

1593 Nov. 7, Roger Clarke, son of Edward Clarke, of Coliton.

1600 Nov. 1, Agnes Clarke, dafter of Edmund Clarke, of Coliford.

BURIALS.

1585 Apr. 9, "John Clarke the elder of Coliton marchant was buried the 9th day of Aprill who in his life tyme was the cheftest traviler of the purchas of the mannor of Colliton and the marketts with other lyberties p'tayning to the same as aperieth by the pattern (patent) and decessd the 6th day of Aprill 1585."

MARRIAGES.

1544 June 9, John Clarke, of Colyford, to Anne Macye, dau: of William Macye, of Colyton.

1563 Jan. 23, John, the son of John Clarke, of Colyton, to Mary, dau: of Simon Repington.

1574 Nov. 22, John, son of John Clarke, of Colyford, to Margaret, dau: of John Smyth, of Sidbury.

1575 John, son of John Clarke, of Colyton, to Ellenor, dau: of John Flower, of Abbott's Isle, Co. Somerset.

1578 Rychard Connett, the sonne of John Connett, of Easte Budleye, was wedded unto Agnes Clarke, the daught. of John Clarke, senior, of Collyton, the iiij day of ffebruary.

PAROCHIAL REGISTERS OF EAST BUDLEIGH, CO. DEVON.

BURIALS—(Records begin 1562.)

1596 Mch. 30, John Conant.

1625 Sep. 3, Richard Connant, Junr.

1627 Dec. 15, Phillip Wotton, an infant.

1630 Sep. 22, Richard Conant, Gent, and Agnes, his wiffe.

1644 May 15, Martha Connant.

1677 Feb. 14, Mary, the wife of Richard Conant, vic.

1688 Dec. 6, Mr. Richard Conant, Vicar of this p's'h.

1699 July 2, Henry Connant.

1740 Apr. 6, Mary Conant.

MARRIAGES*—(Records begin 1556.)

1558 Nov. 26, William Conante.

1578 Feb. 4, Richard Conante.

1607 Oct. 14, Robert Conant, Elizab. Morris.

1609 Sep. 18, Richard Conant & Jane Slade.

1609 Sep. 18; Tho. Knolles & Jane Conant.

1615 Jan. 16, Edmund Coombe & Anne Conant.

1626 Apr. 19, Jane Knolles and Philip Wotton.

1681 July 7, John Mercer, Gent, & Mary Conant.

1698 Aug. 4, George Cross and Joanna Conant, both of this parish.

1806 Aug. 7, Robert Conant and Mary Hill Litton, both of this parish.

BAPTISMS—(Records begin 1555.)

1561 Mch. 2, Christine Conante.

1564 Jan. 28, Johane Conante.

1579 Jan. 20, Johane Conante.

1581 Feb. 21, Richard Conannt.

1584 May 9, Jane Conante.

1585 Mch. 18, John Conannt.

1587 Apr. 30, Thomas Conant.

1588 June 13, Christopher Conante.

* The names of females are not mentioned in the Marriage Registers from 1556 to 1605.

1592 Apr. 9, Roger Conant.
1611 June 16, Jane, daughter of Richard Conant.
1615 Nov. 30, Martha, daughter of Richard Conant.
1617 Jan. 20, Mary, daughter of Richard Conant.
1621 Feb. 10, Richard, son of Ric Connant.
1624 Mch. 30, Sara, daughter of Richard Conant.
1626 Dec. 26, Priscilla? daughter of John Conant.
1660 May 7, Elizabeth, daughter of Richard Connant.
1663 Jan. 6, Richard, sonn of Richard Conant.
1668 Sep. 5, Mary, the daughter of Richard Connant.

The Rector of East Budleigh says: "There are people here named Connett, whose name in 1851 is registered as Connant, but in subsequent entries has been changed to Connett."

PAROCHIAL REGISTERS OF BICTON, CO. DEVON.

BURIALS—(Records begin 1557.)

1616 Nov. 5, Richard, son of Robert Conant.
1616 Nov. 14, Thomas, son of Robert Conant.
1638 May 12, Robert Conant.
1647 May 22, ———Conant.
1654 April 1, Elizabeth Conant, widow.
1658 Nov., Elizabeth, the daughter of Richard Conant.
1658 Dec., Joane, his wife, was buried.
1669 Dec. 20, Richard Conante.
1731 Sep. 22, John Conant.
1883 Nov. 16, Mary Conant.

MARRIAGES—(Records begin 1557.)

1624 Nov. 20, Nicholas Conant and Anne (Rosimond?).
1641 Oct. 28, Richard Conantt and Joane Co(—?)t.
1677 Sep. 24, Robert Conant, of this parish, and Mary Gibbons, of Woodbury.

1699 Feb. 23, Joseph Long, of Aylesbear, and Grace Conant, of Collaton Ralegh.

1706 May 9, John Conant, of this parish, and Joan Warren, of Sidmonth.

BAPTISMS—(Records begin 1642.)

1642 Aug. 28, Maria, daughter of Richard and Jane Conant.

1643 Apr. 18, Jane, daughter of Nicholas and Anne Conant.

1645 Nov. 30, Richard Conant, son of Richard Conant.

1651 —— Johanne, daughter of Richard Conatt.

1662 Mch. 31, Sarah, daughter of Richard and Joane Conant.

1666 Nov. 24, Susanna, daughter of Richard Conant and Joan, his wife.

1679 Aug. 8, Elizabeth, daughter of John Conantt and Maria, his wife.

1683 Mch. 5, Johanna, daughter of John Conant and Mary, his wife.

1685 Aug. 9, John, the son of John Conant and Mary, his wife.

1713 Oct. 15, Joan, daughter of John Conant and Joan, his wife.

1714 Dec. 10, Mary, daughter of John Conant and Joan, his wife.

1720 Aug 19, Joan, daughter of John Conant and Joan, his wife.

1721 Oct. 12, John, son of John Conant and Joan, his wife.

PAROCHIAL REGISTERS OF HENNOCK, CO. DEVON.

BAPTISMS.

1592 Enfanor Connant, daughter of Robt. Connant.

1593 Richard, son of Robert Connant, of Knighton.

1600 Benjamin, son of Robert Connant.

BURIAL.

1596 Richard, son of Robert Connant.

PAROCHIAL REGISTERS OF OTTERY ST. MARY AND ALPHINGTON, CO. DEVON.

MARRIAGES.

1629   May 7, Robert Salter and Marie Connott.
1629   May 9, James Connot and Grace Sparke.

BAPTISMS.

1603   May 13, Margaret, dau: Robert Connot.
1604   Jan. 3, James Connot, son of John Connot.
1607   June, Thomasine Connot, dau: John Connot.
1608   Sep. 7, Susan, dau: Robert Connot.
1629   Elizabeth, dau: John Connot, of Alphington.
1630   July 12, James Conant, son of James Conant.
1632   Mch. 3, Susanna, dau: of John Conant.
1635   May 25, Elizabeth, dau: James Conant and Grace, his wife.
1639   May 1, William, son of James Conant and Grace, his wife.

PAROCHIAL REGISTERS OF DUNSFORD, CO. DEVON.

BURIALS—(Records begin 1594.)

1672   Feb. 16, (Melony?), dau: Nicholas Conant.
1675   Oct. 27, Anne, wife of John Connant.
1676   Aug. 9, Elizabeth, dau: John Connant.
1676   Dec. 26, John Conant, Jun.
1683   Oct. 2, John Connett.
1708   Dec. 6, Sarah, wife of Nicholas Conant.

MARRIAGES—(Records begin 1594.)

1673   June 17, John Connant and Katherine White.
1706   Apr. 9, John, son of Charles Connant, of Parish of Brid-
       ford, and Jane Cox, of this parish.

BAPTISMS—(Records begin 1598.)

1632 May 27, Melonge, the dau: John Cunnant.

1634 Aug. 21, Charles, son of John Cunnant.

1637 Mch. 26, Barbara, dau: John Cunnant and Barbara, his wife.

1641 Mch. 28, Christopher, son of John Cunnant and Barbara, his wife.

1668 Aug. 6, Madelot, dau: Nicholas Conant.

1672 Mch. 2, Malothy, son of Nicholas Conant.

1673 Feb. 17, Katherine, dau: John Connant.

1676 Aug. 8, Elizabeth, dau: John Connant.

1682 Sep. 9, George, son of Geo. Conant.

1683 Feb. 5, Elizabeth, daughter of George Connant.

1684 Feb. 8, Nicholas, son of George Connett.

1708 Nov. 28, Robert, son of Nicholas Conant.

1713 Dec. 17, George, son of Robert Conant.

(A Mrs. Conant and her son, John, are now living in Dunsford parish.)

PAROCHIAL REGISTERS OF SIDMOUTH, CO. DEVON.

BURIALS.

1664 Jan. 28, Henry, son of Edwin Conant.

1665 Mch. 28, Grace, daug. of Henry Conant.

1684 June 18, Henry Cunnat.

1692 Feb. 18, Joan Connant.

1694 Mch. 11, Grace Connant.

1703 Dec. 16, Mr. John Conant.

1721 Nov. 20, Mrs. Joan Connant.

1736 Jan. 15, Mr. John Conant.

1775 Dec. 4, Ann Conant.

1780 Apr. 27, Sarah Conant.

1780 Oct. 16, Mary Conant.

1786 Feb. 17, Elizabeth Conant.

BAPTISMS.

1728 Mch. 7, Anna, daughter of Roger and Anna Conant.

2

1750 Aug. 6, John, son of John and Anne Conant.
1752 May 10, Robert, son of John and Anne Conant.
1754 Mch. 10, William, son of John and Anne Conant.
1755 Dec. 21, Henry, son of John and Anne Conant.

MONUMENTAL INSCRIPTIONS.

HERE LYETH YE BODY OF
HENRY CONNANT, GENT., WHO
DYED YE 10TH DAY OF JUNE,
ANNO DOM. 1684.

Arms: CONANT *impaling* DUKE.

HERE LYETH YE BODY OF JOHN
CONANT, ESQ., WHO DIED YE 13TH OF
JAN., 1736.   AGED 38.

The Vicar of Sidmouth says: "The sexton of our church
here and foreman of our bell-ringers is George Conant, no
doubt a member of the family, and a most respectable man;
and we have a good many fisher folk of that name."

From another source it is learned that Henry Conant, the
father of the above George, is living in the parish, aged about
70 years. His brother, John, was accidentally drowned some
years since.

John Cornet succeeded Henry de Oustyn as Vicar of this
parish, 23 April, 1402, on presentation of Sir Peter Courtenay
(Oliver's *Ecclesiastical Antiquities of Devonshire*).

PAROCHIAL REGISTERS OF BUCKERELL, CO. DEVON.

BURIALS.

1705 Dec. 10, Nathaniel Conant.

1708 Jan. 18, Martha Conant.

1708 Jan. 18, Sarah Conant.

1708 Mch. 15, John Conant.

1741 Sep. 19, Agnes Conant.

1742 Feb. 27, Betty, daughter of William Conant and Elizabeth, his wife.

1749 Apr. 13, Nicholas Conant.

1753 Jan. 7, Joseph Conant.

1755 Mch. 2, Thomas Conant.

1767 Jan. 4, Thomas Conant.

1769 Jan. 8, Elizabeth Conant.

1772 Feb. 23, Sarah Conant.

1773 Jan. 31, Elizabeth Conant.

1773 May 15, Henry Conant.

1779 Dec. 19, Elizabeth Conant.

1780 Nov. 20, Mary Conant.

MARRIAGES.

1739 Dec. 17, William Conant and Elizabeth Lane.

1742 Aug. 29, John Conant and Elizabeth Fortescue.

1746 Oct. 21, John Conant and Mary Bishop.

1748 Apr. 11, Thomas Conant and Martha Gould.

1771 Mch. 7, John Conant and Mary Maudit.

BAPTISMS.

1677 Sarah, the daughter of Thomas Conant and Ann, his wife, was born the second day of April and baptised the —— day of the same month, in the year of our Lord 1677.

1686 May 5, Mary, daughter of —— Conant.

1705 May 13, Agnes, dau. John Conant and Martha, his wife.

1706 Feb. 19, Martha, dau. John Conant and Martha, his wife.

1740 Feb. 10, Betty, dau. John and Elizabeth Conant.

1745   Apr. 28, Elizabeth, dau. John and Elizabeth Conant.

1746   Oct. 12, George, son of John Conant and Mary, his wife.

1748   Aug. 15, John, son of John Conant and Elizabeth, his wife.

1750   Nov. 5, William, son of John Conant and Elizabeth, his wife.

1751   Oct. 27, Anne, dau. of John Conant and Mary, his wife.

1753   July 15, Christopher, son of John Conant and Elizabeth, his wife.

1754   Apr. 28, Henry, son of Thomas Conant and Martha, his wife.

1756   Apr. 11, Joseph, son of John Conant and Elizabeth, his wife.

1756   Apr. 25, Joseph, son of Thomas Conant and Martha, his wife.

1758   Apr. 2, John, son of Thomas Conant and Martha, his wife.

1758   May 21, Ann, dau. of John Conant and Elizabeth, his wife.

1760   June 8, James, son of Thomas and Martha Conant.

1762   Mch. 23, James, son of John Conant and Elizabeth, his wife.

1762   June 6, Daniel, son of Thomas Conant and Martha, his wife.

1764   Dec. 2, Susanna, dau. of Thomas Conant and Martha.

1765   Feb. 17, Mary, dau. of John Conant and Elizabeth, his wife.

1767   Nov. 29, Samuel, son of Thomas Conant and Martha, his wife.

1768   Sarah daughter of —— Conant and Elizabeth, his wife, was born Aug. 1st, 1767, and baptised Oct. 11th, 1768.

1772   Jan. 12, Richard, son of John Conant and Mary, his wife.

1779   Oct. 25, Henry, son of Nicholas and Elizabeth Conant.

1780   Feb. 3, John, son of John Conant and Mary, his wife.

1781   Jan. 7, Robert, son of Nicholas Conant and Elizabeth, his wife.

1783 June 1, Aaron, son of Nicholas Conant and Elizabeth, his wife.

1784 Oct. 10, Dinah, dau. of John Conant and Dinah, his wife.

PAROCHIAL REGISTERS OF AWLISCOMBE, CO. DEVON.

BURIALS.

1566 August 20, Winefred Concnannt, the daughter of Nicholas Conant, was buried.

1566 September 11, Nicholas Conannt was buried.

MARRIAGES.

1568 December 6, Ralph Erle and Johane Connant were married.

BAPTISMS.

1562 November 29, John Couenant, the son of Nicholas Counaunt, was baptised.

1566 August 19, Winefred Conannt, the daughter of Nicholas Conannt, was baptised.

PAROCHIAL REGISTERS OF COTLEIGH, HONITON, CO. DEVON.

MARRIAGE.

1756 April 16, Joseph Connant and Mary Paddock.

PAROCHIAL REGISTERS OF POOLE, CO. DORSET.

BAPTISM.

1709 May 17, Anne, ye Daughter of Mr John Conant, Minister, and Elizabeth, his wife, born 10th inst.

BURIAL.

1720   August 6, Mr. John Conant, Minister.

PAROCHIAL REGISTERS OF LYTCHETT MATRAVERS, CO. SOMERSET.

MARRIAGE.

1706   John Conant, widower, and Mrs. Dorothy Culliford,
widow, were married July 24, 1706.

BURIALS.

1696-7   March 5, Edward Culliford.
1719   Nov. 21, the Rev'd Mr. Samuel Conant, ye very
learned and worthy Rector of this Parish.
1721-2   Feb. 15, John Conant was buried.

PAROCHIAL REGISTERS OF ST. ANN'S, BLACKFRIARS, LONDON.

MARRIAGE.

1618   Nov. 11, Roger Conant and Sara Horton.

PAROCHIAL REGISTERS OF ST. LAWRENCE, JEWRY, LONDON.

CHRISTENINGS.

1619   Sept. 19, Sarah, the daughter of Roger Connaute.
1622   May 27, Caleb, the son of Roger Connaut and Sarah,
his wiffe.

BURIALS.

1618   Mrs. Cannaunt was buried the fifth of August.
1620   Oct. 30, Sarah, daughter of Roger Conant.

REGISTERS OF GRAY'S INN CHAPEL, LONDON.

(Taken from Foster's *Collectanea Genealogica*.)

MARRIAGE.

1713-4 Jan. 23, Joseph Conet, of the parish of St. Martin's in the Fields, and Mary Burrace.

PAROCHIAL REGISTERS OF PLYMTREE, CO. DEVON.

CHRISTENINGS.

1672 Feb. 2, Thomas, son of Christopher Conant.
1675 Mch. 12, Christopher, son of Christopher Conant.
1679 April 30, John, son of Christopher Conant.

BURIAL.

1681 Jan. 2, Christopher Conant.

PAROCHIAL REGISTERS OF WOODBURY, CO. DEVON.

BURIAL.

1651 March 5, Priscilla, wife of Mr. Richard Conant, Minister of Otterton.

BAPTISM.

1679 April 30, John, sonne of Robert Cunnatt.

PAROCHIAL REGISTERS OF CREDITON, CO. DEVON.

BURIAL.

1641 Oct. 6, Mr. Christopher Conant, Constable.

MARRIAGE.

1562 Oct. 4, Mr. William Stone and Mrs. Anne Conant.

PAROCHIAL REGISTERS OF KENN, CO. DEVON.

BAPTISM.

1652 John, fil of John and Mary Connett, was baptised ye
       xxv[th] of June, 1652.

PAROCHIAL REGISTERS OF SHOBROOK, CO. DEVON.

MARRIAGE.

1619 Christopher Conant, merchant, of London, and Mrs.
       Anne Wilton were married 14th Sept., 1719.

PAROCHIAL REGISTERS OF ST. MARY MAJOR, EXETER,
CO. DEVON.

BAPTISMS.

1597   Nathaniel, son of Roger Conatt, 5 Sept.
1603-4 Zachery, son of Roger Conant, 29 Jan'y.
1687-8 Joan, dau. of Mr. John Conant, 4 Mch.
1689   Henry, son of John Connet, 14 July.

BURIAL.

1613 Roger Connat, 6 November.

MARRIAGES.

1596 Roger Conett and Joan ffrancis, 10 May.
1614 Richard Shrieff and Joan Connet, 1 May.

VICAR GENERAL'S MARRIAGE LICENSES.

1664-5 Thomas Rowe, of Badcombe, co. Somerset, clerk,
        bachelor, about 30, and Sarah Conant, of Litchet
        Matravers, co. Dorset, spinster, about 30, and at
        own dispose, at Badcombe or (blank).

ARCHBISHOP OF CANTERBURY'S MARRIAGE LICENSES.

1696   July 22, John Conant, of Morden, co. Dorset, clerk, bachelor, 26, and Elizabeth Parker, spinster, 19, dau. of William Parker, of Kibworth, co. Leicester, gent., who consents; at St. Clement Danes, Midd., or (blank).

MARRIAGE LICENSES ENTERED IN THE BISHOP'S ACT BOOKS, EXETER, CO. DEVON.*

1625   Nov. 12, George Hill, of Tedbourne St. Mary, and Joanna Connant, of the same.

1629   Oct. 9, Laurence Puddicombe, of Bovey Tracy, and Alice Connatt, of Bridford.

1633-4   Mch. 7, Charles Adams, alias Forde, of Sandford, and Amy Connatt, of the same.

1640   Dec. 30, George Lacy, of Branscombe, and Grace Conant, of Sidmouth.

1686   Sept. 18, John Conant, of Sidmouth, and Joanna Brown, of Exeter, spinster.

1774   June 10, William Conant, of Dunsford, yeoman, and Mary —— of the same, spinster.

1779   Aug. 3, Robert Conant, of Sidmouth, shipwright, and Mary Bartlett, of the same, spinster.

OBITUARY NOTICE.

"Died (1728) September 24, Thomas Conant, commonly called Beau Conant, well known at Bath, Tunbridge, and to the Beau Monde. He was the son of an eminent divine."

Gent. Mag., viii. (1738) 491.

* These extracts are the result of a casual search; no systematic search has been made.

WILLS AND ADM'ONS IN THE PREROGATIVE COURT OF CANTERBURY, SOMERSET HOUSE, LONDON.

No Conant wills are to be found in the Consistory Court of the Bishop of London. The following is a complete list of Conant wills and adm'ons in the Court of Canterbury, down to the year 1750. The indexes were examined from the beginning in 1383 to 1750.

Richard Conant, the younger, of East Budleigh. Adm'on 3 Jan., 1625-6.

Caleb Conant, late beyond seas, a bachelor. Adm'on 11 Nov., 1633.

Edward Connett, late beyond seas, a bachelor. Adm'on 17 Sep., 1646.

John Conant, of the Close of Sarum, Wilts, clerk. Proved 26 Sep., 1653.

Elizabeth Conant, of Bicton, Devon. Adm'on 19 June, 1654.

Zachary Conant, of Hennock, Devon, yeoman. Proved 18 May, 1658.

Benjamin Conant, of Hennock, Devon, gent. Proved 22 Feb., 1663-4.

John Conant, of Northampton, D. D. Proved 19 May, 1694.

George Conant, of Queen's Ship, Pembroke. Adm'on 4 July, 1706.

Elizabeth Conant, of Northampton, widow. Proved 2 Dec., 1707.

Jeremias Cannon, al's Conant. Proved Mch., 1708, (Barrett 57).

John Conant, of Kidlington, Oxford, LL. D. Proved 13 Sep., 1723.

John Connett, of London. Proved July, 1726, (Plymouth 141).

Elizabeth Conant, of the Close of Sarum, Wilts, widow. Proved 11 May, 1733.

Anna Hougham, al's Conant, of London. Adm'on 26 July, 1733.

ABSTRACTS.

EDWARD CONNETT, late beyond seas, bachelor, dec'd. Adm'on 17 Sep., 1646, to Eleanor Billett, a creditor.

(Adm'ons 1646, fo. 152.)

ZACHARY CONANT, of Hennock, co. Devon, yeoman, sick in body, etc. Will dated 1 Jan., 1657; proved 18 May, 1658, by Anne Conant, the relict. To the poor of Hennock, £6— of Bovitracy, £3—of Newton Abbott, 20s. To my sister, Susan Comyn, and her daughter, Susan Nosworthy, £5 each. To my kinswoman, Mary Hynes, and her children, Joseph, Benjamin and Grace, £5 each. To my kinswoman, Elizabeth Conant, and her sister, Susan, daughter of John Conant, of Alphington, dec'd, £4 each, and to their brother, John Conant, 20s. To John Conant, of Buckrell, 40s, and to his daughter, Sarah, £4, and to Joseph Conant, brother of John, 20s. To Alice Aishford, daughter of my uncle, Edward Conant, dec'd, and to her sister, Elizabeth, 10s each. To Margaret Conant and her sister, Susan, daughters of Robert Conant, of Alphington, dec'd, 10s each. To Martin Salter and Robert Salter, sons of my kinswoman, Margaret Salter, of Alphington, 10s each. To my kinsman, John Reynell, of Totnes, 20s, and to his brothers and sisters, children of Richard Reynell, of Newton Abbott, dec'd, 10s each. To William Reynell, son of my kinsman, Henry Reynell, 10s. To Oliver Oram and his sister, Margery, 5s each. Elizabeth, Florence, Anne and Grace, daughters of my cousin, John Hore, 10s each. John Woolcott, Dorothy Martyn, Joane Oxenham and Rose Boond, 5s each. Joane, wife of John Prouse, of Chudleigh, ——. To my brother, Thomas Maurie or Maurye, lands called Woodland in Bovitracy. I forgive Henry Westlake £3. To my kinsman, Robert Conant, son of my brother, Benjamin Conant, dec'd, certain bonds. To my cousin, John Hore, of Hennock, wearing apparel. Residue to my wife, Anne, sole Executrix. My friend, Mr. Francis Southcott, and my cousin, John Hore, to be overseers. Witnesses, John Hore and William Nosworthy.

(252 Wootton.)

BENJAMIN CONANT, of Hennock, co. Devon, gentleman, dated 2 July, 1653; proved 27 Feb., 1663, by Susan Hoare, al's Nosworthy; power reserved to the other executors. To be buried near my father, Robert Conant, if I die in co. Devon. To the poor of Hennocke, £20—of Bovitracie, £10—my wife, Martha, £5—my son, Robert Conant, £5 at age of 21. To Mary King, sometime wife of Andrew King, and her daughter, Grace King, £10 each. To Joseph King, son of the aforesaid Mary, all my interest in a tenement in Knighton, now in tenure of my brother, Zachary Conant. To my brother-in-law, Thomas Mawry, £5. The children of Augustine Osborne, late of Culme Stoke, clerk, £25. To Bryan Duppa, sometime Bishop of Chichester, £200. To Charles Danverse, son of Sir John Danverse, of Chelsey, near London, £100. To Christopher Lynes, of Bovitracie, and his children, £25. Thomazine, wife of William Pethebridge, of Hennocke, £5. The residue to my cousin, Henry Westlake, of Dawlish, clerk. Thomas Westlake now Town Clerk of Exon, and my niece, Susan Hore, executors. Witnesses, John Leaker, the elder, and Robert Marlin.

(12 Bruce.)

GEORGE CONANT, of Queen's Ship, Pembroke, but in the Queen's Ship, Bedford. Adm'on 4 July, 1706, to John Conant, junior, son and lawful attorney of John Conant, senior, father of deceased.

(Adm'ons 1706.)

LIST ON WILLS AND ADM'ONS AT EXETER.

1544 Jan. Thomas Connett (will missing).
1583 Apr. Elyen Connaunte, Colyton, Ranlegh, widow.
1585 Mch. Roger Connett, Whimple (adm.).
1585 Apr. Joane Conet, Christow.
1586 Sep. John Connante, Gitsham.
1590 May Peter Connant (will missing).
1591 Feb. Elizabeth Connante (will missing).
1605 Aug. Henrie Conante (will missing).

1607		William Conante (will missing).
1613	Nov.	Roger Conatt, St. Mary Major, Exeter (missing).
1616	Apr.	Richard Connet, Alphington (adm.).
1616	Dec.	Joane Connot, Doddescombleigh (adm.).
1617		Robert Conant, Hennocke.
1618		John Connett, Coliton Rawleigh.
1619		Ellery Connett, Ashburton.
1621	Jan.	John Connatt, Alphington.
1621	Apr.	Edith Connatt, Coliton Rawlegh.
1625	Mch.	Mary Carnet, Otrey.
1626	Feb.	Robert Conant, Ottery St. Mary.
1628	Sept.	Nathaniel Connett, Exeter.
1629		William and Susanna Conett (or Covett?) (adm.).
1631	Oct.	Richard Conant, East Budleigh.
1638	May	Robert Connant, Bicton.
1643	Feb.	Robert Connet, Ashton (adm.).
1661	Sept.	Anna Conant, Hennock.
1663	Apr.	Josies Connet, Bridford.
1664	Apr.	William Connatt, Doddescombleigh.
1669	Jan.	Richard Connant, Briston.
1670	Mch.	John Connett, Doddescombleigh.
1670	Mch.	Barbara Connett, Bridford.
1675	Jan.	Jonathan Connett, Colyton Rawleigh.
1676	Jan.	Richard Connett, Plympstock.
1676	Dec.	John Cunnett, Dunsford (adm.).
1679	Jan.	Grenica Counent, Ottery St. Mary.
1680	Oct.	John Cunnett, Sidmouth (adm.).
1681	Jan.	John Connet, senior, Kenn.
1682	Feb.	Maria Connent, Alphington.
1682		Robert Conant, Woodbury.
1684	Aug.	Henry Conent, Sidmouth.
1688	Feb.	Joanna Conant, Bicton.
1688	Feb.	Richard Conant, East Budleigh.
1690	Jan.	Jacobus Cunnett, Stokenteinhead (adm.).
1692	Apr.	John Cunnent, Combe Rawleigh.
1704	July	John Conant, Sidmouth (adm.).
1706	June	Salter Connet, Gittisham.
1709	Jan.	George Connet, Dunsford.

1710 Dec. ffrancis Cunnet, Limpstone (adm.).

1713 Oct. Henry Cunnet, Gittisham (adm.).

1714 July John Conant, Colyton Rawleigh.

1720 Mch. Elizabeth Cunnet, Tedbourne (adm.).

1722 July Jonathan Cunnet, Exeter (adm.).

1725 May Robert Cunnet, Holcombe Burnell.

1727 Sept. Susanna Conant, Colaton.

1732 July John Conant, Bicton (adm.).

1732 Sept. Joseph Connatt, Colyton Rawley.

1734 Dec. George Conant, St. Nicholas (adm.).

1736 Zachary Connett, Kingskerswell.

1736 Jan. Thomas Connett, Gittisham (adm.).

1737 John Conant, Sidmouth.

1740 July Joseph Conant, Gittisham (adm.).

1747 Mch. Robert Connett, Dunsford (adm.).

1747 Apr. John Connett, Dunsford.

1756 Oct. George Connett, Dunsford.

1776 Jan. Elizabeth Connett, Dunsford.

1777 Dec. John Connett, Bridford.

1778 Feb. William Connett, Dunsford.

1785 May John Connett, Dunsford (adm.).

1786 Apr. Mary Connett, Dunsford.

1788 Apr. Nicholas Connett, Tedbourn St. Mary.

1791 Sept. Mary Connett, Tedbourn St. Mary.

1797 Feb. Joan Cunnett, East Tawton.

1797 July Jeremiah Cunnet, Dunsford.

1798 June Margery Cunnett, Whitstone.

1798 Oct. Jeremiah Connett, Exeter.

1801 Mch. George Connett, Dunsford.

ABSTRACTS.

ARCHDEACONRY COURT OF EXETER.

ELYEN CONANT, of Colyton Rawlegh, widow, dated 20 Feb., 1583, proved 5 Apr., 1583. To the four children of my son-in-law, John King. To Jane, dau. of sd. John King. To Jane, dau. of Jno. Bocher. To Margaret, dau. of James Eliott. To Thos. Hidon, the younger. Owes "my ladye

Dennys" and John Connante. Residue to my dau., Elizabeth, who is sole executrix. Overseers, Robert Ballement and Thomas Hidon, who are the witnesses.

ROGER CONNETT, late of Whimple, deceased. Adm'on granted 31 Mch., 1585, to Joan, his widow. James Brodheare joins in the bond. Sum, £16 5s. 4d.

JOANE CONETT, of Christowe, widow, dated 27 May, 1583, proved 17 Apr., 1585. Mentions son Robert Lendon, son John Connett. Residue to son Richard Lendon, who is sole executor. Witnesses, Christopher Townsente, John Syñone and John Taverner. Sum, £4 17s. 2d.

JOHN CONNETT, of Colyton Rawlegh, dated Sep., 1618, proved Oct., 1618; mentions wife, Ede, sons, Nicholas and John, daughters, Mary and Joan, and the three children of his son, John.

EDITH CONNATT, of Colyton Rawlegh, widow, dated 30 May, 1620, proved Apr., 1621, inventory 31 May, 1620; mentions the same children as above.

JOHN CONNOT, AL'S GREGORYE, of Alphington, dated 3 Dec., 1620, proved 21 Jan., 1620-1. To John Parr, "me platter dishe." To John Connot, my kinsman, "my Byble." To my son, Robert Connot, "my best cloake." To my kinswoman, Agnes Whyte, 20s. To my daughter, Barbara Downe, "my crocke." To my daughters, Agnis Connett and Mary White, "all the goods knowen to be myne." The rest of all my goods not given nor bequeathed, to Edward Downe, whom I make my whole executor. Thomas Drew, and Robert Connot, my son, to see my will performed. "Item, my will is that if Lawrence Whyte doe come and trowbell my Executor for the Legacie given unto Mary, his wife, that then the legacie shall be given unto Agnis, my daughter, or the Executor." Witnesses, John Vincent, Ebbett Hamlin and Thomas Drewe.

ROBERT CONANT, of Otery St. Maries, co. Devon, dated 11 Feb., 1626-7, proved Mch., 1626-7. To my wife, Elizabeth, daughters, Susan, Mary, Margaret, son, John, and two children of my daughter, Jone Tees, various small bequests.

NATHANIEL CONNETT, of Exeter, co. Devon, cutler. Will proved Sep., 1628, by Phillippe Connett. Witnessed by Elizabeth Jewell and —— Jewell. No others mentioned.

JOHN CONNETT, of Bridford, co. Devon, dated 1658, proved Apr. 1658, inventory returned Mch., 1662. To my daughter, Barbara, two debts of £20 éach due from my son, John Connett, of Dunsford, to his brother, Christopher, now dec'd. My son, Charles Connett, to be executor. My wife, Barbara.

JONATHAN CONNETT, of Colyton Rawleigh, co. Devon, proved Jan., 1675. My sons, Jonathan and Henry Connett; my daughters, Jane and Amy Connett. Jonathan Connett and Amy Connett to be executors. Witness, Nicholas Hooper.

JOHN CONNETT, of Kenn, co. Devon, Jan., 1681. His entire estate given by his son, John, to Thomas Gould, a creditor.

HENRY CONNETT, of Gittisham, co. Devon, dated Dec., 1669, proved Mch., 1669-70. My sons, Thomas and Salter Connett; daughters, Joan Mitchell and Catherine, wife of Robert Mitchell. Witnesses, Thomas Hooper and Salter Connett.

JOAN CONNETT, of Doddescombleigh, co. Devon, proved Mch., 1670. Legacies to several persons named Crispin. To my granddaughter, Rebecca Teyley (or Taly); my brother, William Smith.

BARBARA CONNETT, of Bridsford, co. Devon, widow, proved Mch., 1670. Resigns all rights in estate of her daughter, Barbara Connett, spinster, to the brother of said Barbara, Charles Connett.

HENRY CONENT, of Sidmouth, co. Devon, proved Aug., 1684. Inventory dated July, 1684; value, £2219. Life interest to wife, Jane, then to my daughter, Jone, or if she die unmarried to my son, John. My grandson, Abraham Kerslake. My son, John to be executor. Witnesses, Nicholas Hooper and others.

JOHN CONNANTT, of Sidmouth, co. Devon, dated 14 Apr., 1657, proved Oct., 1680. Poor of Sidmouth, £4. My wife to have the use of all my goods during her life. To Jonathan, my son, "my chattle lease of Colleton after my wiffes decease, and five pounds yearlie of that my write due from him." "To Henry, my sonn, ffee of my land and close called fforlande." "The rest of my rent of Colleton, wch is fifteen pounds yearlie I give to my wiff and Johana Lacy for & towards ther housekeeping." * * * * "The rest of my goods except corne I give to my childrens children to be equally divided." Witnesses, Charles Lee, Joanna Lacy and Mary Swaine. As his wife, who was executrix, predeceased him, adm'on was granted to his grandson, John Conant.

SALTER CONNET, of Gittisham, dated 1702, proved 2 June, 1606. Mentions his sons, Benjamin, James, Henry, Matthew, Thomas and John; daughter, Mary Capron. Sons, Thomas and John, executors. Witnesses, John Connon and Gideon Hodge. Thomas Capron was a witness to the inventory.

HENRY CUNNET, of Gittisham. Adm'on granted to his daughter, Sarah, Oct., 1713.

JOHN CONANT, of Bicton. Adm'on granted to his widow, Joanna Conant, of Bicton, 1732.

THOMAS CONNETT, of Gittisham. Adm'on granted 17 Jan., 1736. Among the papers are deeds of lands at Awliscombe from the Bishop of Exeter to Thomas Connett and others.

JOSEPH CONANT, of Gittisham, yeoman, d. 3 July, 1740. Adm'on granted to his sister, Margaret Conant.

COURT OF DEAN AND CHAPTER OF EXETER.

ELLERY CONNETT, of Ashburton, co. Devon, proved 1619. Leaves a legacy to John Helde's eldest daughter, and *her* entire estate to her master.

ARCHDEACONRY COURT OF TOTNES.

ANNA CONNANT, of Hennocke, co. Devon, widow, proved Sep.,
1661. Mentions her brother Richard Renell's children.

RICHARD CONNETT, of Plympstock, co. Devon, proved Jan.,
1676. Leaves legacy to his brother, Nicholas, and residue
to his wife, Willmot. Witness, Jane Ellery.

EXTRACTS FROM RECORDS IN THE PUBLIC RECORD
OFFICE, FETTER LANE, LONDON, E. C.

SUBSIDY ROLLS.

Tax of a twentieth in the County of Devon.
Alexander Conaunt, in the Hundred of Exmystr',   -   -   6d.
Exchequer Lay Subsidies, Devon, 1 Edward III.
(1327), Roll $\frac{95}{6}$

Roll of the tax of a Tenth and a Fifteenth in the County of
Devon.
From Alan Conaunt, in the Hundred of Axminster, - - 8d.
Ibid., 6 Edward III., Roll $\frac{95}{7}$

Assessments of the inhabitants of Exminster and Tyne-
bridge for the first payment of the subsidy granted 14, 15
Henry VIII.
Hundred of Exmyster.   Parish of Doddyscomb Leght.
John Cownat, in goods 40s—to the subsidy,   -   -   12d.
John Cownat, senior, in goods £6—to the subsidy,   -   3s.
John Cownat, junior, in goods £4—to the subsidy,   -   - 2s.
Mychaell Conant, in wages 20s—to the subsidy,   -   -   4d.
Ibid., 14-15 Henry VIII. (1522), Roll $\frac{96}{140}$

Assessment dated 20 December, 15 Henry VIII., for the payment of the subsidy granted 15 Henry VIII. upon the inhabitants within the Hundreds of Eastbudleigh, Colyton and Otery
Saint Mary.

Hundred of Eastbudlegh. The Parish of Wodebury.

John Connant, cessed at the subsidy for his wages at
20s—assessment, - - - - - - - 4d.

Same Hundred. Parish of Colaton Ralegh.

Henry Conant, cessed at subsidy for wages at 20s—assessment, - - - - - - - 4d.

Same Hundred. Parish of Gyttysham.

John Conant, senior, cessed at subsidy for his goods at
£7—assessment, - - - - - - 3s 6d.

John Conant, junior, cessed at subsidy for his goods at
£4—assessment, - - - - - - 2s.

Nicholas Conant, cessed at subsidy for his wages at
26s 8d—assessment, - - - - - - 8d.

Ibid., 15 Henry VIII. (1523), Roll $\frac{96}{183}$

Certificate of the assessment of the second subsidy, dated
10 December, 16 Henry VIII. (1524).

Hundred of Estbudlegh. Parish of Wodebury.

John Conant, for wages 20s, - - - - - 4d.

Same Hundred. Parish of Gyddysham.

John Conant, senior, for goods £7, - - - - 3s 6d.

John Conant, junior, for goods £4, - - - - 2s.

Nicholas Conant, for wages 26s 8d, - - - - 6d.

Roger Conant, for wages 20s, - - - - - 4d.

Ibid., Roll $\frac{96}{151}$

Dated 30 January, 16 Henry VIII. (1525).

A list of the inhabitants of Exminster and Teinbridge, with
the sums to be paid by each towards a subsidy.

Hundred of Exminster. Parish of Dodyscumblegh.

John Conat, senior, in goods and chattels, - - - 2s 6d.

John Conat, junior, in goods and chattels, - - - 2s.

John Conett, in goods and chattels, - - - - 12d.

Same Hundred. Parish of Exminster.

John Conatt, in goods and chattels, - - - - 12d.

Thomas Conott, in wages, - - - - - - 4d.

Same Hundred. Parish of Ayscheberton Manor.

Robert Conett, in goods and chattels, - - - - 2s 6d.

Ibid., Roll $\frac{96}{184}$

Assessment of the second payment of the subsidy granted 34-35 Henry VIII. *

Parish of (Ottery Saint M?)ary.

John Connante, - - - - - - - - 10d.
John Connante, - - - - - - - - 2d.
John Connante, - - - - - - - - 1d.

Parish of Ottery St. Mary.

John Connante, - - - - - - - - 1d.

Parish of Colaton Ralegh.

James Connante, - - - - - - - 10d.
George Connante, - - - - - - - 1d.

Ibid., Roll $\frac{98}{258}$

Assessment of the payment of the subsidy granted 35 Henry VIII. (1543-1544).

Hundred of Hartlond.   Parish of Lamerton.

John Connett, in goods £5, - - - - - 10d.

Ibid., Roll $\frac{97}{234}$

Assessment dated 2 April, 13 Elizabeth (1571).
Parish of Estbudleigh.

From John Conant, for goods £4, - - - - 6s 8d.

Parish of Gytisham.†

From John Conant, for lands £4, - - - 10s 85.

Parish of Combralegh.   Hundred of Axminster.

John Conant, in lands 20s, - - - - - - 16d.

Parish of Ottery St. Marye.

John Conant, in land 20s, - - - - - - 16d.

Manor of Aishburton.   Hemiocke Hundred.

Thomasina Conant, for lands 20s, - - - - 16d.

Ibid., Roll $\frac{100}{369}$

23 Elizabeth (1580-1581).

Assessment of the second payment of the subsidy on the inhabitants of the whole county.

Parish of Estbudlegh.

John Conant, in goods £4 - - - - - - 4s.

---

* This Roll is much injured.
† The last part of the Assessment on this Parish is quite obliterated.

Parish of Gyttisham.

John Conant, in lands £4, - - - - - - 5s 4d.

Henry Conant, in goods £3, - - - - - 3s.

Ibid., Roll $\frac{100}{387}$

31 Elizabeth (1588-1589).
Assessment for the second payment of the second subsidy.
Parish of Ottery St. Mary.

John Conant, in lands 40s, - - - - - 2s 8d.

Parish of Asheberton.

Thomasina Conant, in lands 20s, - - - - 16d.

Parish of Estbudleigh.

Lands. Richard Conant, £4, - - - - - 4s.

Parish of Collaton Raleigh.

Lands. George Conant, 20s, - - - - - 16d.

Parish of Gittesham.

Goods. Henry Conant, £3, - - - - - 3s.

Parish of Harpforde. Hundred of Estbudlegh.

Lands. William Conant, 40s, - - - - - 2s 8d.

Ibid., Roll $\frac{101}{408}$

Assessment of the subsidy granted 7 James I. (1609-1610), upon the inhabitants within the Hundreds of Axminster and East Budleigh.

Hundred of East Budleigh. Parish of Sydmouth.

In goods. John Connant, £3, - - - - - 3s.

Same Hundred. Parish of Gyttisham.

In goods. Henry Conant, £3, - - - - - 3s.

Same Hundred. Parish of Bickton.

In goods. Robert Conant, £3, - - - - - 3s.

Same Hundred. Parish of Collaton Rawleigh.

In lands. John Conant, £1, - - - - - 1s.

Ibid., Roll $\frac{101}{453}$

Assessment of the third subsidy, 21 James I (1623-1624).
Hundred of Wonford. Bridford Parish.

In lands, George Conant. - - - - - - -

Parish of Hemiock.

In lands. Zachery Conant, 20s. - - - - - -

Parish of Sydmouth.

In lands. John Connatt, £4.   · - · - - - - - -

Parish of Gittesham.

In goods. Henry Conett.   -   -   -   -   -   -   -

Hundred of Ottery St. Marie.

Lands. Robert Conant, £1. - -   -   -   -   -   -

Ibid., Roll $\frac{102}{463}$

James I.

Parish of Mortonhampsteed.

In lands. Andrew Conant, 20s—therefor, -   -   -   16d.

Ibid., Roll $\frac{102}{469}$

James I.

Hundred of Hemiocke. Parish of Buckrell.

Thomas Cunnante, £1. -   -   -   -   -   -   -   -

Ibid., Roll $\frac{102}{474}$

PATENT ROLLS.

Appointment of John de Oketon and Elias de Beckingham to take the assize of novel disseisin arraigned by Ismannia, daughter of Conan de Ridmere, against Reginald, son of Conon de Ridmere, touching a tenement in Ridmere, Yorkshire.

Patent Rolls, 1 Edward I., m. 7, dors.

Appointment of G. de Preston and another to take assize of novel disseisin arraigned by Hugh le Tollere, of Peterborough, against Conian, son of (Fitz) Guy, touching a tenement in Peterborough, Northamptonshire.

Ibid., 1 Edward I., m. 2.

Appointment of Nicholas de Stapleton and Elias de Beckingham to take assize of novel disseisin arraigned by Petronilla, daughter of Conan de Lenham, against Simon de Markham and others, touching a tenement in Wormeston, Nottinghamshire.

Ibid., 2 Edward I., m. 9, dors. (57).

Appointment of Guichard de Charrun and William de Northburgh to take the assize of mort dancestor arraigned by Henry, son of Roger de Kelkefield (Kelfield), against Henry, son of Conan, touching land and rent in Kelfield and Shytehou, Yorkshire.

Ibid., 3 Edward I., m. 23, d. 39.

Appointment of Guichard de Charrun and William de Northburgh to take the assize of novel disseisin arraigned by Hasewic de Glesby against Henry, son of Conan, touching a tenement in Mansfield, Yorkshire.

Ibid., 3 Edward I, m. 15, d. 43.

Appointment of John de Reigate and William de Northburgh to take assize of novel disseisin arraigned by Henry Fitz-Couany against Thomas de Derwentewater and William Fitz-Hughtred, touching a tenement in Belton, near Appleby, Westmoreland.

Ibid., 5 Edw. I, m. 19, (70).

Appointment of Solomon de Rochester and Master Thomas de Sodington to take the assize of novel disseisin arraigned by Robert Couenaunt against Filota, late wife of Richard Couenaunt, and others, touching a tenement in Alton, Staffordshire.

Ibid., 5 Edw. I., m. 9, d. (72), A. D. 1277.

PARTICULARS FOR GRANTS. 18 MAY, 35 HENRY VIII., NO. II.

PARCEL OF THE POSSESSIONS OF RICHARD DUKE,

OTTERTON AND HARFORD, CO. DEVON.

Firm (rent) of the 10th of the corn of Harford, aforesaid, leased to John Conant for a term of 60 years by an Indenture made by the said Richard Duke and Elizabeth, his wife, bearing date 15th day of March, in the 34th year of Henry VIII. Rendering therefor by the year, 106s. 8d.

(These particulars for grants were made at the time of the dissolution of the Monasteries.)

EXCHEQUER COURT OF AUGMENTATIONS. COURT ROLLS, P. 21, NO. 27.

m. 1.

Ottery St. Mary.

Court held 14 October, 27 Elizabeth (1585). From William Batt, for license to agree with Thomas Conant in a plea of debt, 6d.

m. 3.

Court held 7 November, 31 Elizabeth. Edward Conant, for license to agree with John Brown in a plea of trespass.

m. 5.

Court held 13 April, 34 Elizabeth. The jurors present that Edward Conant resides with his father and lives within the manor, and is not sworn for allegiance and fealty toward the Lady the Queen.

ASSIZE ROLLS.

In a plea of customs by tenants of the Manor of Horncastle against the Bishop of Carlisle, the name Robert Conet appears.

Assize Roll, Lincoln, $\frac{M}{\frac{3}{16}}$ } 1, 9 Edward I.

Assizes taken at Lincoln on Monday next before the Exaltation of the Holy Cross. The name of Philip Conet, of Maryng, occurs as a Recognitor (i. e., one of the jury) in a plea between John, son of Richard de Tynton, and Richard, son of the same John.

Assize Roll, Divers Counties, $\frac{N}{\frac{2}{18}}$ } 5, 2 Edward II.

INSTITUTION BOOKS, VOL. 2, P. 70, CO. SOMERSET.

| Lymington. | Henricus Rosewell, Milit. 30 Dec. 1619. | Jōhes Conant. |
| £21 6s. 5d. | idem. 24 Nov. 1645. | Robtus Bryen. |

This shows that John Conant was instituted in the living of Lymington on Dec. 30, 1619, that he was succeeded by Robert Bryen, and that Sir Henry Rosewell was the patron.

EXCHEQUER OF ACCOUNTS. FIRST FRUITS.
LIBER COMPOSITION.

Jan. 8, 1618, to 31 Dec., 1623, fol. 38.

Here it is recorded that John Conant compounded for the First Fruits of the Rectory of Lymington, on Jan. 20, 1619, (O. S.) his sureties being Christopher Conant, grocer, and Roger Conant, salter, both of the parish of St. Lawrence, Jewry, London.

NORMAN ROLLS.

5 Henry V. Safe conduct to Nicholas Conen and others "in villa Regis Falesiae (Falaise)."

6 Henry V. Part I., m. 5. Caen, May 22. Grant to William Barrys, of Caen, of the house in Caen of John Conarte, a rebel, together with such lands as were held by the said John Conarte within the vicomté of Caen, but not within the town of Caen, by homage and the rendering yearly a pound of pepper to the king.

6 Henry V. Part II., m. 26, d. Rouen Castle, Feb. 22. Appointment of John Cannet as wine broker at Rouen. Also on the same membrane, March 1, following, is the appointment of William le Conete and various other persons, all of Rouen, as wine brokers at Rouen.

6 Henry V. Part II., m. 15. Rouen Castle, March 14. Grant to John Connart, of Caen, and Egidia, his wife, of the lands they held in Normandy before Aug. 1, 1417.

STATE PAPERS.

LETTER FROM CHALLONER TO JOHN CUERTON.

Madrid 27 May 1562

Mr. Cuerton, with my most herty recomendacons

* * * * If any good barrell butter be at Bilboa to be bought I pray you send me one Fyrken oute of hande and likewise the fardell of cloth for my servants lyvereys and the doblett that my servant sent me in James Connants shippe. * * * *

State Papers, Foreign, 1562, No. 84.

LETTER FROM JOHN CUERTON TO CHALLONER.

Bilboa 5 June 1562

Right Honorabul

Unto your honor I have me recomendyd * * * your servants Goyher and Wynssla who came in good tyme the did depart as 4 days past in a ship of London wt on Jamys Conant * * *

Ibid., No. 107.

LETTER FROM CUERTON TO CHALLONER.

Bilboa 12 Sept 1562

Right Honorabul

* * * * Master White departed from Sensebasteans in James Conats ship and the be in heylth no dowt but by Gods helpe the be in Ingland er this * * * *

Ibid., No. 462.

LETTER FROM CUERTON TO CHALLONER.

Bilboa 7 March 156⅔

Right Honorabul

I * * * * send you sertyn letters * * * * this our resyvyd one from sir Thomas Chamberleyne with anodr for you he wryts that his guardemeselles were dystroyd wᵗ salt water james conant denyes hit and the had byn so at the our the shold a laid hit to his charge ther * * * * *

Ibid., 1563, Vol. LII., No. 381.

LETTER FROM CUERTON TO CHALLONER.

Bilboa 11 July 1564

Right Honorabul

* * * * this shall be to advertyse you that as the syxt of this month James conant made seyle from Portegerleyt wherein went Mistress Adrea & the rest that

came w^t her & more yor servant Robert Farneham & Harvey
came a dey before the ship did depart and went w^t them * *
Ibid., 1564, Vol. LXXIII., No. 468.

MISCELLANEOUS RECORDS.

William Coinan, or Conian, was living in the parish of Coly-
ton Ralegh, Devon, in the year 1456.
Duchy of Lancaster, Court Rolls, 34 Henry VI.,
Bundle 57, No. 692.

Robert de Ros, of Scorborough (Scorreby), Richard de
Breus, of Thorganby, Henry, son of Conan, of Kelfield, and
others, maintain a warren in the wapentake between Ouse and
Derwent, co. York.
Rotuli Hundredorum, Temp. Henry III., Ed-
ward I., Vol. I., p. 122.

The Archbishop of York, Henry, son of Conan, and the
Prior of Drax maintain a fish weir in the river Ouse, by which
the said river is much contracted, to the injury of those passing.
Ibid., p. 135.

Thomas de Wyketoft imprisoned Conan at Lincoln and
took from him 28 shillings by way of a pledge.
Ibid., p. 306.

Yorkshire, Edward I. Henry, son of Conan, holds the
Manor of Liverton, in Cleveland, of the king, and the Manor
of Kelfield, of the Abbey of Selby. Action of Petronilla,
mother of said Henry (who is under age and in custody of the
King), against William de Roseles and Margaret, his wife, to
recover the Manor of Kelfield.
Placitorum in domo capitulari Westmonast.
asservatorum abbreviatio, p. 210.

The sheriff of Lincolnshire returns account of an amerce-
ment of 9sh. 9d. paid by Conan, son of Ely.
Rotuli Cancellarii, 3 John, p. 175.

Conan, son of Brian, held half a knight's fee in Lincolnshire, of the honor of Brittany.

Ibid., p. 192, 3 John.

Hampshire. "De oblatis." Gilbert Conan renders account of 20 shillings.

Ibid., p. 255, 3 John.

Norfolk and Suffolk. Third scutage of King Richard. The sheriff renders account of 70sh. 7d. due from Count Conan, of which he paid 27sh. 4d. and owes 43sh. 3d.

Ibid., p. 328.

Rotuli de Finibus, 15 John, m. 3. Suit by Conan, son of Ely, and Robert, son of Mendred, on the part of their wives, Avicia and Isabella, against Henry de Neville and Geoffrey de Cogneriis, concerning certain lands in the county of Durham.

Rotuli de Oblatis et Finibus in Turri Lond.

asserv. temp. Reg. Joh. p. 509.

Lincolnshire. Suit of Alan de Bosco against John de Bosco concerning certain lands in Ledsham and Fulbeck. Alan claims that the lands were given to Alan, son of Geoffrey (maternal uncle of the said Alan), by Counts Alan and Conan of Brittany, and that the gift was confirmed by King Henry I. John claims the lands were given to himself by Count Geoffrey of Brittany and Constance, his wife.

Rotuli Curiæ Regis, Vol. 1, p. 56, (m. 7, d.)

Conan, chaplain to Count Conan, pays 5 marks into the treasury.

Magnum Rotulum Pipæ, Lincoln. 31 Henry I., p. 114.

Warwickshire and Leicestershire. Conan, son of Daniel, compounds for service; pays 2sh. and owes 4sh. 8d.

Great Roll of the Pipe, 1189-1190, 1 Richard
I., (1189-1190), p. 123.

Charter of King John confirming to Henry, son of Hervey, certain lands granted to him by Walter, son of Zachary, Henry, son of Conan, Warren de Scaregile, Robert de Rokeby and Agnes, his wife, and land granted to Hervey and his heirs by Conan, Duke of Brittany. Dated 21 Feb., 2 John.

Rotuli Chartarum in Turri Londinensi. Vol. 1, Part ?., 1199-1216, p. 88ᵇ, (m. 10.)

Conan, son of Guiomar de Leon, going on a pilgrimage to Jerusalem, is taken prisoner at Mirabel and ransomed by the payment of 400 marks in silver. Anno 4 John.

Rotuli Litterarum Patentium in Turri Londinensi. Vol. 1, Part 1, 1201-1216, p. 15ᵇ, (m. 11.)

Safe conduct to Conan, son of Ely, and others. Anno 17 John (1216).

Ibid., p. 169.

Thomas Conan, one of the adherants of Thomas, Earl of Lancaster, obtains a pardon by consent of Parliament, for all felonies and trespasses committed by him up to the 7th August then last, the robbery of the Cardinal Legates only excepted. Tested at York, 1 Nov., 12 Edward II.

Parliamentary Writs, Vol. 2, Div. 3, p. 712.

Fitz Conan, Henry. Henry, son of Henry, son of Conan, certified, pursuant to writs tested at Clipston, 5 March, as Lord of the Townships of Kelfield and Little Halton, in the county of York. 9 Edward II.

Ibid., Part 2, p. 407, No. 8.

Fitz Conan, Henry (Henricus fil' Conani), returned from the wapentake between Ouse and Derwent, in the county of York, as holding lands, either in capite, or otherwise, to the amount of £40 yearly value, and upwards, and as such summoned under the general writ to perform military service against the Scots. Muster at Carlisle, on the Nativity of St. John the Baptist, 24 June, 28 Edward I.

Ibid., Vol. 1, p. 332, No. 17.

Recognizance of debt from Stephen de Edesworth to Gilbert Conan. Bedfordshire and Buckinghamshire.

Rotuli Litterarum Clausarum, 3 Edward I., (m. 13, d.)

Nottinghamshire. Nicholas Toxte and Christopher Conet presented themselves on the 4th day against Adam le Paumer of a plea that he render to them £10 which he owes them and unjustly detains, etc.

De Banco Roll, 9-10 Edward ⸫. (1281), No. 45, (m. 3, d.)

Thomas Conan was Knight of the Shire for Kent, 46 Edward III.

EXTRACT FROM RECORDS IN THE GUILDHALL, EXETER, DEVON.

Document 950, 6 June, 1379.   Lease of land from the Mayor and Corporation to William de Molton and Joan, his wife, of a tenement called "la Woodhaye," without the Westgate. The boundaries fully described. "Bounded on the south by the garden of Hugh Conaunt."

RECORDS OF THE GROCERS' COMPANY, LONDON.

Apprenticeship of Christopher Conant to Thomas Allyn for vii. years from Michaelmas last. Received and entered 29 Nov., 1609.

Admission to freedom of Christopher Conant, late apprentice to Thomas Allyn. Entered and sworn the xiv. day of March, 1616.

"THOMAS CONETT: lo: goings sonn in law," is mentioned as an inhabitant of the Tower Ward, London, 1640 (*Miscellanea Genealogica et Heraldica*, 1886, p. 114).   This is probably a misprint.   Burke says that Diana, fifth daughter of Sir George Goring, Knt., created Baron Goring 1632, married Thomas *Covert*, Esq., of Slaugham, Sussex (*Hist. of the Com-*

moners, Vol. 1, p. 387-8). Dallaway, in his *History of the Western Division of Sussex*, says, that Diana, *third* daughter of Sir George Goring, married Thomas Covert, Esq.

HALSTED's *History of Kent*, Vol. 4, p. 140, mentions Thomas Conant, A. M. as Rector of Great Mongeham, co. Kent, in 1604. This is also a misprint. Thomas *Consant* compounded for the First Fruits of the living 21 Nov., 1604 (First Fruits Composition Books, 2 James I.). Thomas *Consant* was admitted to the Rectory 11 Oct., 1604 (Bishop's Certificates).

GRADUATES OF ENGLISH COLLEGES.*

1609 John Conant, B. A., of Exeter College, Oxford.

1631 John Conant, B. A., of Exeter College, Oxford.

1645 Richard Conant, B. A., of Emanuel College, Cambridge.

1648 Thomas Conant was an undergraduate of Magdalen Hall, Oxford (not identified). †

1649 Samuel Conant, B. A., of Exeter College, Oxford.

1654 Malachi Conant, B. A., of Exeter College, Oxford.

1673 John Conant, B. A., of Trinity College, Oxford.

1687 John Conant, B. A., of Exeter College, Oxford.

1697 Samuel Conant, B. A., Magdalen College, Oxford.

1700 Philip Conant, B. A., of Exeter College, Oxford (not identified).

1727 John Conant, B. A., of Pembroke College, Oxford.

1757 John Conant, B. A., of Lincoln College, Oxford.

1783 Culpepper Conant, B. A., of Trinity College, Cambridge.

1806 William Conant, B. A., of Trinity College, Cambridge.

1842 Edward Nathaniel Conant, B. A., of St. John's College, Oxford.

1847 John William Conant, B. A., of St. John's College, Oxford.

* Richard Cognett was admitted D. C. L. of Oxford, 20 Feb., 1450-1. Roger Connard, already B. A., became M. A. 1534, M. B. 1559. George Connard, B. A. 1565. Boase's *Reg. Univ. Oxon.*

† Burrows' *Register of the Parliamentary Visitors.*

FAC-SIMILE OF AN INDENTURE OF LEASE from John Ley, Abbot of the Monastery of St. Mary of Dunkeswell, co. Devon, to Nicholas, John, senior, and John, junior, sons of John Cowaunt, farmer, of a tenement and appurtenances belonging to Wessington Manor, with a tenement upon Glittisham down, for the term of their lives at a rent of 12 shillings: in renewal and extension of a previous lease, dated 30 May, 13 Henry VIII. (1521), to John Cowaunt, junior, and Isabella, his first wife (presumably deceased). Attorneys to make livery: John Rode, William Aprior, John Waren and John Tawne. Witnesses: John Galpe, Thomas Riley and William Harris. Dated at Dunkeswell, on the feast of St. Catharine the Virgin, 11 Henry VIII. (25 Nov., 1529). The original, on parchment, now in possession of the compiler, is 10 in. in height and 16 in. broad.

EAST BUDLEIGH, CO. DEVON, ENGLAND.

ALL SAINTS CHURCH, EAST BUDLEIGH, CO. DEVON, ENGLAND.

THE CONANT FAMILY IN ENGLAND.

A. John Conant,[1] with whom the authentic genealogy of the family begins, lived in the parish of East Budleigh, Devonshire, England, but was probably born about the year 1520 at Gittisham, some ten or twelve miles north-east. The Life of Dr. John Conant, written about the year 1700, states that John Conant of East Budleigh "was descended from ingenuous parents of Gittisham, near Honiton, whose ancestors for many generations had been fixed here but were originally of French extraction." Gittisham (pronounced Gitsham) is a small parish on the river Otter, between Honiton and Ottery St. Mary, and about fourteen miles from Exeter, the capital city of the county. In Domesday Book the name appears as Gidesham. A Roman road passed through the parish, traces of which may still be seen.

In the 13th year of the reign of Queen Elizabeth (1571), he was assessed for goods of the yearly value of £4.* In 1581 he was still taxed at East Budleigh, but in 1588 the tax was paid by his son, Richard, and it is probable that between these dates a transfer of property had taken place.

In 1577 John Conant and Edmond ffowler were church-wardens of East Budleigh. In those days the office of church-warden was of considerable importance, and only members of the leading families and such as were of recognized ability were elected to this important office.

John Conant was buried at East Budleigh, 30 Mch., 1596.† It is most unfortunate that many early Conant wills, proved in the court at Exeter, which might throw light on the ancestry of John Conant, are now missing. Although no legal evidence of the fact has yet been found, it seems likely that he was the

---

* Subsidy Rolls.
† Parish Registers of East Budleigh.

son of the John Conant who was buried at Gittisham 4 Sept.,
1559.* In the 15th year of the reign of King Henry VIII.
(1523), John Conant, senior, of Gittisham, was assessed for
£7 in goods, and John Conant, junior, for £4 in goods.† The
latter was perhaps the one who died in the year 1559.

In the Will Office at Exeter there is a copy of the will of
John Connante, of Gittisham, dated 21 June, proved 20 Sept.,
1586. The testator desires to be buried in Gittisham church-
yard. He bequeaths his "cubborde" to Nicholas, his son, and
his "table board" to John, his son; to Matthew, his son, he
leaves a bed. The residue is left to Marie, his wife, who is
sole executrix. Persons named Smith, Crabb, Turling and Vann
are also mentioned. No record of the burial of this John is to be
found in the Parish Registers of Gittisham, although careful
search has been made. A Nicholas Conant was baptized at
Gittisham in the year 1574; if he was the one mentioned in
the will it indicates that the testator died before middle age.
Or, if this was not the Nicholas of the will—and this is the
only ground for supposing the testator died in middle age—it
may be that the son John mentioned in the will was John Conant of East Budleigh, and the testator was the John Conant,
junior, of the Subsidy Roll. In this case the testator must
have died at an advanced age, say eighty-five or six years.
And the burial of the John Conant in 1559 may be that of the
John Conant, senior, mentioned in the Subsidy Roll in 1523.

The ancestry of John Conant, of East Budleigh, may never
be established by legal evidence, but the fact that his parents
lived in Gittisham, and the similarity of names, renders it probable that he was the son of the John Conant who was buried
1559, or the one who died 1586.

Child of JOHN CONANT :—

B. Richard.

B. Richard[2] (*John*) was probably born in the parish of
East Budleigh, about the year 1548. In 1588 he was assessed
for lands in East Budleigh of the yearly value of £4.‡ Richard

* Parish Registers of Gittisham.
† Subsidy Rolls.
‡ Subsidy Rolls.

Conant and Henry Cowde were church-wardens of the parish in 1606, and in 1616 Richard Conant again filled the office. In the year 1600 he paid a "malt rate" of 4s. In 1630 he is rated at 2s. 6d., his rating being next to the highest in the parish, which was paid by a member of the Arscot family, and the only other who paid over one shilling.

The parish of East Budleigh gives its name to the Hundred. It is situated on the west side of the river Otter, about two miles from its mouth, and about fourteen miles south-east of Exeter. The manor belonged to Otterton priory, and in the year 1260 was valued at £13 13sh. 6d.; its mill alone then rented for £1 14sh. 4d. In 1337 the lordship was granted to Hugh de Courtenay, Earl of Devon. In 1536 the manor and advowson of Budleigh belonged to the Benedictine Convent of St. Catherine of Polsoe, and in this year Margaret Trewe, Prioress of Polsoe, leased the rectory with the tithes to John Drake for fifty years at a rental of £26 17sh. 3d. In 1540 the manor and advowson came into possession of Richard Duke, Esq., who purchased from Henry VIII. The church of East Budleigh, dedicated to All Saints, and consecrated by Bishop Lacy about A. D. 1430, is situated on a hill behind the village. It consists of a nave and chancels, and north and south aisles. It is 80 feet long and 48½ feet broad, and the tower, containing five bells, is 72 feet high. In the east window are to be seen the arms of Courtenay, Bishop Lacy, St. George, Holland and Bonville. The pew ends are curiously carved with arabesques, figures, heads and the armorial bearings of local families, among them Ralegh, St. Clere, Grenville, Arscot, Ford, Courtenay and others. The first vicar was Stephen de Budleigh, admitted 11 July, 1261, on presentation of the Prioress and Convent of Polsoe (see Oliver's *Ecclesiastical Antiquities of Devon*).

Sir Walter Ralegh was born at Hays House, in East Budleigh, and his father was one of the church-wardens in 1561. The tales of adventure of Ralegh and Sir Francis Drake—for the Drakes were also connected with this parish—must have had an important influence in leading Roger and Christopher Conant to embark for America.

The Marriage Registers of East Budleigh lack the names of females from the beginning to 1605; but the date of Richard Conant's marriage is given: "4 Feb., 1578." Luckily this omission is supplied by the Registers of Colyton where the marriage took place. There it is recorded that "Rychard Counnett, the sonne of John Counnett, of Easte Budleye, was wedded unto Agnes Clarke, the daught' of John Clarke, senior, of Collyton, the iiij. daye of ffebruary, 1578." Colyton is a market town of Devonshire, twenty-two miles east of Exeter and about eight miles east of East Budleigh.

The Manor of Colyton was part of the possessions of Henry Courtenay, Earl of Devon, and Marquis of Exeter, who was beheaded in 1538. His estates, of course, reverted to the Crown, and a number of the wealthy inhabitants of Colyton purchased from King Henry a portion of the manor. These citizens were enfeoffed by the King, who also granted them the management of fairs and markets. The name of John Clarke stands first on the patent from the King, and also appears on the patent of the second incorporation of enfeoffment, which was granted by Queen Mary. He d. 6th and was buried 9th Apr., 1585.* He m. 9th June, 1544,† Anne, daughter of William Macye, of Colyton, and their daughter Annes, or Agnes, was born 16th May, 1548.‡

Richard and Agnes Conant were buried on the same day, 22 Sep., 1630.§ Both are spoken of in the *Life of John Conant* as persons of "exemplary piety," and judging from what is known of the character of their children this was undoubtedly the case. His will, which is printed in full, is preserved in the Archdeaconry Court of Exeter, and was proved 13 Oct., 1631.

WILL OF RICHARD CONANT.

"In the name of God, Amen. on the twentieth day of November, in the year of our Lord God 1629. I, Richard Conant, of East Budleigh, in the countie of Devon, yeoman,

---

* Parish Registers of Colyton.
† Ibid.
‡ Ibid.
§ Parish Registers of East Budleigh.

knowing the certenty of death, but of the time and hour most
uncertain, and therefore preparing myselfe ready whensoever
it shall please the Lord to call mee out of this transitorie life
into his celestiall kingdome, whereunto p'swaded by faith I shall
aspire in and by the death, meritts and previous bload sheding
of Christ Jesus, my onlie Lord and Saviour and Redeemer, doe
by this my Testament containing therein my last will in manner and forme as followeth: ffirst I bequeath my soule into ye
hands of Almightie God and my body for Christian buriall, and
as touching my worldlie goods: ffirst I give and bequath unto
my grandchild, Richard Conant, sonne of Richard Conant, of
East Budleigh, my silver Bowle, only reserveing the use thereof to my wife dureinge her life tyme: Item, I give and bequeath unto my sonne, John Conant, my silke grogren dublet
and turkie grogren hose: Item, unto my sonne, Robert Conant,
I give and bequeath my second best clokes and myne other apparell (except the worst) and the other before mencioned.
Item, I give the poor of the parish of Eastbudleigh the sume
of twentie shillings to bee disposed according to the discretion
of myne executrix: Item, I give and bequeath further unto
my sonne, John Conant, my gold ringe with a Turkies in it:
Item, I give and bequeath unto Sarah Conant, daughter unto
my sonne, Roger Conant, the sume of five pounds: Item, I
give and bequeath unto Jane Knowles and Susan Knowles,
children unto my daughter, Jane Knowles [Knowles erased
and Wotton written over it], namely to each of them five
pounds to bee paid unto them at their day of marriage if soe
they marrie with the consent and likeing of their friends, par-
ticularlie of the fatherinlawe, Phillippe Wotton, of their
mother, and onkle, John Conant. If they marry not: to be
paid untoe them they being of the age of thirty yeares. And
if in the meantyme, before their said age or marriage, it hap-
pen that any of them dye, then that her portion of ffive
pounds bee likewise paid to the sister surviveing: Item, I give
and bequeath unto all my childrens children (vizt. to every of
them in p'ticular except such as have a larger portion given
them) five shillings: All the residue of my goods, as well moveable as immoveable, or chattels whatsoever is myne or in me
for to give in Budleigh or elsewhere, my debts being paid funeralls discharged and respect had to my promise made to Phillippe Wotton, my sonneinlawe, and my daughter Jane, his
wife, I give and bequeath unto my said daughter Jane Wotton
(onelie reserving the use thereof unto my wife, Agnes Conant,
during her life tyme), and doe make my said daughter whole
and sole executrix: And I doe also ordaine my sonne, John
Conant, of Lymington, in Somersetshire, to be this my overseer to see this my will and testament to be fulfilled. In wit-

ness whereof, I, the aforesaid Richard Conant, have hereunto put my hand, seale, even the day and yeare first above written.

(Signed) *Richard Conant*

Witness:
JOHN CONANT,
ROBERT CONANT.

Probatu fuit huoi testatum apud exon 13 die mense Octobris 1631. Coram mgre Robto Parsons clerico, etc.

The inventory, which is too long to print in full, is also preserved. As of interest for comparison with values of the present day, many of the items are here given. The inventory was taken 30 Sept., 1631, by John Richards (probably a son-in-law), Robert Conant and John Leye; the total amount was £129 14s. 4d.

	lbs. s. d.
"Imprimis: his owne and his wifes wearing apparel,	xx.-00-0
Item: 13 old sheepe and 4 lambs, - - - -	v.-iii.-iiij.
In the Hall:	
Item: one long tableborde, 1 square tableborde, 2 formes, 3 chairs and 6 joynt stools, - - -	0-xxxiij.-0
Item: 1 muskett with all its furniture belonging to the same, - - - - - - - - -	0-xxvi.-iiij.
Item: 1 Iron Barr and 1 Clarke bill, - - -	0-iiij.-iiij.
In the new parlour:	
Item: 1 feather bed, 2 feather boulsters, 2 feather pillows, 1 yard of blankett and one coverlett, -	vi.-0-0
Item: a Laundry Cobbert and 2 Coupetts [?] -	0-xxv.-0
Item: an Eargon [?] Salte and Cups, the moity of 1 mapp, sand glasses with some other small things,	0-vi.-0
Item: one Chair and Cushon, - - - - -	0-xvi.-0
In the old parlour:	
Item: 1 standing bedsted and 1 trundle bedsted, xx. s., one tablebord, vi. s., - - - - -	0-xxvi.-0
In the Buttery:	
Item: 2 dozen and fouer of pewter dishes, 4 porringers, 3 saussers, 1 plate, 1 bason, all of pewter,	0-xxxvi.-0
Item: 4 pewter Cupes, 2 Saltes, one paint pott, 3 Chamber potts, all of them of pewter, - -	0-x.-0
Item: 3 dozzen of Tranchers, - - - -	0-iij.-0
Item: 6 brasse Candlesticks, - - - - -	0-x.-0
Item: 1 pessel and morter, - - - - -	0-v.-0
Item: 6 Stonnige Fuggs [jugs?] and cups, - -	0-i.-0
Item: 1 pipe, 3 hogsheads, 5 beare barrells, -	0-xxii.-0

lbs. s. d.

In the Shoppe next to the Hall:

Item: 2 beames and skales with some brass and leadden waights, - - - - - - -   0-v.-0

Item: one Counter, a chest, the shelves with some other odd implements, - - - - -   0-x.-viij.

In the longe Entery and in the Kitchen:

Item: 2 Cubbords, - - - - - - -   0-x.-0

In the brewinge House:

Item: 1 pare of Iron Racks, 1 pare of And Irons, 2 hearth irons and 6 spetts, - - - - -   0-xxviij.-vì.

Item: 2 hand Irons, 2 fire picks, 1 fire pan, 3 little iron dogs, a flesh pike, a frying pan, a gridiron, -   0-v.-iiij.

Item: 1 dozen wooden dishes and one dozen of spoones, - - - - - - - - -   0-ij.-0

Item: 1 Breweinge fornace, - - - - -   0-L.-0

Item: 3 brasse pots and 2 brass posnetts, [?] -   0-xliij.-0

Item: 3 brasse Caldrons, skillets and a brasse ladle,   0-xx.-0

Item: 5 breweing fates [vats] and 1 boate trundle,   0-xv.-0

Item: 3 dowe [?] and a bowle, - - - - -   0-v.-iiij.

Item: a Clever, a shreeding knife, 2 lettle berrells with some earthen potts, - - - -   0-iiij.-0

In the Milk house:

Item: 10 brass milk pannes with some other old brasse there, - - - - - - - -   iiij-ij.-0

Item: one still to distill water w'thall, - -   0-vj.-0

Item: 4 cheese fates [vats], - - - -   0-ij.-0

In the Weaving Shopp:

Item: 2 old bedsteads, 2 doust [?] beds, 2 doust boulsters with sheets, blanketts, and coverletts,   0-xx.-00

Item: 2 old Coffers with some bords and other small triffells, - - - - - - - -   0-ij.-0

In the new parlour:

Item: one silver bowle, - - - - - -   0-L.-0

Item: 5 silver spoones, - - - - - - -   0-xxviij.-0

Item: 5 glass bottles, - - - - - -   0-v.-0

Item: 1 little Table with a liberry table and 2 little formes, - - - - - - - - -   0-xxij-0

Item: 2 Chests and one Coffer, - - - -   0-xiiij.-0

Item: 2 great deskes and one lesser one with small things in them, - - - - - - -   0-xxvij.-viii.

Item: one greate byble and a deske, - - -   0-xxx.-0

Item: all other bookes, - - - - -   iij.-0-0

In the Chamber over the Shopp:

Item: one bedsted and vallens, a feather bed and a flocke bed, 1 feather boulster, 2 feather pillows, 1 blankett and 1 couerlett, - - - - -   0-xl.-0

Item: Eleven pare of shitts and 4 pare of pilotyes,   iiij.-xxi.-0

Item: 3 large table Clothes & 4 lesser table clothes,

	lbs. s. d.
2 dozen of Table napkins, - - - - -	iij.-viij.-0

Item: 1 warminge pan, vi. s., a sherhook and other
small things, ij. s.,   -   -   -   -   -   -   -   0-viij.-0
In the Chamber over the Hall:
Item: 1 hamper with old iron and other things in
the same,   -   -   -   -   -   -   -   -   0-vi.-viij.
Item: 2 Swords, with an Alment [helmet?], Revett,
an old edd [head] peece and some small things,   0-vi.-viij.
In the Chamber over the entry:
Item: 2 pare verginalls,   -   -   -   -   -   -   0-viij.-0
In the small Chamber:
Item: 2 Sidsaddles and one Couring [covering],   -   0-xiij.-iiij.
Item: a Skaymer, a cheese Racke, etc.,   -   -   -   0-iiij.iiij.
Item: a crosbowe and bender,   -   -   -   -   0-v.-0

*   *   *   *   *   *   *   *

Item: all the small tooles in the toole house, -   -   0-x.-0
Item: some tooles fitt for the use of Husbandry,   0-vi.-viij.
Item: some plane stuffs, a manger, some Racks, 2
ladders, draught fatts, troughs, some peeces of
Timber and all other things about the Court,   -   0-0-ix.
Item: Certaine Implements belonging to a Mill, 0-xxvj.-viij.
Item: three Cellings [?] with bynches to them, a
new millston and Certain other things, -   -   -   ix.-0-0
Item: Certain debts dew unto Richard Conant, now
deceased,   -   -   -   -   -   -   -   -   -   viij.-0-0 "

Children of RICHARD and AGNES (CLARKE) CONANT:—

Joan, baptized 20 Jan., 1579-80; m. —— Richards.
C. Richard, baptized 21 Feb., 1581-2.
D. Robert, b. ——.
    Jane, baptized 9 May, 1584; m. 18 Sept., 1609, Thomas Knowles;
    had Jane, Susan and perhaps others. She m. 2nd, 19 April,
    1626, Philip Wotton; had Philip, who·d. Dec., 1627, and per-
    haps others.
E. John, baptized 18 Mch., 1585-6.
    Thomas, baptized 30 April, 1587, supposed to have d. y.
    Christopher, baptized 13 June, 1588. In 1609 he went to Lon-
    don where he became an apprentice to Thomas Allen, a
    grocer, and after an apprenticeship of seven years was ad-
    mitted to the freedom of the Grocers' Company on 14 Mch.,
    1616*. The Grocers' Company is one of the twelve Great
    Livery Companies of London, and was incorporated by King
    Edward III. in 1345. The next record of him is found at
    Shobrook, Devon, 14 Sept., 1619, where "Christopher Conant,
    merchant, of London, and Mrs. Anne Wilton were married."
    On 20 Jan., 1619-20, he signed the composition bond of his

* Records of the Grocers' Company.

brother, John, and is there described as "grocer, of the parish of St. Lawrence, Jewry, London." In 1623 he came to Plymouth, Mass., in the ship Ann, and shared in the division of land in that year. He had one acre "lying beyond the brooke toward Strawberry hill."[*] From this it may be conjectured that he brought no family, as, if he had had a wife or children his share of land should have been larger. In 1627 he was not at Plymouth, for he had no share in the division of cattle in that year. Possibly he was at Salem with his brother, Roger; but if in England he returned, for he was on the first jury for criminal trial in this country, impanneled for the trial of Walter Palmer for manslaughter, Nov., 1630. This is the last record of him found. He may have returned to England, or gone southward, but if he had died in Massachusetts some record of the fact would most likely have been preserved.

Roger, baptized 9 Apr., 1592. The emigrant to America. See beyond. _(? oc.)_

C. **Richard**[3] (*Richard, John*), baptized at East Budleigh, 21 Feb., 1581-2; m. 18 Sept., 1609, Jane Slade, and was buried at East Budleigh 3 Sept., 1625. His will was proved in the Prerogative Court of Canterbury, Somerset House, London (9 *Hele*). The following is an abstract:

Richard Conant, the younger, of East Budleigh, co. Devon. Will dated 1 Sept., 1625; administration granted 3 Jan., 1625-6, to Jane Conant, the relict, and Robert Conant, the brother. "My lands in Culliton, called Chaple lands, to be sold to satisfy claim of Thomas periam for £76, or else the sd lands to be granted to him. My lands at Poole Hayes, now in possession of George Mico for term of his life and that of his wife. My brothers, John Conant and Robert Conant, and my brothers-in-law, Wm. Slade and Roger Slade, to sell the fee simple of my said lands at Culliton and Poole Hayes to pay my debts, and the overplus to be employed for the benefit of such of my children as they shall think fit. Witnesses, Richard Swetland, Robert Conant, Jane Knowles, Elizabeth Duke, Johan Richards."

Children of RICHARD and JANE (SLADE) CONANT:

Jane, baptized 16 June, 1611, at East Budleigh.
Martha, baptized 30 Nov., 1615, (d. 15 May, 1644?).

---

[*] Records of Plymouth Colony.

F. Mary, baptized 20 Jan., 1617-18.
G. Richard, baptized 10 Feb., 1621-2.
    Sarah, baptized 30 Mch., 1624.

D. Robert[3] (*Richard, John*), b. ——; was of Bicton, a
parish adjoining East Budleigh. He m. at East Budleigh 14
Oct., 1607, Elizabeth Morris, who was buried 1 Apr., 1654.
Administration granted on her estate 19 June, 1654, to her son,
Richard Conant, of Bicton (*P. C. C. Adm'ons* 1554, *fo.* 92).
He was buried 12 May, 1638, at Bicton. His will, dated May,
1638, was probated 23 May, 1638, in the Archidiaconal Court
of Exeter. He leaves most
of his estate to his oldest
son, John Conant, clerk, with   (1629.)
legacies to his son, Richard Conant, and servant, Jane Upham.
     Children of ROBERT and ELIZABETH (MORRIS) CONANT:—

H. John, born 18 Oct., 1608 (Life).
    Richard, buried 5 Nov., 1616.
    Thomas, buried 14 Nov., 1616.
I. Richard, b. ——.

E.   John[3] (*Richard, John*), baptized 18 Mch., 1585-6,* at
East Budleigh, Devon. He was matriculated at Exeter College, Oxford, 15 Nov., 1605; B. A., 5 May, 1609; elected Probationer 30 June, 1611, in place of Vilvaine, and admitted 5
July following; full Fellow 10 July, 1612; B. D., (2 Dec., 1619)
or 28 June, 1620.† The resignation of his Fellowship is as follows: "Ego Johannes Conant sacrae theologiae Baccalaureus,
et scholaris perpetuus Collegii Exon infra universitatem Oxon,
omne meum ius et interesse quod habeo in dicto Collegio, in
manus venerabilis viri Johannis Prideaux sacrae theologiae
Professoris Rectoris dicti Collegii et scholarium eiusdem Collegii in his scriptis resigno. In cuius rei testimonium pre-
sentibus manu mea propria nomen subscripsi meum et sigillum
aposui. Data tricesimo die mensis Junii A. D. 1620.
                    (Signed)   JOHANNES CONANT."

* Registers of All Saints, East Budleigh.
† Boase's *Reg. Col. Exon.*

THE
WOE AND WEALE
OF
GODS PEOPLE.

DISPLAYED
IN A SERMON PREACHED
before the Honourable Houſe of
COMMONS at their late ſo-
lemn Humiliation on *Iuly* 26.
1643.

By *Iohn Conant* B.D. and Paſtour of
Limington in Somerſet-ſhire.

Publiſhed by Order of that Houſe.

LAMENT. 3. 31, 32.
For the Lord will not caſt off for ever. But though he cauſe
grief, yet will he have compaſſion according to the multitude
of his mercies.

LONDON,
Printed by G. M. for *Chriſtopher Meredith* at the Signe of
the Crane in *Pauls* Church-yard. 1643.

On Dec. 30, 1619, he was instituted Rector of Lymington, a country parish near Ilchester, Somersetshire, on the presentation of Sir *John Conant.*
(1629.)
Henry Rosewell (Public Record Office, Institution Books, Vol. 2, p. 70), and on the 20 January following compounded for the First Fruits of the living, the sureties of his bond being his brothers, Christopher and Roger. The rectorship of this parish was the first preferment of Cardinal Wolsey. The appointment to a living in the gift of Sir Henry Rosewell is not without its significance, as Rosewell, or Rowswell, is well known to students of Massachusetts' history, his name standing first among the grantees in the Patent from the Council of Plymouth. It indicates that Conant had already espoused the cause of the Puritans. He remained at Lymington until the troubles of the civil war forced him to leave the parish, when he repaired to London; this was probably toward the close of the year 1642. During his enforced absence his nephew, Rev. John Conant, D. D., then Fellow of Exeter, attempted to perform his duties for him, but was also driven away. It is not likely that he returned to Lymington, and on Nov. 24, 1645, Robert Bryan was instituted in the rectory as his successor.

On July 26, 1643, he preached a sermon before the House of Commons for which he received the thanks of the House with a request that he print the sermon. The sermon was printed in 1643 and copies of it are now excessively rare. The facsimile of the title page here given is from a copy now in possession of the compiler. As it is probably the earliest printed work by a Conant, full particulars are here given. The pages are $7\frac{1}{4}$ in. x $5\frac{3}{4}$ in. in size. There are 28 leaves, or 56 pages. The signatures are A, B, C, D, E, F and G, with four leaves to each letter.

Signature A 1, r°, is blank.

Signature A 1, v°, the order "by the House of Commons, that Master Rous do from this House give thanks unto Master Conant, for the great pains he took in the Sermon he preached (at the intreaty of the House) at S. Margaret in the Citie of Westminster, being a day of publike humiliation, and they desire him to print his Sermon."

Signature A 2, r°, is the title page.

Signature A 2, v°, is blank.

Signature A 3, r°,—A 4, v°. The dedication "To the Honourable House of Commons now assembled in Parliament. * *
* * your hearts being ingaged to approach nigh unto God,
your resolutions and endeavours fixed, with all possible self-
deniall, to advance his honour, to promote his cause, to
establish his truth, further the much desired happiness of
Church and State." Signed "John Conant."

Signature B 1, r°,—G 3, v°. The Sermon.

"A Sermon preached at a late Fast before the Honourable
House of Commons." (paged 1-46.)

Signature G 4, r°, is blank.

Signature G 4, v°, order by the "Commons House of Parliament that M. Rous do give thanks to Mr. Covant, (sic) and
Mr. Blackstone to Master Simpson, for the great paines they
tooke in the Sermons they this day preached * * *."

ABSTRACT OF THE SERMON.

p. 1.   Jer. 30 7.

"*Alas, for that day is great, so that none is like it:
it is even the time of Jacobs trouble; but he shall be
saved out of it.*"

"These words are the words of the Lord, which he
spake by *Jeremiah* the Prophet, concerning *Israel* and
Judah * * *. He prophesied * * * under five
Kings * * *.

p. 2. "He is in his writings Historicall, Propheticall, Reprehensorie, Hortatorie, Deploratorie, Consolatorie. 1.
Historicall, recording the acts and occurrences of the
times * * *. 2. Propheticall, foretelling partly what
should betide this people * * *. 3. Reprehensorie,
crying out against the idolatries, oathes, falshoods, and
other abominations of the land. 4. Hortatorie, earnestly
perswading them to forsake their former evill ways *
* *. 5. Deploratorie, bewailing the heinous and horrible transgressions * * *. 6. Consolatorie, intermix-

ing sweet revivings and refreshings, for supporting the drooping spirits of Gods contrite ones * * *.

p. 3. "A specimen of these two later we have in the words of my Text, which are * * * A mixture of dolefull and joyfull tidings. And these are the Parts thereof, namely: 1, a Lamentation * * *. 2, a Consolation * * *.

p. 4. "It is even the time of Jacobs trouble * * *.

p. 5. "There is * * * *a threefold great day.* First, the time of Christs first coming and continuance here on earth * * *. Secondly, the time of Christs second coming * * *. Thirdly, the time of Gods more especially visiting or punishing a sinfull people *in this life,* bringing on them some heavy calamitie, or great destruction, * * *.

p. 6. "That day will evidently appear to be a great day * *.

p. 7. "That day, on which God visits his people by the hand of their enemies, being a great day, how great is their inadvertency, how brutish their stupidity, who overlook & passe by that day, as if not worthy to be regarded. * * *.

p. 9. "Neither is there any cause of questioning such Gods proceedings against his own Church, and people, for, 1. There he doth more especially love and therefore there he will assuredly visit * * *. 2. There God more especially hates likewise. As he loves their persons, so he hates their sinnes * * *.

p. 10. "3. God is very tender and jealous of his own honour * * *.

p. 11. "This consideration calleth on us for dispositions suitable there unto: namely, for great Preparation before that day cometh, and great Observation when it is come * * *.

p. 12. "As for the parts of Preparation, I shall name but two, viz: Repentance and Prayer * * *.

p. 14. "But great dayes call also for great Observation, especially if such great dayes be great dayes of affliction. And here three things are especially to be observed, namely: 1. What is done. 2. By whom it is done. 3. To what end it is done * * *.

p. 16. "Dayes of affliction betiding the Church of God, are unto Gods people justly days of mourning and lamentation * * *.

p. 22. "Touching the afflicted condition of Gods Church at this day * * *. I shall but intreat you to look over the Maps of *Germanie*, *Ireland*, and *England*, you have the summe of what I would say: * * * you shall find there a roll like that in Ezekiel, written within and without in capitall letters; and with a pen dipped in bloud, and the writings as there, lamentations, and mourning, and woe. In *Germanie* and *Ireland* (for I joyne those together), what robberies, and spoiles, what sackings, and burnings, what devastations, and depopulations have there been? what horrible oathes, and blasphemies, what ravishing of wives, and deflowring of virgins, what irreverent carriages toward the gray-head? * * *

p. 23. "But I return ere I goe too far, this field being too wide for me to walk through it * * *. As for *England*, we have here had our Aceldama's also, the sword having well nigh gone through the land * * * and many thousands having fallen by the dirt thereof * * *. The judgement of the sword hath its beginning amongst us * * * were it drawn against a forraigne enemie, it were more eligible, more tollerable; but civil war is of all els most dangerous & dolefull, when within the same Princes dominions * * * .

p. 26. "Our sins as well as other mens, have acted their part in provoking Gods indignation against the land; and is it not requisite that our sorrow and humiliation should do their part likewise in appeasing the same? * * *

p. 28. "The troubles or afflictions of Gods people are not perpetuall. As they have a day of trouble, so also of salvation and deliverance * * *.

p. 35. "As duties of Humiliation concern every soul here present, so also duties of Reformation, as we all desire to make and maintain our peace with God, and enjoy his favour, which is the very life of our souls. Howbeit you who are called to be our Senators and Worthies in the Parliament are more especially concerned herein, and that in a two-fold relation. First, as by your example you are to encourage others in duties of Reformation. Secondly, as by wholesome Ordinances and Sanctions you are to compel others thereto * * *.

p. 37. "I desire to mention one or two generals whence, I conceive, abuses mostly in Church and State do either take their first rise, or at least are to much fomented thereby. That in the State seems to me to be the want of due execution of wholesome lawes enacted.

p. 38. "That other generall in the Church, I can but briefly touch at neither. I conceive the chief Hydra of abuses there to lodge in the Ministerie.

p. 41. "Deliverance corporall * * *.
"Deliverance spirituall * * *.
"Deliverance eternal * * *.

p. 44. "Grounds of apprehending deliverance neer approaching, taken from the Church and people of God, may be these: 1. When in the way of humiliation they throw themselves at Gods footstoole * * *.

p. 45. "2. When they do renew their covenant with God to hear his voice * * *. 3. When they do wholly rest themselves on Gods protection * * *. But (to conclude) whether deliverance be neer at hand, or further off, certain it is that, 1. The rage and power of the adversarie is limited * * *. 2. The draught of affliction is measured * * *. 3. The strength of Gods people is fitted thereto * * *.

p. 46. "4. Whatever extremeties they are put to, it shall assuredly be well with those that fear God * * *. 5. Such have a promise from Christ himself * * *. But contrariewise, *The end of transgressours is that they shall be destroyed together*."

According to Wood, the Oxford historian, he also published a sermon the same year on Lamentations iii. 31. 32; but apparently Wood is mistaken, as this text appears on the title page of the Fast Sermon of July 26. There is, however, in the Library of the British Museum, an imperfect copy, lacking all after p. 8, of a sermon on Isaiah xiii. 24. 25. In 1644 he wrote a preface to the *Thesaurus Biblicus* published in that year by R. Barnard, Rector of Batcombe, co. Somerset, and a noted Puritan.

Three MS. sermons preached by John Conant in Oxford, 1618-19, on 1 Kings xxi. 20; one on Psalms iv. 1; one on 2 Chron. xxxv. 6; and one in Latin on Mal. ii. 7, are preserved in the "Rawlinson MSS." in the Bodleian Library.

In 1643 he was constituted by Parliament one of the Assembly of Divines* which met at Westminster July 1, of that year, and remained in session till Feb., 1649. The "Confession of Faith" and the "Catechisms" recommended by this Assembly and adopted by Parliament, are to this day the standard of the Presbyterians in England and the United States, and are recognized by the Congregationalists, as a body, as substantially expressing their doctrines.

While he was in London he acted as Curate of St. Botolph, Aldersgate, but about Apr., 1646, he became Rector of St. Thomas à Becket, Salisbury, co. Wilts, where he remained till his death.

A view of his house in the Close of Salisbury is here presented, together with a description of the same taken from a contemporary MS. belonging to the Dean and Chapter of Salisbury; on the same page is a view of St. Thomas Church:

"A survey of certaine houses with gardens, orchards and Backsides to them belonging, together with certaine p'cells of Lande called by the name of Options lyeing and being in the Close of ye Canons of the Cathedrall Church of the Virgin Mary of New Sarum, in the county of Wilts, late parcell of the possessions or late belongings to the late Deane and Chapter of the sayd Cathedrall. Made and taken by us whose names are hereunto subscribed in the moneth of June, 1649. By virtue of a Commision to us graunted (grounded upon an

---

* Fuller's *Church History*, Vol. xi., p. 198.

HOUSE IN THE CLOSE OF SALISBURY.
(Once the residence of John Conant, B. D.)

ST THOMAS À BECKET, SALISBURY, CO. WILTS. ENGLAND.

Act of the Com'ons of England assembled in Parliament for the abolishing of Deanes, Deanes and Chapters, Cannons, P'bends and other Offices and Titles of and belonging to any Cathedrall or Collegiate Church or Chappell within England and Wales) under the hands and scales of five or more of the Trustees In the same Act named and appoynted:

* * * * * * *

The Mansion Howse of Doctor Ogborne one of the late Canons now inhabited by and in the possession of Mr. John Conant Minister of St. Thomas Church in Sarum:

This Howse hath for its entrance a great gate and conteyneth a large Hall a Kitchen a lowe gallery about 80 foot long and 9 foot broad two larders two woodhouses a pantry waynescoted three cellers two waynescoted Parlors a Buttery 12 chambers whereof 4 are waynescoted eight other rooms besides Garretts. A stable conteyning six Bayes of building two gardens with an Orchard conteyning one Acre all which are worth perannum— } XVIII. £

The premises are bounded with the highway or Common Passage between the Cathedrall Churchyard and the sayd Howse on the Eastpart with the river of Avon on the West parte with a Ditch betweene the Deanry and the same howse on the South part and with the howse and Orchard now in the possession of Mr. Richard Davyds on the North.

The premises we find to be graunted by the Committee of Wills (Wiltshire) unto the sayd John Conant in Augmentacon for his better livelyhood * * *.

One peece of pasture ground abutting upon the Close Wall on the South upon a ditch severing it from the high way that leadeth to Harnham Gate on the East by another ditch sevring it from the walke planted with young Elmes that leads to the howse that did lately belong to D'cor Hinchman on the West and by another ditch sevring it from another peece of pasture lyeing on the North thereof being another Option appertayneing to one of the late Canons through wch there is a foot path and Cartway that leadeth to the howse lately belonging to Doctor Hinchman conteyneth p'estim' two acres more or less and is worth per annum— } £ s IIII. X.

Memorandum that in this Close or Option is yearly kept a Sheepe Fayre upon the first Tuesday after Pentecost graunted by Lease from the Deane and Chapter to Roger Upton.

One other peece of pasture ground abutting upon the last before named peece of pasture on ye South upon the highway leading to Harnham Gate on the North and East and upon a ditch lyeing before the howse that was lately D'cor Thorneborough's on the West being another option through wch lyeth a way leadeing to the sevrall howses lately belonging to D'cor Thorneborowe D'cor Mason and Doctor Hinchman conteyneth p'estemat one Acre more or lesse and is worth p'annum— $\left. \begin{array}{cc} £ & s \\ 2 & x. \end{array} \right.$

Memorandum that within this Close or option there is an other faire or fayre for Cattle yearly kept upon the first Tuesday after Pentecost and the proffitts are graunted by Lease from the Deane and Chapter to Roger Upton.

Memorandums

That the before ment'o'ed peece of pasture ground conteyneing one two acres valued at iiii. £ x. s. and one other peece of pasture ground conteyneing one Acre valued at ij. £ x. s. are likewise in the possession of Mr. John Conant one other of the ministers of the sayd Citty given him likewise by the sayd Committee for his augmentac'on.

Examts & Approb^ts per	WALT. FOY
Will: Webb Supvs^r Gen^els	JO: SQUIBB
1649	CHR: WEARE
	GEO: FAIRLEY.

Although Wood says nothing of his character or ability, it is evident that he was a man of high character and much ability; for at this time (1649), on the death of Dr. George Hakewill, Rector of Exeter College, the choice of a new Rector lay between him and his nephew, John Conant. But he absolutely declined the position, and the latter was elected.

He d. 13* and was bur. 15 Apr., 1653.†   In the chancel of

---

* Miscellaneous Collections of Malachi Conant, B. D., Rawlinson MSS., Bodleian Library.
† Parish Registers of St. Thomas, Salisbury.

St. Thomas Church, until the restoration of that church in 1868, was to be seen a flat stone bearing the inscription, "John Conant, died 1653." His funeral sermon (on Matt. xxv. 23) was preached by Mr. Gower. A copy of the sermon is to be found in the Rawlinson MSS., Bodleian Library.

WILL OF JOHN CONANT.

John Conant, of the Close of Sarum, Wilts, clerk, weak in body, etc. Dated 8 Apr., 1653; proved 26 Sept., 1653, by the executors. My dwelling house in the Close of Sarum to my eldest son, John Conant, to whom also lands called Options, if he will buy them. Lands, etc., in Huntspill [Huntsfell?], co. Somerset, to my son, Samuel Conant, my executors to take the rents for 7 years for his better maintenance at the University. To my sons, Richard Conant and Malachi Conant, the lease demised to my brother, Malachi Dewdney, merchant, and Edward Pele, clerk. My daughter, Sarah Conant, £200 at age 21, or marriage. My two sisters, Mrs. Richards and Mrs. Wootton, 20 shillings each. My son-in law, Timothy Sacheverell. Poor of Budley, Devon, where I was born, 20s., poor of New Sarum, 40s. The residue to my friends and executors, Mr. John Strickland, of the Close of Sarum, clerk, the aforesaid Malachi Dewdney and Timothy Sacheverell, and William Stone, of New Sarum, Gent. Witnesses, Richard Combe, John powell, John Vining and Ambrose Ringwood.

(P. C. C. 285 Brent.)

Children of JOHN and —— (DEWDNEY) CONANT:—

J. John.

Samuel, b. —— 1627. He was admitted into Emanuel College Cambridge, 15 Jan., 1645-6; appointed by Board of Visitors, Fellow of Exeter Coll., Oxford, 20 July, 1648; B. A. 26 May, 1649; allowed to incept 29 Apr., 1652; M. A. and B. D. 8 Apr., 1657.* In 1657 he was one of the Proctors of the

1657.

University. Professor Burrows states that he was a delegate of Visitors, 1649, but therein seems to confound Samuel with his cousin, John, then Rector of Exeter.† He was removed from his Fellowship 1662; presented by the University to the Rectory of Brown Candover, Hants; was Chaplain to Dr. Reynolds, Bishop of Norwich. In 1662 he was instituted

---

* Boase's *Reg. Col. Exon.*

† Burrows' *Register of the Parliamentary Visitors*, p. 501.

Rector of Litchet Matravers, Dorset, on the expulsion of Thomas Rowe for non-conformity. In 1673 he was presented to the Rectory of Child Ockford, Dorset; and in 1704 or 1705 to the Rectory of Holy Trinity, Dorchester, which he resigned 1706. On Jan. 24, 1695, he was elected Rector of Exeter College, by the votes of five Fellows who had been expelled for adhering to Dr. Arthur Bury, but never got possession. (See Boase's *Reg. Col. Exon.*; Cassan's *Bishops of Salisbury*, iii. 149; Wood's *Life*, p. cxx., *Athenæ*, iv. 397; Hutchins' *Dorset*, iii. 333, 334, iv. 84.) As is learned from a contemporary letter, he d. 18 Nov., 1719, having been Rector of Litchet Matravers for 57 years. He left £10 towards building a front gate for Exeter Col., and some books to the College Library, among which is an annotated copy of Prince's *Worthies of Devon*. He was buried 21 Nov., 1719, in Litchet Matravers churchyard, where his tomb still exists. The tombstone bears a coat of arms (gules, ten billets or) and a long inscription in Latin.

Richard, living 1677. (See will of Roger Conant.)

K. Malachi.

A daughter, name unknown, who married Timothy Sacheverell.

Sarah, b. about 1637, in Lymington, Somersetshire, and d. 31 Aug., 1719. On 22 Mch., 1664-5, license was granted for her marriage with "Thomas Rowe, of Badcome, co. Somerset, clerk, bachelor, about 30;" she was then of Litchet Matravers. He is probably the same Thomas Rowe who was expelled from the Rectory of Litchet Matravers, co. Dorset, in 1662, for non-conformity. They had several children, among whom were:—

John, who was an "upholsterer" of London.

Samuel.

Thomas. Two very interesting letters written by him have been preserved. They are written on one large sheet of paper which is now in possession of Hon. Zalmon A. Storrs, of Hartford, Conn., and are here given in full:

Lichet, May 13, 1721. Dear Cousin Exercise Conant: I rejoice to hear by yr son's Letter yt you are yet in ye land of ye living and with yr son Josiah since ye death of yr dear wife. Tis a mercy yt you have such a son to be a comfort to ye in your old age. I'm pleased to hear yt ye things I sent you some years since came safe to yr hand and was of such singular use and service to you. My good old Uncle Conant (who bore a part in yt present to you) is now safe in Glory at ye age of above 91 wn. he departed this Life. as is my good hond mother too. I pray God I may follow both their pious steps who thro' faith and patience are now inheriting ye promises. My mother was near abt yt age when she died. I hope God will in mercy continue yr Life to a good old age: and yt twill be rendered to ye last comfortable to you. You

have experienced God's great care and goodness all your life
long hitherto and I hope he will not fail you to the last, but
be ye strength of ye Heart evn when ye Heart and strength
is ready to fail you, and also be yr portion forever. Another
Relative of ours Mr. Conant who was minister of Pool in this
country is suddenly dead too since my uncle Conant: who
has left a widow and 6 or 7 children. So death is at work we
see every where abt. us is a loud call to us to be also ready
and to see yt ye sting of death in particular be taken away
and yt wn our turn comes to pass throu' ye valley of death
we need feer no Ill. I have not heard from Dr. John Conant
lately, but I hear he is indiffert well. One of my Brothers
now in this country joins with me in wishing you and yours
all Health and Happiness and tendering our kind Respects &
Service to you &c. with wh desiring yr. Prayers, concludes in
great Haste from

Yr most Affectionate and truly
loving Kinsman and Servt
Thos. Rowe.

Directed ffor Mr. Exercise Conant at Mr. Josiah Conants
at Windham in New England.

Lichet, May 13, 1721.

Dear Cousin Josiah Conant: Yours bearing date Sep. 12,
1720, came safe to my hands tho' twas not rightly directed for
my brother John (ye upholster) lives at ye sign of ye Angel
by ffleet ditch near ffleet Bridge, Londn, and so any Letter
for ye future will come to us. I wondered for a great while
yt no letter came from you or yr ffather to give an account of
ye Recept of those things yt were sent some years since
which made me fear either ye things never came to hand or
yt else my good old cousin yr. ffather was not in ye Land of
ye living, but I learn to my great satisfaction yt both of ym
are not so: wch. I am glad of. My cousin yr ffather I find recd
all ye particulars of ye Things wch. I sent Him & there was
no mistake neither as to ye Persn. from whose Hands He had
ym. for (ye parcell of things being so small) I desired a ffriend
of mine in London to send ym for me in his things to Mr.
Pitt his correspondent wch accordingly he did and delivered
ym as desired safe ye same to yr ffather. I chose this way
of sending not knowing whether your ffather might be living, for no letter had come over ffrom him for a great while
before: But I'm glad to hear he is still alive and with you
I hope in tolerable good health for his great Age. I did not
know as I remember yt you had buried yr mother before ye
last made mention of it. I dont remember yt I've either
heard from you or writ to you since ye death of my good
old mother and Uncle, who departed this Life ye first of ym
on the last day of Augst & ye other on Nov. 18th 1719: they
both lived to a good old age viz. my uncle above 91 and my

mother was 82 years of Age. My brother Samuel enjoys not
his Health very well by reasn. of an Astma and dropsy & so
proposes to lead for ye future a county Life somewhere in
these parts—but my other Bro. John lives as I mentioned
above in London. Im at present here yet in this country but
propose in some little time to return to London where I have
Lodgings: for I'm not yet married: Dr. Conant lives still at
Kidlington near Oxford. I suppose you know he has buried
his wife some years since. His two Brothers lived both of
ym in London who were all pretty well when I heard from
ym last. You don't mention cousn in yr last what Business
at present you follow and wt yr family consists of &c. wch I
should be glad to know. I send this under cover to Dr. Cotton Mather according to yr order. You will remember me I
hope very kindly to all Relatves as if particularly named and
I hope we shall mutually share in each others Prayers & often meet yt way at ye throne of Grace. I am (being in Great
Haste) Dear Cousin
Yr most Affectionate & Truly
loving Kinsman and Servt.
THOS. ROWE.

F. **Mary**[4] (*Richard, Richard, John*), baptized at East
Budleigh 20 Jan., 1617-8. She came to New England and m. at
Salem, 12 April 1641, Hilliard Verin. He was son of Philip
Verin, of Salisbury, Wiltshire, England, and baptised there 3
Mch., 1621-2. He came to New England with his father in
1635; joined the first church of Salem 1648, and was chosen
deacon 1680. He was clerk of writs for Essex co. for several
years. In Oct., 1663, was appointed by the General Court,
commissioner of customs to enforce the observance of the
Navigation Act in Salem, Marblehead and Gloucester. May
18, 1664, he was chosen ensign of the Salem foot company.
During the last twenty-five years of his life he performed the
duties of clerk of writs, clerk of courts, register of deeds,
register of probate and collector of customs. The first books
of the Probate Records of Essex co. are in his hand-writing,
and begin in 1671. About 1650 he built the house later known
as the Henfield house, which stood back of the old First Meeting House at Salem, and which was taken down when the
Eastern Railroad tunnel was constructed about 1839. He d.
20 Dec., 1683, and was buried in the Charter street burying
ground, where his grave-stone still stands. Mary Verin survived her husband.

Children of HILLIARD and MARY (CONANT) VERIN:—

Mary, b. 15 Feb., 1641; m. 2 Apr., 1662, Samuel, son of George Williams, of Salem. Children:—Samuel, b. 26 Dec., 1662, d. y.; Samuel, b. 21 Nov., 1664; Mary, b. 7 Mch., 1667, d. y.; Hilliard, b. 26 Dec., 1668; George, b. 12 Feb., 1670, d. y.; Sarah, b. 15 July, 1672; Mary, b. 27 Nov., 1674, d. y.; Richard, b. 3 Mch., 1679; Mary, b. 2 Mch., 1681; Joshua, b. May, 1683; Nathaniel, b. 25 Jan., 1687.

Deliverance, b. 23 Feb., 1644; (m. Benjamin Marston. Their son, Benjamin, graduated at Harvard College, 1689, and was a prominent merchant of Salem; his son, Benjamin, was Sheriff of Essex, Justice of the Court of Common Pleas, and frequently Deputy to the General Court?)

Hilliard, b. Apr., 1649; m. 4 May, 1670, Hannah, dr. of Walter Price. He was a merchant of Barbadoes and was lost at sea between Nov., 1679, and June, 1680, leaving children.

Sarah, b. ——; m. 9 Dec., 1673, Deliverance, son of Elias Parkman, who d. 1681. She d. 14 Jan., 1687. Children:—Deliverance, b. 10 Jan., 1676, d. aged 5; Sarah, b. 29 July, 1678; Verin, b. 15 Feb., 1681.

Dorcas?

Abigail?

G. **Richard**[4] (*Richard, Richard, John*), baptized 10 Feb., 1621-2, at East Budleigh. He graduated B. A. at Emanuel College, Cambridge, 1645. During the Commonwealth he was probably settled in the parish of Otterton. Dr. Oliver (*Ecclesiastical Antiquities of Devon*) states that Richard Venne, Vicar of Otterton from 6 Dec., 1625, was buried 28 June, 1662, and adds, "Of Venne's barbarous treatment for his loyalty, for the sequestration of his living and the intrusion of one Conant, see pages 386-7, part 2, of *Walker's Sufferings*." Walker relates that the Parliamentary Committee sequestered the living and ordered a "Troop of Horse to give Mr. Conant, whom they had appointed to succeed him [Venne] Induction to, and Possession of, the Living," and adds that Venne lived to repossess his Vicarage after the Restoration, and recover the fifths from Mr. Conant, "who could not forbear discovering how loath he was to pay them by throwing the money upon the Floor. At which Mr. Venne, smiling, said, 'Well, well, I will take the pains to pick it up.'" The conduct of Mr. Conant in this matter seems rather childlike, but religious prejudice was strong and party feeling violent in those days.

Some years later Mr. Conant must have conformed to the Established Church, for he succeeded Henry Evans as Vicar of East Budleigh 17 July, 1672, on presentation of Richard Duke, Esq., of Otterton. The sureties of his Composition Bond were Thomas Duke, of the parish of St. Peter le Poer, London, merchant, Richard Neve, of London, merchant, and Henry Austin, of Clifford's Inn, gent.

From this time till his death his name is frequently mentioned in the church-warden accounts. During the year ending Apr. 20, 1674, there was paid 10d. "for a booke for Mr.

Richard Conant Vicar,

1674.

Conant to register gift money;" and 5s. "for an order from the Bishop for Mrs. Conant's seat." At this time there was a controversy about the seat of the Vicar's wife. It seems that the use of the pew in the chancel, occupied by the wives of former Vicars, was denied to Mrs. Conant, whereupon the Vicar made complaint to the Bishop who ordered that certain pews erected without license should be removed, and "that a seate bee therein erected accordingly for the use of your said Vicars wife, and to bee continued henceforward for the use of the Vicars wives of the said Parish of East Budleigh aforesaid successively." This order, dated July 17, 1673, was directed to John Upham and Abram Bollen, church-wardens. Other items from the accounts are: Apr. 5, 1675 (year ending), "paid Mr. Conants expenses at the Visitation, 8s. 2d." Apr. 1, 1678, received for "buriing Mrs. Conant in the Church 6s. 8d.," and "laid out by Mr. Conant on travelers, 4d." "Sep. 25, 1680. Then collected In the p'rish of East Budleigh In the County of Devon ffrom house To house ffor the Generall Redemption of Captives. The sum off three pounds fifteen shillings and sixpence witness our names subscribed. Richard Conant, Vicar, John Channon Jun. and Zachens Simms, Wardens." During the year ending April 1, 1689, 6s. 8d. was received "for Mr. Conants Buriell in the Church."*

He was buried at East Budleigh, 6 Dec., 1688.

ABSTRACT OF THE WILL OF RICHARD CONANT.

Richard Conant, minister, of East Budleigh; dated 29 Sept., 1688; proved 15 Feb., 1688-9, in the Principal Registry at Exeter. To the Poore of this parish 40s.; to the poore of the Parish of Witticome Rawleigh 10s. To my Godsonne and grandchild John Mercer 20s. To my grandchild Malachy Mercer 5s.; to my granddaughter Jael Mercer 5s.: to be paid to their parents. To dear daughter Mary Mercer one feather bed performed: that is to say A Bed and bolster and two pillows, one pair good sheets and pillowties and the Rugg and Blanket thereunto belonging. The oaken chest that stands in the middle chamber. Two green window cushions that doe ly in the great Island chest in my chamber. One black forreld bound in quarto written by Mr. Baxter entitled A Saint or a Bruto which stands in the upper shelfe of the middle row of bookes in my study. To my dear sister Mrs. Mary Veren of Salem, in New England (if she be living at the time of my decease) another book of Mr. Baxter's in quarto with blew leaves entitled the Life of Faith. To servant Martha Margary £3. To her sister Jane Clappe of Otterton 5s. 8d., and to Mr. Archelaus Achcot and his wife 6s. All the rest to my dear sonne John Conant whom I make executor. Witnesses, Richard Upham, senior, Thomas Saunders, and Richard Upham, junior.

(Signed)   RICHARD CONANT.   (seal)

Books valued at £40 by Charles Tarlton, Rector of Bicton, and Thomas Upton, Curate of Withycombe Rawleigh. Total value of estate £122 3s. 6d.

He m. 1st, Priscilla —— who was buried at Woodbury 5 Mch., 1651, and 2nd, 1654,† Mary —— who was buried at East Budleigh 14 Feb., 1677.

Child of RICHARD and PRISCILLA (————) CONANT:—

John (probably son of the first wife), the executor of his father's will. In 1694 Abraham Bollen was one of the churchwardens of East Budleigh, as "Debuty for Mr. Jno. Conant." He probably left descendants.

Children of RICHARD and MARY (————) CONANT:—

Elizabeth, bapt. 7 May, 1660, at E. Budleigh.

* These facts from the church-warden accounts are furnished by the kindness of T. N. Brushfield, M. D., of Budleigh-Salterton.

† Polwhele's *Hist. of Devonshire*, Vol. II, p. 231.

Richard, bapt. 6 Jan., 1663, at E. Budleigh.

Mary, bapt. 5 Sept., 1668, at E. Budleigh; m. at E. Budleigh, 7 July, 1681, John Mercer, gent., and had John, Malachi and Jael.

H. John[4] (*Robert, Richard, John*) b. 18 Oct., 1608, at Yeatenton, in Bicton parish, Devonshire. At an early age, having shown a desire and aptitude for study, his uncle, Rev. John Conant, of Lymington, Somersetshire, took charge of his education, first placing him in the free school at Ilchester, and afterwards under the tuition of Mr. Thomas Branker, a learned schoolmaster in the neighborhood. In Lent term, 1626, his uncle took him to Oxford and entered him of Exeter College, placing him under the charge of Lawrence Bodley, B. D., nephew of Sir Thomas Bodley, founder of the Bodleian Library. He was matriculated 18 Feb., 1626-7; B. A. 26 May, 1631; allowed to incept 12 Jan., 1634-5; M. A. and B. D. 29 May, 1654.* He applied himself diligently to his studies and in a short time became known as one of the shrewdest disputants in his college, then one of the most celebrated in the University. He soon became proficient in Latin and Greek, and his knowledge of the latter was so perfect that he was able to dispute publicly in that language in the schools. These accomplishments brought him to the notice of Dr. John Prideaux, then Regius Professor of Divinity, whose saying "*Conanti, nihil est difficile,*" gives evidence of his high opinion of him.

He was chosen Probationer June 30, 1632, and actual Fellow of Exeter College July 3, 1633. For the next ten years his time was fully occupied with his duties as Fellow and tutor, and in the study of the Oriental languages. "He became proficient in Hebrew, Syriac, Chaldee and Arabic. All of which he thought necessary to a thorough understanding of the scriptures. Nor was there any man of his time more remarkable for being a solid and sound expositor, or for clearing the true sense of such texts as were misinterpreted by the Socinians and other heretics."†

In 1642, owing to the troubles of the civil war, he was

---

* Boase's *Reg. Col. Exon.*

† *Biographia Britannica.*

.REV. JOHN CONANT, D. D.,

Rector of Exeter College and Vice Chancellor of Oxford University.

obliged to leave the University, leaving there a large library, which was stolen during his absence.

Before leaving Oxford he had taken Deacon's orders, and finding that his uncle had been driven from his living at Lymington, he performed his duties for him until he also was obliged to leave the parish. He then joined his uncle in London and assisted him in his pastoral duties at St. Botolph's, Aldersgate.

About this time he was offered and accepted the position of domestic chaplain in the family of Lord Chandos, where he remained until elected Rector of Exeter College. During his stay at Harefield, or Harvill, the home of Lord Chandos, he gained the esteem of the family and others by his piety, learning and exemplary life. His salary, though small, was largely expended in charity; and his labors were not confined to the household, for he preached regularly at Uxbridge, the neighboring market town, where great numbers came to hear him. In 1647 he was called upon to relinquish his Fellowship or to sign the Covenant and submit to the Parliamentary Visitation. His resignation in the College Register bears date at Harefield, Sept. 27, 1647. This he preferred rather than "abjure the good order that was established in this church ever since the Reformation, and was perfected under Queen Elizabeth."*

In the spring of 1649, the Rectory of Exeter College became vacant by the death of Dr. George Hakewill, and on the 7th of June Mr. Conant was chosen to that office, and admitted the 29th of the same month. At this time he must have signed the Covenant, which he had before refused. Contemporary judgment might, in this course, accuse Mr. Conant of self-interest, but we may safely follow the opinion of an eminent Oxford Professor† of to-day, who says:

"As his whole conduct acquits him of self-seeking, we must suppose he felt that matters had now gone too far to justify him in declining to do the work to which he had been called by those who knew him best. The points of difference which agi-

---

* *Life of the Rev. John Conant, D. D.*
† *Register of the Visitors of the University of Oxford, 1647-1658.* By Montagu Burrows, Chichele Professor of Modern History.

tated religious men at this time were not so clear as they now seem to us, nor did they always obscure the honest judgment of strong and decided High Churchmen in relation to the actors in these scenes. The famous Robert Nelson was well acquainted with all the facts about Conant, yet he calls him 'a great man, who encouraged learning during his government, and gave an example of piety to those under his care.'* There is nothing except the pronounced Calvinism of Prideaux' earlier works to distinguish the theological principles of that divine from those of Reynolds and Conant. All three of them, acknowledged to be among the most learned men of their day, believed that they represented the Primitive Church and the Elizabethan Establishment. Two of them were bishops, one an archdeacon. Yet the first, strenuously resisting the Laudian theology, but accepting (in some sense) the Divine right of Kings and Bishops, threw himself, in spite of the persecutions he had undergone from Charles and Laud, into the cause of Church and King, and died a martyr for his principles: the second, unable to accept the claims of the English Episcopate, joined the Parliament in the Great Rebellion, but giving up all when his King was dead, rather than put his hand to the 'Engagement' which postulated a Commonwealth, gradually returned to Church and King: the third, agreeing more nearly with Reynolds than with Prideaux on questions of Church and State, yet too much attached to the Constitution to join the Parliamentarians during either their war or their victory, was ready, when things had gone so far that nothing else could be done, to co-operate with them in working the institutions which he was summoned to administer. On the other hand, he carried his objections to the re-organization of the Church at the Restoration further than Reynolds. Though heartily working with him for that great event, connected with him by marriage, standing by his side at the Savoy Conference, and offered 'an ecclesiastical dignity, supposed to be the Bishopric of Exeter,' he again preferred to give up everything rather than conform, taking his place among the Philip Henrys, and that numerous moderate section of Presbyterians who were Churchmen in everything but the recognition of English Episcopacy. His mind would seem to have been an essentially practical one, agreeing on this point, no doubt, with Stillingfleet and Reynolds, who are reported to have held that 'no Church-government is determined in the word of God, but is variable as occasion requireth.' It took ten years to convince him that the Church, as settled at the Restoration, unsatisfactorily as he thought, had attained that stability which gave a promise of national acceptance. Following much the same course of anxious inquiry as before, when he joined the Non-conformists, he

---

* *Life of Bull*, Works, Vol. vii., p. 10.

at last made up his mind, in 1670, to rejoin the Communion in which he had formerly ministered so successfully. Some years later he became Archdeacon of Norwich and Prebendary of Worcester, dying in old age, admired and beloved for his Apostolical simplicity and devotion, 'a worthy member of the Church of England.' * "

When he assumed the Rectorship, he found the College greatly in debt and the number of students much reduced; but by his good management the debt was soon discharged and the number of students largely increased; indeed, it is said that: "Exeter College flourished so much under the government of Mr. Conant, that the students were many more than could be lodged within the walls; they crowded in here from all parts of the nation, and some from beyond the sea, where the fame of Exeter College discipline had reached."† His system of government was truly paternal and, no doubt, fitted to the times. We are told that "his first and chief care was to plant the fear of God in the youth there, to see that they had well laid the foundation of sincere piety and true religion. * * * The public prayers in the College chapel, he would constantly attend upon, whatever other business he neglected, and was strict in obliging the whole College to a constant attendance. * * * He took care that the inferior servants of the College * * * should be instructed in the principles of the Christian Religion, and would sometimes catechize them in his own lodgings. * * * He looked strictly himself to the keeping up all exercises, and would often step into the hall, in the midst of their lectures and disputations, to see that they were performed with that accuracy and exactness as they ought to be. * * * He would often go into the chambers and studies of the young scholars, observe what books they were reading, and reprove them if he found them turning over any modern authors, and sent them to Tully, that great master of Roman eloquence, to learn the true and genuine propriety of that language. Such as were idle, or of suspected morals, were sure to have his company very often, especially at late hours; and he would admonish

* *Life of Bull.*
† *Life of Conant.*

such to keep company with none but those he should recommend, which always were such whose learning and virtuous inclinations had distinguished them in the house, and who might be a check to them as well as a guide."*

Soon after he was settled as Rector, he was in danger of losing this, and all other public employment, through his refusal to take the "Engagement." Time was given for him to reconsider, and it is evidence of the high appreciation in which he was held, that accompanying his acceptance he was allowed to lodge a protest, as follows: "Being required to subscribe, I humbly premise: I. That I be not hereby understood to approve of what hath been done in order unto, or under this present government, or the government itself; nor will I be thought to condemn it; they being things above my reach, and I not knowing the grounds of the proceedings. II. That I do not bind myself to do anything contrary to the word of God. III. That I do not so hereby bind myself; but that if God shall remarkably call me to submit to any other power, I may be at liberty to obey that call notwithstanding the present engagement. IV. In this sense and in this sense only I do promise to be true and faithful to the present government, as it is now established, without King or House of Lords." †

As Rector of Exeter College, he was Vicar of Kidlington, a large parish near Oxford, where he preached regularly twice every Sunday, for a while, but later nominated a curate. Besides attending to his regular duties, he preached very frequently in the three parishes adjoining Exeter College. At All Saints church he preached at seven o'clock every Friday morning for more than ten years; at St. Michael's almost every Sunday; and at St. Mary Magdalen's at four o'clock in the afternoon every other Sunday during the summer months.

On Oct. 28, 1652, he was ordained Priest at Salisbury, and May 29, 1654, was admitted to the degree of Doctor of Divinity. In Dec., 1654, on the death of Dr. Hoyle, Dr. Conant became Regius Professor of Divinity. His lectures while he occupied this chair "were received with the general approba-

* *Life of Conant.*
† See Prince's *Worthies.*

tion of the learned," and he was urged by many to publish them, but could never be induced to do so. In 1655 he had a presentation to the Rectory of Ewelme, in Oxfordshire, but as he was already Rector of Kidlington, refused it. In 1657, however, he accepted the impropriate Rectory of Abergeley, in Denbighshire, which he held till 1660.

From 1651 till 1657 he was one of the "Board of Visitors" established by the Long Parliament for the regulation of the University, and continued by Cromwell. Indeed, he was appointed a delegate to the first Board of Visitors in Sept., 1647, only a few days after he had resigned his Fellowship, but did not serve till 1651, in which year his signature is first found in the Visitors' Register. The fact that Dr. Conant was one of the Parliamentary Visitors of Oxford is nowhere mentioned in his Life. His son, writing at a time when every act of Cromwell or the Puritans was looked upon as odious, shrunk from mentioning it; but Dr. Conant bore himself in this position, as in others, in a manner which commends itself to all impartial observers.

On October 5, 1657, Dr. Conant was appointed, by Richard Cromwell, Vice-Chancellor of the University of Oxford, and

18 Nov., 1657.

admitted on the 9th of the same month. His service in this honorable office continued till August, 1660, and in it he exercised "the most beneficial influence"* during a most trying period. "Upon his receiving the insignia of that office, laid down by Dr. Owen, there was such a universal shout of a very full convocation, as has hardly ever been known on the like occasion. This was owing to the general esteem the University had for him, and to their expectation of something extraordinary from his government. Nor did he disappoint their hopes. The first Lent he made a surprising reform in their public disputations, which for some years had been man-

* Prof. Burrows' Introduction to the *Register of the Visitors.*

aged with such vehemency and disorder as had created several unhappy divisions in the University. By degrees he so corrected these disorders, and prevailed upon the philosophical gladiators, that they were willing to be reduced to a just temper. * * * He used frequently to take his rounds at late hours to ferret out the young students from public and suspected houses. It was not the quality or degree of the persons taken in these circuits that would excuse them to the Vice-Chancellor, who could not betray the trust which the University had deposed in him, or wink at what was punishable by the Statutes."* In 1659 he was largely instrumental in preventing the establishment of a college at Durham, a movement in which Cromwell had been deeply interested, which at that time would have been a serious injury to the old Universities. During the same year the Selden collection of books was added to the Bodleian Library largely through his influence.

On the restoration of King Charles the second, the University sent a deputation, at the head of which was Dr. Conant, to London, to present an Address of Welcome and volume of poems to the King. His Latin speech to His Majesty on this occasion is unfortunately lost, but his Latin poem has been preserved and a copy of the verses is here given:

AD SERENISSIMUM REGEM.†

Accipe pacato, princips celissime vultus,
    Quæ tibi dat tremula, Musa togata manu.

* *Life of Conant.*

† The following translation of the verses is taken from *Biographia Britannica*, Vol. 3, p. 1437, Edition 1750:

TO HIS SACRED MAJESTY.

Kindly accept, that tribute, best of Kings,
The college muse, with trembling rev'rence brings,
The first essays of her unpractis'd song,
Whom war's harsh clamour doom'd to silence long.
But, now reviv'd, the lamps of learning burn,
And, arts returning, wait on thy return.
Heav'n has thy rights restor'd; do thou restore
The rights of heav'n! religion's sacred power!
Return the sceptre GOD bestows again,
And CHARLES reigning; let his Maker reign.
Thrice happy BRITONS, whom you thus shall sway,
And only rule that they may Christ obey.
Our slaughter's past, no longer we deplore,
Nor ills regret that such a PRINCE restore.

Prima offensantis capias tontamina linguae,
Quænon ausa diu, marte strepente, loqui.
Jam solitos rescisse modus patiare Camaenas,
Agnoscunt artes, te redeunte, suas.
Quæ tua sunt cœlum tibi reddidit; ipse vicissim
Jam cælo reddas, Carole magne, sua:
Sceptra Deo tradas, illum regnare jubeto,
Inclyte rex, quo tu sceptra jubente tenes.
O ter felices, te sic regnante, Britannos,
Christus ut emeneat, teque regente regat!
Ipsa sibi tristes gratabitur Anglia clades,
Pensari tanto quæ potuere bono.

On the 25th of March, 1661, the King appointed a commission, known as the Savoy Conference, for the review of the Book of Common Prayer. Dr. Conant was one of this commission on the Puritan side, as was also Dr. Reynolds, whose daughter he had married. Upon the passage of the Act of Uniformity he refused to conform, and thereupon lost the Rectory of Exeter College, which was pronounced vacant Sep. 1, 1662. And now, though he was offered "an ecclesiastical dignity of considerable note," supposed to be the Bishopric of Exeter, he resolved to consider coolly and carefully what line of conduct to adopt, whether to conform or to remain firm in his present conduct. He therefore studied the whole controversy relating to conformity, and having decided on his course was reordained on Sept. 28, 1670, by Dr. Reynolds, Bishop of Norwich. Being now qualified for public service, he was nominated to the Vicarage of All Saints in the town of Northampton, where he had lived for some years, and was instituted on the 15th Feb., 1670-1. In 1675 the town of Northampton was almost entirely destroyed by fire, though his house was unharmed. A very interesting account of the fire, which is too long to reproduce, is given in his Life; the original letter is preserved in the Bodleian Library at Oxford.

As to his ministerial labors, it is said that in preaching he avoided "rhetorical flowers, lofty epithets, pompous quotations, &c., always esteeming it the truest rhetorick in the church to

speak a language different from that of the schools, to deliver
God's word in his own phrase to the capacity of common
hearers. In the pulpit he rarely touched upon curious and
disputable questions of divinity, but applied himself in earnest
to the inculcating the substantials of religion; those solid
truths which all sides agree in, and which every Christian
ought to know and understand. Though he rarely made cere-
monious visits, none visited the sick oftener than he did. In
his visits to the sick, where he found any of them indigent and
necessitous, he would always liberally bestow his relief. His
skill in casuistical divinity was so very singular, that strangers
came to him from distant parts, and he received several letters
from foreigners to remove their inward troubles, and to solve
cases of conscience."

On the 8th of June, 1676, he was installed Archdeacon of
Norwich, and discharged the duties of this office as long as
his health would permit. The beautiful description of charity
which follows is taken from his farewell address to the clergy
of his Archdeaconry:

"He that would successfully promote the salvation of souls,
should be a person of universal charity. By which I understand not such a large and unlimited charity as should dispose
him to think well of the spiritual estate of all men; that
were charity mistaken and misplaced, many were so bad and
so apparently wicked and ungodly, that no such charity is due
to them, or can warrantably be exercised towards them. The
Word of God represents the condition of such as most dangerous and fearful, and therefore we cannot judge otherwise of
them, if we frame our judgment according to the Scriptures,
which give us the rules and assign the measures of our charity.
By an universal charity, therefore, I understand a love of be-
nevolence and goodwill towards all men, an unfeigned desire
of the good of all, with a readiness of mind to do what in us
lies for promoting the good of all, the happiness and welfare
of all, both temporal and eternal. Such a charity, I mean, as
makes us glad of opportunities of performing offices of love to
all, even to the worst, to the most wicked and profligate among
men, as well as to the best, to enemies as well as friends; to

such as have been most vexatious and injurious in their carriage towards us, as well as to such as have been kind and beneficial to us. Such a charity, I mean, as makes us willing and ready upon all occasions to lend our help and best assistance to all that may stand in need thereof; as makes us always ready and willing to relieve them that are in want according to our ability, to counsel and advise such as need our help that way, to instruct the ignorant, to reduce the erroneous, to reclaim the vicious, to strengthen and support the weak, to settle and establish the wavering, to succour and uphold the tempted, to resolve the doubtful, to disentangle the scrupulous, to quiet and satisfy the troubled, to comfort the sorrowful, to sympathize with others in every condition, mourning with them that mourn and rejoicing with them that rejoice."

On Nov. 17, 1681, he was appointed by King Charles II. (see 46th Report of the Deputy Keeper of the Public Records, p. 40), and installed Dec. 3rd of the same year, a Prebendary of Worcester. This preferment came to him wholly unsought, and was procured by the Earl of Radnor, who, it is said, recommended him to the King in these words: "Sir, I come to beg a preferment of you for a very deserving man, who did never beg anything for himself."

In his personal conduct Dr. Conant practiced the virtues he constantly preached. His charity was great; no one seeking assistance was turned away from his door without relief, for he believed it better to give to nine undeserving beggars rather than to let one honest indigent person suffer. At Northampton, for twenty years, he constantly furnished the means whereby never less than twenty, and sometimes as many as forty, poor children received an elementary education; and these children were placed in the families of needy widows so that the money expended for them might indirectly help others also.

He was small in stature, and, though of a delicate constitution by his temperate course of life, his senses were preserved even in extreme age, except that by constant study he lost his eyesight seven years before his death.

The modesty of Dr. Conant was so great that he could not

be prevailed upon to publish either his lectures or sermons, though repeatedly urged to do so. Six volumes of his sermons, preached during the latter part of his life, have, however, been published, and thirty manuscript volumes of sermons are preserved in the Bodleian Library. The following of his sermons have been published: Vol. I., 8vo., London, 1693, edited by Dr. John Williams, contains eleven sermons, with a dedication by Dr. Conant to the inhabitants of Northampton. Vol. II., 8vo., London, 1697, edited by Dr. John Williams, Bishop of Chichester, contains fifteen sermons. Vol. III., London, 1698, edited by Dr. Williams, contains fourteen sermons. Vol. IV., London, 1703, by the same editor, contains thirteen sermons. Vol. V., London, 1708, by the same editor, contains fourteen sermons. Vol. VI., Oxford, 1722, edited by Digby Coates, M. A., Principal of Magdalen Hall, contains thirteen sermons.

Dr. Conant died 12 Mch., 1693-4, and was buried in All Saints Church, Northampton. At the east end of the church, on the north side of the entrance into the chancel, is a white marble monument, supported by two pillars of the Ionic order, bearing the following inscription:

(*Arms:* CONANT, *impaling* REYNOLDS.)

Hic juxta requiescit
JOHANNES CONANT, S. T. P.
E Devonia ortus,
Apud Oxoniensis enutritus:
Ibidem
Collegii Exoniensis Rector,

Academiæ Professor Regius,
Et tertio Vice-cancellarius;
Collegio valedixit anno 1662:
Postea
Archidiaconus Norvicensis,
Ecclesiae Vigorniensis Prebendarius,
Et hujus Ecclesiæ Vicarius.
Vir omnibus hisce muneribus,
(Quorum nullum ambivit, plura refugit)
Par et superior.
Doctrina, Moribus, Pietate, non minus quam annis,
Consummatus, obiit
Anno ætatis suæ 86, Domini 1693,
Mensis Martii die 12 mo.
Elizabetha Uxor mæstiss: Viro charissimo
Hoc marmor, amoris et observantiæ ergo,
Posuit.

ABSTRACT OF THE WILL OF DR. JOHN CONANT.

Will dated 4 Oct., 1693; proved 19 May, 1694. To wife Mrs. Elizabeth Conant, Edward Reynolds, of Kingsthorp, co. Northampton, D. D., and son John Conant, of Kidlington, co. Oxon, Dr. of Laws, all my lands in Kingsthorp, Long Buckby and Quinton, co. Northampton, in trust for wife for life, and to pay £400 each to daughter Francis and son Edward within 12 months from my decease. Also £400 to son Robert 3 months after he shall come out of his apprenticeship. All these sums to be over and above my children's legacies under the wills of their grandfather and grandmother Reynolds. To son John Conant, LL. D., my lands, etc., in co. Norfolk, holden of the Bishop of Norwich by lease for three lives, whereof I have already made a settlement. To son Payntor, and my daughters Dix and King and their husbands, £5 each for mourning. My wife executrix. £5 to the poor of All Saints, Northampton. Witnesses, John Farr, John Massey and Bridget Shortland.

(P. C. C. Box 97.)

Dr. Conant married, Aug., 1651, Elizabeth, youngest daughter of Rev. Dr. Edward Reynolds, then Rector of Braunston, co. Northampton, afterwards Dean of Christ Church College, Vice-Chancellor of Oxford, and Bishop of Norwich.

ABSTRACT OF WILL OF ELIZABETH CONANT.

Dated 9 Jan., 1706; proved 2 Dec., 1707. To son Robert Conant £200 and to his children £5 each. To daughters Mrs. Sarah King and Mrs. Frances Travell £200 each. The four children of my daughter Travell £5 each, and the two children of my daughter Paynter, deceased, £5 each. To my grandchildren Mary and Susanna Paynter my great silver salver and cup and other plate. To my son John Conant and his wife, £10 each for mourning. My five other children, Edward Conant, Robert Conant, Elizabeth Dix, Sarah King and Frances Travell £10 each for mourning. My sons-in-law Dr. William Paynter, Mr. Jonathan Dix, Dr. Benjamin King, and Mr. John Travell; and my son Robert's wife £5 each for mourning. Poor of Braunston, co. Northampton, the place of my birth, £5. Poor of Allhallows, in the town of Northampton, where my dear husband was long minister, £5. Poor of Kidlington, co. Oxon, £5. Residue to son John Conant, of Kidlington, LL. D., executor. Witnesses, Elizabeth Williams, Marg. Gregory and Edward Conant.

(P. C. C. Paley, 257.)

Children of JOHN and ELIZABETH (REYNOLDS) CONANT:—

John, b. —— 1653. B. A. of Trinity College, Oxford, 17 Oct. 1673; Fellow of Merton College, Oxford, 1676; M. A. of Merton, 12 July, 1677; * B. and D. C. L. 22 June, 1683. He settled in London and became an eminent advocate of Doctor's Commons, but was compelled by delicate health to seek retirement in the country. He then settled in Kidlington, co. Oxford, where he died 23 Aug., 1723.† He married Mary Strut, a widow, but left no children. He wrote a life of his father which was published in 1823 under the following title: The | Life | of the | Reverend and Venerable | John Conant, D. D., | Rector of Exeter College, Oxford, Regius Professor of | Divinity in that University, Archdeacon of Norwich, | Prebendary of Worcester, and Vicar of | All Saints, Northampton, | at the time | that town was destroyed by fire: | of which dreadful catastrophe, a particular account is given, | in a private letter to a friend. | The whole written by his son, | John Conant, LL. D., | and now first published by the | Rev. William Stanton, M. A. | London: | Printed for C. and J. Rivington, | St. Paul's Churchyard, | and Waterloo Place, Pall Mall. | 1823. | A monument to his memory in Kidlington Church says: "Johannes Conant, LL. D., obiit Aug. 25, 1725, ætatis suae 71." The date is evidently a mistake for 1723. His will is dated 20 Aug., 1723; proved 13 Sept., 1723 (P. C. C. Richmond, 186). To my brother Mr. Edward Conant, of London,

---

* Broderick's *Merton College.*
† Hearne's MS. Collections, XCVII. p. 122.

an annuity of £100. Sister King an annuity of £15, if she survive her husband, Dr. King; her sons Mr. Benjamin King, of Northampton, and Mr. John King, of Gloucester, £10 apiece in books out of my study. Cousin John Travell £10 in books out of my study; mourning rings to brother Travell and his wife; their sister Mrs. Jane Travell, a pair of silver salvers. My cousin Mary Nanson £20, and her sister Warnford £20. My cousin Frances Dix, when she comes out of her time, £20; her brother and sister that are beyond the seas £10 each when they return to England. Dr. Lane, of Banbury, £2 and a spring clock. My brother Mr. Robert Conant, of London, all my real estate and the residue of my personal estate; mourning rings to him and his wife. His son John, my godson, £50 and £300 in books from my study, proper for him being designed for the Ministry. To Ann, daughter of my brother Robert, £100, and to her sister Mary my plain silver sugar dish. My three servants that used to constantly attend me, £3 each, and to my housekeeper and her husband, the gardener, £3 each. My other three servants, Ann Nown, Richard Penn and James Hunt, who have not long lived with me, 30 shillings each. Poor of Kidlington £10. Every particular in my dear wife's will to be performed. My brother Robert to be executor. Witnesses, John Travell, ffrances Travell, James Wiggington and Lidia Wiggington.

Samuel, b. 1654; d. 1681.

Mary, b. —— 1657. She m. 1st, M. Pool, M. D., and 2nd, Rev. William Paynter, D. D., and had a family. She d. 7 May, 1693. There is a M. I. to her memory in the parish church of Wootton, co. Northampton.*

Elizabeth, b. —— 1658; d. 1709. She m. 1682, Jonathan Dix, and had a family.

Sarah, b. 1661; d. 1751. She m. 1684, Rev. Benjamin King, D. D., afterward Rector of All Saints, Northampton.

Frances, b. 1667; d. 1757. She m. 1695, John Travell, Esq.

Edward, b. —— 1669; d. 1739. He m. 1697, Mary Pocock, who d. 1698, and is buried in the church of All Hallows, Bread Street, London.

L. Robert, b. —— 1670.

There were also two sons and two daughters who died young.

I. Richard⁴ (*Robert, Richard, John*), born in Bicton parish, where he lived. When his father died, in 1638, he left most of his estate to his son, John Conant, then Fellow of Exeter College, who gave his share to his brother Richard.

He m. at Bicton, 28 Oct., 1641, Joane Co(?)rt, who, accord-

*Bridges' *Hist. of Northamptonshire.*

ing to the Rector of the parish, was buried Dec., 1658; but he seems to have mistaken the date 1688 for 1658. Her will is dated 31 Dec., 1686; proved Feb., 1688-9. She mentions her daughter, Mary Guddridge; sons, Robert and John Conant; daughters, Joanna and Rebecca Conant; grand-children, John, son of Robert, and Elizabeth, daughter of John. Daughter Joanna executrix. Witnesses, Clement Peryim, John Tewleake and Roger Bagwell.

He was buried 20 Dec., 1669.

ABSTRACT OF THE WILL OF RICHARD CONANT.

The will of Richard Connantt, of Bicton, co. Devon; dated 11 Nov., 1668; proved Jan., 1669-70, in the Archidiaconal Court of Exeter. To the poor of Bicton. To my daughter Mary, wife of Joseph Gutteridge, of Otterton, £12. To my oldest son Robert Connantt, £12. To my son John Connantt £12. To my son Richard Connantt £12. To my daughter Rebecca Connantt £12. To my daughter Joanna Connantt £12. To my daughter Sarah Connantt £12. To my daughter Susannah Connantt £12. Residue to my wife Joan. Witnesses, John Turleak, Richard Upham and Roger Bagwell. Amount of estate, £441 9s. 0d.

Children of RICHARD and JOAN (———) CONANT:—

Maria, bapt. 28 Aug., 1642; m. Joseph Gutteridge, of Otterton.
Robert, called oldest son in his father's will. He m. 24 Sept., 1677, Mary Gibbons, of Woodbury. They had a son, John, bapt. at Woodbury, 30 April, 1679. Administration on his estate was granted at the Woodbury Peculiar Court, 1682, to his wife, Marie. William Gibbons and Richard Upham, appraisers.
John; m. Maria ———. He was buried 22 Sep., 1731; adm'on granted on his estate July, 1732. Children: i. Elizabeth, bapt. 8 Aug., 1679; ii. Joan, bapt. 5 Mch., 1683; iii. John, bapt. 9 Aug., 1685, m. 9 May, 1706, Joan Warren, of Sidmouth, and had Joan, bapt. 1713, Mary, bapt. 1714, Joan, bapt. 1720, and John, bapt. 1721.
Richard, bapt. 30 Nov., 1645.
Rebecca.
Joanna, bapt. 1651, month and day wanting.
Elizabeth, d. Nov., 1658.
Sarah, bapt. 31 Mch., 1662.
Susanna, bapt. 24 Nov., 1666.

J. John[4] (*John, Richard, John*), b. about 1625. It is presumed that this John was the father of Rev. John Conant, of Poole, for the following reasons: Rev. John Conant, B. D., of Salisbury, left his lands called "options" and his dwelling house in the Close of Salisbury to his son, John Conant. When Elizabeth Conant, widow of Rev. John Conant, of Poole, died, she is described as "of the Close of Sarum." 2nd, John Conant, of Poole, is mentioned in a letter written by Thomas Rowe, nephew of this John Conant, as a relation.

In the parish records of Lytchett Matravers, where Samuel Conant, brother of this John, was Rector, we find the following entries: "John Conant, widower, and Mrs. Dorothy Culliford, widow, were married July 24, 1706;" and also, "John Conant was buried Feb. 15, 1721-2."

Child of JOHN CONANT:—

M. John, b. —— 1670.

K. Malachi[4] (*John, Richard, John*), born probably in Lymington, Somersetshire. He was matriculated at Exeter College, Oxford, 13 Mch., 1650-1; B. A. 12 Oct., 1654; M. A. 28 May, 1657; B. D. 18 Dec., 1665. He was elected Demy of Magdalen College 1652; resigned his Demyship 1655. He was Fellow of Magdalen 1655-1657; Librarian 1665; Clerk of the Market 1659. Antony Wood says of him: "This Theologist, who was a Somersetshire man born, became by the presentation of the President and Society of his College, Minister of Beeding, alias Seal, in Sussex, where and in the neighborhood he was esteemed a good and godly preacher. He hath written and published '*Urim and Thummim; or the Clergy's Dignity and Duty, recommended in a Visitation Sermon preached at Lewes in Sussex*, 27 *April*, 1669, *on Matthew v. 16*. 4to, Oxford, 1669.'"

In Bloxam's Magdalen College Register, Vol. v., p. 218, the following particulars of him are found: In 1668 he was Prebendary of Middleton, in the Cathedral of Chichester. He was presented to the Vicarage of Seale, alias Beeding, 24 Jan., 1666-7.

"A monumental inscription, painted upon wood, remained on
the south-east corner of the chancel of Beeding Church till
the east end was rebuilt in 1852, when the tablet was taken
down and apparently destroyed, for it no longer exists. I had
visited the church and copied the inscription a short time
previously:

'Hic obdormivit in Beatæ Spe Resurrectionis Corpus Mala-
chiæ Conant, S. T. B. qui non magis suis quam bonis, omnibus
flebilis occidit. Cujus eximia eruditio et haud aequanda pietas
omnium venerationem conciliarunt. Cujus indefessum con-
cordiae studium, et singularis modestia, et amabilis animi
candor, nulli non acceptum reddiderent. Socius olim
dignissimus fuit Collegii Divae Magdalenae Oxon. unde in
Ecclesiam hanc vicarius ascitus per xiii. annos officio suo dili-
genter invigilavit. Tandem in virtute non annis senescens ac,
coelo maturus, ardentissimam lapsus febrim, qua cum fortissime
summā cum patientia colluctatus animam ex ignibus hisce vere
purgatoriis immaculatam reddidit Maii MDCLXXX. Ergo hanc
- - - - μνημοσυνον.'

"EXTRACT FROM THE BURIAL REGISTER OF BEEDING.

"Died A. D. 1680, May 24, Mr. Malachi Conant, Bachelor of
Divinity and Vicar of Beden.

"In the Parish Registers are also notices of the baptisms of
Mary and Jane, and Samuel, children of Malachi Conant and
Jane, his wife; and of the burials of the above mentioned Jane
and Urith, their daughters. There is a manuscript note-book
of Malachi Conant in the Bodleian Library, which is remarkable for containing an early copy of the College Grace, in which
the 100th Psalm takes the place of the *Hymnus Eucharisticus*,
afterwards composed by Dr. Thomas Smith."

The note-book mentioned by Dr. Bloxam, is to be found
among the Rawlinson MSS. in the Bodleian Library, C. 945,
under the title "Codex chartaceus, in 4to, manibus variis, sac.
xvii. ff. 269. Miscellaneous collections, chiefly theological, of
Malachi Conant, B. D., dated 1661." The following are some
of the chief articles among the 46 of which the volume is com-

posed: 1. A preservative against Popery by Scriptures; under 47 heads. 2. Sermon (on Matt. xxv. 23) preached by Mr. Gower at the funeral of John Conant, minister at Salisbury, the father of Malachi Conant, p. 1. 3. Prayers before University Sermons at Oxford, pp. 5, 180, 327. 4. Directions and forms for private prayers and graces at meals, pp. 16, 80, 91, 93. 5. Baxter's Directions for the study of Divinity. 6. "Pii concionatoris officium," a transcript of a treatise printed at Cambridge in 1655. 7. The last will and testament of John Conant, of Sarum, who d. 13 Apr., 1653, p. 95. 9. Three sermons preached in Oxford in 1618-19, by a member of Exeter College, no doubt the above mentioned John Conant, pp. 129-221. 10. List of Malachi Conant's pupils, p. 184. 11. Statuta Collegii Magdalenensis, p. 225. 13. A brief survey of the new platform of Predestination, p. 393. 14. Confession of faith made by Dr. John Conant, Rector of Exeter College, when he was ordained, 28 Oct., 1652, p. 425. 15. A short catechism for communicants, p. 420. 17. Classified list of all the School-men. 18. Gratiarum actio apud Magdalenses, p. 501 (Psalm 100 occupies the place of the "Hymnus Eucharisticus" as now sung). 19. Directions of Mr. Thomas Barlow, Keeper of the Public Library, for the Study of Civil and Canon Law. 20. A sermon by Malachi Conant, on Rev. iv. 8, preached on Trinity Sunday at St. Mary's, Oxford, p. 517.

Children of MALACHI and JANE (———) CONANT:—

i. Mary.
ii. Jane.
iii. Samuel. He was matriculated at Magdalen Hall, Oxford, 29 May, 1694, aged 16; elected Demy of Magdalen College 1696, and Probationer in 1703. He d. 18 May, 1706. He received the degree of B. A. 16 Oct., 1697, and M. A. 1 June, 1700. "In the church of Holy Trinity, Cambridge, there is, or was, against a pillar near the end of the Nave, a memorial of Samuel Conant, M. A. of Magdalen College, Oxford. Arms: Gules, ten billets, or." (Extract from a letter from Rev. J. R. Bloxam, D. D., Vicar of Upper Beeding, Sussex.)
iv. Urith.

L. Robert[5] (*John, Robert, Richard, John*), b. —— 1670, probably at Northampton, where his father then resided. He was a citizen and merchant of London, where he d. 1756. He m. 1700, Mary Medlicott.

Children of ROBERT and MARY (MEDLICOTT) CONANT:—

Ann, b. 1703; m. Culpepper Hougham, of London, by whom she had: 1. Mary, who m. Robert Udney, Esq.; 2. Ann, who m. 1769, Spencer Compton, 8th Earl of Northampton, as his second wife. Adm'on on her estate granted 26 July, 1733, to her husband. (*P. C. C. Adm'ons* 1733.)

N. John, b. 1706.
Robert, b. 1707.
Mary.
Frances, b. ——; d. 1798; m. Joseph Woolston.
Susanna, who m. George Tompson, Esq.
Seven other children, names unknown.

M. John[5] (? *John, John, Richard, John*), b. 1670. He received the degree of B. A. from Exeter College, Oxford, 17 Oct., 1687, and M. A. 20 Apr., 1690. On July 22, 1696, license to marry was granted to "John Conant, of Morden, co. Dorset, clerk, bachelor, 26, and Elizabeth Parker, spinster, 19, dau. of William Parker, of (?) Kibworth, co. Leicester, gent., who consents; at St. Clement Danes, Middlesex, or (blank)." *

He was Rector of Poole, co. Dorset, as early as 1704,† and was buried there 6 Aug., 1720.

ABSTRACT OF THE WILL OF ELIZABETH CONANT.

Elizabeth Conant, of the Close of New Sarum, co. Wilts, widow; dated 26 Feb., 1732-3, and proved 11 May, 1733. To sons William and Richard, if living, 1sh. each. To daughter Alice, all my lands, etc., in Kibworth or elsewhere in co. Leicester, and all my other lands whatsoever, upon trust to sell and pay my debts. Residue to my four daughters, Alice, Elizabeth, Anne and Parker, to be divided four years after my death, or on the marriage or death of daughter Alice. Daughter Alice, executrix. Witnesses, —— De la Moore, M. Dyke and Dan'l Dyke, junior.

(P. C. C. Price, 144.)

Children of JOHN and ELIZABETH (PARKER) CONANT:—

William.
Richard.

* *Marriage Licenses, Faculty Office of the Archbishop of Canterbury.*
† Hutchins' *Hist. of Dorset.*

Alice, b. 1700. On a Keinton tombstone, in the south cross aisle of Salisbury Cathedral, is an inscription to the memory of Alice Conant, as follows: "Here lyeth Alice, | Daughter of the Rev'd John Conant | late Rector of Pool, Dorset, | who died July 5, 1745, aged 45 years." *

Elizabeth.

Anne, bapt. at Poole, 17 May, 1709.

Parker.

N. John[6] (*Robert, John, Robert, Richard, John*), b. 1706. He was of Pembroke College, Oxford, B. A. 3 June, 1727, M. A. 20 Apr., 1730. He was Prebendary of Llanvair, in the Church of Bangor (collated 11 Oct., 1735); Vicar of Elmstead, co. Kent (May, 1736); Rector of Hastingleigh, co. Kent; and Rector *sine cura* of Elgingdon-Wroughton, co. Wilts.

He d. 2 Apr., 1779, and was buried in the cemetery of St. George the Martyr, Brunswick Square, London.†

He m. ―― 1733, Mary, dr. of Rev. William Wake, Rector of Hannington and of Waldgrave, co. Northants, Master of the Hospital of St. John, in Northampton, Prebendary of Sarum and of Lincoln, and first cousin of Archbishop Wake. She was b. 1712, d. 1773.

Children of JOHN and MARY (WAKE) CONANT.

John, b. 1734; d. in infancy.

John, b. 1735. He was of Lincoln Coll., Oxford; B. A. 7 Feb., 1757; M. A. 17 Mch., 1775; Fellow of Lincoln. In 1763 he was appointed by that College (in which the nomination is vested by the will of Sir Roger Marwood, the founder,) Master of the Free Grammar School of Sandwich, co. Kent.
On July 5, 1766, he was presented to the Rectory of St. Peter's Church by the Corporation of Sandwich; was instituted to the Vicarage of Sellinge-by-Lympne, co. Kent, 13 Apr., 1778; and was made Vicar of Teynham, 1805. He m. 1766, Anne, dr. of George and Sarah Nairne, of Sandwich, b. 1731, d. 1811. He d. 21 Mch., 1811.‡

William, b. 1737; d. 1753.

Nathaniel, b. 1739; d. 1741.

Herbert, b. 1743; d. 1759.

---

* *Cathedral Church of Salisbury*, p. 113.

† *Epitaphs of St. Pancras*, p. 207.

‡ *Gentleman's Magazine*, Vol. LXXXI. (1811, i. 400).

O. Nathaniel, b. 1745.
    Culpepper, b. 1748. He was B. A. of Trinity Coll., Cambridge,
    1783; M. A. 1786. He d. about May, 1815,* at Mortlake.
    Elias, b. 1750; d. 1765.

O. **Nathaniel**[7] (*John, Robert, John, Robert, Richard, John*), b. —— 1745. He was for a long time Magistrate of the Police Office in Marlborough Street; in Oct., 1813, promoted to be Chief Magistrate at Bow Street, London. In 1813 the honor of Knighthood was conferred on him, and the same year had a grant of arms. The lithographic frontispiece of this volume represents the arms granted to Sir Nathaniel Conant, Knt., quartered with the arms of Wake; the escutcheon of pretense bears the arms of Whiston.

THE GRANT OF ARMS
TO SIR NATHANIEL CONANT, KNIGHT.

To ALL AND SINGULAR to whom these presents shall come Sir Isaac Heard Knight Garter Principal King of Arms and George Harrison Esquire Clarenceux King of Arms of the South East and West Parts of England from the River Trent Southwards send Greetings:—Whereas Sir Nathaniel Conant of Portland Place in the County of Middlesex and of Mount Nugent in Bellingham in the County of Buckingham Knight hath represented unto the most Noble Charles Duke of Norfolk Earl Marshal and Hereditary Marshal of England that the Armorial Ensigns hitherto borne by him and his Ancestors are Gules ten Billets Or but not finding on examination that the said Arms have been duly Established to his family in the College of Arms and being unwilling to continue the use thereof without lawful Authority he therefore requested the favor of His Grace's warrant for our devising granting and confirming such Arms and Crest as may be proper to be borne by him and his Descendants according to the Laws of Arms: And the Memorialist being desirous that Arms for Whiston may in the same Patent be assigned in Memory of his late wife Sarah Conant deceased Daughter and Coheir of John Whiston late of Great Ormond Street in the Parish of St. Andrew Holbourn in the said County of Middlesex Esquire also deceased he farther requests the favour of His Grace's Warrant for our granting and assigning such Arms accordingly to be borne by her Issue by the Memorialist the whole according to the Laws of Arms: And forasmuch as the said Earl Marshal did by Warrant under his Hand and Seal bearing the date of the twenty fifth day of November last authorize and direct us

* *Gentleman's Magazine*, Vol. LXXXV. (1815 i. 475).

to grant such Armorial Ensigns for Conant and Whiston accordingly: Know ye therefore that we the said Garter and Clarenceux in pursuance of His Grace's Warrant and by Virtue of the Letters Patent of our several offices to each of us respectively granted have devised and do by these Presents grant exemplify and confirm unto the said Sir Nathaniel Conant the Arms following that is to say Per Saltire Gules and Azure Billety Or and for Crest on a Wreath of Colours on a Mount Vert a Stag proper the dexter foreleg resting on a Shield Gules Billety Or as the same are in the Margin hereof more plainly depicted to be borne and used for ever hereafter by him the said Sir Nathaniel Conant and his Descendants: And by the Authority aforesaid we do further grant and Assign the Arms following for Whiston that is to say Ermine on a Bend Vert between three Lions Heads Erased two and one Azure as many Roses Or as the same are here depicted to be borne by the Issue of the said Sarah Conant deceased by the Memorialist the 'whole with due and proper differences according to the Laws of Arms. In Witness Whereof we the said Garter and Clarenceux Kings of Arms have to these Presents subscribed our Names and affixed the Seals of our Several Offices this tenth day of December in the Fifty fourth year of the Reign of our Sovereign Lord George the third by the Grace of God of the United Kingdom of Great Britain and Ireland King Defender of the Faith &c and in the year of our Lord One Thousand Eight hundred and thirteen.

(Signed)　　ISAAC HEARD, Garter Principal King of Arms.
　　　　GEORGE HARRISON, Clarenceux King of Arms.

Sir Nathaniel Conant d. —— 1822.

He m. —— 1776, Sarah, dr. of John Whiston, Esq., of London, granddaughter of the celebrated mathematician and divine, Rev. William Whiston. She d. 3 Dec., 1811.* She is described as a woman of great piety, inflexible integrity, highly cultivated understanding, and singular tenderness and sincerity in her attachments.

Children of Sir NATHANIEL and SARAH (WHISTON) CONANT:—

P.　John Edward, b. 18 Oct., 1777.
　　Eliza, b. 27 July, 1779. She m. at St. Marylebone, London, 13 Oct., 1814, Rev. George Robson, of Erbistock, co. Flint. (*Gentleman's Magazine*, Vol. LXXXIV. (1814) ii. 392.)
　　Frances, b. 1 Oct., 1780.
　　William, b. 13 Sept., 1783. He was B. A. of Trinity College, Cambridge, 1806.
　　　　On the death of a Mrs. Elizabeth Stainsby, who was a

family friend of his father, he became heir to her property, and assumed the name Stainsby-Conant.

He d. 1836, leaving no family, and the estate left by Mrs. Stainsby passed to Paynton Pigott, Esq., (of Archer Lodge, co. Hants, and Banbury, co. Oxford,) then of Trunbewell House, Beech Hill, co. Bedford, who according to the conditions of the will of Mrs. Stainsby assumed the name and arms of Stainsby-Conant in addition to his own. He d. 1862. Mr. Paynton Pigott-Stainsby-Conant married Maria Lucy, dr. of Richard D. Gough, Esq., and had children:

I. Francis Pigott-Stainsby-Conant, b. 1810. He was M. P. for Reading, J. P. for Hants, Lieut. Gov. of the Isle of Man. He m. 1833, Frances Phillips, dr. of Gen. Sir Francis T. C. Wilder, by whom he had: (a) Francis Paynton Pigott-Stainsby-Conant, Esq., of Archer Lodge and Heckfield, b. 1837. He m. 1864, Hon. Henrietta Anna, eldest dr. of the Right Hon. Guy Carleton, Baron Dorchester, when he as-* sumed the surname of Carleton in lieu of Stainsby-Conant.* He d. 1883, leaving two sons, Guy Francis Pigott Carleton and Dudley Massey Pigott Carlton. (b) Stainsby Henry Pigott-Stainsby-Conant. (c) Pelling Hugh Gough Pigott-Stainsby-Conant, now of ———, Victoria, Australia. (d) Frances Lucy. (e) Gertrude Elizabeth. (f) Emily Charlotte.

II. Richard Paynton Pigott, Rector of Ellisfield, co. Hants; m. Emma, dr. of Gen. Sir Francis T. C. Wilder.

III. Spencer Botry Pigott, Vicar of Wilbraham, co. Cambridge; m. Eliza McMahan, dr. of Gen. Sir Francis T. C. Wilder.

IV. Sir Gillery Pigott, of Sherfield Hill, co. Hants; m. 1836, Frances, dr. of Thomas Drake, Esq., of Ashday, co. York. He was called to the Bar at the Middle Temple, 1839; appointed in 1856 a Sargeant at Law; Recorder of Hereford, 1859; one of the Judges of the Court of Exchequer, 1863; M. P. for Reading, 1863; Knighted 1863.

V.   John Pelling Pigott, Major in the Army.

VI.   Charles Stainsby Pigott.

VII.   Frederick William Pigott.

VIII. Anna Dolby Pigott; m. Bernard Brocas.

IX.   Elizabeth Mary Pigott.

X.   Lucy Pigott; m. Rev. T. T. Vaughan, Rector of Gotham, Notts.

XI.   Charlotte Archer Pigott.

XII.   Isabella Pigott; m. Charles Eversfield, Esq.

P. John Edward[8] (*Nathaniel, John, Robert, John, Robert, Richard, John*), b. 18 Oct., 1777. In Oct., 1817, he was appointed one of the Magistrates of Worship Street Police Court, London.

He d. 13 Oct., 1848.

He m. 4 Dec., 1817,* Catherine, second daughter of Edward Brown, Esq., of Stamford and Horbling, co. Lincoln.

Children of JOHN EDWARD and CATHERINE (BROWN) CONANT:—

Q. Edward Nathaniel, b. 15 May, 1820.
  Catherine, b. ——; m. Chas. Ellis, Esq., of Wallham Place, Berkshire.
R. John William, b. —— 1824.

Q. **Edward Nathaniel**[9] (*John Edward, Nathaniel, John, Robert, John, Robert, Richard, John*), b. 15 May, 1820. Mr. Conant was educated at Rugby, and St. John's College, Oxford, (B. A. 1842, M. A. 1845,) and was called to the Bar at the Inner Temple, 1845. He succeeded to the estate of his uncle, Rev. Edward Brown, of Lyndon, co. Rutland, 1862. He was High Sheriff of co. Rutland, 1867; is a J. P. and D. L. for co. Rutland, and was chairman of Quarter Sessions for the county 1885. Mr. Conant is Lord of the Manor of Lyndon, and of Aslackby and Dowsby, co. Lincoln, and patron of one living. His residence, Lyndon Hall, near Oakham, a view of which is here given, was built by his maternal ancestor, Sir Abel Barker, in 1673.

He m. 27 Aug., 1844, Gertrude Mary, 2nd dr. of Rev. Charles Proby, Vicar of Twickenham and Canon of Windsor. She d. 27 Mch., 1866.

Children of EDWARD N. and GERTRUDE M. (PROBY) CONANT:—

Gertrude Catherine.
Frances Ann, m. 24 Sep., 1875, Byam Martin, son of Gen. Francis John Davies, of Danehurst, co. Sussex, by Elizabeth, dr. of Sir Thomas Byam Martin, G. C. B.
Edward Henry, b. 20 Oct., 1847; late Lieut. 5th Dragoon Guards.
Emily Agnes, who m. F. Vandeleur, Esq.
Ernest William Proby, b. 7 Mch., 1852.
Cecelia Eva, m. Capt. Frederick G. Fowke, son of Sir Frederick T. Fowke, Bart., of Lowesby, co. Leicester.

---

* *Gentleman's Magazine*, LXXXVII. (1817) ii. 554.

R. John William[9] (*John Edward, Nathaniel, John, Robert, John, Robert, Richard, John*), b. 1824, d. 1884. He was educated at St. John's Coll., Oxford; B. A. 17 Nov., 1847. He m. ——— Frances Groves.

Children of JOHN W. and FRANCES (GROVES) CONANT :—

i. Harry, who m. 1st, Emily Murray, who d. 1882, and had two sons, Erick and Charles; m. 2nd, E. Grimshawe, and had a son.
ii. Edward.

LYNDON HALL. OAKHAM. CO. RUTLAND, ENGLAND.

THE CONANT FAMILY IN AMERICA.

1. **Roger[1] Conant** (see p. 57), the immigrant and ancestor of most of those bearing the name in America, was baptized at All Saints Church, in the parish of East Budleigh, Devonshire, England, 9 April, 1592. He was youngest of the eight children of Richard and Agnes (Clarke) Conant, "who were esteemed for their exemplary piety."[*] His parents evidently instilled into their youngest son the principles for which they themselves were noted, for during his whole life he bore a character of strict integrity and devotion to principle. Richard Conant was one of the leading men of East Budleigh, a church-warden, as was his father before him, and evidently in good circumstances; his wife, Agnes Clarke, was the daughter of the leading merchant of Colyton, a neighboring parish. One of their sons was educated at Oxford, and Roger must have received a good education for the times, for he was frequently called upon to survey lands, lay out boundaries and transact public business. On Jan. 20, 1619-20, Christopher Conant, grocer, and Roger Conant, salter, both of the parish of St. Lawrence, Jewry, London, signed the Composition Bond of their brother, John, for the "first fruits" of the Rectory of Lymington. The records of the Salters' Company have been destroyed by fire, so legal evidence cannot be adduced to show that Roger Conant was a freeman of that company; but the records of the Grocers' Company prove that Christopher Conant was apprenticed in 1609 and admitted to freedom Mch. 14, 1616. The fact that Roger signed this legal document as "salter, of London," is strong presumptive evidence that he was free of the Salters' Company[†] and a citizen of London.

---

[*] Prince's *Worthies of Devon.*

[†] The London Guilds or Livery Companies are divided into twelve great and fifty-eight minor companies, some of which have an authentic history of more than five hundred years. Their joint annual income is about $4,000,000, of which over one-third is expended for charity, and about $500,000 for banquets. There are from thirty to forty thousand members; their

He was married in London in Nov., 1618, and as an apprenticeship of seven years was necessary to gain the freedom of a company, he most likely went to London in 1609 with his brother, or soon after, for he would wish to be well settled in business before marrying. He probably remained in London until he emigrated to New England in 1623, a total residence, if it is assumed that he was a citizen, of about fourteen years. The name of the vessel in which he came is not certainly known but it is extremely probable that it was the Ann, which arrived at Plymouth about July, 1623, and in which his brother, Christopher, was a passenger. In a petition to the General Court, dated May 28, 1671, he says that he has been "a planter in New England forty-eight years and upwards," which would fix the date of his arrival early in 1623. In the allotment of land to the passengers of the Ann, ten acres were allotted to "Mr. Ouldom & those joyned with him."* "Those joyned with him" may have included, and probably did include, Roger Conant, his wife, Sarah, and son, Caleb. The colonists with John Oldham (Mr. Ouldom) were "particulars," that is to say, they came at their own charge, while the "generals" came at the expense of the general stock or Company of Adventurers in England.

He did not remain long at Plymouth, owing to a difference of religious belief between himself and the Pilgrim Fathers. They were Separatists and he a Non-conformist or Puritan. The ship Charity arrived in March, 1624, bringing supplies to the colonists, and also the Rev. John Lyford, a Puritan minister, who was sent at the company's expense. Soon Oldham, leader of the "particulars," and Lyford, who was countenanced by some of the associates in England until they discovered his true character, began an intrigue against the colonists which ended in their expulsion in July, 1624.

widows and descendants being the chief recipients of charity. The freemen of the Livery Companies enjoy various privileges—one of which is citizenship of the city of London— which were formerly more numerous and valuable than at present, and a freeman was considered equal in social position to all but the leading country gentry. The Salters' Company is the ninth of the twelve great Livery Companies; it was chartered by Queen Elizabeth in 1558, and has a Hall in St. Swithin's Lane.

* *Plymouth Records*, Vol. I.

Roger Conant was not expelled with them, as is stated by Rev. J. B. Felt, in his "Notice of Roger Conant,"[*] but joined them soon afterward at Nantasket (Hull), where they had settled, from dislike of the "principles of rigid separation"[†] which prevailed at Plymouth.

It was probably while at Nantasket that he made use of the island in Boston harbor, now called Governor's Island, but then and for sometime after known as Conant's Island. In 1632 it was granted to Gov. John Winthrop for life, he agreeing to plant a vineyard and orchard on it.

During the winter of 1624-5 Rev. John White, of Dorchester, and his associates, under the name of the Dorchester Company, hearing of the settlement at Nantasket and of Roger Conant, "a pious, sober and prudent Gentleman,"[‡] chose him to manage or govern their affairs at Cape Ann. This settlement was commenced in 1622-3 by the Dorchester Company, who sent fourteen men to winter there. In 1623-4 more settlers, with supplies and some cattle, were sent over. John Tilley was made overseer of planting, and Thomas Gardiner had charge of the fishing operations. Their management failed to give satisfaction[§] and Conant was selected as agent or governor for the company, Lyford as minister, and Oldham to trade with the natives. "The information they had of him was from one Mr. Conant, a brother of his, and well known to Mr. White. And he was so well satisfied therein that he engaged Mr. Humphrey, the Treasurer of the joint adventurers, to write to him in their names and to signify that they had chosen him to be their Governor in that place, and would commit unto him all their affairs as well fishing as planting." (Hubbard.)

He, with Lyford, accepted, but Oldham remained at Nantasket. It was late in the fall of 1625[||] that he took charge of the Cape Ann settlement, the location of which was on the west side of what is now Gloucester harbor, near Stage Head.

[*] *New England Historical and Genealogical Register*, Vol. II. p. 234.
[†] Hubbard's *General Hist. of New England*, pp. 102, 106, 116; Young's *Chron. of Massachusetts.*
[‡] Hubbard.
[§] *Planters Plea*, p. 41, reprinted in Vol. II. of Force's *Hist. Tracts.*
[||] Prince's *New England Chronology*, p. 157.

This point projects a few hundred feet into the sea, and on it may still be seen the remains of a rude fort, now called Stage Fort, but named Fort Conant by its constructors.*

While he was at Cape Ann a difficulty occurred between Capt. Miles Standish and a Capt. Hewes, who had been sent over by Lyford and Oldham's friends, which he was instrumental in settling peaceably. It seems that Hewes on his arrival had seized a fishing stage which had been built by the Plymouth colonists. Capt. Standish was sent to regain possession of it. The dispute grew warm and might have ended in bloodshed, for Hewes had fortified his position, had it not been for the friendly advice of Roger Conant and Capt. Pierce, whose vessel lay near by. They counseled prudence and the ship's crew promised to help build a new stage for the Plymouth people, and so the difference which seemed likely to cause serious trouble was settled.† "The magnanimity as well as justice of Conant, in this emergency, is worthy of notice. Though he had been obliged to leave Plymouth for an ecclesiastical diversity of views, he had no wish to encourage hostility against them, or any unrighteous application of their property. He knew the rights of individual judgment in others, and, however different it was from his own, he had no heart to treat them as enemies." ‡

At this time, 1625-6, the number engaged at Cape Ann, over whom he had charge, was about 200,§ and the settlement must have presented a busy appearance. It was soon found, however, that the cargoes sent to England brought less than cost, and the location was a poor one for planting. Could any care on his part have made the effort successful we cannot doubt it would have proved so; but he had disliked the location from the first. Hubbard says: "It must here be noted, that Mr. Roger Conant, on the foresaid occasion made superintendent of their affairs, disliked the place as much as the adventurers disliked the business, and therefore in the mean

* Woodbury's *Old Planter in New England.*
† Prince and Hubbard.
‡ *N. E. Hist. and Gen. Register*, Vol. II., p. 236.
§ Balch's Deposition. Woodbury's *Old Planter in New England.*

while he had made some inquiry into a more commodious place near adjoining, on the other side of a creek called Naumkeag, a little more to the westward, where was much better encouragement as to the design of a plantation, than that which they had attempted upon before at Cape Anne." *

The Dorchester Company had lost about £3000 by their adventure,† and some retired from the company. At the same time a large part of the settlers were sent home, the company paying their wages and providing a passage to England for such as desired it; a small number of the better class remained. When he had fixed upon Naumkeag (Salem) as a suitable place for a settlement, he wrote to White informing him of the discovery. He was induced to remain, not only by hope of gain, but by strong religious motives, as may be seen by the following:

"Secretly conceiving in his mind, that in following times (as since is fallen out) it might prove a receptacle for such, as upon the account of religion, would be willing to begin a foreign plantation in this part of the world, he gave some intimation of it to his friends in England. Wherefore that Reverend person, Mr. White, (under God, one of the chief founders of the Massachusetts Colony in New England,) being grieved in his spirit that so good a work should be suffered to fall to the ground by the adventurers thus abruptly breaking off, did write to Mr. Conant not so to desert his business; faithfully promising, that if himself with three others, (whom he knew to be honest and prudent men,) viz., John Woodbury, John Balch and Peter Palfreys, employed by the adventurers, would stay at Naumkeag, and give timely notice thereof, he would provide a patent for them, and likewise send them whatever they should write for, either men or provisions, or goods wherewith to trade with the Indians. Answer was returned that they would all stay on those terms, intreating that they might be encouraged accordingly." ‡

During his stay at Cape Ann, which lasted about a year,§ he

---

* *Hist. of New England*, p. 107.
† *Planters Plea.*
‡ *Hist. of New England*, p. 107.
§ Hubbard. Baylies' *Hist. of New Plymouth*, Vol. I., p. 113.

occupied "the great frame house" which had been built by
the "old planters" in 1624. Lot, his second son, was probably born in this house or at Nantasket. After the arrival of
Endicott the house was taken down and removed to Salem for
his use. It afterwards became a parsonage, then an inn.
The frame, which, it is said, was brought from England, is still
in use, forming part of a stable. It stands on the northern
side of Church, near Washington street; the timbers are of
oak, yet sound, and after 260 years' usage look equal to the
battles of another century. The engraving of the house here
given is taken from a drawing made in 1775, before it was altered from its original appearance. A full and very interesting
account of the house may be found in the Historical Collections of the Essex Institute, for Feb., 1860.

The removal to Naumkeag was made in the fall of 1626, the
number of settlers being reduced to about forty.* The best
authorities claim that the landing was made not far to the east
of the Eastern Railroad station, near what is now the foot of
Elm street.†

The exact site of his house, which was the first house built
at Salem, cannot be ascertained: Maynes' Block, on Essex
street, opposite the market and Derby square, is supposed to
cover it.‡

---

* *Hist. Col. of the Essex Institute*, Vol. I., p. 105.
† *Old Naumkeag*, p. 24.
‡ Id., pp. 117-119.

Soon after the removal to Salem the settlement was in danger of being abandoned through the invitation of their minister, Rev. John Lyford, to settle in Virginia, and the decision of most of the colonists, including Woodbury, Balch and Palfrey, to accompany him. They tried to induce Conant to go with them, but "he had taken his position, and pledged his faith conditionally, that here he would stand, though perils from savage and hardship of a new settlement clustered around him,"* and could not be moved. On the contrary, he so placed the importance of continuing the undertaking before them, that all, except Lyford, remained. Concerning this period of the history of the colony, he says, in his petition to the General Court, "when in the infancy thereof, it was in great hassard of being deserted, I was a means through grace assisting me, to stop the flight of those few that there then were heere with me, and that by my utter deniall to goe away with them, who would have gone either for England or mostly for Virginia, but hereupon stayed to the hassard of our lives." On the same subject Hubbard (p. 108) says: "God who is ready to answer his people before they call, as he had filled the heart of that good man, Mr. Conant, in New England, with courage and resolution to abide fixed in his purpose, notwithstanding all opposition and persuasion he met with to the contrary, had also inclined the hearts of several others, in England, to be at work about the same design."

In the fall of 1627 John Woodbury, who had been connected with the colony nearly three years, was sent to England as an agent of the colonists. His mission was to present the condition and prospects of the settlement to those interested, and urge them to procure a patent before others should acquire a legal title to lands they had rendered valuable by their toil. Woodbury found that Mr. White had succeeded in interesting some of the members of the old Dorchester Company, and a few gentlemen of London. These gentlemen hastened to procure a charter, and the Council for New England, on March 19, 1627-8, granted to Sir Henry Rosewell, Sir John Young, John

* Felt's *Notice of Roger Conant.*

Humphrey, John Endicott and others, a patent "of some lands in the Massachusetts Bay." Woodbury soon after sailed for America; he arrived in June, 1628, bringing news of the patent, and satisfactory promises for the support of the undertaking.

After Woodbury left England, a new party, of which Matthew Cradock was the leading spirit, acquired control of the patent. John Endicott, one of the patentees, was sent over at once with about fifty colonists, and superseded Conant as Agent or Governor. The new-comers numbered but few more than the old planters, who were greatly dissatisfied at the changed aspect of affairs. Conant undoubtedly expected to continue at the head of the colony under the new patent, according to the previous arrangement with Mr. White. He had been Governor of the colony for upward of three years, or since the spring of 1625, and must have been sorely disappointed on the arrival of Endicott to find himself superseded. The old planters appear to have sustained a separate organization for some months. The company in England was informed of the state of affairs by Endicott, and in a letter dated April 17, 1629, in answer to his, proposed to allow the old planters to become members of the corporation, hold the land already allotted to them, with still further grants which were to be equal to the grants allotted to the adventurers who had put £50 into the company. This sum was as much as most of the adventurers furnished; the whole stock raised by the Massachusetts Company was at first £1035, which was increased the next year by £745. The adventurers contributed £25 generally, some £50, a few £75, and the Governor alone £100.*
They were also to have a reduction on goods transported in the company's vessels, the privilege of cultivating tobacco, which was denied the other colonists; lastly, they were permitted to elect two of their number who should become members of the Council.

Hon. Charles Levi Woodbury says: "These old planters knew the legal status of the coast, and most of them had been

---

* Holmes' *Annals.*

led to settle here as associates of the Dorchester Company in the expected patent from the Great Council. They needed no lawyer to inform them that the company whom Endicott represented had no authority to set up a government or make laws for them. * * * Who could oust them without a previous judgment of the Great Council of Plymouth, or of the courts of Westminster, decreeing their title bad and that of the London company good? * * * There was 'check' in this effort of 'they of London' to freeze out the old planters who had taken and held by their own energy these lands for two years, and were of 'the associates' to whose use an English title for the land had been sought for and granted. To reduce them against their will to 'tenants holding at quit-rents' was a unique way of 'providing them with a patent,' not consonant with the equitable principles on which the Great Council of Plymouth had protected the Plymouth Pilgrims from the rapacity of the trustee of the patent for their use, or which the Lord Chancellor of England enforced in his court."*

The new company were moved to grant these privileges as much by the fact that Oldham held the Gorges patent and was trying to plant a settlement on the Massachusetts territory, which might prove a formidable rival had not these claims been amicably settled, as by the equity of the demands.†

At this trying time, when Conant had just cause for complaint, his self-denial and upright character are clearly shown. He might have led away the greater part of the old planters to Oldham's colony, where doubtless they would have been gladly welcomed, but he preferred to give up his own interest to the public good. He used his influence to preserve harmony; how great it was is to be seen by the following extract: "The late controversy that had been agitated with too much animosity betwixt the forementioned Dorchester planters and their new Agent and his company being by the prudent moderation of Mr. Conant, Agent before for the Dorchester merchants, quietly composed that so *meum* and *tuum* which

---

* *An Old Planter in New England.* Memoir of John Woodbury.
† See letter to Endicott, dated 17 April, 1629; *Hazard's Hist. Collections.*

divide the world, should not disturb the peace of good christians."*

Although he is not universally recognized as the first Governor of Massachusetts, Roger Conant is fairly entitled to that honor; for the colony of which he was the head made the first permanent settlement in the Massachusetts territory, and was the germ from which the Massachusetts Bay Colony sprung. His influence in calling the attention of influential persons in England to the advantages of Massachusetts for purposes of colonization, was greater than has been previously recognized; and we have seen that but for him the colony would have been abandoned. His letters to White and others are mentioned by Hubbard. Sir Henry Rosewell was his brother John's patron, and no doubt knew Roger personally before he left England.

John Wingate Thornton, in his interesting and valuable work,† contends that he was the first and only Governor under the Sheffield or Cape Ann Charter, as Endicott was the first under the second or Massachusetts Charter. The case presented by Thornton, briefly stated, is this: The Council for New England, chartered by King James, 1620, with powers of government, published a platform of government and division of their territories in 1622. In 1624 they divided their territory among the twenty patentees, in the presence of the King. Lord Sheffield, one of the patentees, granted his share to Edward Winslow, Robert Cushman and their associates. This patent was discovered by Mr. Thornton and may now be seen at the rooms of the Essex Institute, in Salem. The same year the Dorchester Company, holding of the Plymouth Associates, began a settlement at Cape Ann, and appointed Roger Conant Governor, who remained at the head of the colony until Endicott came over representing a new company who had purchased the interests of the Dorchester Company.

This work gave rise to an animated discussion among antiquaries at the time it was published. Those who did not

---

* Hubbard.

† *The Landing at Cape Anne;* or the Charter of the First Permanent Colony on the Territory of the Massachusetts Company. Now discovered and first published from the original manuscript. With an inquiry into its authority and a History of the Colony. 1624-1628. Roger Conant, Governor. By John Wingate Thornton. Boston, 1854.

admit the validity of the conclusions reached by Thornton, while admitting that Sheffield held rights under the patent and division, and that he gave a patent to the Plymouth settlers,* state their case as follows:

That if any government was established at Cape Ann it would be by the Plymouth settlers, and that Conant and Lyford were not likely persons to be entrusted with power by the Pilgrims: that the Plymouth Pilgrims made no transfer to the Dorchester Company, notwithstanding Smith's statement that the Dorchester Company held of Plymouth:† that Conant was not appointed Governor by the Dorchester Company: that when Hubbard says "they appointed him to be their Governor in that place" he did not mean Governor but Agent: that Conant never exercised any civil authority, notwithstanding he was the undisputed head of the colony for three years: that if Conant was Governor in the true sense of the term, he was not elected in accordance with the provisions of the charter which provided that the Governor should be elected on the soil.

The fact seems to be that the settlement at Cape Ann was on territory which actually had been granted to Capt. John Mason, so that any argument based on a charter from Lord Sheffield is without weight. However this may be, Roger Conant was at the head, and *de facto* Governor, for over three years, of a colony settled first at Cape Ann and afterwards at Salem. The occupation of the soil was continuous: after the dissolution of the Dorchester Company and the return of the greater part of the colonists to England, some forty or fifty

---

* John Gorham Palfrey holds that the transfer by Sheffield, purchase by Winslow and Cushman, and conveyance to the Dorchester Company were valid. *Hist. of New England*, Vol. I., p. 285.

† Smith's words are these: "And by Cape Anne, there is a plantation a beginning by the Dorchester men *which they hold of those of New Plymouth*, who also by them have set up a fishing worke." Smith's *Gen. Historie*. Ed. 1624, p. 247.

And also: "They procured new Letters patent from King James, drawing in many noblemen and others to the number of twenty, for Patentees, dividing my map and that tract of land from the North Sea to the South Sea. All this they divided in twenty parts for which they cast lots but no lot for me but Smiths Iles."

"March, 1629, six ships go with 350 men, women and children to a place called Naumkecke by the natives, Bastable by King Charles, by the planters Salem. At this place they found some reasonable good provision and houses built by some few of Dorchester with whom they are joined in Society."

remained under his leadership, and for them a charter was procured by friends in England. Upon this foundation the Massachusetts Bay Colony arose. When Endicott arrived, and after the settlement of differences, Conant resigned his authority into his hands.

Contrasting the characters of Conant and Endicott, Thornton says: "Besides strict integrity, there was little common to them. Each was peculiarly fitted for the duties and periods assigned to him, and had the order been reversed the result would have been fatal. Conant was moderate in his views, tolerant, mild and conciliatory, quiet and unobtrusive, ingenuous and unambitious, preferring the public good to his private interests; with the passive virtues he combined great moral courage and an indomitable will: * * *. Governor Conant's true courage and simplicity of heart and strength of principle eminently qualified him for the conflicts of those rude days of perils, deprivation and trial. * * * Endicott was the opposite of Conant, arbitrary and sometimes violent, he ruled with a determined hand, and carried the sword unsheathed, quick to assert and ready to maintain his rights: firm and unyielding: * * *. A man of theological asperity and bigoted." *

It is to be noticed that the form of worship begun by Lyford at Cape Ann was that of the Established Church, and so continued until after the arrival of Endicott and Higginson. The expulsion of the Browns, prominent supporters of Episcopacy, in the fall of 1629, seems to have ended this form of worship for many years. It was the form preferred by Conant, but seeing he could not be gratified he yielded to the majority.

He became a freeman at the term of court beginning May 18, 1631,† and it would appear that the last difference was settled before that date.

At about this time he formed a partnership with Peter Palfrey, Anthony Dike and Frances Johnson, for trade with the Indians along the coast. They had a station or truck-house, as it was called, at Blue Point, near Saco, which was after-

* *Landing at Cape Anne*, p. 66.
† *Records of the Governor and Company of Mass. Bay*, Vol. I., p. 79.

wards sold to Richard Foxwell, together with certain debts due from the Indians. Dike was lost in a storm off Cape Cod while on a trading trip. There was a disagreement among the partners in settling their affairs, as in 1655 Conant, Palfrey, and Nathaniel Pickman as successor to Dike, brought suit in the court at Salem against Francis Johnson to recover the value of a quantity of beaver and otter skins, sent by Foxwell to Johnson, and not accounted for by him. The following testimony is found on the Court files of Essex county. Johnson wrote Foxwell Feb. 12, 1635, acknowledging the receipt of the beaver, otter, etc. "Geo. Taylor sworn June 18 1654 saith that about eighteen years since I dwelling with Mr. Cleeves in Casco bay. Mr. Richard Tucker and I was going to Boston ward, and at Sako, we met with Mr. Richard Foxwell, he desired me and Mr. Tucker to carry a great packet of beaver and otter for him to Mr. Francis Johnson, which we did deliver him in the bay."

Richard Tucker of Falmouth (now Portland) deposed July 1, 1654, that "about eighteen or twenty years since Mr. Richard Foxwell delivered me in my boat then bound for Massachusetts, a great fardel of beaver and another of otter, value to the best of my remembrance seventy or eighty pounds sterling."

DEPOSITION OF LOT CONANT.

"This deponent testifieth that about Seven yeers since that going eastward I was desired to carry a letter by Nathaniel Pickman to Mr. Richard ffoxwell of blue point. This deponent testifieth that afors'd ffoxwell had read ye letter that was sent to him by Nathaniel Pickman and answered that he owed nothing to Nathaniel Pickman but what he owed to Mr. Johnson and to Anthony Dike and it was for goods he had of them at ye trading house.

By me Lot Conant.

Testified upon oath ye 14: 5 mo. 1654.
Before me John Endecott, Deputy Governor."

On 24: 1 mo: 1655-6 Lot Conant testified

"That he heard his father Mr. Roger Conant and Mr. Francis Johnson speaking about the business between Mr. Foxwell and them about putting it to arbitration, but they both declared not by any means to put bills of Debt to arbitration."

DEPOSITION OF TABITHA PITTMAN.

"This I Tabitha Pittman doe testify that at my husband Dikes last going away from me when he was taken away att Cape Codd by the hard winter being the last words he ever spake to me, he said 'wife when thee hast paid Peter Palfrey such a sum (but att present I know not the amount) then there is due to thee from Richard Foxwell onn the bills, three and twenty pounds or there-abouts and all for each partner and that itt was due and oweing to them at the time of the date of the bills."

"Taken upon oath 30: 1: 1657 before me Edmond Batter."

Francis Johnson deposed "that about twenty-four or five years since Mr. Roger Conant, Peter Palfrey, Anthony Dike and myself formed a partnership for a trade to the eastward in which trade they left the sole business of management unto me Francis John-son. * * * At the end of three years or thereabouts I sold unto Mr. Richard Foxwell all the interest in the house with the Debts due from the Indians, household stuff and trading goods for all which I took two bills of debt under his hand payable at two set days one in December the other June after. As I do remember some time after I sold to said Foxwell a small parcel of goods and took his bill for that sum, so that there were three bills of debt made in my name and pertains to what sum I know not. Some-time after the sd. Foxwell sends some beaver and otter by a boat which I received debts to our selves and other men which the trade was indebted to, this beaver and otter was disposed of for that. Two or three or more years after seeing no more pay came from the said Foxwell the above said parton'rs came to account to see how they stood upon which we found Mr. Foxwell so much in-debted to us as amounted to 23 lbs. or thereabouts to every par-tener. the bills which we accounted desperate were delivered into the hands of Peter Palfrey at that time (being in my hands before) by Mr. Conants desire and our consent. * * * "

The original reply of the partners to this declaration, which appears to be in the hand-writing of Roger Conant, is now in possession of the compiler. A fac-simile is here presented, and as the hand-writing of the seventeenth century is difficult to decipher, the text is given in full, as follows:

"ffor awnswer to mr. Johnsons declaration we desire the court and Jury to have knowledge

"1 that as for the matter of these bills it was never denied, only on of them was lost 2 And as for the quantity of the bill lost none of vs can affirm, neither can mr. Johnson, but only by suppo-sition, but whether the bills be or were more or less, we suppose it littell to the purpose or to what we looke after wch is our pts of that beaver and otter wch mr. Johnson hath received as witness

his two letters dated long after the bills. 3. As for the twenty
three pounds wch we accounted due to each of vs, it was so much
disbursed by each of our pticuler statements so must our dis-
bursements even in the trad wch was long before the time that
mr. Johnson received this forementioned beaver & otter, and for
what might be further due by bills if it came to hand to be equally
divided among vs. 4 for the fowerth pticular there is no need of
awnswer to it. 5 As for the arbitrators of Boston they did fully
considder and debate of the bill lost, and of what mr. Johnson had
rendered of our joynt debt, and of what mr. Johnson had pmised
to mr. ffoxwell of land and house to be secured, proofs being produced to the arbitrators by ffoxwels agent.

ROGER CONANT
PETER PALFREY
NATHANIEL PICKMAN "

The verdict was as follows:

"At a Court held in Salem ye 27th 9 mo 1655. Mr. Roger Conant
Peter Palfrey and Nathaniel Pickman ptfs. against Mr. Francis
Johnson defendt: in an action of the case for detaining a parcel
of Beaver cont. 141½ lbs and a parcel of otter nere as bigg in bulke,
wch he received twenty yeers since wth due damages for forbear-
ance. Jury finds for the plfs. in the hands of the defendt 141 lbs
of Beaver vallued at 70 lbs 10s and 70 lbs of otter at 5s per lb: 17 lb
10 sh. three parts whereof we find for the plts. bothe of the beaver
and the otter wh. ¾ amounts to 66 pounds, and costs of Courts wch
is 36s 2d "

In 1631 he signed the bond of John Ellfords, for £40, for his
appearance at the Nov. Court on a charge of murder. Ellfords
was acquitted.

The same year he promised to deliver four bushels of corn
to Thomas Dudley before the end of Oct. (Mass. Col. Records, Vol. I., p. 87.)

"Roger Conant of Salem in New England, planter, makes a
letter of attorney to Mr. Thomas Weston, merchant, to receive
of Captaine (———) Fleet £7 14s. by bill owing him seven
yeares. 16: 8: 1639. (6 d.)" *

He was frequently called to offices of honor and trust by
his fellow townsmen and the General Court, as is shown by
the following records:

At a Court held at Boston, May 9, 1632, it was ordered that
there should be two persons chosen from each plantation to

---

* *Lechford's Note Book*, p. 209.

confer with the Court about raising a general stock for purposes of trade. Roger Conant and Peter Palfrey were the delegates from Salem.*

On November 7, 1632, Capt. Trask, Mr. Conant, Wm. Cheeseborough and John Perkins were appointed to "sett down the bounds between Dorchester and Roxbury." † The same day, "It is referred to Mr. Turner, Peter Palfrey and Roger Conant, to set out a proportion of land in Saugus to John Humfrey, Esq."

Down to the year 1634 the freemen had left the transaction of nearly all business to the Court of Assistants; but that year they elected twenty-four of their own number as deputies to the General Court which met at Boston on May 14th. This was the second representative assembly which met in this country, that of Virginia being the first. Roger Conant was one of the deputies from Salem,‡ and thus assisted in laying the foundation of that form of government which remains to-day our noblest heritage.

In 1635-6 he was one of the committee to oversee the landed interests.   (Felt's Annals of Salem, p. 525.)

In 1636 he was among those selected to examine and mark the canoes belonging in Salem.   (Felt's Annals, p. 526.)

In 1637 he was foreman of the Jury of Trials.

The same year Mr. Edward Howe, Capt. Turner, Mr. Roger . Conant and Mr. William Hathorn were chosen by the General Court to be Justices of the Quarterly Court at Salem.§ The district under their jurisdiction is now embraced in Essex county; he held this office three years.

The Book of Grants for the 11th 7 mo., 1637, is in his handwriting.   (Salem Town Records.)

On Nov. 20, 1637, Capt. Turner, Richard Right, Mr. Conant and George Woodbury were chosen "to certify the bounds between Salem and Saugust." ‖

---

* *Records of the Governor and Company of Mass. Bay,* Vol. I., p. 95.
† Ibid., p. 102.
‡ Ibid., p. 117.
§ Ibid., p. 197.
‖ Ibid., p. 211.

In 1639 a new meeting house was built. A committee of five, of which Conant was one, contracted with John Pickering to build "a meeting house of 25 feet long, the breadth of the old building with a gallery answerable to the form, one catted chimney twelve feet long, etc." (Felt's Annals, p. 119.)

In 1642 he was one of the Grand Jury.

In 1643 he was on a committee to settle the bounds between Salem and Ipswich. (Mass. Col. Records, Vol. II., p. 36.)

On the 13th 4 mo., 1644, it was ordered "that Mr. Conant and Goodman Scruggs shalbe Survayers of the highways towards Wenham and that wayes."

The 16th 10 mo., 1644, he was one of the Jury of Trials.

In 1645 he was one of the "ratters" (assessors of taxes).

In 1646 he was on the Jury of Trials and also the Grand Jury.

On the 26th 8 mo., 1646, "Mr. Woodbury, Richard Brackenbury, Ensign Dixie, Mr. Conant, Lieut. Lothrop and Lawrence Leach, shall forthwith Lay out a way between the Ferry at Salem and the head of Jeffrey's Creek."

In 1655 he was appointed referee to settle a difficulty between Ensign Dixie and Richard Slackhouse.

The 17th 6 mo., 1655, he was again on the Grand Jury; and in 1657 on the Jury of Trials.

He was one of the "eleven men," "seven men" or selectmen in each of the following years: 1637-8-9-40-1-51-2-3-4-7 and 8. (Salem Town Records.)

In 1663 Rev. John Higginson, Mr. Roger Conant and Mr. Lothrop were delegates to the ordination of Rev. Antipas Newman, at Wenham. (Felt's Annals, p. 220.)

In 1671 Roger Conant, William Dixey and Richard Brackenbury were joined with the selectmen to seat all the "married persons in the meeting house."*

The foregoing will show how frequently he was called on to give his services and the benefit of his experience to his townsmen.

Both he and his wife were among the original members of

---

* *Hist. of Beverly*, p. 251.

the first church at Salem, and in 1637 both signed the renewed
covenant.   Hugh Peters was pastor at that time.*

On Feb. 10th, 1649-50, the residents of Beverly finding it
inconvenient to attend church at Salem, petitioned that they
might be permitted to have preaching among themselves.
They were soon allowed this privilege, but not till 1667 were
they dismissed from the Salem church and organized as a separate church with Rev. John Hale as pastor.   The name of
Roger Conant is first on the list of members, and he was on
the committee to fix Mr. Hale's salary.   (Hist. of Beverly, p. 205.)

In 1668 the part of Salem known as Bass river, on Cape Ann
side, was incorporated under the name of Beverly; this name
was not acceptable to Conant, as appears by the following petition; the original is still among the Mass. Archives:†

(The 28th of the 3rd month, 1671.)

"To the honorabel Generall Court, consisting of Magistrates and
Deputies.

"The umble peticion of Roger Conant of Basriuer, alias Beuerly,
who haue bin a planter in New England fortie eight yeers and vp-
ward, being one of the first, if not the very first, that resolued and
made good my settlement vnder God, in matter of plantation with
my family, in this collony of the Massachusetts Bay, and haue
bin instrumentall, both for the founding and carring on of the
same, and when in the infancy thereof, it was in great hassard of
being deserted, I was a means, through grace assisting me, to stop
the flight of those few that then were heere with me, and that by
my vtter deniall to goe away with them, who would haue gon
either for England or mostly for Virginia, but hereupon stayed to
the hassard of our liues.   Now my umble sute and request is vnto
this honorabel Court onlie that the name of our towne or plantation may be altred or changed from Beuerly and be called Budleigh.   I have two reasons that haue moued me to this request.
The first is the great dislike and discontent of many of our people
for this name of Beuerly, because (wee being but a small place) it
hath caused on us a constant nickname of beggarly, being in the
mouths of many, and no order was giuen or consent by the people
heere to their agent for any name vntill they were shure of being
a town granted in the first place.   Secondly: I being the first that
had house in Salem (and neuer had any hand in naming either that
or any other towne) and myself with those that were then with me,
being all from the western part of England, desire this western

* *Hist. Col. of the Essex Institute*, Vol. I., p. 38.
† Mass. Arch., Towns, Vol. I, p. 217.

name of Budleigh, a market towre of Deuonsheer and neere vnto
the sea as we are heere in this place and where myself was borne.
Now in regard of our firstnesse and antiquity in this soe famous a
colony, we should umblie request this littell priuelidg with your
fauors and consent, to giue this name abouesaid vnto our town. I
neuer yet made sute or request vnto the Generall Court for the
least matter, tho' I thinke I might as well have done, as many
others haue, who haue obtained much without hassard of life or
preferring the publick good before theire own interest, which I
praise God, I haue done. If this my sute may find acceptation
with your worships, I shall rest vmbly thankfull and my praires
shall not cease vnto the throne of grace for God's guidance and his
blessing to be on all your waightie proceedings and that iustice and
righteousness may be euerie where administred and sound doctrine,
truth and holiness euerie where taught and practised throughout
this wildernes, to all posterity which God grant, Amen.

Your worships' vmble petitioner and servant,

ROGER CONANT,

It is likewise the umble desire and request of us, whose names ar
heere underwritten, that the name of our town may be changed as
above said.

WILLIAM DODG Sen.	ROBERT MORGAN
WILLIAM DODG Jun.	PETER WOODBERRY
EXERCISE CONANT	JOHN DODG
EDWARD BISHOP	EPHRAIM HERRICK
LOT CONANT	OSMOND TRASKE
HENRY BAILEY	JOHN SAMPSON
JOHN RAYMENT	WILLIAM RAYMENT
JOHN LOVET Sen.	ROBERT HIBBARD
WILLIAM DODG	HENRY HERRICK
BENJAMIN BALCH	JOHN BLACK
CORNELIUS BAKER	ISAAC HULL
EDMUND GROVER	RICHARD HAYNES
JOHN HILL	JOHN GALLOP
JOHN GROVER	JOHN WOODBERRY
JOHN LEECH Sen.	ZACHARIAH HERRICK
JOHN LEECH Jun.	JOHN BENNETT
JOHN CONANT	JOHN LOVETT Jun.

June 1, 1671. The magistrates having perused and considered
this request, see no cause to alter the name of the place as desired,
their brethren the deputies hereto consenting

EDWARD RAWSON *Secretary*

Consented to by the Deputyes

WILLIAM TORREY *Cleric*"

How dear the name of Budleigh was to our ancestor is easily
imagined; there he passed the happy days of his boyhood, and
there in the quiet churchyard were the graves of his ancestors;

though he had been absent nearly half a century the memory
of his birth-place was not effaced. The 200 acres granted him
at this time were a poor substitute for the refusal of his request, and the wish that his last days might be passed amid
surroundings reminding him in name as well as nature of his
"old home" in Devonshire.

The amount of land held by him must have been considerable, for in addition to that acquired at various times by purchase we find by the town Book of Grants on the "25th of 11
mo., 1635-6, that Capt. Trask, John Woodbury, Mr. Conant,
Peter Palfrey and John Balch are to have five farms, viz:
each two hundred acres apiece, to form in all, a thousand acres
of land together lying, and being at the head of Bass river,
one hundred and twenty-four poles in breadth, and so runin
northerly to the river by the great pond side, and soe in
breadth making up the full quantity of a thousand acres, these
limits laid out and surveyed by us

JOHN WOODBERRY
JOHN BALCH"

He moved to this grant at this time, for in 1637 it was ordered "that Mr. Conants house with the half acre of ground
and corn standing on the same should be bought at the town
expense for the use of old Mr. Plase and wife."* The grant
was in that part of the town afterwards set off as Beverly and
was divided according to the quality of the land, and the various qualities equally among the grantees, so that each should
have 200 acres. Conant built his house on an Indian path
leading from the sea around the head of Bass river to the
"great pond" (Wenham lake). As near as can be determined
the house stood on the east side of Cabot street, near Balch
street, and was near the division line between the land of
Joseph L. Standley and Eben H. Moulton; both are descended
from Roger Conant. Jonathan[5] Conant was probably the last of
the name who lived in it. He is said to have sold the northern
part of the homestead farm to Dr. Ingalls Kittredge, who
built a brick house which is still standing, and the southern

---

* Salem Town Records, Vol. I, p. 55.

part, with the old house, to Simon Brown, who took down the house about 1788. There is no record of either of these conveyances in the records of Essex co.; possibly the homestead passed by inheritance, to Jonathan's daughter, Sarah, who married Dr. Kittredge, and was sold by her to Brown at a later period than that mentioned. The position of the house is designated on the map which is given later.

In 1637 Roger Conant held 44 acres in the vicinity of Salem village. (*Hist. Col. of the Essex Institute*, Vol. 19, p. 173.)

The 7th of the 3rd mo., 1638, John Balch, Mr. Conant and John Woodbury were granted five acres of meadow land.

The 7 June, 1671, the General Court granted him 200 acres in consideration of his being a "very ancient planter."* This was not laid out till three years later as is seen by the following:

"Layd out to Mr. Roger Conant of Beverly alias Bass Riuer one parcell of land in the wilderness, on the Eastern side of Merrimack Riuer, two hundred acres, and begins at a great pine tree marked wth. E wch. is the N. W. Corner of Mr. Edwd. Tyngs farm and from this pine it runs eighty three degrees and a half westward from the north, one hundred and thirty pole, which reacheth to Beaver Brooke: and frō the first pine it runs Eleven degrees westward from the South, two hundred and fiuety poles: from thence it runs eighty fower degrees and a half westward from the south one hundred and thirty two pole: the last line parralel to the second line, and closeth to Beaver Brooke. the lines are all true, and seueral trees bounded with and the rest well marked, it lyeth in the form of a long square, laid out by Jonathan Danforth Surveyr 22-3 mo. 1674. The court approves this return 22 May 1679."†

At the 17th Quarter Court, held 1st 5 mo., 1640, "Augustin Calom [Cullum,] pl. agt. Mr. Connant and diuers others that were (mentioned in ascdule) defend'ts in an act. of case. Jury finds for pl. as he shall make it appear by the Towne orders and eight shillings damages and the costs."

"The 26th 4 mo. 1649 Mr. Rodger Conant, William Dodg and Benjamin Balsh plant'fs against Esaurus Reed, ffineas ffiske and William ffiske def'nts in behalf of the towne of Wenham in an action of trespas and upon the case for damages done unto them in a p'sell of meadow. the pla't's beinge defective

---

* *Records of the Governor and Company of Mass. Bay*, Vol. IV., part 2, p. 504.
† Id., Vol. V., p. 227.

in testimony the acyon fell." (Essex County Court Records.)

The 24 :4: 1652, he witnessed a deed from Margaret Scruggs to her son-in-law, John Raymond.

On June 24, 1654, Roger Conant, Nicholas Patch and William Dodge returned the inventory of Thomas Scruggs' estate.

The 27th 9 mo., 1656, "Roger Conant, William Dodge, Benjamin Balch and John Raymond executor of Thomas Scruggs, all of Salem, planters, in consideration of £5, sell Edmond Patch of Salem ten acres of land it being a part of their joint farm and lies next adjoining to Richard Dodge's lands." Recorded 2: 10: 1656. (Essex Deeds, Vol. I., p. 81.)

On the 26 Jan., 1658, Roger Conant witnessed the deed of Osmond Trask to Sam'l Corning.

The inventory of the estate of Samuel Porter, deceased, was taken June 22, 1660, by Roger Conant and John Raymond; and the inventory of John Balch's estate March 19, 1662.

"The deposition of Roger Conant being one of the first Inhabitants of the towne of Salem do testify to my best knowledge that there was never any hi way layd out above the lot that was John Swetts lott: because then the town had noe nead of any hi waye ther: & that there was no hi way layd out between the water side & the upland

ROGER CONANT

one of the layers out that then were

Sworn in Court at Salem 30: 9: 64

Ateste   HILLIARD VEREN, Cleric."

Roger Conant and William Walton witnessed the deed of Samuel Friend to John, son of Lawrence Leach, 7 Sep., 1665.

Roger Conant witnessed the deed of Edward Patch to Richard Dodge, 9 July, 1666.

The following deed is given verbatim as it occurs in Vol. 3, p. 28, Essex Deeds:

10: 12 mo 1667

To all people to whome these pr'sente writings shall come Roger Connant of Salem in the County of Essex in New England, yeoman, sendeth greeting, Know yee that I ye sd. Roger Conant for ye love and natural affection which I beare & have vnto my sonne Lott of ye same Town and County as also for divers good causes and considerations me there unto moving haue given and granted

& by these pr'sents doe freely cleerely & absolutely give, grant and
confirm vnto ye sd Lott Conant my now dwelling house and all
that my land adjoining thereto with the orchard and all appurtenances there to belonging scittuat and lying on Bass River so called
belonging to Salem aforsd all the sd land containing about 20 acres
be it more or less, and is bounded with a bridg in the high way and
the brook to the South and ye land of Edward Bishop on ye north
ye land of Henry Herrick senior on ye brooke side to ye east, together with some land of me ye sd Roger at the north end on the
east and the highwaye to the west also twelve acres more or less
adjoining on east side to the north end on the easterne side of the
brooke & further bounded with ye land of Henry Herrick senior to
the south & north with ye land of Benjamin Balch and east with
the land of the Woodberrys, abbutting as aforesd to ye west against
ye aforesd twenty acres near ye brooke: Alsoe about ten acres of
meddow lying in the great marsh against Wenham river, bounded
east and north with ye Woodberrys marsh on ye west with Benjamin Balch & south with ye land of me ye sd. Roger alsoe sixty
acres of vpland lying neere Richard Dodges farme, bounded with
ye land of Humfrey Woodberry on ye east the land of Wm.
Dodg on ye west a highway on the north and the land of William
Dodg senior and Roger Hascall on the south: also one acre of salt
marsh bounded with the milne river south, with Benjamin Balch
east and north and the Woodberrys west: also one acre of marsh
at the thatch pond, lying in the midle of it. To have and to hold
ye sd house with ye severall p'cells of land to saye ye house and
twenty acres adjoining and twelve acres adjoining towards ye north
end, alsoe the ten acres of meddow and sixty acres of upland, and
one acre of salt marsh and one acre of fresh marsh with all the appurtenances to all ye several p'cells belonging therevnto, unto ye
sd Lott Conant his heires executors administrators and assignes
from the daye of date hearof forever freely without any manner
of reclaim or contradiction of me ye sd Roger Conant my executors or administrators or any other p'son whatsoever by any means
title or p'curement in any maner of wise or without any acount
reckoning or answer therefor to me or any in my name to given
rendered or don in time to come soe that neither ye sd Roger Conant my executors or administrators nor any p'son or p'sons for us
by in or in our names or in the name or names of us or any of us
at any time or times heareafter may aske, claim or demand in or to
the pr'mises or any p't thereof any interest rite, title, use or possession, and demand we and every of us to be utterly excluded and
forever debarred by these p'ssents to ye sd Roger Conant my executors and administrators and sd p'cells of land given and granted
as abovesaid against all people shall and will warrant and defend,
by these pr'sents as witness my hand this twentieth daye of November in ye yeare of our Lord God one thousand six hundred and

sixty six, being ye eighteenth year of ye Raigne of our Sovereign
Lord King Charles ye Second &c

signed sealed &   ROGER CONANT
delivered in ye pr'sents   with a seale
of us, the marke of
 JOHN I VEREN
 HILLYARD VEREN

Roger Conant acknowledged this to be his act and deed 10: 5 mo
67 before

       WM HATHORNE Assistant

The same day Lot Conant leased to Roger Conant and Sarah,
his wife, "a dwelling house, an orchard or orchards and garden,
containing about three acres on Bass river Side bounded with
a brook near the bridge to the south, the land of Henry Herrick senior to the east, the land of said Lot on the north and
the highway to the west being the house and orchard formerly
of said Roger Conant and now in his occupation and also one
acre of marsh for their lives, they paying to sd Lot one Indian
corne at ye first day of January if the same be lawfully demanded." (Essex Deeds, Vol. 3, p. 29.)

At this time he also transferred to his son, Exercise, "forty
five acres of upland being scituated and lying in ye Township
of Salem toward Wenham and is bounded on the northeast
with a high waye, on the southwest with the land of William
Dodg Jr. on the southeast also with Wm. Dodg Jr. and on ye
northeast with som land of me ye sd Roger and about three
acres and a halfe of fresh meddow lyeing in Wenham great
meddow, bounded on ye south with Wenham river soe called
on ye west with meddow of Benjamin Balch, on east with ye
Woodberrys on ye north with ye upland alsoe one acre and a
quarter lying at the great pond marsh bounded between Ben.
Balch his marsh and the marsh of Peter Woodbery."

On 23 Mch., 1670, Roger Conant, Jno. Raymond, and Benjamin Balch, of Bass river side, or Beverly, planters, sold to
Isaac Hull, cooper, nine acres, "which lyeth neer his now
dwelling house." The same day, Wm. Dodge, John Raymond,
Roger Conant, Benjamin Balch and Peter Woodbury each
gave him one acre lying near "the south east corner of the great
pond." Both these deeds are recorded the 13th April, 1670.

The following deposition is recorded in Vol. 3, p. 281, Essex Deeds, Ipswich Series:

"The deposition of Mr. Roger Conant, farmer William Dodge and Exercise Conant. These deponants witnesseth that Edward Bishop of Beverly in the year 1670 did pas an act of deed of gift to his Grandson William Rayment, concerning his houseing and lands, all of them on the west syde of the country Road from Salem fferry to Wenham wards with all the preveledjes and app't'nances thereunto belonging which lands now bounding upon John Rayment, John Woodbery, Ben. Balch, Wm. Raymond. Also these deponents witnesseth that the above mentioned Wm. Rayment is to enjoy it at the decease of his grandfather and grandmother now living if he live there unto. If not that his next Brother or Sister shall enjoy it also these deponents testifyeth that the above mentioned p'misses was given signed and sealed & delivered in the p'ssence of us and we were witnesses to it.

Sworn at Court held at Ipswich the 30 Sep. 1673 by ffarmer Wm. Dodg and Exercise Conant as

Attest   ROBT. LORD Cleric."

The following deed is recorded in Vol. 4, p. 50, Essex Deeds: Roger Conant, of Beverly, in consideration of his love and natural affection for his kinsman, John Conant, of Beverly, house carpenter, conveys to him twenty acres "near Wenham great pond bounded with the pond north-westerly, the high way on the south, northerly with land of Roger Conant and westerly with land of Ben. Balch." It is dated Feb. 4, 1673, and witnessed by Daniel Eppes and Exercise Conant.

In 1674 his name occurs in a list of the house-holders of Marblehead.

Roger Conant died Nov. 19, 1679, in the 88th year of his age; the place of his burial is not known. He left a will which is recorded in the Probate Records of Essex co., Vol. I., p. 75. The original will is preserved among the County Court Files; it runs as follows:

"At Salem Court, 25: 9: 1679. The Last will and testament of Roger Conant, dated the 1st of the 1 mo. [March] 1677. I Roger Conant aged about eightie fiue yeares, being of perfect vnderstand-

ing, though weak & feeble in body, doe hereby declare my will
and minde wherein in the first place I doe bequeath my soule vnto
God that gaue it & my body to the graue, in hope of a blessed
Resurrection: & for my outward estate and goods, I giue vnto
my Sonne Exercise one hundred and fortie acres of Land lyeing neer
adjoining vnto the new towne of Dunstable a part of two hundred
acres granted me by the General court: also I giue & bequeath
vnto him ten acres of Land next adjoining vnto his p'sont home lott
and land Lying by the side of william Dodgeses his land, and butts
one the land of thomas Herrick: also I give him two acres of
marsh at the south end of the great pond by whenham, or if my
daughter Elizabeth Conant will exchange to have soe much at the
great marsh neer wenham: also I give him my swamp at the head
of the railes * which is yet undivided betwixt me and Benjamin
Balch adjoining vnto william Dodgeses swamp: also I giue him
my portion of land Lying by Henry Haggats on wenham side:
now out of this fore mentioned Land he is to pay seaven pounds
toward the discharge of such Legassis as I have given & bequeathed: according as is hereafter sett down

more I giue vnto my grandchild John Conant sonne of Roger
Conant ten acres of Land adjoining to his twenty acres by the great
pond side he paying twenty pounds for the same towards the payment of legassis as after mentioned

more I giue vnto my grandchild Joshua Conant seaventeen acres
of Land Lying by the south side of the great marsh neer wenham and bounding unto the land of peeter woodbery: and the rest
to return to my Executor.

also I giue vnto my Daughter Sarah two acres of Land lying between the head of the railes & Isaac Hull his ground as part of
six acres betwixt me and Benjamin Balch: this to her and her
children.

also sixtie acres of Land out of my farm granted me by the General Court neer the new town of Dunstable I giue and bequeath
unto the hands of Capt Roger Clap of the castle neer Dorchester
for the use of a daughter of one mrs. pitts deceased whose daughter
now Liueth in culleton a towne in Devon in old England and is in
lue for certaine goods sold for the said mrs. pitts in London and
was there to be paid many years since but it is alleaged was neuer
paid and the aforesaid capt clap to giue a discharge as theire attur-
ney according as he is impowered and intrusted in theire behalfe:

furthermore as legacies I doe giue vnto my sonne lott his ten
children twenty pounds to be equally divided: to my daughter Sa-
rahs Children to John five pounds to the foure daughters fiue
pounds betwixt ym: to my daughter Mary Dodge to herself fiue
pounds and fiue pounds to her fiue children equally divided: to Exercise his children foure pounds betwixt them: to Adoniron Veren
three pounds to his sister Hannah twenty shillings and her two

---

* In Beverly, near Wenham.

children each ten shillings: to my cozen Mary Veren wife to Hillie veren three pounds as also three pounds unto the daughters of My Cozen Jane Mason deceased to be divided amongst them including Loue steevens* her children a share:

my wearing apparell I giue and household implements not otherwise disposed of and my Gray horse and cattle to my sonn Exercise and sheepe I giue to Rebacka Connant my grandchild and one sheep to Mary Leach:

and whereas there remains in my hands a certain portion of cattle belonging vnto one Mr Dudeney in England and by him assigned vnto his nephew Richard Conant valued at twenty fiue pounds and now left in the hands of my sonne exercise Conant that there be a rendering vp of such cattle or theire valuation mentioned unto the said Richard Conant upon seasonable demand he giuing a full discharge for the same.

and further my will is that my sonn Exercise be my executor to my will and Testament and for further help in seeing these things forementioned my sonne william Dodge and my grandchild John Conant Senior to be overseears of the same. In witness whereof I haue here vnto sett my hand the day and yeare aboue written. The blotting out of part of a line and a whole line under the part was before signing hereof

The mark X of
ROGER CONANT his seale

JOHN BENNET
BENJAMIN BALCH

Sealed in the presence of the aforesaid witnesses and delivered

JOHN BENNET
BENJAMIN BALCH

25-9-mo 1679 Benjamin Balch and John Bennett gave oath in Court at Salem that they signed as witnesses to the within written that then the said Roger Conant declared the same to be his last will and testament and there is no later will of his that they know of

Attest   HILLIARD VEREN Cler:"

"The estate of Roger Conant deceased a true Inventory there of appraised by John Rayment and William Rayment this 24th 9 mo 1679

200 acres land lying at Dunstable not improved   £ 060 s 00 d 00

more land sold to Elizabeth Conant not paid for   040 00 00

* " Love Stevens bapt. 4: 11: 1665, born in the church or received in her minority with her parents." John Stevens m. Love Holyroad 2 July 1661; their children were Mary b. 1 May 1662; John b. 1 June 1664; Joshua b. 15 July 1666; Benjamin, bapt. 12: 5: 1668: Love b. 29 Oct. 1669; Elizabeth b. 20 Oct. 1671; Stephen b. 4 Nov. 1673; and perhaps William, bapt. 4 Nov. 1677. Love the mother d. 7 Dec. 1675. (See *Hist. Col. of the Essex Institute*, Vol. 3, and also Vol. 16, p. 8.)

more land 10 acres and more 10 acres 20	-	-	040	00	00
more land 23 acres	-	-	-	-	-	-	-	059	00	00
more two acres of meddow	-	-	-	-	-	010	00	00
swampy land 20s 2 acres of land £5	-	-	-	006	00	00
more land	-	-	-	-	-	-	-	-	001	00	00
2 cows and a horse 10£ cattell 15£ 4 sheep 1£	-	026	10	00
a bed and furniture 5£ wearing cloathes and linen £9	-	-	-	-	-	-	-	-	014	00	00
a chest trunk and box 20s other things 20s -	-	002	00	00
								258	10	00

JOHN RAYMENT
WILLIAM RAYMENT

Exercis Conant the executor gaue oath to the truth of the aboue written Inventory and is allowed of in Court at Salem 28: 9 mo: 1679

Attest   HILLIARD VEREN Cler:

For a description of the Salem of Roger Conant's time, one cannot do better than to read Hawthorne's description of "Main Street:" "You perceive, at a glance, that this is the ancient and primitive wood,—the ever-youthful and venerably old,—verdant with new twigs, yet hoary, as it were, with the snowfall of innumerable years, that have accumulated upon its intermingled branches. * * * * In more than one spot, among the trees, an upheaved axe is glittering in the sunshine. Roger Conant, the first settler in Naumkeag, has built his dwelling, months ago, on the border of the forest-path; and at this moment he comes eastward, through the vista of woods, with his gun over his shoulder, bringing home the choice portions of a deer. His stalwart figure, clad in a leathern jerkin and breeches of the same, strides sturdily onward, with such an air of physical force and energy that we might almost expect the very trees to stand aside, and give him room to pass. And so, indeed, they must; for, humble as is his name in history, Roger Conant still is of that class of men who do not merely find, but make, their place in the system of human affairs; a man of thoughtful strength, he has planted the germ of a city. There stands his habitation, showing in its rough architecture some features of the Indian wigwam, and some of the log cabin, and somewhat too, of the straw-thatched cottage in Old England, where this good yeoman had his birth and breeding.

The dwelling is surrounded by a cleared space of a few acres, where Indian corn grows thrivingly among the stumps of the trees; while the dark forest hems it in, and seems to gaze silently and solemnly, as if wondering at the breadth of sunshine which the white man spreads around him. An Indian, half hidden in the dusky shade, is gazing and wondering too. Within the door of the cottage you discern the wife with her ruddy English cheek. She is singing doubtless a psalm tune, at her household work; or, perhaps she sighs at the remembrance of the cheerful gossip, and all the merry social life, of her native village beyond the vast and melancholy sea. Yet the next moment she laughs, with sympathetic glee, at the sports of her little tribe of children; and soon turns round, with the home-look on her face, as her husband's foot is heard approaching the rough-hewn threshold. How sweet must it be for those who have an Eden in their hearts, like Roger Conant and his wife, to find a new world to project it into, as they have, instead of dwelling among old haunts of men, where so many household fires have been kindled and burnt out, that the very glow of happiness has something dreary in it."

Roger Conant married in the parish of St. Ann's, Blackfriars, London, Nov. 11, 1618, Sarah Horton. Her parentage has not been ascertained; there was an ancient Devonshire family of the name to which she may have belonged. She was living in 1666, as at that date she is mentioned in a deed, but probably died before her husband as she is not mentioned in his will.

Children of ROGER and SARAH (HORTON) CONANT:—

i.   Sarah, christened 19 Sept., 1619, in the parish of St. Lawrence, Jewry, London, England; buried there 30 Oct., 1620.

ii.   Caleb, christened 27 May, 1622, in the same parish. From the following extract it appears that he came to Massachusetts with his parents, and afterwards returned to England (probably for an education) where he died: "Caleb Conant, late beyond seas, dec'd, a bachelor. Adm'on granted 11 Nov., 1633, to his uncle by the father's side (patruo), John Conant, clerk. (P. C. C. Somerset House, Adm'ons, 1633, folio 204.) It is probable that letters of administration were taken for the reason that he was entitled to a small portion under the will of his grandfather, Richard Conant.

2. iii.   Lot, b. about 1624, either at Nantasket or Cape Ann.
3. iv.   Roger, b. 1626. The first white child born in Salem, Mass.
4. v.   Sarah, b. about 1628. She is mentioned in the will of her grandfather, Richard Conant, dated Nov. 20, 1629.
5. vi.   Joshua, b. ——.
6. vii. Mary, b. ——.
   viii. Elizabeth, b. ——; living unmarried in 1679.
7. ix.   Exercise, bapt. 24 Dec., 1637. (Salem First Church Records.)

That the seven last named were all the children of Roger and Sarah Conant that reached maturity is quite sure, for about 1640 the family was composed of nine persons, as is recorded in the Salem "Book of Grants" in Roger Conant's hand-writing. (Hist. Col. of the Essex Institute, Vol. 9, p. 103.)

SECOND GENERATION.

2.   **Lot^2** (*Roger*), b. about 1624 at Nantasket or Cape Ann. He seems to have lived at Marblehead as early as 1657; was selectman in 1662; had one cow's commonage in 1667, and on May 25, 1674, is recorded as one of the 114 householders.* On Nov. 20, 1666, his father gave him the homestead at Beverly with 32 acres adjoining and 72 acres in other parts of the town (Essex Deeds, Vol. 3, p. 28. For deed in full see p. 120 of this Genealogy). On the same day Lot leased the homestead with three acres adjoining, composing the southern part of the home farm, to his father and mother for an annual rent of "one Indian corn." About this time he probably moved to Beverly and built a house near his father's, for "a dwelling house and orchard containing about 4 acres, with an old house of his father" is mentioned in the inventory of his estate. On July 4, 1667, he was one of those dismissed from the First Church of Salem to form a church at Bass River, or Beverly.

In 1669-70, Mch. 10, with consent of his wife, Elizabeth, he sold to Vinson Stilson, of Marblehead, "all that his messuage, tenement or dwelling house with the land on which it stands & land belonging being ¼ acre in Marblehead bounding unto

* Roads' *Hist. of Marblehead*, p. 26.

the lands of John Trebye and Richard Thisle." (Essex Deeds, Vol. 3, p. 181.)

On the 20 Mch., 1671, "Lott Conant of Beverly, yeoman, sells John Treby of Marblehead a dwelling house with land adjoining and orchard and garden *Lot Conant* (Petition, 28 May, 1671.) bounded by the highway or street westerly and some land of Vinson Stilson westerly and Richard Hanaver north-westerly, the marsh of Nathaniel Walton north-easterly and land of said Lott Conant south-easterly." Signed by Lot and Elizabeth Conant, and witnessed by Hilliard Veren and Francis Johnson. (Essex Deeds, Vol. 3, p. 140.)

On the 20 Mch., 1672, "Lot Connet attacting Matthew ffairfield and not p'secuting the Court allows the said ffairfield costs 4s." (County Court Records.)

He died 29 Sep., 1674, leaving the following will:

"I Lot Conant aged about fiftie yeers being sicke and weak, yet of p'fit understanding doe hereby declare my last will and testament wherein in the first place I doe bequeth my soule unto god that gave it, and my body to the grave in hope of a blessed resurrection: and for my outward estate and goods I doe bequeath and give unto my five sonns to each of them fiftie pounds and unto my sonn nathaniel the shop and tools over & above the rest, and unto my five daughters twenty pounds to each of them and this estate I leave to be whole and unbroken till they come to full age or to marriage estate and in the meane time the whole to rest in the hands of my wife, and for the bringing up of the children and further more my will is that my wife be executrix and that the land be not at all disposed off from the children and that my wife have the dwelling house and orchard for her life time. and also that my kinswoman mari Leach have a cow or heifer at her being married or going from my wife. And for help unto my wife in this matter I doe instruct and designe mr. John Hale, Captaine Lathrop and my brother Exercise Conant to be assisting. hereunto I have subscribed my hand this 24 of the 7 month 1674.

Witness (signed) LOT CONANT
  ROGER CONANT
  EXERCISE CONANT

Roger Conant and Exercise Conant sworn in Court at Salem the 26: 9 mo: 1674 that they were present as witnesses when Lott Conant signed and proclaimed the above written as his last will and testament and there is no later will they know of, the said Lott being of good understanding.

Attest HILLIARD VEREN Cl."

9

The original will is preserved in the Court Files of Essex county. A fac-simile of it is here presented.

"An Inventory of the land and goods of Lott Conant deceased the 29: 7 mo 1674

	£ s d		£ s d
3 oxen at 4£ apiece -	12.00.00	a bedstead, bed, bolster and furniture -	7.00.00
10 cows at 3£ 10s p-piece	35.00.00	a livery, cubboard and cloath - - -	2.00.00
5 heifers 2£ - - -	10.00.00	sheets 7 pr. - - -	8.00.00
2 calves 15s ye piece -	1.10.00	a fine piece of pillow	
20 sheep at - - -	7.00.00	[beere ?]- - -	0.08.00
5 swin great and small	10.00.00	2 chests and boxes -	2.00.00
a horse - - -	5.00.00	a table and six stools	1.10.00
2 beasts killed and salted for ye house -	5.00.00	2 leather chaires - -	10.00
land 60 acres not improved - - -	150.00.00	a peace of searge -	3.00.00
land improved 19 acres	104.10.00	2 chaire - - -	0.06.00
meddow land 12 ackers	61.00.00	a feather bed, rugge and blankets - -	5.00.00
mow land 9 ackers -	40.00.00	a bedsted, downe bed & furnitur - -	4.00.00
a dwelling house and orchard containing about 4 acres with an old dwelling house of his father - -	160.00.00	a trundle bed & furnitur - - -	2.00.00
		waring apparrell -	8.00.00
more land 5 acres and 6 ackers purchased but not yet paid -	40.00.00	a carpet - -	1.00.00
		curten cloath - -	2.00.00
		cushion cloath - -	0.06.00
an old barn and cattle houseing - - -	5.00.00	spinning wheel - -	0.10.00
a shop where Nathan Conant works - -	5.00.00	sheeps wool and yarn	1.00.00
		cotten wooll - -	1.14.00
now a 3d pt. of a shed and house - -	2.00.00	flax and linen yarn -	1.00.00
		pewter and plates -	1.10.00
now an eighth of a catch - - -	20.00.00	earthern ware - -	0.10.00
land lying at Marblehead by Darly fort 2 ackers and ½ - -	5.00.00	a copper, 2 skillets a warming pan - -	2.00.00
a house at Marblehead	5.00.00	2 iron potts, and 2 skilletts - - -	2.00.00
corn Indian and English 127 bu. - -	13.00.00	2 musketts, 3 swords -	2.00.00
hay and fodder 32 load	20.00.00	pot hooks, andirons and spitt - - -	2.00.00
a cart and a putt and sleade - - -	2.00.00		
plowe tackling and chaines - - -	2.00.00		61.04.00
axes, hoes, & sithes -	1.00.00		721.00
	721.00.00	sum totall is - -	782.04.00

This inventory prised by
Mr. William Dodge Sen
and John Raiment

The relict and executrix of said Lott Conant gave oath to the truth of the above Inventory to the best of her knowledge and what she shall come to have knowledge of afterwards to be added to the foregoing and the apprisers did declare yt they made a true apprisal of ye estate above written according to their best understanding in Court Salem 26: 9: 74

Attest   HILLIARD VEREN Cl."

Lot Conant married Elizabeth, daughter of Rev. William Walton, who took his degrees at Emanuel College, Cambridge, in 1621 and 1625, and was settled over the parish of Seaton, Devonshire, where his daughter was baptized 27 Oct., 1629. William Walton was from Essex county, England, and is thought to have been at Hingham, Mass., as early as 1635. He was made a freeman 3 Mch., 1636; settled at Marblehead as early as 1639, and was pastor there until his death in 1668. Josiah Walton, son of Rev. William, died leaving a will dated 23 June, 1673, by which his estate was divided among his brothers, Nathaniel and Samuel, and his sisters, Martha Munjoy, Elizabeth Conant and Mary Bartlett. (Essex County Probate Records.)

Elizabeth, widow of Lot Conant, married 10 Jan., 1681-2, as his third wife, Andrew, son of Robert and Elizabeth Mansfield, of Lynn. He was b. 1623; made his will 1 June, 1679, which was proved 25 Nov., 1683.

Children of LOT and ELIZABETH (WALTON) CONANT:—

```
 8.  i.   Nathaniel, b. 28 July, 1650, ⎫
 9.  ii.  John, b. 15 Dec., 1652,      ⎬ baptized 1st Ch. Salem, 26
10. iii.  Lot, b. 16 Feb., 1657-8,     ⎭   May, 1662.
     iv.  Elizabeth, b. 13 May, 1660,
11.  v.   Mary, b. 14 July, 1662.
12.  vi.  Martha, b. 15 Aug., 1664; bap. 12: 8: 1664.
13. vii.  Sarah,   ⎫ twins, b. 19 Feb., 1666-7; bap. 3: 5: 1667, at
14. viii. William, ⎭   First Church, Salem.
15.  ix.  Roger, b. 10 Mch., 1668-9; bap. 23: 3: 1669.
16.  x.   Rebecca, b. 31 Jan., 1670-1; bap. 28: 9: 1671.
```

3. **Roger**[2] (*Roger*), b. 1626 at Salem, and was the first

white child born there, as the following record from the "Book of Grants"* shows: "21 : 11 : 1639 [Jan. 21, 1640] Granted to Roger Conant the son of Roger Connant being the first borne Child in Salem the som of twenty acres.

> WILLIAM HATHORN
> JOHN WOODBURY
> JEFFREY MASSEY
> MR. CONANT"

He lived at Marblehead in 1648, at which date he had a lot laid out to him. In 1656 he was one of the "seven men," or selectmen. Savage (*Genealogical Dictionary*) says that his wife's name was Sarah, but the following records seem to show that it was Elizabeth: "22: 11 mo: 1661. Ye church consented to ye baptizing of Mrs. Elizabeth Conants child upon ye letter from ye church at Cork testifying to her membership there." and "11th: 1: 1684, Mrs. Roger Conant was admitted to the first church by letter from the church in Ireland." (Salem First Church Records.) "13 Aug., 1684, Elizabeth Conant was one of those set off to form a church at Marblehead." (Felt's *Annals of Salem*, p. 558.)

A bible once the property of Roger Conant is still in existence, in possession of Chas. W. Palfray, Esq., of Salem. In it appears the following touching record: "The 4 day of May 1672 being Saturday, my dere littel sone Samuel Conant dyed. The 15 day of June 1672 being Saturday—my dere, dere dere husband Roger Conant dyed." The bible is now much defaced, being nearly three hundred years old; it is the third English, or Geneva edition, commonly called the "Breeches Bible."

No will or administration on the estate of Roger Conant remains in the Probate Records of Essex county.

Children of ROGER and ELIZABETH (———) CONANT:

i. Samuel, d. 4 May, 1672.
ii. John, b. 1650; bapt. 26: 3: 1662; m. ———, Elizabeth ———. She d. 3 July, 1711, aged 59, and her g. s. remains at Marblehead. They had no children so far as known. He was a house carpenter and later a trader at Marblehead, where he

also had a fishing stage. His first purchase of land appears to have been 2 July, 1676, when "William Williams late of Beverly now of Wenham" sells "John ye son of Roger Conant deceased one acre and 3 poles of land in Beverly" for 55sh. (Essex Deeds, Vol. 5, p. 20.) On 4 Sep., 1677, "John Bennett of Beverly weaver in consideration of £100 paid by John Conant of Beverly carpenter" sells him "one half acre of upland with the dwelling house thereon standing situated in Beverly and bounded north with land of David Thomas, east by Edward Grover, south by Antony Wood and west by the highway." (Essex Deeds, Vol. 5, p. 20.) On 8 Nov., 1678, he buys "one acre of upland and one acre of meddow" of Thomas Tuck, of Beverly, blacksmith, for £16. (Vol. 5, p. 13.)

On 11 Jan., 1688-9, "John Conant formerly of Beverly now of Marblehead for a consideration of £70, conveys to Philip English of Salem ¾ acres bounded by the road yt goes to Ipswich, south by Antony Wood, west by Thomas Gage with dwelling house thereon," and "30 acres between Beverly and Wenham bounded west by Wenham Pond, south and east by the county road, north by common land, with the building thereon." This was a mortgage which was afterward released. (Essex Deeds, Vol. 8, p. 397.)

On 3 Nov., 1692, Samuel Dutch, of Salem, conveys 12 poles of land in Salem to John Conant, of Marblehead. (Vol. 10, p. 123.) On 5 Dec., 1702, Samuel Ward, of Ipswich, mariner, son of Major Samuel Ward and Sarah, his wife, sells him a small lot of land in Marblehead "under the Great Rock before Mr. Walton's house." (Vol. 15, p. 127.) At about the same date he paid Nathaniel Walton £20 for one acre of marsh and upland near Little Harbor (Vol. 21, p. 134), and a short time after Henry Russell and Elizabeth, his wife, Thomas Rolls and Mary, his wife, James Trefey and Sarah, his wife, all of Marblehead, with the consent of Amos Dennis and Elizabeth, his wife, children of Henry Russell, deceased, sold him 1-5 acre in Marblehead. (Vol. 21, p. 188.) On 31 Mch., 1713, he paid £18 to Francis Hains for "a small parcell" of land which Hains purchased of Mary Lindall, it being the tenement of George Peek and Charles Green. (Vol. 32, p. 120.) On 5 Nov., 1718, "John Conant of Marblehead yeoman or trader," sells land which he bought "of Francis Hains deceased and his wife Elizabeth now living," to Eben Hawkes of Lynn. (Vol. 35, p. 210.)

In 1724 he shared in the division of Marblehead Great Neck, of which he was one of twenty-eight proprietors, among whom 300 acres were divided.

He died at Marblehead 19 Apr., 1738, aged 88 years. His gravestone still remains.

WILL OF JOHN CONANT.

"In the Name of God Amen. I John Conant of Marblehead in the County of Essex, yeoman, being Aged and Infirm do make my last will and Testament in Manner ffollowing. Impr. I make my good ffriends and Kindsman Messrs Deac. William Dodge and Jonathan Conant both of Beverly my Executors of this my will and order them in due time after my Decease to pay and discharge all my Debts and funeral Charges.

Item, I give and bequeath to my Cousin John Conant Jr. of Beverly in the County of Essex, weaver, one moiety or half part of all my Homestead consisting of about two acres of Land and Two old Houses in Marblehead, with all my cows commonage on the greate neck in Marblehead aforesd. To him the sd John Conant and to his Heirs forever.

Item I give to my several kindred ffollowing the several sums ffollowing in Bills of Credit, viz. To Deacon William Dodge before mentioned Fifty pounds. To Jonathan Conant of Beverly Fifty pounds. To Sarah Trow wife of George Trow Fifty pounds. To William Conant Twenty pounds. To Roger Conant Fifty pounds, To Ebenezer Conant son of the sd Roger Twenty pounds. To Daniel Conant Twenty pounds. To Joshua Dodge Twenty pounds. To Lott Conant Ten pounds. To Mary Kimball widow Ten pounds. To Rebecca wife of Nathaniel Rayment Ten pounds. To Caleb Conant living in the County of Barnstable Twenty pounds. To John Conant living in the same County Twenty pounds. To Joshua a minor son of the sd Caleb Conant Fifty pounds and to each of the children of Caleb Conant late of Mansfield in Connecticut Colony dec'd Ten pounds.

In witness whereof I have hereunto set my hand and seal the sixth Day of October A. D. 1737 and in the Eleventh year of His Majesties Reigne (The words Twenty pounds above the last on the other side being first Interlined)

(signed)   *John Conant*

Signed sealed Published and declared by the sd John Conant to be his last will and Testament in presence of us

WILLIAM ROBINSON
NATHAN BOWEN
EDWARD BOWEN

Ipswich Apr. 42, 1738. Before the Hon John Appleton Esq. Judge of Probate of Wills in the county of Essex Nathan Bowen and Edward Bowen Personally appeared and made oath that they were present and saw John Conant late of Marblehead signe, and seal and heard him publish and de-

clare the within written Instrument to be his last Will and
Testament and when he so did he was of sound understanding and of a Disposing mind to the best of their Discretion
and that together with Wm. Robinson they sett their hands
att the same time in his presence as witnesses.

(Sig)   DANIEL APPLETON Reg.

Upon which this will is proved and allowed—"

The inventory was taken 3 May, 1738, by Joshua Orme,
John Howard and Thomas Kimball. Amount as follows:

Real estate in Beverly, - - - - -	£148–00–00
Real estate in Marblehead, - - - - -	201–00–00
Personal estate, - - - - - - -	687–09–00
Notes and debts due, - - - - - -	20–17–00
	£1057–06–10
Debts due from the estate, - - - - -	107–05–10
	£950–01–00
An additional inventory, - - - - -	148–12–00
Total, - - - - -	£1098–13–00

4. **Sarah**[2] (*Roger*), born about 1628; married John, son
of Lawrence and Elizabeth Leach. Although there is no direct documentary evidence to prove that she married John
Leach, the circumstances indicating such a marriage are considered sufficient to warrant the statement; viz.: 1st, John
Leach's wife was named Sarah; 2nd, there is no record of
the marriage of either of them to anyone else; 3rd, John
Leach was a near neighbor of Roger Conant; 4th, John
Leach's eldest surviving child was John, and there were at
least four daughters, one of whom was named Mary, who, at
the time of Lot and Roger Conant's death, was unmarried;
5th, in Lot Conant's will Mary Leach is called kinswoman;
and in Roger Conant's will she is mentioned in connection
with his granddaughter, Rebecca; he also mentions his daughter, Sarah, and her son, John, and four daughters. Lawrence
Leach came to New England in the fleet with Higginson, in
1629; took the freeman's oath 18 May, 1631, and died June,
1662, aged about 82.

John Leach had a grant of land 1637, and was made freeman 1681 (Savage).

Y

Sarah Leach was admitted to the First Church, 1648, and dismissed to the Beverly church, 1667; she died about 1681.

Children of JOHN and SARAH (CONANT) LEACH:

i.   John, bapt. 3 Sept., 1648;
ii.   John, } twins, bapt. Nov., 1648. married and had family.
iii. Sarah, }
iv.   Rachael, bapt. 6 Apr., 1651.
v.   Sarah, bapt. 6 June, 1652.
vi.   Elizabeth, bapt. 27 Nov., 1653.
vii. Mary, bapt. 3 Sep., 1654; m. 2 Mch., 1680, Thos. Field, and
      probably then received the cow or heifer left her by Lot Co-
      nant, 1674, "at her being married or leaving my wife."
viii. Richard, bapt. 15 June, 1656, d. y.
ix.   Remember, } bapt. 3 Nov., 1661.
x.   Hannah,   }

> For descendants see Leach Genealogy, in preparation, by Josiah Granville Leach, Esq., of Philadelphia, Pa.

5. Joshua[2] (*Roger*), b. about 1630, in Salem. Very little can be ascertained about him except that he was a sea captain; lived in Marblehead 1657, and d. in England in 1659. It seems probable that he was the person referred to in the following extract from a letter of Rev. John Davenport to John Winthrop, junior, dated New Haven, 14th, 2nd, 1655: "Captaine Coñant is better, they have putt such household stuffe as they shall have use of into a vessel bound hitherward purposing to keepe house here."[*] If the family removed to Connecticut their stay was short, for no record of the name remains in the New Haven Colonial Records.

He m. Seeth [Gardner, d. of Thomas, bapt. at Salem, 25: 10: 1636. After his death she m. (2) John Grafton, as appears by the following record: "John Grafton and Seeth his wife were married 1: 10 mo: 1659."?]

The inventory of his estate was taken 28 May, 1659, by John Poor and Richard Prince; the amount was £189 17s.; charges due John Gardner, £35 7s. 11d. In 1659 (Nov.): "This court doe appoynt Thomas Gardner administrator to the Estate of Joshua Conant who dyed intestate in England and is to be accountable for said Estate." (County Court Records.)

---

[*] *Col. of the Mass. Hist. Society,* 3rd Series, Vol. X., p. 8.

Child of JOSHUA and SEETH (GARDNER?) CONANT:—

17. Joshua, b. 15 Apr., 1657, at Salem; bap. 4 June, 1657.

6. **Mary**[2] (*Roger*), b. about 1632, in Salem. She m. (1)
John, son of John and Agnes Balch. John Balch, senior, was
one of the first settlers of Massachusetts, and one of the com-
pany who removed from Cape Ann to Salem with Roger
Conant. The family is a very ancient one, the name appearing on the roll of Battle Abbey (see *N. E. Hist. and Gen.
Register*, Vol. IX., p. 233). John Balch, senior, is said to
have come from near Bridgewater, Somersetshire, Eng., with
Robert Gorges in 1623. John, jr., was drowned while crossing
the ferry from Salem to Beverly during a violent storm, 16
Jan., 1662. Administration on his estate was granted at the
Mch. term, 1662, of the court held at Ipswich. His estate
amounted to £189 17s.; he owed £30; the inventory was returned at Salem June, 1662, by Roger Conant and Samuel
Corning. John and Mary (Conant) Balch had one child, as
appears by the following: "Whereas there was administration granted to Mary Balch of the estate of her husband Jo.
Balch and the Court at Salem the 4th mo [1662] did divide the
estate between the said Mary Balch and Mary the daughter of
John Balch: Now the sd daughter being deceased by the consent of the parties it is ordered : That Benj. Balch shall after
the end of seven years next coming enjoy all the lands that
did belong to the said John Balch, being 50 acres in all, more
or less, only the said Mary to enjoy all the improved land upland and meadow during the said term of seven years, the rest
to be in his possession." (Probate Records.)

She was admitted to the First Church 30 Mch., 1663, and one
of those dismissed to form the church at Beverly, July 4, 1667.

She m. (2) William, son of William Dodge, born 19 Sep.,
bapt. 4 Oct., 1640, at Salem. William Dodge, senior, was of
an ancient Cheshire family,* and arrived at Salem in 1629, in
the Lion's Whelp. Concerning him the company at London
wrote to Governor Endicott "that William Dodge, a skillful

---

* *Dodge Memorial*, pp. 22, 23.

husbandman may have ye charge of ye teame of horses."
William Dodge, jr., was made a freeman 1683, and was representative to the General Court 1690. He gained, says Savage,
considerable reputation in the Indian wars. The following
story of him is told by Hubbard: * One day he was riding
with a friend when they were attacked by two Indians; Dodge
succeeded in killing his Indian, but the pistol of his friend
missed fire; the Indian was about to kill him with a knife
when Dodge came to his aid and dispatched the second Indian.
Thus, says Hubbard, "he did three good offices at once, saved
the life of one friend and slew two of his enemies."

Mary Dodge was one of the original members of Beverly
church (1667).

Child of JOHN and MARY (CONANT) BALCH:—

i.   Mary, died in infancy.

Children of WILLIAM and MARY (CONANT) DODGE:—

i.   William, b. 20 Mch., 1663-4,
ii.   Mary, b. 26 May, 1666,
iii. Joshua, bap. 29 Aug., 1669, } in Beverly.
iv.   Hannah, bap. 9 July, 1671,
v.   Sarah, bap. 8 Mch., 1677-8,

7. **Exercise**[2] (*Roger*), b. 1637, in Salem (Bass river side);
bapt. at First Church, Salem, 24 Dec., 1637; was freeman 27
May, 1663. In 1667 was one of the original members of the
Church at Beverly. In 1680 (9 June), John Clap (nephew of
Capt. Roger Clap of Dorchester), of Colyton, Devonshire, England, brought a suit to recover
of Exercise Conant, of Beverly,
land in Dunstable, left by said
Clap's father in his will, "for
the use of my wife in lieu of a debt oweing her mother ye widdo
Pitts of Lyme." (Mass. Archives, Vol. 16, p. 186.) This
suit was successful, for Exercise sold, some time after, to John
Moulton, of Wenham, for £8, "all that tract of land containing two hundred acres bee it more or less as it was laid out by
Jonathan Danforth unto Roger Conant deceased, excepting

(1674.)

---

* *Narrative of the Troubles with the Indians in New England, or Indian Wars.*

sixty acres sold by ye sd Exercise, and laid out to Jono. Clapp of Boston." Acknowledged at Ipswich Sep. 5, 1699.

In 1682-3 he was representative from Beverly to the General Court.

Apr. 20, 1682, "at a town meeting Mr. John Hale, Farmer William Dodge, Samuel Corning Sen. John Rayment Sen. Exercise Conant and John Hill were chosen to go to Ipswich, on the 21st to take notice of an address framed unto his Majesty in the name and behalf of themselves and others called parties unto Mr. Mason's claim." (See *Mass. Hist. Col.*, 3rd series, Vol. 7, p. 268.)

6 Feb., 1663-4, Exercise Conant, of Beverly, yeoman, and Sarah, his wife, sell John Balch, of Beverly, carpenter, "my whole portion of land given me in my father's will lying between the head of the Rails and Isaac Hull his ground, upon the right hand of the county road leading from Beverly to Wenham." Bounded on the south by John Leech, east by William Dodge, north by Isaac Hull and west by the county road. Acknowledged at Boston 1714. (Essex Deeds, Vol. 28, p. 90.)

28 May, 1683, he witnessed the will of John Gallee.

4 Oct., 1687, Exercise and Sarah Conant, of Beverly, sell William Elliot four acres of meadow situated in Wenham. Deed witnessed by George Wyatt, William Gedney and Francis Glover; recorded 16 Feb., 1692-3. (Essex Deeds, Vol. 9, p. 76.)

18 Jan., 1689-90, Exercise, Sarah and Abia Conant witness the deed of Benjamin Balch to his son, Freeborn Balch. (Essex Deeds, Vol. 8, p. 446.)

1 Apr., 1690, Exercise Conant, of Beverly, yeoman, with consent of Sarah, his wife, in consideration of £35 paid by Peter Woodbury, sells a parcel of land in Beverly containing 20 acres, "bounded west by the Herricks, southerly by land of Wm. Dodge, east with Cornelius Baker and me sd Conant and northerly bearing on ye east with Capt. William Rayment and me said Conant, with a corner of said land cornering up to the towne way." Witnessed by Jno. Harvey and Sam'l West. (Essex Deeds, Vol. 8, p. 169.)

27 Jan., 1691-2, Exercise and Sarah Conant sell John Conant, of Beverly, carpenter, 7 acres of land "wherein ye sd John Conants house now standeth bounded by Philip White on ye north and east with Freeborn Balch and south with high way; also 100 rods where the barn of said John now stands." Witnessed by John Fisk and Joshua Wallis. (Essex Deeds, Vol. 21, p. 230.)

23 May, 1695, "Exercise Conant of Beverly, yeoman, with consent of Sarah my wife for consideration of £9 10s paid by Joshua Wallis

Exercise Conant
(1679.)

our son-in-law of same town, cordwainer, and our promise to his wife Abia for a portion," sells a parcel of meadow and upland in Beverly, containing four acres, "bounded north-east and north-west by the county road and south-east and south-west by said Conants own land on which sd Wallis his dwelling house now stands." Witnessed by Jo. Abbey and Nathaniel Rayment. (Essex Deeds, Vol. 11, p. 101.)

25 May, 1695, Exercise Conant, of Beverly, sells his cousin, John Conant, "my now dwelling house, orchard, and field adjoining, and barn, containing in all 10 acres, bounded east and south by Wm. Dodge, west and north partly against Joshua Wallis his four acres and partly against two roads." Witnessed by Lot Conant and George Trow. (Essex Deeds, Vol. 22, p. 192.)

These last transfers seem to have been preparatory to his removal to Windham, Conn., for he bought a house and lot of Jonathan Crane, at Windham Centre, on 11 Apr., 1695. He was admitted an inhabitant of Windham 4 Nov., 1695. His stay there was short, for 13 July, 1696, he sold his house and lot No. 7, with the 1000 acre right belonging to it, for £70 in silver, and removed to Lebanon, Conn., where he had been granted half a lot on 1 Nov., 1695. He was one of the earliest settlers of Lebanon.

Dec., 1697, he was granted 1½ acres in the Clark and Dewey purchase.

In 1700 he appointed his son-in-law, Richard Hendee, his attorney to sell lands in Lebanon, and in 1701 sells house and lot in Lebanon to Daniel Clark, of Hartford, for £37.

At about this time he removed to Boston, Mass., for the following records are found in the Records of the Selectmen (see Boston Record Commissioners' Reports, Vol. 11): "June 30, 1701, Exercise Conant his Petition for a License to Sell all Sorts of Strong drinck out of door by Retaile is approved by the Select men" (p. 6). Sep. 15, 1702, "Ordered that Exercise Connet shall be joyned with the watch he to take his turn with the eight watch men to watch one night in eight in each of their Sted and to be allowed out of their pay twelve pence p' night for each night wch he Shall watch in their Sted" (p. 27). June 24, 1706, "At a meeting of the Select men Mr. Exercise Connunt is nominated and appointed to Inform against and prosecute all persons who shall hereafter Transgress the Town order relating to Regulateing of buryalls, and the Select men will take care that he shall be allowed a competent recompence for his Service therein. Ordered that the Several bell ringers within this Town at their Tolling of Bells for funeralls, Shall Turn up an Hour glass at the beginning of the Second bell for funeralls on week dayes, and at the beginning of the first bell for funeralls on Lords dayes and by their Information to assist Mr. Exercise Connunt or whom else the Select men Shall appoint of what they shall know relateing to the breach of the Town order for regulating buryalls" (p. 51). Jan. 21, 1706, "Exercise Conant appointed one of the Select watch" (p. 55). Nov. 4, 1709, "James Thornbery and Exercis Connant to Serve as overseers of the watch at forty five shill. p. mo." (p. 96). Feb. 28, 1711, "Exercise Conant and Ezekiel Cleasby appointed Inspectors of funerals" (p. 126). Sep. 6, 1715, "Ordered That the Town Watch men whereof Mr. Exercise Conant is at present Overseer do each morning for the space of six moneth ensuing give Seasonable notice to James Williams Bell ringer to Ring the Bell at five of the clock, in as much as at present there is no Town Clock" (p. 234).

On 12 Jan., 1706-7, the First Church of Beverly dismissed Exercise and Sarah Conant to the North Church of Boston, but the records of that church contain no mention of him.

The following depositions are recorded:

"Exercise Conant aged 72 years sworn saith, his Father Mr. Roger Conant late of Beverly about 32 years since was seized of certain Farm in Beverly next adjoining and abutting the farm of Henry Herrick and died seized of it then when it passed to his son Lott Conant his heir then living and now possessed by his son Lott Conant. the deponant lived many years with his father upon the said farm and the dividing line between Mr. Conant and Mr. Herrick was a certain brook. Sometime denominated the brook that comes out of the new [–?] and sd Conant and Herrick respectively improved land on either side of the brook. Boston 28 Mch., 1710." (Essex Deeds, Vol. 21, p. 180.)

In a case of "Inhabitants of Beverly vs. Dodge," Exercise Conant, aged 72 years, sworn, deposes "that he was born in Salem w'thin the county of Essex in New England. And for the greater part of his time lived in Beverly formerly part of Salem, and is well Knowing of the Lands and highways in Beverly afores'd and as long as he can Remember upw'ds of fifty years past that where the stone or Stones lye at the Corner of the Right hand going up Capt. Herricks Lane (so called) was ever the reputed bounds of the Field of Farmer Wm. Dodge dec'd running on a line to Mr. Hascalls hill * * * Further saith not.

Boston 19 June 1710." *Exercise Conant*

He returned to Windham about 1718, and his wife dying that year, he afterwards lived with his son, Josiah.

In some way not known, he gained the title of Lieutenant, and was commonly known as Lieut. Exercise Conant.

Exercise Conant died 28 Apr., 1722, in his 85th year, at Windham; his grave stone still remains in the part of the town now Mansfield.

He m. Sarah ———, who died 4 Dec., 1718. Their children were all born in Beverly and baptized at the First Church.

Children of EXERCISE and SARAH (———) CONANT:

18. Sarah, bap. 14 Feb., 1668-9.
19. Abiah, bap. 21 June, 1672.
20. Jane, bap. 20 June, 1675.
21. Elizabeth, bap. 29 July, 1677.
22. Josiah, bap. 4 July, 1680.
23. Caleb, bap. 29 Apr. 1683.

THIRD GENERATION.

8. Nathaniel[3] (*Lot, Roger*), born 28 July, 1650, in Beverly; married Hannah, dr. of Andrew and Bithiah Mansfield, and g. dr. of Robert and Elizabeth Mansfield. By the will of his father he was left £50 and the shop in which he worked, together with the tools in it. He was a cordwainer or shoemaker. He appears to have moved to Bridgewater, Plymouth county, as early as 1687, for on 18 Apr., 1688, Philip White, of Beverly, sold to Sir William Phipps, of Boston, "all his messuage or tenement, yards, orchard, upland and swampy ground thereto belonging, containing six acres, in Beverly, which I lately purchased of Nathaniel Conant, cordwainer, bounded by the highway called Woodbury's Lane and by land of Benj. Balch, together with shops, houses," etc. (Essex Deeds, Vol. 8, p. 177.)

The first mention of him in Bridgewater records is on the 3rd Monday of May, 1688, when "Goodman" Conant was to see to the repairs of the road leading from South brook to Comfort Willis'. (Mitchell's *Hist. of Bridgewater*, p. 66.)

In 1691-2 (7 Jan.), Nathaniel Conant, of Bridgewater, sells his brother, John Conant, of Beverly, "ten acres of land in Beverly lying towards Wenham near the great marsh, bounded west and south on William Dodges lying by Brimble hill, easterly on land of Jo. Woodbury, northerly on land of my two brothers John and Roger Conant, and two and one half acres near Wenham bounded by the Woodberrys east, Freeborn Balch on the west, north by Samuel Balch and south by John Conant." Witnessed by Benjamin Balch and Samuel Conant. (Essex Deeds, Vol. 21, p. 226.)

Mch. 14, 1693, he was one of the Jury of Trials. Dec. 6, 1694, and Mch. 8, 1698, he was one of the Grand Jury.

In 1703 a way was laid out beginning at Jonathan Washburn's, running "by the west end of old Goodman Conant's house."

On Mch. 7, 1708, he sells William Orcutt 25 acres of land for £14. (Plymouth Deeds, 2nd Series, Vol. 15, p. 56.)

In 1711 (20 Mch.), in consideration of his parental affection, etc., he conveys fifty-three acres of land in Bridgewater to his son, Nathaniel. (Plymouth Deeds, Vol. 11, p. 12, 2nd Series.)

In 1712 (3 July) he conveys 50 acres to his youngest son, Lot; this was the homestead and was situated in what was afterwards the South Parish.

In 1715 he was one of the petitioners for a second parish; this was incorporated 1716, and was called the South Parish.

On May 20, 1720, he sold Francis Woods ¾ acre of land. (Plymouth Deeds, Vol. 20, p. 119.)

On Dec. 5, 1729, he sold James Allen 11¾ acres of land for £20.

He died 1732, leaving the following will:

In the name of God Amen. July the third 1712 I Nathaniel Conant Senior of the Town of Bridgewater in ye County of Plymouth in New England, yeoman. Being of Sound Judgement and Disposing mind and memory Praised be God therefore yet calling to mind my mortality and knowing that it is appointed for all men once to die do make and ordain this my last will and Testament. That is to say Principally and first of all I do Recommend my Soul unto the hands of God yt gave it. My Body I recomend unto ye Earth to be buried in decent Christian Burial att ye Discretion of my Executors. Nothing doubting that at ye General Resurrection I shall Receive ye same by ye mighty power of God and as for such worldly goods and Estate wherewith it hath pleased God to bless me in this life, I give and Bequeath unto Hannah my dearly beloved wife one third part of my home living both housing and land. Together with 2 cows one bed and bedding necessary household goods for her use and Comfort during her widowhood. Then I have already given to my eldest son Nathaniel Conant that tract of land whereon he now dwelleth by a conveyance under my hand and seal wʰ I do hereby confirm to him and his heirs forever and my will is that he therewithall rest contented.

Then to my son Josiah Conant I give about 20 pounds which he hath already received partly toward the purchasing of his land where he first settled and partly in help towards Building and fencing and my will is that he therewithal rest contented.

Then to my youngest son Lot Conant I have given by deed my homestead to be by him fully and freely possessed and enjoyed after my decease and my wifes decease and my will is that he shall enjoy two thirds thereof during my wifes life after me wherewith he is to rest contented.

Then as for my 3 eldest daughters Bethiah, Hannah, and Martha, who have been disposed of in marriage I done for each of them respectively according to my ability about to the value of 12 pounds each and my will is that both they and their heirs do rest themselves contented therewith.

Then to my two youngest daughters Lydia and Rebecah I give all my moveable estate which shall remain after my wifes decease to be equally divided betwixt them.

Finally I nominate and appoint Hannah my well beloved wife Executrix and my eldest son Nathaniel Executor of this my last will and testament. Hereby renouncing, Revoking and Disallowing all other wills, testaments, Legacies, bequests or executers by me heretofore made, devised or named. Ratifying and establishing this and none other my last will and testament. In witness whereof I have hereunto set my hand and seal the day and year above written.

Signed, sealed, pronounced, and declared by the said Nathaniel Conant as his last will and testament. In presence of us

JOSEPH HAYWARD
NATHANIEL BRETT
SETH BRETT

This will was proved 24 Aug., 1735. The estate amounted to £711 10s. 0d.

Children of NATHANIEL and HANNAH (MANSFIELD) CONANT:—

24. Bithiah, b. 8 Nov., 1677, bap. 17 Mch., 1677-8, at Beverly.
25. Nathaniel, b. 3 Jan., bap. 7 Mch., 1679-80, at Beverly.
26. Josiah, bap. 27 Nov., 1680, at Beverly.
27. Hannah, b. 25 Jan., 1683-4, bap. 14 Sep., 1684, at Beverly.
   Martha, b. 24 Feb., 1686-7, bap. 3 July, 1687, at Beverly; m. 10 Mch. 1711, Thomas Knowlton, of Ipswich.
28. Lot, b. 27 Mch., 1689, bap. 20 Oct., 1689; birth recorded at Bridgewater.
   Lydia, b. 8 Nov., 1692; m. 1712, Andrew Lovell. Her birth recorded at Bridgewater.
   Rebecca, b. 4 Oct., 1694; m. 15 June, 1714, Shubael, son of Thomas and Elizabeth (Lovell) Ewer, of Barnstable, Mass. Thomas Ewer was son of Thomas, who was son of Thomas, of Charlestown, Mass.

9. **John³** (*Lot, Roger*), b. 15 Dec., 1652, in Beverly. He was a farmer and weaver. He settled in Beverly on the "60 acres of upland lying near Richard Dodge's farme" (see p. 121), given by Roger¹ to Lot,² his father, in 1666, and built a house at the point marked "4" on the map here presented. The

10

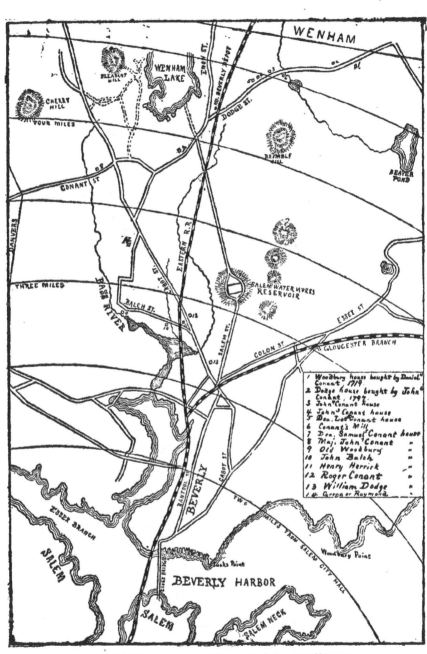

MAP OF BEVERLY, SHOWING LOCATION OF ANCIENT HOUSES.

(NOTE. 14 Gregg or Raymond, should be Scruggs or Raymond.)

house stood on the north side of the road, now called Dodge street, about one-third of a mile from North Beverly station, on the Eastern railroad. This house was taken down about 1830 and a new house built at "5," which is now occupied by Mr. Andrew Dodge, whose mother, Nancy[7] Conant, was John's great-great-granddaughter.

During King Philip's war he served in Capt. Samuel Appleton's company, and on 10 Dec., 1675, £4 16s. 10d. is allowed him as wages.* It is not probable that he took part in the attack on the Narraganset fort, as the men under Appleton were mostly employed in garrison duty at Hadley and Springfield.

He was admitted to the First Church of Beverly 23rd Aug., 1691.

In 1692 he purchased part of the farm of his brother, Nathaniel, who had moved to Bridgewater. (Essex Deeds, Vol. 21, p. 226.)

In 1715 (6 Sep.) John Conant, of Beverly, yeoman, in consideration of £197, sells John Chipman, of Beverly, one messuage or tenement containing 12 acres, bounded north-east by the town road and land of Jabez Baker, north-west by said Baker and the county road leading to Boston, south-west and south-east by land of William Dodge. The deed is signed by John and Bithiah Conant, and witnessed by Edward Rayment, Jonathan Herrick and Mary Rayment. (Essex Deeds, Vol. 30, p. 3.)

He died Sep. 30, 1724, leaving the following will:

"I John Conant of Beverly in the County of Essex in his Majesties Province of the Massachusetts Bay in New England, Yeoman, being through Divine goodness of Sound minde and memory but sick and weak in Body and not knowing how soon my change shall come, Do make and ordaine this my Last will and testament that is to say in the first and chief place I give my Immortal Spirit up unto the hands of God who gave it hoping through the merritt of my Dear Lord and Savior Jesus Christ to Receive Remission of Sins and Life Eternal and my body I commit to the earth to be buried Deacently att the Discression of my Executors hereafter named not doubting but that I shall Receive the same att the Resurrection in the Last Day. And as touching the worldly Estate with which it hath pleased God to bless me, I Demise and dispose of the same in manner as followeth.

* *N. E. Hist. and Gen. Register*, Vol. 38, p. 441; and *Mass. Arch.*, Vol. 68, p. 104.

First: My will is that all my just debts and funeral charges be first paid by my Executors hereafter named not out of my moveable estate but said Debts and funeral charges to be raised and Levied out of the Lands which I Do herein give to my Executors and paid by them in an equal portion.

Item. I will and bequeath to my well beloved son Lott Conant one piece of Land Lying in the township of Marblehead Containing three acres and a half be it more or less and being all the land I have in said township and also one piece of woolen cloth which is now at the fulling mill which together with what I have already given him is his full Part or Portion of my estate.

Item. I will and bequeath to my well beloved son John Conant all that piece of Ground which he hath for some years improved Lying Northwesterly from my orchard containing six acres be it more or less and bounded as the fence now stands and likewise ye one half of my field lying southward of the Highway before my door that part of the field lying next to the land which my son Daniel bought of the widow Alice Woodberry. Saving and accepting the breadth of one Rod and an half from the highway to the fence at the lower end of the field on the fence att Brimble Hill swamp this rod and a half lying next to the western most half of the field, I reserve for my son Benjamin, saving and accepting also a way and place convenient for watering cattle to and att the spring which is in Johns Part of the field which convenient watering place I like wise reserve for my son Benjamin, he making all the fence which shall be occasioned thereby.

Item. I give likewise to my son John the one half of my wood and land in Manchester woods and likewise the little orchard between his house and mine and one third part of ye cider house and mill thereon standing. Saving and accepting a way from the land att the back part of my house along by the end of my house to the high way which way I reserve to Benjamin a way six foot wide.

Item. I will and bequeath to my well beloved son Daniel Conant the Land which his part of the house stands on, and the land about his part of the house beginning at the back part of the house att the Distance of six feet from the house and extending a line westerly untill you come of against ye fence on ye eastward side of my old garden and from thence on a line as said fence stands to the highway. Daniel having six foot on the back part of the house and the land within that line att the end of his house and before his door. Including the little garden and half ye yard before his house I likewise give to Daniel the westernmost part of my old garden, the Divisional line between his and the other part being on the North side of the Garden eastward of the apple trees therein and extending thence on a straight line to the highway taking in all the appletrees to Daniels part. I likewise give to Daniel my land next to Brimble Hill Pasture and Brimble Hill swamp, the upland meadow ground and swamp, containing about ten acres in the whole, be it more or less. I likewise give to Daniel the one half of my Barn in the westernmost part thereof together with a convenient way and room Round his part of the Barn for his cattle and other occasions and the Barn floor to be for the both of Daniel and Benjamin in common and likewise one third part of my cider house and mill I give to Daniel.

Item. I will and bequeath to my well beloved son Benjamin Conant my part of the house, together with the House I now Dwell in and the one half of the yard before the door together with the way reserved for him att the end of the house next to my son Johns and likewise the orchard Lying to the back part of my house and the easternmost part of my old garden and also the one half of my field Lying southward from the Highway before my door Namely the westernmost half together with the Rod and a half from the County Road to the Lower end of the field and also the watering place reserved for him out of my son Johns part as aforesaid, and also the other half of the Barn, Reserving to Daniel as aforesaid. I likewise give to Benjamin the one half of my wood land in Manchester woods.

Item. I will and bequeath to my three sons John, Daniel and Benjamin Conant all my meadow in the great marsh to be equally divided between them and likewise all of my wearing clothes, and also my cart, plows, chains and Tools and all manner of Husbandry Implements to be equally divided between those three sons.

Item. I likewise bequeath to Benjamin all my Barley and two bushells of Beans and the one third part of my cider House and mill.

Item. In as much as I judge Daniels portion to be somewhat less than Johns and Benjamins I will and order that my sons John and Benjamin shall each of them pay to my son Daniel the sum of six pounds in good Province Bills within the space of seven years next after my decease.

Item. I will that tho my well is in that part of my land which I gave to John yet Daniel and Benjamin shall have the use of it together with free egress thereto and therefrom.

Item. I will and bequeath to my five well beloved daughters, viz Elizabeth Coburn, Bethiah Herrick, Deborah Darby, Rachel Cleaves and Jemima Batchelder all my Indian Corn, my man and all my cattle and sheep and swine and all my household goods in a word all my moveable estate not herein before disposed of to be equally divided between them only in case it shall please the Sovereign God to remove me by death before the first day of next, then I would have my stock kept where they are till that time and until that time I reserve to my son Benjamin the use of such cattle as he shall have occasion of.

Item. I will and Bequeath to each of my three sons Liberty of going over Each others Part of land with Horse or foot or team as they shall have occasion att any time and at all times forever that is to say over any part of each others land which I have herein given them Respectively. furthermore as to all and every Part that I have herein given to my children Respectively I do hereby give and Bequeath the same as above mentioned to them their heirs, executors, administrators and assignes forever.

Item. I do hereby constitute and ordain my three sons John, Benjamin and Daniel Conant joynt executors of this my will and testament. Revoking and Disannulling all other and ordaining and confirming this only as my last will and testament. In testamony whereof I Do hereunto sett my hand and seal this twenty first Day of September Anno Domini one thousand seven hundred and twenty and four. Anno Reg. Reg. Georgius undecimo.

(seal)

In presence of
              her
     EMMA X WILLIAMS
              mark

Signed Sealed and Declared by the said John Conant to be his last will and testament. In presence of

> ELISHA DODGE
> NATHANIEL DODGE
>   her
> EMMA X WILLIAMS
>   mark

Essex ss. Ipswich, October 26, 1724. Before the Honorabl John Appleton Esq. Judge of Probat of Wills &c Just. County of Essex. Elisha Dodge, Nathaniel Dodge and Emma Williams all personally appeared and made oath that they were present and saw John Conant Late of Beverly Deceased signe seale and heard him publish and Declare ye above and within written Testament in the several Pages thereof to be his last will and testament and when he did so he was of good understanding and of Disposing mind to the best of their Discerning and that they all at the same time sett their hands in his presence as witnesses

Sworn attest   DAN'L APPLETON Reg.

Upon which this will is Proved approved and Allowed itt being Presented by the executors therein named, who accepted the said trust and gave Bonds to Pay all Debts Due from sd Estate and Legaceys according to the will

Attest   DAN'L APPLETON, Reg."

John Conant married 7 May, 1678, Bithiah, dr. of Andrew and Bithiah Mansfield, of Lynn. She was born 7 Apr., 1658, admitted to the First Church of Beverly 6 Nov., 1681, died 27

July, 1720. Andrew Mansfield was son of Robert and Elizabeth Mansfield, who are said to have come from Exeter, Devon, Eng. On 10 June, 1650, Robert Mansfield "with consent of his wife Elizabeth in consideration of their son Andrew living with them until ye time of his marriage as a faithful and obedient child hath given to sd. Andrew as a childs portion, a house and house lot, 6 acres of land," beside a very large estate in various parts of Lynn.

20 Nov., 1663, Andrew Mansfield and wife, Bithiah, deed land to Charles Gott.

Andrew m. 2nd, Mary, widow of John Neal and dr. of Francis Lawes, who died at Lynn 27 June, 1681. He m. 3rd, 10 Jan., 1681-2, Elizabeth, widow of Lot Conant and dr. of Rev. William Walton. He was deputy to the General Court 1680-3. His will is dated 1 June, 1679; a codicil is added dated Boston, 19 Nov., 1683; proved 25 Nov., 1683. The will and codicil combined are quite long; in it occurs the following paragraph: "I give my Quarter part of Sloop which Jonathan Hart goeth master of equally betwixt my two sons and four daughters Andrew and Daniel Mansfield, Hannah and Bethia Conant, Lydia and Deborah Mansfield."

Robert, the father of Andrew Mansfield, died 1666; his wife, Elizabeth, d. 8 Sep., 1673, aged about 87 years (Savage). Her will is dated 20:2:1667; proved 26:9:1673; in it are mentioned sons, Joseph and Andrew, and daughter, Elizabeth.

Children of JOHN and BITHIAH (MANSFIELD) CONANT:—

29. Lot, bapt. 1 June, 1679, at Beverly.
30. Elizabeth, b. 14 Jan., 1681-2.
31. Bithiah, b. 14, bapt. 26 Oct., 1684.
32. John, b. 7 July, bapt. 15 Aug., 1686.
33. Deborah, b. 20 Feb., 1687-8.
    Mary, b. 20 Oct., 1689 (probably died before her father as she is not mentioned in his will).
34. Daniel, b. 19, bapt. 25 Nov., 1694.
35. Rebecca, b. 29 Mch., bapt. 5 Apr., 1696.
36. Benjamin, b. 22, bapt. 23 Oct., 1698.
37. Jemima, b. 9 Nov., 1701.

10. Lot[8] (*Lot, Roger*), born in Beverly 16 Feb., 1657-8, where he lived till 1717, when he moved to Ipswich. He was a farmer. He was in Capt. Joseph Gardiner's company in

King Philip's war, and took part in the attack on fort Narraganset on Dec. 19, 1675. He was admitted to the First Church of Beverly 1 Mch., 1701-2, and to full communion 19 July, 1702.

On the 28 May, 1717, Lot Conant and Elizabeth, his wife, sold ¼ acre of land in Beverly to Henry Herrick, jr., bounded east by the county road, south, west and north by Capt. Jos. Herrick's land. His wife signed by mark. (Essex Deeds, Vol. 33, p. 175.) On the same date "Lot Conant of Beverly yeoman with consent of Elizabeth my wife" in consideration of £186 13sh. conveys to Joseph Herrick, senior, "a parcel of land and marsh or meadow lying in Beverly containing 12 acres and 135 poles, bounded on the east by land of Ebenezer Rayment, south by said Herrick, on the west it comes to George Trows land." This deed is witnessed by Edward Rayment and John Herrick. (Essex Deeds, Vol. 34, p. 170.)

On the 30 July, 1717, he buys the homestead of Daniel Foster, of Ipswich, for £460, containing 90 acres of upland and 17 acres of fresh meadow; "also one old common right in the common land of Ipswich." Deed witnessed by Thomas Poor and Jona. Rayment. (Essex Deeds, Vol. 33, p. 16.)

On the 11 May, 1721, a committee on the part of the town of Ipswich, sell Lot Conant and others 111 acres of land on Turner's Hill. (Essex Deeds, Vol. 40, p. 156.)

On 18 Apr., 1735, Lot Conant was one of the grantees of the Narragansett Townships. (*N. E. Hist. and Gen. Reg.*, Vol. 19, p. 145.)

He left a will which was proved 10 Jan., 1744-5; it runs as follows:

"In the Name of God Amen. the Thirteenth Day of January Anno Domini 1743-4 I Lott Conant of Ipswich in ye county of Essex, New England being weakly in body but of perfect mind and memory, thanks be given to God therefor, calling to mind the mortality of my body knowing that it is appointed for all men once to Die. Do make my last will and testament viz. Principally and first of all I give and bequeath my Soule unto ye hands of God who first gave it being and my body I recommend to be buried in Decent Christian burial at the Discretion of my executors nothing doubting but that I shall Receive the same again at the General Resurrection by the mighty power of God. and as for Such worldly Estate as it hath pleased God to bless me with in this Life, I give, Demise and Dispose of the same in the following manner and form.

Item. I Give to my beloved wife Elizabeth all my indoor moveables, viz. Corn of all sorts: and wooll and flax and Cider as well as other household goods to use and dispose off as she shall think most convenient and I give her the improvement and benefit of one third part of my Real Estate both buildings and lands as fully as she could have it if I made no will. and give sd. wife the use and proffit of one third part of my live stock which shall be Left after my Debts and funeral charges shall be paid, During her natural Life and she is to have her firewood brought to the door and cut fit for the fire one half thereof by my son Joshua and the other half by my son William so long as she shall remain my widow, and my said sons Joshua and William are to find a horse for my said wife to ride to meeting on and other where as she shall have occasion so Long as she shall continue my widow. furthermore I give to my said wife all my money or bills of Public credit that be left at my Decease for her own use.

Item. I give to my son Jonathan all my buildings and Lands in Beverly and all my interest in Land Lying in Marblehead.

Item. I give to my son Joseph one hundred pounds in old Tenor bills of Credit or so much in money or bills of Public Credit as to be equal thereto and to be paid by my son Joshua within five years after my Decease.

Item. I give to my son Joshua one half of all my Lands and meadow lying in Ipswich and Topsfield both for Quantity and Quality with half of the buildings thereon and half of my utencels of husbandry only reserving liberty in my now Dwelling house as may hereafter bee mentioned for my daughter Elizabeth.

Item. I give to my son Samuel one hundred pounds in old Tenor bills of Credit or such money or other bills of Credit as to be equal! to said hundred pounds to be paid by my son William within five years after my Decease.

Item. I give to my son William one half of all my Lands and meadow lying in Ipswich and Topsfield with half the buildings thereupon reserving liberty in my now Dwelling house as may hereaftar be mentioned for my daughter Elizabeth and I give to my son William half of my Utencels of Husbandry and all Sheep that shall be left at my Decease.

Item. I give to my Daughter Abigail Thorndike twenty pounds in old Tenor bills of Credit or so much money or other bills of Public Credit as to be equall in value to the said Twenty pounds (besides what she has already had) and to be paid by my son Jonathan within two years after my Decease.

Item. I give to my Daughter Ruth Woodbury (besides what she hath already had) twenty pounds in old Tenor bills of public Credit or so much money or other bills of Credit as to be equal in vallue to the said Twenty pounds and to be paid by my son Joshua within two years after my Decease.

Item. I give to my Daughter Johannah Hutchinson (besides what she hath already had) Twenty pounds in old Tenor bills of Public Credit or so much money or other bills of Credit as to be equal in Vallue to said twenty pounds and to be paid by my son William within two years after my Decease.

Item. I Give to my Daughter Elizabeth Seventy pounds in old Tenor bills of Public Credit or so much money or other bills of Credit as to be Equal in Vallue to said Seventy pounds and to be paid by my two sons Joshua and William within three years after my Decease and my sd Daughter shall have Liberty to live in my now Dwelling house so long as she continue a single Woman and in case my said Daughter shall stand in need of some further help to support her besides her portion then my son Jonathan shall pay three pounds in old Tenor bills of public Credit or so much money or other bills as to be equal in Vallue to said three pounds, and to be paid yearly and every year to my son Joshua or my son William for or towards the support of my said Daughter so long as She shall stand in need of help from others to support her: and farther if my sd Daughter shall not be able to mantain herself after her mothers Decease that then my two sons Joshua and William shall take care of her and provide all things needful for her according as her circumstances shall require as long as she shall remain a single woman.

Item. I Give to my three Grandchildren hereafter named Twenty pounds in old Tenor bills or so much money or other bills of Credit as to be equall in Vallue to said Twenty pounds viz. to Abigail Thorndike six pounds, To William Ober six pounds and to Johannah Ober Eight pounds, and to be paid by my son Jonathan within three years after my Decease.

And my will is that my Executors hereafter named shall sell so much of my Stock of Cattle or horses as to pay my Just Debts and funeral Charges.

And also I Give to my two sons Joshua and William all the rest of my Live Stock to be Equally divided between them two thirds thereof as soon as the aforesaid Debts and charges are paid and the other third at my wifes Decease.

And I Do hereby Constitute make and ordain my well beloved Wife Elizabeth and my son Jonathan Conant to be Executors of this my Last Will and Testament. Ratifying and Confirming this to be my Last Will and Testament and none other. In witness whereof I have hereunto set my hand and affixed my seal the day and year above written.

Signed, Sealed, Pronounced and Declared by the said Lott Conant to be his last Will and Testament in presence of us witnesses

Lott Conant (seal)

JOHN DAVIS
ANDREW BRADSTREET
JACOB PEABODY"

He married (1) Abigail ———; m. (2) Elizabeth, dr. of John and Mary Pride, bapt. 12 Dec., 1686, and admitted to the church 23 Feb., 1706-7.

Children of LOT and ABIGAIL (———) CONANT:—

Samuel, b. 30 Mch., 1687; bapt. 10 June, 1688; died young.
38. Abigail, b. 6 Feb. 1689-90; bap. 3 July, 1690.
39. Jonathan, b. 8, bapt. 16 Oct., 1692.
Sarah, b. 2, bapt. 9 Nov., 1693; d. y.
Roger, b. 18, bapt. 24 Feb., 1694-5; prob. d. y. Not mentioned in his father's will.

Children of LOT and ELIZABETH (PRIDE) CONANT:—

40. Joseph, b. 9, bapt. 16 Nov., 1701.
41. Ruth, b. 18, bapt. 22 Nov., 1702.
Joshua, b. 2, bapt. 3 Dec., 1704; d. y.
Elizabeth, bapt. 28 Apr., 1706; d. y.
42. Joshua, b. 19 Oct., 1707; bapt. 2 May, 1708.
43. Joanna, b. 15, bapt. 27 Nov., 1709.
Bartholomew, b. 4 Feb., 1711-2; d. y.
Elizabeth, b. 27 Mch., bapt. 3 Apr., 1715.
44. Samuel, b. 18, bapt. 24 Nov., 1717. All above born in Beverly.
45. William, b. 8 Mch., 1720, in Ipswich.

11. **Mary**[3] (*Lot, Roger*), b. 14 July, 1662, in Beverly. She married for her first husband, 14 Mch., 1681-2, Andrew, son of Giles and Elizabeth Burley, of Ipswich, where he was born 5 Sep., 1657. He died 1 Feb.. 1718-9. Giles Burley was an inhabitant of Ipswich as early as 1648; made his will 18 July, 1668. (See Burleigh Genealogy.)

Children of ANDREW and MARY (CONANT) BURLEY:—

i. Rebecca, b. at Ipswich 29 Mch., 1683; published 5 May, 1705, to Robert, son of Robert and Mary (Boreman) Kinsman. He was representative to the General Court 1692; moved to Norwich, Conn., 1721; was selectman 1725-1728; died 7 June, 1761. (See Burleigh Gen.; also Kinsman Gen.)
ii. Andrew, b. 5 Apr., 1686; d. 5 Aug., 1686.
iii. Martha, b. 3 Mch., 1692-3; d. 26 Sep., 1693.
iv. Andrew, b. 15 June, 1694; d. 15 Dec., 1753. Published 1st, 9 Nov., 1717, to Lydia Pengry; she d. 27 Aug., 1736, leaving six children. Married 2nd, 9 Jan., 1738, widow Hannah Burnham; she d. 15 Sep., 1759. He was a Justice of the Court of Sessions, and representative to General Court 1741 and 1742. Left an estate valued at £2549 14s. 11d. (For family see Burleigh Genealogy.)

v.   Mary, b. 28 Apr., 1696; published 28 Sep., 1716, to Samuel
     Adams, son of Nath'l.
vi. Sarah, b. 6 Oct., 1698; published 12 Feb., 1725, to Richard
     Kimball.
vii. Elizabeth, b. 25 Aug., 1700; published 13 Jan., 1725, to Daniel,
     son of Dillingham and Mary Caldwell. (For children see
     Burleigh Genealogy.)
viii. John or Jonathan, b. 1700; m. 24 Nov., 1714, Mary, dr. of Sam-
     uel Eastman. He removed to Exeter, N. H., where he died
     1724, leaving three children. His wife was b. 1691. (The
     youthful age at which he was m. is somewhat remarkable.
     Charles Burleigh, Esq., author of the Burleigh Genealogy,
     vouches for the accuracy of the statement.)

The widow Mary (Conant) Burley m. (2) Sergeant Caleb Kimball,
b. 8 Sep., 1662, at Ipswich; published 14 Apr., 1722; she d. 23 Nov.,
1743. He was son of Caleb and Anna (Hazeltine) Kimball, of Ipswich. Caleb, senior, b. 1639, was son of Richard and Ursula
Kimball, who came from Ipswich, England, to Watertown, Mass.,
1934, and subsequently removed to Ipswich; he m. 7 Nov., 1660,
Anna, dr. of Robert and Anna Hazeltine, of Bradford; she d. 9
Apr., 1688. He was killed, says Savage, at Bloody Brook, 18 Sep.,
1675, being one of the Flower of Essex, under Capt. Lathrop;
others say he d. 1662; the latter are probably right, for the Caleb
killed at Bloody Brook appears to have been a son of Henry and
Mary (Wyatt) Kimball and to have died unmarried.

12.   **Martha**[3] (*Lot, Roger*), b. 15 Aug., bapt. 12 Oct., 1664,
at Beverly; m. 31 May, 1688, Luke, son of Luke and Hannah
(Long)* Perkins. He was born in Charlestown, Mass., 18
Mch., 1667-8, baptized at 1st Church there 19th 4 mo., 1669 or 70,
and lived successively in Marblehead, Beverly, Wenham, Ipswich (1704) and Plympton, where he moved about 1714. In
each of the places he lived he put on record the date of his
marriage and birth of his children. He died at Plympton 27
Dec., 1748, aged 82. His wife was dismissed from the church
in Beverly to that at Plympton, Oct., 1716; she d. 2 Jan., 1754.
Luke Perkins, senior, was son of Abraham † and Mary Perkins, of Hampton, N. H. (See Genealogy of the Perkinses
of Hampton, in preparation by Joseph W. Porter, Esq., of
Bangor, Maine.)

---

* She was widow of Henry Cookey, and dr. of Robert Long, of Charlestown.
† He was from Newent, co. Gloucester, Eng. His will was proved 18 Sep., 1683. His
wife, Mary, d. 29 May, 1706.

*

Children of LUKE and MARTHA (CONANT) PERKINS:—

i.   John, b. 5 Apr., 1689, bapt. 30th 6 mo., 1691; m. Mercy Jackson, 18 Apr., 1721, by Rev. Isaac Cushman, in Kingston. He d. about 1727. Children: 1. John, of Middleboro', m. 1745 Patience Páddock. 2. Mercy. 3. Eleanor. 4. Elizabeth. (See Davis' *Ancient Landmarks of Plymouth*.)
ii. Martha, b. 19 Sep., 1691; d. young.
iii. Hannah, b. 12 Mch., 1692-3, bapt. 8 May, 1693.
iv. Luke, b. 17 Sep., bapt. 17 Nov., 1695; m. Ruth, dr. of Robt. Cushman, in Plympton, 28 Jan., 1716-17, by Rev. Isaac Cushman. He removed from Kingston to some place unknown. Children: 1. Ignatius, b. 1720. 2. Hannah, b. 1723; m. Nathan Shaw. 3. Mary, b. 1726.
v.   Mark, b. ——, bapt. at Beverly 30 Apr., 1699; m. Dorothy, dr. of Matthew Whipple, of Ipswich; published as both of Ipswich, 4 June, 1721. Lived in Plympton and North Bridgewater (1741); was a blacksmith; he d. 20 Dec., 1756, and his widow m. 5 Oct., 1760, Solomon Packard, of B. Children:
1.   Dorothy, b. 4 Feb., 1721-2; m. 1742, Jacob Packard, who was descended from Samuel Packard, who came from Windham, near Hingham, Eng., and settled in Hingham, Mass., 1638. Their son, Rev. Hezekiah Packard, D. D., graduated at Harvard 1787, and was settled over the church at Chelmsford, Mass., and later in Maine; he was the father of: i. Rev. Alpheus S. Packard, D. D., who was tutor and professor of Bowdoin College for sixty-five years: ii. Charles, a minister at Lancaster and Middleborough, Mass.: iii. George, an Episcopal minister at Lawrence, Mass.: iv. Hezekiah, a teacher, died in Portland, Maine, 1867, aged 62: v. Rev. Joseph Packard, D. D., professor in the Episcopal Seminary in Fairfax co., Va.: and vi. William, who died aged eighteen. All the sons were graduates of Bowdoin College.
2.   Matthew, b. 25 June, 1723, d. 10 Mch., 1724.
3.   Sarah, b. 27 June, 1725; m. Ebenezer Packard. (See Mitchell's *Hist. of Bridgewater*, p. 256.)
4.   Josiah, b. 4 Jan., 1727-8; m. 17 Aug., 1755, Abigail, dr. of Benj. Edson. (See *Hist. of Bridgewater*, p. 268.)
5.   Jonathan, b. 5 Jan., 1729-30; m. 1752 Abigail, dr. of Jonathan Packard. (See *Hist. of Bridgewater*.)
6.   Isaac, b. 27 Apr., 1731; m. 2 May, 1754, Joanna, dr. of Benj. Edson.
7.   Martha, b. 30 Dec., 1733; m. 1763, Nathan Packard.
8.   Ebenezer, b. 7 May, 1736, d. 9 Nov. following.
9.   Jemima, b. 17 Feb., 1738-9; m. Levi Keith, 8 Nov., 1759. (See *Hist. Bridgewater*, p. 212.)
10. Mary, b. 16 Feb., 1739-40; m. 6 July, 1761, Simeon Packard. (See *Hist. of Bridgewater*, p. 257.)

    11. Capt. Jesse, b. 6 Dec., 1742; m. 5 June, 1769, Susanna, dr. of
Dr. Daniel Field.

 vi. Josiah, b. ——, bapt. 16 Nov., 1701, at Beverly; m. 1st, Debora,
dr. of Nehemiah Bennett, of Middleboro'; she d. 19 May,
1751, and he m. 2nd, a sister of Rev. Jona. Parker. He d. 15
Oct., 1789. Children:

    1. Nathan, b. 1723; m. Mary, dr. of Jonathan Sampson.
    2. William, b. 1724; m. Eliza ——.
    3. John, b. 1726; m. Mehitable Shaw.
    4. Martha, b. 1727.
    5. Joshua, b. 1729; m. Hannah, dr. of Geo. Sampson.
    6. Abner, b. 1731.
    7. Josiah, b. 1732; m. Debora, dr. of Ebenezer Soule.
    8. Luke, b. 1733; m. Eliz. dr. of Isaac Churchill.
    9. Abner, b. 1735.
  10. Debora, b. 1737.
  11. Hannah, b. 1740.
  12. Zephaniah, b. 1742; m. Patience, dr. of William Ripley.
  13. Isaac, b. 1744; m. 1771, Molly, dr. of Barnabas Shurtleff.
      (See *Ancient Landmarks of Plymouth*.)

 vii. Martha, b. 14 Aug., 1707; m. 1 Jan., 1729-30, Elisha Washburn,
of Kingston. He d. 1734.

    13. Sarah³ (*Lot, Roger*), b. 19 Feb., 1666-7; bapt. 3 July,
1667; d. 1 Nov., 1750, aged 84 (Hale's Notes). She m. ——,
George Trow, who d. 1751, in camp (Beverly Records), aged
84 (Hale's Notes).

Children of GEORGE and SARAH (CONANT) TROW:—

i. George, b. 3 Dec., 1686, at Beverly.
ii. Sarah, b. 22 Feb., 1688-9; d. 25 Jan., 1700-1.
iii. William, b. 24 Oct., 1691; m. Elizabeth Raymond, and had:
Sarah, b. 1722; William, b. 1725; George, b. 1727, m. Anna
Brown, of Salem, 1757; he d. 1789; Anna, b. 1733, d. y.; Elizabeth, b. 1735, d. y.; Elizabeth, b. 1736; Anna, b. 1741; Hannah, b. 1742. William, the father, d. 24 Oct., 1745, and the
widow m. Ebenezer Trask.
iv. Bartholomew, b. 9 Apr., 1694.
v. Roger, b. 13 June, 1696; d. 2 July, 1707.
vi. Ann, b. 5 Sep., 1698.
vii. Richard, b. 6 Feb., 1701-2; m. Hannah Raymond (See p. 161.)
viii. Martha, b. 14 Mch., 1703-4.
ix. Josiah, b. 5 Mch., 1706; his son, Josiah, m. 25 Feb., 1758-9,
Elizabeth Batchelder, by Rev. John Chipman. Children:
1. Mary, m. Zachariah Batchelder. 2. Sarah, m. 1st, Trask,
2nd, Amos Brown. 3. Rebecca, m. Abner Coffin. 4. Betsey, m. John Trow. 5. William, m. Joanna Baker. 6.
Capt. James, m. 1st, Mary Woodbury, 2nd, Eunice Smith,

for answeare to vs
and fully to take knowledg was not denied, only
And as for the quantitie of
neither vine nor Johnson
the Bill was worn more
the ___ onto what
___ and after a ___ Joh
two letters dated ___

As for the ___
of vs, it was so much
so make our ___
the ___ Johnson
and ___ might be ___
be equally done and ___
for the ___ ___

As for the arbitration
and debt of the Bill ___
not of our ___ debt ___
___ in the ___
being produced to the arb

declaration we desire the court
at vor the matter of their bill
on of them was left

All ___ mine of vs ___
only by supposition, but ___
___ suppress it, ___
___ ___
the Bill

___
___ by way of our ___
___ in the ___
___ it ___
___ by Bill if ___
___

___
men they did fully consider
of what mr Johnson ___
of what mr Johnson ___
and ___ be ___
both they ___ agreed

Roger ___
Andrew ___
Nathaniel Pickman

and had James, Mary and Sabrina, by 1st wife; William, John Francis, a merchant of Beverly, who has a fam., Sabrina, Jane Elizabeth, who m. Sam'l Trask, of Peabody, and Amos, by 2nd wife. 7. Elizabeth. 8. Josiah. 9. Nathaniel.

14. William³ (*Lot, Roger*), b. 19 Feb., 1666-7; bapt. 3 July, 1667, at Beverly. He was admitted to full communion with the First Church of Beverly, 5 Sep., 1703, and dismissed to the church at Bridgewater 12 Jan., 1706-7.

In 1706 he bought land of Nath'l Allen, in East Bridgewater, on the north bank of Satucket river. (Plymouth Deeds, 2nd Series, Vol. 10, p. 103.) On this purchase he built a house the same year; the house stood on sloping ground, and was two stories in front and one story on the back side. He occupied this house till his death; it was taken down in 1811. In 1715 the town "allowed thirty hands to build a bridge at William Conant's, they to be freed of all other highway work so long as they keep said bridge in good repair." On August 13, 1717, he sold six acres of land on the west side of Satucket river to Joseph Washburn, sen., for £9. (Plymouth Deeds, 2nd Series, Vol. 13, p. 101.) On June 3, 1723, William Conant, of Bridgewater, and Mary, his wife, sold to "my cousin, John Conant, of Beverly, weaver, three acres of land in Beverly, it being 1-11 of the land not disposed of, of the homestead of our father, John Woodbury, late of Beverly." (Essex Deeds, Vol. 58, p. 96.) On Mch. 16, 1729-30, he with others sold 20 acres of land to John Kingman, jr., for £30.

(Deed, 1723.)

His will is dated 1748, proved at Plymouth 1754, for which see Plymouth Probate Records, Vol. 13, p. 279.

He m. ———, Mary, dr. of John Woodbury, of Beverly. She was admitted to the First Church of Beverly, 5 Sep., 1703, the same day as her husband, and was dismissed to the church at Bridgewater at the same time he was.

Children of WILLIAM and MARY (WOODBURY) CONANT:—

46. Mary, b. 4 Apr., bapt. 17 June, 1694.
    William, b. 30 Jan., bapt. 2 Aug., 1696; prob. d. y.

47. David, b. 11 Dec., 1698; bapt. 1 Oct., 1699.
48. Elizabeth, b. ———; bapt. 16 Nov., 1702.
    Abigail, b. ———.
    Hannah, b. ———; bapt. 5 Aug., 1705; d. 1773; unm.
    Sarah, b. ———, 1708, in Bridgewater, Mass.
    Ruth, b. ———, 1711, in Bridgewater, d. 1780; unm.

15. **Roger**[3] (*Lot, Roger*), b. 10 Mch., 1668-9; bapt. 23
May, 1669, at Beverly. He lived in that part of the town
known as the "Precinct of Salem and Beverly," and was admitted to the Second, or North, Church May 4, 1718. In Mch.,
1719-20, he bought land at Concord, Mass., and soon after
moved there with his family. On May 6, 1721, Roger Conant,
of Concord, sells John Conant, weaver, Daniel Conant, mason,
and Benjamin Conant, tailor, all of Beverly, 16 acres of land
for £90. (Essex Deeds, Vol. 58, p. 95.) In Nov., 1724, he
sells his house and barn in Beverly to ——— Bucknam. (Essex Deeds, Vol. 44.) On March 8, 1736, he gives 4 acres of
meadow land to his son, Israel, and during the same year gave
land to his son, Ebenezer. He lived in that part of the town
called "Concord Village," now Acton.

He d. 1745, leaving a will dated Sep. 16, 1745. The inventory of his estate was taken May 26, 1746; amount, £355
14s. 7d.

ABSTRACT OF THE WILL OF ROGER CONANT.

Roger Conant, of Concord, yeoman, being sick and weak in body,
do make and ordain the following will and testament. To son
Ebenezer £20; to son Israel 20 acres of land out of my homestead,
"lying next to his present dwelling house;" to son Thomas, the
house he lives in and 30 acres adjoining the land given my son Israel, "containing in it my now Dwelling house and barn which I
give to said Thomas;" to son Josiah, 20 acres of land adjoining the
30 acres given Thomas. He mentions, also, wife Mary, daughters
Wheeler, Adams, Mehitable Piper and Sarah Piper, and three children of his son Roger, deceased. Witnesses, Samuel Heywood,
Ephraim Wood and Joseph Lee.

He m. 25 Apr., 1698, Mary, dr. of Capt. Thomas and Mary
Raymond, or, as then frequently written, Rayment. She was
admitted to the First Church of Beverly Nov. 8, 1702, and
dismissed to the Second Church April 22, 1716. Capt. Thomas

Raymond d. 1735, and his son-in-law, Roger Conant, was appointed administrator of his estate.

(1735.)

Children of ROGER and MARY (RAYMOND) CONANT:—

49. Ebenezer, b. 30 Dec., 1698; ⎫
50. Roger, b. 6 Dec., 1701; ⎬ bapt. at First Church, 1 Aug.,
51. Mary, b. 20 June, 1703; ⎭ 1703.
52. Abigail, b. 25 May, bapt. 2 July, 1705.
53. Israel, b. 4 Apr., bapt. 2 Sep., 1707.
    Lydia, b. 27 May, 1709; m. ——— Adams.
54. Josiah, b. 12 Dec., 1711; bapt. 20 July, 1712.
    Sarah, b. 25 Apr., 1714; bapt. 2 May, 1714, at First Church
    of Beverly; m. ——— Piper.
    Mehitable, b. ———, bapt. 5 Feb., 1715, at Second Church of
    Beverly; m. 14 Mch., 1744-5, Josiah Piper, of Stratham, N. H.
55. Thomas, b. 29 Mch.; bapt. 6 Apr., 1718, at Second Church of
    Beverly. ·

16. **Rebecca**[3] (*Lot, Roger*), b. 31 Jan., 1670-1, at Beverly; d. 5 Dec., 1760; m. Nathaniel, son of John and Judith (Woodbury) Raymond. He was b. 15 Mch., 1670-1, bapt. 6 Aug., 1671, in Beverly. He d. 8 Jan., 1749-50. His will dated 13 May, 1747, proved 29 Jan., 1749-50; the inventory was taken by Daniel Conant, Benjamin Jones and Peter Woodbury, and amounted to £1400 13s. 6d.

Children of NATHANIEL and REBECCA (CONANT) RAYMOND:—

i. David, b. 13 Jan., 1692.
ii. Rebecca, b. 20 Nov., 1694; m. ——— Sears.
iii. Elizabeth, b. 26 May, 1697; m. 1721, Wm. Trow.
iv. Benjamin, b. 1 Dec., 1699; m. Mary, dr. of Joseph Trask.
    Children: Joseph, Benjamin, Elizabeth, Mary and Rebecca.
v. Judith, b. 20 Nov., 1702; m. 6 Feb., 1723, Benjamin Corning.
vi. Hannah, b. 8 Oct., 1705 (m. 1st, 1735, Richard Trow?); m. 2nd,
    Joseph Corning.
vii. George, b. 21 Dec., 1707.
viii. Mary, b. 31 Jan., 1710; m. ———, William Preston.
ix. Nathaniel, b. 1 Apr., 1712.
x. [John, b. 9 Feb., 1716. ·

17. Joshua[8] (*Joshua, Roger*), b. 15 Apr., bapt. 4 June,
1657; was of Salem. The following is an abstract of the only
deed in his name recorded in the Essex Registry: 20 Dec.,
1684, Joshua Conant, of Salem, for the consideration of £30 paid
by Freeborn Balch, of Beverly, conveys to him "a certain p'cel
of 17 acres of land lying in Beverly, being bounded easterly by
Peter Woodberry and marsh that was formerly Mr. Conant's,
westerly by land sold by Exercise Conant to John Conant senior, southerly by the Jebacco Roade and north by Benjamin
Balch senior, it being all the land given me by Roger Conant
in his will, reserving the priviledg to pass to Lot Conant."
(Vol. 8, p. 146.)

In the spring of 1689 news of the landing of William and
Mary in England, and the Revolution against King James,
reached Boston, and the colonists deposed Sir Edmund Andros—then Governor of all New England—who was supposed
to be plotting with France. Andros was sent to England for
trial. The trouble with France continued and on Sep. 17,
1689, several vessels belonging in Salem were captured by a
French fleet and carried to Port Royal; among the prisoners
was Joshua Conant, whose statement of the capture follows:

"Joshua Conant testifieth: That he being Commander of the
Ketch Thomas and Mary of Salem, he was taken by three French
Ships off from Torbay near Cansir upon Tuesday the 17th of September last, two of which were Ships of War the other a Merchant-
man, and being put on board the Admiral viz the Lumbuscado and
therein carried to Port Royal a Prisoner. Mr. Mero told me that
the French on board told him, that there was ten sail of them ships
of war came out in company together from France, and that they
came directly from France and were bound to Boston in New England and that Sir E. A. had sent to the French King for them and
that the Countrey was to be delivered up unto their hands: but
hearing that Sir E. A. was taken and now held should not proceed
at present but threatened what they would do next summer.

JOSHUAH CONANT.

Joshuah Conant personally appeared before me and made oath
to the truth of the above said evidence. Salem, Nov. 23, 1689.

JOHN HATHORNE, Assistant.

Joshua Conant Testifies that on Board the Lumbuscado: one
Peter Gott told him there were thirteen Ships of them came out

of France in Company together, and that they were bound directly for Boston in New England Expecting that the Country was before or would be delivered up to the King of France: and told him before they could get clear of the Coast of France: several of their Ships were taken by the English Ships of War and the rest of their Fleet taken or dispersed and lost about Newfoundland. Sworn Nov. 23, 1689." (See Publications of the Prince Society, Andres Tracts, Vol. 1, p. 204.)

✓ Joshua Conant removed about 1700 to the north part of Eastham, now Truro, Barnstable co., Mass., with his family. No further record of him has been found.

He married (1) 31 Aug., 1676, Christian, dr. of Richard Mower, or More. She was bapt. 5 Sep., 1652, at Salem, and d. 30 May, 1680. Her g. s. remains in the Charter Street Burial Ground, at Salem, and bears the following inscription: "Christian Conan[t], wife of Joshua, and daughter of Richard More, died May 30, 1680, aged 28 years." Richard More came in the Blessing, 1635, aged 20 yrs.; was a mariner; joined the church 1642; freeman 28 Feb., 1643. (Savage.)

Joshua Conant m. (2) 9 Jan., 1690-1, Sarah Newcomb.

Child of JOSHUA and CHRISTIAN (MORE) CONANT:—

Joshua, b. 12 May, 1678 (bapt. 13 Nov., 1678?).

Children of JOSHUA and SARAH (NEWCOMB) CONANT:—

Kezia, b. 8 Nov., 1691.
56. Caleb, b. 13 Nov., 1693 (bapt. 2 Dec., 1693?).
Sarah, b. 12 Apr., 1695.
57. John, b. 19 Apr., 1700.

18. **Sarah**[8] (*Exercise, Roger*), bapt. 14 Feb., 1668-9, in Beverly; m. by Rev. John Hale, of Beverly, 16 Aug., 1693, John, son of James, g. s. of James Moulton, of Salem and Wenham. James Moulton, the immigrant, joined the church at Salem, 31 Dec., 1637. His son James was bapt. 7 Jan., 1638; made freeman 1666. He moved from Salem to Wenham before 1667.

Children of JOHN and SARAH (CONANT) MOULTON:—

i. Mary, b. 10 June, 1696; m. John Bingham, of Windham, Conn., 6 Dec., 1721.
ii. John, b. 1 Oct., 1698; m. int. pub. 28 Jan., 1729, to Hannah, dr.

of Samuel Kilham, of Wenham; m. 2nd, Sarah ———, who
d. 3 Jan., 1744. He d. 1755; estate settled 8 Dec., 1755.
Children:

1. Jonathan, b. 1730; farmer of Wenham; served in Revolutionary army; d. 1806 or 7. He m. Mary, dr. of Capt. Samuel Tarbox, and 2nd, —— Cue. His children were: Thomas; John, b. 1762; Jonathan, b. 1765; Tarbox, b. 1769; Samuel; Daniel, of Amherst, N. H., who was the father of
the late Francis Moulton, of Brooklyn, N. Y.; Capt.
William, b. 1775, who was father of Samuel, who was
Representative to Congress three terms from Illinois.
2. John.
3. Sarah, b. 1732; m. Bartholomew Dwinell.
4. Hannah, b. 1735.
5. Josiah, b. 1739.

iii. Abigail, b. 27 Mch., 1701.
iv. Josiah, b. 16 July, 1703; d. 17 Mch., 1730.
v.   Hannah, b. 1 Apr., 1706; m. 1737, Joseph Ayres.
vi. Sarah, b. 29 Aug., 1709; m. 1728, Moses May.
vii. Samuel, b. 19 Oct., 1710; m. 1733, Sarah Fisk.
viii. Benjamin, b. 7 July, 1711; m. 1740, Tabitha Howard.

19. **Abiah**[3] (*Exercise, Roger*), bapt. 21 June, 1672; m. 1
June, 1691, Joshua, son of Nathaniel and Margaret Wallis.
Nathaniel Wallis was b. 1632, in Cornwall, Eng., and in 1658
was living at Casco Bay, (now Portland, Me.,) where he signed
the submission to Massachusetts. In 1660 Robert Jordan was
summoned before the General Court for baptizing the children
of Nathaniel Wallis "after the exercise was ended upon the
Lord's day, in the house of Mrs. Mackworth in the town of
Falmouth," and was required "to desist from any such prac-
tises for the future." (Mass. Records.) During the French
and Indian war the family was driven away from Falmouth
and settled at Beverly, Mass., where Nathaniel d. 18 Oct., 1709,
leaving, by will, his farm of 309 acres in Falmouth to his sons,
Joshua and Caleb. His wife, Margaret, d. 14 May, 1711,
aged 81. (Willis' *Hist. of Portland*, pp. 92, 301.)

12: 2: 1691, Joshua Wallis admitted to the First Church
of Beverly. 10: 10: 1692, Abiah, wife of Joshua Wallis, admitted to church.

On Mch. 10, 1696, Joshua Wallis, with consent of Abiah,
his wife, sold the four acre lot given them by her father, Exercise Conant, to Jonathan Baker. The deed was witnessed by

Nathaniel Wallis and Samuel Hardie. In 1698 (Dec.) Joshua Wallis buys land in Beverly of Henry Haggerty. Witnesses, David and Sarah Maxee. (Essex Deeds, Vol. 25, p. 188.)

May 14, 1739, Joshua Wallis, of Sherburne, Mass., cordwainer, sells to his son-in-law, Jacob Cozens, of Holliston, "all rights in Falmouth and Yarmouth." Witnessed by Abraham and Joshua Cozens. (York Co. Deeds, Vol. 23, p. 231.)

Child of JOSHUA and ABIAH (CONANT) WALLIS:—

i. Mary, b. 4 Sep., 1694; the only child recorded at Beverly.

20. Jane[3] (*Exercise, Roger*), bapt. 20 June, 1675, at Beverly; m. 4 July, 1695, as his second wife, William, son of James Moulton, of Wenham. They removed to Windham, Conn., where he was admitted an inhabitant 1698. After a stay of about five years the family moved again, this time to Ipswich, Mass., where William Moulton died, 1763.

Children of WILLIAM and JANE (CONANT) MOULTON:—

i. William, b. 1696; d. same year.
ii. William, b. at Windham, Nov., 1697; husbandman.
iii. James, b. at Windham, July, 1700; shoemaker.
iv. Daniel, b. at Ipswich, Jan., 1703; was m. and had two children, Sarah and Elizabeth.
v. Sarah, b. at Ipswich, 1705; m. Jonathan Clinton.
vi. Caleb, b. at Ipswich, 1709; cooper.
vii. Lucy, b. at Ipswich, 1712.
viii. Nathaniel, b. at Ipswich, 1715; a shoemaker, of Andover, Mass.
ix. Joseph, b. at Ipswich 1716; d. 1735.

21. Elizabeth[3] (*Exercise, Roger*), bapt. 29 July, 1677, at Beverly; m. 17 Oct., 1695, as his second wife, Richard, son of Richard Hendee, of Norwich, Conn. Richard Hendee was one of the first proprietors of Killingworth, Conn. In 1689 he purchased land in Joshua's Tract of Joseph Fitch, on which he settled as early as 1691. Joshua's Tract took its name from the fact that it was given by Joshua, grandson of Uncas, to a company of gentlemen of Norwich; the name was soon changed to Windham. In 1692 he was granted the privilege of building a dam and saw mill on Beaver brook, also half a mile of land adjoining for timber and pasture. Richard Hendee was admitted an inhabitant 30 May, 1693. He d. 6 Feb.,

1743; his wife d. 23 Sep., 1762. By his first wife, Sarah Smith, he had one son, Jonathan, who is the ancestor of the Pittsford, Vt., Hendees.

Children of RICHARD and ELIZABETH (CONANT) HENDEE:—

i. Hannah, b. 25 Dec., 1697; m. —— Hurd, of Stratford.
ii. Sarah, b. 16 Apr., 1700; m. —— Casey, of Mansfield.
iii. Caleb, b. 12 Mch., 1704 (d. young?).
iv. Josiah, b. 25 Apr., 1707; lived in Ashford; left a large family. One of his descendants (Caleb) was one of Gen. Washington's Life Guards. Many of his descendants still live at Ashford.
v. Elizabeth, b. 28 Apr., 1710; m. —— Brown, of Windham.
vi. Barzillai, b. 18 June, 1713; lived and died at Woodbury, Conn. Left a large family who, it is supposed, removed to western New York.
vii. Asa, b. 25 Aug., 1715; settled in Coventry, Conn., where he died leaving children:
1. Asa, removed to Utica, N. Y., where he died leaving Asa, Cyrus, Cloa, Zoa, Lota and Esther.
2. Eliphalet, m. Mary Loomis, of Bolton; settled in Coventry where he d. 1827, leaving (a) Abner, now of Hebron, Conn.; (b) Mary, now of Andover, Conn.; (c) Eliphalet, of Andover, Conn., m. Amelia Babcock, of Columbia; is the father of Lucius J. Hendee, President of the Ætna Fire Insurance Company of Hartford; (d) Leonard, of Andover.
3. Lydia.
4. Mary.
5. Esther.
viii. Nathaniel, b. 10 Aug., 1718.
ix. Mary, b. 6 July, 1720; m. —— Dudley, of Woodbury, Conn.

22. Josiah[3] (*Exercise, Roger*), bapt. 4 July, 1680, at Beverly; removed to Connecticut with his father; lived in Windham, afterwards Mansfield. He was admitted an inhabitant of Windham, 12 Dec., 1701; bought land in Memeaguague, a tract south-east of Windham, but afterwards included in it, 27 Jan., 1702. In 1710 he purchased 96 acres of land of his brother, Caleb, in Windham.

In 1720 he united with the church of Mansfield, and in 1730 was chosen deacon.

In 1722 he was one of a committee appointed by the legislature "to view the proper lines for Voluntown." The committee met Sep. 17, 1722, at the house of John Amos, in Preston.

In May, 1726, he was chosen surveyor of lands for Windham county.

Josiah Conant d. 1 Nov., 1765, in the 86th year of his age. He m. 6 Oct., 1709, Joanna, dr. of Deacon Shubael and Joanna (Bursley) Dimmick. She was b. Mch., 1682, in Barnstable, Mass., and removed to Mansfield about 1695, with her parents; she d. 17 May, 1766. Shubael Dimmick was bapt. at Barnstable, Sept. 15, 1644; he was son of Elder Thomas Dimmick who came from Barnstable, Eng., to Dorchester, Mass., 1635, and in 1640 removed to Barnstable, in which year he was representative from that town. Shubael Dimmick was prominent in the public affairs of Barnstable and Windham, being selectman, deputy to the general court and ensign of militia at Barnstable, and selectman and deacon at Windham. He died 29 Oct., 1732.

Child of JOSIAH and JOANNA (DIMMICK) CONANT:—

58. Shubael, b. 15 July, 1710.

23. **Caleb**[3] (*Exercise, Roger*), bapt. 29 Apr., 1683; settled in Windham where he purchased a right of land of his brother, Josiah, in 1703. He was a member of the First Church of Windham.

Apr. 29, 1717, he sold his house and land on Mountain Meadow hill to Jabez Huntington.

He d. Apr., 1727; the inventory of his estate taken 1 May, 1727.

He m. 23 Aug., 1714, Hannah, dr. of Ensign Jonathan Crane, an early and prominent settler of Windham. She d. 11 Oct., 1726.

Children of CALEB and HANNAH (CRANE) CONANT:—

59. Malachi, b. 12 June, 1715.
60. Benajah, b. 13 Feb., 1716-17.
    Sarah, b. 20 Dec., 1718; d. at Mansfield 8 Sep., 1742; unmarried.
    Ruth, b. 28 Oct., 1720; m. Shubael Conant (see 58).
    Mary, b. 6 Jan., 1722-3; d. 23 Nov., 1726.
61. Josiah, b. 9 Dec., 1724.
62. Hannah, b. 25 Sep., 1726.

FOURTH GENERATION.

24. Bithiah[4] (*Nathaniel, Lot, Roger*), b. 8 Nov., 1677, at Beverly; removed to Bridgewater with her parents; m. 14 Dec., 1696, Nathaniel, son of Deacon Samuel and Sarah (Partridge) Allen, of East Bridgewater. They lived at Conant's Bridge, and afterwards in South Bridgewater. She d. between 1704 and 1710, and he m. 2nd, Abigail ———, and had other children.

Samuel Allen was b. 1632, at Braintree, and moved to E. B. about 1660; his wife, Sarah, was dr. of George Partridge, of Duxbury.

Children of NATHANIEL and BITHIAH (CONANT) ALLEN:—

i. Andrew, b. 1698. ⎱ It is thought that they moved to Cape Cod.
ii. Hannah, b. 1700. ⎰ (See Mitchell's *Hist. Bridgewater.*)
iii. James, b. 1704; m. 1732, Mary, dr. of Daniel Packard, and had Children:
    1. Nehemiah, b. 1733, of Oakham, Mass.
    2. Maj. James, b. 1735; m. Martha, dr. of Jacob Hayward, and had family.
    3. Ruth, b. 1738; m. Ichabod Packard and went to Oakham.
    4. Bithiah, b. 1740; d. y.
    5. Susanna, b. 1742; m. Capt. Jonathan Willis.
    6. Jesse, b. 1744; m. Abigail, dr. of Stoughton Willis; went to Oakham; had James and Chloe.
    7. Bithiah, b. 1749; m. George Black.
    8. Caleb, b. 1751; of Conway, Mass.
    9. Silas, b. 1754; of Heath, Mass.
    10. Hannah, b. 1756; m. 1773, Ebenezer Keith.

25. Nathaniel[4] (*Nathaniel, Lot, Roger*), b. 3 Jan., 1679-80, in Beverly. In 1711 his father gave him a farm in South Bridgewater, upon which he built the house in which he lived.

On Dec. 5, 1718, he sold 9 acres of land to Josiah Aldrich and John Aldrich, jr., for £10. (Plymouth Deeds, Vol. 20, p. 210.) On Sep. 1, 1732, for a consideration of £130, he sold his son, Thomas, 36 acres of land "whereon his dwelling house now stands." (Plymouth Deeds, Vol. 28, p. 106.) On Nov. 20, 1741, for £100, he sold his son, Jeremiah, 16 acres of land in "the south precinct of Bridgewater with the dwelling house and barn standing thereon, between the dwelling house of my son Jeremiah and my now dwelling house." (Vol. 35,

p. 72.) On the same day he conveyed 6 acres to his son, Thomas, for £25 (Vol. 37, p. 107), and "40 acres of land in south precinct of Bridgewater with the dwelling house where I now live and the barn and malt house," to his youngest son, John, for £100. (Vol. 37, p. 160.)

He d. 8 Sep., 1745, leaving a will dated 1743, for which see Plymouth Probate Rec-

nathaniellconant

ords, Vol. 10, p. 19; the
inventory is also record- (Will, 1743.)
ed in same Volume, p. 21.

He m. (1) Mary ———, who died without children; m. (2) (intention published at Lynn, 5 June, 1701,) Margaret Laughton, of Lynn; m. (3) 17 Dec., 1716, Elizabeth Hains (or Hinds?); she died 27 Feb., 1757.

Children of NATHANIEL and MARGARET (LAUGHTON) CO-NANT:—

63. Thomas, b. 29 Feb., 1704-5.
    Nathan, b. 10 May, 1706.
64. Bithiah, b. 26 July, 1709.

Children of NATHANIEL and ELIZABETH (HAINS?) CONANT:—

65. Jeremiah, b. 5 Oct., 1720.
66. Margaret, b. 3 June, 1722.
67. John, b. 20 Apr., 1725.
68. Elizabeth, b. 25 Dec., 1727.

26. Josiah[4] (*Nathaniel, Lot, Roger*), b. 26, bapt. 27 Nov., 1681,[*] in Beverly; moved to Bridgewater with his parents; about 1712 settled in Middleborough, where he lived till his death.

In 1711 (May 25) Josiah Conant, of Bridgewater, sells Nathaniel Allen 100 acres on "the northerly or northwest side of Setaquat river," for £110. (Plymouth Deeds, Vol. 9, p. 343.) In 1712 (June 9) Josiah Conant, of Middleborough, sells Thomas Little "one whole share of land in ye south purchase of Middleboro', and two lots in south purchase numbered 129 and 196, also 3 acres of mowing land in the south meadows

---

* This date is probably correct and not that given on p. 145.

in the township of Plympton." (Plymouth Deeds, Vol. 10,
p. 344.) On June 9, 1718, he sells Benjamin Hayford 30 acres
"being the 14th lot in the south purchase." (Vol. 16, p. 115.)

He d. intestate a short time before the 11 Oct., 1721; his
widow was administratrix of his estate. Many papers relating
to the settlement of his estate are preserved in the Plymouth
Probate Records, some of which follow:

"An Inventory of the Real and Personal Estate of Josiah Conant,
late of Middleboro', deceased, which he died seized of, apprised at
Middleboro' afores'd ye 11 day of Oct., Anno Dom. 1721, by us ye
subscribers, as followeth:

	£	s.	d.
Imprimis, to his Homestead with his dwelling house and all other Buildings, thereon and fencing - -	250	00	00
Item, 5 acres of meadow lying at Perchade Purchase	20	00	00
Item, one lot of Land in ye 16 sh. purchase - -	14	00	00
To one Lott of Land in Perchade Purchase - -	7	00	00
To one Lott of Land in sd Perchade Purchase - -	14	00	00
To one half lot Land in Perchade Purchase being near Nath. Allens - - - - - - -	5	00	00
1-8 part of a Saw Mill, - - - - - - -	11	00	00
To his apparrell or wearing cloath and Books - -	14	00	00
his arms and ammunition - - - - - -	4	00	00
Beds Bedding & Bedstead - - - - - -	21	15	00
To his Table Linen - - - - - - -	2	00	00
To his Pewter, earthern ware & glass bottles - -	2	19	00
To his Iron Pots & Iron and all other iron ware, -	3	19	00
To his warming pan - - - - - - -		08	00
Item, to his swine - - - - - - -	6	05	00
Item, to his geese - - - - - - -		13	06
Item, to his cart and cart tackling & cart wheels -	8	07	00
horse & one mare & Furniture - - - -	15	16	00
To his plough & Plough Irons - - - - -	1	01	00
7 cows 23£ 2 sters 5£ 10s. - - - - -	28	10	00
4 yearlings 5£ 4 calves 3£ - - - . - -	8	00	00
Axes, saws & husband tools - - - - - -	3	08	00
one pair of worsted Lambs - - - - - -	1	00	00
Raisor, Inkhorn 3s. & 3 Bells 14s. - - - -		17	00
Chests, tables & chairs - - - - - - -	1	17	00
Wollen & linen yarn - - - - - - -	4	03	00
his Lombe & Lombe tackling - - - - -	3	00	00
Spinning wheels & cards - - - - - -	1	00	00
Tubs, Pails & wooden ware - - - - - -	3	17	00
Corn Flax & Tobacco - - - - - - -	13	18	00
hay and other Foddering - - - - - -	16	10	00
Cyder Caske & Provision - - - - - -	3	05	00

Feathers, malt & Salt - - - - - - -	3 00 00
760 Ft. Pine boards - - - - - - - -	3 00 00
Sheep & lambs - - - - - - - -	1 10 00
Item, to his negro boy - - - - - - -	50 00 00
To a Quarter of a (Lac?) and whale Bone - - -	06 00
Rec'd from Joseph Sturdivant - - - - -	12 00 00
Due from Joseph Bumpus to ye estate - - -	09 05
Due from Abraham Burden Sen. - - - -	· 06 00
Due from Samuel Bennett - - - - -	08 00
Due from Estate of Thos. Bignall Jr. - - -	2 00 00
Rec'd from Samuel Pratt - - - - -	1 17 04
Rec'd for 1-2 bu of Rye - - - - - -	03 00
To a Negro sold for more than Prised at - - -	10 00 00

576 08 03

Taken by Ichabod Southward, Samuel Barrows and Samuel Pratt.

June 3, 1723. Elizabeth Conant, administratrix on ye estate of her husband Josiah late of Middleboro' in ye county of Plymouth, deceased, made oath that ye within and above is a just and true Inventory of her husbands estate as far as cometh to her knowledge.

Before me ISAAC WINSLOW, Judge."

"The accompt of Elizabeth Conant admx. of ye estate of Josiah Conant late of Middleboro' is as followeth:

	£ s. d.
Imprimis, To ye widdows Bed Bedding & Bedstead	8 00 00
To corn & Tobacco spent in ye family - - -	13 18 00
To a fat cow spent in ye family - - - - -	3 10 00
To pork spent in ye family - - - - - -	3 00 00
" Funeral charges - - - - - -. -	18 00
" Paid Benjamin Hayford - - - - - -	5 18 00
" " S. Pratt Jr. - - - - - - -	1 00 00
" " Henry Wood - - - - - -	03 00
" " Ephraim Sampson - - - - -	15 06
" " Eleazer Carver Jr. - - - - -	2 00 00
" " Abraham Burden - - - - - -	10 00
" " Nathanell Conant - - - - -	1 10 00
" " Mess. Watson & Bartlett - - - -	19 03
" " Nathaniel Eames - - - - -	1 02 00
" " Thomas Knowlton - - - - -	19 06
" " Joshua Bramhall - - - - -	4 04 04
" " Sam'l Eaton - - - - -	14 02 06
" " Lydia Cushman - - - - -	05 11
" " Ebenezer Wood - - - - -	13 00
" " James Partridge - - - - -	08 00
" " Clemment Weaver - - - - -	12 10 02
" " Thos. Palmer - - - - - -	5 10 00
" " Thomas Witherell - - - - -	07 04

To Paid Enoch Lovell - - - - - - - -	2 10 00
" " Eben Fuller - - - - - - -	6 05 00
" " Capt. Thomson - - - - -	03 10
" " Nathaniel Conant Jr - - - - -	12 00
" " Abigail Leonard - - - - -	06 00
" " Timothy Washburn - - - - -	03 00
Due to estate of Thos. Bignall - - - - -	3 11 00
" " Wm. Thomas Sen - - - -	1 00 00
" " Isaac Peirce - - - - -	12 00
Pd. to Nath. Thomas Esq. - - - - - -	1 03 00

The charges of Administration - - -	90 13 01
Pd. to the apprisers - - - - - - -	1 10 00
To ye letter & bonds of adm. warrant and apprais- ment taking & allowing ye accompts - - -	1 00 00
To ye admx. for ye trouble - - - - - -	3 00 00
The widdow desireth a further allowance as followeth:	
Pd to Joshua Turner a debt which was due - -	7 09 01
To a yearling colt - - - - - - - -	1 05 00
To a debt Pd. to Clement Weaver - - - -	1 11 05
More Paid to Clement Weaver being a Remainder of labor - - - - - - - - -	2 09 05

June 3, 1723. The above written accompt is allowed by me.

ISAAC WINSLOW, Judge."

On June 1, 1729, the estate was divided among the heirs, the widow taking the homestead; the remainder of the estate was divided into seven shares, Joseph, the eldest son, taking a double portion. (Plymouth Probate Records, Vol. 5, p. 696.)

Josiah Conant m. 1 Sep., 1701, Elizabeth, dr. of Thomas Washburn, of Bridgewater. Thos. Washburn m. 1st, Abigail, dr. of Jacob Leonard; 2nd, Deliverance, dr. of Samuel Packard; he was son of John and Elizabeth (Mitchell) Washburn, of Bridgewater.

Children of JOSIAH and ELIZABETH (WASHBURN) CONANT:—

Jerusha, b. 8 Jan., 1701-2; bapt. Middleboro' 1721: m. Samuel Pratt, of M.

Mary, b. 20 Dec., 1703; m. 26 Apr., 1725, John, son of John Cobb, jr., as his second wife. His first wife was Joanna Thomas. Mary d. 16 Aug., 1795, aged 92.

Prudence, b. 3 Mch., 1706-7.

69. Joseph, b. 30 Aug., 1709.

Susanna, b. 7 Aug., 1711; m. (1) 1733, James Winslow; m. (2) 1744, Jesse Bryant. She d. 17 Apr., 1801, aged 90.

Josiah, b. 20 Jan., 1717-18 (d. 8 Sep., 1745?).

27. Hannah[4] (*Nathaniel, Lot, Roger* `. 25 Jan., 1683-4, in Beverly; m. (1) at Bridgewater, 30 May, 1710, Nathaniel, son of Jonathan and Mary Hill. His father was an early settler of E. B., and was probably son of John, of Dorchester.

She m. (2) 1732, Samuel, son of Nathaniel and Hannah (Willis) Hayward.

Children of NATHANIEL and HANNAH (CONANT) HILL:—

i. David, b. 1712; m. Mary, dr. of Thomas Buck; had 1. Anna. m. Joseph Vinton; 2. Eunice, b. 1749, m. 1769, Abraham Joslyn; 3. Molly, b. 1751, m. (1775, Nehemiah Shaw?); 4. Jerusha, b. 1753, m. 1776, William Snow; 5. Tiley, b. 1755.
ii. Abijah, b. 1714; m. 1747, Sarah Lawson, of N. Bridgewater, and had James and Robert.
iii. Mary, b. 1717; m. 1738, Benaiah Smith, of Easton.
iv. Ebenezer, b. 1719; m. Abigail Stoddard, of Hingham; had 1. Jonathan; 2. Joseph; 3. Solomon; 4. John.
v. Josiah, b. 1722; m. Mary ——; had 1. Mary, m. Nath. Ames; 2. Huldah; 3. Josiah, m. Abigail Beal; 4. Noah, m. Hannah Beal; 5. Abigail; 6. Sarah, m. Samuel Codding; 7. William; 8. Elizabeth; 9. Prudence; 10. Barnum, m. Mary Ellis.
vi. Hannah, b. 1725; m. 1743, William Snow; had Calvin and Salome.

28. Lot[4] (*Nathaniel, Lot, Roger*), b. 27 Mch., 1689, probably at Bridgewater. Lived on the paternal homestead at South B. given him by his father in 1712; he d. 6 June, 1774.

He m. 1 Feb., 1710-11, Deborah Lovell, of Barnstable; she d. 16 Sep., 1773.

Children of LOT and DEBORAH (LOVELL) CONANT:—

Hannah, b. 2 Aug., 1712; m. 1745, as his second wife, Nathaniel, son of Joseph Pratt, of B.; his first wife was Sarah Snow, who d. 1743; he d. 1749.
70. Gershom, b. 10 July, 1714.
71. Lot, b. 5 May, 1718.
72. Sylvanus, b. 17 Nov., 1720.
73. Phinehas, b. 4 Feb., 1726-7.
74. Deborah. b. 8 Sep., 1728.
75. Timothy, b. 21 Nov., 1732.

29. Lot[4] (*John, Lot, Roger*), bapt. 1 June, 1679, at Beverly. He removed to Concord, Middlesex co., about 1716, as appears by deeds recorded in the Essex Registry of Deeds.

3 Apr., 1710, Lot Conant, of Beverly, buys 15 acres in Man-

chester of Benj... 'i Edwards, of Wenham. Witnessed by
John Newman and Benjamin Edwards, Jr. 4 Feb., 1716-17,
Lot Conant, of Concord, yeoman, sells "to my father John
Conant and brother Daniel Conant both of Beverly," 15 acres
of land in Manchester. Witnessed by John and Deborah
Darby. (Vol. 31, p. 191.)

In 1738 Lot and Susanna Conant sell land to their son, John
Conant, of Townsend. In 1751 he sells land to his son, Ezra,
and in 1757 to his grandson, Andrew Conant, jr. (Middlesex Deeds.)

The house he lived in at Concord was afterwards occupied
by Col. Brown.

He d. 20 Sep., 1767, in his 90th year.

He m. (1) 15 May, 1698, Martha Cleaves. She was admitted to the First Church of Beverly 31 May, 1701, and d. 15
Feb., 1725, at Concord, aged 44, where her grave stone is still
to be seen. He m. (2) Susannah Clark, probably dr. of Samuel
and Rachael Clark, b. 29 Apr., 1689. He m. (3) Mary ———.

Children of Lot and Martha (Cleaves) Conant:—

76. Robert, b. 26 Apr., bapt. 7 May, 1699.
77. Andrew, bapt. 25 Jan., 1702-3.
78. William, bapt. 6 July, 1707.
    Dinah, bapt. 20 Aug., 1710.
    Ezra, bapt. 15 June, 1712; d. y.
79. John, bapt. 4 Oct., 1713.
    Elizabeth, bapt. 3 Apr., 1715 (m. 5 Mch., 1746, William Brown,
        of Framingham?). All above born in Beverly.
80. Martha, born 10 July, 1716, in Concord.
81. Bithiah, b. 1720.

Children of Lot and Susannah (Clark) Conant:—

82. Ezra, b. 19 Sep., 1730.
    Sarah, b. 29 Apr., 1732; m. 18 Dec., 1753, in Concord, Jonathan
        Hodgman, of Concord.

30. **Elizabeth**[4] (*John, Lot, Roger*), b. 14 Jan., 1681-2, in
Beverly, Mass. She m. Daniel Coburn; intention published
21 Sep., 1700. He was probably son of Robert and Mary
(Bishop) Coburn, of Chelmsford, and b. 1678.

Children of DANIEL and ELIZABETH (CONANT) COBURN:—

i.   Daniel, b. 17 July, 1704, in Beverly.
ii. Robert, bapt. 1 Sep., 1706, in Beverly.
iii. Andrew, bapt. 7 Nov., 1708, in Beverly.

31.   Bithiah⁴ (*John, Lot, Roger*), b. 14, bapt. 26 Oct., 1684; she was admitted to First Church of Beverly, 16 Oct., 1702; m. 13 Sep., 1713, Jonathan Herrick, as his second wife. His first wife was Elizabeth, dr. of Wm. Dodge. He removed from Beverly to Concord, Mass. He was descended from Henry Herrick, one of the early settlers of Beverly, who is supposed to have been the fifth son of Sir William Herrick, of Bean Manor, co. Leicester, England.

Children of JONATHAN and BITHIAH (CONANT) HERRICK:—

i.   Israel, b. 1714.
ii. A son b. 1715; d. y.
iii. Mary, b. Sep., 1717.
iv. Lucy, b. ——.
v.   Joseph, b. 1720.

32.   John⁴ (*John, Lot, Roger*), b. 7 July, 1686, in Beverly. He was admitted to the First Church of Beverly 6 Aug., 1704, and chosen deacon 23 Feb., 1723. He was a farmer and weaver. About the year 1732 he built a house on the northerly side of Dodge street, in Beverly, some twenty rods east of his father's house and near the spot marked "3" on the map presented on page 146. The house was taken down in 1884 by Mr. Charles E. Riva, who built a house near and west of the old house.

By the provisions of his father's will he came into possession of the east half of the field south of the highway (Dodge street), the orchard between his house and his father's, and "that piece of ground which he hath for some years improved lying north-westerly from my orchard." The fulling mill where he plied his trade of "weaver" was at the spot marked "6" on the map.

On Mch. 2, 1722-3, John Conant, weaver, and Benjamin Conant, tailor, both of Beverly, buy 7 acres of land in Beverly of

John Conant ʒa

(1721.)

Zachariah Hubbard, of Lynn. (Essex Deeds, Vol. 40, p. 168.)

On Mch. 15, 1722-3, Samuel Balch, senior, Paul Thorndike, John Lovett, junior, and John Ober, all of Beverly, sell three acres of land belonging to Patience Woodbury (non compos), to John Conant, husbandman and weaver. (Essex Deeds, Vol. 58, p. 97.) On Apr. 28, 1727, he bought land of his brother, Benjamin. (Essex Deeds, Vol. 58, p. 99.) On Mch. 19, 1722-3, he bought three acres of land of Humphrey Woodbury, "which formerly belonged to my father, John Woodbury." (Essex Deeds, Vol. 58, p. 98.) On 29 Jan., 1739, John Conant, junior, of Beverly, weaver, sells Jonathan Conant, currier, 20 acres of land and two old houses in Marblehead. (Essex Deeds, Vol. 109, p. 185.)

His will is dated 28 May, 1754, proved 26 May, 1755; recorded in Essex Co. Probate Records, Vol. 333, p. 44. He left a legacy to the second parish of Beverly, to which other sums were added in 1760, and a silver tankard for communion service purchased. His will mentions: wife, Mary; sons, John, Samuel and Lot; daughters, Martha Friend, Bithiah Dodge, Sarah Waldron, Mary Baker and Elizabeth Conant. His cousin, Jonathan Conant, and son, Samuel, are appointed executors. The inventory of the estate was returned 8 July, 1755, and amounted to £628 15s. 8d.

He m. (1) 30 Jan., 1713-4, Martha, dr. of Richard and Mary (Eaton) Dodge, of Wenham. She was admitted to First Church 8 Aug., 1714, and d. 5 Oct., 1721. Richard Dodge was son of Richard the immigrant.

He m. (2) 2 June, 1722, Mary (Lovett) Cressy, widow of John Cressy; she d. 1766.

Children of JOHN and MARTHA (DODGE) CONANT:—

    Samuel, b. 29 Dec., 1713; bapt. 2 Jan., 1713-14; d. 29 Jan., 1715.
83. Martha, b. 22 Apr., 1716.
84. John, b. 6 Mch., 1717-18 (bapt. 9 Feb., 1717-18?).
    Bithiah, b. 29 Jan., bapt. 7 Feb., 1719-20; m. —— Dodge.

Children of JOHN and MARY (LOVETT) CONANT:—

    Elizabeth, b. 6 May, bapt. 9 June, 1723.
    Sarah, b. 20 July, 1725 (bapt. 18 July, 1725?); m. —— Waldron.
    Mary, b. 31 Aug., bapt. 3 Sep., 1727; m. —— Baker.

85. Samuel, b. 14 Apr., bapt. 19 Apr., 1730.
   Benjamin, b. 9 Apr., 1732 (bapt. 2 Apr., 1732?); d. 16 May, 1736.
86. Lot, b. 2 Oct., bapt. 9 Nov., 1735.

33. **Deborah**[4] (*John, Lot, Roger*), b. 20 Feb., 1687-8; m. ———, John, son of John and Alice Derby, b. 8 Oct., 1681, at Marblehead. He removed to Beverly and was a church member there.

Children of JOHN and DEBORAH (CONANT) DERBY:

i. John, b. 27 Dec., 1704.
ii. Andrew, b. 26 Jan., 1706-7.
iii. Benjamin, b. 12 Mch., 1710-11; d. y.
iv. Ebenezer, b. 23 Nov., bapt. 7 Dec., 1712.
v. Deborah, b. 11 Apr., 1714.
vi. Benjamin, b. 28 Nov., 1715.
vii. Joseph, b. 10 June, 1718.
viii. Mary, b. 12 June, 1720.

34. **Daniel**[4] (*John, Lot, Roger*), b. 19 Nov., 1694, in Beverly. He was a farmer and mason, and lived in Beverly on Dodge street. At the time of his father's death he and his brother, Benjamin, seem to have occupied a house near their father's, but the indefinite terms of John's will in describing the land, make it difficult to determine whether the house was at the spot marked "3," "4" or "5" (see p. 146).

On 29 June, 1717, he bought 14 acres of land in Beverly, of Samuel Woodbury and others, "it being part of the homestead of our father, John Woodbery." On 1 Oct., 1719, John and Richard Woodbury, of Beverly, in consideration of £170, sell Daniel Conant, of Beverly, a lot of land containing 12 acres, with dwelling house, barn and orchard, "bounded northerly by the highway, easterly partly upon land of Elisha Dodge and partly *Daniel Conant* (1721.) on Trask's meadow, and westerly on said Woodberry's land" (Essex Deeds, Vol. 37, p. 42). May 17, 1730, Daniel Conant, mason, of Beverly, buys 6½ acres of land of Daniel Raymond (Essex Deeds, Vol. 58, p. 102). Apr. 12, 1750, Daniel Conant, senior, of Beverly, sells Daniel Conant, junior, "one third of a grist mill on Elwive brook, near the road which leads from

12

the house of John Conant to the house of Elisha Dodge, with liberty of ingress and egress into and from the said mill as he shall have occasion, with liberty of flowing the land above the mill from the middle of September to the last day of April." Witnesses, John Conant and Rufus Herrick   (Essex Deeds, Vol. 120, p. 248).

He was representative from Beverly to the General Court two years   (Stone's *Hist. of Beverly*, p. 193).

He d. intestate 1751, and his sons, Daniel and Nathaniel, were appointed administrators on May 13, 1751; account rendered Oct. 10, 1753: real estate, £771 18s., personalty, £172 14s. 8d., debts paid, £370 12s. 9d.; an additional inventory: real estate, £60, debts collected, £2979 15s. 11d., and certain lands in Coxhall, province of Maine, not appraised.

The intention of marriage of Daniel Conant, of Beverly, and Lucy Dodge, of Ipswich, was published 16 Dec., 1716, at Beverly.   They were m. by the Rev. Samuel Wigglesworth, at Hamilton, 23 Jan., 1716-17.   She was daughter of Richard and Martha Dodge.   Richard Dodge was b. 1643, in Salem, and d. about 1734.   He was son of Richard Dodge, the immigrant, who d. at Beverly, 15 Jan., 1672, and Edith, his wife, who d. 27 Jan., 1678.

Children of DANIEL and LUCY (DODGE) CONANT:

87.   Lucy, b. 2 Apr., bapt. 6 Apr., 1718.
88.   Daniel, b. 19 July, bapt. 28 Aug., 1720.
      Mary, b. 15, bapt. 22 Apr., 1722; m. (int. pub. 3 Feb., 1745) Jonathan Baker, junior, of Salem.
89.   Margaret, b. 15, bapt. 28 June, 1724.
90.   Nathaniel, b. 23, bapt. 31 July, 1726.
91.   Hephzibah, b. 16, bapt. 26 Oct., 1729.
92.   Josiah, b. 5, bapt. 12 Nov., 1732.
      Elizabeth, b. 13, bapt. 18 Apr., 1735 (m. 30 Dec., 1787, Nath'l Cressy, as his 2nd wife; she d. 23 Feb., 1803?).
      Martha, b. 27 Sep., 1739.

35.   **Rebecca**[4] (*John, Lot, Roger*), b. 29 Mch., 1696, in Beverly; m. 2 June, 1719, Benjamin, son of William and Martha (Corey) Cleaves; she d. 13 Sep., 1770.   He was b. 23 July, 1686, d. 14 Sep., 1775, leaving an estate appraised at £896 16s. 3d.   His will mentions sons, Benjamin, Joshua and Andrew,

daughters, Bithiah Ober, Deborah Dodge and Lydia Ober (Essex Co. Probate Records).

Martha (Corey) Cleaves was daughter of Giles Corey, who was an early settler of Salem; he m. (1) Margaret ———; (2) Mary Britz, who d. 1684. He m. (3) Martha ———, who was admitted to Danvers church 27 Apr., 1690. On 1 Mch., 1692, she was committed to Boston jail on a charge of witchcraft, and executed 22 Sept. of the same year. On the 13th May Giles Corey was committed to Boston jail; on Sep. 9, he was brought before the jury. He refused to answer the questions of the court, and for this conduct was sentenced to be pressed to death; this inhuman punishment was executed on the 19th Sept. He was excommunicated by the church the day before his death. Nearly twenty years afterward the church voted to erase the record of his excommunication, "humbly requesting the merciful God would pardon whatsoever sin, error or mistake was in the application of that censure, and of the whole affair." On 25 July, he confirmed his will made 24 Apr., giving his estate to his son-in-law, Wm. Cleaves, and John Moulton, of Beverly. (For other particulars of the witchcraft delusion, see Calef's *More Wonders of the Invisible World*, Hutchinson's *Hist. of Mass.* and Felt's *Annals of Salem*.)

Children of BENJAMIN and REBECCA (CONANT) CLEAVES:—

i.   Bithiah, b. 25 July, 1720; m. William Ober (see p. 181).
ii. Benjamin, b. 4 Jan., 1722; his will, 1808, mentions drs. Rebecca Bowles, Hannah and Anna Cleaves.
iii. Joshua, b. 2 Feb., 1724.
iv. Deborah, b. 2 Feb., 1725; m. ——— Dodge.
v. Rebecca, b. 29 Feb., 1728.
vi. Lydia, b. 29 Aug., 1731; m. 1753, Capt. James Ober. He d. 3 Mch., 1790. She d. 1814. Their children were Mary, b. 1754, m. Jacob Hooper, of Manchester; Hannah, b. 1757, m. John Stone; Woodbridge, 1759; Elizabeth, b. 1761, m. Benj. Briant; and Lydia, b. 1765, m. John Graves.
vii. Andrew, b. 1 Oct., 1735.

36. **Benjamin**[4] (*John, Lot, Roger*), b. 22 Oct., 1698, in Beverly. He lived on Dodge street, in the house with his brother, Daniel, till about 1728, when he removed to Dudley,

Worcester co., Mass.   27 Apr., 1727, he sold 5½ acres of land
in Beverly to his brother,
John Conant, "bounded
North by Daniel Conant,
east by Thomas Blower and partly by John and Benjamin
Conant, South by John Conant and West by land of said
Benjamin."   On 13 Apr., 1728, Benjamin Conant, of Beverly,
tailor, in consideration of £150, sells John Conant, 9½ acres of
land, bounded west by Jonathan Dodge, north and south by
Daniel Conant, east by John and Daniel Conant, and 1-2 acre
of orchard, bounded west and north by John Conant, east and
south by Daniel Conant (Essex Deeds, Vol. 58, p. 100).

In 1732 he was one of the incorporators of Dudley.   He
was an active and enterprising citizen, and prominent in the
public affairs of the town.   He was town clerk for 26 years,
from 1737 to 1763, and chairman of the board of selectmen
13 years, from 1743 to 1756.

He removed to Warwick, Mass., in his old age, and d. there
20 Sep., 1767.

He m. (1) Martha Davidson; published 4 Dec., 1720; she d.
at Dudley, 5 Jan., 1745-6; m. (2) 17 Sep., 1746, Lydia Lamb.

Children of BENJAMIN and MARTHA (DAVIDSON) CONANT:—

    Lydia, b. 5, bapt. 11 Feb., 1721-2, at Second Church of Beverly;
      m. in Dudley, 14 Feb., 1744, Andrew White.
93. Ezra, b. (9 Mch., 1723?) bapt. 8 Mch., 1723-4, at Second Church.
    A child (d. 12 Mch., 1726.   Second Church Record).
    Abigail, bapt. 12 Mch., 1726-7, at Second Church of Beverly;
      d. 29 Dec., 1736, at Dudley.
    Benjamin, b. 6 June, 1729; d. 6 Jan., 1737, at Dudley.
    Ebenezer, b. 2 Nov., 1731; d. 8 Jan., 1737, at Dudley.
    John, b. 6 June, 1733; d. 5 Jan., 1737, at Dudley.
    Asa, b. 26 Apr., 1736; d. 7 Jan., 1737, at Dudley.
    Martha, b. 8 Jan., 1738; m. ——, Josiah Conant (92).
94. Benjamin, b. 20 Oct., 1740.

Children of BENJAMIN and LYDIA (LAMB) CONANT:—

    Abijah, b. 9 Aug., 1747; m. Bathsheba Nichols, dr. of John;
      after his death she m. Ebenezer Brown.
95. Asa, b. 29 June, 1750.
    Abigail, b. 4 Mch., 1752.
    Lucy, b. 26 Jan., 1754; d. 19 Sep., 1756.
    Jemima, b. 20 Dec., 1755; d. 20 Oct., 1756.

37. Jemima[4] (*John, Lot, Roger*), b. 9 Nov., 1701; m. 6 Nov., 1720, John, son of John and Sarah (Rea) Batchelder, of Salem.

Child of JOHN and JEMIMA (CONANT) BATCHELDER:—

> John, bapt. 1724; m. Mary Rea; had John, who m. Hannah Woodbury, and had a dr. Hannah, b. 26 Sep., 1775, m. 29 Apr., 1798, John Dutch; their children were: 1. Alfred, b. 1800; m. Susan B. Felt; he was a merchant of Boston, removed to Illinois, 1834, editor of a Whig paper, and d. at Chicago, Ill., 1878; 2. Francis Jones, m. Thomas Lord, of Boston; 3. Sarah Nichols, m. William Davis Messer; 4. Maria, m. Joel Priest; 5. Henry; 6. William Nichols, m. Martha J. White. (See Fowler Family, by M. A. Stickney.)

38. Abigail[4] (*Lot, Lot, Roger*), b. 6 Feb., 1689-90; m. (1) Nicholas, son of Richard and Abigail (Woodbury) Ober; published 16 Nov., 1710. He was born at Beverly, 1686, d. 9 June, 1730; his widow was appointed administratrix, 4 Mch., 1731; returned account of estate 1740: real estate, £353 15s., personal and increase, £193 7s. He is styled "weaver" and "shoreman." The widow, Abigail (Conant) Ober, m. for her second husband, (Herbert?) Thorndike.

Children of NICHOLAS and ABIGAIL (CONANT) OBER:—

i. Abigail, bapt. 3 Aug., 1712; m. before 1740, (John?) Thorndike; had Abigail.
ii. Sarah, bapt. 6 Nov., 1715; d. aged 7 mo.
iii. William, bapt. 21 June, 1724; m. 1 Jan., 1739, Bithiah Cleaves (*ante* p. 179); she d. 1805, aged 85. He was buried 17 Feb., 1786, aged 66. Their children were: 1. An infant, d. 1746; 2. Rebecca, bapt. 5 Feb., 1748-9, m. James Lovett; 3. Nicholas, bapt. 20 Oct., 1751, a private in Coast Guards, 1775, prize master on brig Saratoga, 1780, m. 1772, Mary Tuck; 4. William, bapt. 13 Oct., 1754, m. Hannah ———, had William, b. 1762, Nicholas, b. 1764, Hannah, b. 1765, and Elizabeth, b. 1768; he then moved to Bluehill, Me., and had other children.
iv. Joanna, bapt. 29 Mch., 1724.
> (Above dates given on authority of J. Foster Ober, Esq., of Boston.)

39. Jonathan[4] (*Lot, Lot, Roger*), b. 8, bapt. 16 Oct., 1692; currier, lived in Beverly. In 1713 he was the largest contributor towards building the Second Parish meeting house, paying £25 13s. 3d. (*Hist. of Beverly*, p. 257). Mch. 31, 1716, he bought 1¼ acres of land, with the house and barn standing on it, of Jonathan and Jerusha Dodge for £20, bounded west by the county road, south and east by Lot Conant, north by George Trow (Essex Deeds, Vol. 33, p. 216). Feb. 18, 1718-9, Jonathan Conant, of Beverly, currier, with consent of Abigail, his wife, for a consideration of £85 sells Jonathan Herrick, of

Jonathan Conant

(1738.)

Beverly, practitioner, one acre and forty poles of land, with the dwelling house and barn thereon, bounded north by the county road and east by George Trow (Essex Deeds, Vol. 34, p. 187).

Mch. 16, 1718-9, Jonathan and Abigail Conant admitted to the Second Church, of which he was afterwards chosen deacon.

He lived in Cabot street, on the old Roger Conant homestead.

He d. 18 June, 1749, leaving a will dated 17 June, 1749 (Essex Probate Records, Book 328, p. 285), of which he made

Abagill Conant

(1749.)

his cousin, Deacon John Conant, executor; his estate amounted to £962 18s.

He m. 25 Dec., 1715, Abigail, dr. of Peter and Mary Woodbury, bapt. 16 Sep., 1694; she d. 1 Feb., 1750.

Children of JONATHAN and ABIGAIL (WOODBURY) CONANT :—

Sarah, b. 10 Sep., 1716; d. y.
Abigail, b, 10 June, 1719; d. y.
Lot, bapt. 16 July, 1721.
Mary, b. 14 Nov., 1722.
Mercy, bapt. 21 Aug., 1726.
Lydia, b. 3 July, 1729.
Sarah, } bapt. 10 Sep., 1732.
Abigail, }
Joanna, b. 3 Aug., 1735.
96. Jonathan, b. 9 Aug., 1737.

(Jonathan Conant's dr. d. 1732. Jonathan Conant's 2nd, 3rd, 4th and 5th child d. 1736. From "Hale Notes" in *Hist. Coll. Essex Inst.*)

40.   Joseph[4] (*Lot, Lot, Roger*), b. 9, bapt. 16 Nov., 1701, in Beverly. He moved to Falmouth, Maine, where he was admitted an inhabitant on 22 Apr., 1728, on the payment of £10. In 1728 the proprietors laid out for him two lots, one of 30 and one of three acres, and 18 Mch., 1729-30, a one acre lot. On 5 Feb., 1730-1, the proprietors laid out for him a ten acre lot at the head of Fore river, and 10 Aug., 1734, they laid out for him 43 acres on the Presumpscot river, in lieu of the 30, 10 and 3 acre lots, which he returned to them (Falmouth Proprietors' Records, Vol. 1, p. 223). On the last named date they *Joseph Conant* (1731.) also laid out to him 60 acres on the southerly side of Presumpscot river.

He is said to have been the first settler of Saccarappa village,* which he reached by going up Presumpscot river in a canoe. He built his house on the north side of the river, near the falls.

On 10 June, 1740, Joseph Conant, "husbandman," sold Thomas Haskell, "my dwelling house that stands on the Northeasterly side of Presumpscot River near Saccarappa Falls in Falmouth."

In 1744, Apr. 9, his name appears on the roll of a "snow shoe" company enlisted by Dominicus Jordan.

Nov. 16, 1744, Joseph Springer mortgages his house and land at Ipswich, for £100 12s., to Joseph Conant, Zachariah Brackett and Thomas Stickney (Essex Deeds, Vol. 86, p. 250).

Feb. 18, 1754, the proprietors laid out 30 acres to him in right of Jonas Knapp.

Feb. 4, 1755, he sold one-eighth of his saw mill at Saccarappa falls, to Enoch Freeman, for £16 13sh. 4d., lawful money (York Deeds).

May 25, 1758, he sold to Francis Peabody, of Middleton, "one half of one thirtieth part of the mill privilege at Saccarappy Falls with the privilege of setting mills on both sides of

---

* Ray's *Hist. of Westbrook*, and *Hist. of Cumberland County.*

the river, which was granted to Benjamin Larraby, Benjamin Ingersoll, Robert Pearse and John Bailey, together with half the dwelling house and one half the grist mill thereon standing, being part of the privilege I purchased of Thomas Smith."

He owned the mill privilege in common with his younger brother, Samuel, who also moved to Falmouth.

On Nov. 27, 1764, he conveyed his lands at Duck Pond to his sons, Joseph and Bartholomew. These transfers were in anticipation of a surgical operation, which in those days few survived. The following extract from the diary of Rev. Thomas Smith will explain: 1764, Nov. 27. "I rode with Mr. Deane to Conant's and Proctor's; I prayed with the former, who had his leg amputated by Nathaniel Coffin, and Mr. Deane with the latter, who had his arm broken in two places." He did not survive this operation long, and probably died Dec. 31, 1764, as a note from Rev. Samuel Deane's diary indicates: "1765, Jan. 2. Attended the funeral of Mr. Conant" (see Journals of the Rev. Thomas Smith and the Rev. Samuel Deane, pp. 201 and 309).

He m. at Boxford, Mass., 9 Dec., 1725, Sarah Jewett; published 7 Nov., 1725; she was dr. of Thomas and Hannah Jewett; bapt. 12 July, 1702. Thomas Jewett was son of Ezekiel, g. s. of Maximilian; m. Hannah, widow of Richard Swan (dr. of William Story?).

Children of JOSEPH and SARAH (JEWETT) CONANT:—

Hannah, b. 27 Dec., 1726, at Ipswich, Mass.
Lot, b. 7 Nov., 1728, at Falmouth, Me.; d. y.
Thomas, b. 2 Dec., 1731; d. y.
97. Elizabeth, b. 3 Oct., 1733. } twins.
Sarah, b. 3 Oct., 1733. }
98. Bartholomew, b. ———.
99. Joseph, b. ———.

41. **Ruth**[4] (*Lot, Lot, Roger*), b. 18, bapt. 22 Nov., 1702, in Beverly, Mass.; d. (1751?). She m. 14 Dec., 1721, Benjamin Woodbury; the service was performed by Rev. John Chipman.

Children of BENJAMIN and RUTH (CONANT) WOODBURY :—

i. Joseph, b. 27 Sep., 1722.
ii. A child, b. 27 Apr., 1725 (still born.)

iii. Benjamin, b. 5 Feb., 1726-7.
iv. Joshua, b. 25 Mch., 1728-9.
v. Elizabeth, bapt. 1 Nov., 1730.
vi. Lot, bapt. 14 Oct., 1733.

42. Joshua[4] (*Lot, Lot, Roger*), b. 19 Oct., 1707, in Beverly. He moved to Ipswich with his parents; was a farmer.

He d. intestate 3 Apr., 1749, and his wife was appointed administratrix. She presented an account 30 May, 1757, and an additional account 6 Dec., 1763, in which she charges herself with various sums paid: to brothers—William, for interest in his father's house; to Samuel, for bringing up three children, $12\frac{1}{2}$ years in all; to Joseph, for legacy the deceased was to pay him by their father's will. The estate was appraised at £604 16s. 3d.

He m. Jerusha Cummings; published 1 Jan., 1736-7; she d. about 1796.

Children of JOSHUA and JERUSHA (CUMMINGS) CONANT:—

Jehoaddan, b. 10 Oct., 1737. 8 Apr., 1777, Jehoaddan Conant, spinster, sells $8\frac{1}{2}$ square rods of land, in Ipswich, to Nathaniel Day, jr. (Essex Deeds, Vol. 136, p. 213.)
Peletiah, b. 19 Jan., 1739-40; d. y.
Jerusha, b. 7 Sep., 1743; m. Daniel Chapman.
100. Lot, b. 21 Dec., 1746.
101. Joshua, b. 6 Feb., 1749-50.

43. Joanna[4] (*Lot, Lot, Roger*), b. 15, bapt. 27 Nov., 1709, in Beverly; d. at Sutton, Mass., 1802, aged 93; m. 1733, Nathaniel, son of Benjamin and Jane (Phillips) Hutchinson. He was b. at Salem Village, 3 May, 1698; lived on the farm given him by his father until about 1733, when he moved to Sutton, Worcester co., Mass., having sold his farm to his brother, Benjamin. He was descended from the immigrant, Richard Hutchinson, who came from North Muskham, Eng., 1634, with his wife, Alice (Bosworth), and settled at Salem Village, now Danvers; he was of the ninth generation from Barnard Hutchinson, of Cowlam, Yorkshire, Eng., living A. D. 1282 (*Essex Hist. Coll.*, Vol. X.).

Nathaniel Hutchinson left a will, dated 5 May, 1756, proved 24 Oct., 1757.

Children of NATHANIEL and JOANNA (CONANT) HUTCHINSON:—

i.   Bartholomew, b. 28 June, 1734; d. 1820; m. Ruth Haven.
ii. Elizabeth. b. 1 Nov., 1736, at Sutton.
iii. Nathaniel, b. ——; d. 1755, in French war, at Skeensboro', now Whitehall, N. Y.
iv. Lot, b. 1 Aug., 1741; m. Hannah Morse; removed to Braintree, Vt.; d. 24 Mch., 1818.
v.   Benjamin, b. 30 Jan., 1744; d. at Royalston, Mass., 7 Jan., 1840, where he had removed prior to 1770. He settled on a tract of wild land about 1½ miles from the centre of the town. He m. (1) Judith Libby, who d. 19 May, 1795; m. (2) widow Mary (Hill) Partridge.
vi. Jonathan, b. 2 Sep., 1746; removed to Royalston, Mass., and thence to Concord, Vt., in 1789. He m. Ruth Underwood; she d. 14 May, 1834; he d. 1 Sep., 1807.
vii. Sarah, b. Aug., 1752; d. 8 June, 1834; m. Samuel Rich, of Sutton.

For record of these families see *Essex Inst. Hist. Collections,* Vol. 10, in which is a full genealogy of the family, by Perley Derby, Esq., of Salem, Mass.

44. Samuel[4] (*Lot, Lot, Roger*), b. 18 Nov., 1717, probably in Beverly. It is thought that he moved to Falmouth while a young man, and lived for a time in the family of his brother, Joseph. Judge Ray, in his *History of Westbrook*, thinks that he built a house on "Pork Hill," at Saccarappa, in which he lived till his death. Apr. 9, 1744, his name appears on the roll of the "snow shoe" company.

In 1748, Feb. 27, Parson Smith makes the following entry in his journal: "Went to Saccarabig. Mr. Conant tells me he

Samuel Conant

(1749.)

has ground one thousand bushels of corn this winter, there being no other mill than his between North Yarmouth and Saco" (Smith's and Deane's Journals). There is some doubt as to which of the brothers this entry refers to, but it is thought to be Samuel.

Mch. 24, 1756, he deeds to Joseph Noyes, of Falmouth, one-half of a grist mill "at a place called Saccarappa on the

Western side of Presumpscot river, the other half belonging to my brother Joseph Conant." In this deed he calls himself "millman" (York Deeds).

On Sep. 15, 1758, "Samuel Conant is presented for selling drinck without a lisence." David Webb, of Gorham, "blacksmith," and Samuel Cole, his "brother-in-law," became sureties. On the 2nd Tuesday of July, license was granted by the Court of Sessions at York, to Samuel Conant, innholder, "to keep a House of Publick Entertainment and likewise to Retail Spirituous Liquors in Falmouth" (York Co. Court Records).

Nov. 15, 1782, Samuel Conant, "miller," conveys to his son, Daniel, one-half the house in which he lives, together with his right in the mill privilege adjoining said house (Cumberland Deeds).

He m. (1) Hannah Wooster; published at Falmouth, 26 Feb., 1741; m. (2) 9 Aug., 1744, Mary, dr. of Francis Peabody; published 19 Mch., 1744; she was b. at Middleton, Mass., 10 Aug., 1718.

Children of SAMUEL and MARY (PEABODY) CONANT:—

102. Elizabeth, b. 1745.
103. William.
104. Daniel.
     Mary, m. David Partridge.
     (Rebecca, m. Jesse Partridge?)

45. **William**[4] (*Lot, Lot, Roger*), b. 8 Mch., 1720, in Ipswich, where he lived till his death. 12 Mch., 1752, John and Mary Lefavor sell William Conant, of Ipswich, 53 acres of land with buildings thereon *William Conant* (1757.) (Essex Deeds, Vol. 121, p. 37). 7 Jan., 1774, John Chapman, of Ipswich, sells William Conant, yeoman, 16 acres of land, bounded by Isaac Davis, Joseph Metcalf, Silvanus Lakeman and Jeremiah Stanford (Essex Deeds, Vol. 136, p. 16).

Apr. 1, 1765, he was appointed guardian of Joshua and Lot, sons of his brother Joshua.

He d. 1 July, 1784, leaving a will dated 24 Mch., 1777, proved 5 July, 1784, which mentions his wife, Elizabeth, sons, William, Moses and Aaron, daughters, Elizabeth Cummings and Eunice Foster (Essex Probate Records, Vol. 357, pp. 35, 36 and 106).

He m. ———, Elizabeth Potter.

Children of WILLIAM and ELIZABETH (POTTER) CONANT:—

105. William, b. 3 Sep., 1747.
106. Moses, b. ———.
107. Aaron, b. 25 Nov., 1752.
      Elizabeth, b. ———; m. ——— Cummings.
      Eunice, b. ———; m. ——— Foster.

46.   Mary[4] (*William, Lot, Roger*), b. 4 Apr., 1694, in Beverly; moved to Bridgewater with her parents; m. 19 Nov., 1719, Nicholas, son of Thomas Whitman, as his third wife.

John Whitman (father of Thomas) came from England, was one of the first settlers of Weymouth, was ensign of militia, deacon in church, and appointed by the Governor one of three persons "to end small controversies;" he d. 1692.   Thomas Whitman was b. in England, about 1629, came to Mass., 1641; he m. Abigail Byram, and settled in East Bridgewater about 1662.   Nicholas Whitman was run over by a cart and killed, 1746, aged 70; his wife d. 1770, aged 77.

Children of NICHOLAS and MARY (CONANT) WHITMAN:—

i.   Mary, b. 1720; d. y.
ii.   William, b. 1722; b. y.
iii.   Josiah, b. 1724; m. Elizabeth, dr. of Ezekiel Smith, of Hingham, 1747; he lived on the homestead; his children were: 1. Levi, b. 1748, graduated at Harvard, 1779, settled at Wellfleet, Mass.; m. 1st, Sarah Thomas; had (a) Levi, grad. Harvard, 1808, a lawyer, lived at Norway, Me., had ch.; (b) Sarah, b. 1790, m. Albion K. Parris, the second Governor of Maine, who had been a member of the General Court of Mass. (1803), Senator for Oxford and Somerset (1814), twice elected member of U. S. Congress, and Judge of the U. S. District Court of Maine; after five terms as Governor he was elected to the U. S. Senate; they had a family; (c) Charles, b. 1791, a lawyer of Waterford, Me., and Washington, D. C.; (d) Josiah, b. 1793, a merchant of Portland, Me.; (e) Ruth, (f) Eliza G. and (g) Hope. 2. Lemuel, b. 1750, settled at Kinderhook, N. Y., and had a family. 3. Abigail, b. 1751, m. Dea. John Whitman. 4. Josiah, b. 1753, m. Sarah, dr. of Caleb Sturdivant, and had (a) Ezekiel, b. 1776, grad. at Brown Univ., 1795, m. Hannah, dr. of Cushing Mitchell, and lived at New Gloucester, Me.; he was elected to Congress four times, 1808, 1816, 1819 and 1821; a member of the Exec-

utive Council of Mass.; he was Judge of the Court of Common Pleas for 19 years, was then appointed Chief Justice of Supreme Court of Maine, and held that office a full term of seven years; he moved to Portland, Me., and subsequently to East Bridgewater, Mass., where he died; his dr., Julia, m. William Willis, the historian, of Portland, Me.; (b) Betsey, who m. a Hawes, of Wellfleet.

iv. Sarah, b. 1726; m. Eleazer Alden, and d. aged 94.
v. Abigail, b. 1728; d. y.
vi. Nicholas, b. 1731; m. Mary House, of Hanover, Mass.; had Isaiah, Elijah, Mary and Eunice.
vii. Susanna, b. 1734; d. y.
viii. Ebenezer, b. 1736; m. Abigail Freelove; had Abigail, Ebenezer, Jephthah.

(See Mitchell's *Hist. of Bridgewater.*)

47. David⁴ (*William, Lot, Roger*), b. 11 Dec., 1698, in Beverly.   He moved to Bridgewater with his parents while a child; occupied the house built by his father in 1706, till about 1780, when it passed into the possession of the Whitman family, and he moved to Lyme, N. H. He d. at Lyme, N. H., 3 Apr., 1789.

(1762.)

He m. 1723, Sarah, dr. of Benjamin and Sarah (Aldrich) Hayward; she was b. 1705, d. 26 Jan., 1755, at Bridgewater. Benjamin Hayward was grandson of Thomas Hayward, who came from England and settled at Duxbury; he was one of the original proprietors and first settlers of Bridgewater.

Children of DAVID and SARAH (HAYWARD), CONANT :—

William, b. 12 Sep., 1724; d. y.
108. David, b. 6 Apr., 1726.
Jemima, b 12 May, 1732; d. 7 June, 1755.
109. Jonathan, b. 25 Oct., 1734.
Solomon. b. 24 Sep., 1737; d. 9 Mch., 1755.
(Benjamin?)
William, b. 29 Jan., 1742. He graduated at Yale College, 1770; settled in the ministry at Lyme, N. H., 1773. Through his influence, in the course of ten years some thirty families removed from Bridgewater to Lyme, among whom were his brother, Jonathan, and Arthur Latham. He was the first minister of the Congregational Church at Lyme, and continued there till his death, in 1810. He m. (1) a Cook; m. (2) Martha Perkins, widow of Theodore, and dr. of

Nathan Conant.   If they had children all died young.

48.   Elizabeth[4] (*William*, *Lot*, *Roger*), bapt. 16 Nov.,
1702, at Beverly; moved to Bridgewater with her parents; m.
1724, Benjamin, son of Benjamin and Sarah (Aldrich) Hayward, and brother of Sarah Hayward, who m. her brother,
David. He d. 1741.

Children of BENJAMIN and ELIZABETH (CONANT) HAY-
WARD :—

i.   Sarah, b. ——; m. Isaac Buck, son of Matthew.
ii.   Rebecca, b. 1729; m. Thomas Parris, of East Bridgewater; she
      d. 1806; he d. 1797.   Their children were Benjamin and
      Thomas. Thomas Parris was grandson of Thomas Parris
      who came to Long Island, 1683, thence to Newbury, Mass.,
      and Pembroke. The latter was son of John Parris, a Dis-
      senting minister of Devonshire, Eng.
iii. Hannah, b. 1736.
iv.   Ruth, b. 1741.

49.   Ebenezer[4] (*Roger*, *Lot*, *Roger*), b. 30 Dec., 1698, in
Beverly; moved to Concord with his parents about 1719.   His
first purchase of land was in Jan., 1723; another is recorded
May, 1724; the first sale was in 1728.   In 1730 he bought land
in Billerica, and Mch. 13, 1732, sold a house with land adjoining to his brother, Israel, for £112.   In 1737 he and his wife,
Ruth, join in a conveyance of land in Sudbury.   He appears
to have been an active and enterprising man of business, and
frequent conveyances of land are recorded in his name (see
Middlesex Deeds).

His son, Ebenezer, settled in Ashburnham, Mass., about 1770,
where he also removed.

He m. ——, Ruth Pierce, who d. 19 Nov., 1797, very aged;
he d. 24 Oct., 1794; both at Ashburnham.

Children of EBENEZER and RUTH (PIERCE) CONANT:—

　　　Mary, b. 17 Feb., 1734 (m. —— Fuller, of Fitchburg?).
　　　Lydia, b. 12 Aug., 1737.
110.　Hannah, b. 12 Feb., 1740.
111.　Ebenezer, b. 11 Aug., 1743.
　　　Eunice, b. 4 Dec., 1745 (m. —— Hacket, of Westmoreland,
　　　N. H.?).

Abigail, b. 27 Oct., 1749; m. ———— Sellingham, of Ashburnham
and Ashley; he was of German origin.

Ruth, b. 11 Apr., 1752; m. by Rev. John Cushing, 3 Sep., 1774,
Moses Ware, of Ashburnham. They removed to Fitzwilliam, N. H.

Elizabeth, b. 18 Apr., 1755; m. ———— Kendall.

50. Roger[4] (*Roger, Lot, Roger*), b. 6 Dec., 1701, in Beverly. He settled in Charlestown, Mass.; was a "joiner." His
estate taxed 1727, 1729, 1730. He d. 22 Nov., 1731 (g. s.).

He m. 18 Apr., 1727, Abigail, dr. of Thomas and Hephzibah
(Crosswell) Harris, b. 16 Sep., 1705; she was admitted to the
church 28 Jan., 1727-8. In 1738 she, with her sister, Silence
Harris, buys one-half of a pew "in lower front gallery next
the men's seats." She d. 7 Oct., 1761, and her g. s. remains.

Children of ROGER and ABIGAIL (HARRIS) CONANT:—

112. William, b. 23 Feb., bapt. 25 Mch., 1727-8.
       Samuel, b. 8 Mch., 1728-9; d. 28 Aug., 1729.
113. Samuel, b. 24 May, 1730.
114. Abigail, b. ————; bapt. 9 Apr., 1732.

51. Mary[4] (*Roger, Lot, Roger*), b. 20 June, 1703, in Beverly; went to Concord with her parents; m. Ebenezer, son of
Jonathan Hubbard, of Concord. He d. 1755, aged 54.

Child of EBENEZER and MARY (CONANT) HUBBARD:—

Ebenezer, b. 1727; d. 1 Oct., 1807. In 1775 68 bbls. of flour
were stored on his premises, which were partly destroyed
by the British on the memorable 19th Apr., 1775. His son
was the Rev. Ebenezer Hubbard; grad. at Harvard, 1777,
ordained at Marblehead, 1 Jan., 1783, where he continued
till his death, 15 Dec., 1800, aged 43.

52. Abigail[4] (*Roger, Lot, Roger*), b. 25 May, 1705, in
Beverly; moved to Concord with her parents. Married ————,
Nathaniel, son of William and Sarah Wheeler, of Concord.
He was b. in Concord, 8 Sep., 1702. They probably moved
out of Middlesex co., as the record of death of neither of
them appears in Concord or Acton records, nor can any will
or settlement of estate be found in the county records. Wil-

liam Wheeler was son of William and grandson of George
Wheeler, one of the first settlers of Concord.

Children of NATHANIEL and ABIGAIL (CONANT) WHEELER:—

> Nathaniel, b. 27 May, 1734.
> Roger, b. 22 July, 1737; m. Eunice Gilbert. He lived in Ac-
> ton. They had a family of nine children, the last born
> 1784.

53. **Israel**[4] (*Roger, Lot, Roger*), b. 4 Apr., 1707, in Beverly; moved to Concord Village (now Acton) with his parents.
In various deeds he is termed "scythe maker." On Mch. 13,
1732, he buys a house and lot of his brother, Ebenezer, for
which he paid £112, and on Mch. 8, 1736, Roger Conant deeds
4 acres of meadow to "my son Israel" (Middlesex Deeds).
In 1732 he is mentioned as one of the proprietors of Walpole,
N. H., and on 29 Dec., 1736, drew lot No. 20 "on ye plain"
(New Hampshire Town Papers). On 6 May, 1743, he sells
land in Canterbury, N. H., to Robert Pope, of Boston, for
£20 (Rockingham Co. Deeds, Vol. 26, p. 479).

July 4, 1747, he and his wife, Martha, relinquish all rights in
the estate of her father, Ebenezer Lamson, of Concord, for a
payment of £150. Jan. 5, 1749, he sells a house and lot "in
the southerly part of the town," to Dr. Joseph Lee, for £512
(Middlesex Co. Deeds).

He d. 1753, intestate and insolvent. The papers relating to
the settlement of his estate mention several small children, but
not by name.

He m. 14 July, 1732, Martha, dr. of Ebenezer Lamson.

Children of ISRAEL and MARTHA (LAMSON) CONANT:—

115.   Jonathan, b. 3 Feb., 1732-3, at Acton.
>   Mary, b. ———; m. 8 Feb., 1753, Seth, son of Woodis and
>   Elizabeth (Wood) Lee, b. 15 Oct., 1728, in Concord.
116.   Israel, b. ———.
>   (There were two or three other children.)

54. **Josiah**[4] (*Roger, Lot, Roger*), b. 12 Dec., 1711, in Beverly. He settled in West Dunstable, afterwards incorporated
as Hollis, N. H., as early as 1744. At the second town meeting held June, 1746, it was "Voted, that the selectmen provide

stocks," and at a town meeting the Jan. following, "Voted to Accept the Account of Josiah Conant for making the Stocks."

In 1736 (Dec. 29) he drew lot No. 19 at a meeting of the proprietors of Township No. 3 (Walpole, N. H.); it does not appear that he ever settled there (N. H. Town Papers, Vol. 13, p. 594).

On Jan. 20, 1745-6, he bought land in Dunstable, of Daniel Emerson, for which he paid £67 10s. (Rockingham Co. Deeds, Vol. 53, p. 28). Aug. 27, 1747, Josiah Conant, "housewright," of Hollis, deeded 20 acres of land in Concord, for £20, to his brother, Thomas, "it being part of a farm which my honored father, Mr. Roger Conant, deceased, bequeathed to me in his last will, bounded by land given him, the said Thomas." This deed is signed by Josiah and Catherine Conant, and witnessed by his brother, Ebenezer (Middlesex Co. Deeds).

On Mch. 7, 1748, he was chosen "tithing man," and in 1751 selectman; the latter office he held five years (Worcester's *Hist. of Hollis*).

He d. at Hollis 17 Dec., 1756.

A statement of his granddaughter, Mrs. Catherine (Conant) Bradbury, found among the papers left by Dr. J. F. Worcester to the Essex Institute of Salem, is as follows:

"My grandfather, Josiah, came from Reading or Malden to Hollis. Bought the place where Elias Conant, of Hollis, now lives, which was then a wilderness. He built a part of the house now standing. He married Catherine Emerson, sister of the Rev. Daniel Emerson, and had five children; three lived to adult age—Josiah, Catherine and Abel. The two latter moved to Hardwick, Vt. Catherine married a Goss. My grandfather died young, when Deacon Josiah was ten years old. His widow married a Thurston."

Josiah Conant m. 9 Feb., 1745-6, Catherine, dr. of Peter Emerson, of Reading; she was b. 20 Dec., 1718, d. 2 Aug., 1809. Peter Emerson was son of Joseph, and grandson of Thomas, the immigrant. She m. (2) 18 Dec., 1777, Moses Thurston.

Children of JOSIAH and CATHERINE (EMERSON) CONANT:—

117. Josiah, b. 17 Oct., 1746.

13

Catherine, b. 23 Dec., 1748; d. y.
118. Catherine, b. 10 Sep., 1753.
119. Abel, b. 3 Oct., 1755.

55. **Thomas**[4] (*Roger, Lot, Roger*), b. 29 Mch., 1718, in
Beverly; moved to Concord (now Acton) with his parents.

On Aug. 28, 1747, he sold ten acres of woodland and upland
to his brother, Ebenezer, for £25. On Dec. 18, 1749, he sold
90 acres of land, with the house and barn thereon, bounded by
land of "my brothers, Israel and Ebenezer," also 2 acres of
meadow, to John Savage, for £1900. Oct. 26, 1778, Thomas
Conant, of Westminster, Mass., buys land in Fitzwilliam, N.
H., of John Mellen, for £320 (Cheshire Deeds, Vol. 5, p. 373).
He removed to Westminster, Worcester co., Mass., about
1749, where he d. 20 July, 1813, aged 95.

He m. ———, Hannah ———.

Children of THOMAS and HANNAH (———) CONANT:—

Hannah, b. 13 Nov., 1750, in Westminster, Mass; m. 5 July,
1790 (by Rev. Aseph Rice), John Estabrook, jr.
120. Josiah, b. 19 Nov., 1758, in Westminster.
121. Thomas, b. 6 Aug., 1763, in Westminster.

56. **Caleb**[4]* (*Joshua, Joshua, Roger*), b. 13 Nov., 1693, in
Beverly; moved to Truro, Barnstable co., with his parents,
soon after 1700.

Caleb Conant, "living in the county of Barnstable," is mentioned in the will of John Conant, of Marblehead (1737).

He m. ———, Hannah (Lombard?); she was admitted to
the church at Truro, 16 Oct., 1726, and was probably dr. of
Capt. Thomas Lombard.

Children of CALEB and HANNAH (LOMBARD?) CONANT:—

Kezia, b. 5 Nov., 1721; bapt. 9 Apr., 1727, in Truro.
Joshua, b. 14 Sept., 1724; bapt. 9 Apr., 1727, in Truro; (he is
mentioned in the will of John Conant, of Marblehead,
1737).
Caleb, b. 12 Mch., 1726; bapt. 9 Apr., 1727, in Truro. On 25

---

* Caleb Cunnit was in Capt. John Robertson's company in the French war; taken prisoner
by the French, June 10, 1711; was at Annapolis Royal from 10 Oct., 1710, to 10 Oct., 1711;
is credited with 244 days' service. (New Hampshire State Papers, Vol. 15.)

May, 1744, his father was appointed administrator of his estate (Barnstable Probate Records).

Hannah, b. 26 Apr., 1729, in Eastham; bapt. in Truro, 14 June, 1729; admitted to the church, 23 June, 1749; m. 29 Apr., 1753, Benjamin Green, of Eastham, by Samuel Smith, J. P.

Solomon, b. 23 Apr., 1733, in Eastham. He served during the Revolutionary war in Capt. Tobey's company of Col. Willard's regiment; was discharged at Fort Edward (Mass. Muster Rolls, Vol. 23, p. 203).

John, b. 13 Dec., 1737; bapt. 5 Mch., 1738, in Truro.

57. **John**⁴ (*Joshua, Joshua, Roger*), b. 19 Apr., 1700, in Beverly; moved to Cape Cod with his parents, and settled in Provincetown. Feb. 16, 1730, he was one of the proprietors of Truro (Freeman's *Hist. of Cape Cod*). In 1737 he is mentioned in the will of John Conant, of Marblehead.

Perhaps he moved to Truro, for 14 Mch., 1760, Joshua Atkins, of Truro, was appointed administrator of the estate of John Conant, of Truro. This may refer to his nephew, John, son of his brother, Caleb (Barnstable Probate Records).

He m. 18 Oct., 1725, Kezia, dr. of Capt. Thomas and Mary (Newcomb) Lombard, b. 1705. The ceremony performed by Rev. John Avery, of Truro. Thomas Lombard was son of Jedediah, and grandson of Thomas, the immigrant.

Children of JOHN and KEZIA (LOMBARD) CONANT:—

Elizabeth, b. 30 Sep., 1726 (m. Thomas Kilbourn, 14 July, 1764?).

122. John, b. 17 Aug., 1730.

Sarah, b. 30 Sep., 1732.

Mary, dr. of Kezia Conant, bapt. 4 May, 1746. (Truro Church Records.)

58. **Shubael**⁴ (*Josiah, Exercise, Roger*), b. 15 July, 1711,* in Windham, Conn. He settled in Mansfield, where his parents had removed when he was a boy. In 1731 he joined the Congregational Church, of which he was afterwards deacon. In 1732 he graduated from Yale College, and was licensed to preach, by the Windham County Association, May 21, 1734, but never settled in the ministry, though he was invited to

* The year here given is correct, not that on p. 167.

succeed his father-in-law, Rev. Eleazer Williams, of Mansfield. In 1735 he began his career as a lawyer, in which he was eminently successful. In 1739 he was appointed Lieut. Colonel of Militia; in 1746 Justice of the Quorum; in 1760 Associate Justice of the County Court; and in 1766 Judge of Probate for Windham District. He represented his town in the state assembly for thirty sessions, before 1760, and was speaker twenty-one sessions. He was a member of the Governor's council from 1760 to 1775, and on the breaking out of the Revolution one of the members of the Council of Safety. It is related that when Gov. Fitch called the council together to decide upon the course to be pursued in regard to the Stamp Act, it was found that there was a difference of opinion. After a day of fierce debate, Gov. Fitch decided to enforce the Act, whereupon Judge Conant, Col. Dyer, with four other members, withdrew, thus emphasizing their belief that the Act was contrary to the chartered rights of the colony.

His homestead was the "Phillips place," afterwards the residence of George Cummings at Mansfield Centre. He was a man of great ability, much dignity of character, and trusted and confided in on account of his superior mental endowments. Probably no one exerted a more wide or healthy influence on the community than he. (See Waldo's *Hist. of Mansfield*, pp. 15, 16, 29; Hinman's *Early Tolland*, p. 116; *Williams Family*, p. 69; Centennial Discourse in *Puritan Settlers*, p. 691; and *Hist. of Yale College Graduates*.)

He d. at Mansfield, 16 Sep., 1775; estate valued at £1637.

He m. (1) 8 Jan., 1734, Eunice, dr. of Rev. Eleazer Williams, the first settled minister of Mansfield, who graduated at Harvard College, 1708; and granddaughter of Rev. John Williams, of Deerfield. She d. 10 Sep., 1736, aged 25. Rev. Eleazer Williams was b. 1 July, 1688, and m. Mary Hobart; he d. 21 Sep., 1742. He m. (2) 20 Apr., 1738, his cousin, Ruth, dr. of Caleb Conant; she d. 27 July, 1766. She was admitted to the church at Mansfield, Sept., 1739.

Ruth Conant

(1740.)

He m. (3) 21 July, 1774, Sarah, widow of Samuel West,

jr., of Tolland, and dr. of Ichabod Lothrop, who survived him.

Child of SHUBAEL and EUNICE (WILLIAMS) CONANT:—

123. Eunice, b. 28 May, 1736.

Children of SHUBAEL and RUTH (CONANT) CONANT:—

> Shubael, b. 10 Aug., 1739; grad. Yale College, 1756; m. ——;
> family unknown.
> Joanna, b. 11 Oct., 1741; d. 14 Aug., 1743.

124. Roger, b. 8 Mch., 1743-4.

> John, b. 12 Oct., 1746; m. ——, Martha, dr. of Thomas
> Storrs, and removed to Middlebury, Vt. She d. at Monroe,
> Mich., at the residence of Dr. Harry Conant, her nephew.
> They had no children.

125. Ruth, b. 1 Feb., 1748-9.
126. Eleazer, b. 29 June, 1751.

> Joanna, b. 21 Sep., 1753; m. Simeon Hovey.
> Augusta, b. 22 Jan., 1756; m. —— Evans; both died in N. Y.
> state.
> Fidelia, b. 8 June, 1760; d. y.
> Origen, b. 25 Oct., 1763; d. y.

59. Malachi[4] (*Caleb, Exercise, Roger*), b. 12 June, 1715,
in Windham. He settled in the eastern or north-eastern part of Mansfield, about 1½

(1740.)

miles south-easterly of Gurleyville; he was a farmer.

He d. 23 Jan., 1783.

He m. 15 Feb., 1738-9, Sarah, dr. of Edmund and Kezia
(Presbury) Freeman, b. 18 Jan., 1720, in Sandwich, Mass.; d.
7 May, 1791, in Mansfield, Conn. Edmund Freeman was son
of Edmund and Sarah Freeman, and g. s. of Edmund Freeman
who m. Rebecca, dr. of Governor Thomas Prince, the fourth
Governor of Plymouth Colony.

Children of MALACHI and SARAH (FREEMAN) CONANT:—

> Lydia, b. 26 Aug., 1739; m. Ebenezer Fenton.
> Mary, b. 22 Mch., 1741-2; m. James Parker.
> Priscilla, b. 1 May, 1743; m. Elisha Hopkins.
> Kezia, b. 25 Sep., 1745.
> Malachi, b. 11 Oct., 1747; d. 8 Dec., 1747.

127. Seth, b. 5 Dec., 1748.

128. Sylvanus, b. 10 Feb., 1750-1.
      Sarah, b. 3 Mch., 1753; d. 30 Jan., 1780.
      Malachi, b. 25 Apr., 1755; d. 30 Aug., 1775, at Cambridge,
         Mass., in Continental army.
      Abigail, b. 20 Feb., 1757; d. 17 Feb., 1777.
129. Edmund, b. 19 Apr., 1759.
130. Nathaniel, b. 28 Sep., 1761.
      Hannah, b. 19 June, 1764; m. Amasa Wright and had a family.

60. Benajah[4] (*Caleb, Exercise, Roger*), b. 13 Feb., 1716-7,
in (Windham?); settled in Mansfield. He d. 16 Feb., 1798.
He m. 8 Jan., 1740, Jemima, dr. of Edward Bosworth.

(1740.)

Children of BENAJAH and JEMIMA (BOSWORTH) CONANT :—

131. Caleb, b. 12 Oct., 1741.
      Sarah, b. 7 Sep., 1743; d. 7 July, 1810; m. ——— Smith, of Ash-
         ford, Conn.
      Mehitable, b. 3 Oct., 1745; d. 31 Jan., 1754.
      Edward, b. 16 Jan., 1746-7; d. 1 Mch., 1746-7.
      Beersheba, b. 19 Feb., 1747-8; d., unmarried, at Lebanon, N.
         H., 16 Apr., 1814.
      Miriam, b. 17 Dec., 1749; d. about 1839.
      Edward, b. 30 Sep., 1752; d. 21 Oct., 1754.
      Samuel, b. 14 June, 1754. He had property at Barrington, R.
         I. He d. at the hospital at Valley Forge, 1777.
      Hannah, b. 2 June, 1756.
      Mehitable, b. 16 Oct., 1758; d. 1850, aged 91 years, 6 mo.
132. Jonathan, b. 16 Apr., 1761.
      Peter, b. 9 July, 1763; d. 25 Sep., 1764.

61. Josiah[4] (*Caleb, Exercise, Roger*), b. 9 Dec., 1724, in
Mansfield. He
lived in the North
Parish of Mans-
field; m. 14 Apr.,
(1740.)
1752, Ann Ames, who d. 21 May, 1807. He d. 10 July, 1807.

Children of JOSIAH and ANN (AMES) CONANT:—

Anna, b. 22 Dec., 1752; d. 25 Oct., 1757.
Josiah, b. 15 Sep., 1754; said to have m. and had a family.
Lot, b. 25 July, 1758; d. 15 Dec., 1759.
Augusta, b. 18 July, 1760.
Anna, b. 22 Jan., 1763.

62. Hannah⁴ (*Caleb, Exercise, Roger*), b. 25 Sept., 1726,
in Mansfield; m. Daniel Bingham, who settled in Salisbury,
Conn. She d. 25 Feb., 1804.

Child of DANIEL and HANNAH (CONANT) BINGHAM:—

Caleb, who was a celebrated teacher and bookseller of Boston, Mass. He was the compiler of the "*Columbian Ora-
tor*." He m. a daughter of Thomas Kemble, of Boston.

FIFTH GENERATION.

63. Thomas⁵ (*Nathaniel, Nathaniel, Lot, Roger*), b. 29
Feb., 1704-5, in Bridgewater, Mass., where he lived and died.
In 1725 (Jan. 23), Thomas Conant, of Bridgewater, cordwainer, and Martha, his wife, sell all their right in real estate
"which our father, William Ames, died seized of," to her
brother, William Ames, for £50 (Plymouth Deeds, Vol. 27,
p. 203). On Sep. 8, 1729, Joshua Forbes and Thomas Conant,
"owners in common of a lot of land in the southerly part of
Bridgewater," agree upon a division, by which Thomas Conant
received 16½ acres (Vol. 28, p. 106). In 1732 he bought the
lot of land upon which his house stood, of his father, Nathaniel (Vol. 28, p. 106). On Dec. 5, 1729, he sold four acres of
land to James Allen, for £14 (Vol. 32, p. 55).

He d. 1787; his will,
dated 1774, is recorded   *Thomas Conant*
in Vol. 30, p. 157, of   (1774.)
Plymouth Co. Probate Records.

He m. (1) Martha, dr. of William and Mary (Haywood)
Ames, who was b. 7 Mch., 1704-5, and d. about 1743. (She

was, perhaps, widow of —— Bryant.)   William Ames was
son of John and Sarah (Willis) Ames, early settlers of West
Bridgewater.   John Ames was son of William, who came to
New England as early as 1640, and settled at Braintree; he
was son of Richard Ames, of Bruton, Somersetshire, England
(*Mitchell's Bridgewater*, p. 99).

He m. (2) 29 Oct., 1745, Mary, dr. of Francis and Mary
Wood, of Bridgewater; she was b. 25 July, 1712, and d. 1802.

Children of THOMAS and MARTHA (AMES) CONANT :—

133.   Nathan, b. 12 Apr., 1731.
    Sarah, b. 2 May, 1733; m. 1754, J. Heiford, of Middleboro'.
    Martha, b. 8 Feb., 1735; m. 11 Sep., 1755, Seth, son of Mark
      and Hannah Lothrop.
    Rebecca, b. 20 July, 1737; m. 1761, Robert Randall.
    Bithiah, b. 19 Sep., 1738.
    Mary, b. 19 Feb., 1740; m. 1767, Zebulon Bryant.
134.   Zilpah, b. 15 May, 1742.

Children of THOMAS and MARY (WOOD) CONANT :—

    Abner, b. 11 Oct., 1746; never married; settled in Hardwick;
      was a cordwainer.   He boarded with Timothy Paige, Esq.,
      the latter part of his life; d. 29 Oct., 1807.
135.   Zenas, b. 6 Nov., 1748.·
136.   Ezra, b. 22 July, 1750.
    Jedediah, b. 22 Feb., 1752; m. 1777, Roland Sears, of Ashfield.
    Abigail, b. 3 Jan., 1754.
    Keturah, b. 13 Dec., 1756; m. 5 Dec., 1782, Barnabas, son of
      Jeremiah Washburn, and went to Pomfret, Vt.

64.   Bithiah[5] (*Nathaniel, Nathaniel, Lot, Roger*), b. 26
July, 1709, in Bridgewater; m. 15 Oct., 1733, Elkanah Rickard (or Record), of South Bridgewater; he d. 1777.

Children of ELKANAH and BITHIAH (CONANT) RICKARD :—

    Seth, b. 1735; m. 1757, Susanna Packard.
    Amasa, b. 1738; m. 1759, Deliverance, dr. of Joseph Pratt.
    Uriah, b. 1740; m. 1761, Zilpah White.
    Keturah, b. 1744.

65.   Jeremiah[5] (*Nathaniel, Nathaniel, Lot, Roger*), b. 5
Oct., 1720, in Bridgewater.   In 1741 he bought 16 acres of
land, with the house and barn, of his father, for £100 (Plymouth Deeds, Vol. 35, p. 72).

Perhaps the family moved to Easton, where two of his sons lived, about the time of the Revolution; the record of his death is not to be found at Bridgewater. He d. about 1755.

He m. 26 Apr., 1739, Martha, dr. of Daniel and Mary (Harris) Packard. After the death of Jeremiah, she m. (2) 5 Oct., 1757, James Dunbar, and had other children. Daniel Packard was son of Ensign Samuel and Elizabeth (Lathrop) Packard, and grandson of Samuel, who came from Windham, near Hingham, England.

Children of JEREMIAH and MARTHA (PACKARD) CONANT:—

137.   Azubah, b. 18 Feb., 1739.
      Lydia, b. 23 Apr., 1742.
138.   Nathaniel, b. 24 Oct., 1743.
139.   Daniel, b. 7 Dec., 1744.
      Betty, b. ———; m. 1769, Noah Phinney, of B.
140.   Roger, b. 22 June, 1748.
      Lydia, b. 10 June, 1751; m. 1773, Zephaniah Smith.
      Martha, b. 8 Jan., 1753; m. 1779, Josiah Mehurin, as his second wife.
      Chloe, b. 18 Nov., 1755; m. ——— Walker.

66. Margaret[5] (*Nathaniel, Nathaniel, Lot, Roger*), b. 3 June, 1722, in Bridgewater; m. 1739, Abel, son of Samuel Edson, son of Samuel, son of Deacon Samuel, one of the first settlers of Bridgewater. (See *Mitchell's Bridgewater.*)

Children of ABEL and MARGARET (CONANT) EDSON:

i.   Rachael, b. 1744.
ii.   Abel, b. 1750; m. 1771, Betty, dr. of Wm. Trask.
iii.   Levi, b. 1754; m. Sarah Hayward, of Raynham; he d. of small pox, 1777.
iv.   Daniel, b. 1756.
v.   Elizabeth, b. 1756; m. Rodolphus Borden.
vi.   Kezia, b. 1758.
vii.   Rufus, b. 1765; m. Mary Cole.

67. John[5] (*Nathaniel, Nathaniel, Lot, Roger*), b. 20 Apr., 1725, in Bridgewater. He lived on the homestead of his father in the southern part of Bridgewater. He d. about 1816, and his son, Zenas, was appointed administrator of his estate.

He m. 3 Mch., 1746, Abihail, dr. of Dea. Solomon and Sarah (Johnson) Pratt; she was b. 8 Dec., 1724. Solomon Pratt

was son of Joseph Pratt, who went from Weymouth to S.
Bridgewater in 1705.

Children of JOHN and ABIHAIL (PRATT) CONANT:—

141.   Abihail, b. 10 Dec., 1746.
       Zenas, b. 6 Nov., 1748; d. y.
142.   John, b. 25 Jan., 1749-50.
       Zenas, b. 25 Apr., 1751. On 4 Mch., 1776, he was in Capt.
       Abram Washburn's company, in the Revolutionary army
       (Mass. Ar-
       chives, Vol.
       24, p. 20),
       and in 1780
       was in the   (1816.)
       expedition to Rhode Island, in Capt. James Allen's com-
       pany of Carey's regiment (Mass. Archives, Muster Rolls,
       Vol. 1, p. 15).
143.   Lucy, b. 29 Aug., 1753.
       Silvia, b. 3 Sep., 1755; m. 1773, (146) Silvanus Conant.
144.   Jeremiah, b. 28 Jan., 1758.
       Bithiah, b. 18 Jan., 1760.
145.   Thomas, b. 1 Mch., 1766.

68.   Elizabeth[5] (*Nathaniel, Nathaniel, Lot, Roger*), b. 25
Dec., 1727; d. before 1754; m. 14 June, 1744, Daniel, son of
John and Hannah (Washburn) Keith; b. 2 May, 1725; d.
1775. After the death of Elizabeth, he m. (2) Lydia Keyzer
and had other children. They lived at Bridgewater.

Children of DANIEL and ELIZABETH (CONANT) KEITH:—

i.   Isaiah, b. 1745; m. 1773, Sarah, dr. of John Burr.
ii.   Daniel, b. 1747; m. 1776, Melatiah, dr. of James Hooker.
iii.   Jeremiah, b. 1749; m. 1776, Agatha Bryant.
       See Mitchell's *Hist. of Bridgewater* for descendants.

69.   Joseph[5] (*Josiah, Nathaniel, Lot, Roger*), b. 30 Aug.,
1709, in Bridgewater, Mass. He removed to Middleboro' with
his parents; removed to Stafford, Conn., about 1733, where he
was one of the earliest settlers. He was a miller. No mention of the family is to be found in Stafford records after 1755,
and it is probable that they removed to some place unknown.
No other children than those mentioned below are recorded at
Stafford; perhaps William, of Wareham, and Timothy, of
Norton, were his sons. He m. (1) Mary ——, who d. 6
Mch., 1735; and (2) Thankful ——.

Child of Joseph and Mary (———) Conant:—

Mary, b. 6 Jan., 1735, in Stafford, Conn.

Child of Joseph and Thankful (———) Conant:—

Susanna, b. 7 Feb., about 1750, in Stafford.

70. **Gershom**[5] (*Lot, Nathaniel, Lot, Roger*), b. 10 July, 1714, in Bridgewater, where he lived and died. On 17 June, 1779, he sold five acres of land in Bridgewater to Ezra Conant, of Bridgewater, for £13 10s., "it being part of my homestead." The deed is signed by Gershom and Anna Conant, and witnessed by Thomas Conant and Nathan Orcutt (Plymouth Deeds, Vol. 65, p. 194). He d. 1792, aged 78; his will is recorded in Vol. 33, p. 136, and the inventory Vol. 33, p. 218 (Plymouth Probate Records).

He m. 1738, Anne, dr. of Henry and Bithiah (Howard) Kingman, b. 1710, d. 1791; granddaughter of John and Elizabeth

Gershom Conant

(1745.)

Kingman; g. g. dr. of Henry and Joanna Kingman, of Weymouth.

Children of Gershom and Anne (Kingman) Conant:—

Anne, b. 26 June, 1740; m. 1764, Joseph Muxam, and had family.
Eunice, b. 21 Aug., 1743; m. 1783, Barnabas Snell.
146. Silvanus, b. 23 May, 1747.

71. **Lot**[5] (*Lot, Nathaniel, Lot, Roger*), b. 5 May, 1718, in Bridgewater, where he lived. He m. (1) 1743, Betty Holmes, of Middleboro'; she d. 1772; m. (2) 1780, the widow Rhoda Perry, who d. 1790.

Children of Lot and Betty (Holmes) Conant:—

Sarah, b. 25 Dec., 1743; d. 2 June, 1744.
147. Lydia, b. 2 Sep., 1746.
Luther, b. 10 Feb., 1751; d. 1753.
Betty, b. 30 May, 1754; m. (135) Zenas Conant.
148. Benjamin, b. 29 Aug., 1756.
149. Rebecca, b. ———.

72. **Sylvanus**[5] (*Lot, Nathaniel, Lot, Roger*), b. 17 Nov.,

1720, in Bridgewater. He graduated from Harvard College, 1740, and was ordained as fourth pastor of First Congregational Church at Middleboro', 28 Mch., 1745, where he continued in the ministry nearly 33 years, or till his death.*

He was a man of great ability, and a steadfast patriot, serving as chaplain in two of his country's wars. In 1755 he was in the expedition against Crown Point, as is shown by the following extract from the diary of Rev. Samuel Chandler: "Nov. 10, I read and visited. Mr. Conant came up to camp who is chaplain of Col. Thatcher's regiment. He prayed upon parade." In 1775 he served as chaplain of Col. Cotton's regiment, in the Revolutionary army (Mass. Arch., Muster Rolls, Vol. 26, p. 5), and in 1776 as chaplain of Col. Cushing's regiment (Ibid., p. 14).

In 1759 he preached a sermon which was published under the title, "The Art of War the Gift of God: a Discourse before the Military Companies, Middleborough, April 6, 1759" (8vo. pp. 16. Boston, 1759). In 1763 he published a sermon preached at Taunton: "The Blood of Abel and the Blood of Jesus. Sermon delivered at the Execution of Bristol, a Negro Boy, for the murder of E. McKinstry. Taunton, Dec. 1, 1763" (8vo. pp. 36. Boston, 1763). In 1768 he preached the funeral sermon of Daniel Oliver, eldest son of Hon. Peter Oliver, Chief Justice of Massachusetts (published at Boston the same year). On Dec. 23, 1776, he delivered the sermon at Plymouth, at the celebration of the anniversary of the landing of the Pilgrims (also published at Boston, 1776).

He d. 8 Dec., 1777, of small pox, leaving a will of which his brother, Phinehas, was appointed executor (Plymouth Probate Records, Vol. 25, p. 25; inventory p. 27).

He m. (1st, Bithiah ———, of Boston?); m. 2nd, Abigail, dr. of Col. Hezekiah Huntington, of Norwich, Conn., widow of Thomas Frink; she b. 22 June, 1731, d. 3 Jan., 1759; a memorial of her was published at New London, Conn.; m. 3rd, Hannah (Williams?), who survived him.

---

* *Mass. Hist. Coll.*, Vol. 3, p. 149.

Children of SYLVANUS and ——— (———) CONANT:—

Rispah, }
Sylvanus, } both died in infancy.

73. **Phinehas[5]** (*Lot, Nathaniel, Lot, Roger*), b. 4 Feb., 1726-7, in Bridge-water. He was *Phinehas Conant* (1771.) executer of the will of his brother, Rev. Sylvanus Conant, and as such sold 10 acres of land in Middleboro', on 22 Dec., 1794, to Isaac Thompson, for £13 1s. (Plymouth Deeds, Vol. 78, p. 237).

He d. at Bridgewater, 1798. For his will see Plymouth Probate Records, Vol. 36, p. 383.

He m. 1749, Joanna, dr. of David and Joanna (Allen) Pratt, of Bridgewater.

Children of PHINEHAS and JOANNA (PRATT) CONANT:—

Peter, b. 7 Mch., 1751; d. 22 June, 1752.
Sarah, b. 17 Apr., 1752.
150.   Peter, b. 3 Aug., 1753.
Joanna, b. 6 Apr., 1755; m. (229) Elias, son of David Conant.
Martha, b. 11 Jan., 1757.
151.   Phinehas, b. 25 Jan., 1759.
152.   David, b. 1 Sep., 1762.
Jacob, b. 22 July, 1768; d. 14 Oct., 1778.

74. **Deborah[5]** (*Lot, Nathaniel, Lot, Roger*), b. 8 Sep., 1728, in Bridgewater; m. 1753, Isaac, son of Gideon and Mary (Perkins) Washburn, of Bridgewater.

Children of ISAAC and DEBORAH (CONANT) WASHBURN:—

i.   Elijah, b. 1753; moved to Hardwick.
ii.   Nathaniel, b. 1757.
iii.   Edmund, b. 1759.
iv.   Isaac, b. ———.

75. **Timothy[5]** (*Lot, Nathaniel, Lot, Roger*), b. 21 Nov., 1732, in Bridgewater. He moved to Oakham, Mass., about 1765. On Jan. 1, 1776, he was in camp at Roxbury, as corporal in Capt. Samuel Dexter's company of Col. Learned's regiment (Mass. Arch., Muster Rolls, Vol. 24, p. 135). He d. after serving one year and four months (Continental Army Rolls, Mass. Archives).

Sep. 16, 1761, Timothy and Hannah Conant, of Bridgewater, and Elijah Blackman, sell one-quarter of one-half of all divisions laid out to house lot No. 27 in North Yarmouth, Maine, that came to them as heirs of Thomas Blackman, of Stoughton (Cumberland Deeds).

He m. 1754, Hannah Blackman; after his death she m. (2) 1803, Hezekiah Hooper.

Children of TIMOTHY and HANNAH (BLACKMAN) CONANT:—

153. James, b. 3 Sep., 1755, in Bridgewater.
      Susanna, b. 5 Aug., 1756; d. 16 Apr., 1758.
154. Luther, b. 7 Jan., 1758.
      Susanna, b. 5 Aug., 1760.
      Lucy, b. ———, 1762.
155. Deborah, b. 6 Aug., 1764.
      Timothy, b. 20 Feb., 1770; m. 1788, Nancy, dr. of Solomon
        Pratt. They probably removed to Fitzwilliam, N. H., as
        indicated by the following records: "1795, Feb. 6, a child
        of Timothy Conant and Nancy, his wife, died. 1795, Feb.
        15, a child of Timothy Conant and Nancy, his wife, died."
        Neither the town or church records give any further record
        of the family.
156. Sylvanus, b. 23 Apr., 1773.
      Abigail, } twins, b. 26 Oct., 1774.
      Sarah,   }
   · Hannah, b. 4 Mch., 1777.

76. **Robert**[5] (*Lot, John, Lot, Roger*), b. 26 Apr., bapt. 7 May, 1699, in Beverly. He moved to Concord with his parents; settled in Chelmsford as early as 1726. "Oct. 31, 1726. A town way laid out issuing out of the road at the easterly end of Robert Cunnants dwelling house, running northerly through a corner of Robert Cunnants land" (Chelmsford Town Records). He lived near where the house of Charles F. Fletcher now stands (*Hist. Westford*, p. 9). He removed about 1754 to Stow, where he d. 27 Mch., 1773. He was a farmer and carpenter. His will is recorded in the Middlesex Co. Probate Registry, as follows:

"In the name of God, Amen. 25 Mch., 1773, in the thirteenth year of his Majestie's Reign, I Robert Conant of Stow in the County of Middlesex in his Majesties Province of Massachusetts Bay in New England, yeoman, being far advanced in life and very sick and weak in body but of perfect mind and memory, thanks be to God,

therefore calling to mind the mortality of my body and knowing
that it is appointed for all men once to die do make and ordain this
my last will and testament that is to say principally and first of all I
do give and recommend my Soul to the hands of God that gave it and
my body I recommend to the earth to be buried in decent christian
burial at the discretion of my Executor hereinafter named nothing
doubting but at the general resurrection I shall receive the same
again by the mighty power of God: and touching such worldly estate wherewith it hath pleased God to bless me in this life I give and
dispose of the same as followeth:—I give to Sarah my wife one
half of the produce of the lands I now possess together with the
easterly end of my dwelling house and one quarter of the barn
during her natural life, the said produce to be delivered to her in
the house and barn respectively properly managed and harvested
by the said Executor during the natural life of my said wife. My
will also is that she be provided with Doctors, nurses and what
may be otherwise necessary to make her life comfortable by my sd.
Executor hereafter named. the above provision I make for my
sd. wife in lieu of Bond given to me by my son Daniel Conant
dated the 20 of April, A. D. 1771.

Also I give to my eldest son Samuel Conant or his heirs forty six
pounds thirteen shillings and four pence to be paid him within one
year after my decease by my sd. Executor.

Also I give to Josiah, Benjamin, Robert, Shebuel and Rachel,
the children of my son Josiah Conant late of Pepperell deceased
forty six pounds, thirteen shillings and four pence lawful money to
be equally divided between them to be paid them in two years after my decease.

Also I give to my son Peter Conant or his heirs forty six pounds
thirteen shillings and four pence to be paid him within three years
after my decease by my sd. Executor.

Also I give my daughter Esther Parlin or her heirs thirteen
pounds six shillings and eight pence to be paid her by my Executor in four years after my decease.

Also I give to my daughter Martha Taylor or her heirs thirteen
pounds, six shillings and 8 pence to be paid her by my said Executor within four years after my decease.

Also I give to my daughter Rebecca Walcott or her heirs thirteen pounds six shillings and eight pence to be paid her by my said
Executor within four years after my decease.

Also I give to my youngest daughter Lydia Haynes or to her
heirs thirteen pounds six shillings and eight pence to be paid her
within four years after my decease by my said Executor.

Also all the residue of my estate real and personal (after my just
debts and the above Legacies are paid) I hereby give to my youngest son Daniel Conant and his heirs and also all and any that is
herein heretofore assigned to Sarah my wife for term of life after
her decease. And I do hereby appoint the said Daniel Conant Executor of this my last will and testament and revoking all other

wills by me at any time heretofore made, do ordain this to be my last will and testament. In witness whereof I have hereto set my hand and seal the day and year first above written.

(seal)

Signed, sealed delivered published pronounced and declared by the said Robert Conant to be his last will and testament in presence of us

Henry Gardner
John Adams
Luke Brooks "

Robert Conant m. (1) Esther ———; m. (2) Sarah ———.

Children of Robert and Esther (———) Conant :—

157. Samuel, b. ———, 1722.
158. Josiah, b. ———.
159. Peter, b. ——————— , 1727.
     Esther, b. ———; m. ——— Parlinor.
     Martha, b. ———; m. ——— Taylor.
     Rebecca, b. ———; m. ——— Walcott.
     Lydia, b. ———; m. ——— Hayes.
160. Daniel, b. ———, was perhaps son of second wife.

77. Andrew[5] (*Lot, John, Lot, Roger*), bapt. 25 Jan., 1702-3, in Beverly; moved to Concord with his parents. In 1723 he bought a farm in Concord, adjoining his father's, upon which he lived. In various deeds he is described as a "clothier." 3 Jan., 1765, Samuel Gardner, of Danvers, and Andrew and Anna Conant, of Concord, sell lands formerly belonging to Daniel Gardner, deceased (Essex Deeds, Vol. 129, p. 56).

He m. (1) at Charlestown, 2 May, 1723, Elizabeth Taylor; she d. 10 Sep., 1758, aged 54; m. (2) at Concord, 6 June, 1759, Mrs. Mary Hubbard (or Hibbert), who d. 30 Nov., 1763, aged 60; m. (3) in Danvers, Mass., 19 July, 1764, Anna, widow of Daniel Gardner.

Children of ANDREW and ELIZABETH (TAYLOR) CONANT:—

(All born in Concord.)

    Elizabeth, b. 10 Feb., 1723-4.
161. Andrew, b. 22 Aug., 1725.
    Lydia, b. 22 Dec., 1728; d. 26 Oct., 1731.
    Nathan, b. 2 Feb., 1730-1; drowned 30 July, 1733.
    Kezia, b. 1 Feb., 1732-3.
    Nathan, b. 18 Mch., 1734-5; d. y.
    Lydia, b. 29 Oct., 1737.
162. Silas, b. 15 Aug., 1740.
163. Eli, b. 16 Mch., 1741-2.
    Ruth, b. 25 Mch., 1744-5; d. 14 Mch., 1760.
164. Abel, b. 5 Apr., 1747.
    Nathan, b. 23 June, 1751.

78. William[5] (*Lot, John, Lot, Roger*), bapt. 6 July, 1707, in Beverly; moved to Concord with his parents. He settled in Acton about 1734, where he died 21 Apr., 1756, intestate. In the papers relating to the settlement of the estate (Middlesex Probate Records) the widow, Dorothy, sons, William, Asa and Oliver, and daughters, Lois, Lucy and Molly, are mentioned.

He m. (1) in Concord, 15 June, 1731, Mary Lamson, who d. 3 Dec., 1744; m. (2) Dorothy Wooley, intention published 9 Mch., 1745-6.

Children of WILLIAM and MARY (LAMSON) CONANT:—

165. William, b. 26 Apr., 1732, in Concord.
    Asa, b. 19 Aug., 1735, in Acton.
    Lois, b. 23 Aug., 1738; m. int. pub. 11 Aug., 1759, to Nathan Green, of Concord.
    Lucy, b. 27 Mch., 1740; m. int. pub. 27 Nov., 1761, to Josiah Hayward.
    Oliver, b. 1 Mch., 1741-2.
    Molly, b. 14 Nov., 1743; m. 19 Feb., 1767, Seth Brooks, of Acton.

79. John[5] (*Lot, John, Lot, Roger*), bapt. 4 Oct., 1713, in Beverly; moved to Concord with his parents when very young. He settled in Townsend before 1739 (perhaps had lived at Stow for two or three years previous), having purchased a saw and grist mill at Townsend Harbor from John Stevens and John Pratt, the builders. This mill was located a short dis-

tance west of the place where the leather-board factory now
stands, and was the only mill in the town till about 1768, when
a mill was erected at West Townsend (Sawtelle's *Hist. of
Townsend*, p. 242). He built a large two story house, which is
now standing (1878), near the south end of the dam. This
house was used as a tavern, and is frequently mentioned in the
records as the meeting-place of committees. In 1765 it was
kept by his widow, Sarah Conant, as is shown by the following: "At a meeting of the proprietors of the common and
undivided lands in the township of Townsend, legally assembled at the house of Mrs. Sarah Conant, Innholder, in said
Townsend, upon Tuesday, the twenty-sixth day of February,
1765." The tavern was afterwards kept by Nathan Conant,
second son of John, and later by John Conant, his youngest son.

The mill remained in possession of his descendants for many
years, and passed out of the family about 1830.

In early days some of the colonists owned slaves; whether
"Caesar" referred to in the following extract from the church
records was a slave or "hired help," is not shown by the records: "Whereas Caesar a negro servant of Mr. John Conant,
a member of the church of Townsend, has for some time in a
disorderly and schismatical way withdrawn and separated from
the communion and public worship of said church, to the
breach of his solem covenant engagements, when he joined in
full communion with said church, and to their great offence
and grief, which practice of his tends to the dissolution and
destruction of the church and the order of the gospel among us.

"Said church therefore met December 18, 1751, to consider
and act upon this case, and after prayer to God for direction
and assistance, and hearing what he had to say in vindication
of his conduct, in writing and by word of mouth, the church
voted unanimously:

"1. That Caesar's misconduct in separating from the communion and worship of our church in Townsend is in our
judgment matter of public scandal.

"2. Voted, that until said Caesar gives good grounds of repentance for his misconduct, we suspend him from our communion."

"Caesar's commentaries" do not appear on the records. (*Hist. of Townsend*, p. 86.)

On 18 Apr., 1752, John Conant, of Townsend, sells land in New Ipswich, N. H., to Joseph Bates, of Westford, for £80 (Rockingham Co., N. H., Deeds, Vol. 51, p. 452).

From the Town Records of Townsend it appears that John Conant was selectman in 1745, 1754 and 1755; town treasurer from 1739 to 1746; and held the offices of "hog-reeve" and "deer-reeve."

He d. 1756, intestate, and his widow, Sarah, was appointed administratrix. The children mentioned are William, Molly, Sarah, and Nathan, Daniel, Hannah and John, minors, under 14 years of age. The final settlement of the estate was made in 1798, when various sums were paid—to his daughter, Sarah; to Thomas, son of his daughter, Hannah, who m. Thomas Hubbard; to the children of his son, John, deceased, viz.: John, Daniel, Hannah, Joel, Polly, Noah, Sarah, Olive and Jonas; to the children of his son, Daniel, deceased, viz.: Millie, Daniel and Lovey; and to the children of his daughter, Mary, deceased, viz.: Samuel, Sally, Hannah and Simon.

He m. in Concord, 28 Jan., 1734-5, Sarah, dr. of Jacob and Sarah (Wood) Farrar, b. in Concord, 19 Jan., 1715-6; g. d. of Jacob and Susan (Rediat) Farrar. Sarah Wood was dr. of Josiah, who was killed at Lovewell's fight, 1725. Jacob Farrar was also killed in the battle.

In 1762, May 8, Sarah Conant, administratrix of the estate of John Conant, bought land of Jonathan Stevens, for £450 (Rockingham Co., N. H., Deeds, Vol. 68, p. 322). In 1772 she was the only woman among thirty-five inhabitants of Townsend who shared equally the expense of building pews in the new meeting house. On Oct. 20 her name appears on the town records as having drawn pew No. 16 (*Hist. of Townsend*, p. 144). 12 Nov., 1800, her son, Nathaniel, was appointed administrator of her estate.

Children of JOHN and SARAH (FARRAR) CONANT:—

166.   William, b. ———.
    Sarah, b. ———; m. in Concord, 17 Nov., 1757, Ephraim Heald,
      of Townsend, afterwards of Peterboro', N. H.

Molly, b. ——; m. 29 May, 1764, Sam'l Douglass, of Ship Town, N. H., and had Samuel, Sally, Hannah and Simeon.

167. Nathaniel, b. 1743.

168. Daniel, b. 1745.

Hannah, b. ——; m. Nov., 1770, Thomas Hubbard; had a son, Thomas.

169. John, b. ——.

80. Martha[5] (*Lot, John, Lot, Rogér*), b. 10 July, 1716, in Concord, Mass.; m. Jonathan, son of Stephen and Prudence (Billings) Hosmer, g. s. of Stephen and Abigail (Wood) Hosmer, g. g. s. of James Hosmer, the immigrant. He was b. 29 Mch., 1712; was deacon of the Acton church; town clerk of Acton, 1744-55 and 1758-61.

Children of JONATHAN and MARTHA (CONANT) HOSMER:—

i. Jonathan, b. 28 Aug., 1734.
ii. Martha, b. 2 Apr., 1736.
iii. Ruth, b. 8 May, 1738.
iv. Stephen, b. 1 Feb., 1740.
v. Sarah, b. 7 July, 1745; m. 1 Apr., 1766, Oliver Stevens.
vi. Lucy, b, 14 Nov., 1752.
vii. Abner, b. 26 Aug., 1754, who was killed Apr. 19, 1775, in the Concord fight; one of the first victims of the Revolution.
viii. Jonas, b. 26 Oct., 1758.

81. Bithiah[5] (*Lot, John, Lot, Roger*), b. ——, 1720, in Concord; m. 12 Apr., 1739, Daniel Hosmer. She d. 6 Feb., 1801. The late Commander Edward P. Lull, U. S. N., was a great-great-grandson of Daniel and Bithiah (Conant) Hosmer.

Children of DANIEL and BITHIAH (CONANT) HOSMER:—

Lot, b. ——.
Rebecca, b. ——.
And others.

82. Ezra[5] (*Lot, John, Lot, Roger*), b. 19 Sep., 1730, in Concord, where he lived. Ezra Conant, of Concord, was in Capt. Hunt's company of Col. Brook's regiment in the Continental army (Mass. Arch., Muster Rolls, Vol. 45, p. 320).

He d. 20 Jan., 1806 (Town Records), or, as given on his grave stone, 21 Jan., 1805.

He m. in Littleton, 20 Dec., 1753, Lucy, dr. of Esquire Russell, of Littleton; she d. 22 May, 1828, aged 95 years.

Children of Ezra and Lucy (Russell) Conant:—

170. Lot, b. 24 Dec., 1754, in Concord.
Lucy, b. 8 Jan., 1757; d. unmarried, 3 Apr., 1829.
Mary, b, 28 July, 1758.
Susanna, b. 26 Jan., 1760; d. unm., 9 Sep., 1819.
Elizabeth, b. 21 Sep., 1761; d. unm., 3 Apr., 1829, within fifteen minutes of the death of her sister, Lucy.
171. Ezra, b. 18 Sep., 1763.

83. **Martha**[5] (*John, John, Lot, Roger*), b. 22 Apr., 1716, in Beverly; m. John Friend, of Wenham.

Children of John and Martha (Conant) Friend:—

i. John, b. 1738 in Wenham; a farmer; m. 1st, Sarah Wallis, m. 2nd, Hannah Wells, who d. 1829. Children: by Sarah—1. John; 2. Benjamin: by Hannah—3. Isaac; 4. Sarah, who m. ⸺ Merrill, of Georgetown; among her children were Rev. James Merrill, of North Andover, and Rev. Daniel Merrill; 5. Israel; 6. Martha; 7. Nathaniel; 8. Simeon, b. in Dracut, 7 May, 1780, m. 1810, Hannah Palmer, and had Mary Elizabeth, b. 1816, Juliette, b. 1820, m. Elijah Baker, of Hudson, N. H., and John Palmer, b. 1823, now of Peabody, Mass.; 9. Samuel, b. 25 Mch., 1782, m. Dorcas Hovey, had Samuel, b. 1806, Louisa, John K. W., Sarah H., Martha H., and Elbridge G., now of Gloucester, Mass.; 10. Hannah; 11. Daniel.

ii. Daniel, who graduated at Harvard, served in the Revolution on a privateersman; was lost at sea.

84. **John**[5] (*John, John, Lot, Roger*), b. 6 Mch., 1717-8 (bapt. 9 Feb., 1717-8?), in Beverly. He lived on Dodge street, Beverly, probably at spot marked "3" (see map, p. 146); was a farmer, and deacon of the Congregational Church. It is related that while getting in a load of hay one Saturday night he found that the

John Conant
(1755.)

sun had already set. As Sunday began, in those days, at sunset of Saturday, the good deacon unyoked his oxen and left the hay in the field till Monday morning.

On 10 June, 1776, John Conant, yeoman, and Mary, his wife, Anna Batchelder, widow, Mehitable Batchelder, widow, and Benjamin Cleaves, yeoman, and Anna, his wife, all of Beverly, sell land bequeathed to them by Benjamin Meacham (Essex Deeds, Vol. 135, p. 207).

He d. 1780, and his son, John, was appointed administrator Feb. 5, 1781.

He m. July, 1739, Mary, dr. of James and Elizabeth (Cue) Meacham (sometimes written Meacon).

Children of JOHN and MARY (MEACHAM) CONANT:—

    Mary, b. 18 July, 1740; m. ——— Perkins.
172. John, b. 23, bapt. 26 June, 1743.
    Elizabeth, b. 29 Feb., bapt. 29 Sep., 1745; d. unmarried.
    Martha, bapt. 2 Oct., 1747; d. unm. (of a cancer).
    Bithiah, bapt. 26 Nov., 1752; d. unm. (insane).

85. Samuel[5] (*John, John, Lot, Roger*), b. 14, bapt. 19 Apr., 1730, in Beverly. He was a farmer and lived on the north-western side of Dodge street, Beverly, near Conant street, at " 7 " (see map, p. 146). The house he lived in is now owned by descendants of his daughter, Hannah, who m. Cornelius Batchelder. He was a deacon of the Second Congregational Church.

(1755.)

On 9 Mch., 1772, Samuel Conant, of Beverly, yeoman, and his wife, Mary, sell Lot Conant, of Beverly, weaver (his brother), nine acres of pasture land (Essex Deeds, Vol. 136, p. 172).

He d. 29 Dec., 1811.

He m. 8 Mch., 1749, Mary Brown.

Children of SAMUEL and MARY (BROWN) CONANT:—

173. Samuel, b. 6 Jan., 1750-1; } bapt. at Second Church, 26 Nov.,
    Sarah, b. 1 Aug., 1752; }   1752.
174. Hannah, b. 6, bapt. 9 May, 1756, } twins.
    Jonathan, b. 6, bapt. 9 May, 1756. }
    Mary, b. 27 Feb., bapt. 1 Mch., 1761.
175. Nathaniel, bapt. 14 Apr., 1765.

86. Lot[5] (*John, John, Lot, Roger*), b. 2 Oct., bapt. 9 Nov., 1735, in Beverly, and lived on Dodge street, at " 5 " (see p. 146), near his father. He was also a farmer, and deacon of the Second Church.

On 29 Mch., 1760, Samuel and Lot Conant, of Beverly, weavers, with consent of their wives, Mary and Abigail, sell Abigail Trask eight acres of woodland in Manchester, "which formerly belonged to our father, Deacon John Conant, deceased" (Essex Deeds, Vol. 109, p. 23).

He m. 20 Jan., 1756, Abigail Perkins.

Children of LOT and ABIGAIL (PERKINS) CONANT:—

Nabby, b. 25 Feb., 1756; d. y.
Sarah, b. 23 Feb., bapt. 26 Feb., 1758.
176. Nabby, b. 6, bapt. 9 Mch., 1760.
177. Benjamin, b. 9, bapt. 10 Feb., 1765.
Jonathan, bapt. 17 Feb., 1771.

87. **Lucy**[5] (*Daniel, John, Lot, Roger*), b. 2 April, 1718, in Beverly; m. 1738 (int. pub. at Beverly, 24 Sept., 1738), Samuel Brimblecome, of Marblehead. Her grave stone remains at Marblehead, with the following inscription: "Lucy Brimblecome, wife of Samuel Brimblecome, Jr., with seven small children by her side. Dyed June 12, 1757, æ 39 years 1 month and 30 days."

Child of SAMUEL and LUCY (CONANT) BRIMBLECOME:—

Samuel, d. at Marblehead, 4 Mch., 1807, aged 64 years, 4 months and 8 days.

88. **Daniel**[5] (*Daniel, John, Lot, Roger*), b. 19 July, bapt. 28 Aug., 1720, in Beverly. He was a farmer and lived in Beverly, on Dodge street. A tradition exists among some of his descendants that he shipped on an English war ship and was never heard from afterwards. Parsons, in his *Hist. of Alfred, Maine*, says that he bought land in Alfred, of John White, settled there, and was buried in what is called the "White field." It seems very probable that the Daniel referred to by Parsons was this Daniel's nephew, son of his brother, (90) Nathaniel.

On Apr. 18, 1753, he bought one-sixth of the grist mill known as Conant's Mill, of Jacob Dodge (Essex Deeds, Vol. 125, p. 247). Many deeds executed by him jointly with his brother, Nathaniel, are recorded in the Essex Registry, for which see under (90) Nathaniel.

He m. 31 Dec., 1743, Elizabeth Dodge.

Children of DANIEL and ELIZABETH (DODGE) CONANT:—

Daniel, b. 3 Aug., 1744; m. 1766, Anna Tarbox. He was a sea
captain, sailing for Capt. Richard Derby and his brother,
Elias Hasket Derby. A number of original letters and
papers relating to his transactions with the Derbys were
presented to the compiler by Matthew Adams Stickney,
Esq., of Salem, among which are the following receipt and
letter:

"Salem, Nov'r 28th, 1770. Rec'd of Rich'd Derby Sixteen
Pounds & Eight Pence Lawfl Money to pay advance Wages
Days Works & ct for ye Sloop Sally

St Lucia Apr'l 16 1771

Capt Derby

Sir: thes are to Inform you of my Proceedings hear. I
Rote not the Prises in my Last Letter because I Hade not
Received the proseeds nor Dide I at that time know wather
Ever I should But Sense have hade the Good Luck To Receive fish at 21 horses at aboute Twenty three pounds 10s
Rice at 100 pr Tarse porke Ninety five Lumber 115—This
Seson has proved Very bad for Drogers Bute I have Left
with Capt. Putnam Cash for fifteen hundred Gallons of
molasses & Like wise Cask to Pute it in as pr. Recept.
Shall Sail In About two howers for Martinica Whare I hope
to full Lode in Aboute four Weakes from this Date then
shall Procede for Sallem for father particklers I Refair you
to Capt. Dodge   In hast

I Remain yours to Sarve

DANL CONANT"

He d. 1786, in the West Indies; his will was probated 3
Oct., 1786; he leaves his property to his wife; no children
are mentioned.

178.   Jonathan, b. 8 Jan., 1745-6.
Eleanor, b. 8 Jan., 1747-8; m. James Babson, of Wenham.
Betsey, b. 17 Nov., 1749; d. unm.
Barnibas, b. 7 Nov., 1751; d. y.
Hannah, b. 9 Nov., 1755; m. Nathaniel Batchelder.
Esther, b. 10 Nov., 1758; m. Timothy Batchelder.
179.   Barnibas, b. 16 Mch., 1761.
180.   Josiah, b. 21 Aug., 1763.

89.   **Margaret**[5] (*Daniel, John, Lot, Roger*), b. 15 June,
1724; m. 17 Oct., 1743, Joshua Dodge, of Beverly.

Children of Joshua and Margaret (Conant) Dodge:—

Huldah.
Lucy.
Margaret.

90. Nathaniel[5] (*Daniel, John, Lot, Roger*), b. 23, bapt. 31 July, 1726, in Beverly. On May 13, 1751, he was appointed one of the administrators of his father's estate.

On 13 Dec., 1753, Daniel Conant, yeoman, and Nathaniel Conant, tanner, both of Beverly, sell Joshua Cleaves and Peter Shaw, of Beverly, 6 acres of land in Topsfield (Essex Deeds, Vol. 106, p. 18).

On 18 Jan., 1754, Nathaniel Conant, tanner, and Daniel Conant, yeoman, buy the homestead of John Dodge.

On 23 Oct., 1754, Daniel and Nathaniel Conant sell Joshua Cleaves 9 acres and 115 poles of land, bounded south by Jonathan Dodge, east, north-west and south-west by Freeborn Balch, and west by the County road (Vol. 106, p. 10).

On 22 Nov., 1755, the name of Nathaniel Conant appears in a list of soldiers stationed at Lake George (Mass. Archives).

On 4 Jan., 1761, Daniel Conant, yeoman, and Nathaniel Conant, gentleman, both of Beverly, sell 6 acres, 100 poles of land in Wenham to John Dodge (Essex Deeds, Vol. 125, p. 17).

On 4 June, 1761, Daniel Conant, husbandman, and Nathaniel Conant, tanner, joint administrators of the estate of Lieut. Daniel Conant, late of Beverly, deceased, for the consideration of £430, sell various parcels of land, viz.: 16 acres and 140 poles in Beverly, bounded west by Raymond and others, thence 96 poles on Jno. Conant's land, thence 29 poles east on the widow Lucy Conant's right of dower, thence 47 poles south-east on Deacon John Conant's land, thence 14 poles east on said Conant's land, thence 46 poles north to the highway, thence 17 poles to the beginning; also, 20 acres of land in Wenham; also, 9 acres of orchard and tillage land; also, 14 acres and 91 poles of pasture; also, 6 acres of meadow and two-thirds of a barn on the first described piece of land, and

1 acre and 40 poles of land whereon the dwelling house now stands, and two-thirds of the dwelling house on the remaining part of land, not set off to the widow (Vol. 125, p. 18).

On 21 Oct., 1761, John Low and Nathaniel Conant, both of Beverly, gentlemen, in behalf of the proprietors of Coxhall (afterwards incorporated as Lyman), sell ten fifty acre lots in Coxhall to Benjamin Stevens (York Co. Deeds, Vol. 40, p. 173).

The original of the following receipt was presented to the compiler by Matthew Adams Stickney, Esq., of Salem:

"Salem, Dec. 5, 1764. Rec'd of Rich'd Derby 32¼ galls. of Rum the excise of wich is to be accounted for by Nath'l Cimbal [Kimball] of Wells, In the county of York he being a Licensed Person there.

NATHEL CONANT."

On 27 Feb., 1765, Daniel Conant, yeoman, and Nathaniel Conant, gentleman, both of Beverly, sell John Conant, weaver, a piece of upland and swamp, containing 7 acres and 56 poles, bounded south on Joshua Herrick's land, 35 poles, east on Lot Conant's land, 3 poles, north on Samuel Conant's land, 31 poles, and west on John Dodge's land, 45 poles (Essex Co. Deeds, Vol. 117, p. 258).

On 15 Dec., 1767, Daniel Conant, yeoman, and Nathaniel Conant, gentleman, both of Beverly, sell Benjamin Raymond and William Green 23 acres in Wenham and Beverly, 20 acres in Wenham (Vol. 117, p. 252).

On 1 Mch., 1768, Daniel and Nathaniel Conant sell Benjamin Raymond 5 acres of land, "bounded east on Elisha Dodge, north on the highway, the west side extending so far south on our own land as to make up 5 acres, together with our part or share, viz.: one-half part of the Grist and Saw Mill that stands on the premises" (Vol. 117, p. 252).

On 30 Mch., 1768, Daniel and Nathaniel Conant, both of Beverly, sell Deacon John Conant, weaver, for the consideration of £140 13sh., 21 acres and 110 poles of land, in Beverly, bounded as follows: "Beginning at the gate in the Highway and bounding south-westerly with land of Lot Conant, 46 poles, then south-easterly on land of Ebenezer Frances, 3 poles, then north-westerly on land of said Frances, 6 poles, then north-westerly on land of said Frances, 24 poles, then south-easterly on land of Samuel Conant, 3 poles, then south-westerly on land of said Conant, 19 poles, then south-east on land of Lot and John Conant, 48 poles, then north-easterly on land of Retire Trask, 41 poles, then east 28 poles to the Mill Dam, then north-easterly on land of Benjamin Raymond, 37 poles, then east on land of said Raymond to the highway, and thence to the first named bounds" (Vol. 123, p. 159).

On 30 Mch., 1768, Daniel and Nathaniel Conant sell Ebenezer Francis two parcels of land in Beverly; the first containing one acre and 60 poles, with a dwelling house upon it, situated northward of the highway, beginning at the highway and bounded easterly with land of Lot Conant on several courses, about 24 poles, thence northerly with land of Samuel Conant, 8 poles, west with land of said Conant as the wall stands to the highway, and thence to the first mentioned bounds. The second containing 14 acres and 23 poles, with the barn thereon, lying to the south of the highway, bounded as follows: Beginning at the corner against the highway, thence south-west on land of John Dodge, 96 poles, thence south-east on land of Samuel Conant, 28 poles, thence east on land of Deacon John Conant, on several courses, 48 poles, thence north on land of said John and Lot Conant, 17 poles, thence east on land of said Lot Conant to the highway, and thence to the first bounds; also, one-half part of a cider mill standing on Lot Conant's land (Vol. 121, p. 252).

On 12 Apr., 1768, Nathan Conant, gentleman, and Daniel Conant, yeoman, both of Beverly, sell George Dodge, of Salem, 100 acres of land in Coxhall; also, a dwelling house and 50 acres of land adjoining, and one-third part of a saw mill, with privileges and appurtenances thereto belonging (York Co. Deeds, Vol. 40, p. 152).

These transfers seem to have been preparatory to his removal to the, then, Province of Maine; for soon afterward we find him settled in the North Parish of Sanford, in York co., now Alfred, Maine. The births of the four eldest of his children are recorded at Beverly; the dates of the others are taken from the family bible, now in possession of John H. Conant,

Esq., of Watertown, Mass. The last deeds in which he is styled "of Beverly," are dated 1768, but it seems probable that he removed to Alfred some two years before. Very likely the family were left at Beverly until he had cleared land and built a home in Alfred.

On 10 July, 1777, Nathaniel Conant, of Sanford, in the county of York and state of Massachusetts Bay, gentleman, sells 50 acres of land in Coxhall, to Frances Parsons, "single-woman," of Bradford (York Deeds, Vol. 40, p. 88).

"An act for annexing a certain triangular piece or parcel of land to the Town of Sanford, which Nathaniel Conant purchased of this Commonwealth. Passed Mch. 11, 1786" (Acts and Resolves of the Gen. Court of Mass.).

Alfred was first settled in 1764, by Simeon Coffin, so that Nathaniel Conant was one of the earliest settlers. He purchased land freely and soon became the largest land-owner in the town. He lived in a wooden house, near the mill, which he purchased of one Ellenwood; it stood opposite the present brick house built by his son, Andrew. To this one-story house he employed Seth Peabody to add a two-story house, which, on the erection of the brick house by his son, was moved half a mile north, and was afterwards the residence of Rev. Mr. Douglass, Chas. Paul and Israel Chadbourn. The mill before mentioned was situated on the stream running from Shaker Pond, on the road leading from Alfred to Kennebunk; it was used as a saw and grist mill. Mr. Conant was also the first trader of Alfred. (Parson's *Hist. of Alfred.*)

The town of Sanford was divided into two parishes, July 5, 1782; the first meeting of the North or Alfred parish was held at the house of Nathaniel Conant, on Tuesday, Aug. 27, 1782, who, with eight others, signed the first covenant. "Sanford North Parish, Sep. 29, 1783. Voted to postpone erecting a meeting-house till next spring. Mr. Nathaniel Conant then and there gave an acre of land to set the meeting-house and school-house on." (He had purchased this land, which is the site of the present Congregational meeting-house and graveyard, of Jeremiah Eastman.) "April 6, 1784. Voted to purchase two barrels of Rum, 1 barrel of Pork, 4 bushels of beans,

10 gall. of molasses, 10 pounds of coffee, and 28 pounds of sugar, to raise the meeting-house. Voted that Mr. Nathaniel Conant be requested to furnish said articles." "May 29, 1788. Chose Mr. Nathaniel Conant, Dan'l Gile and Thomas Williams a committee to Look out a man To preach amongst us in order for a settlement." "Apr. 2, 1792, at a sale of the pews Mr. Nath'l Conant bought No. 2 for £4, No. 5 for £4 and No. 18 for £4 2sh." (Records of the First Congregational Church of Alfred.)

He d. 6 Jan., 1808, and was buried in the church-yard at Alfred, where his g. s. remains.

He m. 16 Dec., 1756, Abigail, dr. of Joshua and Hannah (Raymond) Dodge, born in Beverly, 3 July, 1732; d. in Alfred, 30 Sep., 1813. Joshua Dodge was son of Joshua and g. s. of William and Mary (Conant) Dodge (see p. 138). Hannah Raymond was dr. of George and Jerusha (Woodbury) Raymond and g. dr. of William and Hannah (Bishop) Raymond (*Raymond Genealogy*, p. 123). Jerusha Woodbury was dr. of Peter and Sarah (Dodge) Woodbury, g. d. of John Woodbury, the immigrant.

Children of NATHANIEL and ABIGAIL (DODGE) CONANT:—

181. Lucy, b. 11 Sep., 1757, in Beverly.
182. Hephzibah, b. 3 Feb., bapt. 16 Mch., 1760.
       Nathaniel, b. 27, bapt. 28 Mch., 1762; d. 12 Aug., 1764.
183. Joshua, b. 7 Apr., 1764, in Beverly.
184. Nathaniel, b. 30 June, 1766, in (Alfred?).
185. Daniel, b. —— Apr., 1768.
186. John, b. 10 Sep., 1771.
187. Andrew, b. —— Sep., 1773.

91. Hephzibah[5] (*Daniel, John, Lot, Roger*), b. 16, bapt. 26 Oct., 1729, in Beverly; m. 21 Mch., 1744-5, Jonathan, son of Jonathan Batchelder, of Salem; published 3 Feb., 1744-5. He was b. 1720, d. 18 Oct., 1776.

Children of JONATHAN and HEPHZIBAH (CONANT) BATCHELDER:—

i.   Timothy, b. ——; m. Esther Conant.
ii. Samuel, b. 1 Jan., 1755, in Beverly; m. 1783, Elizabeth, dr. of Peter Woodbury. He moved to New Ipswich, N. H., where he d. 17 Feb., 1814; she d. 1835. Children:

A. Samuel, b. 8 June, 1784, in Jaffrey, N. H.; d. 5 Feb., 1879, in Cambridge, Mass. He was a manufacturer; lived in New Ipswich, N. H., Lowell, Mass., Saco, Me., and Cambridge, Mass.; was a member of the N. H. and Mass. legislatures. He m. 1810, in Granville, N. Y., Mary Montgomery. Children: 1. William; 2. Horace; 3. Edward E.; 4. Francis Lowell; 5. Mary Anne; 6. Isabella, who m. Thomas Potts James, of Philadelphia, and has (a) Mary Isabella, b. 1852, m. 1885, Silvio Gozzaldi, of Denno, Austria; (b) Montgomery, b. 1853, who was a captain in the British army, under Col. Buller, at the time of the Zulu war, and is now (1885) at the head of a station on the Congo; (c) Clarence Gray, b. 1856, of Philadelphia, Pa.; (d) Frances Batchelder, b. 1859, who has shown a most lively interest in the compilation of this Genealogy, and whose co-operation in procuring copies of English records has been an invaluable assistance to the compiler; she is now living with her mother at Rockbeare Manor, near Exeter, Devon, only a few miles from East Budleigh; 7. Eugene; 8. Samuel.

B. Peter, b. 1786. C. Betsey, b. 1789. D. William, b. 1791. E. Nancy, b. 1793.

iii. Nathaniel.

iv. Jonathan.

v. Asa.

vi. Ruth, b. 3 Aug., 1763; m. 1st, Andrew Thorndike, brother of Col. Israel Thorndike; 2nd, William Leech. She d. 4 Jan., 1794. Her children by her second husband were : 1. Frank; 2. Andrew; 3. Sarah, m. Elisha Whitney; 4. Elizabeth, m. Elisha Whitney, and had Sarah, who m. Dr. Charles Haddock, of Beverly, and had Dr. Charles Whitney Haddock; 5. Ellen.

vii. Daniel.

92. **Josiah**[5] (*Daniel, John, Lot, Roger*), b. 5 Nov., 1732, in Beverly. He removed to Dudley, Mass., and there m. 25 May, 1757, his cousin, Martha, dr. of (36) Benjamin Conant. He was a farmer and lived in the northern part of the town, near Charlton. It is supposed that he built the house and mill afterwards owned and occupied by his son, Josiah.

Children of JOSIAH and MARTHA (CONANT) CONANT:—

Lucy, b. 8 Oct., 1758, in Dudley; m. 15 Apr., 1779, John White.

188. Rufus, b. 16 Aug., 1760.

189. Lodema, b. 12 Nov., 1762.

Hephzibah, b. 17 May, 1767; m. 16 Feb., 1792, Asa Mann.

190. Josiah, b. 30 Sep., 1770.

93. **Ezra**[5] (*Benjamin, John, Lot, Roger*), bapt. 8 Mch., 1723-4, in Beverly; moved to Dudley with his parents. He was town clerk at Dudley from 1763 to 1769, when he moved to Warwick, Mass., and was town clerk there nine years, selectman one year.

Aug. 30, 1774. "Voted and chose Mr. Ezra Conant moderator. Voted the sum of eight shillings, being this town's proportion of the sum agreed on by the Honorable Council and House of Representatives in their session to pay a committee of Congress. Voted to get two barrels of powder, and lead and flints, answerable for a town stock; and that the selectmen be a committee to procure the same. Voted to adhere strictly to our chartered rights and privileges, and to defend them to our utmost capacity; and that we will be in readiness that if our brothers in Boston or elsewhere should be distressed by the troops sent here to force a compliance to the unconstitutional and oppressive acts of the British Parliament and will give us notice, that we will repair to their relief forthwith. Voted to choose a captain, lieutenant and ensign, and that they enlist fifty men in this town to be ready at a minutes warning to go if called for, to the relief of our brethren in any part of the Province. Voted and chose Samuel Williams captain, James Ball lieutenant, and Amzi Doolittle ensign. Voted that the expenses of said company (if called to go) shall be paid by the town, an account thereof being exibited to the town by the officers thereof" [*Hist. of Warwick*, p. 44].

Signed by EZRA CONANT, Moderator.

Aug. 29, 1774, Ezra Conant, of Warwick, buys land in Claremont, from Josiah Willard, for £60 (Cheshire Co., N. H., Deeds, Vol. 1, p. 107).

Sep. 9, 1778, Ezra Conant, of Warwick, Mass., sells land in Claremont, N. H., to Ebenezer Conant, for £30 (Cheshire Co., N. H., Deeds, Vol. 6, p. 212). Nov. 29, 1780, Ezra Conant, of Warwick, sells land in Claremont, N. H., to Stephen Fisk, of Claremont, for £60 (Cheshire Deeds, Vol. 6, p. 91). Oct. 10, 1781, Ezra Conant, of Warwick, sells land in Claremont, to C. Atkins, for £122 10s. (Cheshire Deeds, Vol. 7, p. 146).

He d. 7 Dec., 1804.

He m. (1) in Dudley, 1 Jan., 1745, Millicent Newell, b. 19 Dec., 1725, d. July, 1769; m. (2) in Warwick, int. pub. 16

Jan., 1770, Anna Fisk. In 1772, Anna Conant, formerly Fisk, guardian of Stephen and James Fisk, sons of Stephen Fisk, late of Greenwich, in Hampshire county, petitions to sell lands of her late husband (Cheshire County Court Records).

Children of EZRA and MILLICENT (NEWELL) CONANT:—

    Asa, b. 14 Oct., 1746.
    John, b. 21 July, 1748; d. y.
191. Ezra, b. 7 Apr., 1751.
192. Amos, b. 8 Jan., 1753.
193. Millicent, b. 25 Aug., 1754.
    Ebenezer, b. 12 Apr., 1756.
194. John, b. 29 Aug., 1758.
    Jemima, b. 1 Oct., 1760.
    Stephen, b. 19 June, 1762; on Dec. 25, 1778, he was in Capt. Enoch Chaplin's company of Col. Gerrish's regiment, stationed at Springfield (Mass. Archives, Vol. 25, p. 173). On July 6, 1780, "Stephen Conant, aged 18, hight 5 ft. 10 in., Ruddy complexion," marched from Springfield under Lieut. Taylor, "to reinforce the Continental army" (Vol. 35, p. 186), and was discharged Dec. 8, 1780, receiving £11 1s. 4d. (Vol. 4, p. 259). In 1781 he was in the 6th regiment, under Capt. Daniels (Coat Rolls).

(1780.)

195. Benjamin, b. 28 Mch., 1764.

Children of EZRA and ANNA (———) (FISK) CONANT:—

    Anna, b. 26 May, 1771; m. (197) Charles Conant.
196. Clark, b. 23 June, 1773.

94. **Benjamin**[5] (*Benjamin, John, Lot, Roger*), b. 20 Oct., 1740, in Dudley. He moved to Warwick with his father about 1770; was selectman at Warwick five years.

He m. (1) 1 May, 1768, Mary Davis; she d. 16 Sep., 1786; m. (2) (widow Jemima Hill? int. pub. 12 Nov., 1788).

(1779.)

Children of BENJAMIN and MARY (DAVIS) CONANT:—

197. Charles, b. 29 July, 1769.
    Mercy, b. 23 July, 1771.
    Polly, b. ———; m. 18 Feb., 1795, Samuel Goss.
198. Benjamin, b. 14 Sep., 1775.
    Samuel, b. 30 July, 1777; d. 2 Apr., 1779.

199. Ebenezer, b. 3 July, 1779.
200. Samuel, b. 22 Apr., 1781.
     Sarah, b. 15 Aug., 1783; m. George Bancroft, of Barre.
     Eunice, b. 10 Apr., 1785; m. David Ball, of Warwick, and had
       a dr., who m. Edward Mayo.

95. **Asa**[5] (*Benjamin, John, Lot, Roger*), b. 29 June, 1750,
in Dudley. He moved to Warwick; was an inn-keeper.

On Dec. 21, 1789, he bought land in Winchester, N. H., of
Solomon Willard (Cheshire
Co., N. H., Deeds, Vol. 15,
p. 299); and on Dec. 25, of
A. Scott, of Winchester
(1779.)
(Vol. 15, p. 298). On Feb. 20, 1793, he bought land in Winchester from Edward Houghton (Vol. 25, p. 159). Dec. 12,
1793, he sold land in Winchester to Philip Goss (Vol. 25, p.
161). Nov. 27, 1794, he bought land in Winchester of John
Hutchins (Vol. 25, p. 158). In 1802 he was one of a committee appointed by the town "to look into the state of the
treasury, and to make a report what sums there are that belong
to the ministry."

He d. 21 Feb., 1832.

He m. (1) Martha Merriam, pub. 2 Dec., 1769; she was dr.
of Joshua and Susanna (Gleason) Merriam, of Oxford, b. 30
June, 1752. Her father was born in Lexington and settled in
Oxford North Gore in 1729. He was of the fifth generation
from William Merriam, of Hadlon, co. Kent, England (Joshua,[5]
John,[4] Joseph,[3] Joseph,[2] William[1]). She d. 12 Mch., 1812, and
he m. (2) Elona Daniels, who d. 1 Sep., 1820 (he m. (3) the
widow Lydia Ball?).

Children of ASA and MARTHA (MERRIAM) CONANT:—

     Mercy, b. 19 Sep., 1771, in Warwick; m. Isaac Robbins.
201. Asa, b. 22 Sep., 1773.
202. Jonas, b. 18 Aug., 1775.
     Abijah, b. 17 Apr., d. 2 Oct., 1777.
203. Jemima, b. 1 Aug., 1778.
     Martha, b. 19 Mch., 1781.
204. Susanna, b. 29 May, 1783.
205. Patty, b. 23 Oct., 1786.
     Miriam, b. 16 Oct., 1792; m. 4 Oct., 1827, Amory Bartlett, of
       Chesterfield, N. H.

15

96. **Jonathan**[5] (*Jonathan, Lot, Lot, Roger*), b. in Beverly, 9 Aug., 1737. He lived in Beverly, on the Roger Conant homestead, till about 1783, when he removed to a farm on Cherry Hill. In 1791 he sold the "Cherry Hill" farm and removed to Amherst (now Mt. Vernon), N. H. He was the last of the name who lived in the original Roger Conant house. This statement is made on the authority of Mr. E. H. Moulton, of Beverly, who writes: "Soon after I bought the house where I now live, in 1858, my wife's grandfather, Major John [Conant, b. 1771], called to see me; going to the window and looking south, he said: 'Your land is a part of the old Roger Conant estate. The house that he built stood a little more than half way between this house and Mr. Lovett's [now Joseph Lovett Standley's]. Jonathan Conant was the last of the name that lived in it: he sold the northern part of the farm to Dr. Kittredge, who married his daughter, and built the brick house; the homestead he sold to a Mr. Brown, who pulled the old house down. Then he bought the Cherry Hill farm. I remember him well—he went to Mt. Vernon when I was a boy.'" There seems to be no reason to doubt the substantial accuracy of this statement, though no transfer from Jonathan[5] to Brown is recorded in the Essex Registry previous to 1800. Possibly there was an intermediate owner, or Major John's memory may have failed as to the purchaser of the old house.

On 17 Mch., 1759, Jonathan Conant and Mercy, his wife, sell 20 acres of land in Beverly, to Joshua Dodge, 2nd, "bounded east upon the town's road which leads from the house of John Baker's heirs, late of Wenham, to Burch plain, northerly upon Caleb Dodgeses land, west upon Deacon Joshua Dodge, and south upon Joshua Dodge, 2nd" (Essex Co. Deeds, Vol. 124, p. 9). On the same day, Edward Raymond, of Beverly, gentleman, in consideration of £250, sells Jonathan Conant, of Beverly, currier, 25 acres of land in Beverly, "bounded south by land of Trow's and Balch's heirs, east by land of Peter Shaw, north by said Shaw till it comes to the county road, running on said road till it comes to the first bounds" (Essex Deeds, Vol. 125, p. 214). On 25 Jan., 1770, Jonathan and Mercy Conant sell

Ebenezer Francis, 8 acres of land, "beginning at the county road, at a willow bush, and running east, 52 poles, to land of Henry Herrick, thence north, 24 poles, to land of Trow's heirs, thence west, 42 poles, to land of Joseph Raymond, thence southerly to the road, and thence to the first bounds" (Essex Deeds, Vol. 148, p. 232). On 15 Apr., 1774, Jonathan Conant, currier, sells to Benjamin Beckford, 6 acres and 124 poles of land, bounded north-east by a private way and south-west by Capt. Henry Herrick's garden (Vol. 133, p. 81). On 1 June, 1782, Jonathan Conant, gentleman, of Beverly, sells John Francis, 70 poles of land in Beverly (Vol. 140, p. 73). About this time he sold 4 acres and 105 poles of land in Beverly to John Lovett, 4th (Vol. 141, p. 162).

On 29 May, 1783, Jonathan and Mercy Conant sell Richard Quarterman "a parcel of land in Beverly, containing 11 acres and 8 poles, with the dwelling house, barn and all out buildings thereon, bounded southerly on land of Capt. John Francis on two courses, 108 poles, till it comes to land of Peter Shaw, thence east by land of said Shaw, 16 poles, thence north on land of Peter and Benjamin Shaw till it comes to the county road, thence west with said road, 22 poles. And also one-fourth of a pew in the Second Parish Church" (Essex Co. Deeds, Vol. 141, p. 39). On 11 Apr., 1783, Jonathan Conant, Esquire, of Beverly, buys of George Dodge, 114 acres and 145 poles of land, with the buildings thereon, for the consideration of £1378 17sh. (Essex Deeds, Vol. 155, p. 148). On 27 Dec., 1786, Jonathan Conant, Esquire, and Mercy, his wife, sell Joseph Wood 2 acres of salt marsh (Vol. 146, p. 242). On 18 Dec., 1787, Jonathan Conant, currier, buys of Simon Brown 2 acres of land with the west half of a dwelling thereon, which Brown bought of Nathaniel Raymond, administrator of the estate of Benjamin Raymond (Vol. 147, p. 77). On 23 Mch., 1789, Jonathan Conant, Esquire, and Joseph Wood, both of Beverly, sell Judith Francis, spinster, "2 acres of land with the west half of the dwelling thereon, in Beverly, bounded east by the county road, south by land of the heirs of Ebenezer Raymond, west by Samuel Dodge and north by land of John Low. It being the same land which we bought of Simon

Brown, as per his deed dated 18 Dec., 1787" (Vol. 151, p. 201).
On 26 May, 1791, Jonathan Conant sells the land bought of
George Dodge, to Israel Thorndike, Esquire (Essex Deeds,
Vol. 166, p. 174). 21 Sep., 1795, Jonathan Conant, of Am-
herst, N. H., sells Joseph Wood and Capt. Hugh Hill, 20 acres
and 100 poles of land in Beverly (Essex Deeds, Vol. 164, p. 95).

On the breaking out of the Revolutionary war he was chosen
as one of the "Com-
mittee of Corre-
spondence and
Safety." At the Lexington alarm he marched to Boston under Capt. Peter Shaw (Mass. Archives, Lexington Alarm Lists,
Vol. 13, p. 128); he was afterwards paymaster in Col. Francis'
regiment, and then in Col. Tupper's regiment, serving four
years or more (Continental Army Rolls). He was in the battle of Monmouth (Stone's Hist. of Beverly, p. 177). Jonathan
Conant and Larkin Thorndike were the first representatives
from Beverly after the adoption of the Constitution.

In 1787 he was one of the selectmen of Beverly, and soon
after moved to Mt. Vernon, N. H., where he died.

He m. 30 Jan., 1758, Mercy Lovett.

Children of JONATHAN and MERCY (LOVETT) CONANT:—

206. Jonathan, b. 11 Apr., 1760, in Beverly.
207. Lot, b. 18 June, 1764.
      Joseph, bapt. 28 Sep., 1766 (d. y.?).
208. Israel, b. 15 Nov., 1767.
209. Sarah, bapt. 3 June, 1770.
      Josiah, bapt. 7 July, 1776 (d. y.?).
      Joanna? (added by Dr. J. F. Worcester, who seems to have
      mistaken a dr. of (208) Israel for a sister).

97. Elizabeth[5] (*Joseph, Lot, Lot, Roger*), b. in Falmouth,
3 Oct., 1733; m. Ezekiel Jones before July, 1759. On 27 July,
1759, "Joseph Conant, of Falmouth, yeoman, for the good
will and affection I bear to my son-in-law, Ezekiel Jones, and
Elizabeth, his wife, and in consideration of £13 6s. 8d. paid by
him do sell * * * him a certain parcel of land containing
about 5 acres, it being part of the 60 acres laid out to me by
the Proprietors of Falmouth, 10 Aug., 1734." The deed is
witnessed by Moses Pearson and Samuel Conant (Cumberland

Co., Me., Deeds, Vol. 1, p. 364). On 19 Jan., 1771, Ezekiel and Elizabeth Jones, of Falmouth, in consideration of £21, sell the above 5 acres to Stephen Waite, of Falmouth, mariner (Cumberland Deeds, Vol. 5, p. 364), and soon after moved to Royallsborough, afterwards incorporated as Durham. Feb. 10, 1786, Ezekiel Jones, of Royallsborough, buys 14 acres of land in R., of Samuel Brown (Cumb. Deeds, Vol. 16, p. 243). Nov. 28, 1800, Ezekiel and Elizabeth Jones, of Durham, sell 77 acres of land in Durham to Thomas Pierce, of Scituate (Cumb. Deeds, Vol. 35, p. 532). Oct. 23, 1799, Abigail Lyman, widow, of York, sells land in Durham to Joshua, son of Ezekiel Jones, of Durham (Cumb. Deeds, Vol. 85, p. 133). July 20, 1836, Joshua Jones, Abijah Collins, with his wife, Dorothy, in her right, Thomas Austin and Sarah, his wife, in her right, Samuel and Ezekiel Jones, sell land in Durham to Moses Jones, of Durham, it being their part of the homestead of Joshua Jones, late of Durham, deceased (Cumb. Deeds, Vol. 170, p. 24). Mch. 18, 1836, Joel Jones, and others, sell land in Durham (Cumb. Deeds, Vol. 147, p. 221). June 27, 1836, William Jones, of Mexico, sells Moses Jones, of Durham, "all my right in real estate which my father, Joshua Jones, died possessed of" (Cumb. Deeds, Vol. 147, p. 223).

Child of Ezekiel and Elizabeth (Conant) Jones:—

> Joshua, who had Ezekiel, William, Joel, Samuel, Joshua, Sally, Abigail and Dorothy.

98. Bartholomew[5] (*Joseph, Lot, Lot, Roger*), b. in Falmouth, Me., about 1736. He lived near Duck Pond, in the part of the town now Westbrook.

On 31 Aug., 1761, Joseph Conant, of Falmouth, sells "my son, Bartholomew Conant, labourer," one-half of about 55 acres of land, "it being the remainder of my 60 acre lot laid out to me by the Proprietors of Falmouth, Aug. 10, 1734 * * * that is to say, the northerly half of said 55 acres, next to and adjoining the Presumpscot river, said 60 acres lying between Samuel Proctor's land on the east and John Waite's on the west." Deed witnessed by Joseph Pride and Enoch Freeman (Cumberland Co. Deeds, Vol. 1, p. 367). This lot of land Bartholomew and Joseph sold on 28 Feb., 1765, to John Waite (Vol. 3, p. 118).

On 27 Nov., 1764, Joseph Conant conveyed to his sons, Bartholomew and Joseph, " a certain tract of land containing about 16 acres, lying in Falmouth, beginning at the south-easterly side of the Great Pond, on the northern side of Presumpscot river, including the meadow ground at the end of said pond." On Aug. 12, 1768, Bartholomew Conant, of Falmouth, millman, sells one-sixteenth part of a saw mill and one-quarter of one acre of land, situated upon the stream which runs out of Duck Pond, to James Torrey (Vol. 6, p. 256); on Apr. 5, 1779, one-sixteenth of the saw mill to Ebenezer Mayo (Vol. 6, p. 261); on Aug. 12, 1768, one-sixteenth to Jacob Morrell (Vol. 7, p. 172). On Jan. 2, 1804, Daniel Lunt, administrator of the estate of Bartholomew Conant, deceased, sells land at Duck Pond to Thomas Winslow (Vol. 49, p. 606).

He served 35 months and 23 days during the Revolutionary war, in Capt. Mayberry's company of the 11th Mass. regiment, and was discharged an invalid (Mass. Archives, Continental Army Rolls).

He d. 14 Jan., 1802.

He m. in Falmouth, 6 Mch., 1760, Anna Frink; int. pub. 15 Feb., 1760. She d. 2 Oct., 1794, aged 65.

Children of BARTHOLOMEW and ANNA (FRINK) CONANT:—

      Sarah, b. 10 May, 1761; m. —— Gibbs.
210,   Eunice, b. 12 July, 1763.
      Abigail, b. 18 Nov., 1765; m. 3 Feb., 1785, Ichabod Varney, by Rev. Thomas Smith.
211.   Joseph, b. 3 Feb., 1767.

99. Joseph[5] (*Joseph, Lot, Lot, Roger*), b. in Falmouth, about 1738. He lived at Duck Pond, in Falmouth (Westbrook), until about 1810, when he moved to Lisbon, in Androscoggin co., where he engaged in the lumber business.

On Aug. 31, 1761, his father deeded him one-half of 55 acres of land in Falmouth (Cumberland Deeds, Vol. 1, p. 366), which he sold Feb. 28, 1765, to John Waite (Cumb. Deeds, Vol. 3, p. 118). Oct. 15, 1809, Joseph Conant, of Falmouth, yeoman, sells land in Falmouth to Samuel Sawyer, containing

1 acre and 36 rods, "bounded thus: the said piece with ¾ of the saw mill which stands thereon is part of the 104 acres on which I now dwell, which the Duck Pond brook runs through, and adjoins the 16 acres deeded to me and my brother, Bartholomew, by our father, Joseph Conant, deceased" (Cumb. Deeds, Vol. 57, p. 377).

He d. 27 June, 1816, in Portland, while there as witness at a trial.

He m. 10 June, 1762, Anna Shackford.

Children of JOSEPH and ANNA (SHACKFORD) CONANT:—

> Hannah, b. ——; m. 4 Oct., 1781, Joseph Elder.
> Anne, b. ——; m. 1 Mch., 1781, Nathan Partridge.
> 212. Bartholomew, b. ——.
> 213. Thomas, b. about 1773.
> George, b. ——; d. y.

100. **Lot**[5] (*Joshua, Lot, Lot, Roger*), b. 21 Dec., 1746, in Ipswich, Mass., where he lived on the homestead of his father. He was in Capt. Brown's company at Providence, R. I., 1 Jan., 1779 (Mass. Arch., Muster Rolls, Vol. 41, p. 92).

Lot Conant
(1797.)

He m. (19 Mch., 1768?), Hephzibah Wildes.

Children of LOT and HEPHZIBAH (WILDES) CONANT:—

> Bartholomew, said to have settled in Bridgton, Me.
> Israel, m. ——, Martha Gould.
> Moses, m. and had a child, who d. y.
> Joshua.
> 214. Joseph.
> Eunice, b. 25 Dec., 1769; m. ——, Dudley Wildes, and d. in Ipswich, 19 Sep., 1864.
> Sarah.

101. **Joshua**[5] (*Joshua, Lot, Lot, Roger*), b. in Ipswich, 6 Feb., 1749-50. 24 May, 1771, Joshua Conant, of Ipswich, husbandman, sells land "formerly belonging to my father, Joshua Conant, late of Ipswich, bounded by land of my uncle, William Conant, my sister, Johoaddan, and brother, Lot" (Essex Deeds, Vol. 136, p. 211). He settled in Londonderry, N. H. He was one of the signers of the "Association Test," 1776. Enlisted 20 July, 1777, in Capt. Daniel Reynold's company,

and was at the battle of Bennington, where he received a wound from which he died 10 Sep., 1777 (N. H. State Papers, Vol. 15, p. 201). His wife was Mary Henderson, of Rowley, Mass.

Children of JOSHUA and MARY (HENDERSON) CONANT:—

215.   Nathaniel, b. 6 Oct., 1776.
216.   Joshua, b. 2 June, 1779.
       Abiah, b. ——; m. (int. pub. 28 Jan., 1811,) Reuben Coburn.

102.   Elizabeth[5] (*Samuel, Lot, Lot, Roger*), b. in Falmouth, about 1745; m. before 1770, William, son of James Babb. In a deposition given in 1805, he says that he is 63 years old and was born within one mile of a place called Saccarappa. His wife, in a deposition given at the same time, says that she is 60 years old, that when a girl she had often heard Moses Pearson, Esq., converse with her father, Samuel Conant (Cumberland Deeds, Vol. 45, p. 507).

Children of WILLIAM and ELIZABETH (CONANT) BABB:—

i.   Solomon.
ii.   Alexander.
iii.   Elizabeth, m. —— Woodbury.
iv.   A dr., m. —— Plummer.
v.   Daniel.
vi.   Henry, m. Elizabeth, dr. of Jonathan Webb.
vii.   William.
viii. George.

103.   William[5] (*Samuel, Lot, Lot, Roger*), b. in Falmouth. He lived in Saccarappa village, near the corner of Maine and Bridge streets. On 9 Sep., 1783, he gave bonds to keep the peace towards William Westcoat, of Falmouth, innholder, but was discharged at the October term of court, Westcoat not appearing (Cumberland Co. Court Records). He d. about 1805, and Peter Thatcher was appointed administrator of his estate.

He m. 23 Sep., 1779, Ruth Chapman (by Rev. Thomas Browne), who survived him.

Children of WILLIAM and RUTH (CHAPMAN) CONANT:—

i.   Samuel, lived unmarried, in the family of his uncle, Daniel;
       d. about 1870.
ii.   Lydia, d. aged 21 (Newspaper of 7 Apr., 1810).
iii.   Edward. On June 11, 1808, Samuel, Lydia and Edward, heirs

of Wm. Conant, sell land to William Webb (Cumb. Deeds, Vol. 55, p. 128).

iv.   Polly.

v.   Shoah.

104. Daniel[5] (*Samuel, Lot, Lot, Roger*), b. in Falmouth, about 1760; lived at Saccarappa. In Oct., 1797, the jury presented Jonathan Webb, Daniel Conant and Jonathan Winslow, all of Falmouth, "for erecting a boom on Presumpscot river, on or about Mch. 1, 1795, about 100 rods above the uppermost falls at Saccarappa, which prevented persons from passing, and which still remains to the interference of travel." Verdict, "not guilty" (Cumberland County Court Records).

From a deposition given in 1840, it appears that he was then 80 years old; he says that he was born and had always resided in Saccarappa, and that he had been for many years engaged in "lumbering and driving the river."

He d. 10 Dec., 1853, aged nearly 93 years.

He m. 26 Oct., 1786, Anna, dr. of Solomon Haskell, senior, who d. 21 Sep., 1844.

Children of DANIEL and ANNA (HASKELL) CONANT:—

    Eunice, b. 3 Oct., 1786; m. Joseph Hawes.

    Ann, b. 19 Oct., 1788; m. Mark Babb.

217.   Elizabeth, b. 15 Feb., 1791.

    Daniel, b. 12 Feb., 1794; d. unm. 16 July, 1874. An enterprising farmer and lumberman of Saccarappa, noted for his fine oxen.

    Mary, b. 24 Aug., 1796; d. 9 Feb., 1881, aged 84 years, 5 mos.; never married.

    Nathaniel, b. 10 June, 1799; d. unm., 21 Oct., 1871, aged 72 years and 3 mos.

218.   Solomon, b. 30 Mch., 1801.

105. William[5] (*William, Lot, Lot, Roger*), b. in Ipswich, 3 Sep., 1747, where he lived.

On 3 Feb., 1787, he witnessed the will of John Fowler, of Ipswich (Essex Probate, Vol. 71, p. 55). Apr. 18, 1789, Joseph Fowler and Lydia, his wife, John Smith and Hannah, his wife, sell 38 acres of land to William Conant, of Ipswich. Apr. 4, 1810, John Fowler, of Ipswich, sells 90 acres of land, and buildings, in Linebrook parish, to William Conant, William Conant, jr., and Daniel Conant, of Ipswich.

He d. 8 May, 1826.

He m. ———, Mary Perkins.

Children of WILLIAM and MARY (PERKINS) CONANT:—

      John, b. ———, 1770; d. y.
219. William, b. 11 July, 1772.
220. Daniel, b. 11 Jan., 1774.
221. John, b. Aug., 1776.
222. Joseph, b. 4 June, 1782 (or 1790?).

106. Moses[5] (*William, Lot, Lot, Roger*), b. in Ipswich, about 1749. He lived in Ipswich; m. 27 June, 1779, Mary Wildes. At the news of the battle of Lexington, he marched to Boston, under Capt. Abraham How (Mass. Archives, Lexington Alarm Lists, Vol. 12, p. 146).

Children of MOSES and MARY (WILDES) CONANT:—

223. William, b. 1785.
224. Asa Wildes, b. 1788.
      Lois.
      Matty.

107. Aaron[5] (*William, Lot, Lot, Roger*), b. 25 Nov., 1752, in Ipswich. He was a tailor. He removed from Ipswich to Topsfield, where he d. 14 Jan., 1816, from a wound inflicted by his shears while sitting on his bench.

He served during the Revolutionary war in Capt. John Dodge's company of Col. Gerrish's regiment (Mass. Archives, Muster Rolls, Vol. 18, p. 147).

He d. intestate. The inventory of his estate is recorded in Essex Probate Records, Vol. 89, p. 233.

He m. 18 Mch., 1779, in Topsfield, Eunice Dorman, who d. 21 June, 1823.

Children of AARON and EUNICE (DORMAN) CONANT:—

      Eunice, b. 28 Feb., 1780; d. 24 Jan., 1868.
225. Samuel, b. 17 June, 1784.
226. Aaron, b. 13 May, 1787.
227. Nathaniel, b. 5 Oct., 1795.
228. William, b. 24 July, 1801.

108. David[5] (*David, William, Lot, Roger*), b. 6 Apr., 1726, in Bridgewater. He built and lived in a one-story house, near his father's, at South Bridgewater. He d. 1760, intestate. The inventory is recorded in Vol. 16, p. 136, of Plymouth Probate Records. He m. 1748, Rhoda, dr. of Thomas and Deborah (Harden) Latham.

Children of DAVID and RHODA (LATHAM) CONANT:—

229. Elias, b. ———, 1749.
  Mary, b. ———, 1752; m. (136) Ezra Conant.
230. Solomon, b. ———, 1756.
231. Rufus, b. ———, 1757.
232. David, b. 10 May, 1759.

109. Jonathan[5] (*David, William, Lot, Roger*), b. 25 Oct., 1734, in Bridgewater. He removed to Greenwich, Mass., thence to Lyme, N. H., and thence to Orange, Vt., where he d. 1820. He was a carpenter. During the Revolution he served seven years, wintered at Valley Forge and took part in the battle of Brandywine. At one time he was in Capt. David Kingman's company of Col. Mitchell's regiment, as sergeant (Mass. Archives, Muster Rolls, Vol. 2, p. 173).

In 1788 he was selectman of Lyme, N. H.

He m. 1759, Jane, dr. of Arthur and Alice (Allen) Latham, g. dr. of Capt. Chilton and Susanna (Kingman) Latham, g. g. dr. of Robert and Susanna (Winslow) Latham. Susanna Winslow was dr. of John, brother of Gov. Edward Winslow; her mother was Mary Chilton, who is said to have been the first woman who landed at Plymouth, 1620.

Children of JONATHAN and JANE (LATHAM) CONANT:—

  Jane, b. 7 Mch., 1760; m. Deacon (150) Peter Conant.
  Sally, b. 20 Nov., 1761; m. 1782, Abisha, son of Nehemiah Besse.
  Jerusha, b. 26 Mch., 1764.
233. Josiah, b. 19 Feb., 1768.
  Lydia, b. 13 July, 1770.
  Alice, b. 17 June, 1773.

110. Hannah[5] (*Ebenezer, Roger, Lot, Roger*), b. 12 Feb., 1740, in Concord, Mass.; m. there Josiah Dodge, and settled in Ashburnham. They removed about 1780 to Machias, Me.

Children of JOSIAH and HANNAH (CONANT) DODGE:—

i.   Eunice, b. ——,
ii.   Mary, b. ——,
iii. Josiah, b. ——,
iv.   Anna, b. ——,   } in Ashburnham.
v.   Betty, b. ——,
vi.   Reuben, b. ——,
vii. Daniel, b. ——,
viii. Ebenezer, b. 30 June, 1779,

III. **Ebenezer**[5] (*Ebenezer, Roger, Lot, Roger*), b. 11 Aug., 1743, in Concord, Mass.; settled in Ashburnham, before 1768. A manuscript volume, written jointly by Ebenezer Conant and his son, John, is in existence, or was in 1868, to which Ebenezer contributed about 100 pp., mostly of a theological nature. The titles of the theological works are: 1. A Piece wrote upon some Jarring Sentiments among my Brethren about Predestination and Election. 2. A Profession of Faith. 3. A Letter to Mr. Lee. 4. A Discourse on the Fall and Recovery of Man. 5. Thoughts upon a Man's Spirit being generated with his Body. 6. A Covenant. 7. Thoughts upon the New Birth. These works show that Mr. Conant was a man of deep religious convictions, and intensely interested in the nice points of theology. The story of his conversion as told by his son, John, is this: "About 1780 a Baptist preacher (named Fletcher) came to our town. The people mocked him and hooted at him; but some, out of curiosity, went to hear him. Among others my father and mother went and they came home pricked to the heart. Long before this, on the birth of their first child, they had joined the Congregational Church by what is called the half-way covenant, so that they might have their children sprinkled. This mock baptism was performed on myself when I was only eight days old. Now they were dissatisfied with the half-way covenant religion, and followed the Baptist minister no longer from curiosity, but to obtain salvation."

At the news of the battle of Lexington he was elected lieutenant in Capt. Davis' company of Col. Whitcomb's regiment (Mass. Archives, Lexington Alarm Lists, Vol. 2, p. 37). In 1777 he was adjutant of Col. Stearns' regiment, at Saratoga, and was allowed £10 for 25 days' service, £1 10s. 6d. for rations, and £1 13s. 6d. for a horse (Mass. Arch., Muster Rolls, Vol. 26, p. 30). In 1779, June 9, "Ebenezer Conant, aged 36, heighth 5 ft. 9 in., dark complexion, of Ashburnham," enlisted for 9 months in Capt. Lane's company of Col. Rand's regiment (Muster Rolls, Vol. 45, p. 282).

The same year he was one of the selectmen of Ashburnham.

In possession of his great grandson, John Conant Merriam, of Logansport, Ind., is an old horn drinking flask carried by him during the Revolution. It is inscribed, "Eben Conant's Bottle. In Col. Shepard's Company and Reg't. Salem, Sept. 11, 1779," and is carved with trees, houses, a ship, chickens, etc.

Again let his son tell the story: "In 1781 my father fell sick; he was sick two years, which made us very poor. I can never forget his last address to us, made the week before he died. My poor mother was in very great distress about her large family of little children. She could not tell how we should live when he was gone, and begged my father to give some of his children away to friends who would gladly receive them if he gave them on his death bed. But when she had done speaking, he looked up into her face with such a joyful look as I never saw before in my life, and said, 'I have given away all your children to the dearest Friend in the world; I have given them away to God.'"

He d. 3 Aug., 1783, in Ashburnham.

He m. Lydia Oakes, of Harvard, who was b. 6 June, 1743, in Stow.

Children of EBENEZER and LYDIA (OAKES) CONANT:—

    Lydia, b. 21 Nov., 1768; d. Sep., 1776, in Ashburnham.
234. Sarah, b. 17 Oct., 1770, in Ashburnham.
235. John, b. 2 Feb., 1773,   "
236. Elizabeth, b. 15 Mch., 1775,   "
237. Eben, b. 6 June, 1777,   "
238. Calvin, b. 30 May, 1779,   "
239. Luther, b. 24 Jan., 1782.   "

112. **William**[5] (*Roger, Roger, Lot, Roger*), b. 23 Feb., 1727-8, in Charlestown, Mass. He was taxed at Charlestown, 1756 to 1773; bought land of Jona. Sprague's executor, 1773; claimed for loss, 1775 (Wyman's *Genealogies and Estates of*

Charlestown). He was selectman of Charlestown, 1767 to 1771. On Feb. 12, 1770, was one of a committee "to inquire whether any inhabitant had imported or bought or sold goods contrary to the agreement of the merchants of Boston, and to prepare such resolves on the above affairs as they think proper" (Frothingham's *Hist. of Charlestown*). He was prominent in military affairs, and at a meeting of the officers of the First Regiment of militia, held Nov. 29, 1774, Thomas Gardner was chosen Colonel, Wm. Bond, Lieut. Col. and William Conant, 2nd Lieut. Col. (Boston Gazette, Oct. 19, 1772, and Dec. 5, 1774).

It was with Col. Conant that Paul Revere planned the hanging of the signal lanterns in the steeple of the North Church, to give warning of any movement of the British army toward Concord, where the patriots had gathered their stores. Revere says: "I agreed with a Col. Conant and some other gentlemen, that if the British went out by water, we would show two lanterns in the North Church steeple, and if by land, one, as a signal." It seems that Dr. Warren had sent Revere with a message to Hancock and Adams, in Lexington, where they passed their nights while attending the sessions of the Provincial Congress, at Concord. On his return from this errand he met Col. Conant, at Charlestown, and made the arrangement to show the signals on any movement of the British. On Tuesday evening (Apr. 18, 1775), about ten o'clock, Dr. Warren discovered the movement of the troops, "sent in great haste," says Revere, "for me, and begged that I would immediately set off for Lexington." He went at once and directed the hanging of the lanterns in the steeple; took his boat and rowed over to Charlestown. He says: "They landed me on the Charlestown side. When I got into town I met Col. Conant and several others; they said they had seen our signals. I told them what was acting, and went to get me a horse" (Mass. Hist. Col., 1st Series, Vol. V., p. 107). He then set out on his "midnight ride." From the above statements the historical inaccuracies of the poem are apparent. The lanterns were not displayed for Revere's information—for he already knew all they were intended to convey—but for the information of Col.

Conant and his friends. Neither did Revere reach Concord, but was seized after leaving Lexington.

He d. July, 1811.

He m. (1) 1 Feb., 1759, Sarah Morecock, of Dorchester, who was admitted to the church, 20 Apr., 1760; m. (2) Anne ———.

Children of WILLIAM and SARAH (MORECOCK) CONANT:—

    Sarah, b. 30 May, 1760.
240. William, b. 2 Apr., 1762.
    Silence, b. 22 Feb., 1764.
241. Thomas, b. 16 May, 1765.
    Mary, b. 1 Jan., 1767.
    Samuel, b. ———, 1769; d. unm.
    Rebecca, bapt. 27 Dec., 1772.

113. Samuel[5] (*Roger, Roger, Lot, Roger*), b. 24 May, 1730, in Charlestown, where he lived. His estate taxed 1756-73; claimed for loss, 1775; buys 9 rods of land of S. Bailey, "towards the ferry," 1755; buys of Mary Phillips, 1755; of T. Jenner, 1760; of J. Hopkins, mowing land on south side of town hill, 1759; of S. Greenleaf, 4 acres on Moulton point, 1763; of E. Cheever, 1765; of Joanna Jenner, executrix of Thomas, $4\frac{3}{4}$ acres on south-west of the way over Bunker's Hill, 1770; of S. Henley, 2 acres, 1798; buys pew No. 53 in 1800 (Wyman's *Genealogies and Estates of Charlestown*). He was a baker by trade. "Samuel Conant took into the church Mch. 25, 1759" (Diary of Robert Cally, of Charlestown).

He d. 27 May, 1802 (g. s.). His will is dated 4 June, 1794,

(1794.)

proved 2 June, 1802; he devised to his wife (the executrix) the use of estate for life, then one-half to his daughter, Abigail, and one-half to his grandchildren, Samuel and Polly.

He m. Rebecca Coffin, int. pub. at Boston, 24 Jan., 1754; she admitted to church, 5 Jan., 1755, and d. in New Bedford, 20 Aug., 1813, aged 80.

Children of SAMUEL and REBECCA (COFFIN) CONANT:—

242. Samuel, bapt. 16 Feb., 1755.
    Rebecca, b. 6, bapt. 8 Aug., 1756.
    Jacob, b. 1, bapt. 3 Sep., 1758; graduated at Harvard, 1777; no
        further record.
    John, bapt. 10 Aug., 1760.
243. Abigail, bapt. 20 June, 1762.
    Rebecca, b. 10 Sep., 1763; d. of small pox, 22 Apr., 1764.
    John, bapt. 31 Jan., 1768.
    William Harris, bapt. 8 Apr., 1770.

114. Abigail[5] (*Roger, Roger, Lot, Roger*), bapt. in Charlestown, 9 Apr., 1732; m. 23 Jan., 1731-2, Samuel, son of Philip and Tryphena Lord, of Ipswich. She was admitted to the church at Charlestown, 4 Mch., 1753; d. 6 Apr., 1781, in Ipswich. Samuel Lord, bapt. in Charlestown, 23 Jan., 1725-6. The family moved to Ipswich.

Children of Samuel and Abigail (Conant) Lord :—

    Samuel, b. 26 Mch., 1753, in Charlestown.
    And others b. in Ipswich.

115. Jonathan[5] (*Israel, Roger, Lot, Roger*), b. in Concord, 3 Feb., 1732-3; settled in Ashburnham; removed to Reading, Vt. Feb. 12, 1753, Jonathan Conant, of Concord, sells land "called Monadnock No. 8," to Peter Prescott, of Concord (Rockingham, N. H., Deeds, Vol. 45, p. 139). The name of Jonathan Conant, of Concord, appears in a list of those who took part in an expedition to Nova Scotia, in May, 1755 (Shattuck's *Hist. of Concord*, p. 72). He also served a short time in the Revolutionary army (Mass. Arch., Lexington Alarm Lists, Vol. 12, p. 129). Apr. 1, 1790, Jonathan Conant, of Reading, Vt., sells land in Flint's Town, (Baldwin) Maine, "formerly belonging to my father, Israel Conant," to Elisha Jones, of Concord, Mass. (Cumberland Deeds, Vol. 19, p. 410).

His wife was Eunice ———.

Children of Jonathan and Eunice (———) Conant:—

    William, b. 17 Aug., 1765, in Ashburnham, Mass.
244. Jonathan, b. 14 Jan., 1767,   "   "
    Israel, b. 3 Oct., 1768,   "   "
    (Henry, b.———; was a Justice of the Peace at Reading, Vt.;
        d. about 1850?)

116. Israel[5] (*Israel, Roger, Lot, Roger*), b. about 1738, in

Concord, Mass. Settled in Merrimack, N. H., where he d.

He m. in Concord, 15 Apr., 1767, Mary Haywood.

Children of ISRAEL and MARY (HAYWOOD) CONANT:—

> Mary, b. 16 Feb., 1768.
> Joel, b. 22 Feb., 1770; d. 20 Feb., 1799. On June 3, 1794, Joel
> Conant, of Litchfield, N. H., signed a petition for a bridge
> at Cromwell's Falls (N. H. Town Papers, Vol. 12, p. 424).
> 245. John, b. 1 Jan., 1773.
> Israel, b. 11 Dec., 1775; d. 26 May, 1808.
> Sarah, b. 1 Mch., 1779; d. 2 Nov., 1808.

117. Josiah[5] (*Josiah, Roger, Lot, Roger*), b. in Hollis, N.
H., 17 Oct., 1746. He settled in Hollis; was a farmer; was a
member of the church, and deacon from 1787 till his death.
He was town treasurer in 1780. In 1774 (the last tax collected
under the king) he paid a tax of 7s. 6d.; only one person in
the town paid over £1.

He enlisted Dec., 1775, in Captain Worcester's company;
was at Cambridge three months. On Aug. 6, 1778, he enlisted
in Capt. Emerson's company, of which he was sergeant, for
service in Rhode Island (Worcester's *Hist. of Hollis*, pp. 158,
173 and 181; and N. H. State Papers, Vol. 15, p. 510).

He d. 21 Aug., 1807.

He m. (1) 9 Jan., 1769, Elizabeth Elliot, of Mason, N. H.,
who d. 23 July, 1788; m. (2) 16 Dec., 1788, Zerviah Fox, of
Hollis, b. 23 Dec., 1755, d. 12 Feb., 1816.

Children of JOSIAH and ELIZABETH (ELLIOT) CONANT:—

> 246. Josiah, b. 5 Feb., 1770.
> Elizabeth, b. 10 Nov., 1771; m. —— Whitney, and had a
> family.
> 247. Catherine, b. 28 Nov., 1773.
> 248. William, b. 16 Jan., 1776.
> Mary, b. 7 Jan., 1778.
> 249. Abigail, b. 30 Aug., 1780.
> Ruth, b. 31 Dec., 1782; d. 1853.
> Elias, b. Sep., 1785; d. 6 July, 1788.

Children of JOSIAH and ZERVIAH (FOX) CONANT:—

> Sarah, b. 24 Sep., 1789; d. 24 July, 1799.
> Joseph, b. 4 July, 1791; d. 28 July, 1798.
> 250. Elias, b. 11 Sep., 1792.
> Hannah, b. 29 Feb., 1794.
> Sophia, b. 16 Feb., 1796.
> 251. Elizabeth, b. 4 July, 1800.

118. Catherine[5] (*Josiah, Roger, Lot, Roger*), b. in Hollis, 10 Sep., 1753; m. 10 Feb., 1774, Capt. John Goss, who d. 26 Sep., 1821, aged 82. He was b. in Salisbury, Mass., 13 Feb., 1739; first taxed at Hollis, 1770. About 1805 the family removed to Hardwick, Vt., where he died.

The news of the battle of Lexington was received at Hollis on the afternoon of Apr. 19. The minute men immediately assembled, elected Reuben Dow, captain, John Goss, lieutenant, and started for Cambridge next morning. He was at the battle of Bunker Hill, and in 1777 was captain of the Hollis company at the battle of Bennington.

Children of John and Catherine (Conant) Goss :—

i. John, b. 7 Jan., 1775.
ii. Samuel, b. 29 Nov., 1776.
iii. Abel, b. 23 Oct., 1780.
iv. Catherine, b. 11 Oct., 1782.
v. Lucy, b. 30 Dec., 1784.
vi. Anna, b. 15 Aug., 1787.
vii. Mark, b. 10 Oct., 1789.
viii. Luke, b. 13 June, 1792.
ix. Elizabeth, b. 19 Nov., 1795.

119. Abel[5] (*Josiah, Roger, Lot, Roger*), b. 3 Oct., 1755, in Hollis. He was deacon of the Hollis Church from 1787 to 1813. In 1775 he enlisted in Capt. Dow's company, and was in the battle of Bunker Hill, where he lost "one knapsack, value 1s. 8d., one tumpline, value 1s. 4d.;" served eight months that year; is described as "aged 19 years, light complexion, height 5 ft. 6 in." In 1776 he enlisted for one year, and in 1778 was in service as corporal (Worcester's *Hist. of Hollis*, pp. 149, 150, 155, 164 and 181; and N. H. State Papers, Vol. 15, p. 510).

In 1783 Abel and Margaret Conant, of Hollis, sell all the right that belonged to "our father, Josiah Conant, who was one of the original proprietors of a new Township on the east side of the Saco river," to Oliver Prescott, of Groton (Cumberland Co., Me., Deeds).

In 1813 he moved to Hardwick, Vt., where he d. 2 May, 1844.

He m. (1) 20 Nov., 1781, Margaret, dr. of James and Margaret Jewett, of Hollis; b. 18 Oct., 1758, d. 25 July, 1788; m. (2) Lydia Thurston.

Children of ABEL and MARGARET (JEWETT) CONANT:—

    Margaret, b. 30 Aug., 1782, in Hollis.
252. Abel, b. 1 June, 1784.
253. James, b. 7 Apr., 1786.
    Catherine E., b. 29 Dec., 1787.

Children of ABEL and LYDIA (THURSTON) CONANT:—

    Susanna S., b. 26 May, 1791.
    Joseph, b. 24 Nov., 1792.
    Daniel, b. 11 Dec., 1794; d. 21 Feb., 1795.
    Lydia, b. 26 Apr., 1796.
    Rebecca, b. 28 Nov., 1798.
    Moses Thurston, b. 3 Feb., 1801.
    John Calvin, b. 30 Jan., 1803.

120. Josiah[5] (*Thomas, Roger, Lot, Roger*), b. in Westminster, Mass., 19 Nov., 1758; lived in that part of the town now Gardner. He d. 1835. He m. Annis Derby, published 3 Oct., 1784.

Children of JOSIAH and ANNIS (DERBY) CONANT:—

    Aaron, b. 15 Mch., 1785, in Westminster.
    Lucy, b. 19 Feb., 1787, in Gardner.
    Nancy, b. 6 Feb., 1789,   "
    Betsey, b. 8 Apr., 1791,   "
254. Farwell, b. 12 Apr., 1793,   "
    Abigail, b. 11 June, 1795,   "
    Mary, b. 30 Aug., 1797,   "
    Josiah, b. 30 July, 1799,   "
    Emily, b. 17 Aug., 1801,   "
    Susanna, b. 18 July, 1803,   "
    Lyman, b. 12 Aug., 1805,   "
    Maria, b. 16 June, 1807,   "
    Lawson, b. 2 May, 1809,   "
    Sylvester, b. 20 June, 1810, "

121. Thomas[5] (*Thomas, Roger, Lot, Roger*), b. in Westminster, Mass., 6 Aug., 1763, where he lived. He m. (1) 21 Dec., 1784, Ruth Rice, of Gardner Farms, who d. 25 July, 1797; m. (2) Polly Brown; m. (3) Betsey Morse.

Children of THOMAS and RUTH (RICE) CONANT:—

    Polly, b. 16 Apr., 1785, in Westminster.

Sally, b. 16 Aug., 1787; m. —— Estabrook.
Nathan, b. 30 Apr., 1790; d. y.
Levi, b. 7 Apr., 1791; d. aged 8 yrs.

Children of THOMAS and POLLY (BROWN) CONANT:—

John Sherlock, b. 15 Aug., 1799; m. but left no children.
Lurinda, b. ——; m. Elmer Baker, of Princeton.

122. John[5] (*John, Joshua, Joshua, Roger*), b. 17 Aug., 1730, in Provincetown, Mass. "May 5, 1765, John Conant and Abigail, his wife, of Provincetown, owned the covenant" (First Church of Truro Records). John Conant and Silas Newcomb buy a pew in Truro church, 1 Dec., 1774, and 22 Feb., 1779, John Conant buys a pew (Freeman's *Hist. of Cape Cod*).

Children of JOHN and ABIGAIL (——) CONANT:—

John, b. 19 Dec., 1763; bapt. 12 May, 1765.
255. Samuel, b. 22 Aug., bapt. 15 Oct., 1765.
Elizabeth, b. 20 Sep., bapt. 6 Nov., 1768.
Abigail, b. 6 Aug., 1770; bapt. 14 Apr., 1771; d. 1772.
Sarah, b. 6 Oct., 1772; bapt. 13 June, 1773.
256. Simeon, b. 4 June, 1780, in Provincetown.
    (Dates of births from Provincetown Records; dates of baptisms from Truro Church Records.)

123. Eunice[5] (*Shubael, Josiah, Exercise, Roger*), b. 28 May, 1736, in Mansfield, Conn., "on Friday, half an hour and half a quarter after one in ye morning" (Family Record).

She d. in Southold, L. I., and was buried in the Presbyterian churchyard, where her g. s. with the following inscription, remains: "The remains of Mrs. Eunice Storrs, daughter of ye Honorable Shubl. Conant, Esq., of Mansfield, and wife of ye Rev'd John Storrs, pastor of ye first church of Christ in Southold, who died March 27, A. D. 1767, ae 31."

She m. (1) Dr. Samuel Howe, of Mansfield; m. (2) Rev. John Storrs, the sixth pastor of the First Congregational Church, of Southold. After her death he m. and had other children.

Child of JOHN and EUNICE (CONANT) STORRS:—

i. Richard Salter, b. 30 Aug., 1763; was named for his uncle, Dr. Rich. Salter, of Mansfield, in whose family he was brought up, his mother having died while he was an infant. He was the pastor of the church of Longmeadow, Mass., and d. there 3 Oct., 1819. He m. in West Haven, Conn., 12 Oct., 1785, Sarah, dr. of Rev. Noah Williston, b. 14 June, 1765, d. 27 Jan., 1798; m. 2nd, Sarah Williams. Children:

1. Richard Salter, b. in Longmeadow, 6 Feb., 1787, who was pastor of the church of Braintree, Mass. He m. 1st, Sarah Woodhull; 2nd, Harriet Moore; 3rd, Anna Stebbins. By his second wife he had Rev. Richard Salter Storrs, D. D., of Brooklyn, N. Y., who m. Mary Jenks, and has three daughters, all married.

2. Sarah Williston, b. 28 Nov., 1788; m. in Longmeadow, 1808, Col. Charles Eugene Billings, of Conway, Mass. He was a farmer and merchant of C.; represented the town in Gen. Court, and was colonel of militia in the War of 1812. Children: (a) Jerusha W., b. 1809, m. Prof. Bela B. Edwards, of Andover, Mass., had Sarah, who m. Rev. William Edwards Park, and had Prof. Edwards A. Park, of Andover Theological Seminary, and Marion E.; (b) Sarah W., d. y.; (c) Charles, b. 1812, m. Hannah Egert, and has Charles, Hannah L. and Kate; they live at Beloit, Wis.; (d) William W., b. 1821, a physician, d. unm.; (e) Storrs; (f) Richard Salter, who is pastor of the Congregational Church at Somersville, Conn.; (g) Maria L., m. Rev. W. G. Mosher; (h) Edward Payson, living in San Francisco; (i) Elizabeth Storrs, b. 1832, m. Rev. Hiram Mead, of So. Hadley, Mass.; he was Professor of Homilities at the Theological Seminary at Oberlin, Ohio; she is a teacher at Abbott Academy, Andover, Mass.; (k) Hannah Storrs, unm.

3. Charles Backus, b. in Longmeadow; m. and had Charles and Henry Martyn, who m. Katherine, dr. of Pres. Hitchcock, of Amherst College, and has Charles, Richard Salter and Katherine.

4. Jonathan, d. unm.

5. David, m. Rachel James, and d. leaving a son, William, now living in Chicago, Ill.

6. (By second wife) Eleazer Williams; m. Lucy C. Burt, and had Richard Salter, d. y., Lucy, m. Judge L. Barbour, and Sarah.

7. Eunice Conant, d. 1883, unm.

8. Lucy, who m. —— Dunham, and d. without children.

124. Roger[5] (*Shubael, Josiah, Exercise, Roger*), b. 8 Mch., 1743-4, in Mansfield, Conn. He graduated at Yale College, 1765; studied medicine, and was a surgeon in the Revolutionary army. He d. 1777, of fatigue, at the battle of Long Island. He m. 14 July, 1774, Elizabeth Bronson.

Child of ROGER and ELIZABETH (BRONSON) CONANT :—

Clarissa, b. 4 Oct., 1775; d. Apr., 1777.

125.   Ruth[5] (*Shubael, Josiah, Exercise, Roger*), b. 1 Feb., 1748-9, in Mansfield, Conn.; d. 18 Apr., 1792.   She m. 6 Jan., 1774, Daniel, son of Thomas Storrs, jr., b. in Mansfield, 7 Feb., 1748; d. 5 Jan., 1831.   He was a farmer of Mansfield, and an officer in the Revolutionary army.

Children of DANIEL and RUTH (CONANT) STORRS :—

i.   Origen, b. 11 Oct., 1774.
ii.   Zalmon, b. 18 Dec., 1779; he was a prominent citizen of Mansfield, and a graduate of Yale College (1801).   Among his children were, Daniel P. Storrs, of Mansfield Center, Conn., Hon. Z. A. Storrs, of Hartford, Conn., Treasurer of Society for Savings, and Hon. Origen Storrs, formerly Mayor of Lockport, N. Y.
iii. Juba, b. 9 Mch., 1782.
iv.   Sophronia, b. 2 Mch., 1784.
v.   Selina, b. 29 June, 1786.
vi.   Lucius, b. 23 June, 1789.   He moved to Buffalo, N. Y., 1811; was a merchant and later in the insurance business; an alderman of Buffalo for many years; was appointed Major General of militia by Gov. DeWitt Clinton.   He d. 1875. He m. Lucy Young, dr. of Benj. and Susan (Young) Caryl. Children: 1. Selina, b. 1826; 2. Maria, m. —— Bigelow; 3. Susan, b. 1831; 4. Charlotte, b. 1834; 5. Lucius Caryl, b. 1837; 6. Origen Seymour, b. 1840; 7. William Hamilton.
vii. Egbert, b. 7 Feb., 1792.

126.   Eleazer[5] (*Shubael, Josiah, Exercise, Roger*), b. 29 June, 1751, in Mansfield, Conn.   He graduated at Yale College, 1776, after which he studied theology, but never settled in the ministry.   He was a paymaster in the Revolutionary army.   About the year 1800 he removed from Mansfield, Conn., to Middlebury, Vt.

He d. 13 Sep., 1819, in Maumee, Ohio, while on a visit to his son, Horatio.

He m. (1) Eunice, dr. of Thomas Storrs, 10 July, 1777, in Mansfield; she d. 19 Aug., 1790; m. (2) 19 Nov., 1791, Betsey Cummings, who d. in Maumee, 12 Sep., 1819.

Children of ELEAZER and EUNICE (STORRS) CONANT :—

Fidelia, b. 26 July, 1779; d. 5 Mch., 1783, } twins.
257. Amelia, b. 26 July, 1779,   }
Eunice, b. 22 May, 1781; d. 24 Aug., 1781.

Shubael, b. 1 Aug., 1783; was apprenticed when 14 years old to learn the watchmaker's trade, to A. Storrs, of Northampton, Mass.; returned after three years to Middlebury. He traded in Burlington and Walpole, N. H., where his business capacity attracted the attention of some merchants who in 1807 sent him West to buy furs. He continued in their employ till the War of 1812, when he was taken prisoner with a valuable cargo of furs, at Mackinaw, by the British. He was released after the capture of Detroit by Gen. Brock. He then settled in Detroit, where he became prominent in business and social circles, and acquired a large property. He was J. P. and Judge. He d. 17 July, 1867, unm., at the residence of his niece, Mrs. Martha Tillman.

258. Horatio, b. 24 Nov., 1785.

Clara, b. 30 Jan., 1788; m. 1815, Elisha Martindale; she d. 1860, in 'Maumee, O. Children: 1. Clara; 2. Shubael; 3. Eliza, m. —— Gunn; 4. Louisa, m. —— Van Tassel.

259. Harry, b. 19 Apr., 1790.

Children of ELEAZER and BETSEY (CUMMINGS) CONANT:—

Alma, b. 26 May, 1795; d. 11 Mch., 1796.

260. Caroline, b. 11 Jan., 1798.

Elizabeth, b. 9 Dec., 1799, in Mansfield, Conn.; m. Leander Sackett, as his 2nd wife. His first wife was Rebecca Conant, descended from George, of Plymouth (*vide postea*).

Charles, b. 15 Aug., 1803, in Middlebury, Vt., where he d. aged 9 years.

127. **Seth**[5] (*Malachi, Caleb, Exercise, Roger*), b. 5 Dec., 1748, in Mansfield, Conn., where he lived. He d. 12 Aug., 1815.

He m. (1) 17 Nov., 1771, Eunice, dr. of David Royce, who d. 1 July, 1799; and he m. (2) Mrs. Martha (Wing) Fay; she d. 31 Jan., 1816.

Children of SETH and EUNICE (ROYCE) CONANT:—

David, b. 2 Oct., 1772; d. 31 Aug., 1774.
Mary, b. 29 Oct., 1774; d. 1 Sep., 1775.
David, b. 31 Aug., 1775; d. y.
Malachi, b. 7 Dec., 1776; d. y.

261. David, b. 15 Mch,, 1779.
262. Seth, b. 11 Oct., 1782.

Daniel, b. 8 May, 1785; d. 2 June, 1806.
Edmund, b. 7 June, 1787; d. y.

Children of SETH and MARTHA (WING) CONANT:

Eunice, b. ——; m. Daniel Crane, of Willimantic, Conn.; left a son, Edmund, now of Willimantic.

263. John W., b. 19 Dec., 1803.
      Mary, b. ———; m. Julius Hovey, of Gurleyville, Conn., and
      had three daughters.
      Elizabeth, b. ———; m. Geo. R. Hanks, a silk manufacturer,
      of Mansfield, Conn.

128. Sylvanus⁵ (*Malachi, Caleb, Exercise, Roger*), b. 10
Feb., 1750-1, in Mansfield, Conn.; lived on the homestead of his
father. He was a member of the Congregational Church. He
d. 2 Sep., 1843. He m. (1) 22 Oct., 1778, Anna, dr. of James
Royce; she d. 5 May, 1802, aged 42; m. (2) 12 Apr., 1807,
Elizabeth Utley, of Ashford, who d. 5 Jan., 1836, aged 72.
      Children of SYLVANUS and ANNA (ROYCE) CONANT:—

      Abigail, b. 7 Oct., 1779; d. unm., Oct., 1862.
      Sarah, b. 12 Dec., 1780; m. Nathan Utley, and had children.
264. Sylvanus, b. 26 Dec., 1782.
265. James, b. 15 Feb., 1784.
      Abiah, b. 10 Dec., 1785; buried 25 Dec., 1787.
      Kezia, b. 4 Jan., 1788; m. Asa Symonds, of Mansfield.
266. Chester, b. 23 May, 1790.
267. Joseph, b. 22 Mch., 1792.
268. Edmund, b. 22 Nov., 1796.
269. Lucius, b. 29 Sep., 1799, } twins.
      Lois, b. 29 Sep., 1799,   }   m. Elisha Fenton, and had
      one son, who d. y.; she d. 21 Jan., 1884.

      Child of SYLVANUS and ELIZABETH (UTLEY) CONANT:—

      Roxa, b. 24 Apr., 1808; d. unm., 6 Apr., 1864.

129. Edmund⁵ (*Malachi, Caleb, Exercise, Roger*), b. 19
Apr., 1759, in Mansfield. He settled in Hanover, N. H.; removed to Washington, Vt., thence to Farnham, Canada, where
he died 1 July, 1831. He m. in Hanover, N. H., Dec., 1787,
Asenath Jacobs, b. 11 Aug., 1766, in Ashford, Conn.; she d.
in Washington, Vt., 4 Mch., 1827.
      Children of EDMUND and ASENATH (JACOBS) CONANT:—
                    (Born in Hanover, N. H.)
270. Antha, b. 9 Dec., 1789; d. 19 June, 1851.
      Asenath, b. 2 Jan., 1792; d. 1 Apr., 1860.
271. Arta (or Arba?) b. 30 Mch., 1794.
      Edmund, b. 22 May, 1796.
272. Elam Lucius, b. 14 June, 1798.
273. Estes, b. 1 Apr., 1800.
      Elizabeth, b. 23 Mch., 1803.

274. Samuel Malachi Augustus, b. 24 Mch., 1805.
275. Matthew Watson Marcy, b. 7 June, 1807.

130. Nathaniel[5] (*Malachi, Caleb, Exercise, Roger*), b. 28 Sep., 1761, in Mansfield, Conn.; was a miller. He d. 1819, at Saratoga Springs, N. Y.

He m. (1) ——— ———; m. (2) Lois Royce.

Children of NATHANIEL and LOIS (ROYCE) CONANT :—

276. Gideon, b. ———, in Mansfield.
Polly.

131. Caleb[5] (*Benajah, Caleb, Exercise, Roger*), b. 12 Oct., 1741, in Mansfield, Conn. He settled at German Flats, N. Y., about 1801. He m. 15 May, 1760, Susanna Bibbins.

Children of CALEB and SUSANNA (BIBBINS) CONANT :—

Mehitable, b. 27 Aug., 1760.
Ebenezer, b. 12 Oct., 1762.
Amos B., b. 7 Feb., 1765.
Tryphena, b. 25 Jan., 1767.
John, b. 12 Oct., 1769.
277. Timothy, b. 19 Apr., 1772.
Guerdon, b. 20 Nov., 1775.
Samuel, b. 5 Oct., 1779.

132. Jonathan[5] (*Benajah, Caleb, Exercise, Roger*), b. 16 Apr., 1761, in Mansfield, Conn. When he was about ten years old he went to live with Benjamin Hutchings, of Mansfield, with whom he remained till the breaking out of the Revolution, when he returned to his father's. Fearing that he would enlist, his father apprenticed him to a cousin, John Slapp, of Lebanon, N. H., with whom he remained only a short time, and enlisted Sep. 3, 1777, for three years, in Capt. House's company of Col. Cilley's regiment, in the Revolutionary army. He is described as "aged 17, light complexion, 5 ft. 5 in. tall" (N. H. Town Papers, Vol. 12, p. 373). At the close of the war he settled in Lebanon; removed to Chelsea, Vt., and d. 23 Oct., 1810, in Shelburne, N. Y.

He m. 25 Nov., 1786, Irene Bennet, who d. 20 Mch., 1815, in Chelsea, Vt., in the 56th year of her age; she was born 25 Nov., 1759.

Children of JONATHAN and IRENE (BENNET) CONANT :—

278. William, b. 25 Aug., 1787.
279. Samuel, b. 28 May, 1789.
280. Caleb, b. 18 Apr., 1791.
281. Sarah, b. 6 Mch., 1794.
    Jonathan, b. 11 Mch., 1796, } d. 31 Mch., 1796.
    Irene, b. 11 Mch., 1796, }
    Myra, b. 10 Mch., 1800; d. 18 July, 1804.

SIXTH GENERATION.

133. Nathan[6] (*Thomas, Nathaniel, Nathaniel, Lot, Roger*), b. 12 Apr., 1731, in Bridgewater, Mass. In Mass. Court Records, Vol. 28, p. 370, is the petition of Nathaniel Conant, of Bridgewater, stating that in 1762 he enlisted in Col. Harris' regiment, and was at the retaking of Newfoundland; that he there contracted an illness from which he is a cripple. He was granted an annuity of £3.

He d. 1778, and his will is recorded in Vol. 30, p. 157, of Plymouth Probate Records.

He m. 14 June, 1753, Hannah, dr. of Isaac and Mary (Hudson) Lazell, b. 1729. Isaac Lazell was son of Isaac and g. s. of John and Elizabeth (Gates) Lazell, of Hingham.

Children of NATHAN and HANNAH (LAZELL) CONANT:—

   Hannah, b. 23 May, 1754; m. 1778, Jonathan Washburn, jr., of Middleboro'.
   Lois, b. 12 July, 1756; m. (230) Solomon Conant.
   Martha, b. 25 Feb., 1760; m. (1) Theodore Perkins, and had a son, Thomas, b. 1785; she m. (2) Rev. William Conant (see p. 189).
282. Caleb, b. 26 Jan., 1762.
   Rebecca, b. 9 Mch., 1764.
   Mary, b. 29 July, 1768; m. Isaac Smith, of Braintree.

134. Zilpah[6] (*Thomas, Nathaniel, Nathaniel, Lot, Roger*), b. 15 May, 1742, in Bridgewater; m. 1766, Samuel, son of Samuel and Hannah (Ames) Keith, b. 1745.

Children of SAMUEL and ZILPAH (CONANT) KEITH:—

i. Kezia, b. 1768; d. unm.
ii. Barzillai, b. 1770.

iii. Ruth, b. 1772.

iv. Abner, b. 1774; m. 1803, Eunice Benson, and had Zilpah, Anna, Eunice, Lurania, Abner and Elvira Benson.

v. Cyrus, b. 1776.

vi. Samuel, b. 1779.

vii. David, b. 1782; m. 1806, Ruth Wilbur.

viii. Jonathan, b. 1782; m. 1805, Polly Gushee.

135. Zenas[6] (*Thomas, Nathaniel, Nathaniel, Lot, Roger*), b. 6 Nov., 1748, in Bridgewater, where he lived. He m. 29 Nov., 1774, Betty, dr. of (71) Lot Conant, b. 30 May, 1754.

Children of ZENAS and BETTY (CONANT) CONANT:—

283. Oliver.

284. Betty, b. 1779.

285. Sarah, b. ——.

     Olive, b. ——; m. (318) Jacob Conant.

136. Ezra[6] (*Thomas, Nathaniel, Nathaniel, Lot, Roger*), b. 22 July, 1750, in Bridgewater. He was a farmer of Bridgewater, and d. 2 Feb., 1840. He m. 29 June, 1773, Mary, dr. of (108) David Conant, b. 3 July, 1752; d. 1835.

Ezra Conant

(1780.)

Children of EZRA and MARY (CONANT) CONANT:—

     Mary.

     Ezra.

286. Gaius, b. 6 Sep., 1776.

     Mehitable.

287. Thomas, b. 5 Oct., 1785.

137. Azubah[6] (*Jeremiah, Nathaniel, Nathaniel, Lot, Roger*), b. 18 Feb., 1739, in Bridgewater; m. 1762, Jesse, son of James and Experience (Hayward) Dunbar, of Bridgewater.

Children of JESSE and AZUBAH (CONANT) DUNBAR:—

i. Susanna, b. 1763; m. Caleb Alden, of Middleboro'.

ii. Jeremiah, b. 1764.

iii. Martha, b. 1768.

iv. Elias, b. 1772; m. Roxilinia Leach.

v. Lydia, b. 1777.

vi. Dinah, b. 1780.

vii. Kezia, b. 1782; m. 1809, Simeon Wood, of Boston.

138. Nathaniel[6] (*Jeremiah, Nathaniel, Nathaniel, Lot,*

Roger), b. 24 Oct., 1743, in Bridgewater. He enlisted in the
Continental army for
three years in 1777 *Nathaniel Conant*
(Mass. Arch., Mus-   (1812.)
ter Rolls, Vol. 27, p. 156). He d. 1812, and his will is recorded in Plymouth Probate Records, Vol. 44, p. 97.

He m. 1772, Silence, dr. of Ephraim and Susanna (Willis)
Forbes, b. 1745.

Children of NATHANIEL and SILENCE (FORBES) CONANT:—

288. Andrew, b. 25 Mch., 1774.
      Susanna, b. 10 July, 1777; m. 1812, Wm. Durkey, of Hampton,
        Conn.
      Silence, b. 16 July, 1781.

139. **Daniel**[6] (*Jeremiah, Nathaniel, Nathaniel, Lot, Rog-*
er), b. 7 Dec., 1744, in Bridgewater. He moved to Pelham
(Mitchell's *Hist. of Bridgewater*). May 8, 1779, Daniel Conant, of Bridgewater, sold 8 acres and 12 rods of land in the
southerly part of Bridgewater, to Nathaniel Orcutt, for £454
10s. (Plymouth Deeds, Vol. 60, p. 6). The same day he sold
8 acres, 12 rods, to Moses Orcutt; Joanna, his wife, releases
dower (Plymouth Deeds, Vol. 60, p. 157).

He m. 1767, Joanna, dr. of Cornelius and Experience Washburn, of Bridgewater.

Children of DANIEL and JOANNA (WASHBURN) CONANT:—

289. Robert, b. 24 June, 1768.
      Experience, m. Jedediah Ayer.
290. Daniel.
291. Cornelius.
      Archibald.
292. Jeremiah.
      Anna.

140. **Roger**[6] (*Jeremiah, Nathaniel, Nathaniel, Lot, Rog-*
er), b. 22 June, 1748, in Bridgewater, Mass. The name of
Roger Conant, of Easton, appears on the "Muster Roll of
Capt. Abial Mitchell's company, which was down at the
Alarm" (Mass. Arch., Lexington Alarm Lists, Vol. 13, p. 16),
and Roger "Conent" served one month and twelve days as corporal in Scott's company of Ashley's regiment, "which marched

from Westmoreland, Chesterfield and Hinsdale to Ticonderoga, on the alarm May 8, 1777" (N. H. State Papers, Vol. 15, p. 6). On Oct. 7, 1776, Roger Conant, of Westmoreland, N. H., sold Samuel Guild, of Easton, "land that was set off to Rhoda, his wife, the daughter of Thomas Randall" (Bristol Co. Deeds, Vol. 60, p. 496). Soon after the latter date he appears to have settled in New York State, near Saratoga, but on-ly remained there a short time. He ac-quired a large tract of land there, which he sold, and removed with his family to Canada, induced by the fact that the Canadian government made large grants to settlers. He received a Royal grant, being termed an United Empire Loyalist. A grant was also issued to his son, Eliphalet, dated 31 Dec., 1778, for the east half of lot number 30 in Darlington, co. Durham, Canada West (now Ontario). It does not appear that he settled in Canada as early as 1778; family tradition fixes the date as 1792.

Roger Conant (1777.)

He settled on this grant (a large part of which remains in possession of his great-grandson, Thomas Conant, Esq., of Oshawa), taking his household goods and cattle from N. Y., crossing the Niagara river at Niagara, then the capital of Canada West. According to tradition* in one branch of the family, he lived for a time in Boston, and took part in the "Boston tea party." But this, like many family traditions, appears to be unreliable.

In 1812 he was fined £80 for speaking against the English government. At his death he left a large property to his children. His will is dated 13 June, 1821; proved 20 Aug., 1821.

He m. in Easton, Mass., 27 July, 1772, Rhoda, dr. of Thomas and Rebecca (Phillips) Randall, b. 17 Aug., 1755. Thomas Randall was son of Thomas, son of Thomas, son of Robert, of Weymouth, Mass.

Children of ROGER and RHODA (RANDALL) CONANT:—

293. Abel,
294. Eliphalet, } said to have been born in Massachusetts.
     Barnabas,) d. 1812, on Lake Champlain.

---

* Another tradition is, that this Roger was born in England about 1727, was sent to America as a land agent; lived in Boston and married there a Crandall. Evidently Roger of the sixth generation is confounded with Roger the immigrant.

295. Jeremiah.
296. Polly.
     Fanny.
297. Rhoda.
298. Thomas.
     Sarah.

141. Abihail[6] (*John, Nathaniel, Nathaniel, Lot, Roger*), b. 10 Dec., 1746, in Bridgewater; m. 1774, John, son of Joab and Martha (Bolton) Willis, of Bridgewater.

Children of JOHN and ABIHAIL (CONANT) WILLIS:—

i.   John, b. 1777.
ii.   Asa, b. 1779.

142. John[6] (*John, Nathaniel, Nathaniel, Lot, Roger*), b. 25 Jan., 1749-50, in Bridgewater, where he lived. He was a deacon of the church. John "Conet," of Bridgewater, was in Capt. Abijah Bangs' company, in Oct., 1777, in the expedition to Rhode Island (Mass. Arch., Muster Rolls, Vol. 1, p. 49).

He d. 4 May, 1844.

He m. 1772, Deborah, dr. of Nathan and Sarah (Pratt) Perkins, who d. 6 Nov., 1843.

Children of JOHN and DEBORAH (PERKINS) CONANT:—

299. Marlborough, b. 14 Oct., 1775.
300. Martin, b. 1777.
301. Seth.
     Lucy, b. ——; m. (1) 1794, Jacob Pierce; m. (2) Andrew Tucker.
     Deborah, b. ——; m. 1807, Ansel, son of Samuel Leonard.
     Lucinda.

143. Lucy[6] (*John, Nathaniel, Nathaniel, Lot, Roger*), b. 29 Aug., 1753, in Bridgewater; m. 1773, Ziba, son of Hezekiah and Huldah (Edson) Hayward, who d. 1830.

Children of ZIBA and LUCY (CONANT) HAYWARD:—

i.   Ziba, m. Sally Bosworth, of Halifax.
ii.   Lucy, m. Wm. Bosworth, of Halifax.
iii. Calvin, m. Mary Forbes.
iv.   Jeremiah.
v.   Huldah.

144. Jeremiah[6] (*John, Nathaniel, Nathaniel, Lot, Roger*), b. 28, Jan., 1758, in Bridgewater.

In 1777, (Apr. 21), Jeremiah Conant, of Bridgewater was in Capt. Ed. Cobb's company "that marched to Bristol," (Mass. Arch., Muster Rolls, Vol. 6, p. 139). From July 25 to Sep. 9, 1778, he was sergeant in Capt. Packard's company, of Col. Carpenter's regiment (Muster Rolls, Vol. 22, p. 50).

About 1783 he removed from Bridgewater to Pomfret, Vt., where he settled as a carpenter and farmer. He was a member of the Congregational Church, and deacon many years; also a Justice of the Peace, and member of the Vermont Legislature for several years. He d. in Pomfret, Jan. 1828.

He m. (1) 1782, Mary, dr. of Capt. Solomon and Joanna (Washburn) Leonard; b. 19 July, 1759; d. 20 Dec. 1791; m. (2) 1793, Chloe, dr. of Dea. Seth and Hannah (Washburn) Pratt, b. 25 Feb., 1768, d. 29 Apr., 1851.

Children of JEREMIAH and MARY (LEONARD) CONANT :—

302. Leonard, b. 27 Sept., 1783, in Pomfret, Vt.
303. Polly, b. 8 July, 1785.
304. John, b. 19 June, 1787.
305. Jeremiah, b. 2 Aug., 1789.
    Hannah, b. 17 Dec., 1791; m. Frederick H. Ware, of Pomfret and had Lucy and two sons.

Children of JEREMIAH and CHLOE (PRATT) CONANT :—

    Chloe, b. 24 Feb., 1795, d. 27 May, 1795.
306. Seth, b. 3 Oct., 1796.
    Ophir, b. 19 Nov., 1798; he studied medicine with Dr. Waterhouse, to whose practice he succeeded. He removed to Malone, N. Y., where he d. 7 March, 1842 (sine prole).
    Marshall, b. 5 Jan., 1801, m. in Woodstock, Vt., 1 Sept., 1835, Roxanna, dr. of John and Asenath (Vaughan) Darling, b. 6 Oct., 1806, and still living at Bridgewater, Mass. He taught school for more than twenty-five years. First at Woodstock, Vt., then Boston, where he went immediately after his marriage. It is said he was designed to learn the carpenter's trade, but injured his health by hard labor so that he was confined to his bed for over a year. During his sickness he studied astronomy and other natural sciences. After his marriage he entered Dartmouth College and graduated 1839. While at Boston he was Assistant Engineer of the Boston Water Works. After leaving Boston he went to Bridgewater as the second Principal of the Bridgewater Normal School, but resigned after seven years' service, on account of failing health. He was afterwards in the Internal Revenue Department at Washington for ten years. He

published "The Year Book, an Astronomical and Philosophical Annual. Boston, 1836." And in the Boston Athe-
neum Library, is a MS. by him, entitled, "Investigations in
Regard to the Concavity of Surface of Incompressible Fluids
contained in Vessels in Moton on Verticle Axes," dated
Farmington, N. H., 1850.   Mr. Conant had no children;
he d. 10 Feb., 1873.

Lucia, b. 5 Mch., 1803; d. 19 Nov., 1822, in Pomfret.

Achsah, b. 28 Mch., 1805; d. 28 June, 1832.

307.   Thomas, b. 6 Aug., 1807.

145. Thomas[6] (*John, Nathaniel, Nathaniel, Lot, Roger*),
b. 1 Mch., 1766, in Bridgewater, Mass.   He removed from
Bridgewater to Oakham, Mass., 1794, and thence in 1825 to
Westford, Vt., where he d. 19 July, 1839.   He was a carpenter and farmer, held various town offices, and was a Captain
of militia in the war of 1812.

He m. 1789, Lydia, dr. of Calvin and (147) Lydia (Conant)
Edson; she d. in Westford, Vt., 19 Sep., 1864.

Children of THOMAS and LYDIA (EDSON) CONANT.

308.   Edson, b. 6 Aug., 1790, in Bridgewater.

Marshall, b. 3 July, 1792; d. 27 Mch., 1863, at Saratoga Springs.
He never married.   Engaged in business for a time in Boston, and afterwards went to N. Y. as a teacher.

Salmon, b. 11 Feb., 1795, in Oakham; d. Aug., 1819.   Supposed
to have been drowned in Hudson river.

309.   Thomas, b. 13 Apr., 1797.

Sumner, b. 29 Aug., 1799; he was a cripple; removed to Dorset, Ohio; m. Esther Basset, but left no children.

310.   Lewis, b. 22 Dec., 1802.

John Avery, b. 1 June, 1805, who d. at Honolulu, S. I.

Dwight, b. 19 Sep., 1809; m. Emily McCallen, of Westford,
Vt.   He was a farmer and teacher of music.   He d. 30
June, 1870.

311.   Gardner, b. 18 Oct., 1818.

146. Silvanus[6] (*Gershom, Lot, Nathaniel, Lot, Roger*),
b. 23 May, 1747, in Bridgewater, Mass.   He served in Capt.
Packard's company
of Col. Carpenter's   *Silvanus Conant*
regiment, from 25   (1792.)
July to 9 Sept., 1778, in the Revolutionary war (Mass. Arch.,
Revolutionary Rolls, Vol. 22, p. 50); also 11 days in 1780 in
the expedition to Rhode Island, in Capt. Allen's company

(Mass. Arch., Revolutionary Rolls, Vol. 1, p. 15). He removed to Turner, Me., where he d. 22 June, 1828.

He m. 1773, Silvia, dr. of (67) John Conant; she d. 20 Jan., 1842, in Turner, Me.

Children of SILVANUS and SILVIA (CONANT) CONANT:—

Silvia.
312. Sylvanus, b. 20 Jan., 1787.

147. Lydia[6] (*Lot, Lot, Nathaniel, Lot, Roger*), b. 2 Sep., 1746; m. in Bridgewater, 1756, Calvin, son of Dr. Elijah and Anne (Packard) Edson. They removed to Oakham, Mass.

Child of CALVIN and LYDIA (CONANT) EDSON:—

Lydia, who m. 1789, (145) Thomas Conant.

148. Benjamin[6] (*Lot, Lot, Nathaniel, Lot, Roger*), b. 29 Aug., 1756, in Bridgewater, Mass. In Apr., 1775, he was one of Capt. Nathan Mitchell's company "that marched to Cambridge on the Lexington alarm" (Mass. Arch., Lexington Alarm Lists, Vol. 12, p. 191). Mch. 4, 1776, he was in Capt. Washburn's company "that marched to Braintree" (Muster Rolls, Vol. 24, p. 20). In 1777 he served 7 months in Capt. Randall's company (Muster Rolls, Vol. 22, p. 187). And on July 31, 1780, Benjamin Conant, of Bridgewater, age 23 years, height 5 ft. 7 in., of dark complexion, was in Lieut. Pike's company (Muster Rolls, Vol. 35, p. 214). About 1795 he removed from Bridgewater to Turner, Me., where he died. He m. 1783, Elizabeth, dr. of Hezekiah and Elizabeth (Leonard) Hooper.

Children of BENJAMIN and ELIZABETH (HOOPER) CONANT:—

Temperance, b. 15 Nov., 1783, in So. Bridgewater, Mass.
313. Marcus, b. 24 Oct., 1785, " "
Winslow, b. 15 Jan., 1788, " "
314. Benjamin, b. 24 Sep., 1790, " "
315. Hooper, b. 10 July, 1793, " "
316. Hezekiah, b. ———, in Turner, Me.

149. Rebecca[6] (*Lot, Lot, Nathaniel, Lot, Roger*), b. about 1759, in Bridgewater; m. 1782, Benjamin, son of Dr. Daniel and Joanna (Harlow) Snell, b. 1752.

Children of BENJAMIN and REBECCA (CONANT) SNELL:—

i. Rebecca, m. George Baker, of Duxbury.

17

ii.   Benjamin, n. m.
iii.   Susannah, m. John Carver.
iv.   Stella, n. m.

150.   Peter[6] (*Phinehas, Lot, Nathaniel, Lot, Roger*), b. 3
Aug., 1753, in Bridgewater, where he lived.   He was sergeant
of Capt. Mitch-
ell's company,
in the Revolu-
tionary army,

(1793.)

in June, 1776 (Mass. Arch., Muster Rolls, Vol. 36, p. 80).   He
was deacon of the church at Bridgewater.   Perhaps the family removed to Northfield, N. H.

He m. 1777, Jane, dr. of (109) Jonathan Conant.

Children of PETER and JANE (CONANT) CONANT:—

317.   Peter, b. 1778.
        Silvia, who m. 1814, Joseph Hayward.
        Ruth, who m. 1800, Daniel Keith.
318.   Jacob.
319.   Liba, b. 1793.

151.   Phinehas[6] (*Phinehas, Lot, Nathaniel, Lot, Roger*),
b. 25 Jan., 1759, in Bridgewater, where he lived.   In Nov.,
1776, he was a private in Capt. Washburn's company, stationed
at Newport, R. I. (Mass. Arch., Muster Rolls, Vol. 3, p. 260).
In 1777 he was in Capt. Jos. Keith's company of Col. Cotton's
regiment (Muster Rolls, Vol. 2, p. 137), and July 27, 1780, he
enlisted for three months in Capt. Packard's company (Muster
Rolls, Vol. 3, p. 40).   He m. 1785, Joanna, dr. of Daniel and
Experience (Harlow) Washburn; she d. 1829.

Children of PHINEHAS and JOANNA (WASHBURN) CONANT:—

        Sally, b. 22 Oct., 1786.
        Betsey, b. ——.
320.   Galen, b. 6 Feb., 1790.
321.   Ira, b. ——.
        Allen, b. 22 Apr., 1798.

152.   David[6] (*Phinehas, Lot, Nathaniel, Lot, Roger*), b.
1 Sep., 1762, in Bridgewater, where he lived.   He d. 1792.   For
will see Plymouth Probate Records, Vol. 33, p. 249.   He m.

1783, Silvia, dr. of Samuel and Susanna (L e o n a r d) Whitman. After his death

(1793.)

she m. (2) 1798, Azariah Hayward, jr., and had children.

Children of DAVID and SILVIA (WHITMAN) CONANT:—

> Martha, b. 14 Jan., 1785.
> Susanna, b. 27 Mch., 1787.
> David, b. 2 Nov., 1790.

153. James[6] (*Timothy, Lot, Nathaniel, Lot, Roger*), b. 3 Sep., 1755, in Bridgewater; moved to Oakham with his parents. In Aug., 1777, he was a private in Capt. Crawford's company, in the Revolutionary army (Muster Rolls, Vol. 18, p. 14). July 1, 1778, he was promoted to sergeant in Capt. Scott's company (Vol. 26, p. 418). He afterwards enlisted for three years (Continental Army Rolls). He was afterwards a captain of militia. After his return from the army he built a large two-story house, which he occupied as innkeeper and merchant for many years. He was selectman of Oakham from 1788 to 1796; constable in 1794; tax collector in 1796; and held other minor offices. He m. 29 Aug., 1778, Dorothy Bullard.

Children of JAMES and DOROTHY (BULLARD) CONANT:—

> Luther, b. 20 July, 1779, who was a farmer of Oakham; d. 2 Apr., 1839.
> 322. Deborah Lazell, b. 23 June, 1781.
> 323. Elijah, b. 12 Mch., 1783.
> 324. Lot, b. 8 May, 1785.
> Lucy, b. 7 May, 1786; d. 1866, unm.
> Elizabeth, b. 6 Mch., 1789; m. Benjamin Reed, of Oakham.
> 325. Abigail, b. 16 Nov., 1791.
> 326. James, b. 5 Dec., 1793.
> Lydia, b. 1 Aug., 1796; m. Luke Stone, of Rutland.
> Charles, b. 5 Dec., 1798; m. (1) 15 Mch., 1829, Eliza Kelly; m. (2) —— Maynard. Was of Oakham.
> John, b. 8 May, 1801; m. (1) Lois Conant (p. 260); m. (2) Mary Francis. Was of Oakham and Worcester, Mass.

154. Luther[6] (*Timothy, Lot, Nathaniel, Lot, Roger*), b. 7 Jan., 1758, in Bridgewater; moved to Oakham. Luther Conant, of Oakham, served three years in Capt. Reed's company (Mass. Arch., Continental Army Rolls). July 7, 1780, Luther Conant, of Hardwick, is described as 22 years old, 5 ft. 7 in.

tall, light complexion (Muster Rolls, Vol. 35, p. 188). In 1781 he was a sergeant, and discharged in New York state, 240 miles from Hardwick (Id., Vol. 4, p. 84).

In 1800 he was selectman of Oakham.

He m. (1) Molly White; m. (2) 4 May, 1787, Susanna Allen.

Child of LUTHER and MOLLY (WHITE) CONANT:—

327. Justus.

Children of LUTHER and SUSANNA (ALLEN) CONANT:—

328. Sullivan, b. 26 Feb., 1801.
Nathan.
Abiah, m. —— Beaman.
Louisa, m. (1) —— Raymond; m. (2) —— Leonard.
Susan, m. —— Wheeler.
Hannah, m. —— Spear.
Lois, m. John Conant (see p. 259).

155. Deborah[6] (*Timothy, Lot, Nathaniel, Lot, Roger*), b. 6 Aug., 1764, in Bridgewater; m. 1783, Nathan Lazell, of Bridgewater. He was son of Isaac and Bithiah (Alger) Lazell; g. s. of Isaac, who was son of Isaac and g. s. of John, of Hingham. He d. 1832.

Children of NATHAN and DEBORAH (CONANT) LAZELL:—

i. Hannah, m. 1818, Nathan Nye, of Freeport (second wife).
ii. Susan, m. 1807, Nathan Nye.
iii. Sally, m. 1809, Jonathan Cushing, of Boston.
iv. Deborah, n. m.
v. Nathan, m. Anna, dr. of Abraham Wilkinson, of Pawtucket. He was a prominent citizen of Bridgewater.
vi. Caroline, m. 1816, Paul Revere.
vii. Harriet, m. 1814, Dr. Paul Lewis Nichols, of Kingston.
viii. Julia, m. George W. Norwood, of Boston.

156. Sylvanus[6] (*Timothy, Lot, Nathaniel, Lot, Roger*), b. 23 Apr., 1773, in Oakham, Mass. He removed to Medina, N. Y., where he was a farmer and merchant. He d. Sept., 1853.

He m. Eleanor dr. of Eleazer and Mehitable (Allen) Spooner, b. 1770; d. 24 Jan., 1832. (See Spooner Genealogy.)

Children of SYLVANUS and ELEANOR (SPOONER) CONANT:—

Caroline, b. 25 June, 1797; d. 22 June, 1867. She m. Samuel Grant, and had a family.
Vesta, b. 5 Jan., 1799; m. Mordecai Leighton, and had children.
Ruby, b. 2 Oct., 1803; d. 14 Sept., 1807.

Sarah, b. 31 Mch., 1806; d. 11 Jan., 1813.
James, b. 27 Jan., 1809; d. 28 Feb., 1809.

157. Samuel[6] (*Robert, Lot, John, Lot, Roger*), b. in Concord (part now Acton), about 1722. Lived in Chelmsford and Stow with his parents. He settled in Stow as a farmer. He is named as the oldest son, in his father's will. He d. 19 May, 1785. He m. Sarah Holman, who d. 1 Feb., 1804.

Children of SAMUEL and SARAH (HOLMAN) CONANT:—

329. Silas, b. 31 May, 1747.
330. Oliver.
331. Samuel.
332. John, b. 3 Jan., 1758.
Levi, was killed by the fall of a tree when about 20 years old.
A dr., who m. John Eaton, of Farmington.

158. Josiah[6] (*Robert, Lot, John, Lot, Roger*), b. in Concord about 1724. Lived in Stow with his parents, and settled in Pepperell, Mass. He d. about 1770. He m. 12 May, 1748, Rachael Hobart, of Groton (see Butler's *Hist. of Groton*).

Children of JOSIAH and RACHAEL (HOBART) CONANT:—

Rachael, b. 29 May, 1749, in Groton.
333. Josiah, b. 21 Aug., 1750.
334. Benjamin, b. 27 June, 1752.
Robert, b. 5 Nov., 1754; m. and had a daughter, Lydia.
335. Shebuel, b. 23 Dec., 1756, in Pepperell.

159. Peter[6] (*Robert, Lot, John, Lot, Roger*), b. in Chelmsford, Mass., about 1732. He settled in Stow, Mass. In 1776 he was in Capt. Barrows' company in the Continental army (Muster Rolls, Vol. 1, p. 16). In the same year he was at the battle of White Plains (Vol. 18, p. 23). His will was proved 1785, and mentions his wife, Sarah; sons, Ephraim, of Temple, N. H., Peter, of Stow, Isaac, of Stow,

Peter Conant

(Will, 1783.)

Josiah, and Abraham a minor; daughters, Mary Gates and Sarah Jewell. Amount of inventory, £983 16s. 3d. (see Middlesex Probate Records).

He m. Sarah (Gibson?), whose will, dated 12 Jan., 1818, mentions daughters, Mary Gates and Sarah Whitney, sons, Ephraim and Peter, grandson, Phineas.

Children of PETER and SARAH (GIBSON?) CONANT:—

336. Ephraim, 16 Jan., 1757.
337. Peter, b. 10 May, 1760? (27 May, 1756, Town Records).
      Isaac, b.——; m. 26 Mch., 1781, Mercy Whitcomb. He was in
         the Revolutionary army, 1777 (Mass. Arch., Muster Rolls,
         Vol. 41, p. 113); in Taylor's co. of Reed's regt., "age 17,
         height 5 ft. 4 in., light complexion," 1778 (Vol. 28, p. 160).
338. Ebenezer? not mentioned in father's will.
339. Josiah.
      Abraham, m. 21 July, 1789, Eunice Merrill, of Concord, and
         settled in Waterford, Me.; had children.
340. Mary.
341. Sarah.

160. Daniel[6] (*Robert, Lot, John, Lot, Roger*), b. in Chelms-
ford, Mass., about 1740; is mentioned in his father's will as the
youngest son. He was wounded in the battle of Lexington, 19
Apr., 1775 (Mass. Hist. Col., 2nd Series, Vol. 8, p. 45). On
Sep. 22, 1777, Daniel Conant, of Stow, was sergeant in Capt.
Silas Taylor's company in the Continental army (Mass. Arch.,
Muster Rolls, Vol. 23, p. 179). He died 20 July, 1808, and his
son, Abraham, was ap-
pointed administrator, 8
Dec., 1808. A division of   *Daneel Conant*
                                         (1773.)
the estate was made in 1812, by Augustine Tower, Silas
Brooks and Aaron Jones; heirs mentioned: widow, Mar-
tha, sons, Abraham, Benjamin and Simeon (a minor), daughters,
Sarah Conant and Mary, wife of Simeon Puffer (Middlesex
Probate Records).

He m. 14 Jan., 1772, Martha Cole, of Acton, where they
were married; mar. int. published 10 Apr., 1771. She d. 21
Feb., 1815.

Children of DANIEL and MARTHA (COLE) CONANT:—

      Hannah, b. 3 Jan., 1773.
      Daniel.
      Maria H., m. Simeon Puffer.
342. Abraham.
      Sally, m. Joseph Wild, and had Joseph, William, George and
         Sarah.
343. Benjamin, b. 19 October, 1786.
344. Simeon.

161. Andrew[6] (*Andrew, Lot, John, Lot, Roger*), b. in

Concord, 22 Aug., 1725. He is called in the records Lieutenant
Andrew, and later
Capt. Andrew, but
his name has not been
found in the Mass.
Archives as serving

(1803.)

in the Revolutionary army; probably his connection was with
the militia.

His will is dated 27 Apr., 1803, proved 6 Dec., 1805. He d.
17 Sep., 1805. His will mentions his wife, Mary, sons, Zebulon
and Andrew (Middlesex Probate Records, Vol. 98, p. 208).

He m. (1) 30 Nov., 1748, Ruth Brooks, who d. 3 Feb., 1770,
aged 41; m. (2) Mary ——, who d. 20 June, 1818, aged 84.

Child of ANDREW and RUTH (BROOKS) CONANT:—

345. Zebulon, b. 29 Oct., 1749.

Children of ANDREW and MARY (———) CONANT:—

Thaddeus, b. 1 Nov., 1771; d. in West Indies, Jan., 1803.
346. Andrew, b. 7 May, 1773.
Nathan, b. 30 Sep., 1777.

162. Silas[6] (*Andrew, Lot, John, Lot, Roger*), b. 15 Aug.,
1740, in Concord or Acton. He was a farmer of Acton. He
d. 3 Apr., 1803. He m. 30 Dec., 1762, Lois Potter, b. 2 May,
1744, d. 12 Nov., 1815.

Children of SILAS and LOIS (POTTER) CONANT:—

Betsey,* b. 7 Oct., 1764, in Acton; d. 12 Oct., 1799; m. Jacob
French.
347. Samuel Potter, b. 27 Mch., 1767.
Keziah,* b. 29 Sep., 1769; m. 29 Dec., 1791, Elisha Jones, of
Hopkinton.
Charlotte, b. 4 Apr., 1772; d. 1 Feb., 1823; m. 22 Apr., 1791,
Joseph Dole.
Lois, b. 5 July, 1774; m. 27 Aug., 1795, Capt. Reuben Hayward.
She d. 31 Oct., 1841. He d. 1 Dec., 1838.
348. Silas, b. 25 Oct., 1776.
Andrew, b. 9 Mch., 1782; d. 8 Feb., 1803.
349. James, b. 26 May, 1788.

163. Eli[6] (*Andrew, Lot, John, Lot, Roger*), b. 16 Mch.,

* Betsey and Keziah are given in records as children of Silas and Elizabeth Conant.

1741-2, in Acton. He lived in Concord. Jan. 15, 1776, Eli
Conant, of Concord, was sergeant in Capt. Wheeler's company,
in the Revolutionary army (Mass. Arch., Muster Rolls, Vol. 24,
p. 73). The next year
he was lieutenant in the
expedition to R. I. (Vol.
18, p. 21). He was dis-
charged Oct. 11, 1778; there was then due him 9 mo. and 11
days' pay, £75 17s. 5d., "ration money," £43 10s. He d. 26
May, 1801. He m. 23 Dec., 1767, in Concord, Elizabeth Gardiner.

Children of ELI and ELIZABETH (GARDINER) CONANT:—

350. John Gardiner, b. 30 Aug., 1768.
      Mary, b. 26 Oct., 1769.
351. George, b. 7 Apr., 1771.
      Pamela, b. 7 Oct., 1772.
      Sarah, b. 2 Jan., 1774; m. 20 Oct., 1799, Reuben Durrant, of
          Bedford. She d. 1832.
      Anna, b. 17 Oct., 1775.
      Betty, b. 9 Mch., 1777.
      Artemus, b. 19 Feb., 1779.
      Rufus, b. ——; removed to Enfield, N. H., thence to Paw-
          let, Vt.; m. (1) Fanny Laythe; m. (2) Nancy Goodwin.

164. **Abel**[6] (*Andrew, Lot, John, Lot, Roger*), b. in Acton,
5 Apr., 1747. He settled in Concord, where he d. 31 Dec.,
1833, aged 87 (g. s.). He m. (1) 7 May, 1771, Catherine Johnson, who d. 24 Mch., 1780, aged 28 (g. s.); m. (2) 7 Feb., 1785,
Abigail Davis, who d. 1840; she was of Acton (Acton Records).

Children of ABEL and CATHERINE (JOHNSON) CONANT:—

      Anna, b. 23 Dec., 1771; d. 10 Feb., 1796.
352. Abel, b. 11 July, 1773.
      Ruth, b. 29 Apr., 1775.
      Lydia, b. 12 Mch., 1777 (m. Joel Durrant?).
      Hannah, b. 14 May, 1779.
353. Ebenezer, b. 1780.

Child of ABEL and ABIGAIL (DAVIS) CONANT:—

354. Luther, b. about 1790.

165. **William**[6] (*William, Lot, John, Lot, Roger*), b. in

Concord, 26 Apr.,1732.
He was a farmer of
Acton. In 1765 he re-
moved to Harvard,
Mass., where he d.

(1756.)

1804. He m. Huldah Puffer, of Sudbury; int. pub. 6 Nov.,
1756; she d. 1818, aged 84.

Children of WILLIAM and HULDAH (PUFFER) CONANT:—

355. Reuben, b. 15 Jan., 1757, in Acton.
     Mary, b. 10 Feb., 1759; m. Zacheus Dudley, of Harvard.
356. Simeon, b. 27 Aug., 1762.
     Louisa, b. ——; m. Jonathan Reed, of Harvard.
     A daughter, who m. Israel Longley, of Shirley.
357. Levi, b. 7 Aug., 1767.
     A daughter, b. ——.

166. William⁶ (*John, Lot, John, Lot, Roger*), b. in Townsend, about 1738. He settled in Shirley at an early period of
its organization, on land now owned by Lyman Eaton, in the
easterly part of the town. The date of his death is unknown.
He m. Eunice, dr. of William and Sarah (Parker) Farwell, of
Shirley (*Hist. of Shirley*).

Child of WILLIAM and EUNICE (FARWELL) CONANT:—

358. William, b. 17 Aug., 1765.

167. Nathaniel⁶ (*John, Lot, John, Lot, Roger*), b. in
Townsend, 1743. At the Lexington alarm he was one of the
Townsend minute men who marched to Cambridge (Mass.
Arch., Lexington
Alarm Lists); and
in 1777 he was
lieutenant in Capt.

(1799.)

Gates' company (Id., Vol. 22, p. 164). His elder brother having removed from the town, he appears to have succeeded to
the tavern and mill business of his father.

"Public notice is hereby given, that there will be a Lett at
Public Auction, to the highest bidder, on Thursday, the 16th
day of March next, at One of the Clock afternoon, at the

house of Nathan Conant, Innholder, in said Townsend: the
Real Estate of Joseph Adams, physician.

Townsend, Feb. 8, 1780.   JAMES LOCK, Agent."
(Boston Gazette, Feb. 14, 1780.)

He was selectman, 1791-2. He m. (1) 13 June, 1765, Betty
Stevens; m. (2) 4 Feb., 1773, Esther Emery.

Child of NATHAN and BETTY (STEVENS) CONANT:—

359. Nathan, b. 17 Aug., 1766. ⸺

Children of NATHAN and ESTHER (EMERY) CONANT:—

> Gardner, b. 9 Aug., 1775; had a son, J. G. Conant, b. 1807, who
> lived in 1875 at Grove, Geauga co., Ohio.
> John, b. 27 Oct., 1777.

360. Levi, b. 19 Feb., 1779.
361. Betsey, b. 10 Apr., 1781 (birth recorded in Town Records as
      Esther).

168. Daniel⁶ (*John, Lot, John, Lot, Roger*), b. about 1745,
in Townsend, where he lived; was selectman 1802, 1805, 1806
and 1807. He
was one of the
Townsend "min-
ute men" who
marched to Cam-   (1798.)
bridge at the Lexington alarm. He afterwards enlisted for
three years in the Continental army, and was in the 1st company of the 2nd regiment (Mass. Archives, Continental Army
Rolls). Milley Conant was appointed administratrix of his
estate, 25 Mch., 1799. The appraisers were Daniel Adams,
Isaac Mulliken and Peter Manning. Division made 20 Oct.,
1802, by Milley Conant, now Milley Wallis. Payments made
to Daniel, Milley and Lovey (Midd. Probate Records).

He m. 19 June, 1782, Millicent Farrer.

Children of DANIEL and MILLICENT (FARRER) CONANT:—

> Millicent, b. 8 Sep., 1782; m. 7 June, 1801, Jonathan Wallis.

362. Daniel, b. 16 July, 1784.
> John, b. 5 Dec., 1786; d. y.
> Isaac, b. 15 Mch., 1789; d. y.
> Lovia, b. 9 July, 1791; m. 18 Apr., 1815, John Warner.

169. John⁶ (*John, Lot, John, Lot, Roger*), b. in Townsend. In 1756 he was under 14 years old (Middlesex Probate Records). He was select-man of Townsend in 1770 and 1771. In 1771 he pur-

J ohn Conant

(1762.)

chased pew No. 2 in the Townsend church (Sawtell's *Hist. of Townsend*, p. 144). In 1775 he was sergeant in Capt. James Hasley's company of minute men (Mass. Arch., Lexington Alarm Lists). He succeeded, with his brother, Nathan, to the mill and inn of his father. Feb. 22, 1793, he sold land in Jaffrey, N. H., to John Joslyn, of Jaffrey, for £60 (Cheshire Deeds, Vol. 23, p. 535). He d. before 1798. He m. 15 Aug., 1771, Sarah Farrer, who d. 1827.

Children of JOHN and SARAH (FARRER) CONANT:—

363. John, b. 24 Oct., 1772.
      Daniel, b. 12 Oct., 1774.
      Hannah, b. 4 July, 1776; m. 1798, Joseph Wallis.
364. Noah Farrar, b. 26 May, 1778.
      Sarah, b. 10 Sep., 1780; m. 11 Oct., 1801, Samuel Keep.
365. Joel, b. 4 May, 1783.
      Polly, b. 27 Oct., 1785.
      Olive, b. 19 Feb., 1788; m. 17 Sep., 1807, James Swann, of Bradford, N. H.
      Jonas, b. 6 Apr., 1791.

170. **Lot**[6] (*Ezra, Lot, John, Lot, Roger*), b. in Concord, 24 Dec., 1754. He removed from Concord, Mass., to Reading, Vt. He m. Hannah Johnson, of Sudbury.

Lot Conant

Children of LOT and HANNAH (JOHNSON) CONANT:—

366. Mary, b. 8 Nov., 1783, in Concord.
367. Catherine, b. 20 Oct., 1784.
368. Hannah, b. 19 Oct., 1789.
369. Lot, b. 15 July, 1792.
370. Thaddeus, b. 1 Sep., 1795.
371. Elisha Lockwood, b. 30 Apr., 1801.

171. **Ezra**[6] (*Ezra, Lot, John, Lot, Roger*), b. in Concord, 18 Sep., 1763. He graduated at Harvard College, 1784; studied theology and was ordained at Winchester, N. H., 19 Feb., 1788; dismissed 13 Oct., 1806.

Ezra Conant

(1816.)

He was afterwards settled over a church at Roxbury, Mass.
He d. 24 Oct., 1844, at the residence of his son, Caleb, in
Roxbury, Mass.

He m. (1) 16 Jan., 1791, Sarah, dr. of Col. Reuben and
Sarah (Foster) Alexander, b. 26 June, 1767; d. in Winchester,
N. H., 27 Nov., 1801. Col. Reuben Alexander was the sixth
generation from John Alexander, who came from Scotland to
America in 1650, bringing his family with him (Col. Reuben,[6]
Ebenezer,[5] Ebenezer,[4] John,[3] George,[2] John[1]). He m. (2) 1803,
Anna, dr. of Asa Alexander, of Winchester, b. 4 Mch., 1781;
d. 30 Nov., 1844.

Children of EZRA and SARAH (ALEXANDER) CONANT:—

> Lucy Russell, b. 24 Aug., 1791; m. Benjamin Kimball, and
> had Charles. She d. 9 Sep., 1817.
> 372. Sarah Foster, b. 5 Sep., 1793.
> 373. Pamela, b. 19 Sep., 1795.
> Andrew Buckley, b. 28 Oct., 1796.
> Reuben Buckley, b. 9 Nov., 1801; d. 28 Aug., 1819.

Children of EZRA and ANNA (ALEXANDER) CONANT:—

> Caleb Alexander, b. 14 Aug., 1804; a merchant of Roxbury;
> d. 17 Aug., 1875.
> Elizabeth Amelia, b. 30 Mch., 1808; d. 7 Feb., 1887, unm., at
> the residence of her brother, Ezra, in Roxbury.
> 374. Ezra, b. 4 July, 1812.

172. John[6] (*John, John, John, Lot, Roger*), b. 23 June,
1743, in the house at "3" (see p. 146) on Dodge street, Beverly; when mar-
ried, moved into
the house at "4,"
and in 1797 bought
the house at "2"

John Conant

(1781.)

of Nathaniel G. Dabney. At the time of the "Lexington
alarm" he marched to Cambridge in Capt. Peter Shaw's company (Mass. Arch., Muster Rolls, Vol. 13, p. 128); and in
1778 was in Capt. Francis Brown's company, in service in
Rhode Island (Mass. Arch., Muster Rolls, Vol. 1, p. 90). He
d. 20 June, 1809. He m. 14 Jan., 1764, Emma, dr. of Herbert Thorndike; she d. 25 July, 1824.

Children of JOHN and EMMA (THORNDIKE) CONANT:—

Sally, b. 10 Nov., 1765; d. 20 July, 1850, unm. (insane).
Martha, b. 8 Sep., 1767; d. unm.
Emma, b. 4 May, 1769; d. 14 Aug., 1770.
375. John, b. 11 Mch., 1771.
Emma, b. 3 Jan., 1773; d. Apr., 1773.
Herbert, b. 6 Oct., 1774; d. 6 Oct., 1787.
376. Emma, b. 2 May, 1776.
Mary, b. 28 Feb., 1778; m. Jonathan Foster.
377. Ezra, b. 28 Feb., 1780.
Nicholas, b. 17 Nov., 1783; d. 6 Oct., 1795.

173. Samuel[6] (*Samuel, John, John, Lot, Roger*), b. 6 Jan., 1750-1, in Beverly. He lived on Dodge street. In 1775

Samuel Conant

(1812.)

he was one of Capt. Peter Shaw's company of minute men (Mass. Arch., Muster Rolls, Vol. 12, p. 34). He m. Esther Kelley.

Children of SAMUEL and ESTHER (KELLEY) CONANT:—

Mary, b. 23 Sep., 1784; m. (1) —— Elliot, of Beverly, and had two daughters, who d. y.; m. (2) Major Eaton.
Esther, b. 18 Dec., 1787; m. (1) —— Prescott, and had a dr., Adeline, b. 1811, who lives in New York city; m. (2) —— Whittrege.

174. Hannah[6] (*Samuel, John, John, Lot, Roger*), b. 6, bapt. 9 May, 1756 in Beverly; m. Cornelius Batchelder of Beverly.

Children of CORNELIUS and HANNAH (CONANT) BATCHEL-DER:—

i.   Samuel? m. and had a dr. Abigail Ann, who m. Samuel White.
ii.   Cornelius, m. and had William, of Beverly Farms; Sarah, m. James Dunn, of Beverly, and had Levi A. and Francis; Eliza Ann, who m. —— Stott, and had a son, Walter.
iii. Hannah, aged nearly 90, lives on the old homestead, at Beverly. (Mch., 1885).

175. Nathaniel[6] (*Samuel, John, John, Lot, Roger*), bapt.

Nathaniel Conant

1812.

in Beverly, 14 Apr., 1765. He moved from Beverly to New Salem, N. H. He m. 1789, Sarah Burnham.

Children of NATHANIEL and SARAH (BURNHAM) CONANT:—

378. Nathaniel, b. 3 Oct., 1790.
    Mercia, b. 23 Mch., 1792; m. Benjamin Woodbury. She d. of consumption. Children.
    Mary, b. 3 June, 1794; m. Andrew Dodge, of Wenham, and had a child; both mother and child d. y. of consumption.
    William, b. 11 July, 1796; d. Sept., 1802.
    Sally, b. 11 July, 1798; d. 28 Sept., 1812.
    Samuel, b. 23 Jan., 1801.
    William, b. 27 Aug., 1803.
379. Eunice, b. 27 Jan., 1807.
    Samuel, b. 15 Sept., 1811; m. and had two sons.

176. **Nabby**[6] (*Lot, John, John, Lot, Roger*), b. 6, bapt. 9 Mch., 1760, in Beverly; d. 25 Oct., 1842. She m. David, son of David Perkins, b. in Topsfield, Mass., 11 May, 1756; they were published 2 Nov., 1783. He d. 27 July, 1827. (See *Perkins Genealogy*, Essex Inst. Hist. Coll. 1886.)

Children of DAVID and NABBY (CONANT) PERKINS:—

i.   Nabby, b. 24 Oct., 1786; d. 13 Mch., 1857; unmarried.
ii.   Sarah, b. 27 Mch., 1788; m. John Dwinell.
iii. David, b. 20 Aug., 1791; m. Hannah Green.
iv. Ebenezer, b. 4 July, 1794; m. Amelia Parish.
v.   Mercy, b. 17 Aug., 1800.
vi. Benjamin Conant, b. 18 May, 1804; m. Lucy Peabody, and died childless.

177. **Benjamin**[6] (*Lot, John, John, Lot, Roger*), b. in Beverly, 9 Feb., 1765; he was a farmer of Beverly; he lived on the farm on Dodge street, left him by his father. He m. Abigail Shaw.

Children of BENJAMIN and ABIGAIL (SHAW) CONANT:—

380. Nancy.
    Jerusha, who m. Jacob, son of William Dodge, of Wenham; he was a pump maker; she was killed by the fall of a pump which he was lowering into a well, through the breaking of a rope.

178. **Jonathan**[6] (*Daniel, Daniel, John, Lot, Roger*), b. in Beverly, 8 Jan., 1745-6; he removed from Beverly to Dudley, Mass. He m. in Dudley, 9 July, 1772, Lucy Corbin; she d. 6

Mch., 1826 (Town Records), (6 Nov., 1824, Family Record).

Children of JONATHAN and LUCY (CORBIN) CONANT:—

Hervey, b. 10 Apr., 1773 (d. 21 May, 1848?).
Molly, b. 9 Jan., 1775; m. 30 June, 1796, David Nichols, jr.
Lucy, b. 5 Mch., 1777.
Jonathan, b. 4 Jan., 1779.
Daniel, b. 1 Nov., 1781.
Sarah Healy, b. 2 Sep., 1784.

179. Barnabas[6] (*Daniel, Daniel, John, Lot, Roger*), b. in Beverly, 16 Mch. 1761; he was a ship carpenter and cooper. He moved from Beverly to Wendell, N. H. Barnabas Conant of Beverly, buys land in Wendell, N. H., of John Wendell, of Portsmouth, N. H., Nov. 9, 1793, for £60 (Cheshire Deeds, Vol. 23, p. 232). He d. 27 Feb., 1847.

He m. 1786, Mary Batchelder, who d. 10 Nov., 1804.

Children of BARNABAS and MARY (BATCHELDER) CONANT:—

381. Mary, b. in Beverly, 1 Mch., 1787.
Elizabeth, b. 21 Feb., 1791.
Josiah, b. 17 Dec., 1793.
William, b. 19 July, 1797, in Sunapee, N. H.

180. Josiah[6] (*Daniel, Daniel, John, Lot, Roger*), b. in Beverly, 21 Aug., 1763. He moved from Beverly to Warwick, Mass; was a miller and farmer; he d. 19 Jan., 1855. He m. 28 Dec., 1788, Olive, dr. of David and Elizabeth Gale, who d. 15 Jan., 1852. They were married at Warwick, by Rev. Samuel Reed.

Children of JOSIAH and OLIVE (GALE) CONANT:—

Polly, b. 11 Sep., 1789; d. unm., 12 Mch., 1870.
Philena, b. 12 Oct., 1791; m. (413) Benjamin Conant.
382. Gardner, b. 30 Jan., 1794.
383. Josiah, b. 21 June, 1796.
384. Hiram, b. 10 Jan., 1799.
Daniel, b. 19 Apr., 1801; d. Sep., 1803.
385. Samuel, b. 21 Aug., 1803.
Lucinda, b. 4 June, 1806; m. Horace Gale, of Winhall, Vt.
Children: Melinda, b. 24 Oct., 1832; Maria, b. 7 Oct., 1834;
and Gardner, b. 20 Sep., 1837.

181. Lucy[6] (*Nathaniel, Daniel, John, Lot, Roger*), b. in Beverly, Mass., 11 Sep., 1757; m. 1778, Capt. Jeremiah Roberts, of Lyman, Me.

Children of JEREMIAH and LUCY (CONANT) ROBERTS:—

i.   John, m. Hannah Chadbourn, and had Andrew, Elizabeth, Thomas, Hannah, Nathaniel, and others who d. y.

ii.   Hannah, m. John Gile, of Alfred, and had Lucy, Hephzibah, John, Daniel, Eliza, Jeremiah, Nathaniel, d. y., and Nathaniel.

iii.   Larkin, m. Susan Roberts, and had Hephzibah, Nathaniel, Larkin and Harriet.

iv.   Nathaniel, m. ——; had Lizzie, Abigail and Israel.

v.   Lucy, m. John Brock, of Lyman; no children.

vi.   Ebenezer, d. y.

vii.   Ichabod, d. y.

viii.   Hephzibah, d. y.

ix.   Jeremiah, b. 27 May, 1798; m. Olive Roberts, and had Harriet, Martha, Elizabeth, Albert, Drusilla, John, Lucy, Olive and Lucy.

x.   Daniel, was of Saco; m. Sarah Whitney, and had John, Sarah, Lyman, Jeremiah, Rose, Daniel and Thomas.

182. Hephzibah[6] (*Nathaniel, Daniel, John, Lot, Roger*), b. 3 Feb., 1760, in Beverly; m. Tobias, son of Capt. Tobias Lord, as his second wife (his first was Mehitable Scammon). Tobias Lord was b. in Wells; he was a lieutenant in the Revolutionary army, under Capt. Joseph Littlefield, at Burgoyne's surrender, 1777. In 1778 he went to Kennebunk, Me., built·a store and engaged in trade and ship building. He moved to Alfred in 1803, returned to Kennebunk in 1808, and died suddenly Jan. 16, 1808, at the house of his daughter, Mrs. Francis Watts.

Children of TOBIAS and HEPHZIBAH (CONANT) LORD:—

i.   Mehitable, b. 1782, in Kennebunk; m. Francis O. Watts.

ii.   Abigail, b. 1785; m. Charles W. Williams, of Kennebunk. Children: 1. Capt. William; 2. Capt. Charles, m. Diantha Fiske; 3. Capt. Claudius; 4. Capt. Albert; 5. Capt. Tobias; 6. Rev. Francis; 7. Abigail; 8. Harriet, m. Dr. Sawyer, of Fort Wayne, Ind.; 9. Serena, m. Rev. George Campbell, of Millbury, Mass., and had Serena, and Lucy, who m. a nephew of George Peabody, the philanthropist.

iii.   Hephzibah, b. 1787; m. Robert Waterston, a merchant of Boston; had: 1. Rev. Robert C., a Unitarian minister, who m. a dr. of Josiah Quincy; 2. Helen; 3. Lucy; 4. Mariah, who m. George C. Lord (her cousin).

iv.   Betsey, b. 1790; m. Francis O. Watts (his second wife), of Boston.

v.   George, b. 23 Sep., 1791; m. 23 Apr., 1816, Olive Jefferds, dr.

of William and Olive (Gilpatrick) Jefferds. Children: 1. Hannah C., b. 1817; 2. Lucy Hayes, b. 1819, d. y.; 3. Olive, b. 1821, d. y.; 4. George Clement, b. 1823, of Newton, Mass., m. 1846, Marion Waterston, and has Robert, Marion, Caroline and Charles E. Mr. Lord has been for a number of years past, President of the Boston and Maine Railroad; 5. Charles Howard, b. 1825; 6. Edward Watts, b. 1830.

vi. Ivory, b. 1793; m. (1) Louisa, dr. of Hugh McCulloch; (2) Olive (Bourne) Emerson. Children: 1. Ivory; 2. Augusta; 3. Louisa, m. Joseph Dane, jr., of Kennebunk.

vii. Francis A., b. ——; m. Francis Smith.

viii. Lucy, b. 1797; m. Hercules M. Hayes, of New York city.

ix. William, b. 1799; m. Sarah, dr. of Col. Daniel Cleaves, of Saco. Children: 1. William; 2. Hartley; 3. Sarah; 4. Mary; 5. Betsey, m. Francis O. Watts, of Boston, and has Francis, a lawyer, of Boston, and Augusta.

183. Joshua⁶ (*Nathaniel, Daniel, John, Lot, Roger*), b. 7 Apr., 1764, in Beverly, Mass.; moved to Alfred, Me., with his parents; lived in Shapleigh and Lyman, where he d. 4 Oct., 1842. He m. Adelia, dr. of Dea. —— Gile, of Alfred, who d. 30 Sep., 1842, in Lyman, Me.

Children of JOSHUA and ADELIA (GILE) CONANT:—

386. Ruth, b. 8 Oct., 1787.
387. Nathaniel, b. 15 Dec., 1789.
Hephzibah, b. 15 Nov., 1791; m. (1) Benjamin Dunnell, a lawyer, of Wells; m. (2) William Dunnell, of Wells; m. (3) Luther Emerson, of Parsonsfield.
388. Theodate, b. 18 Sep., 1793.
389. Joshua, b. 1 Aug., 1796.
390. Daniel, b. 7 May, 1798.
Abigail, b. 20 Mch., 1800; m. John Roberts, of Lyman.
391. William Green, b. 25 Dec., 1806.
392. Thomas Gile, b. 15 Dec., 1815.

184. Nathaniel⁶ (*Nathaniel, Daniel, John, Lot, Roger*), b. 30 June, 1766, in (Beverly?); moved to Alfred, Me., with his parents. He bought a lot near his father's mill, of Benjamin Tripe, and built a house, which is still standing. After his death it was occupied by his son-in-law, B. J. Herrick, and is now (1886) owned by C. H. Roberts. He was a well known and esteemed citizen of Alfred, where for many years he was engaged in mercantile pursuits. He held various town offices, and was for many years a Justice of the Peace. In 1806 and 1807 he represented the town in the Massachusetts legislature.

He was the second representative from Alfred, John Holmes, afterwards U. S. Senator, being the first. He d. 12 May, 1842.

He m. ——, Hephzibah, dr. of Joshua and Martha Dodge, of Danvers, Mass.; she was born 30 Aug., 1771; d. 1 Feb., 1859, at the residence of her son-in-law. "She was among the last survivors of a large number of persons who emigrated from Essex co., Mass., to Alfred and vicinity, and she took great pleasure in relating reminiscences of her early life in Massachusetts, and particularly of the public men of that time. It is believed that few persons had as extensive and exact knowledge of the course of public events as Mrs. Conant. Few persons had a purer or better cultivated literary taste; she read much, and what is better, she read well. She was a constant reader and true lover of the Bible, and committed large portions of it to memory. As an example of the great tenacity of her memory, the following fact is related: At the age of seventy she repeated a eulogy on Washington, pronounced by her old pastor, Rev. Benjamin Wadsworth, which she had not seen for forty years. The writer has in his possession a copy of the eulogy, written also from memory, by her own hand, when she was 82 years of age, the chirography of which is almost as plain as print." [From an obituary notice by H. G. H(errick?).]

Child of NATHANIEL and HEPHZIBAH (DODGE) CONANT:—

393.   Mary, b. 15 Nov., 1799.

185. Daniel[6] (*Nathaniel, Daniel, John, Lot, Roger*), b. Apr., 1768, in Alfred, Me.; was a farmer. He d. 14 Sep., 1807.
He m. Ruth, dr. of Dea. Gile, of Alfred.
Children of DANIEL and RUTH (GILE) CONANT:—

Ivory, b. 31 Aug., 1795; d. unm., 1841.
Abigail, b. 1 June, 1798; d. 1810.
Daniel, b. 5 Mch., 1801; m. —— Williams, but d. 1842, without children.
Louisa, b. 2 July, 1805; pub. 16 June, m. 22 Aug., 1827, James Griffin.

186. John[6] (*Nathaniel, Daniel, John, Lot, Roger*), b. in Alfred, Me., 10 Sep., 1771. About 1795 he moved to Kennebunk, where he engaged in trade for a short time, then returned

John Conant

to Alfred. He succeeded to the mill and store of his father, at Conant's Mills (now called Littlefield's Mills), and afterwards occupied the brick store near the meeting-house. He was the second postmaster of Alfred, and active and enterprising in commercial pursuits. He lived in the house now owned by Hon. Ira T. Drew, where he d. 27 Feb., 1850. The portrait here presented is from a painting in possession of John H. Conant, Esq., of Watertown, Mass.

He m. ———, Lydia, dr. of Benjamin and Anna (Merrill) Farnum, of Concord, N. H.; she was born 25 Dec., 1776, d. 28 May, 1842. Benjamin Farnum was son of Ephraim and Molly (Ingalls) Farnum, grandson of Ephraim, son of Ralph, who was son of Ralph Farnum (or Farnham), the immigrant. Anna Merrill was b. at Concord, 20 Dec., 1743; dr. of Deacon John and Lydia (Haynes) Merrill, of Haverhill, Mass., and Concord, N. H.; her grandfather, John Merrill, was son of Nathaniel and grandson of Nathaniel Merrill, the immigrant, one of the earliest settlers of Newbury, Mass. Molly Ingalls was dr. of Henry and Abigail (Emery) Ingalls, g. dr. of Henry and Mary (Osgood) Ingalls, g. g. dr. of Edmund Ingalls, of Andover, the immigrant.

Lydia, wife of John Conant, was admitted to the church about the first of Oct., 1807 (Alfred Church Records).

Children of JOHN and LYDIA (FARNUM) CONANT :—

394. Nancy Merrill, b. 27 Dec., 1796; bapt. 24 Jan., 1803.
     Cyrus, b. 17 May, 1799; d. 19 Jan., 1803.
395. Alvah, b. 17 Dec., 1800, in Kennebunk; bapt. 24 Jan., 1808, in Alfred.
396. Cyrus King, b. 1 Jan., 1803; bapt. 24 Jan., 1808, in Alfred.
     Lucinda, b. 19 Nov., 1804; d. 2 Jan., 1808.
397. Caroline, b. 16 Apr., 1809; bapt. 2 July, 1809.
     George Dow, b. 2 Feb., 1811; bapt. 19 May, 1811; he never married. Was engaged in commercial pursuits at Alfred with his father and brother, Alvah, for a number of years. He d. 29 Dec., 1880, at Alfred.
398. Lucy Maria, b. 7 Dec., 1812.
399. Lydia Haynes, b. 25 Apr., 1816.

187. Andrew⁶ (*Nathaniel, Daniel, John, Lot, Roger*), b. in Alfred, Sep., 1773. He was a prominent and well known citizen of Alfred. In 1820-1 he was a member of the first legislature of Maine, after the separation of the state from Massachusetts, and was re-elected 1822. He held various town offices, and was Justice of the Peace many years, and also a captain of militia. In 1836 he removed to Kennebunk and purchased the farm of Robert Towne, Esq. Soon after he removed to Dexter, Me., where he d. 1848.

He m. 4 Mch., 1797 (pub. 16 Jan., 1797), Sarah, dr. of Joseph Emerson. She d. in Tonica, Ill., 13 Sep., 1856, aged 82.

Children of ANDREW and SARAH (EMERSON) CONANT:—

  Hannah, b. 1797; d. in infancy.
  Eliza, b. 1798; d. aged 12.
400. Lucinda, b. 9 Feb., 1806.
401. Sarah P., b. July, 1811.
402. Andrew Emerson, b. 7 Dec., 1815.

188. Rufus[6] (*Josiah, Daniel, John, Lot, Roger*), b. 16 Aug., 1760, in Dudley, Mass. He was a farmer, and lived near his father's homestead. He m. 11 May, 1790, Dolly White, of Charlton.

Children of RUFUS and DOLLY (WHITE) CONANT:—

  Clarissa, b. 22 Feb., 1791; m. 23 Apr., 1814, William Foskett. She d. 1 Apr., 1869.
403. Hosea, b. 2 Mch., 1793.
  Dolly, b. 14 May, 1795; m. 24 Oct., 1816, Andrew King.
  Pattie, b. 7 Apr., 1797; m. 20 Jan., 1824, Jacob Smith. She d. 13 Mch., 1855.
  Asa, b. 4 July, 1800; m. (1) 15 Nov., 1827, A. L. Cleveland; m. (2) Abigail ———.
  Lodema, b. 19 Aug., 1802; d. 6 Oct., 1808.
404. Rufus, b. 16 Mch., 1805.
  Matilda, b. 22 July, 1807; m. 23 July, 1840, M. L. Burnat. She d. 5 Dec., 1875.
  Abiel, b. 15 May, 1811; d. 12 Aug., 1814.

189. Lodema[6] (*Josiah, Daniel, John, Lot, Roger*), b. 12 Nov., 1762, in Dudley; m. (pub. 5 May, 1787) Joseph, son of Elisha and Mary (Davis) Rich; he was b. 6 Mch., 1759, in Sutton; was a farmer, later a miller. He settled in Charlton, removed to Stockbridge and thence to De Ruyter, N. Y. He d. 25 Mch., 1813; she d. 25 Oct., 1814.

Children of JOSEPH and LODEMA (CONANT) RICH:—

i. Sarah, b. 20 June, 1789, at Charlton; m. 19 Aug., 1805, David

Benjamin; they removed to Conneaut, Ohio. She d. 18
Feb., 1873. He died 18 Feb., 1825. They had ten children.
He was a farmer, merchant, and owner of a flouring-mill.

ii. Martha, b. 11 July, 1792; m. 25 Dec., 1811, Elias P. Benjamin
(bro. of David). He was a miller and farmer of De Ruyter,
N. Y. She d. 22 Nov., 1866. He d. 27 Nov., 1866. They
had eleven children.

190. Josiah[6] (*Josiah, Daniel, John, Lot, Roger*), b. 30
Sep., 1770, in Dudley, Mass. He settled in the northern part
of Dudley, afterwards known as Tuft's Village, on a farm, and
also owned a saw and grist mill, driven by the stream flowing
from Baker's Pond. His house, of which an engraving is

given, is supposed to have been built by his father. He d. 16
Sep., 1813. He m. ———, Lucy Foskett.

Children of JOSIAH and LUCY (FOSKETT) CONANT:—

405. Hervey, b. 3 June, 1796.
Sylvia, b. 8 Aug., 1798; m. 14 Dec., 1817, Capt. Lemuel, son
of Maj. Lemuel and Dolly (Corbin) Healy. He was born
24 Nov., 1792; d. 2 Sep., 1866. He was town clerk, assessor
and selectman many years. They had two children. She
d., and he m. (2) Eliza Warden.

406. Josiah, b. 7 Dec., 1804.

191. Ezra[6] (*Ezra, Benjamin, John, Lot, Roger*), b. 7
Apr., 1751, in Dudley, Mass.; moved to Warwick with his
parents. He was town clerk at Warwick one year. He was

a physician; settled at Oxford, where he d. 9 May, 1789. He m. 27 Oct., 1773, Ruth, dr. of Capt. Samuel and Ruth (Learned) Davis, of Oxford, where she was born 25 Nov., 1752. Capt. Samuel Davis was b. in Roxbury, Mass.; son of Samuel, g. s. of John, g. g. s. of William Davis, an early settler of Roxbury. He was a captain of militia in the French and Indian war, and a prominent citizen of Oxford. After the death of Dr. Ezra Conant, his widow m. Joseph Healy, of Dudley.

(1779.)

Children of EzRA and RUTH (DAVIS) CONANT:—

> Ruth, b. 8 Jan., 1775, in Warwick; d. 8 Sep., 1777.
> 407.   Sally, b. 15 May, 1777.
> Samuel, b. 29 Aug., 1780, in Oxford. He was drowned at Brookline or Roxbury, where he was employed, 5 Aug., 1805.
> Learned, b. 27 Sep., 1784; d. unm., at Oxford.

192. **Amos**[6] (*Ezra, Benjamin, John, Lot, Roger*), b. 8 Jan., 1753, in Dudley; moved to Warwick with his parents, thence to Barre, Vt., where some of his children were born. He then removed to Claremont, Sullivan co., N. H., where his name appears on the tax list of 20 Dec., 1783 (N. H. Town Papers). During the Revolution he served a short time as corporal in Capt. Ashley's company of Col. Bellows' regiment (N. H. State Papers, Vol. 15, p. 27). Thence he moved to Irasburg, Orleans co., Vt., finding his way by marked or "spotted" trees. He selected a farm of 110 acres, cleared it and died there 21 June, 1847.

He m. in Winchester, N. H., 27 Aug., 1776, Elizabeth Erskine, b. in Bridgewater, Mass., 6 May, 1755, d. in Irasburg, Vt., 14 June, 1820.

Children of AMOS and ELIZABETH (ERSKINE) CONANT:—

> Betsey, b. 14 May, 1778, in Barre, Vt.
> Amos, b. 9 Jan., 1780, in Barre, Vt.
> 408.   Samuel, b. 8 Mch., 1781, in Claremont, N. H.
> Betsey, b. 12 Dec., 1782.
> 409.   Ebenezer, b. 20 May, 1785.
> 410.   Charles, b. 30 Sep., 1787.
> Cynthia, b. 21 Mch., 1790.
> Ezra, b. 16 Oct., 1792; lived in Irasburg, Vt.; had a family; a

son was in the employ of the Fairbanks Scale Co., of Chicago, Ill.

Ralph, b. 29 Apr., 1794.

193. Millicent[6] (*Ezra, Benjamin, John, Lot, Roger*), b. 25 Aug., 1754, in Dudley; moved to Warwick, with her parents; m. in Warwick, 9 Aug., 1770, Thomas, son of Elisha and Mary (Davis) Rich. He was born in Sutton, 29 Oct., 1738, was one of six brothers who went from Sutton to Warwick, Mass. At the "Lexington alarm," he was first lieutenant in Capt. Wright's company. He moved to Shoreham, Vt., in 1786, having bought land at Richville, the previous year. He built a saw mill near the falls in 1787.

Children of THOMAS and MILLICENT (CONANT) RICH :—

i.   Charles, b. 13 Sep., 1771; m. 24 Sep., 1791, Molly Watts, of Hartwick, N. Y. They had a large family of children. He d. 24 Oct., 1824, in Shoreham, of which he was one of the most prominent citizens. He was many years a member of the State legislature, and in 1813, was elected to Congress as a democrat; was re-elected from 1817 to 1824. His son, Davis Rich, was a member of the Vermont legislature, and assistant Judge of the County Court (See Genealogy of Samuel Davis, of Oxford, p. 38).

ii.   Judith, who m. 1792, William Pitt Bailey. She d. 1827, in Potsdam, N. Y.

iii.   Eben, b. 1775, m. 6 Sep., 1798, Elizabeth Stockwell. They lived in Shoreham; had a family.

iv.   John, b. 12 Dec., 1777; m. 29 Jan., 1801, Betsey Williams. He entered the U. S. army, and d. at Green Bay, Wis.

v.   Millicent, b. 18 Nov., 1779; m. 5 Feb., 1801, Moulton Needham, of Whiting, Vt.

vi.   Anna, b. 14 Oct., 1781; m. Peter Ripley Leonard, and d. at Pierrepont, N. Y.

vii.   Clarissa, b. 29 Jan., 1784; m. Christopher Willson, of Canton, N. Y. They had no children.

viii. Samuel, b. 16 June, 1785; m. 29 Jan., 1804, Polly Bailey. He was a lieutenant in the war of 1812, and d. in Prescott, Canada, 18 Dec., 1828.

ix.   Betsey, b. 27 July, 1787; m. 29 Jan., 1804, Ezekiel Willson, of Potsdam, N. Y.

x.   Lucinda, b. 31 July, 1789; m. Reuben Willson, of Canton, N. Y.

xi.   Luretta, b. 5 Aug., 1791; m. Benj. Healy, of Potsdam, N. Y.; no children.

xii.   Ezra, b. 13 Nov., 1792; m. Esther Rich. He d. 1869, in New London, Wis.

194. John[6] (*Ezra, Benjamin, John, Lot, Roger*), b. 29 Aug., 1758, in Dudley; moved to Warwick, with his parents; was town clerk of Warwick, 9 years. He served in the Revolutionary army, in Capt. Wm. Campbell's company of Col. Learned's regiment (Mass. Arch., Coat Rolls), and was afterwards captain of militia. He moved from Warwick to Glover, Vt., and thence to Craftsburg, where he is buried. He m. (int. pub. (1775.) 30 Jan., 1779, in Warwick) Sarah Leonard.

Children of JOHN and SARAH (LEONARD) CONANT:—

> Sarah, b. 24 Nov., 1779.
> Millicent, b. 29 Jan., 1781.
> 411. Newell, b. 5 Nov., 1782.
> Beulah, b. 3 Aug., 1784.
> Lucy, b. Apr., 1786.
> 412. Ezra, b. 1 Feb., 1788.
> Mercy, b. 8 Jan., 1790.
> Anna, b. 2 Apr., 1793; m. James Caldwell, of Lowell, Vt.; moved to Rochester, N. Y.

195. Benjamin[6] (*Ezra, Benjamin, John, Lot, Roger*), b. 28 Mch., 1764, in Dudley; moved to Warwick, with his parents; was a deacon of the church. He d. 11 Jan., 1815, in Warwick.

He m. (1) 24 Oct., 1784, Mary, dr. of David and Elizabeth Gale; m. (2) 1 Dec., 1803, Eunice Watts.

Children of BENJAMIN and MARY (GALE) CONANT:—

> 413. Benjamin, b. 28 Mch., 1785.
> Betsey, b. 30 Nov., 1786; m. int. pub. 25 Jan., 1805, to Joseph Barber, Jr.
> Polly, b. 30 Nov., 1788; (m. int. pub. 13 Sept., 1824, to Rufus Wheelock?) (see p. 282).

196. Clark[6] (*Ezra, Benjamin, John, Lot, Roger*), b. 23 June, 1773, in Warwick, Mass.; settled in Windsor, Vt.

He m. in Warwick, 20 Nov., 1794, Sally, dr. of Jeremiah and Rebecca (Scott) Dean (see *Hist. Charlestown, N. H.*).

Child of CLARK and SALLY (DEAN) CONANT:—

> 414. Dean, b. ——, 1800.

197. Charles[6] (*Benjamin, Benjamin, John, Lot, Roger*), b. in Warwick, Mass., 29 July, 1769. He was a tailor. He moved from Warwick, to Shoreham, Vt., after 1796. He m. in Warwick, 13 Sep., 1791, Anna, dr. of (93) Ezra Conant.

Children of CHARLES and ANNA (CONANT) CONANT :—

> Louisa Anna, b. 4 July, 1792.
> Davis, b. 15 May, 1794.
> Stephen, b. 18 June, 1796.

198. Benjamin[6] (*Benjamin, Benjamin, John, Lot, Roger*), b. 14 Sep., 1775, in Warwick, Mass., where he lived. He d. 8 July, 1867. He m. 25 June, 1805 (Family Records), int. pub. 9 May, 1805 (Town Records), Betsey, dr. of Wilder Stevens; she d. in Hartland, Vt., 3 Nov., 1876.

Children of BENJAMIN and BETSEY (STEVENS) CONANT:—

415. Samuel, b. 20 June, 1808.
416. Harvey, b. 28 June, 1811.

199. Ebenezer[6] (*Benjamin, Benjamin, John, Lot, Roger*), b. in Warwick, 3 July, 1779, settled in Winchester, N. H. He d. 20 Jan., 1832. He m. in Winchester, N. H., 22 Nov., 1806, Dolly Thayer, b. 23 July, 1779.

Children of EBENEZER and DOLLY (THAYER) CONANT :—

> Eana, b. 8 Sep., 1807.
> Huldah P., b. 4 May, 1809.
> Hezekiah, b. 17 Feb., 1811.
> Louisa, b. 6 Jan., 1814; d. 10 Aug., 1816.
> Philena, b. 1 May, 1816.
> Louisa, b. 16 Sep., 1818.
> Eunice, b. 26 Dec., 1821.
> Ebenezer, b. 23 Nov., 1823.
> Sarah Davis, b. 11 Apr., 1826.
> Charles Bennett, b. 11 Sep., 1828.

200. Samuel[6] (*Benjamin, Benjamin, John, Lot, Roger*), b. 22 Apr., 1781, in Warwick, Mass. He was a clothier; settled in Troy, Pa., while a young man; afterwards moved to Cuba, N. Y., where he d., 1853.

He m. in Troy, Pa., Aug., 1814, Amy Powell; she d. 1876, in Cuba, N. Y.

Children of SAMUEL and AMY (POWELL) CONANT :—

.   Lucy, b. 29 Oct., 1815, in Troy, Pa.
      Mary Ann, b. 20 Nov., 1816.
      Dolly, b. 9 Jan., 1819.
417. Samuel H., b. 14 July, 1822, in Troy, Pa.
418. Charles L., b. 25 Aug., 1827, in Cuba, N. Y.
      James P., b. 22 June, 1829, in Cuba, N. Y.; d. unm.

201.   Asa[6] (*Asa, Benjamin, John, Lot, Roger*), b. 22 Sep.,
1773, in Warwick; was a farmer of Warwick. He d. in Winchester, N. H., 1865. He m. in Warwick, 2 May, 1805, Divine,
dr. of Joseph and Ann (Hopkins) Goodell; b. 15 Mch., 1779.

Children of ASA and DIVINE (GOODELL) CONANT :—

419. Sabrina, b. 6 May, 1807.
420. Asa Hopkins, b. 23 May, 1811.
      Divine Ann, b. 3 Nov., 1816; m. —— Swan, has 1. Olive, m.
      —— Martin, of Granville, Vt.; 2. Conant, who was killed in
      the army; 3. Winfred.

202.   Jonas[6] (*Asa, Benjamin, John, Lot, Roger*), b. 18
Aug., 1775, in Warwick. He was a farmer of Warwick, served
in the U. S. army in the war of 1812. He d. 18 Sep., 1856.
He m. (1) Sarah Leonard, who d. 23 July, 1823; m. (2) (int.
pub. 31 Dec., 1824) Mrs. Anna Barker, of Brattleboro', Vt.

Children of JONAS and SARAH (LEONARD) CONANT:—

      Polly, b. 17 June, 1804 (m. 1824, Rufus Wheelock, see p. 280).
      Almira, b. 21 Apr., 1806; mar. int. 5 Jan., 1830, to Shebnah
        Paine.
      Jonas Leonard, b. 2 Oct., 1808.
      Rufus, b. 7 Sep., 1810.

Child of JONAS and ANNA (————) (BARKER) CONANT :—

      Charles Merriam, b. 4 Feb., 1827, now living in Gill, Mass.

203.   Jemima[6] (*Asa, Benjamin, John, Lot, Roger*), b. 1
Aug., 1778, in Warwick; m. Samuel Melendy. They settled
in Bainbridge, N. Y.

Children of SAMUEL and JEMIMA (CONANT) MELENDY :—

      Asa.
      Sophronia.

204.   Susanna[6] (*Asa, Benjamin, John, Lot, Roger*), b. 29
May, 1783, in Warwick; m. 3 Nov., 1799, James Blake, of
Warwick.

Children of JAMES and SUSANNA (CONANT) BLAKE:—

Alexander.
Eliza.
Susan.
James.
Thomas.
Jonathan.

205. Patty[6] (*Asa, Benjamin, John, Lot, Roger*), b. 23 Oct., 1786, in Warwick; m. 18 Jan., 1803, Jonathan, son of Jonathan and Sarah (Pierce) Blake (see *Blake Family*, p. 56). He was born in Dorchester, Mass., 29 May, 1780, and moved to Warwick, with his father, 1781. In 1831-2 he wrote a history of the town of Warwick, to be read before the Lyceum. This history was transcribed at a later period (1854) by his brother, Samuel, and published by the town in 1873, under direction of a committee chosen for the purpose. He also wrote many poems on various subjects, some of which were published in the *History of Warwick;* and kept a voluminous diary for nearly sixty years. He was a distinguished surveyor of land, a profession in which many of his ancestors were noted. He was town clerk of Warwick fifteen years; selectman nine years; justice of the peace forty-two years; representative to the General Court two years; senator two years; county commissioner in Franklin county nine years; and a member of the Unitarian Church of Warwick over fifty years. Patty (Conant) Blake d. in Warwick, 21 Oct., 1819, and he m. as his second wife, Mrs. Betsey (Howland) Ballard. He d. 13 Apr., 1864, in Brattleboro', Vt.

Children of JONATHAN and PATTY (CONANT) BLAKE:—

i. John.
ii. Jonathan.
iii. James.
iv. Edward.
v. Mary Ann.
vi. Martha.

206. Jonathan[6] (*Jonathan, Jonathan, Lot, Lot, Roger*), b. 11 Apr., 1760, in Beverly, Mass.; moved to Mt. Vernon, N. H., with his parents, where he d. 28 Oct., 1829. In 1803 his name appears in a list of inhabitants of Amherst (N. H. Town

Papers).   In 1811 he settled in Antrim, N. H., where he remained till 1816, when he returned to Mt. Vernon.   He m. Polly Baker, of Wenham, Mass., who d. 26 Apr., 1834.

Children of JONATHAN and POLLY (BAKER) CONANT:—

421.   Israel Elliot, b. 6 Oct., 1789.
       Mehitable.
       Ruth.
       Nancy.
       Mary.
422.   William, b. 31 Oct., 1802.
       Fanny.

207.   Lot[6] (*Jonathan, Jonathan, Lot, Lot, Roger*), b. 18 June, 1764, in Beverly, Mass.; moved to Mt. Vernon, N. H., with his parents, where he died.   He m. Mehitable Woodbury, who d. 6 Dec., 1844, aged 77.   She was admitted to the church at Mt. Vernon, 15 May, 1797.

Children of LOT and MEHITABLE (WOODBURY) CONANT:— ·

       Jonathan, d. y.
       Charlotte, bapt. 16 Aug., 1801; m. Hezekiah Wallace, of Beverly, and had children.
       Eliza, b. 1803; m. —— Averill.
       Peter Woodbury, bapt. Oct., 1811; d. 13 Nov., 1826.

208.   Israel[6] (*Jonathan, Jonathan, Lot, Lot, Roger*), b. 15 Nov., 1767, in Beverly.   He went to Mt. Vernon, with his parents, but returned and settled in Beverly.   He was a cooper and wheelwright; built a house and shop on Federal *Israel Conant* (1825.) street, which is still standing.   He was admitted to Dane Street Church, Dec., 1820.   He d. about 1845.

He m. (1) about 1809, Elizabeth, dr. of Capt. Isaac and Joanna (Woodbury) Chapman, b. 24 Sep., 1770.   June 15, 1809, Israel Conant, shoreman, and Elizabeth, his wife, in her right, sell land in Raymond, Cumberland co., to Richard Manning, jr., "left by our father, Isaac Chapman" (Cumberland Co., Me., Deeds, Vol. 57, p. 237).   Aug. 10, 1816, Israel Conant, of Mt. Vernon, and Elizabeth, his wife, sell land in Raymond, "left by our father, Isaac Chapman" (Vol. 76, p. 19).   He m. (2) Mary Cross.

Child of ISRAEL and ELIZABETH (CHAPMAN) CONANT:—

Joanna, b. ——; d. ——; she was admitted to Dane Street Church, 1820.

209. Sarah[6] (*Jonathan, Jonathan, Lot, Lot, Roger*), bapt. 3 June, 1770, in Beverly; m. Dr. Ingalls, son of Solomon and Tabitha (Ingalls) Kittredge, b. in Mt. Vernon, N. H., 10 Dec., 1769. She d. at Beverly, 7 Oct., 1833. After her death he m. Lydia Smith.

Children of INGALLS and SARAH (CONANT) KITTREDGE:—

i.   Ingalls, b. 30 June, 1798, in Townsend, N. H.; studied at Phillips Academy; entered Harvard College, where he graduated, 1820; graduated from Harvard Medical School, 1823; m. 22 Sep., 1824, Augusta Smith, who d. 12 Jan., 1874. He d. 14 Feb., 1867, in Beverly. Children: 1. Sarah Augusta, b. 26 Aug., 1827; m. 1848, Charles W. Galloupe, and had: (a) Sarah K., who m. Hon. Wesley Morton; (b) Wilhelmina, who m. Dr. Samuel J. Mixter. 2. Lydia Smith, b. 25 Aug., 1829; unm. 3. Helen Maria, b. 23 Nov., 1831; unm. 4. Henrietta, b. 14 Jan., 1834; unm. 5. Susan, b. 31 Aug., 1835; m. 1864, Edward Leech Giddings, now a member of the banking firm of Tower, Giddings & Co., of Boston. During the late war he served as captain in the 40th Mass. Volunteers for about one year. Children: (a) Charles; (b) Mabel. 6. Caroline, d. y. 7. Caroline, b. 17 Feb., 1842; unm.

ii. Sarah, b. 1 Oct., 1800, in Beverly, Mass.; m. 22 May, 1835, Francis Woodbury; she d. 1835.

210. Eunice[6] (*Bartholomew, Joseph, Lot, Lot, Roger*), b. 12 July, 1763, in Westbrook, Me.; m. 7 Jan., 1790 (by Rev. Thomas Browne), Capt. Daniel Lunt, as his second wife (his first wife was Molly Frink). He was b. in Kittery, Me., 19 Nov., 1749; son of Samuel Lunt; came to Falmouth about 1760, and settled at Duck Pond (in Westbrook), on the farm where Deering Colly now resides; owned a large amount of land on both sides of the Presumpscot river, and at Blackstrap and Duck Pond (*Hist. Westbrook*). In April, 1775, he was a member of Brackett's company of "minute men;" sergeant in same company, 10 May, 1775. In 1776, in Skillen's company of Francis' regiment; commissioned 2nd lieut., 3 Feb., 1777. Captain in Col. Tupper's regiment, 18 Mch., 1780; in Vose's regiment, 1783 (Memorials of the Mass. Society of the Cincinnati).

A wallet, once Capt. Lunt's, in which he kept a diary for many years, is now in possession of his granddaughter, Mrs. Zelia A. (Lunt) Walker. The first entry is dated May, 1778, at Valley Forge: "Sargt. Small Pr. stockings lent." He seems to have been more lucky than many of the army who passed that terrible winter of 1777-8, at Valley Forge, in having a pair of stockings to lend.

"Sep. 11 1778 on duty officer of day.

"14   No Provision this Day and that has been the case half this month.

"23 Sep. 1780   This day marched to Camp at topend.

"25   This Night at twelve o'clock the whole army was under marching orders on account of the filliny that had been carid on betwix Gen'l Arnold & the Adj't Gen. of the British army. * * * * Arnold diserted to the Enemy before he was able to carry his hellish plot into execution.

"Oct. 26   This day the army was Revued by his Excellency and the Embasador from france I left Camp Lodged in cakitat."

Then follow entries relating to his journey home, the arrival, and the building of a new house. In May, 1781, he left home to join the army again. Among the papers in possession of Mrs. Walker is an invitation to dine with Gen. Washington, as follows: "General Washington presents his Compliments to Cap. Lunt and requests the favor of his Company to Dinner tomorrow at 3 o'clock.

Thursday.   Answer if you please."

From an earlier journal it appears that in 1772 Capt. Lunt made a journey to British Guiana, and worked there as a blacksmith for a short time, but returned the same year. In 1799 he was commissioned "Captain of a Company in the Squadron of Cavalry in the Second Brigade Sixth Division of the Militia" of Mass. The roll of his company is given in full in Ray's *History of Westbrook* (Westbrook Chronicle, Feb. 1, 1884). He d. 27 Nov., 1823; his wife d. 19 Feb., 1841, aged 77.

Children of DANIEL and EUNICE (CONANT) LUNT:—

i.   Francis, b. 16 July, 1790; m. Lydia ——. He settled in Peru, Me. Children: Daniel, Robert, John, Eunice, Lydia, Lodicia and James.

ii. Mary, b. 8 Feb., 1792; d. 11 Oct., 1813; m. Wm. Kyle.
iii. George W., b. 24 Mch., 1794; d. 21 Oct., 1871. Children:
Mary A., m. Henry B. Walker, Esq., of Westbrook; Zelia
A., b. 13 May, 1825, m. Henry B. Walker (his 2nd wife), and
had Calvin S., Edward S., Henry P., Charles B. and Ernest W.
iv. Bartholomew, b. 24 Jan., 1796; d. 14 Feb., 1837. Children:
Mary, Sarah, William and George.

211. **Joseph**[6] (*Bartholomew, Joseph, Lot, Lot, Roger*), b.
3 Feb., 1767, in Westbrook, Me.; moved to Peru, Me., where
he d. 29 Feb., 1833. He was a farmer. He m. Lucinda Tufts,
who d. 1 Feb., 1857, aged 81.

Children of JOSEPH and LUCINDA (TUFTS) CONANT:—

Bartholomew, never married.
John, married and had family.
423. Daniel Lunt, b. 25 Sep., 1807.
424. Thomas, b. 30 Mch., 1809, in Topsham, Me.
Frank.
Hannah.

212. **Bartholomew**[6] (*Joseph, Joseph, Lot, Lot, Roger*),
b. in Westbrook (then Falmouth) about 1768. He d. at Point
à Pître, West Indies, 1805 or 1806. He m. Catherine Whiting, a widow, who d. about 1808.

Child of BARTHOLOMEW and CATHERINE (——) CONANT:—

425. George, b. 13 Dec., 1804.

213. **Thomas**[6] (*Joseph, Joseph, Lot, Lot, Roger*), b. in
Westbrook, about 1773; moved to Bowdoin, thence to Lisbon,
Me.; was a millwright, lumberman and farmer. He was a
corporal in the war of 1812. He d. in Lisbon, 1854. He m.
Rachael, dr. of Oliver McCaslin; she d. about 1847 or 1848.

Children of THOMAS and RACHAEL (McCASLIN) CONANT.—

426. Oliver, b. 20 Feb., 1796.
427. Lot, b. about 1798.
428. Ann, b. about 1800.
429. Lydia, b. about 1803.
430. Daniel, b. Oct., 1806.
Louisa, b. ——; d. 1856 in Topsham, Maine. She m. James
Maxwell, who d. in Lewiston, Me., 1876. Their son William E., lives in Topsham, Me.
431. Elizabeth C., b. 13 Feb., 1814.

214. Joseph[6] (*Lot, Joshua, Lot, Lot, Roger*), b. in Ip-

[signature: Joseph Conant]

(1839.)

swich, Mass., about 1780; settled in Rowley.

He m. Ruth Guildford.

Children of JOSEPH and RUTH (GUILDFORD) CONANT:—

> Samuel; m. Julia W. Morse, and had Julia. He is now (1887) living in Linebrook Parish, Ipswich.
> Dorothy.
> Joseph; m. 16 Oct., 1832, Lucy H. Foster, and had children.
> Martha.
> Joshua; m. Julia Jane Peabody.
> Alvin; d. y.
> Eunice.
> Alvin T.; m. 1848, Melinda, dr. of Daniel Proctor Pingree. He enlisted in Co. K., 40th Regt., Mass. Vols., mustered in 3 Sep., 1862; d. 16 Oct., 1863, on Folly Island, S. C. He left no children.
> Hannah.
> Eliza.
> Rosalind.
> Emeline.
> Sarah.

215. Nathaniel[6] (*Joshua, Joshua, Lot, Lot, Roger*), b. in Londonderry, N. H., 6 Oct., 1776, where he lived; was a farmer. Dec. 26, 1793, Nathaniel Conant, of Londonderry, N. H., sells land to John Dickey (Rockingham Co. Deeds, Vol. 152, p. 159). He d. 12 July, 1863, in Auburn, N. H. He m. (1) Rhoda March, who d. 1847; m. (2) —— Manning.

Children of NATHANIEL and RHODA (MARCH) CONANT:—

432. Henry, b. 17 Dec., 1797, in Londonderry.
> Sarah McAllister, b. 20 Mch., 1800; m. (int. pub. 1820,) Isaac Crowell.
> Mary, b. ——; m. (1) Warren Bancroft, of Derry, N. H.; m. (2) 5 June, 1848, —— McKinley, in Lowell, Mass.; she had several children.
> Rebecca, b. in Londonderry, N. H.; d. in Lowell, Mass.
433. William Heath, b. 29 Dec., 1807, in Londonderry.
> Samuel M., b. 29 May, 1810.
> James, b. ——; m. and had children.
> Jane, b. 19 Aug., 1819; m. and had children.
> John P., b. 4 July, 1823.

216. Joshua⁶ (*Joshua, Joshua, Lot, Lot, Roger*), b. 2 June, 1779, in Londonderry, N. H.; was a farmer. He d. 1 Feb., 1825. He m. 1800, Sybil, dr. of Robert and Polly Adams, of Londonderry; she d. 1864.

Children of JOSHUA and SYBIL (ADAMS) CONANT:—

 Abiah, (Biah), b. ———.
434. Joshua, b. 11 Mch., 1798.
435. Nathaniel, b. 11 Apr., 1802.
 John, d. aged 17.
 Polly, who m. Andrew Bryant, of New Salem, N. H., and
  had a son James.
 Joseph.
 Ephraim; unm.
436. Martha.
437. William, b. 27 Dec., 1810.
438. Enoch.
 Sally, who m. Silas Hall, of Londonderry.
 Rachael; unm.
 Eliza.

217. Elizabeth⁶ (*Daniel, Samuel, Lot, Lot, Roger*), b. in Westbrook, Me., 15 Feb., 1791; m. Jeremiah Clements; she d. 1878.

Child of JEREMIAH and ELIZABETH (CONANT) CLEMENTS:—

 Samuel, b. ———. He was a member of the well known lumber firm of Brigham, Clements & Warren. He d. 17 June, 1877.

218. Solomon⁶ (*Daniel, Samuel, Lot, Lot, Roger*), b. in Westbrook, 30 Mch., 1801. He was engaged with his brothers, Daniel and Nathaniel, in farming and lumbering operations, at Saccarappa, for many years. He d. 4 Sep., 1869.

He m. 24 Feb., 1850, Susan L., dr. of William A. and Susan S. (Small) Libby, b. 14 Oct., 1823, in Gray, Me.

Children of SOLOMON and SUSAN L. (LIBBY) CONANT:—

 Mary Ellen, b. 22 Dec., 1851; m. 19 Oct., 1873, Henry S.
  McLellan, and lives at Saccarappa village.
 Daniel, b. 9 Sep., 1856; lives on the homestead.
 Willie A., b. 3 Oct., 1861; d. 24 Dec., 1862.
 Hattie L., b. 11 July, 1863.

219. William⁶ (*William, William, Lot, Lot, Roger*), b.

11 July, 1772, in Ipswich, where he settled; was a farmer; d. Dec., 1858. He m. Ruth Foster about 1801.

Children of WILLIAM and RUTH (FOSTER) CONANT:—

439. William Foster, b. 17 July, 1802.
440. Gilbert, b. 1 Aug., 1804.
441. Daniel, b. 11 Mch., 1806.
      Elizabeth, b. 14 Mch., 1809; d. 19 Feb., 1810.
      Cyrus, b. 1812; d. 5 July, 1820.
      Harriet, b. 13 Mch., 1818; m. —— Atwood.
      Eleanor, b. ——; m. —— Emerson.
      Abigail, b. 7 June, 1825; d. 8 Jan., 1844.

220. **Daniel**[6] (*William, William, Lot, Lot, Roger*), b. 11 Jan., 1774, in Ipswich; settled in Georgetown, Mass.; d. May, 1849; m. (1) 21 Mch., 1800, Sarah Chapman; m. (2) 26 Mch., 1811, Lucy Hazen.

Children of DANIEL and SARAH (CHAPMAN) CONANT:—

      Joseph Chapman, b. 19 May, 1802.
      Sarah, b. 7 Mch., 1804.

Children of DANIEL and LUCY (HAZEN) CONANT:—

      Lucy P., b. 2 Jan., 1812.
      John Perley, b. 13 July, 1815.
      Mary, b. 16 Oct., 1816.
      Almira, b. 26 May, 1819.

221. **John**[6] (*William, William, Lot, Lot, Roger*), b. Aug., 1776, in Ipswich; was a blacksmith and farmer; settled in Topsfield. Sep. 3, 1799, Enoch Perley, of Bridgton, sells John Conant, of Topsfield, blacksmith, two lots of land in Bridgton, Me. (Cumberland Deeds, Vol. 34, p. 354). He d. 11 July, 1801; m. Dorcas Hubbard.

Children of JOHN and DORCAS (HUBBARD) CONANT:—

      Dorcas. 2 June, 1818, Dorcas Conant, of Topsfield, single woman, sells land in Bridgton, Me., to Elias Berry, of Denmark (Cumberland Deeds, Vol. 79, p. 400).
442. John.

222. **Joseph**[6] (*William, William, Lot, Lot, Roger*), b. 4 June, 1782 (1790?), in Ipswich, where he settled. The following extract is taken from the Boston Traveller of Sep. 28, 1866: "Mr. and Mrs. Joseph Conant, of Ipswich, celebrated

their golden wedding recently, at the old Conant homestead. Their children and grandchildren were present. Mr. Conant conducted a musical entertainment, playing his favorite instrument, the bass viol. He was a musical teacher of some renown, and leader of the church choir for many years." He d. in Ipswich, 14 June, 1870 (the date of his birth given on his g. s. is 7 June, 1790). He m. 24 Sep., 1816 (from his g. s.)— 5 Sep., 1816 (Family Record)—Anna Foster, who d. 13 July, 1877.

Children of JOSEPH and ANNA (FOSTER) CONANT:—

Mary Ann, b. 2 July, 1817, in Ipswich.
John Batchelder, b. 11 Aug., 1819; m. 13 Oct., 1840, Sarah Conant; he d. 25 July, 1841.
Elizabeth, b. 11 Jan., 1822; d. 13 Jan., 1822.
443. Joseph Perkins, b. 10 Mch., 1823.
George Washington, b. 18 Jan., 1826; unm.
Lydia Elizabeth, b. 12 Feb., 1828.
444. Daniel Webster, b. 23 Aug., 1831.
Elias Cornelius, b. 19 Mch., 1834.

223. William⁶ (*Moses, William, Lot, Lot, Roger*), b. 1785, in Ipswich, where he lived. He d. 4 July, 1851. He m. 1808, Elizabeth Foster, who d. 2 Oct., 1844.

Children of WILLIAM and ELIZABETH (FOSTER) CONANT:—

Calvin, b. 21 Feb., 1809; m. 29 Nov., 1836, Hannah Howe. He d. 27 July, 1843.
Elizabeth, b. 8 Mch., 1811; m. Luther Chaplin; has a dr., Caroline L., who m. Benjamin Dodge.
Ruth, b. 11 Dec., 1814.
Lois, b. 29 Nov., 1819.
Eunice, b. 10 May, 1825; m. —— Jackson.

224. Asa Wildes⁶ (*Moses, William, Lot, Lot, Roger*), b. 1788, in Ipswich, where he lived; d. 19 July, 1817. He m. 27 Dec., 1809, Margaret Soward.

Children of ASA WILDES and MARGARET (SOWARD) CONANT:—

Lois, b. 20 Oct., 1810.
Martha, b. 2 Sep., 1812.
Margaret, b. 11 Oct., 1814.
Asa Warren, b. 15 Sep., 1816; d. y.

225. Samuel⁶ (*Aaron, William, Lot, Lot, Roger*), b. 17

June, 1784, in Topsfield, Mass. When a young man he was employed in a hotel in Boston, kept by Col. Ephraim Wildes. He thence went back to Topsfield and kept a hotel and store in company with Solomon Wildes. He then moved to Lynnfield and kept a hotel on the old stage route between Boston and Portsmouth. While at Lynnfield he became financially embarrassed and moved to Topsfield, and thence to Wenham, where he worked as a shoemaker. He joined the church at Wenham, 3 July, 1842, and d. 10 July, 1861. He m. (1) 1817, Joanna Remick, of New Salem, N. H.; she d. 15 Apr., 1833. He m. (2) 18 Oct., 1834, Priscilla (Howe) Bradstreet, widow of John Bradstreet, and dr. of Joseph and Mehitable (Stickney) Howe; she was b. 11 July, 1801; living (1885).

Children of SAMUEL and JOANNA (REMICK) CONANT:—

Aaron, b. 7 Aug., 1817; a sailor; d. of small pox, 22 June, 1848, at Staten Island, N. Y.

445.   Samuel Dorman, b. 14 Aug., 1819, in Topsfield, Mass.
446.   Eunice, b. 3 Aug., 1821, in Lynnfield.
Caroline E.; d. y.
Lydia Ann; d. y.
Woodbury Page, b. 4 June, 1829; he lives at Washington, D. C.; is assistant botanist in the Department of Agriculture.
James Austin, b. 20 Feb., 1833; a sailor; was lost at sea, on the west coast of Africa, 20 Oct., 1855.

Children of SAMUEL and PRISCILLA (HOWE) CONANT:—

Caroline E., b. 24 Mch., 1836; m. 8 Apr., 1857, W. P. Kimball, of Wenham, Mass.
447.   Lydia Ann, b. 2 Dec., 1838.
Benjamin Howe, b. 22 Mch., 1840; d. 12 Aug., 1841.
Benjamin Howe, b. 11 Apr., 1843, in Wenham; never mar.; he lives in Wenham with his mother (1885). During the War of the Rebellion he served in the 2nd co. of 8th regt. of Mass. vols. He is a shoe cutter in Francis Woodbury's shoe manufactory, in Beverly; and also has been organist of the Congregational Church of Wenham, for a number of years past.

226.   Aaron[6] (*Aaron, William, Lot, Lot, Roger*), b. 13 May, 1787, in Topsfield, Mass.; was of Portsmouth, N. H., and Linebrook parish, Ipswich, Mass. He was a famous driver on the old

Aaron Conant

(1816.)

stage route from Boston to Portsmouth. After the advent of railroads he was a shoemaker. He d. in Ipswich, 12 Dec., 1880.

He m. Nov., 1815, Mehitable, dr. of Jonas and Mehitable (Gould) Merriam; b. 12 Apr., 1795; d. 18 Dec., 1878.

Children of AARON and MEHITABLE (MERRIAM) CONANT:—

> William Merriam, b. 15 Mch., 1818; a farmer; m. in Deerfield, N. H., 16 Sep., 1858, Mary Simpson; had a dr., b. 31 Jan., 1860; d. aged three weeks. He lives in Ipswich, Mass.
> 448. Nathaniel Peabody, b. 10 Nov., 1819.
> Aaron Franklin, b. 2 Oct., 1823, in Topsfield; m. in Portsmouth, N. H., Oct., 1845, Catherine Forbish. He d. 18 Nov., 1852.

227. Nathaniel[6] (*Aaron, William, Lot, Lot, Roger*), b. 5 Oct., 1795, in Topsfield; was of Topsfield and Wenham. He d. in Topsfield, 10 Mch., 1872. He m. 4 Oct., 1819, Elizabeth Kilham Dodge, b. in Gloucester, Mass., 31 Aug., 1796; d. in Beverly, 1 Mch., 1884.

Children of NATHANIEL and ELIZABETH K. (DODGE) CONANT:—

> Abraham K., b. 28 Jan., 1821; d. 7 June, 1844.
> Hannah F., b. 27 Aug., 1822; m. Charles A. Kilham, of Beverly.
> Rebecca D., b. 17 Mch., 1828.
> Elbridge F., b. 3 Dec., 1829; d. before 1884.
> Albert Austin, b. 25 Jan., 1833, in Topsfield, where he resides; has been librarian of the Town Library. He is now a member of the firm of March Bros., Pierce & Co., doing business on Summer street, Boston. He m. in Saco, Me., 22 Dec., 1859, Mary Cutts, dr. of Albert G. and Sarah Elizaabeth Lane. She was b. in Machias, Me., 20 Feb., 1836.

228. William[6] (*Aaron, William, Lot, Lot, Roger*), b. 24 July, 1801, in Topsfield. He was a stage driver on the old stage route from Boston to Newburyport; after the railroad was opened he established an express line between Boston and Newburyport. He d. 1885. He m. Deborah Dodge.

Children of WILLIAM and DEBORAH (DODGE) CONANT:—

> Caroline E., b. ———; m. Enoch M. Reed.
> William H., b. ———; d. 11 Dec., 1861.

229. Elias[6] (*David, David, William, Lot, Roger*), b. 1749

in Bridgewater, Mass., where he lived.   He served in the Revolutionary army for a short time; was in Allen's co. of Cary's
regt. (Mass. Arch., Muster Rolls, Vol. 1, p. 15).   He m. 1774,
Joanna, dr. of (73) Phinehas Conant, b. 1755.

Children of ELIAS and JOANNA (CONANT) CONANT:—

> Huldah, d. 1778.
> William, d. 1778.
449. William, b. 1780.
450. Martin, b. 26 Aug., 1787.
> And perhaps others.

230.   Solomon[6] (*David, David, William, Lot, Roger*), b.
in Bridgewater, 1756.   In Apr., 1775, he was a "minute man"
(Mass. Arch., Muster Rolls, Vol. 12, p. 191).   In Oct., 1777,
Solomon Connant was in Bangs' company, in service in Rhode
Island (Id., Vol. 1, p. 49).   The same year Solomon Conett,
21 years old, of Bridgewater, enlisted for three years (Id.,Vol.
27, p. 155).   Afterwards he was a corporal in the 4th co. of
the 2nd regt.; had served 43 months and 16 days (Continental
Army Rolls).   At the close of the war he moved to Lyme, N.
H.   He m. 1783, Lois, dr. of (133) Nathan Conant.

Children* of SOLOMON and LOIS (CONANT) CONANT :—

> Abigail.
> Nathan, d. y.
> Solomon, d. y.
> Zilpah.
> Nathan.
> Latham, was a farmer of Lyme.
> Isaac, settled in N. Y. state.
> Barzillai.

231.   Rufus[6] (*David, David, William, Lot, Roger*), b.
1757, in Bridgewater.   In 1776 he was in Mitchell's company,
Cary's regiment, of the Revolutionary army, from March till
June (Mass. Arch., Muster Rolls, Vol. 36, p. 180).   On 22 June,
1780, he was at West Point, in Allton's co. of Rand's regt.
(Id., Vol. 17, p. 10).   After the war he settled in Lyme, N. H.,
as a trader.   He m. 1783, Thankful, dr. of Nathan and Thankful (Besse) Leonard.

---

* Their names are from an old Family Record. The Town Records of Lyme were destroyed by fire, so it is impossible to give dates. The same remark applies to the three
families following.

Children of Rufus and Thankful (Leonard) Conant:—

451. Ezra, settled in N. Y. state.
      Polly.
      Nancy, m. —— Warner, of Hardwick, Vt.
      Celia.
452. George, b. 28 Apr., 1789, in Lyme, N. H.
      Julia (or India?), m. Amasa Paine, of Hardwick, Vt.
453. Rufus, b. 21 Aug., 1794, in Lyme.
      Betsey.
      John A.
454. Leonard.
      Cassandra (or Clarissa?), m. John Scott, of Lyme, and had
      John, Azel and Mary Ann.

232. David⁶ (*David, David, William, Lot, Roger*), b. 10
May, 1759, in Bridgewater, Mass. On Sep. 12, 1776, he was a
drummer in Turner's co. of Cushing's regt., in the Revolutionary army (Mass. Arch., Muster Rolls, Vol. 3, p. 201). Dec. 8
he was drummer in Kingman's co. of Mitchell's regt. (Id.,Vol.
2, p. 173). Apr. 19, 1777, he was drummer in Allen's co. (Id.,
Vol. 1, p. 29). Oct., 1777, he was a private in Snow's co. of
Howe's regt. (Id., Vol. 22, p. 189). July 22, 1780, he was private in Allen's co. of Cary's regt. (Id., Vol. 1, p. 15). After
the war he moved, with his brothers, to Lyme, N. H. He m.
1782, Lucy, dr. of Nehemiah and Sarah Besse, b. 1762.

Children of David and Lucy (Besse) Conant:—

      Sarah.
      Lucy, b, 1775; d. unm. 1 June, 1873.
455. David, b. 10 Mch., 1787.
      Huldah.
      Rhoda, m. Lewis Cook, of Lyme; had four children, among
        whom is John A. Cook, of Lyme.
      Joanna, m. Oloton Claflin, of Lyme.
      Olive, m. —— Granger, of Lyme.
      John Adams, b. ——; he returned to E. Bridgewater, where
        he kept store; he had a son and two daughters.
      Mary.

233. Josiah⁶ (*Jonathan, David, William, Lot, Roger*), b.
19 Feb., 1768, in Bridgewater; removed to Lyme, N. H., and
Orange, Vt., with his parents. He was of athletic build, about
6 feet tall, and light complexion. He was killed by a falling
tree, 9 July, 1801, in Orange. Some of the family returned to

Lyme about 1807. He m. 1788, Betsey, dr. of John and Esther Sloan; she d. 22 Sep., 1854, aged 88, at the house of her son, Jonathan, in Lyme, N. H. Her parents were the first settlers of Lyme, N. H., where they went from Palmer, Mass.; their g. s. in Lyme church-yard records that each lived to be 96 years old.

Children of JONATHAN and BETSEY (SLOAN) CONANT:—

> Lucy, b. 1789; m. a Nichols, of Barre, Vt.; she d. about 1858.
> Asenath, b. 1790; m. —— Brown, of Orange, Vt.; she d. 1857.
> Isaac, b. 1792; n. m.; was drowned in the Connecticut river, 1815.
456. Jonathan, b. 15 June, 1793.
> Jane, m. —— Raymond; they went to Malone, N. Y.; had two children; she d. 1860.
> David, d. in Strafford, Vt.; unm.
> Elizabeth, who m. a Cook, of Barre, Vt.; she was living, 1883, aged 83.

234. **Sarah**[6] (*Ebenezer, Ebenezer, Roger, Lot, Roger*), b. 17 Oct., 1770, in Ashburnham, Mass.; m. in Ashburnham, 6 Nov., 1788, by the Rev. Jona. Cushing, Jonathan, son of Isaac and Eleanor (Monroe) Merriam. He was born in Concord, 6 July, 1764; was sixth gen. from Joseph Merriam, as follows: Jonathan,[6] Isaac,[5] Isaac,[4] Thomas,[3] Joseph,[2] Joseph.[1] He was a hatter by trade. They removed to Brandon, Vt., about 1795, where he d. 26 Mch., 1825. She d. 2 May, 1839, in Springfield, N. Y.

Children of JONATHAN and SARAH (CONANT) MERRIAM:—

i. Isaac, b. 25 Oct., 1789, in Ashburnham; m. 1818, in Groton, N. H., Mary Powers. He was a Baptist minister in Maine and in the West.

ii. Jonathan, b. 5 Nov., 1791; m. in Leicester, Vt., 1824, Achsah Olin.

iii. Sarah, b. 31 Aug., 1794; m. in Brandon, 9 June, 1818, Rev. Samuel Wait. He was the first President of Wake Forest College, N. C. She d. 16 June, 1871.

iv. Lydia Conant, b. 5 Nov., 1796; m. 28 Jan., 1823, Dea. Jacob Powers, of Brandon. She d. 9 Oct., 1830.

v. Eben, b. 15 Feb., 1800; d. y.

vi. Calvin, b. 16 Sep., 1803; d. y.

vii. Abel Woods, b. 24 Dec., 1804; m. in Bridgeport, Vt., 1833, Lydia Hunt.

viii. Rollin Charles, b. 5 Oct., 1807; d. in Forestville, N. C., 9
Apr., 1837.

ix. Mylon, b. 5 July, 1811; m. in Waterville, Me., 20 Sep., 1842,
Diantha Russell. He is a minister at Providence, R. I.

235. John[6] (*Ebenezer, Ebenezer, Roger, Lot, Roger*), b. 2
Feb., 1773, in Ashburnham, Mass. The particulars of his life
have been taken from the journal already spoken of, kept by
him and his father, the *Life of A. H. Conant*, by Rober Collyer, and the Black River Gazette of July 4, 1876.

His father died when he was quite young, leaving the family
in poor circumstances; but by constant exertion he acquired a
fair education, and at the age of seventeen built a saw mill for
his mother and begun work on his own account as a journey-
man carpenter. In 1794 he determined to settle in western
New York, but while on a visit to Brandon, Vt., he saw the
falls there, and realizing the capability of the place for development, he bought on credit of Simeon King and Joseph
Hawley, "one-half of the mills and water power in the village," for the consideration of £160; the deed is dated 23
Dec., 1796. He returned home and moved his family to Brandon at once. In Brandon he found a small congregation of
Baptists, which he gathered into his house when the weather
was cold and into his shop when it was warm. "In 1800," he
says in his journal, "I myself, I say it with modesty, being the
main man, with eleven others, built a meeting-house forty feet
by thirty-five, and there we worshipped thirty-nine years."
In 1801 he was made justice of the peace, an office he held
many years; in 1806, clerk to the church; in 1809 he was representative to the state legislature, which position he filled at
various times four terms; in 1815, was appointed by government to assess the town for a direct tax; was postmaster from
1814 to 1827; and in 1841 was a member of the Electoral College which elected President Harrison. In 1818 he was chosen
deacon of his church, which office, he says, "I consider the
most honorable and responsible ever conferred on me by mor-
tal man."

His trade of a house-carpenter added to the superior mechanical talents he possessed, was of great service to him in

the important business which he established, and in superintending the erection of the valuable buildings and works of his own, erected in after years. He finally became the owner of the entire water power in the village. In 1816 he built the stone grist mill which is still standing at the head of the falls; in 1839 the brick mill below it, which at the time was one of the best structures of the kind in the state. In 1820 he erected the furnace in the village, the first blast of which was made in October. To this establishment, long known as "Conant's Furnace," Brandon is chiefly indebted for the impetus then given to its manufactures, which has resulted in its continuous growth and prosperity.

"No man's name has been more intimately associated with the town of Brandon for the last half century than John Conant's. In all public measures for the improvement of the place, or for the advancement of literary or religious objects, he took an active part, and where money was needed to carry forward such measures, or for such objects, his zeal was most prominently exhibited in his liberal contributions. In his religious character and life he maintained an unspoken fidelity to the cause which he had publicly espoused, and to the church where his vows were recorded, of which he was long an efficient member and deacon. If in earlier life, his strong denominational attachments led him to be somewhat uncharitable in his views, he became in later life, liberal in his feelings towards all evangelical christians; cordially uniting with them in meetings and measures for the advancement of the common cause. Of the Baptist denomination, however, in the state, and the church in this town, he was while he lived an acknowledged pillar."

In person he was of about the medium height, full build, with plump, muscular limbs. He spoke with a gentle smile and however much in earnest he was unimpassioned in manner and voice and deliberate in his enunciation. His remarks on public occasions were usually brief, but pertinent and sensible. In 1823 he took into partnership two of his sons, John A. and Chauncy W., under the firm name of John Conant & Sons,

John A. Conant,

by whom the business was conducted for many years, and until he withdrew from active business.

In 1843, when seventy years old, he made a journey to the West; travel was not so easy then as now, and he had an impression that he should never return alive, but that did not matter. He first visited his children at Rochester, then went to Buffalo, Cleveland, Cincinnati, St. Louis, Galena, Mineral Point, Milwaukee, Chicago, St. Joseph, Detroit, and thence home again, and says: "So mercifully was one old man of seventy preserved in all this long and dangerous journey."

He d. 30 June, 1856, in Brandon.

He m. (1) in Ashburnham, 19 Nov., 1794, Charity Waite, dr. of Waite and Esther (Breding) Broughton, who d. 12 Dec., 1851, aged 79. "She was earnest, industrious, of good judgment and unwearied perseverance, and contributed largely to the success of her own family and to the welfare of the community. Want never appealed to her in vain, nor were the suffering wont to find her hearth cold or her roof inhospitable." He m. (2) 1853, Mrs. C. Phillips Bowman, of Chicago, Ill., who was living 1876.

Children of JOHN and CHARITY WAITE (BROUGHTON) CO-NANT :—

457. Cynthia, b. 2 June, 1795, in Ashburnham, Mass.
458. Samuel Stillman, b. 26 Mch., 1797, in Brandon, Vt.
459. Chauncy Washington, b. 11 Jan., 1799.
  John Adams, b. 1 Dec., 1800. He received his education in the district schools and village academy of Brandon, and at an early age developed fine business capabilities. At sixteen years of age he was entrusted by his father with almost the sole charge of the store and village post office. In 1822 a partnership was formed under the style of John Conant & Sons; the members were John Conant and his sons, John A. and Chauncy W. The business consisted of a store, a blast furnace, a cupola furnace, with the several processes incident to the mining (for the firm were owners of a rich deposit of iron ore) and manufacture of iron and castings; besides the manufacture of lumber, of pot and pearl ashes, of brick, the mining and cleansing of manganese, agriculture upon a large scale and large transactions in real estate. The undertakings of the firm were attended with marked success—a result traceable to the activity, sagacity and just course of dealing of its members. In 1841

Mr. Conant retired from active business with the firm. He had long recognized the necessity of establishing railway communication with the seaboard, and accordingly turned his attention to securing the desired result. The difficulties were formidable—prejudice must be overcome and money secured. In 1843 a charter was procured for the construction of a railroad between Bellows' Falls and Burlington, which now forms one of the connecting links in the Central Vermont railroad. This was at that time the only enterprise of the kind seriously contemplated in Vermont. The Rutland and Burlington railroad was opened on 18 Dec., 1849, as the result of his exertions. He was the largest contributor to the capital stock of the company, taking one-sixteenth part. He was a member of the first board of Directors, and re-elected many years. In 1851 he declined the presidency of the company. In 1830 and '31 he represented Brandon in the state legislature, and during the years 1833-34 held the office of sheriff of Rutland county. He has been president of the Brandon bank since its organization. Mr. Conant is known as well for private liberality as for public spirit. "His benefactions are distinguished not more by their generosity and their judicious distribution, than by the delicacy and tact with which they are bestowed." Since his retirement from business his favorite pursuit has been agriculture; the superintending his farms, and especially the cultivation of his garden and fruit trees are the never failing amusements of his leisure. He m. (1) Caroline D. Holton; m. (2) May, 1869, Adelia A. Hammond, of Pittsford, who d. 25 Sep., 1881. No children. His portrait is from an ambrotype taken about 1855.

460. Thomas Jefferson, b. 13 Dec., 1802.
461. Sophronia, b. 14 May, 1805.
462. Caroline Cerusa, b. 8 Mch., 1807.
463. Chara Emily, b. 21 May, 1809.
      Frances Maria, b. 29 May, 1812; m. (1) Lucius Smith, of San Francisco, Cal.; m. (2) Rev. B. Brierly, of San Francisco; m. (3) E. N. Stratton, of San Francisco. She now resides, a widow, in San Jose, Cal. Her only surviving child is Conant Brierly.

236. Elizabeth[6] (*Ebenezer, Ebenezer, Roger, Lot, Roger*), b. 15 Mch., 1775, in Ashburnham, Mass.; m. in Brandon, Vt., 10 Feb., 1795, David, son of Isaac and Eleanor (Monroe) Merriam, as his second wife; b. in Concord, Mass., 28 Jan., 1760; m. (1) Phebe Foster, who d. 1794; he d. 15 Feb., 1842. He was of the seventh generation from William Merriam, as follows: William,[1] Joseph,[2] Joseph,[3] Thomas,[4] Isaac,[5] Isaac,[6]

David.[7] He went to Brandon in 1787, from Walpole, N. H.; was deacon in the church, selectman, and held other town offices.

Children of DAVID and ELIZABETH (CONANT) MERRIAM:—

i.   Betsey, b. 13 Sep., 1796; m. 1815, David Kelsey.
ii. Alvin, b. 26 May, 1802; d. 1826.
iii. Angeline E., b. 18 July, 1808; m. 1836, Leonard D. Jenney.
iv. Daniel D., b. 19 Feb., 1821; m. in Pittsford, Vt., 1842, Sarah T. Spencer.

237. Eben[6] (*Ebenezer, Ebenezer, Roger, Lot, Roger*), b. 6 June, 1777, in Ashburnham, Mass.; moved to Brandon, Vt., in 1795, with his family. In 1816 he bought of Elisha Cox the farm he lived on, in Brandon, and built a stone house, since occupied by Junia Sargent. About 1833 he moved to Geneva, Ill., where he d. 16 July, 1870. He m. (1) Rebecca Stuart; m. (2) 4 June, 1807, Fanny, dr. of Edward Clifford, of Pittsford, Vt.; she d. 26 Jan., 1848; m. (3) 17 May, 1849, Polly Olin Wright.

Children of EBEN and REBECCA (STUART) CONANT:—

Rebecca, d. y.
Sophia, d. y.

Children of EBEN and FANNY (CLIFFORD) CONANT:—

Rebecca, b. 6 Mch., 1808; m. Wm. Clay.
Fanny Amelia, b. 6 Feb., 1810; m. Harris W. Phillips, and had Charles, now a resident of Chicago, Ill.
464. Augustus Hammond, b. 16 Oct., 1811.
Calvin, b. in Sheldon, Vt.; d. in infancy.
Harriet Mercy, b. 16 Aug., 1815, in Sheldon; m. David Goodenough, and d. in Illinois, 19 Aug., 1838. They had a son, Alfonso, who lives in California.

238. Calvin[6] (*Ebenezer, Ebenezer, Roger, Lot, Roger*), b. 30 May, 1779, in Ashburnham, Mass.; went to Brandon with his mother, thence to Pittsford, Vt., in 1799. After his marriage he resided for a while with his father-in-law, afterwards built a house on the east side of the Brandon road. He was admitted to the Baptist church, 9 Nov., 1800; was clerk of the church, 1802. His house being large was occupied by the Baptist society as a place of worship for several years. In 1811 he moved to Brandon, thence to Shelburne, thence, in 1816, to Putnam, Ohio. He was an ingenious mechanic and also a skillful physician, which profession he followed for a number of years. He d. in Putnam, 26 Jan., 1829. He m. 24 May, 1801, Esther, dr. of Rev. Elisha and Phebe (Batchelder) Rich; she was b. 15 Jan., 1782, in Pittsford; d. 11 June, 1825.

Children of CALVIN and ESTHER (RICH) CONANT:—

Lydia, b. in Pittsford; d. y.
Melinda, b. in Brandon; d. y.
Betsey, b. in Brandon; d. y.
465. Charles Rich, b. 5 Dec., 1807.
466. Lorenzo, b. 22 Sep., 1812, in Sheldon, Vt.
Cyrus M., b. 22 Mch., 1817. He was for a while in the U. S. Navy. In 1848 started by vessel for California, but d. at sea only two days out from San Francisco.

239. **Luther**[6] (*Ebenezer, Ebenezer, Roger, Lot, Roger*), b. 24 Jan., 1782, in Ashburnham, Mass.; moved to Brandon, Vt., 1795, and thence to Geneva, Ill. He d. 8 Aug., 1835. He m. in Brandon, Reziner Bemis, b. 7 May, 1789; d. in Geneva, Ill., 30 June, 1867.

Children of LUTHER and REZINER (BEMIS) CONANT:—

Polly, b. 8 June, 1806.
Amanda, b. 6 Mch., 1809.
Amelia, b. 8 June, 1812; m. —— Powers.
Mary, b. 14 Sep., 1815; m. —— Enos; has Helen and Emma R., both of Lawrence, Ks.
467. William, b. 13 Mch., 1819.

240. **William**[6] (*William, Roger, Roger, Lot, Roger*), b. 2 Apr., 1762, in Charlestown, Mass.; settled in Boston; d. Sep., 1792; m. at Christ Church, Boston, by Rev. Mr. Montague, Jan., 1791, Polly Butler.

Child of WILLIAM and POLLY (BUTLER) CONANT:—

Mary Butler, b. 1792; m. 1816, David Swift. She d. 27 July, 1879. Children: 1. Mary Elizabeth; 2. William Conant, now in business at 7 Exchange Place, Boston; 3. Henry Wentworth, d. y.; 4. Henry George, d. 1847, unm.

241. **Thomas**[6] (*William, Roger, Roger, Lot, Roger*), b. 16 May, 1765, in Charlestown, Mass.; settled in Boston; m. in Boston, 27 Oct., 1791, Abigail Groin, by Rev. John Lothrop.

Child of THOMAS and ABIGAIL (GROIN) CONANT:—

Peter Groin, b. 24 Aug., 1792; his name was changed by act

of legislature to William. He m. and had several drs. and one son who was killed in the War of the Rebellion. He d. 5 Oct., 1870.

242. Samuel⁶ (*Samuel, Roger, Roger, Lot, Roger*), bapt. 16 Feb., 1755, in Charlestown; a coachmaker; claimed for loss, 1775, as S. Conant & Co. He d. before 1802. He m. 7 Mch., 1782, in Boston, Mary, dr. of Daniel and Margaret (Jarvis) Parker, by Rev. John Elliot. (For her ancestry see Bangor Hist. Magazine, pp. 126-130.)

Children of SAMUEL and MARY (PARKER) CONANT:—

Samuel, a mariner; was lost at sea, leaving a son, Samuel. In 1813, Samuel and Polly sell Abigail Tobey their right in 7½ acres of land. (See Wyman's *Genealogies and Estates of Charlestown, Mass.*)

(1802.)

468.   Polly, b. 17 July, 1785.

243. Abigail⁶ (*Samuel, Roger, Roger, Lot, Roger*), bapt. 20 June, 1762, in Charlestown, Mass.; d. 29 Jan., 1846, in New Bedford, Mass. She m. ———, William, son of Dr. Elisha and Desire (Newcomb) Tobey, b. 20 Mch., 1755, in Dartmouth (now Acushnet), Mass. He was the postmaster of New Bedford from the establishment of the office until 1806. He d. 5 Jan., 1835.

Children of WILLIAM and ABIGAIL (CONANT) TOBEY:—

i.   William C., d. 24 Sep., 1783, an infant.
ii.   Elisha C., d. 6 Aug., 1784,   "
iii. Abigail, d. 20 Aug., 1786,   "
iv.   William C., b. ———; d. in Rochester, N. Y., 4 Jan., 1847, aged 58. He was a sea captain in the merchant service. He m. (1) Eliza, dr. of Col. George Claghorn (who built the frigate Constitution). Children: 1. William Henry, b. 11 Dec., 1810, m. Lucy Worth Fuller, and had Lucy Anne, William Henry Augustus and Nathaniel; 2. Frederick Augustus, b. 24 Jan., 1813, who d. in New Bedford, unmarried; 3. Ann Eliza. b. in New Bedford, d. in Rehoboth.
v.   Samuel, b. ———; d. at sea; unmarried.
vi.   Abigail, b. 18 May, 1793; d. 22 Apr., 1879; m. 9 June, 1812, Capt. Avery Parker, son of John Avery Parker. He went

to sea soon after his marriage and was never heard from afterward.

244. Jonathan[6] (*Jonathan, Israel, Roger, Lot, Roger*), b. 14 Jan., 1767, in Ashburnham, Mass.; moved to Reading, Vt. He m. 6 Nov., 1794, Hannah Shaw.

Children of JONATHAN and HANNAH (SHAW) CONANT:—

i.   Betty, b. 13 Jan., 1795.
ii. Eunice, b. 22 June, 1796.
iii. Lewis, b. 29 Apr., 1798; d. 8 June, 1813.
iv. Filinda, b. 20 Apr., 1802.
v.   William, b. 24 May, 1809.

245. John[6] (*Israel, Israel, Roger, Lot, Roger*), b. 1 Jan., 1773, in Merrimack, N. H.; d. 27 Sep., 1824. He m. (1) Sarah Smith, of Nashua, N. H., b. 30 May, 1778, d. 16 Apr., 1812; m. (2) Sarah Kendrick, of Amherst, N. H.

Children of JOHN and SARAH (SMITH) CONANT:—

469. John Washington, b. 11 June, 1805.
      Sarah Almira, b. 10 Apr., 1807; d. 17 Aug., 1846; m. Jan., 1835, Prentice Cushing, who d. 21 Oct., 1853. Children: 1. Waldo Shepard, b. 14 Feb., 1842, d. 19 Mch., 1864; 2. Mary Sophia, b. 27 Nov., 1844, m. 10 Jan., 1865, Benjamin F. Cilley, of East Weare, N. H., and has Elden G., b. 24 Nov., 1868, and Ernest A., b. 8 Apr., 1872.
470. Benjamin Israel, b. 24 Apr., 1808.
471. Mary Joanna, b. 25 Aug., 1809.
      Caroline Jane, b. 27 Oct., 1810; d. 15 May, 1879; m. Truman Sanborn.
      Ballard Smith, b. 4 Nov., 1811; d. 2 Feb., 1812.

Children of JOHN and SARAH (KENDRICK) CONANT:—

472. Jotham Shepard, b. 18 Aug., 1816.
      Sophia, b. 29 Mch., 1818; d. 26 Mch., 1832.
      Rachael, b. 10 Aug., 1819; m. 14 Apr., 1851, George B. Dupee, of Westford, Mass. He d. 7 Sep., 1881.
473. Stephen Kendrick, b. 10 Feb., 1821; of Boston.

246. Josiah[6] (*Josiah, Josiah, Roger, Lot, Roger*), b. 5 Feb., 1770, in Hollis, N. H., where he settled; was a cabinet maker by trade; built the house now (1876) occupied by Dexter Greenwood, Esq.; was town treasurer from 1818 to 1830; d. 30 July, 1841. He m. 1 Jan., 1797, Lucy Jewett, who d. 22 Nov., 1839.

Children of Josiah and Lucy (Jewett) Conant:—

James Jewett, b. 26 May, 1797; lived in Bellows' Falls, Vt.; d. unm., 20 Oct., 1865.
474. Frederick Josiah, b. 19 Feb., 1799.
475. William, b. 1 June, 1801.
David Jewett, b. 10 May, 1803.
Lucy, b. 18 Mch., 1806; d. unm., in Hollis, 2 July, 1882.
476. Addison Lorenzo, b. 26 May, 1808.
Elizabeth, b. 5 May, 1811; d. in Milford, N. H., 2 Nov., 1884; m. 22 Nov., 1838, Moses Proctor, who d. 12 Nov., 1884. Children: 1. Clara E., b. 1842, m. Owen J. Lewis; 2. Charles M., b. 1844; 3. Frederick J., b. 1847, of Milford, N. H.
477. Clarissa, b. 1 May, 1814.
Sarah, b. 24 Mch., 1818.
Horatio Nelson, b. 6 Oct., 1820.
Ralph Jewett Cummings, b. 1 May, 1824; m. 1850, Elizabeth A. Beckwith.

247. Catherine⁶ (*Josiah, Josiah, Roger, Lot, Roger*), b. 28 Nov., 1773, in Hollis; m. 30 May, 1795, James Bradbury.

Children of James and Catherine (Conant) Bradbury:—

i. James, b. 4 Jan., 1796; m. Louisa Ayers; was of Quincy, Mass.
ii. Catherine, b. 25 Mch., 1798.
iii. William Saunders, b. 14 Feb., 1800; m. 1824, Elizabeth Emerson. He was a merchant of Westminster, Mass.; d. 1881. Children: 1. Elizabeth E.; 2. William Frothingham, b. 1829; he is head master of the Cambridge High School; is author and editor of many mathematical books used in schools; is m. and has a family; 3. Edward E., b. 1832; 4. Charles F., b. 1836; 5. Esther Caroline, b. 1839; 6. Charlotte Ann, b. 1844.
iv. Charles, b. 4 July, 1802; m. Mary Worcester; d. in Oxford, Conn., 1830.
v. Elizabeth, b. 18 Sep., 1804; m. Francis Caverly, of Morrisiana, N. Y.
vi. Samuel Fox, b. 25 Dec., 1806; m. Mary A. Leathe.
vii. Josiah Conant, b. 21 Feb., 1809; m. Almira Hemenway; is of Charlestown, Mass.
viii. Mary Ann, b. 17 May, 1811.

248. William⁶ (*Josiah, Josiah, Roger, Lot, Roger*), b. 16 Jan., 1776, in Hollis, N. H.; settled in Greensboro', Vt., while a young man; a farmer and cabinet maker; was a deacon of the Congregational Church at Greensboro' nearly fifty years. He d. 1868, aged 92. He m. about 1809, Betsey Tolman; she d. Mch., 1859.

Children of WILLIAM and BETSEY (TOLMAN) CONANT:—

Mary Elizabeth, b. 1811.
478. Ebenezer Tolman, b. 13 July, 1813.

249. Abigail[6] (*Josiah, Josiah, Roger, Lot, Roger*), b. 30 Aug., 1780, in Hollis, N. H.; m. 22 Oct., 1812, William E. Rockwood, of Wilton, N. H. He was b. 22 Mch., 1780; d. 16 Apr., 1873. She d. 13 May, 1874.

Children of WILLIAM E. and ABIGAIL (CONANT) ROCK-WOOD:—

i.   William Josiah, b. 1 Apr., 1815; unm.; of Brookline, N. H.
ii.   Elizabeth Elliot, b. 9 Jan., 1819; unm.

250. Elias[6] (*Josiah, Josiah, Roger, Lot, Roger*), b. 11 Sep., 1792, in Hollis, N. H.; lived on the old homestead; a farmer; d. 3 Feb., 1854. He m. Hannah Hazeltine, b. 19 July, 1795.

Children of ELIAS and HANNAH (HAZELTINE) CONANT:—

George, b. June, 1817; d. 13 Feb., 1838.
William Augustus, b. 18 Jan., 1819; d. 2 Feb., 1821.
Jane, b. 11 Dec., 1820.
William Henry, b. 11 Oct., 1835; he lives on the old home-stead, in Hollis. The house built by his g. g. f., Josiah, is still standing.

251. Elizabeth[6] (*Josiah, Josiah, Roger, Lot, Roger*), b. 4 July, 1800, in Hollis; m. Thomas Tarbox, of Rhinebeck, N. Y., and Salem, Mass.

Children of THOMAS and ELIZABETH (CONANT) TARBOX:—

i.   William C.
ii.   James.
iii. Eliza.

252. Abel[6] (*Abel, Josiah, Roger, Lot, Roger*), b. 1 June, 1784, in Hollis, N. H. He studied law with Col. W. Hastings, in Townsend, Mass., and in New Ipswich, N. H., with Benja-min Champney; was admitted to the bar, 1813, at Concord; practiced at Townsend and New Ipswich. In 1834 removed to Lowell, Mass., and, his health having failed, relinquished his profession. He afterwards studied chemistry and mechanics, and became a successful inventor. At an early day he invented the parlor organ and the hollow auger used by wheelwrights; also invented and patented the mortise door lock now in common use. He invented the process of raising bread with cream tartar and other acids, but the difficulty of preventing infringement deprived him of the benefit of his inventions. He invented many other improvements, and to the day of his death was engaged in perfecting several new inventions, which he expected soon to make public. His habits were simple, retired and exemplary, and his mind and memory remarkably clear to his death. He d. in Lowell, 12 Apr., 1875. He m. in New Ipswich, N. H., May, 1822, Harriet Hubbard, dr. of Professor John Hubbard, of Dartmouth College.

Children of ABEL and HARRIET (HUBBARD) CONANT:—

> John H., b. 3 Apr., 1823, in New Ipswich; d. 29 Dec., 1876. He m. 1851, Frances Ann, dr. of Peter and Hannah Crowell, b. 28 Apr., 1831, in Portsmouth, N. H. They lived in Boston. Mrs. Conant was well known as a "medium;" her biography was published in 1873.
> Harriet Maria, b. 20 May, 1825.
> Horace J., b. 17 Sep., 1827, in Pepperell, Mass.
> Sarah Isabella, b. 14 Jan., 1829.
> 479. James Edwin, b. 3 Feb., 1831.

253. **James**[6] (*Abel, Josiah, Roger, Lot, Roger*), b. 7 Apr., 1786, in Hollis, N. H.; moved to Hardwick, Vt. He d. 1875. He m. Sarah, dr. of Joseph and Mercy (Butterfield) Fletcher, of Tyngsborough, Mass., b. 14 Nov., 1788; d. 1872.

Children of JAMES and SARAH (FLETCHER) CONANT:—

> 480. James Augustus, b. 8 June, 1809.
> 481. Joseph Fletcher, b. 16 Nov., 1811.
> Sarah, b. 5 Oct., 1813.
> Rebecca Harding, b. 11 June, 1815; m. Varnum Powers, of Hardwick, and has Selwin.
> 482. Abel E., b. 20 Sep., 1817.
> Sarah A., b. 2 Sep., 1819; m. Myron Kelsey, of Nashua, N. H., and has Edward and Henry.
> Margaret Jewett, b. 5 Feb., 1823; d. 1837.
> Elizabeth Wyman, b. 25 July, 1826; m. Nathan Cummings, of Hudson, N. H., and has children, Frank H. and James.
> Cordelia Ann, b. 2 Mch., 1830; m. George S. Wells, of Hardwick, Vt., and has children, Edward D., Willis and Ernest.

254. **Farwell**[6] (*Josiah, Thomas, Roger, Lot, Roger*), b.

12 Apr., 1793, in Gardner, Mass., where he resided till 1848, when he moved to Shelburne, where he d. July, 1866.   He was a manufacturer of chairs.   He m. 1819, Lucy, dr. of Joseph and Rebecca (Nichols) Wright.

Children of FARWELL and REBECCA (WRIGHT) CONANT:—

Rebecca, b. 11 Dec., 1820.
Mary Ann, b. 13 Jan., 1823.
Calvin, b. 3 Apr., 1825.
John R., b. 25 Oct., 1829; a prominent citizen of Gardner.
Charles W., b. 16 Sep., 1833; a chair manufacturer, of Gardner; m. (1) 13 June, 1866, Hannah C., dr. of Daniel and
Abigail Proctor, of Springfield, Mass.; m. (2) 27 June, 1877,
Sarah R., dr. of Ebenezer P. and Caroline Spear, of Amherst; he has no children.
Lucy Maria, b. 3 May, 1837.

255. Samuel⁶ (*John, John, Joshua, Joshua, Roger*), b. 22 Aug., bapt. 15 Oct., 1765, in Provincetown, Mass.   He m. 6 Nov., 1789, Betsey Smith.

Children of SAMUEL and BETSEY (SMITH) CONANT:—

483.   John, b. 24 Aug., 1793.
484.   Betsey, b. 10 June, 1807.
And five others, who d. y.

256. Simeon⁶ (*John, John, Joshua, Joshua, Roger*), b. 4 June, 1780, in Provincetown, Mass., where he lived.   He was a sea captain, and afterwards kept a hotel in Provincetown. He was selectman of Provincetown for seven years, and representative to the General Court of Mass. in 1812.   He d. 26 July, 1849.   He m. (1) 22 Oct., 1802, Susanna, dr. of Phineas and Susanna Nickerson, b. in Provincetown, 31 Mch., 1780; d. 3 July, 1820; m. (2) Sarah Collins.

Children of SIMEON and SUSANNA (NICKERSON) CONANT:—

Abigail, b. 22 Aug., 1803; d. 6 July, 1834; m. Isaac Paine, and
had Abigail, who m. Silas Lumas and lives in Fernandina,
Florida.
Susanna, b. 13 Oct., 1805.
Simeon, b. 11 Jan., 1811.
485.   Sarah J., b. 29 Jan., 1819.

257. Amelia⁶ (*Eleazer, Shubael, Josiah, Exercise, Roger*), b. 26 July, 1779, in Mansfield, Conn.; moved to Middlebury,

Vt., with her parents; m. Asa Winter, and settled in Adrian, Mich., where she d. about 1862.

Children of ASA and AMELIA (CONANT) WINTER:—

i. E. Conant, settled in Oregon.
ii. William, of Adrian, Mich.

258. Horatio⁶ (*Eleazer, Shubael, Josiah, Exercise, Roger*), b. 24 Nov., 1785, in Mansfield, Conn.; moved to Middlebury, Vt., with his parents. He graduated at Middlebury College, 1810; was a tutor there two or three years, then studied medicine at the Yale Medical School, but did not graduate. His father had intended him for the ministry but he did not feel fitted for it, so settled as a physician at Maumee City (now South Toledo), Ohio. He was also a county magistrate, holding a commission as judge. He d. 9 Dec., 1879.

He m. (1) 17 Dec., 1817; Mrs. (Hull) Forsyth, she was dr. of Isaac Hull, a brother of Gen. Hull; she d. Apr., 1828. He m. (2) 3 Aug., 1832, in So. Toledo, Mrs. Emma (Vinton) Upton; she d. 7 June, 1877.

Children of HORATIO and ——— (HULL) CONANT:—

Hamilton Horatio, b. 26 Aug., 1821; he was killed, 1864, in the Union army; unmarried.
Alice, b. 23 Oct., 1823; m. Albutin Shaw, and had a son, b. 1852.

Child of HORATIO and EMMA (VINTON) CONANT:—

486. Austin Benezette, b. 7 Mch., 1838.

259. Harry⁶ (*Eleazer, Shubael, Josiah, Exercise, Roger*), b. 19 Apr., 1790, in Mansfield, Conn.; moved to Middlebury, Vt., with his parents. He graduated at Middlebury College in 1813; studied medicine and surgery with Dr. Tudor, of Middlebury, and also in New Haven, Vt., and Pittsfield, Mass. In 1816 was examined by the State Medical Censors and admitted as a member of the Medical Society of Vermont. In 1820 he removed to Michigan, and settled in Monroe, then Frenchtown, where he soon acquired a large practice in which he was very successful. In Feb., 1824, he was appointed by Gov. Lewis Cass, county commissioner for Monroe county, and in December of the same year was appointed sheriff of Monroe co. In the spring of 1826 he accompanied Gov. Cass to the

Wabash river, in Indiana, as his attending physician, at a meeting with the Indians for the purpose of signing a treaty. In July, 1826, was appointed by Gov. Woodbridge, surgeon of the 2nd Regular Territorial Militia, and soon after judge of probate for Monroe county. On Sep. 18, 1832, he united with the Presbyterian church, and was elected ruling elder the same year, an office he held until his death. Mr. Conant was a man of strong character, firm to a marked degree, yet winning friends wherever known by his sterling integrity, gentleness and intellectual culture. He d. in Monroe, 2 Sep., 1851.

He m. in Monroe, 4 June, 1821, Maria, dr. of Ambrose and Hezakia Stewart, who was b. 26 Oct., 1804, in Shaftsbury, Vt. She is still (1886) living.

Children of HARRY and MARIA (STEWART) CONANT:—

 Harriet Pierce, b. 4 Mch., 1822; d. 25 Mch., 1844; she m. in Monroe, 15 Aug., 1843, James Armitage, as his first wife.
487. Martha Ann, b. 3 Dec., 1825.
 Helen Maria, b. 9 Sep., 1828; m. 3 Nov., 1852, James Armitage, as his second wife. They reside in Monroe.
488. Sarah, b. 3 Feb., 1832.
 Emily, b. 1835; d. same year.
 Emma Frances, b. 31 Mch., 1838; d. 18 May, 1838.
 Elizabeth Johnson, b. 31 Mch., 1838; d. 15 Sep., 1841.
489. John Shubael, b. 27 May, 1841.
490. Harry Armitage, b. 5 May, 1844.

260. Caroline[6] (*Eleazer, Shubael, Josiah, Exercise, Roger*), b. 11 Jan., 1798, in Mansfield, Conn.; moved to Middlebury, Vt., with her parents, where she m. Emor Hawley. In 1820 they removed to Detroit, Mich., and thence to Kalamazoo, Mich. She d. 3 May, 1884.

Children of EMOR and CAROLINE (CONANT) HAWLEY:—

 Jane, m. (1) Mr. March, and had Susan, who m. a Stevens; m. (2) Mr. Van Der Walker, and had Kittie, who lives with her mother, in Kalamazoo.
 Sherman, dead (1886).
 Edward, " "
 George, " "
 Caroline, who resides in Aiken, S. Carolina.
 Cornelia, dead (1886).

261. David[6] (*Seth, Malachi, Caleb, Exercise, Roger*), b.

15 Mch., 1779, in Mansfield, where he lived. He m. 5 Mch., 1809, Elizabeth, dr. of Capt. James Royce.

Children of DAVID and ELIZABETH (ROYCE) CONANT:—

> David Origen, b. 22 Dec., 1809; m. Sarah, dr. of (264) Sylvanus Conant, jr.; d. 1864, childless.
>
> Harriet Elizabeth, b. in North Haven, 20 Feb., 1812; m. (1) Palmer Knowlton; m. (2) (494) Theodore Delos Conant.

262. Seth[6] (*Seth, Malachi, Caleb, Exercise, Roger*), b. 11 Oct., 1782, in Mansfield, Conn.; moved to Sullivan co., N. Y., and settled near Monticello, about 1815. He was a deacon of the Congregational church of Mansfield, and after his removal to N. Y. an elder in the Presbyterian church. He d. 19 Jan., 1840. He m. Abial Royce, who d. 1 Oct., 1851, in her 67th year.

Children of SETH and ABIAL (ROYCE) CONANT:—

> 491. Erasmus Darwin, b. 30 Aug., 1803, in Mansfield.
>
> Eunice, b. 8 July, 1805; d. 23 Aug., 1858; m. (1) Paul Jagger; m. (2) John Smith.
>
> Sophia Ann, b. 30 Nov., 1807; d. 15 Feb., 1856; m. (1) James Arkills; m. (2) —— Hoyt.
>
> Lydia Atwood, b. 15 June, 1810; m. Robert Kinne. They live in Monticello, N. Y.
>
> Catherine Ruggles, b. 6 June, 1812; d. 11 Mch., 1846; m. William Edmonds.
>
> Amanda Fidelia, b. 3 Dec., 1814; d. 2 June, 1815.
>
> Angeline, b. 9 Aug., 1816; d. 31 Dec., 1856.
>
> Seth Dill, b. 19 Dec., 1818; d. 15 Oct., 1841.
>
> Ann Eliza, b. 14 Sep., 1821; d. 20 Oct., 1851; m. —— Hall.
>
> Mary Jane, b. 17 Feb., 1826; m. Charles Green; lives in Port Jarvis, N. Y.
>
> Eleanor Elizabeth, b. 13 July, 1827; d. 1851.

263. John W.[6] (*Seth, Malachi, Caleb, Exercise, Roger*), b. 19 Dec., 1803, in Mansfield, Conn., where he lived; was a member of the Methodist church. He d. 15 June, 1854. He m. Julia, dr. of Rodney Hanks; after his death she m. (269) Lucius Conant.

Children of JOHN W. and JULIA (HANKS) CONANT:—

> Abba Philena, b. 15 Nov., 1832; d. 21 Mch., 1854.
>
> Mary, d. aged 20.
>
> David A., b. 22 Feb., 1837; m. 1866, Nellie Phillips. He was in co. D, 21st Conn. Vols., in the late Rebellion; is now of Newton Lower Falls. Mass.

Martha W., b. 24 Oct., 1838; m. 4 Dec., 1860, Samuel D. You-
mans, of Columbia, Conn.; has a son, John W.

Olive T., b. 30 Dec., 1840; m. 10 May, 1860, George W. Parker,
of Mansfield; has a family.

264. Sylvanus[6] (*Sylvanus, Malachi, Caleb, Exercise,
Roger*), b. 26 Dec., 1782, in Mansfield, Conn., where he lived;
d. 23 Apr., 1851. He m. (1) Chloe Azard, of Stafford; m. (2)
Anna Dimock.

Children of SYLVANUS and CHLOE (AZARD) CONANT:—

492. Nelson, b. 5 Sep., 1808.

Caroline, b. 7 Mch., 1810; m. Chauncy S. Harris; she d. 26
Apr., 1864.

Anna, b. 17 Dec., 1811; unm.

Sarah, b. 29 Apr., 1813; m. David O., son of (261) David Conant.

Louisa, b. 7 Mch., 1815; m. Abraham Holman. She d. 22
July, 1856.

265. James[6] (*Sylvanus, Malachi, Caleb, Exercise, Roger*),
b. 15 Feb., 1784, in Mansfield, Conn., where he lived; d. 18
July, 1862. He m. (1) 18 Feb., 1808, Sophronia Atwood; she
d. 24 Apr., 1817; m. (2) 17 Dec., 1817, Betsey Campbell, who
d. 24 Apr., 1871.

Children of JAMES and SOPHRONIA (ATWOOD) CONANT:—

Mary Sophronia, b. 28 Nov., 1809; m. 1831, Thomas Hicks, of
Pomfret, Conn.; has family; now of Bridgeport.

Clarissa, b. 8 July, 1812; m. Marcus Sessions, of Chaplin, Conn.

Origen A., b. 3 Apr., 1814; d. unm., 26 July, 1840.

Olive, b. 20 Mch., 1817; m. (1) 1839, Dwight Swift; m. (2) Alfred Hotchkiss; now of New Haven.

Children of JAMES and BETSEY (CAMPBELL) CONANT:—

George, b. 22 Mch., 1820; m. Apr. 2, 1850, Eunice Gurley. He
d. 10 Apr., 1856. No children.

493. Albert A., b. 11 Sep., 1821.

Laura, b. 28 May, 1823; m. 22 May, 1845, Lucius Hendee. She
d. 16 May, 1855. Two children.

Julia, b. 16 Nov., 1824; m. 1849, George Welton, of Watertown, Conn.; has two children.

266. Chester[6] (*Sylvanus, Malachi, Caleb, Exercise, Roger*), b. 23 May, 1790, in Mansfield, Conn., where he lived; d.
7 Aug., 1865. He m. 28 Mch., 1813, Sarah French.

Children of CHESTER and SARAH (FRENCH) CONANT:—

> Sarah Maria, b. 5 Feb., 1814; d. unm., 6 Dec., 1883.
> John Milton, b. 6 Apr., 1817.
494. Theodore Delos, b. 4 Feb., 1819.
495. Henry Washington, b. 14 Jan., 1825.
> Edwin Lysander, b. 26 Feb., 1835; m. 2 Oct., 1854, Sarah Morey. He d. 31 Oct., 1857. No children.

267.   Joseph[6] (*Sylvanus, Malachi; Caleb, Exercise, Roger*), b. 22 Mch., 1792, in Mansfield, Conn.   He engaged in the manufacture of silk thread, and was one of the pioneers of the silk industry in this country.   He lived in Mansfield on the place owned in 1864 by Roger Southworth.   He d. 10 Oct., 1870, in Northampton.   He m. (1) Zerviah Huntley, of Franklin; m. (2) Pamelia Gaylord, of Ashford; (3) Caroline E., dr. of Elisha Williams, Esq., of Willimantic.

Child of JOSEPH and ZERVIAH (HUNTLEY) CONANT:—

> Lucina Amelia, b. 30 Aug., 1814; m. O. S. Chaffee, of Mansfield, Conn., who is engaged with his sons in the manufacture of silk sewings.

268.   Edmund[6] (*Sylvanus, Malachi, Caleb, Exercise, Roger*), b. 22 Nov., 1796, in Mansfield, Conn., where he lived; m. Hannah Anderson, of Willington, Conn.

Children of EDMUND and HANNAH (ANDERSON) CONANT:—

496. Rufus Fielder, b. 27 May, 1827.
497. Julius Edmund, b. 19 Sep., 1829.
> William, b. ——; is in the silk business in Patterson, N. J.

269.   Lucius[6] (*Sylvanus, Malachi, Caleb, Exercise, Roger*), b. 29 Sep., 1799, in Mansfield, Conn., where he lived; a member of the Methodist church.   He m. (1) 6 Dec., 1821, Marietta Eaton; m. (2) Mrs. Julia (Hanks) Conant, widow of (263) John W. Conant.

Children of LUCIUS and MARIETTA (EATON) CONANT:—

498. Harriet Marilla, b. 30 June, 1823.
499. Lydia Amanda, b. 27 Feb., 1825.
> Mary Jane, b. 25 Apr., 1827; m. 19 Aug., 1848, Asa P. Squires. She d. 24 Mch., 1860, leaving Myron P., d. y., and Mary Jane.
500. John A., b. 16 Aug., 1829.
501. David Philo, b. 29 Aug., 1833.
> William L., b. ——.

502. Hiram Ellsworth, b. 13 Sep., 1839.

Juliette, b. 7 Dec., 1843; m. 30 Oct., 1865, James L. Merrick. They live in Mechanicsville, N. Y. Children: Arthur Lucius, b. 4 June, 1867; Mabel Eveline, b. 29 July, 1869.

270. Antha[6] (*Edmund, Malachi, Caleb, Exercise, Roger*), b. 9 Dec., 1789, in Hanover, N. H.; m. 11 June, 1826, Thomas Tucker, a farmer, of Vershire, Vt.

Child of THOMAS and ANTHA (CONANT) TUCKER:—

William, b. 2 June, 1827; m. 25 Nov., 1851, Mary Jane Barker, of Thetford, Vt.; has George W. and Georgianna (twins), b. 20 Feb., 1853. They live in Athol, Mass.

271. Arta[6] (*Edmund, Malachi, Caleb, Exercise, Roger*), b. 30 Mch., 1794, in Hanover, N. H.; m. 27 Dec., 1827, Benjamin, son of Richard Hazen and Ruth (Cochran) Little, who were among the first settlers of Chelsea, Vt. In 1881 he resided in Lowell, Wis.; a farmer. She d. 24 Apr., 1861.

Children of BENJAMIN and ARTA (CONANT) LITTLE:—

i. Silas, b. 31 Oct., 1828.
ii. Caroline Elizabeth, b. 24 Apr., 1833.
iii. Edmund Conant, b. 14 Nov., 1835; m. 1877, Laura, dr. of Reuben T. Lewis. A farmer, of East Hardwick, Vt.; has one son, Malachi Edwin, b. 1880.

272. Elam Lucius[6] (*Edmund, Malachi, Caleb, Exercise, Roger*), b. 14 June, 1798, in Hanover, N. H.; m. in Berlin, Vt., 24 Jan., 1826, Susanna, dr. of Increase and Deborah (Tillotson) Batchelder, of Berlin, b. 19 Aug., 1796; d. 10 June, 1855, in Peacham, Vt. He d. in Barnet, Vt., 9 July, 1878.

Children of ELAM LUCIUS and SUSANNA (BATCHELDER) CONANT:—

A daughter, b. 21 Dec., 1826; d. 22 Dec., 1826.
A son, b. 28 Jan., d. 10 Feb., 1828.
Malachi A., b. 15 Feb., 1829; d. 2 Dec., 1830.
A son, b. 14 May, 1830; d. same day.

503. Susan Asenath, b. 10 June, 1831, in East Farnham, P. Q., Canada.
504. Lucius Malachi Augustus, b. 21 Apr., 1833, in East Farnham, Canada.
505. Rovilla Philura, b. 23 Oct., 1835, in E. Farnham.

Dorinda Elizabeth, b. 16 Aug., 1840, in Hardwick, Vt.; d. 25 Jan., 1867.

273. Estes[6] (*Edmund, Malachi, Caleb, Exercise, Roger*), b. 1 Apr., 1800, in Hanover, N. H.; a shoemaker; d. 7 Apr., 1880. He m. 17 Feb., 1829, Fidelia Webb, of Barre, Vt., b. 8 July, 1800; d. 16 May, 1881.

Children of ESTES and FIDELIA (WEBB) CONANT:—

> Cynthia Asenath, b. 28 July, 1830, in Berlin, Vt.; m. 22 Jan., 1872, Edgar B., son of Reuben and Jane (Saunders) Lewis, of Morristown, Vt.
>
> Hiram Malachi, b. 8 Apr., 1832; m. 11 May, 1858, Augusta Abigail Goodrich, of Hardwick. He was a farmer, of East Hardwick, Vt.; d. 23 July, 1878.
>
> Seth Webb, b. 1 Dec., 1833; m. (1) 15 Sep., 1861, Martha Ann, dr. of Nathaniel and Roxanna Foss, of Barton, Vt.; m. (2) 29 May, 1867, Phebe Thomas, dr. of Aniel and Mary (Thomas) Albee, of Hardwick. He is a farmer, of E. Hardwick (1885).
>
> Abner G., b. 2 Nov., 1842; d. 1845.

274. **Samuel Malachi Augustus**[6] (*Edmund, Malachi, Caleb, Exercise, Roger*), b. 24 Mch., 1805, in Hanover, N. H. He was a merchant, of West Farnham, Canada; d. 6 Oct., 1863. He m. 8 Jan., 1855, Hannah Smith, of Stanbridge, Canada. She d. 16 May, 1862.

Children of SAMUEL M. A. and HANNAH (SMITH) CONANT:—

> Samuel Marshall, b. 4 Jan., 1856; of W. Farnham, Can.
>
> A child, b. 1 Jan., 1858; d. same day.

275. **Matthew Watson Marcy**[6] (*Edmund, Malachi, Caleb, Exercise, Roger*), b. 7 June, 1807, in Hanover, N. H.; was a trader; lived in Franklin, Vt., Durham, Canada, Sutton, Canada, Barre, Vt., Grafton, N. H., Royalton, Vt., and Boston, Mass. He m. (1) in Franklin, Vt., 21 Oct., 1827, Mary Tillotson Batchelder, b. in Berlin, Vt., 25 May, 1806, d. in Berlin, 14 Mch., 1834; m. (2) in Berlin, 12 May, 1836, Mary Baldwin Blanchard, b. in Orange, Vt., 29 July, 1820.

Children of MATTHEW W. M. and MARY T. (BATCHELDER) CONANT:—

> Amelia Maria, b. 13 Apr., 1828, in Franklin, Vt.; m. —— Hawley, and d. in Beloit, Wis., Oct., 1883.
>
> 506. Edmund, b. 27 Dec., 1829, in Durham, Can.
>
> A daughter, b. 25 Mch., d. 9 Apr., 1832, in Brown, Can.
>
> Estes, b. 8 Mch., 1833, in Sutton, Can.; never m.; lives in Chelsea, Vt.

Children of MATTHEW W. M. and MARY B. (BLANCHARD) CONANT:—

507.   Joseph Jacobs, b. 4 Apr., 1837, in Barre, Vt.
       Sarah Stacy, b. 22 Dec., 1838, in Grafton, N. H.
508.   Henry Harrison, b. 11 Nov., 1840, in Grafton, N. H.
509.   George Washington Smith, b. 31 Jan., 1843, in Royalton, Vt.
       Mary Matilda, b. 10 Oct., 1844, in Boston, Mass.; d. 20 Feb.,
          1845.

276. Gideon[6] (*Nathaniel, Malachi, Caleb, Exercise, Roger*), b. in Mansfield, Conn.; was a hat maker; settled in Amsterdam, N. Y.; d. in Schenectady, N. Y., Apr., 1848. He m. in Saugatuck, Conn., Elizabeth, dr. of John and Polly (Buckley) Burr, b. in Green's Farms, Conn.

Children of GIDEON and ELIZABETH (BURR) CONANT:—

       Mary.
510.   William B., b. 14 July, 1816.
       Nathaniel, d. from scalds received on the steamer Swallow,
          on North river, 1841.
       Eliza.
       Henrietta.
       Henry.

277. Timothy[6] (*Caleb, Benajah, Caleb, Exercise, Roger*), b. 19 Apr., 1772, in Mansfield, Conn.; moved to German Flats, N. Y., with his parents, about 1801. He settled in Warren, Herkimer co.; was a carpenter. He d. 15 Mch., 1858, in Chesterville, Monroe co., Ohio. He m. ——, Rhoda Lyons, b. 18 June, 1769; d. in Hinckley, O., 29 June, 1845. Her maternal grandfather was Samuel Marshall, a famous preacher.

Children of TIMOTHY and RHODA (LYONS) CONANT:—

511.   Daniel Marshall, b. 19 Feb., 1796.
       Chester; said to have settled in Michigan, and to have had
          several children; two of his sons served in Union army
          during the war.
512.   Timothy B., b. 22 Sep., 1798, in Warren, N. Y.
513.   Aaron.
       And three daughters.

278. William[6] (*Jonathan, Benajah, Caleb, Exercise, Roger*), b. 25 Aug., 1787, in Lebanon, N. H., and moved to Chelsea, Vt., with his parents. He settled in Laporte, Ind., where he d. 23 Jan., 1855. He m. in Ohio, 18 July, 1822, Rebecca Blue.

Children of WILLIAM and REBECCA (BLUE) CONANT :—

Irene Bennett, b. 19 Sep., 1824.
John, } b. 23 Sep., 1825; d. same day.
Jonathan, }
Warren Scuyler, b. 12 May, 1827.
Sarah, b. 28 Jan., 1829; d. 31 July, 1829.
Alban Slaughter, b. 5 May, 1830.
Cyrus William, b. 14 Mch., 1832; d. 22 Oct., 1833.
Louisa, b. 2 Mch., 1834.
Mary Ann, b. 10 Nov., 1836; d. 2 Aug., 1838.
Edwin Ruthven, b. 24 Oct., 1840; now of Grand Island, Neb.
Maria Josephine, b. 22 Nov., 1845.
Henry Thaddeus, b. 22 Nov., 1845.

279. Samuel Williams[6] (*Jonathan, Benajah, Caleb, Exercise, Roger*), b. 28 May, 1789, in Lebanon, N. H. He was a printer and afterwards a watch-maker. He settled in Boston, Mass., where he remained till 1830, when he removed to Baltimore, Md. On June 26, 1826, his given name was changed, by act of the Mass. legislature, from Samuel to Samuel Williams (*List of Persons whose names have been changed in Massachusetts*, 1780-1883, *p.* 52). He d. in Baltimore, 2 Jan., 1870. He m. in Boston, 24 Mch., 1816, Sally Tyng, dr. of Samuel and Abigail (Orcutt) Winslow, who d. in Baltimore, 1 Apr., 1884.

Children of SAMUEL W. and SARAH T. (WINSLOW) CONANT :—

William Bennett, b. 31 Jan., 1817; d. 7 Feb., 1817.
Albert Williams, b. 14 Apr., 1818; d. 29 May, 1821.
514. Sarah Ann Willis, b. 2 Sep., 1819.
515. Catherine Mary, b. 22 Dec., 1823.
Henry Albert Bird, b. 18 Jan., 1825; d. 12 July, 1825.
516. Samuel Williams, b. 12 Sep., 1832.
Charles Harker, b. 5 Nov., 1834; d. 19 Oct., 1835.
Anna Louisa, b. 17 Nov., 1837; m. 31 July, 1857, Samuel T.
Ball. Child: Charles Edwin Bennett, b. 26 Apr., 1858; d. 13 June, 1858.

280. Caleb[6] (*Jonathan, Benajah, Caleb, Exercise, Roger*), b. 18 Apr., 1791, in Plainfield, N. H. "At the age of six years he went to live with Capt. John Wood—to remain until he was twenty-one. At about the age of nineteen, however, he left the captain's roof, and went to Chelsea, Vt., where he worked at his trade, as a carpenter. While here he built a house and was soon married to Sally Barnes. In 1840 his two oldest children located in North Lawrence, St. Lawrence co., N. Y., and two years later their father and mother followed them, the latter dying at North Lawrence in Nov., 1849. For many years grandfather continued to live with his eldest son, both at No. Lawrence and at Grand Rapids, whither the latter removed in 1857. The later years of his life were spent with his second son, Alban Jasper, at St. Louis, Mo., and Upper Alton, Ill., where he d. 16 Apr., 1877." (See *Genealogy of the Conants*, compiled by Will F. Conant, Detroit, Mich., 1880.)

He m. in Chelsea, Vt., 10 Sep., 1817, Sarah Barnes; she d. in North Lawrence, N. Y., 17 Nov., 1850.

Children of CALEB and SARAH (BARNES) CONANT :—

517. John Harvey, b. 2 Oct., 1818.
518. Alban Jasper, b. 24 Sep., 1821.
      Emily Mary, b. 1 July, 1823, in Chelsea, Vt. She is living, unm., in Upper Alton, Ill.
      Louisa, b. 3 Mch., 1826; d. 25 May, 1826.
519. Henry Albert, b. 7 Aug., 1828.

281. Sarah[6] (*Jonathan, Benajah, Caleb, Exercise, Roger*), b. 6 Mch., 1794, in Chelsea, Vt.; m. (1) 19 Dec., 1815, Daniel Barnes, who d. 6 Mch., 1838. She m. (2) 18 Feb., 1846, Noah Rowe, who d. Oct., 1846. She d. about 1875, in Dover, N. H.

Children of DANIEL and SARAH (CONANT) BARNES :—

i.   Aaron Howe, b. 12 Nov., 1816.
ii.   John Harvey, b. 31 Mch., 1818; d. 2 May, 1818.
iii.   Jonathan Edwards, b. 27 June, 1820; d. 1 Sep., 1834.
iv.   Albert Williams, b. 15 Sep., 1822; d. 18 Sep., 1822.
v.   A son, b. 22 Nov., 1823; d. y.
vi.   Laura J., b. 20 Nov., 1825.
vii.   A son, b. 27 Mch., 1827; d. y.
viii. Ellen M., b. 29 Nov., 1828.
ix.   A son, b. 1829; d. y.
x.   A daughter, b. 1 Dec., 1832; d. y.

SEVENTH GENERATION.

282. Caleb[7] (*Nathan, Thomas, Nathaniel, Nathaniel, Lot, Roger*), b. 26 Jan., 1762, in Bridgewater, Mass. Caleb Conant, of Bridgewater, was in Capt. Jacobs' company, in the Revolutionary army, from Jan. 1, 1778, to Jan. 1, 1779 (Mass. Arch., Muster Rolls, Vol. 1, p. 147) ; and in Allen's company of Cary's regiment 1780 (Id., Vol. 1, p. 15). Feb. 26, 1785, Caleb Conant, of Bridgewater, sells two lots of land in Bridgewater, containing 21½ acres, to Ezra Conant; Hannah, wife of Nathan, relinquishes dower (Plymouth Deeds, Vol. 65, p. 195).

Sep. 5, 1787, Caleb Conant, of Bridgewater, sells 11 acres of land in South Bridgewater, to Ezra Conant. Hannah, mother of Caleb, relinquishes her right of dower. Witnessed by Theodore Perkins and Zenas Conant (Plymouth Deeds, Vol. 71, p. 232). He m. 1789, Olive Thrasher, and moved westward (Mitchell's *Hist. of Bridgewater*).

Children of CALEB and OLIVE (THRASHER) CONANT :—

> Lucy.
> Hannah.
> Nathan.
> Betsey.

283. Oliver[7] (*Zenas, Thomas, Nathaniel, Nathaniel, Lot, Roger*), b. about 1776, in Bridgewater, Mass. He m. 1796, Polly, dr. of Calvin and Rhoda (Hammond) Washburn.

Children of OLIVER and POLLY (WASHBURN) CONANT :—

i.   Oliver.
ii.   Dolly.
iii. Rhoda.
iv.   Nancy.

284. Betty[7] (*Zenas, Thomas, Nathaniel, Nathaniel, Lot, Roger*), b. 1779, in Bridgewater, Mass.; m. 1798, Levi, son of Giles and Deborah (Jackson) Leach, g. s. of John and Betsey (Eddy) Leach. She d. 29 Sep., 1849.

Children of LEVI and BETTY (CONANT) LEACH :—

i.   Deborah Jackson, b. 26 Jan., 1799; m. (319) Liba Conant.
ii.   Giles, b. 1 Apr., 1801; prepared for college at Bridgewater Academy; grad. Amherst, 1829; studied at Andover, 1829-32; ordained at Sandwich, N. H., 5 Feb., 1833, where he

preached many years; afterwards pastor at Wells and Rye, Me., and Meredith Village, N. H.; was a member of the State Board of Education three years. He d. 1885. Children; 1. Elizabeth Hervey, b. 1834; m. John Henry Sanborn, of Sanbornton, N. H.; now of Franklin Falls, N. H.; he served in the 12th N. H. regt. as an engineer; 2. Lucy; 3. Ernera Giles, b. 1847; m. Chester W. Eaton, Esq., a lawyer and editor of the "Wakefield Times;" 4. Clara Amelia; m. F. D. Miller.

iii.   Anna, b. 1807; m. 1832, Hiram Wentworth, of Bridgewater, Mass. She d. 22 Sep., 1865.

iv.   Clarinda, b. 1810.

v.   Betsey, b. 1812; m. Simeon Pratt, of Middleboro'.

vi.   Sarah, b. 1816; m. 1863, James Sullivan Alden.

vii.   Levi, b. 1 Oct., 1818; m. 1845, Catherine, dr. of Dr. John Sanborn. He is of Meredith Village, N. H.; served during the late war; was at the battles of Fredericksburg, Chancellorsville and Gettysburg; discharged on account of wounds received in the last battle. Children: 1. Willis S., b. 1847; enlisted in same company as his father; d. at Falmouth, Va., 1863; 2. Edward G., b. 1849; graduated at Dartmouth, 1871; admitted to the Bar, 1874.

viii.   George Myron, b. 28 Apr., 1821; m. 1844, Betsey Edson; d. 1877, in Middleboro', Mass. Children: 1. George M., b. 1845; 2. Giles, b. 1849; 3. Anna E., b. 1857; 4. Sadie, b. 1866.

285.   Sarah[7] (*Zenas, Thomas, Nathaniel, Nathaniel, Lot, Roger*), b. about 1781, in Bridgewater, Mass.; m. 1805, Dr. Ephraim, son of Ichabod and Penelope (Standish) Leach. Penelope Standish was widow of Nathaniel Cobb, jr., and g. g. g. d. of Miles Standish. Dr. Ephraim Leach moved from Bridgewater to Eaton, N. Y., in 1820, and d. there 3 July, 1873.

Children of EPHRAIM and SARAH (CONANT) LEACH:—

i.   Ichabod Conant, b. 13 Oct., 1805; d. 6 Oct., 1878. He m. 22 Sep., 1834, Clarissa Harlow Shirley, of Bedford, N. H., and had a family. A son is the possessor of a dress sword which Capt. Miles Standish brought over in the Mayflower, and also one of his sleeve buttons. The sword passed from Capt. Miles[1] to Alexander,[2] to Miles,[3] to Miles,[4] to Peneelope[5] (Standish) (Cobb) Leach, to Dr. Ephraim,[6] and from him to his oldest son, Ichabod Conant Leach. The sword was intact until within twenty years, when the handle was destroyed by the burning of a house.

ii.   Penelope Standish, b. 18 Aug., 1808; m. 6 Apr., 1831, Bradshaw White, a farmer and merchant of Morrisville, N. Y. Four of their sons served in the Union army: Francis Lewis, enlisted 1862, lost an arm in battle 1864; Henry

Franklin, enlisted 1862, wounded at Antietam; William Conant, enlisted 1861, served up to Gettysburg, was taken ill after the battle and d. 17 Sep., 1863; Joseph Bradshaw, enlisted 1861, at the first call, was wounded at Bull Run.

iii. Matilda Brackett, b. 27 Sep., 1811; d. 13 Feb., 1850; m. 20 Apr., 1841, Lewis Wentworth, of Bridgewater.

iv. William H., b. 19 Jan., 1814; d. in Eaton, N. Y., 30 Oct., 1861; m. 1836, Emily Graham.

v. Isaac B., b. 19 Sep., 1816.

vi. Zenas Conant, b. 2 July, 1818; m. 1848, Caroline Niles. A farmer, of Eaton, N. Y.

vii. John H., b. 2 Mch., 1821; m. 18 Jan., 1845, Catherine Hickey. He is a merchant, of Troupsburg, N. Y.

viii. Ephraim, b. 23 Nov., 1823; m. 8 Nov., 1860, Margaret Hendricks. A farmer, of Troupsburg.

ix. Cordelia, b. 24 Apr., 1826; m. 20 Apr., 1841, Lewis Wentworth, as his second wife.

x. Lewis, b. 21 Jan., 1830; m. 25 Apr., 1854, Mary Bennett.

286. Gaius[7] (*Ezra, Thomas, Nathaniel, Nathaniel, Lot, Roger*), b. 6 Sep., 1776, in Bridgewater. He graduated at Brown University, 1800, and was ordained at Paxton, Mass., 17 Feb., 1808, where he remained for twenty-two years. On 24 Apr., 1834, he was settled over the Second Congregational Church of Plymouth, where he remained seven years; he was succeeded there by John Dwight. He d. 6 Feb., 1862. He m. (1) Cassandra, dr. of Zachariah and Abigail (Kilbourn) Whitman; pub. 4 Dec., 1802; she d. 8 Mch., 1813. He m. (2) the widow Chloe (Allen) Leonard, dr. of Jesse Allen and widow of Jonas Leonard; pub. 2 Oct., 1813; she d. 4 Dec., 1857.

Children of GAIUS and CASSANDRA (WHITMAN) CONANT:—

520. Cyrus Whitman, b. 27 Nov., 1803.
521. Ezra Styles, b. 9 Nov., 1805.
522. Benjamin Kilbourn, b. 20 Nov., 1807.
523. Mary Angelina, b. 24 Nov., 1809.
     Cassandra Whitman, b. 1812.

Children of GAIUS and CHLOE (ALLEN) CONANT:—

James Allen, b. ——; d. in Worcester.
524. William, b. 11 June, 1816.

287. Thomas[7] (*Ezra, Thomas, Nathaniel, Nathaniel, Lot, Roger*), b. 5 Oct., 1785, in Bridgewater, Mass. In 1860, at the request of the pastors of the Old Colony Baptist Association, he wrote an autobiography, which was published the next year at Boston, by A. T. Graves, from which the following particulars of his life have been gathered. He says:

"I am the seventh generation of *Rogers** Conant, who came to America from England, 1623, and who had in charge, from a company of merchants in London, a colonization establishment at Cape Ann. * * * For *Rogers* Conant was considered Governor of that Company. He was one of twelve brothers,† six of whom, being Protestants, fled into England, from France, at the revocation of the Edict of Nantes, leaving behind six other brothers who were Papists."

He fitted for college at Rochester and Bridgewater academies, and was urged by his brother, Gaius, who had graduated from Brown, to attend that university, and by his father to settle on a farm near his own. He decided, however, to learn the carpenter's trade, which he did, and worked in Boston and Roxbury until he was about twenty-one years of age, when he settled in Bridgewater. He was fond of balls and parties, and had arranged to attend a dance one evening when, he says, " I was seated at the table alone, and no other person in the house except my mother, I was for the first time in my life thoroughly convinced that there was no solid enjoyment in parties of pleasure, or in vain and sinful amusements, whatever; but I now had the conviction that there was something in religion of which I was ignorant, and which alone could furnish true peace of mind." The result was that he spent the night in prayer, and became converted. All his relatives were Congregationalists, but after consideration he determined that immersion was the only proper mode of baptism. He accordingly joined the First Baptist Church of Middleboro', in Oct., 1806, and was baptised by Rev. Isaac Sawyer. During the next three winters he taught school in Sandwich, and lost no opportunity of conversing on religious subjects.

In 1808, he determined to preach, and placed himself under the instruction of his brother (Rev. Gaius Conant), in Paxton, where he remained till July, 1809, when he received

---

* Evidently Mr. Conant did not take the trouble to consult the accounts of the family then in print.

† (The story of the twelve brothers exists in other branches of the family. I am able only to trace it back to (235) John. Its absurdity is apparent. F. O. C.)

from the church in Middleboro' a license to preach. He went then to Barnstable, and finding it difficult to find a place to preach, on account of the prejudice against Baptists, went from door to door, conversing with every one who would listen.

From Barnstable he went to Yarmouth, to Nantucket, to Edgartown; here he says, "I was seized by a mob, while I was preaching, and dragged out of the hall backwards, down the stairs, and out of doors. I continued talking, however, all the time." He then went to Tisbury, then back to Edgartown and Falmouth. As he was entirely dependant on voluntary contributions for his support, he taught school in winters and in 1810-11, taught in Duxbury. While there he walked to Plymouth every Saturday afternoon and held services for a small congregation of Baptists. After leaving Duxbury he preached in Marshfield for about six months, and then for a while in Bellingham. During the winter of 1811-12, he taught school in South Scituate, and preached in Marshfield. In 1812 a Baptist church was organized in Pembroke, and Mr. Conant was ordained as an evangelist, 12 May, 1812. For the next sixteen years he preached three-fourths of the time in Marshfield—with the exception of about two years during the war with Great Britain, when he preached in Westboro' and Shrewsbury—and the other fourth in New Bedford, Scituate, Plymouth, Duxbury, Hingham or So. Abington. In 1828 he was engaged as city missionary in Boston. In 1829 he received a call from the Baptist church in Plymouth, which he accepted, and remained there five years. In 1835 he settled in Brewster, where he remained until 1839, then went to Chatham for a while, then to Hanover. In 1843 he accepted an invitation to take the pastoral charge of the Baptist church in Scituate, where he remained ten years. At the close of his pastorate in Scituate, owing to ill health in his family and his own advanced age, he declined any regular charge, but continued to supply vacant pulpits wherever he felt he was most needed. In 1860, then seventy-five years of age, he preached every Sunday when pleasant in a hall near Beach woods, Scituate, and taught a Sunday school and Bible class. "The Lord employed him in founding the Baptist churches in Bell-

ingham, Westboro', New Bedford, Abington and Hanover;
and in enlarging the churches in Plymouth, Marshfield and
Brewster. He was also among the first who preached evangelical doctrine in Edgartown, Hingham, Cohasset, Duxbury and
North Marshfield" (*Watchman and Reflector*).

He m. 26 Mch., 1812, Annie Leonard, sister of Rev. Lewis
Leonard, D. D., of Cazenovia, N. Y.

Children of THOMAS and ANNIE (LEONARD) CONANT:—

> Thomas Baldwin. He d. in Brewster, Dec., 1835, aged 23
> years, of consumption, having nearly completed his profes-
> sional studies as a physician.
> Annie Leonard.

288. Andrew[7] (*Nathaniel, Jeremiah, Nathaniel, Nathaniel, Lot, Roger*),
b. 25 Mch., 1774,
in Bridgewater,
where he lived.

(1812.)

He m. 1795, Kezia, dr. of Benjamin and Mary Washburn.

Children of ANDREW and KEZIA (WASHBURN) CONANT:—

> Jeremiah, b. 28 Jan., 1796.
> Olive, b. 10 Aug., 1801.
> Thomas Jefferson, b. 21 Mch., 1806.
> Andrew, b. 26 Nov., 1808.

289. Robert[7] (*Daniel, Jeremiah, Nathaniel, Nathaniel,
Lot, Roger*), b. 24 June, 1768. He settled in Fowler, St.
Lawrence co., N. Y., where he d.; was a farmer. He m. in
West Windsor, Conn., Rhoda, dr. of John Thrall; she d. in
Fowler.

Children of ROBERT and RHODA (THRALL) CONANT:—

> Rhoda.
> Robert.
> 525. Chauncy, b. 24 May, 1800, in Fairfield, N. Y.
> Patty.
> Polly.
> Erastus.
> Anna J.
> Truman E.

290. Daniel[7] (*Daniel, Jeremiah, Nathaniel, Nathaniel,
Lot, Roger*), b. about 1773; place unknown; settled in N. Y.

state, near Rochester. (Information given by his nephew, (526) Jeremiah.)

Children of DANIEL and ——— (———) CONANT:—

Benedict.
Jason.
Jemima.

291. Cornelius[7] (*Daniel, Jeremiah, Nathaniel, Nathaniel, Lot, Roger*), b. about 1776; settled near Rochester, N. Y. His descendants are said to be living there still.

Children of CORNELIUS and ——— (———) CONANT:—

Alvah.
Alonzo.
Arvilla.

292. Jeremiah[7] (*Daniel, Jeremiah, Nathaniel, Nathaniel, Lot, Roger*), b. in N. Y. state, probably, about 1780. He moved West, and settled in Athens co., Ohio, about 1822. He was a soldier in War of 1812 (information given by his son). He m. in N. Y. state, Abigail, dr. of Daniel Muncy; she d. in Carl co., Ind.

Children of JEREMIAH and ABIGAIL (MUNCY) CONANT:—

Abigail, b. in Herkimer co., N. Y.
Joanna, b. in Herkimer co., N. Y.
526. Jeremiah, b. in Herkimer co., N. Y.
Daniel, b. in Genesee co., N. Y.; went, it is said, to Mississippi, and d. there.
Horatio, b. in Ontario co., N. Y.
Herman, b. in Ontario co., N. Y.; m. in Ohio, and had family.
Lewis, b. in Ontario co., N. Y.; d. aged 24, unm.
John, b. in Athens co., Ohio; d. unm.
Henry, b. in Athens co., Ohio; d. unm.
Charlotte, b. in Athens co., Ohio.
Cornelius, b. ———; d. 1840, unm.

293. Abel[7] (*Roger, Jeremiah, Nathaniel, Nathaniel, Lot, Roger*), b. about 1773, in Massachusetts, perhaps in Easton; moved to N. Y. state and then to Canada, with his parents. He was a farmer; had a large tract of land in

Darlington and Scarborough. He removed to Pickering, where he d. 17 Jan., 1844. During the War of 1812 his sympathies were with the Americans, and for not turning out with the militia he was imprisoned.

He m. 1799, in Darlington, Canada, Mary, dr. of Daniel and Sarah (Burke) Lightheart, who was born in Sorrel, Canada, 1781. He m. a second wife and had four sons and four daughters, names unknown.

Children of ABEL and MARY (LIGHTHEART) CONANT:—

> David, b. Apr., 1801, in Darlington; m. Lucy Devons. He was sheriff of Toronto, Can., 1841-7; d. 1847, leaving two sons and two daughters.
> Barnabas, b. 1803; m. Electa Wood; left four sons and two daughters.
> 527. Roger, b. 15 Oct., 1805.
> Abel, b. 1808, in Darlington, Canada; d. 1847; m. Fanny Burgess, and had Fanny and Abel.
> Betsey, b. 10 Feb., 1810.

294. Eliphalet[7] (*Roger, Jeremiah, Nathaniel, Nathaniel, Lot, Roger*), b. about 1774, in Massachusetts; moved to New York and Canada, with his father; settled in Darlington, Canada. He d. 1818. He m. Susan Trull.

Children of ELIPHALET and SUSAN (TRULL) CONANT:—

> Eunice.
> Zubia, m. James Snyder, of Darlington.
> Davis, m. and went to Rochester, Mich.
> And perhaps others.

295. Jeremiah[7] (*Roger, Jeremiah, Nathaniel, Nathaniel, Lot, Roger*), b. about 1778; moved to Canada, with his parents, and thence to Michigan, where he d. about 1864. He m. Laney Van de Carr.

Children of JEREMIAH and LANEY (VAN DE CARR) CONANT:—

> Charles, said to have left a large family.
> Sally, m. Wm. Wilson.

296. Polly[7] (*Roger, Jeremiah, Nathaniel, Nathaniel, Lot, Roger*), b. in N. Y. state, about 1780; moved to Darlington, Canada, with her parents; m. John Pickel, as his second wife.

Children of JOHN and POLLY (CONANT) PICKEL:—

i.   John, now living in Oshawa, Canada.
ii.   George.
iii. Wilmot.

297. **Rhoda**[7] (*Roger, Jeremiah, Nathaniel, Nathaniel, Lot, Roger*), b. about 1784, near Saratoga, N. Y.; moved to Canada with her parents; m. Levi Annis (probably a son of Charles and Elizabeth Annis. Charles Annis was a soldier in the Revolutionary army, from Windham, N. H.; was at one time of Methuen, Mass.; he went to Canada).

Children of LEVI and RHODA (CONANT) ANNIS:—

i.   Charles, m. Nancy Nichols and settled in Michigan; had 1. George, a Baptist minister; 2. Ezra, a physician; 3. Hiram, of Grand Centre, Mich., and others.
ii.   David.
iii. Roger.
iv. Matthew.
v.   Andrew.
vi. Jeremiah.
vii. William.
viii. Levi.
ix. Polly, m. Washington Peck.
x.   Sally, m. Wm. Skelton.
xi. Betsey.

298. **Thomas**[7] (*Roger, Jeremiah, Nathaniel, Nathaniel, Lot, Roger*), b. about 1787, near Saratoga, N. Y., or perhaps in Darlington, Canada. He appears to have succeeded to the larger part of the large landed estate left by his father. He was killed 1833, by one of McGraw's dragoons. He m. (1) 3 Mch., 1807, in Darlington, Hannah Stoner; m. (2) Ann Pickel.

Child of THOMAS and ANN (PICKEL) CONANT:—

528. Daniel, b. 4 July, 1818, in Darlington, Can.

299. **Marlborough**[7] (*John, John, Nathaniel, Nathaniel, Lot, Roger*), b. 14 Oct., 1775, in Bridgewater, Mass.; a carpenter; removed to Thomaston, Maine, about 1795; d. 21 Nov., 1822. He m. (1) Mary Dunbar, who d. 1796; m. (2) Petronella Fales, who d. 16 Aug., 1816; m. (3) Mrs. Catherine Keene, 9 Aug., 1821.

Children of MARLBOROUGH and PETRONELLA (FALES) CO-
NANT:—

Emily, b. 30 Mch., 1800; m. W. S. Kimball; rem. to Illinois.
Camilla, b. 30 Mch., 1800; m. (1) —— Hall; m. (2) Edward
   Newlert, and removed to Belfast, Me.
John P., b. 6 Oct., 1801; d. 1 Oct., 1802.

529. David Fales, b. 3 Oct., 1802, in Thomaston, the part now
     Rockland.

Mary, b. 31 Dec., 1803; d. y.
Anna, b. 31 Dec., 1803; m. Nath'l Meservy.
Olivia, b. 16 Mch., 1806; m. Nelson Spear, of Rockland.
Juliette, b. 6 Dec., 1807; m. Samuel Hall, of So. Thomaston.
Oliver, b. 20 Sep., 1809; d. 27 Oct., 1817.
Lucy, b. 11 Jan., 1812; d. 20 Aug., 1820.
Melinda T., b. 1 Apr., 1814; m. James May.
Sarah J., b. 18 Apr., 1816; d. 13 Aug., 1816.

300. **Martin**[7] (*John, John, Nathaniel, Nathaniel, Lot,
Roger*), b. 1777, in Bridgewater, Mass.; a nail maker and
blacksmith. He was one of the first settlers of Canton, Me.;
d. 10 May, 1854. He m. (1) 1797, Olive, dr. of Ebenezer and
Silence (Packard) Benson, of Bridgewater, who d. June, 1835;
m. (2) in Canton Point, Me., Sarah K., dr. of Daniel and Mary
(Knowles) Foster, b. 13 Jan., 1814, in Dixfield, Me.

Children of MARTIN and OLIVE (BENSON) CONANT:—

Otis.
Susan, b. 12 Mch., 1800; m. Aaron Stevens, of Canton.
Irene, m. Thomas Paine, of Jay, Me.
Apollos, of Jay, Me.; d. 1883, in Dixfield, Me., leaving a dr.,
   Flora E., who m. —— Axtell.

530. Ebenezer Benson, b. 16 Oct., 1811, in Bridgewater, Mass.
531. John Martin, b. 9 Nov., 1815, in Canton, Me.

Albert, m. Clarinda T., dr. of Oliver J. Paine; she was b. 19
   Jan., 1837. He d. about 1880.

Children of MARTIN and SARAH K. (FOSTER) CONANT:—

Mary L., b. 7 Oct., 1839;. m. —— Foster.
Anna L., b. 4 Nov., 1843; m. in Portland, Me., 18 Oct., 1869,
   Abiel H. Edwards; she is a widow, living in Strong, Me.
   (1885).
S. Evelyn, b. 7 June, 1846; m. —— Fuller.

301. **Seth**[7] (*John, John, Nathaniel, Nathaniel, Lot, Roger*), b. about 1779, in Bridgewater, Mass., where he lived. He
m. 1801, Hannah, dr. of Nathaniel and Betty (Washburn)
Pratt, of Bridgewater.

Children of SETH and HANNAH (PRATT) CONANT:—

> Enoch, b. 6 Mch., 1803; d. 12 Aug., 1822.
> Hannah, b. 7 Apr., 1805.
> Hephzibah, b. 16 Oct., 1808.
> Alvin, b. 1812; d. 20 Oct., 1821.
> Louisa, b. 1815; d. 1836.
> Sarah, b. 1817.
> 532. Seth Wilder, b. 15 Mch., 1822.

302. Leonard[7] (*Jeremiah, John, Nathaniel, Nathaniel, Lot, Roger*), b. 27 Sep., 1783, in Pomfret, Vt.; a farmer; moved to Franklin, N. Y., and thence to Malone, N. Y., where he d. 24 Apr., 1871. He m. (1) in Pomfret, Vt., 13 Feb., 1810, Lucy Cleveland; m. (2) 13 Jan., 1820, Eunice Bates, of Fort Covington, N. Y.

Child of LEONARD and LUCY (CLEVELAND) CONANT:—

> Lucy, b. 23 May, 1811, in Malone, N. Y.

Children of LEONARD and EUNICE (BATES) CONANT :—

> 533. Azro B., b. 31 July, 1821.
> 534. Marshall, b. 9 Nov., 1822.

303. Polly[7] (*Jeremiah, John, Nathaniel, Nathaniel, Lot, Roger*), b. 8 July, 1785, in Pomfret, Vt.; m. 4 Dec., 1806, Sanford, son of Abijah and Sarah (Mascraft) Child, b. 3 Mch., 1780. She d. 1843, in Malone, N. Y., where they lived. (See *Child Genealogy.*)

Children of SANFORD and POLLY (CONANT) CHILD:—

> i.   Gardiner A., b. 14 May, 1808; of Malone, N. Y.
> ii.   Leonard C., b. 23 July, 1809.
> iii. Lucy, b. 12 July, 1811; m. Enoch Miller.
> iv.   Justin, b. 27 June, 1813.
> v.   Mary, b. 17 Sep., 1816.
> vi.   Benjamin F., b. 14 Jan., 1819.
> vii. Charles, b. 7 May, 1821.
> viii. Thomas J., b. 4 July, 1823.
> ix.   Catherine E., b. 30 Dec., 1827.

304. John[7] (*Jeremiah, John, Nathaniel, Nathaniel, Lot, Roger*), b. 19 June, 1787, in Pomfret, Vt.; a farmer; moved to Bridgewater, Mass., in Mch., 1829, where he d. Feb., 1831. He m. Rebecca Leonard, of Pomfret, Vt., dr. of Nathaniel Washburn, who d. 10 Oct., 1852.

Children of JOHN and REBECCA L. (WASHBURN) CONANT:—

535. Chauncy, b. 18 Aug., 1814, in Pomfret, Vt.
536. Albert, b. 6 July, 1821, in Pomfret, Vt.

305. **Jeremiah**[7] (*Jeremiah, John, Nathaniel, Nathaniel, Lot, Roger*), b. 2 Aug., 1789, in Pomfret, Vt.; a farmer; removed to Malone, N. Y.

Children of JEREMIAH and ——— (———) CONANT:—

Annette.
Sarah.

306. **Seth**[7] (*Jeremiah, John, Nathaniel, Nathaniel, Lot, Roger*), b. 3 Oct., 1796, in Pomfret, Vt.; a farmer. He is still (1885) living there, in good health, but lost his sight some years ago. On his 85th birthday he made a mental calculation of his age, in seconds, which was found to be correct.

He m. (1) ——— ———; m. (2) Mch., 1837, Louisa, dr. of Josiah and Margaret (Aiken) Chandler, b. 1800, d. 10 Sep., 1853 (see *Chandler Genealogy*); m. (3) ——— ———.

Children of SETH and ——— (———) CONANT:—

537. Edward, b. 10 May, 1829.
Lucia, m. ——— Wood.

Child of SETH and LOUISA (CHANDLER) CONANT:—

Abram, b. 14 Dec., 1838; d. Aug., 1850.

307. **Thomas**[7] (*Jeremiah, John, Nathaniel, Nathaniel, Lot, Roger*), b. 6 Aug., 1807, in Pomfret, Vt. He removed to East Bridgewater, Mass., in 1836; was a shoe cutter; in 1859 was a member of the General Court of Mass.; has served on the school committee of E. B.; is still living there. He m. (1) in Pomfret, 12 Sep., 1836, Esther, dr. of Daniel and Abigail (Harding) Chedel, b. 17 July, 1810; d. 24 June, 1846 in E. Bridgewater; m. (2) 24 Mch., 1847, Sarah, widow of Asa Taylor Stickney Hoyt, dr. of Elisha Gassett, of Hopkinton, Mass., b. 16 Apr., 1815.

Children of THOMAS and ESTHER (CHEDEL) CONANT:—

John, b. 4 Aug., 1837; enlisted May, 1861, in company C, 29th Mass. Vols.; served three years. He d. in Portland, Me., 31 May, 1878.

538. Thomas, b. 10 July, 1841.
539. James Scott, b. 4 Jan., 1844.
    Esther, b. 10 June, d. 3 Aug., 1846.

308. Edson[7] (*Thomas, John, Nathaniel, Nathaniel, Lot, Roger*), b. 6 Aug., 1790, in Bridgewater, Mass.; removed to Oakham, Mass., and Westford, Vt., with his parents; settled in Nassau, N. Y. He was a carpenter. He m. about 1815, Polly Cole.

Children of EDSON and POLLY (COLE) CONANT:—

    Jeremiah, who settled in Troy, N. Y.
    Stedman.
    Waldo.
    Lewis.

309. Thomas[7] (*Thomas, John, Nathaniel, Nathaniel, Lot, Roger*), b. 13 Apr., 1797, in Oakham, Mass.; moved to Westford, Vt., with his parents. He removed to Dorset, Ohio, where he is still (1885) living; a farmer. He m. (1) in Oakham, 5 Apr., 1819, Lucy Parmenter, who d. within two years; m. (2) in Westford, Vt., the widow Mary Allen.

Children of THOMAS and MARY (——) (ALLEN) CONANT:—

    Marshall.
540. Rufus.
    Otis.
541. Sidney, b. 17 Sep., 1831.
    Lucy Edson; m. —— Soaland; is of Boston, Mo.
    Lydia.
    Minerva.

310. Lewis[7] (*Thomas, John, Nathaniel, Nathaniel, Lot, Roger*), b. 22 Dec., 1802, in Oakham, Mass. He was a farmer and music teacher, of Westford, Vt. He m. Betsey, dr. of Esquire Evarts, of Georgia, Vt. Her father was a brother of Jeremiah Evarts, of Boston, the father of Senator Wm. Evarts, of New York.

Child of LEWIS and BETSEY (EVARTS) CONANT:—

    Arvilla, who is now living in Minnesota.

311. Gardner[7] (*Thomas, John, Nathaniel, Nathaniel, Lot, Roger*), b. 18 Oct., 1818, in Oakham, Mass.; moved to Westford, Vt., with his parents; learned the shoe makers' trade, at which he has worked some. He settled in Dorset, Ashtabula co., Ohio; has been a mail messenger since 1878, and sexton of the Methodist Episcopal church, of which he is one of the stewards. He is very fond of music, is a good musician, and has taught some. He m. Mary Russ, of Schroon, N. Y.

Child of GARDNER and MARY (RUSS) CONANT:—

Frederick, b. 1868; now in Nebraska.

312. Sylvanus[7] (*Silvanus, Gershom, Lot, Nathaniel, Lot, Roger*), b. 20 Jan., 1787, probably in Bridgewater, Mass.; was a farmer; moved to Turner, Me., with his parents; d. 26 June, 1873. He was a soldier in the War of 1812. He m. (1) in Bridgewater, 1808, Mary Packard, b. 15 June, 1785; d. 26 Nov., 1848. He m. (2) Patience Flagg.

Children of SYLVANUS and MARY (PACKARD) CONANT:—

542.   Everett Quincy, b. 2 Apr., 1809, in Bridgewater.
      Edwin Anthony, b. 3 Sep., 1811, in Bridgewater; m. Louisa Holden, in Woonsocket, R. I., and had one child, who d. y.; both dead (1887).
      Mary Ann, b. 22 Nov., 1813, in Turner, Me.; m. 27 Nov., 1836, Hiram Tuttle, and had Edwin Melville, b. 24 Nov., 1839, d. y., and Solon Chase, b. 4 Nov., 1842, of Buckfield.
      Martha Jane, b. 3 Sept., 1821, in Turner.
      John Anson, b. 27 Sep., 1824, in Turner; a jeweler, of South Attleboro', Mass.; m. in Indianapolis, Ind., 30 Apr., 1856, Charlotte Jane, dr. of Absalom and Ann (Leonard) Roberts, b. in Bristol, N. Y., 30 Aug., 1830; adopted child, Robert McPherson, b. in Maynard, Mass., 21 Apr., 1874.
      Horatio Gates, b. 27 Mch., 1826.

Child of SYLVANUS and PATIENCE (FLAGG) CONANT:—

Sylvanus Melville, b. 10 Sep., 1850, in Turner.

313. Marcus[7] (*Benjamin, Lot, Lot, Nathaniel, Lot, Roger*), b. 24 Oct., 1785, in Bridgewater, Mass.; moved to Turner, Me., with his parents.

Children of MARCUS and ——— (———) CONANT:—

    Ira.
    Laura.
    A daughter, m. ——— Larrabee.

314. Benjamin[7] (*Benjamin, Lot, Lot, Nathaniel, Lot,*

Roger), b. 24 Sep., 1794, in Bridgewater, Mass.; moved to Turner, Me., with his parents; a farmer. He d. 1868. He m. in Turner, 30 Oct., 1816, Alethea Staples, who was b. 8 July, 1793; she d. Oct., 1848.

Children of BENJAMIN and ALETHEA (STAPLES) CONANT:—

543. Alonzo, b. 1817.
544. Leonard, b. 1818.
    Abigail, b. 1821; m. Benjamin Drake.
    Betsey, b. 1823.
545. Benjamin, b. 5 Sep., 1825.
    Clarissa.
    Hezekiah, b. 1827.
    Lewis, b. 1830; of Osceola, Missouri.
    Oscar, b. 1832.
    Almeda, b. 1834.

315. Hooper[7] (*Benjamin, Lot, Lot, Nathaniel, Lot, Roger*), b. 10 July, 1793, in Bridgewater, Mass.; moved to Turner, Me., with his parents, where he settled as a farmer. He m. in Green, Me., Anna Keene.

Children of HOOPER and ANNA (KEENE) CONANT:—

546. Calvin, b. 15 June, 1817.
547. Anna Briggs, b. 31 Aug., 1818.
548. Lot, b. 15 Feb., 1820.
549. Winslow, b. 28 May, 1822.
550. Lucitty K., b. 23 Dec., 1823.
    Isaac, b. 28 June, 1826; of Plymouth, Mass.

316. Hezekiah[7] (*Benjamin, Lot, Lot, Nathaniel, Lot, Roger*), b. about 1795, in Turner, Me., where he lived.

Children of HEZEKIAH. and ——— (———) CONANT :—

    Alexander.
    Lydia.
    Mary.

317. Peter[7] (*Peter, Phinehas, Lot, Nathaniel, Lot, Roger*), b. 1778, in Bridgewater, Mass., where he lived; m. 1809, Lucy Brewster.

Child of PETER and LUCY (BREWSTER) CONANT :—

    Maria; m. 25 Nov., 1837, Alexander, son of Joseph Alden, b. 4 Sep., 1814; had Maria J., b. 30 Aug., 1839; m. 1865, Henry Webster, of Abington, Mass., and had family; he enlisted, 1862, in company C, 38th Mass. Vols.; served three years.

318. Jacob[7] (*Peter, Phinehas, Lot, Nathaniel, Lot, Roger*), b. in Bridgewater, Mass.; m. 1805, Olive, dr. of (135) Zenas Conant. On May 1, 1802, he bought land in Hebron, Me. (Cumberland Deeds, Vol. 36, p. 343). Apr. 5, 1805, Jacob Conant, of Bridgewater, yeoman, sells 60 acres of land in Hebron, Me., to his father, Peter Conant, house-wright (Cumberland Deeds, Vol. 45, p. 396).

They removed to Ohio (Mitchell's *Hist. of Bridgewater*).

Children of JACOB and OLIVE (CONANT) CONANT :—

    Charles, b. 1807, in Bridgewater.
    Jane, b. 1809,   "
    William, b. 1812,   "

319. Liba[7] (*Peter, Phinehas, Lot, Nathaniel, Lot, Roger*), b. 1793, in Bridgewater, Mass. He graduated at Brown University, 1819. He studied for the ministry, and was settled over the Congregational Church of Northfield, N. H., about 1822, where he remained over thirty years. He afterwards preached in Groton and Hebron. He d. 3 Apr., 1881, in Bristol, N. H. He m. 26 Oct., 1820, in Bridgewater, Deborah Jackson, dr. of Levi and Betsey (Conant) Leach, b. 26 Jan., 1799; d. in Bristol, N. H., 14 Apr., 1877.

Children of LIBA and DEBORAH J. (LEACH) CONANT :—

    Elizabeth Jane, b. 13 Nov., 1821, in Bridgewater, Mass.; m. 20 June, 1848, Lucius Wilson Hammond; she d. 25 May, 1885.
    Sarah Ann, b. 8 Feb., 1827, in Northfield, N. H.; m. 7 June, 1853, Joseph Hammond Keyes; she d. Mch., 1882.
    Henry Francis, b. 22 Nov., 1829, in Northfield, N. H.; d. 28 Nov., 1836.
    Ellen McAllister, b. 19 Oct., 1833, in Northfield, N. H.; m. 11 Oct., 1853, Hon. David Everett Willard, of Concord, N. H. He was Railroad Commissioner of N. H., 1878-9-80; State Senator, 1883-4.

320. Galen[7] (*Phinehas, Phinehas, Lot, Nathaniel, Lot, Roger*), b. 6 Feb., 1790, in Bridgewater, Mass., where he lived.

Children of GALEN and HANNAH (———) CONANT :—

551. Hannah Allen, b. 17 Aug., 1814.
    Galen, b. 1 Feb., 1816; m. Sarah ———, and had Anguinette.
    Harriet M., b. 15 Apr., 1823.
    A son, b. 16 Mch., 1829; d. y.

321. Ira[7] (*Phinehas, Phinehas, Lot, Nathaniel, Lot, Roger*), b. about 1792, in Bridgewater, Mass., where he lived. He m. Lucy Leonard.

Children of IRA and LUCY (LEONARD) CONANT:—

Lucy Maria, b. 22 July, 1824; m. George Leonard, of Bridgewater. Children: Ella, Lucy and Anne.
552. Ira M., b. 3 Jan., 1827, in Wareham.
Caroline L., b. 18 Nov., 1831.
553. William Henry, b. 13 Mch., 1834.
Charles C., b. 26 Mch., 1837; d. y.

322. Deborah Lazell[7] (*James, Timothy, Lot, Nathaniel, Lot, Roger*), b. 23 June, 1781, in Oakham, Mass.; m. 20 Nov., 1804, Josiah Burbank. They removed to Winchester, N. H. He d. 14 Oct., 1861. She d. 8 Sep., 1826.

Children of JOSIAH and DEBORAH L. (CONANT) BURBANK:—

i. Angelina Maria, b. 8 June, 1807; d. 1849, in Oakham.
ii. Samuel Adams, b. 10 Feb., 1809; d. 19 May, 1869.
iii. John, b. 18 Apr., 1811; d. 18 Jan., 1872.
iv. James Conant, b. 27 Jan., 1813.
v. Nathan Packard, b. 14 Mch., 1815.
vi. Lucy Bacon, b. 11 Mch., 1820, in Oakham; m. in Winchester, N. H., 12 June, 1839, Charles Mansfield, b. 1839; had 1. Charles Martin, b. 1842; 2. Josephine Lucy, b. 1849; 3. Charles Burbank, b. 1857; 4. Henry Martin, b. 1858.
vii. Daniel Emerson, b. 16 Aug., 1822; d. 1859.

323. Elijah[7] (*James, Timothy, Lot, Nathaniel, Lot, Roger*), b. 12 Mch., 1783, in Oakham, Mass.; a farmer; removed to Barre, thence to New York. He m. Nancy Taft.

Children of ELIJAH and NANCY (TAFT) CONANT:—

554. Robert Taft, b. 1 Sep., 1810.
Mary, b. ———; d. 19 Jan., 1881; m. James R. Parsons.

324. Lot[7] (*James, Timothy, Lot, Nathaniel, Lot, Roger*), b. 8 May, 1785, in Oakham, Mass. He served in the War of 1812 as a drum major; was a farmer; removed to Wheeling, West Va., where he d. 14 Oct., 1868. He m. Mary McClellan, b. 29 July, 1792; d. in Wheeling, W. Va., 29 Dec., 1879.

Children of LOT and MARY (McCLELLAN) CONANT:—

Samuel, b. 3 Oct., 1816, in Mass.; a farmer of Jefferson co., Ohio; not married.

555. Luke, b. 4 June, 1817.
    Henry, b. 8 May, 1819, in Massachusetts; he is a steamboat
      pilot on the Ohio river; not married.
    Walter, b. 17 Mch., 1821; a steamboat pilot; d. 3 Aug., 1848,
      unm.
    Thomas, b. 15 Apr., 1823; d. 20 Dec., 1854.
556. Mary H., b. 8 July, 1825.
557. Abigail S., b. 22 Jan., 1828, in Barre, Mass.
    Louisa L., b. 3 June, 1830; m. 20 May, 1881, Hiram E. Rabe,
      of Clyde, Ohio.
558. Sarah Jane, b. 22 June, 1834, in Wheeling.
559. George W., b. 20 June, 1837.

  325. **Abigail**[7] (*James, Timothy, Lot, Nathaniel, Lot, Roger*), b. 16 Nov., 1791, in Oakham, Mass.; m. 31 Oct., 1810, Asa,
son of Ezekiel and Sarah (Bullard) Shattuck, of Barre, Mass.,
b. 26 Mch., 1789, d. in Hartford, Conn., 12 Dec., 1863; she d.
5 Mch., 1862.

    Children of ASA and ABIGAIL (CONANT) SHATTUCK :—

    Sarah B., b. 1 June, 1812; m. 11 Apr., 1833, Edson D. Cheney.
    Abigail, b. 18 Jan., 1814; d. 11 Mch., 1816.
    Lucy B:, b. 1 Mch., 1816; m. 5 Apr., 1836, Lewis Allen.
    George, b. 11 Apr., 1818; of Woodhaven, L. I.; he m. (1) in
      Worcester, Mass., 1859, Martha A., dr. of Varnum Brig-
      ham; had Edwin and George; m. (2) in New York, 1881,
      Mary C. Teel, dr. of Samuel E. King.
    Mary H., b. 19 Mch., 1820; m. 24 June, 1841, James Hays; she
      d. 11 May, 1851.
    Eliza B., b. 10 May, 1822.
    Dolly Ann, b. 4 Nov., 1825; d. 24 Jan., 1848.
    Henry S., b. 26 Nov., 1827.
    Nathan Lazell, b. 8 Aug., 1832.

  326. **James**[7] (*James, Timothy, Lot, Nathaniel, Lot, Roger*), b. 5 Dec., 1793, in Oakham, Mass., where he lived. He
was a farmer, merchant and innkeeper, and served in the War
of 1812 as captain of militia. He d. 10 Mch., 1867. He m.
22 Dec., 1816, Susan Stone, who d. 30 Jan., 1877.

    Children of JAMES and SUSAN (STONE) CONANT :—

    Harriet Stone, b. 11 Mch., 1817; of Barre; unm.
560. George F., b. 10 Apr., 1819, in New Braintree.
    Joseph, b. 14 Sep., 1821, in Oakham.
561. John, b. 21 Feb., 1823.
    Susan, b. 6 Feb., 1826.
    Louisa, b. 27 Sep., 1828.

Eliza A., b. 6 June, 1831; m. William Smith, of Oakham.
562. Albert S., b. 18 Apr., 1835.
Maria R., b. 1 Aug., 1838; m. Erastus Wood, of Barre.
Henry L., b. 19 July, 1841; m. 1866, Ellen Crawford; lives in Barre.

327. Justus[7] (*Luther, Timothy, Lot, Nathaniel, Lot, Roger*), b. ———, in Oakham, Mass.; a physician; lived in Turner, Me., and Shutesbury, Mass. He d. in Shutesbury, Mass., 13 Jan., 1813. He m. in Turner, Me., 30 July, 1807, Sarah, dr. of Chandler and Sarah (French) Bradford, b. 15 May, 1790, d. 10 July, 1818, in Turner.

Children of JUSTUS and SARAH (BRADFORD) CONANT:—

Roxa, b. 29 Oct., 1807.
Justus, b. 30 Dec., 1809; of Turner, Me.

328. Sullivan[7] (*Luther, Timothy, Lot, Nathaniel, Lot, Roger*), b. 26 Feb., 1801, in Oakham, Mass. After his marriage he settled in Shutesbury, where he remained about three years, then lived in Amherst one year, and returned to Shutesbury. In the fall of 1830 he moved West with his family. They went to Troy, N. Y., by wagon, thence to Rochester by canal, thence by wagon to Olean Point where they took a raft and floated down the river to Pittsburg. They went from Pittsburg to Chester, Ill., by steamboat, and thence to Springfield, Ill., where he arrived Feb. 18, 1831, and there settled. This was the winter of the "deep snow," and when Mr. Conant arrived at Springfield the snow was four feet deep (see Power's *Hist. Sangamon County, Ill.*).

He m. (1) in Shutesbury, Mass., 10 Sep., 1822, Lydia R. Heminway, b. Nov., 1803; d. 30 May, 1867, in Springfield, Ill., and he m. again.

Children of SULLIVAN and LYDIA R.(HEMINWAY) CONANT:—

563. Abigail A., b. 5 July, 1823, in Shutesbury, Mass.
564. William S., b. 27 Feb., 1825, " "
565. Susan E., b. 10 Mch., 1827, " "
566. Levi J., b. 25 Oct., 1831, in Springfield, Ill.
Mary A., b. 20 July, 1833, in Springfield, Ill.; m. Cook S. Hampton.
567. Phineas H., b. 12 Apr., 1837, in Springfield.
Caroline A., b. 1 Sep., 1843; m. Rev. Thomas M. Dillon, of the M. E. church. They lived, in 1874, at Martinsburg, Ill.

22

. Lydia J., b. 19 July, 1845; m. 17 Mch., 1868, George L. Dingle. He served in the War of the Rebellion, and afterwards settled in Santa Fe, New Mexico, where he was deputy postmaster in 1876.

329. Silas[7] (*Samuel, Robert, Lot, John, Lot, Roger*), b. 31 May, 1747, in Stow, Mass.; moved to Sudbury, Mass., about 1782.   He made his will 3 May, 1820; mentions his wife, Dolly; sons, Amos and Levi; daughter, Zerviah, and grandson, Emory.   He d. 20 Sep., 1836, in Sudbury.   He m. in Sherburne, 16 Feb., 1770, Dorothy Brown, b. 24 Feb., 1749; d. 10 Feb., 1832.

(1820.)

Children of Silas and Dorothy (Brown) Conant:—

568. Amos, b. 20 Oct., 1771.
      Dolly, b. 17 June, 1773; m. —— Stone; she d. 19 Oct., 1805.
569. Levi, b. 24 May, 1775.
      Zerviah, b. 29 Oct., 1779; m. —— Stone; she d. 29 Sep., 1862.

330. Oliver[7] (*Samuel, Robert, Lot, John, Lot, Roger*), b. about 1750, in Stow, Mass.; settled in Sudbury, then in Weston.   In 1777 Oliver Conant, of Sudbury, was in Rice's company of Bullard's regiment, in the Continental army, in service in New York (Mass. Arch., Muster Rolls, Vol. 22, p. 178).   On Jan. 15, 1776, Oliver Conant, of Concord, was corporal in Wheeler's company of Niseon's regiment (Id. Vol. 24, p. 73).   He m. Thankful Walker.

Children of Oliver and Thankful (Walker) Conant:—

570. Abraham, b. 2 Sep., 1778.
      Polly, b. 13 Nov., 1779, } twins.
571. Isaac, b. 13 Nov., 1779, }
      Thankful.
      Oliver.
      Sally, m. —— March, of Cambridge.
      Louisa.
572. Asa W., b. 1787.
573. Josiah.
      Betsey.

331. Samuel[7] (*Samuel, Robert, Lot, John, Lot, Roger*), b. about 1752, in Stow; settled in Sterling, where he d. 2 Mch.,

1808. He m. Lydia Walker, of Weston, b. 1754; d. 23 May, 1796, in Sterling. *4 2 yrs*

Children of SAMUEL and LYDIA (WALKER) CONANT:—

574. Nathan, b. 1777.
       Thankful? b. 1780.
575. Jacob, b. 13 Jan., 1783.
       Samuel, b. 1784; was selectman of Sterling; m. Sophia Burpee; no children.
576. Sally. *b. 1785*
       Lydia, b. 1788; was a teacher of a school for young ladies in Sterling, Boston and Plymouth; she d. 23 Feb., 1826, unm.
       Polly, b. 1791; d. 10 Nov., 1814, unm.
       John, b. 1795; d. 7 Dec., 1798.

332. John[7] (*Samuel, Robert, Lot, John, Lot, Roger*), b. 3 Jan., 1758, in Stow, where he lived. He was in Minot's company of Baldwin's regiment, in the Revolutionary army, Jan. 12, 1776, at Cambridge (Mass. Arch., Muster Rolls, Vol. 21, p. 36); and Bowker's company of Webb's regiment, 1781 (Id., Vol. 17, p. 129). He d. 28 Dec., 1829, leaving a will dated 12 Oct., 1824 (Middlesex Probate), in which he men-

John Conant

(1824.)

tions wife, Maria; sons, William, Elijah, Joel, John, Daniel, Jephthah; daughters, Nancy Randall, Huldah Hobart and Sally G.; granddaughter, Mary Hosmer Conant; also John and Betsey Goldsmith and Maria Whitney, children of his present wife by her first husband.

He m. (1) Huldah Hubbard, of Pepperell, b. 10 Dec., 1761, d. 18 Jan., 1802; m. (2) widow Maria Goldsmith, of Concord.

Children of JOHN and HULDAH (HUBBARD) CONANT:—

       William, of Stow; had a son, Albert.
       Elijah, of Waltham; had a son, Frank.
577. Joel, b. 1 Feb., 1788.
578. John, b. 12 Jan., 1790.
       Daniel, d. y.
       Nancy, b. 27 Dec., 1793; m. Luke Randall; she d. 28 Aug., 1828.
       Daniel, b. 8 Dec., 1795; of Stow; had Frederick, now of Hudson, Mass.
       Jephthah, of Leominster; had a son, Daniel.
       Huldah, b. ——; m. —— Hobart.
       Calvin, d. y.

Children of JOHN and MARIA (●———) CONANT:—

Sherman G., b. 1810; of Harvard; had John and Sherman.
Sally G., b. ———; m. Solon Buck, of Stow.

333. ' Josiah[7] (*Josiah, Robert, Lot, John, Lot, Roger*), b.
21 Aug., 1750, in Groton, Mass.; settled in Pepperell. He d.
July, 1808. His will, preserved in the Middlesex Co. Probate
Records, mentions wife, Lydia; mother, Rachael; brothers,
Benjamin and Shebuel; adopted son, John Conant Searle;
Stephen White, jr., of Westford, Rachael Williams and Heph-
zibah Webber; Lydia, dr. of his brother Robert. He m. 5
Oct., 1773, Lydia, dr. of Timothy and Lydia (Fletcher) Pres-
cott, of Westford, b. 15 Jan., 1754. She m. (2) Jonathan
Pierce, of Townsend, and d. 1812.

They had no children (*Hist. of Westford*, p. 467).

Adopted child of JOSIAH and LYDIA (PRESCOTT) CONANT:—

John Searle, b. 14 Sep., 1794, son of Robert Searle, who took
the name John Conant-Searle, and was living in Topeka,
Kan., 1875.

334. Benjamin[7] (*Josiah, Robert, Lot, John, Lot, Roger*),
b. 27 June, 1752, in Groton; miller; moved to Pepperell, with
his parents; settled in Milford, N. H. In 1782 he was an inhabitant of Amherst, N. H. (N. H. Town Papers). Oct. 4,
1809, Nathan Austen, of Salem, N. H., sells Benjamin Conant,
of Milford, N. H., land in Salem (Rockingham Deeds, Vol.
193, p. 5). He m. ———, Lucy Hopkins.

Children of BENJAMIN and LUCY (HOPKINS) CONANT:—

579. Anna, b. about 1780.

A daughter, who m. ——— Burnham; had son, Orasmus, who
lived in Milford.

Benjamin, b. ———; m. and had a son, Walter, who d. aged
7 years.

Abel, b. 17 July, 1793; d. 6 Dec., 1836; graduated at Dartmouth
College, 1815. He was principal of Groton Academy 1815
to 1819, and studied divinity at the same time; was ordained
pastor of First Congregational Church, 24 Jan., 1821, and d.
in office. Two sermons by him have been published: first,
"A Sermon Delivered at Leominster on Leaving the Old
Meeting House," Oct. 12, 1823 (Worcester, 1824, 8vo, pp. 15),
and second, "A Sermon Delivered at Leominster, Oct. 15,
1823, at the Dedication of the New Meeting House"

(Worcester, 1823, 8vo, pp. 20). He m. in Hillsboro', 15 Nov., 1821, Rebecca Adams, of Amherst, who d. in Amherst, Aug., 1854. They had two daughters, both dead (1884). (See Chapman's *Alumni of Dartmouth College; Hist. of Groton; and Hist. of Leominster.*)

335. Shebuel[7] (*Josiah, Robert, Lot, John, Lot, Roger*), b. 23 Dec., 1756, in Pepperell, Mass. Jan. 13, 1776, he was in Capt. Haskell's company of Col. Prescott's regiment, in camp at Cambridge (Mass. Arch., Muster Rolls, Vol. 19, p. 170); and Dec. 18, 1777, he was sergeant in Lakin's company of Robinson's regiment (Id., Vol. 2, p. 184). He m. (1) Anna Farley; (2) Rhoda (Shattuck) Boynton, b. 29 July, 1760, dr. of David and Sarah (Burt) Shattuck, widow of John Boynton.

Child of SHEBUEL and ANNA (FARLEY) CONANT:—

580. Josiah Franklin, b. Apr., 1806.
    And perhaps others.

336. Ephraim[7] (*Peter, Robert, Lot, John, Lot, Roger*), b. 16 Jan., 1757, in Stow. He took part in the battle of Lexington, Apr. 19, 1775; was in Whitcomb's company of Prescott's regiment (Mass. Arch., Lexington Alarm Lists, Vol. 13, p. 168). He moved to Georgetown, Mass., thence to Temple, N. H., where his name appears in a list of inhabitants, 1784 (N. H. Town Papers, Vol. 13, p. 561), thence to Thomaston, Me., and finally settled in Temple, Me., as a farmer. He d. in Temple, Me., 22 Jan., 1826. He m. in Temple, N. H., Rebecca Hayward.

Children of EPHRAIM and REBECCA (HAYWARD) CONANT:—

581. Asa, b. about 1778.
    Simeon, b. 1779.
582. Ephraim, b. 7 Feb., 1781.
583. Joseph, b. 25 Jan., 1783.
    Peter, b. 1785; left home young; went to Ohio, it is said.
    Sarah.
584. Abraham, b. 7 Mch., 1789.
    Rebecca, b. 1790; never m.
585. Isaac, b. 18 Jan., 1793.
    Abigail, b. 1795; m. George Simmons, and had Oliver, Peleg, Stephen, Lucy and Sarah.
    Jacob, b. 1797; was drowned while driving logs.

337. **Peter**[7] (*Peter, Robert, Lot, John, Lot, Roger,*) b. 10 May, 1760, in Stow, where he lived; was a wheelwright; he d, 22 Sep., 1833.   His will dated 2 Sep., 1833; mentions children, Artemus, Peter, Betsey Randall, Francis, Abraham (executor), Mary Gates, Levi, Cyrus, Phineas; children of son Isaac, and wife Elizabeth (Middlesex Probate Records).   He m. 7 Dec., 1780, Elizabeth, dr. of Phineas Fairbanks, of Harvard, who d. 2 Feb., 1847.

Children of PETER and ELIZABETH (FAIRBANKS) CONANT:—

> Isaac, b. about 1781; moved to Hope, Me., where he d. before 1827, leaving a son, Isaac, now (1886) living in or near Princeton, Ill.
586. Phineas.
> Peter, b. about 1785; lived in Charlestown, Mass.; had John, Cornelius, and William who was of Boston, Mass.
> Artemus, b. about 1787; lived in Athol, Mass.; had Sarah, Artemus B. and Elizabeth.
> Betsey, m. —— Randall.
587. Francis, b. 12 Sep., 1789.
> Abraham, a merchant, captain of militia, sheriff; moved to Sycamore, De Kalb co., Ill.; had a son who was killed during the late Rebellion.
> Levi, a school teacher, of Chelsea, Mass.; had a son who d. y.
> Cyrus, a merchant in Boston and New York; had children.
> Sarah, b. ——; a dress maker; d. at Stow, 1830, unm.
> Mary, b. ——; m. Luke Gates; moved to Aurora, Ill.; she d. 1851.

338. **Ebenezer**[7] (*Peter, Robert, Lot, John, Lot, Roger*), b. about 1762, in Stow, Mass.   He moved to Waterford, Me.; was accidently shot in a shooting match.   [He is not mentioned in his father's will or in the Probate Records.   Information furnished by Jonathan N. Conant.]

Child of EBENEZER and —— (——) CONANT:—

> Ebenezer.

339. **Josiah**[7] (*Peter, Robert, Lot, John, Lot, Roger*), b. about 1765, in Stow, Mass., where he lived; d. about 1818. (Information given by Jonathan N. Conant, of West Vienna, N. Y.)

Children of JOSIAH and POLLY (——) CONANT:—

> Josiah, lived in Berlin, Mass.
> Bailey, lived in Stow.

340. Mary[7] (*Peter, Robert, Lot, John, Lot, Roger*), b. in Stow, Mass.; m. Maj. Elisha Gates, and settled in Waterford, Me.

Child of ELISHA and MARY (CONANT) GATES:—

Mary Eliza, b. 29 Jan., 1817; d. 25 Jan., 1882.

341. Sarah[7] (*Peter, Robert, Lot, John, Lot, Roger*), b. in Stow, Mass.; m. (1) Ezra Jewell, who settled in Waterford, Me.; one of the first settlers. She m. (2) —— Whitney.

Children of EZRA and SARAH (CONANT) JEWELL:—

i. Nathan, b. 1780; m. Betsey Pollard.
ii. Sally, b. 1782; m. Oliver Stone.
iii. Lewis, b. 1785; m. (1) Nancy Longley; m. (2) Lydia Spurr.
iv. Mary, b. 1789; m. Nathan Brooks.
v. Charlotte, b. 1791; m. Major William Morse.
vi. Ezra, b. 1794; m. Charlotte, dr. of Nathan and Mary Brooks, and had: 1. Abigail B., who m. Daniel M. Young, of Norway, Me., and Wellesley Hills, Mass., and had Eugene, Augustus H., John B., Fred H. and Annetta H.; 2. Charlotte; 3. Isaac B.; 4. Georgianna.

342. Abraham[7] (*Daniel, Robert, Lot, John, Lot, Roger*), b. in Stow, about 1780; settled in

(1808.)

Acton. He was lieutenant of militia; town clerk of Acton, 1822. He m. in Acton, 6 May, 1813, Eunice Jones.

Children of ABRAHAM and EUNICE (JONES) CONANT:—

588. Winthrop Faulkner, b. 11 June, 1814.
Abigail Martha, b. 15 June, 1816; m. —— Fairbanks.
Charlotte, b. 26 Mch., 1820; m. 13 June, 1843, Stevens Hayward, of Boxboro'.

343. Benjamin[7] (*Daniel, Robert, Lot, John, Lot, Roger*), b. 19 Oct., 1786, in Stow; a farmer, of Stow; m. 9 Aug., 1813, Sarah; dr. of

(1809.)

Josiah and Prudence Randall, who d. 5 Jan., 1858. He d. 8 Nov., 1843.

Children of BENJAMIN and SARAH (RANDALL) CONANT:—

589.   Francis, b. 15 Nov., 1814, in Stow.
         Susan, b. 11 Nov., 1816; d. 22 Aug., 1846.
         Benjamin, b. 22 Feb., 1820; m. 26 Apr., 1848, Charlotte G.
            Barclay, of Danbury, N. H.; no children. He d. 31 Oct.,
            1879.
590.   Mary, b. 3 June, 1822, } twins.
591.   Martha, b. 3 June, 1822, }
         Sarah, b. 5 Dec., 1824; d. 8 June, 1832.
         Betsey, b. 29 Apr., 1827; m. 31 Dec., 1885, John W. Green,
            now of Maynard, Mass.
         Sarah, b. 6 Feb., 1833; d. 3 July, 1860.

344. **Simeon**[7] (*Daniel, Robert, Lot, John, Lot, Roger*),
b. about 1784, in Stow; m. 6 Apr., 1815, Betsey Goldsmith,

(1809.)

who d. 9 Feb., 1872. He d. 8 Mch., 1868, in Stow.

Children of SIMEON and BETSEY (GOLDSMITH) CONANT:—

         Daniel G., b. 10 May, 1816; d. 13 Apr., 1818.
592.   Martha Maria, b. 23 May, 1818, in Stow.
         Mary C., b. 4 Sep., 1820; d. 17 Nov., 1825, in Acton.
         Betsey H., b. 9 Apr., 1823; d. 30 Sep., 1826.
         Hannah, b. 13 Aug., 1825; d. 28 Nov., 1825.
593.   Betsey H., b. 23 Feb., 1828.
         George, b. 12 Sep., 1830; m. 30 Aug., 1854, Harriet Hayward,
            who d. 15 Jan., 1863; m. (2) 25 Nov., 1863, Lore E. Willis;
            no children.
         Nancy, b. 10 Oct., 1833; d. 19 Feb., 1858.
         Lydia B., b. 24 Nov., 1834; m. 29 June, 1858, Luther W. Piper;
            she d. 19 June, 1883.
         John G., b. 2 Dec., 1839; d. 1 Nov., 1840.

345. **Zebulon**[7] (*Andrew, Andrew, Lot, John, Lot, Roger*),
b. 29 Oct., 1749, in Concord. In Apr., 1775, he was in Capt.
Wilder's company of minute men, and at the news of Lexing-
ton marched to Cambridge. He was then of Winchendon
(Mass. Arch., Muster Rolls, Vol. 13, p. 179). He removed to
New Ipswich, N. H., where he was an inhabitant as early as
1785 (N. H. Town Papers, Vol. 12, p. 744). He m. Mary
Wright, b. Feb., 1752.

Children of ZEBULON and MARY (WRIGHT) CONANT:—

         Ruth, b. 2 May, 1772; m. ——— Adams.
         Mary, b. 13 Feb., 1774; m. ——— Clary, of Leominster, Mass.

Zebulon, b. 14 Dec., 1776; drowned 8 July, 1803.
Hannah, b. 4 May, 1779; d. 1802.
594. Joseph, b. 31 Mch., 1781.
Bessie, b. 31 July, 1783; m. —— Spaulding, of Franklin, Vt.
Betsey, b. 13 Sep., 1785; m. —— Thompson, of Grafton, Vt.
Nathan, b. 9 Feb., 1788; d. 3 Oct., 1843.
Kezia, b. 19 June, 1789; m. —— Saunders.
Nancy, b. 10 Aug., 1793; m. —— Wetherbee.
595. Andrew, b. 12 Feb., 1796.

346. Andrew[7] (*Andrew, Andrew, Lot, John, Lot, Roger*), b. 7 May, 1773, in Concord, where he lived. He d. 31 Jan., 1813, and Joseph Miles was appointed administrator of his estate (Middlesex Probate Records). He m. 16 June, 1803, Lydia Miles. After his death she m. Amos Noyes. She d. 15 Nov., 1825, aged 45.

Children of ANDREW and LYDIA (MILES) CONANT:—

William Andrew, b. 30 Nov., 1804; d. before 12 Apr., 1820.
Evelina, b. 26 Oct., 1809 (m. 10 May, 1831, Silas Stow, of Stow?).
Mary Ann, b. 9 Sep., 1810.

347. Samuel Potter[7] (*Silas, Andrew, Lot, John, Lot, Roger*), b. 27 Mch., 1767, in Acton, Mass.; a farmer. He d. 6 Nov., 1815, leaving a will dated 3 Nov., 1815, proved 22 Nov., 1815 (Middlesex Probate Records). He m. 23 Oct., 1789, Rebecca Tuttle, b. 11 Dec., 1766, d. 11 Sep., 1835.

Children of SAMUEL P. and REBECCA (TUTTLE) CONANT:—

Samuel, b. 21 Jan., 1790; m. 2 Aug., 1812, Mehitable Piper, and had a son, who d. 3 Jan., 1815, aged 3 weeks.
596. Nathan, b. 30 Oct., 1791, in Littleton.
597. Paul, b. 23 Jan., 1793, in Acton.
Rebecca, b. 3 Jan., 1798; m. 24 May, 1821, Nathan Brooks, of Acton.
Susanna C., b. 5 June, 1800; m. 7 Nov., 1819, Robert Chaffin, jr.; she d. 26 Nov., 1871.
598. Silas, b. 4 May, 1803.
Charles, b. 1825; d. 16 Apr., 1829.
Simon, b. ——; m. ——; had Mary, d. 17 Nov., 1825, aged 5 years, and a child, d. 30 Nov., 1825, aged 3 months.
599. Nahum, b. 2 Oct., 1810.

348. Silas[7] (*Silas, Andrew, Lot, John, Lot, Roger*), b. 25 Oct., 1776, in Acton; a farmer. He m. (1) 11 Aug., 1796, Abigail Lawrence, who d. 21 Dec., 1805; m. (2) 28 May, 1807,

Mary, dr. of Josiah and Lucy (Conant) Hayward, of Concord.

Children of SILAS and ABIGAIL (LAWRENCE) CONANT:—

Abigail, b. 11 Feb., 1797; d. 27 Nov., 1815.
600. Silas, b. 24 Dec., 1798.
601. Joshua L., b. 3 Oct., 1801.
Lois P., b. 5 Mch., 1803; m. —— Haynes.
Sally F., b. 25 Sep., 1805; m. —— Farmer.

Children of SILAS and MARY (HAYWARD) CONANT:—

Andrew, b. 3 Feb., 1808.
Mary, b. 3 May, 1810; d. 12 Feb., 1812.
Mary Ann, b. 5 Dec., 1812; m. Orville Giles, of Weymouth.
Nancy H., b. 23 Jan., 1814; d. Oct., 1814.
Lucy Abigail, b. 23 Mch., 1816; m. 30 Nov., 1837, Sylvester
Hayward.
Harriet Elizabeth, b. 29 Apr., 1821; d. 19 July, 1837.

349. James[7] (*Silas, Andrew, Lot, John, Lot, Roger*), b.
26 May, 1788, in Acton, Mass. He was a carpenter; served in
the War of 1812 as a private. He d. in Mason, N. H., 26
Oct., 1836. He m. 4 Nov., 1810, Seba, dr. of Jesse Davis, b.
in Acton, 23 June, 1789. She d. 5 July, 1875, in New Ipswich, N. H.

Children of JAMES and SEBA (DAVIS) CONANT:—

Luseba Wright, b. 14 Apr., 1811, in Acton; d. 2 Feb., 1859; m.
9 Dec., 1836, Josiah Webber.
Louisa J., b. 26 Sep., 1812; m. (1) 9 May, 1839, Jonathan Love-
joy, son of William and Rebecca (Lovejoy) Cogswell, of
Rindge, N. H.; m. (2) Emerson Howe, of New Ipswich,
N. H.
602. James Franklin, b. 23 Nov., 1814.
Jesse Davis, b. 22 Oct., 1818; m. Rachael Golopen, and moved
West.
Mary, b. 20 July, 1820; m. (1) 5 Apr., 1845, Walter Davis; m.
(2) James Comee, of Fitchburg.
603. Andrew, b. 13 Nov., 1822, in Acton.
Sarah Ann, b. 1 Feb., 1825, in New Ipswich, N. H.; m. 15
Nov., 1848, George Henry Ramsdell.
George Washington, b. 11 Apr., 1827, in New Ipswich; m. 28
May, 1850, Diana P., dr. of Paul and Hannah R. (Hanna-
ford) Boyce. Now of Peterboro', N. H.
Sylvia Maria, b. 17 Nov., 1829; m. 3 Oct., 1849, David Thomas,
of Claremont, N. H.
Harriet Elizabeth, b. 5 Apr., 1834, in Mason, N. H.; m. 2 July,
1857, Horace Eugene Evans. Now of Townsend, Mass.

350. John Gardiner[7] (*Eli, Andrew, Lot, John, Lot, Roger*), b. 30 Aug., 1768, in Concord, Mass. He removed to Pawlet, Vt., and d. in Wells, Vt., 1830. He m. Rachael, dr. of Ebenezer and Esther Giles, b. in Townsend, Mass., 2 Feb., 1771; d. 1820, in Pawlet.

Children of JOHN G. and RACHAEL (GILES) CONANT:—

604. John.
    Rufus, a blacksmith.
    Samuel, a blacksmith.
605. Wesley, b. May, 1806.

351. George[7] (*Eli, Andrew, Lot, John, Lot, Roger*), b. 7 Apr., 1771, in Concord, Mass.; moved to Enfield, N. H.; m. Eunice Crossman, b. in Bolton, 16 Mch., 1772.

Children of GEORGE and EUNICE (CROSSMAN) CONANT:—

    Sarah, b. 16 Dec., 1791, in Fitchburg, Mass.; m. Bela Johnson, of Enfield, N. H.; she d. July, 1882.
    Andrew G., b. 14 Nov., 1795, in New Chester, N. H.; d. 28 Mch., 1800.
    Mary, b. 21 Nov., 1797, in Enfield, N. H.; d. 23 Oct., 1800.
    Anna, b. 25 Nov., 1799; m. Eben Clark, of Canaan, N. H.; she d. 3 Dec., 1822.
    George, b. 16 Apr., 1802; d. 22 Jan., 1809.
    Mary, b. 5 Aug., 1804; m. Thomas Merrill, Esq., of Enfield.
    Elizabeth, b. 23 Nov., 1807; m. Thomas Goodwin; she d. 6 Sep., 1871.
606. Alpheus, b. 17 Mch., 1810.
607. George W., b. 2 July, 1812.

352. Abel[7] (*Abel, Andrew, Lot, John, Lot, Roger*), b. 11 July, 1773, in Concord, where he lived. He m. Lydia (*Parker*) Wright, of New Ipswich, N. H. (m. int. pub. 13 Aug., 1797, in Lincoln, Mass.), who d. 27 Nov., 1825, aged 51.

Children of ABEL and LYDIA (PARKER) CONANT:—

    Lydia Parker, b. 6 Nov., 1798.
    Abel Johnson, b. 3 Jan., d. 22 Feb., 1801.
    Mary Amanda, b. 3 May, 1802.
608. George Franklin, b. 13 Sep., 1805.
    Isaac Kilbourn, b. 9 Oct., 1807; d. 12 Dec., 1815.
    Albert Henry, b. 19 Aug., 1809.
    A daughter, b. 1810; d. 20 Dec., 1815.
    Abel Wright, b. 4 Mch., 1812. His given name was changed 25 Mch., 1845, by act of legislature, to Arnold William (List of Persons whose names have been changed in Mass-

achusetts, p. 108). He was for many years a member of the dry goods firm of Conant, Elden & Wood, doing business in Boston. He retired from business several years before his death, and spent most of his time in travelling. He d. 5 June, 1884, in Paris, France, leaving a large property, the greater part of which he bequeathed to charitable and religious institutions.

353. **Ebenezer**[7] (*Abel, Andrew, Lot, John, Lot, Roger*), b. about 1780, in Concord, Mass. He d. 7 Apr., 1868 (aged 88 years 9 months?). He m. 6 Dec., 1812, Betsey Hobson, or Hosmer, who d. 31 Jan., 1831, aged 39.

Children of EBENEZER and BETSEY (HOBSON?) CONANT :—

William Augustus, b. 19 Sep., 1813; d. 18 June, 1833.
Darius, b. 6 Nov., 1815.
Harriet Maria, b. 30 July, 1817; d. 30 Apr., 1842.
Cyrus, b. 5 Oct., 1819.
Eliza Ann, b. 22 June, 1822.
Emily, b. 11 Feb., 1824.
Caroline, b. 20 Apr., 1828; d. 7 Feb., 1841.
Elizabeth, d. 26 Feb., 1831, aged 4 months.

354. **Luther**[7] (*Abel, Andrew, Lot, John, Lot, Roger*), b. about 1790, in Concord, Mass.; settled in Acton; m. 3 Jan., 1813, Sukey Edwards.

Children of LUTHER and SUKEY (EDWARDS) CONANT :—

A son, who d. 18 June, 1827.
Augustine, b. 8 Sep., 1828; of Boston.
A child, who d. 28 Nov., 1835, aged 3 years.
Luther, b. 4 June, 1831; lives in Acton, on the homestead. He served in a Mass. regt. during the late war. He was representative to the General Court of Mass., 1887.

355. **Reuben**[7] (*William, William, Lot, John, Lot, Roger*), b. 15 Jan., 1757 (in Acton?); settled in Harvard, Mass. In July, 1777, he was in H. Whitney's company of Col. Josiah Whitney's regiment, in the Revolutionary army; later was corporal in Sawyer's company (Mass. Arch., Muster Rolls, Vol. 24, p. 135, and Vol. 26, p. 419½). He served three years in 1st company of the 10th regiment, in the Continental army (Continental Army Rolls).

Children of REUBEN and ——— (———) CONANT :—

Reuben, m. Hannah Lampson, and had Mary Ann and Lucy.

Mary.
Abel, d. unm.
Lucy.
William, m. Betsey Whitney, and had William and Andrew.
Porter, m. Mary Hapgood, and had Mary Louisa.
Lydia, m. and had family.

356. Simeon[7] (*William, William, Lot, John, Lot, Roger*), b. 27 Aug., 1762, in Acton, or Harvard, Mass. On 22 July, 1780, Simeon Conant of Harvard, " 18 years of age, 5 ft. 9 in. tall, light complexion," was in Capt. Wm. Scott's company, and was discharged 15 Dec., 1780, having served six months in the Revolutionary army (Mass. Arch., Muster Rolls, Vol. 35, p. 206, and Vol. 4, p. 106). 9 Feb., 1786, he bought land in Waterford, Maine, of Silas Holman, which he sold 1792-3 (Cumberland Deeds, Vol. 14, p. 327). He removed from Harvard about 1800, and settled in Grafton, Vt., where he d. 3 June, 1836. He m. 17 Mch., 1788, Betsey Johnson, of Bolton.

Children of SIMEON and BETSEY (JOHNSON) CONANT:—

	Sarah, b. 22 Jan., 1789.
609.	Emery, b. 20 Jan., 1791.
610.	Luther, b. 19 Sep., 1793.
611.	Elizabeth, b. 7 Nov., 1796.
	Nancy, b. 27 Aug., 1799.
612.	Ruxby, b. 23 Mch., 1803.

357. Levi[7] (*William, William, Lot, John, Lot, Roger*), b. 7 Aug., 1767, in Harvard, Mass., where he lived; was a farmer and cooper; d. Nov., 1842. He m. in Bedford, 1794, Abigail Davis, who d. Apr., 1843.

Children of LEVI and ABIGAIL (DAVIS) CONANT:—

613.	Benjamin, b. 13 July, 1795.
614.	Rebecca, b. 23 Jan., 1797.
	Sewall, b. 13 Oct., 1798.
	Abigail, b. 31 Mch., 1800.
	Eliza, b. 6 Aug., 1801.
615.	Lucinda, b. 26 Apr., 1804.
616.	George W., b. 10 Apr., 1805.
	Levi, b. 4 Sep., 1807; d. y.
617.	Levi, b. 6 Feb., 1810.
618.	Henry, b. 18 Sep., 1815.

358. William[7] (*William, John, Lot, John, Lot, Roger*),

b. 17 Aug., 1765, in Shirley, Mass., where he lived;. a carpenter. He committed suicide by hanging, 5 Aug., 1846. He m. 17 Nov., 1796, Sarah Phelps.

Children of WILLIAM and SARAH (PHELPS) CONANT:—

William, b. 2 May, 1797.
Sally, b. 3 Dec., 1798; m. Luke Woodbury, of Bolton, and had May B., b. 1827, who m. 1853, Charles F. Sawtell, of Fitchburg, Mass. She d. 30 Dec., 1832.
Lucinda, b. 23 Dec., 1800; d. 28 July, 1847.
Eunice, b. 20 Mch., 1802; m. (1) Dec., 1823, John Farnsworth; m. (2) Luke Woodbury, of Bolton, who d. 1843.
Lavina, b. 3 July, 1803; m. (1) 3 Oct., 1830, George Spaulding; he d. 1847, and she m. (2) 25 Dec., 1856, John Clement, of Townsend; m. (3) 5 May, 1868, Jonas Parker, of Townsend.
Jefferson, b. 26 Aug., 1809.

359.   **Nathan**[7] (*Nathaniel, John, Lot, John, Lot, Roger*), b. 17 Aug., 1766, in Townsend, Mass.; lived in West Townsend; a miller. He was concerned in "Shay's rebellion" (*Hist. Townsend*, p. 219). He d. 31 July, 1845. He m. (1) 3 Mch., 1791, Mary Dix (Id., p. 402); m. (2) 22 Dec., 1796, Mrs. Hannah Potter (Id.; p. 406), who d. 6 Nov., 1828, aged 49 (Family Record).

Children of NATHAN and HANNAH (————) CONANT:—

Abigail, who d. 24 Apr., 1831, aged 28.
619.   Nathaniel, b. 1805. *
620.   John, b. 15 Apr., 1807.
Samuel; went West; was a surgeon, it is said, under Gen. Rosecrans, at Galliopolis, during the late war. After the war lived in Boston a while, then went West again.

360.   **Levi**[7] (*Nathaniel, John, Lot, John, Lot, Roger*), b. 19 Feb., 1779, in Townsend, Mass., where he lived till 1808, then moved to Cavendish, Vt.; d. July, 1857, in West Townsend, Mass. He m. 27 Nov., 1800, Eunice Saunders, of Lunenburg, Mass., b. 22 Apr., 1781; d. 7 Mch., 1853, in West Townsend.

Children of LEVI and EUNICE (SAUNDERS) CONANT:—

Levi, b. 9 Dec., 1801; of Cambridge, Mass.; m. Eliza Fillebrown. Adopted child: Charlotte Morrison, who m. William P. Greenough, of Cambridge.
Sally, b. 11 June, 1803; d. 30 Dec., 1878; m. 18 Oct., 1825, in

Ludlow, Vt., Isaac Pollard. Children: 1. Emily, b. 22 June, 1826, m. Richard R. Dudley; 2. Adaline, b. 27 Oct., 1828, m. Timothy Hastings, of Mt. Holly, Vt., and had Isaac, Frank and Adda; 3. Isaac, b. 11 July, 1830, m. Viola Brown, now of Nehawka, Neb.; 4. Moses, b. 21 Aug., 1832, of Plymouth, Vt., m. Sarah Miner; 5. Julia Ann, b. 20 Dec., 1834, in Plymouth, Vt., m. Lawson Sheldon, of Nehawka, Neb.; 6. Levi C., b. 10 Feb., 1837; 7. Isadore E., b. 1 Sep., 1845, m. Vilas E. Moore, of Springfield, Mass.

Adaline, b. 39 Jan., 1805; m. Royal Wood, of Brattleboro', Vt. Children: Adaliza, Lucy, Sanford, Philip and Jane.

Eliza, b. 12 Sep., 1807, in Townsend, Mass.; m. Thomas Dodge, of Mt. Holly, Vt.; now of DeKalb, Ill. Children: Warren, Rollin and Lucien.

621. David, b. 8 Apr., 1809, in Ludlow, Vt.

Calvin, b. 12 Oct., 1811.

Roxana W., b. 22 Mch., 1820; m. John Davis, of Townsend, Mass. Children: Eliza, who m. Albert Rogers, and Henry, of DeKalb, Ill.

361. Betsey[7] (*Nathaniel, John, Lot, John, Lot, Roger*), b. 10 Apr., 1781, in Townsend, Mass.; d. 17 Dec., 1862; m. 16 Oct., 1803, Thomas, son of Moses and Martha (Reed) Warren, b. 12 May, 1782, in Townsend; d. 25 Oct., 1859, in West Townsend. He was a dealer in wood and coal, of Boston and West Townsend.

Children of THOMAS and BETSEY (CONANT) WARREN:—

i. Charles, b. 29 Apr., 1804; d. in Balize, Honduras, Nov., 1865.
ii. Varnum, b. 3 Oct., 1806, in Townsend.
iii. Roxana, b. 19 Feb., 1810, in Cavendish, Vt.; d. 12 Aug., 1819.
iv. Moses, b. 23 Feb., 1815, in Cavendish, Vt.; d. 17 June, 1817.
v. Moses Conant, b. 16 Jan., 1817, in Cavendish, Vt.; now of Boston; m. 12 Oct., 1842, Frances Mehitable, dr. of Joseph and Ann (Goss) Bozman. Children: 1. William Henry, b. 21 June, 1843; 2. Joseph Bozman, b. 6 Jan., 1847, d. 1848; 3. George Edward, b. 11 Oct., 1850; 4. Mary Frances, b. 21 Apr., 1852; 5. Charles Gardner, b. 14 Nov., 1854, d. 1855; 6. Charles Bozman, b. 24 Jan., 1856; 7. Nellie, b. 11 Oct., 1859, d. 1868.

362. Daniel[7] (*Daniel, John, Lot, John, Lot, Roger*), b. 16 July, 1784, in Townsend. He taught school in Townsend, 1808 (*Hist. of Townsend*, p. 236).

Children of DANIEL and LOIS (———) CONANT:—

Daniel, b. 29 Mch., 1807.

Fred Plummer, b. 13 Dec., 1808.

363. John[7] (*John, John, Lot, John, Lot, Roger*), b. in Townsend, Mass., 24 Oct., 1772; was of Townsend. He m. 31 Oct., 1793, Rebecca Wallis.

Children of JOHN and REBECCA (WALLIS) CONANT:—

> Rebecca, b. 29 Dec., 1793.
> Asa, b. 23 Mch., 1795.
> Rebecca, b. 7 Aug., 1799; m. 7 May, 1818, Bemsley Lord.
> Hannah, b. 19 July, 1801.
> Mary, b. 15 Nov., 1804.
> Daniel, b. 25 Nov., 1807.

364. Noah Farrar[7] (*John, John, Lot, John, Lot, Roger*), b. 26 May, 1778, in Townsend, Mass.; a miller and farmer. He removed to Deering, N. H., Lowell, Vt., and back to Townsend. He d. 2 May, 1852. He m. in Deering, N. H., 7 Apr., 1810, Polly Stearns.

Children of NOAH F. and POLLY (STEARNS) CONANT:—

622. Noah, b. 11 Aug., 1812, in Townsend.
      John, b. 6 Dec., 1814, in Townsend.
623. Joseph Stearns, b. 16 Feb., 1817, in Lowell, Vt.
      Eliza, b. 18 Feb., 1819, in Lowell, Vt.
      Josiah, b. 7 July, 1821, in Townsend.
      Mary, b. 10 May, 1824, in Townsend.
      Benjamin Hartwell, b. 10 May, 1827.
      George H., b. 15 July, 1831.

365. Joel[7] (*John, John, Lot, John, Lot, Roger*), b. 4 May, 1783, in Townsend, Mass.; m. 11 May, 1813, Charlotte, dr. of Moses and Martha (Reed) Warren, b. 16 June, 1790; d. 11 Jan., 1867.

Children of JOEL and CHARLOTTE (WARREN) CONANT:—

> Charlotte Warren, b. 30 June, 1815; d. 5 Oct., 1870; m. Apr., 1846, Lysander Willard, and had Henry.
> Franklin, b. 1817.
> Henry, b. 1819; d. 1822.
> Mary, b. 1821; d. 9 Sep., 1860; m. 1850, William Emery.
> Henry D., b. 1825; d. 13 July, 1843.

366. Mary[7] (*Lot, Ezra, Lot, John, Lot, Roger*), b. 8 Nov., 1783, in Concord, Mass.; m. 10 Oct., 1805, Elisha Perkins, of Concord.

Child of ELISHA and MARY (CONANT) PERKINS:—

i.   Luke, m. Elizabeth Crosby, and had: 1. Mary; 2. Henry; 3. Jane; 4. William; 5. Ozro.

367. Catherine[7] (*Lot, Ezra, Lot, John, Lot, Roger*), b. 20 Oct., 1784, in Concord, Mass.; m. 10 July, 1808, Henry Hapgood, b. in Marlboro', 20 Nov., 1787.

Children of HENRY and CATHERINE (CONANT) HAPGOOD:—

i.   James Munroe, b. 11 Nov., 1809, in Marlboro'.
ii.   Adaline, b. 27 Apr., 1812; d. 9 Dec., 1846.
iii.   Henry, b. 10 June, 1814; d. 1844.
iv.   Catherine, b. 2 Dec., 1816, in Hingham, Mass.; d. 27 Oct., 1834.
v.   Lucy Ann, b. 4 May, 1819, in Hingham; d. 1845.

368. Hannah[7] (*Lot, Ezra, Lot, John, Lot, Roger*), b. 19 Oct., 1789, in Concord, Mass.; m. 11 Nov., 1811, Col. William, son of William and Rebecca (Brown) Whiting, of Lancaster. He was b. in Sterling, Mass., 20 Oct., 1788; his father, William, was son of Judge Thomas and Mary (Lake) Whiting, of Concord. Judge Thomas Whiting was of the fifth generation from Rev. Samuel Whiting, of Boston, Lincolnshire, England. Col. William Whiting was a member of the Unitarian church. He became interested in the Abolition movement in early days, and was for many years Vice President of the Mass. Anti-Slavery Society.

Children of WILLIAM and HANNAH (CONANT) WHITING:—

i.   William, b. 31 Mch., 1813; graduated at Harvard, 1833; studied law; LL. D., 1872. He was a member of the Electoral College which elected Grant in 1868; was a member of the 43rd Congress from the 3rd Mass. District; Solicitor to the War Department, 1862-5. He took a great interest in genealogical studies, and was President of the New England Historic Genealogical Society many years. He m. 28 Oct., 1840, Lydia, dr. of Hon. Thomas Russell, of Plymouth. Children: 1. Rose Standish, b. 28 Dec., 1843; 2. William St. John, b. 6 Nov., 1848; 3. William Russell, 22 Sep., 1850; 4. Harold, 13 May, 1855.
ii.   Anna Maria, b. 8 Oct., 1814; d. 16 Feb., 1867.
iii.   Louisa Jane, b. 12 June, 1820; m. 14 Sep., 1858, Rev. Spencer Barker, of Leominster, Chaplain of the Mass. Heavy Artillery during the war. He is now of McIndoes Falls.

369. Lot[7] (*Lot, Ezra, Lot, John, Lot, Roger*), b. 15 July, 1792, in Concord, Mass.; removed to Reading, Vt., with his

23

father, where he d. 4 Oct., 1847. He was a carpenter. He m.
in Reading, 11 Feb., 1817, Hannah, dr. of Samuel and Hannah
(Hall) Newton, b. 28 Jan., 1796, d. 9 Sep., 1885.

Children of LOT and HANNAH (NEWTON) CONANT:—

624. Isabella Eliza, b. 30 Dec., 1819.
      Emily Maria, b. 22 Oct., 1821; m. Daniel Crocker, of North
      Bridgewater.
      Elisha Ferdinand, b. 30 Sep., 1823; d. 1836.
    ⸗ Marcella Aurora, b. 9 June, 1824; m. (374) Ezra Conant.
      Mary Amelia, b. 10 Apr., 1828; d. aged 20.
      Harriet Clementina, b. 10 May, 1831; m. 17 Oct., 1874, Theo-
      dore Harding, of Medfield, Mass., where they reside.
      Laura Lovett, b. 10 Aug., 1833; m. 28 Jan., 1851, G. A. Par-
      ker, of Meriden, Conn.; has John Herbert, b. 1857.
625. Thaddeus Elisha, b. 23 June, 1835.
      Electa Ann, b. 23 July, 1837; d. 28 May, 1855.
      Ellen Louisa, b. 23 Apr., 1840; m. John A. Harvey, of Meri-
      den, Conn.

370. Thaddeus⁷ (*Lot, Ezra, Lot, John, Lot, Roger*), b. 1
Sep., 1795, in Concord, Mass.; removed to Reading, Vt., with
his parents, thence to Boston, Mass.; was a merchant. He d.
in Brattleboro', Vt., 1850. He m. Laura Carter Butterfield, b.
1799, in Peterboro', N. H.; d. in Boston, 26 Nov., 1830.

Children of THADDEUS and LAURA C. (BUTTERFIELD) CO-
NANT:

      Laura Ann, b. 28 Oct., 1821; d. 23 Apr., 1845.
626. James Henry, b. 13 July, 1823.
      William Thaddeus, b. 25 Dec., 1825; d. 1845.
      Helen Francis, b. 12 Mch., 1828; d. 19 Feb., 1845.
      Emily Susanna, b. 3 Sep., 1830; m. Charles Jones, of Athol,
      Mass.; had six children, among whom were Nathaniel and
      Wythe.

371. Elisha Lockwood⁷ (*Lot, Ezra, Lot, John, Lot,
Roger*), b. 30 Apr., 1801, in Concord, Mass. He removed to
Reading, Vt., with his parents, and thence to Evansville, Ind.
He was a merchant, and afterwards a banker and real estate
agent. He d. 2 July, 1882, in Evansville. He m. 1829, in
Cincinnati, Ohio, Maria, dr. of Rev. Adain Hurdus; she d. 8
Dec., 1876.

Children of ELISHA L. and MARIA (HURDUS) CONANT:—

Thaddeus Lockwood, b. 10 Mch., 1829. He is unmarried; now resides in Topeka, Kansas; is cashier of the Topeka City R. R. Co. He has adopted George Cottrell Brooks, who was aged 15 in 1884.

627. William Henry, b. 24 Dec., 1834, in Cincinnati.

Maria Louisa, b. 15 Aug., 1837, in Louisville, Ky.; m. William H. Oakley, and has William L. and Ora S.

Matilda Ames, b. 15 May, 1840, in St. Louis, Mo.; unmarried.

Laura Jane, b. 1844, in Memphis, Tenn.; d. y.

372. Sarah Foster[7] (*Ezra, Ezra, Lot, John, Lot, Roger*), b. 5 Sep., 1793, in Winchester, N. H.; m. Lynde Wheelock, of Keene, N. H., where they died.

Children of LYNDE and SARAH F. (CONANT) WHEELOCK:—

i. George, of Keene, N. H. (1885).
ii. Andrew, of Lowell, Mass. (1885).

373. Pamela[7] (*Ezra, Ezra, Lot, John, Lot, Roger*), b. 19 Sep., 1795, (or 19 Apr., 1799,) in Winchester, N. H.; m. 23 Jan., 1816, John H. Fuller, of Keene, N. H.

Children of JOHN H. and PAMELA (CONANT) FULLER:—

i. Lucy C., b. 4 June, 1817.
ii. Sarah A., b. 23 May, 1819; d. 1838.
iii. John Quincy, b. 10 Mch., 1821.
iv. Sophia P., b. 30 Aug., 1823; m. Frederick R. Bartlett; has Ellen, b. 1855, and Theodore, b. 1857.
v. James G., b. 14 Dec., 1825; d. 1852.
vi. Reuben B., b. 3 Oct., 1827.

374. Ezra[7] (*Ezra, Ezra, Lot, John, Lot, Roger*), b. 4 July, 1812, in Winchester, N. H.; moved to Roxbury, Mass., with his parents. He was a manufacturer of morocco and patent leather, but retired from business about 1860, and has since lived in Roxbury (Boston). He m. 28 Sep., 1848, in Roxbury, Marcella A., dr. of Lot and Hannah (Newton) Conant; she d. 22 Mch., 1852.

Children of EZRA and MARCELLA A. (CONANT) CONANT:—

Ezra Russell, b. 6 Aug., 1849, in Roxbury; d. 13 June, 1873.
Emma Elizabeth, b. 6 Aug., 1849; d. 9 Dec., 1858.
Harriet Anna, b. 23 Oct., 1850; d. 15 May, 1871.

375. John[7] (*John, John, John, John, Lot, Roger*), b. 11

Mch., 1771, in Beverly, in the house at "4" (see p. 146).   He
was a farmer and shoemaker;
was major of militia; and rep-   *John Conant*
resentative to General Court,   (1839.)
from Beverly, two years.   He removed from Beverly to Topsfield, where his children were born, but afterwards back to
Beverly and bought a farm on Conant street (at "8," see p.
146), a little to the west of Cabot street, where he d. 30 Mch.,
1859.   He m. (1) 2 Sep., 1792, Sarah W., dr. of Benjamin
Fisk, b. in Topsfield, 1773, d. 25 Feb., 1830; m. (2) in Beverly, Oct., 1831, Rebecca, dr. of Cornelius Baker; she d. 1 May,
1883.

Children of JOHN and SARAH (FISK) CONANT:—

628.   John, b. 5 Oct., 1793, in Topsfield.
629.   Sarah, b. 5 Oct., 1796.
630.   Harriet, b. June, 1799.
          Benjamin, b. 1802; m. 15 Oct., 1835, Sophia Silver; they had
            no children.   He was a sea captain, and d. 17 July, 1839, in
            Madagascar.
          Irene, b. 1808; d. 20 July, 1822.

376.   Emma[7] (*John, John, John, John, Lot, Roger*), b. 2
May, 1776, in Beverly; m. Thomas Dodge.

Children of THOMAS and EMMA (CONANT) DODGE:—

i.   Clara, d. unm.
ii.   Emma, m. Eben Perry, of Dublin, N. H.
iii.   Mary, b. about 1802; m. Benjamin Ludden, of Beverly.   Chil-
         dren; 1. Adaline, d. y.; 2. Benjamin E., who m. Elizabeth
         Woodbury, and had Ella, Charles, William E., Anna and
         Frank.
iv.   Louisa, m. —— Jacobs, of Medford.
v.   Alsira, m. William Lefavor, of Salem.
vi.   Albert T., b. 1817; m. Elizabeth Herrick.   Children: 1.
         Frank; 2. Charles, of Providence, R. I.; 3. Robert Ran-
         toul, of Beverly; 4. Frank; 5. Arthur.   Albert T. Dodge
         was a farmer; held various town offices in Beverly.

377.   Ezra[7] (*John, John, John, John, Lot, Roger*), b. 28
Feb., 1780, in Bev-
erly; was a farmer;   *Ezra Conant*
d. about 1850.   He
m. 26 Mch., 1812,   (1811.)

Mary, dr. of Joseph and Esther Corning; she was b. 2 Dec., 1791; d. May, 1880.

Children of EZRA and MARY (CORNING) CONANT:—

Martha, b. 5 Feb., 1814; m. Francis Edwards, of Wenham. She d. 1884.
631. Joseph, b. 6 May, 1816.
632. John, b. 20 Sep., 1818.
633. Ezra, b. 14 Sep., 1820.
634. Herbert Thorndike, b. 4 Mch., 1823.
Emma T., b. 2 Apr., 1828; d. 29 July, 1829.
Emma T., b. 5 Apr., 1830; d. 2 Oct., 1850; unm.
Charles G., b. 12 Feb., 1826; lives on the homestead in North Beverly; a farmer; unmarried. In 1880 he tore down the old house at "2" (see p. 146), which his grandfather bought in 1797, and built the present house.

378. **Nathaniel**[7] (*Nathaniel, Samuel, John, John, Lot, Roger*), b. 3 Oct., 1790, in Beverly, Mass.; moved to New Salem, N. H., with his parents; settled in Manchester, N. H.; was a cooper; d. 1832. He m. Hannah Graves Whittaker, who d. 11 Aug., 1847.

Children of NATHANIEL and HANNAH G. (WHITTAKER) CONANT:—

Sarah Jane, d. in Cleveland, Ohio.
Mary, d. in Cleveland, Ohio.
Mercy, b. 1823, in Manchester, N. H.
Andrew Burnham, b. 8 Aug., 1828, in Manchester, N. H., where he lives. He is a watchman in the Manchester Mills. He m. 23 Dec., 1868, Lettie Ann Brown. They have no children.
Clarissa Maria, b. 19 Apr., 1830; d. in Cleveland, Ohio.

379. **Eunice**[7] (*Nathaniel, Samuel, John, John, Lot, Roger*), b. 27 Jan., 1807, in New Salem, N. H.; m. 19 Mch., 1832, in Derry, N. H., Washington Haines. She d. 29 Jan., 1837.

Children of WASHINGTON and EUNICE (CONANT) HAINES:—

i. Charles P., b. 7 May, 1834.
ii. Eliza Jane, b. 6 Oct., 1836.

380. **Nancy**[7] (*Benjamin, Lot, John, John, Lot, Roger*), b. ———, in Beverly; m. William, son of Deacon William Dodge. They lived in Wenham.

Children of WILLIAM and NANCY (CONANT) DODGE:—

i.   William.
ii.   Benjamin.
iii. Lydia, m. Francis Jenness, of No. Beverly.
iv. Andrew, of No. Beverly. He owns the western part of the
     old Conant homestead on Dodge street, and lives at "5"
     (see map, p. 146).
v.   Abigail, ⎫
vi.   Martha, ⎬ one of these m. Porter Hamilton.
vii. Joanna, ⎭

381. Mary[7] (*Barnabas, Daniel, Daniel, John, Lot, Roger*), b. 1 Mch., 1787, in Beverly, Mass.; moved, with her parents, to Sunapee, N. H.; m. 12 Apr., 1821, Isaac Eastman, b. in Weare, N. H., 13 Apr., 1775. He was a farmer, of Sunapee; d. 16 June, 1856. She d. 11 Feb., 1874.

Children of ISAAC and MARY (CONANT) EASTMAN:—

i.   Daniel Conant, b. 24 Dec., 1821; m. 3 July, 1855, Sarah Jane
     Messer. Lives in Sunapee.
ii.   David, b. 8 Feb., 1823.
iii. Mary Ann. b. 30 Nov., 1827.

382. Gardner[7] (*Josiah, Daniel, Daniel, John, Lot, Roger*), b. 30 Jan., 1794, in Warwick, Mass., where he lived; d. Jan., 1877. He m. 20 Apr., 1826, Livonia Hodge.

Children of GARDNER and LIVONIA (HODGE) CONANT:—

635. James A., b. 31 Mch., 1827.
636. Samuel D., b. 8 Apr., 1835.
637. Josiah, b. 17 Jan., 1840.
     Melinda L., b. 20 July, 1841; d. 1872; was twice m. but had
     no children.
     Luana A., d. aged 6 years.

383. Josiah[7] (*Josiah, Daniel, Daniel, John, Lot, Roger*), b. 21 June, 1796, in Warwick, Mass., where he lived; d. 6 Apr., 1870. He m. 22 Feb., 1835, Rhoda Gale, who d. 1 Aug., 1861.

Children of JOSIAH and RHODA (GALE) CONANT:—

     Irene, b. 18 Nov., 1835; m. June, 1874, Leonard Fisher, of
     Dana, Mass.
     Tryphena, b. 18 Nov., 1835; d. y.
     Mary E., b. 25 Feb., 1837.
     Elsie, b. 12 Jan., 1841.

384. Hiram[7] (*Josiah, Daniel, Daniel, John, Lot, Roger*),

b. 10 Jan., 1799, in Warwick, Mass. He was a farmer; lived in Holden, Orange and Greenfield. He m. in Oakham, Mass., 31 Mch., 1828, Ruby S. Reed; she d. in Orange, 17 Aug., 1845.

Children of HIRAM and RUBY S. (REED) CONANT:—

> Hiram Reed, b. 28 June, 1829, in Holden.
> Ellen Olive, b. 28 May, 1831,   "
> 638. Edward Everett, b. 9 Mch., 1837, "
> Henry Clay, b. 14 Feb., 1840, in Orange.
> Josiah Gardner, b. 16 Jan., 1845, in Orange.

385. Samuel[7] (*Josiah, Daniel, Daniel, John, Lot, Roger*), b. 21 Aug., 1803, in Warwick, Mass.; removed to Richmond, Vt., in 1826, where he has since resided. He m. (1) 1828, Lucy Barker; m. (2) 19 Apr., 1840, Harriet Melinda Pierce.

Children of SAMUEL and HARRIET M. (PIERCE) CONANT:—

> Polly Jane, b. 15 Nov., 1844; d. before 1884.
> Samuel Pierce, b. 5 Dec., 1848; d. in Newton University Hospital, Baltimore, Md., 7 Mch., 1864.
> Harriet Melinda, b. 28 Aug., 1850.
> 639. Ransom Merritt, b. 20 Aug., 1852.
> 640. Hiram Solomon, b. 20 Apr., 1854.

386. Ruth[7] (*Joshua, Nathaniel, Daniel, John, Lot, Roger*), b. 8 Oct., 1787, in Alfred, Me.; m. 12 Nov., 1809, Richard Thompson, of Kennebunk, Me.

Children of RICHARD and RUTH (CONANT) THOMPSON:—

i.   Caleb.
ii. Daniel.
iii. Franklin, now (1886) of Kennebunk.

387. Nathaniel[7] (*Joshua, Nathaniel, Daniel, John, Lot, Roger*), b. 15 Dec., 1789, in Alfred, Me.; lived in Shapleigh; a farmer; he d. 6 Apr., 1834, in Shapleigh. He m. in Bridgton, Me., 29 Dec., 1817, Rachel, dr. of Nathan and Mary Dodge, b. in Beverly, Mass., 29 May, 1790, d. in Shapleigh, 29 Sep., 1867.

Children of NATHANIEL and RACHEL (DODGE) CONANT:—

> Amanda, b. 5 Oct., 1818.
> Charles, b. 1 Apr., 1821, in Shapleigh; a farmer; has been town treasurer; m. in Springvale, Me., 21 July, 1844, Drusilla, dr. of Joshua and Nancy (Stone) Russell, b. in Alfred, 28 Sep., 1824. They have no children, but have adopted Belle A. Sherburn.

641.   Nathan Dodge, b. 1 Apr., 1825.
       Mary A., b. 24 June, 1828.

388. Theodate[7] (*Joshua, Nathaniel, Daniel, John, Lot, Roger*), b. 18 Sep., 1793, in Alfred, Me.; d. 7 June, 1846. She m. Abiel, son of Nathaniel Farnum, of Alfred.

Children of ABIEL and THEODATE (CONANT) FARNUM:—

i.   George.
ii.   Charles, m. but d. without children.
iii.   William.
iv.   Delia, m. —— Simpson.
v.   Harriet.
vi.   Lucy, m. —— Myrick. He is a judge, in San Francisco, Cal.

389. Joshua[7] (*Joshua, Nathaniel, Daniel, John, Lot, Roger*), b. 1 Aug., 1796, in Alfred, Me. He is now living in Brookline, Mass. The autograph of which a fac-simile is given, accompanying his portrait, was written in June, 1887. He m. (1) 17 Mch., 1824, Theodate Trafton; m. (2) 1 Feb., 1830, Rebecca, dr. of Joseph and Phebe (Hayes) Fogg, of Berwick, Me., b. 31 May, 1800, d. 2 Mch., 1885. Joseph Fogg was fifth in descent from Samuel Fogg, of Hampton, N. H. (see Maine Genealogical and Historical Recorder, Vol. 1, p. 78).

Children of JOSHUA and THEODATE (TRAFTON) CONANT:—

Lydia Ann, b. 12 Dec., 1824; d. 10 Jan., 1837.
William G., b. 28 May, 1827; d. 5 Mch., 1849.

Children of JOSHUA and REBECCA (FOGG) CONANT:—

Mercy Jane, b. 26 Dec., 1830; d. 26 Mch., 1833.
Mary H., b. 28 Jan., 1833.
Edward Card, b. 29 Apr., 1835; graduated at Bowdoin Medical College, 1858, but afterwards studied law with Hon. N. D. Appleton, of Alfred, and was graduated LL. B. 1865, at Harvard Law School. He was admitted to Suffolk Bar, and opened an office in Boston, but in 1866 removed to Little Rock, Ark., and engaged in mercantile pursuits, but became insane, and after thirteen years of illness d. 29 Sep., 1879.
642.   Nathaniel, b. 26 Mch., 1837.
John R., b. 11 Mch., 1839; d. 4 Sep., 1840.
Lydia Ann, b. 17 Dec., 1840.

390. Daniel[7] (*Joshua, Nathaniel, Daniel, John, Lot, Rog-*

Joshua Conant

er), b. 7 May, 1798, in Alfred, Me.; m. (1) Amy, dr. of Henry and Amy (Herrick) Wiggin, b. 27 Oct., 1794; m. (2) Paulina Hasty.

Child of DANIEL and ―――― (――――) CONANT:―

Ellen, who lives in Alfred.

391. William Green[7] (*Joshua, Nathaniel, Daniel, John, Lot, Roger*), b. 25 Dec., 1806, in Alfred, Me., where he has always resided. He was a merchant, but retired a number of years ago. He m. Hannah Jones Herrick, of Beverly, Mass.

Child of WILLIAM G. and HANNAH J. (HERRICK) CONANT:―

643. William Henry, b. 20 May, 1830.

392. Thomas Gile[7] (*Joshua, Nathaniel, Daniel, John, Lot, Roger*), b. 15 Dec., 1815, in Alfred, Me. He moved to near Bloomington, Illinois, and thence to Kansas.

Children of THOMAS G. and ―――― (――――) CONANT:―

Susan.
John.

393. Mary[7] (*Nathaniel, Nathaniel, Daniel, John, Lot, Roger*), b. 15 Nov., 1799, in Alfred, Me.; d. 30 Nov., 1868. She m. 14 Jan., 1819, Benjamin Jones, son of Joshua and Mary (Jones) Herrick, of Beverly, Mass. (see *Herrick Genealogy*). He was b. 9 Apr., 1791; d. 24 May, 1870. Maj. Herrick went to Alfred in 1816 and engaged in mercantile business, but was appointed deputy sheriff soon after, and held that position till 1830. In Sept. of the latter year he was elected a member of the state legislature. In the spring of 1831 he was appointed by Gov. Smith, high sheriff of York county, which office he held till Dec., 1836, when he resigned the office of sheriff to enter upon that of register of deeds. The latter office he held until 1847. He filled for many years the position of brigade major and inspector of militia. For many years was chairman of the board of selectmen. He was an active and prominent member of the Masonic order. In religious and educational matters he took an active interest, being a member of the Methodist Episcopal Church, and for many years a trustee of the Maine Wesleyan Seminary. He was for a long period an influential member of the Democratic party, and was widely and favorably known throughout the state.

Children of BENJAMIN J. and MARY (CONANT) HERRICK:—

i.   Benjamin Jones, b. 29 Dec., 1819; d. 20 Mch., 1820.
ii.   Benjamin Jones, b. 13 Feb., 1821; d. 6 Mch., 1821.
iii. Mary Caroline, b. 17 Aug., 1822; m. (1) 3 Sep., 1847, Isaac N. Burton, of Boston, Mass., who d. 4 July, 1849; m. (2) Hon. Sylvester Littlefield, of Alfred. He was a member of the state legislature in 1857 and 1862; county treasurer, 1866 and 1867; assistant assessor of Internal Revenue, 1871, 1872 and 1873; presidential elector, 1876. He d. 24 Sept., 1886.
iv.   Horatio Gates, b. 28 Oct., 1824; A. B., Bowdoin College, 1844; studied law with Hon. N. D. Appleton, of Alfred, and was admitted to the Bar, 1847, and commenced practice in No. Berwick, Me. In 1857 removed to Saugus, Mass., and entered upon the practice of law in Boston. In 1862 was appointed draft commissioner for Essex co., and in May, 1863, was commissioned provost marshal of the 6th district of Mass. In Nov., 1865, he was elected sheriff of Essex co., and has held that office until the present time (1887) by repeated elections. In 1871 was appointed a member of the board of prison commissioners for the Commonwealth, and has held many other offices of honor and trust. He is now of Lawrence, Mass. He m. 28 Aug., 1848, Isabella Sewall, dr. of Hon. John T. and Mary E. R. (Goodwin) Paine, of Sanford, Maine; she d. 12 Jan., 1857. Children: 1. Frederick St. Clair, b. 13 Mch., 1850, of Methuen, Mass., m. Isabel J. Ball, and d. 1884, leaving two daughters; 2. John St. Clair, b. 13 Mch., 1855, d. y.; 3. Alice Bigelow, b. 7 Oct., 1856, d. y.
v.   Nathaniel Jones, b. 8 Feb., 1827. He was several years clerk in the public offices of York county, and afterwards in the office of the secretary of state, at Augusta. During the war he held an important position in the Quartermaster's Department at Washington, and at Bowling Green, Ky., and during the administration of President Johnson was storekeeper at Kittery Navy Yard. Has for many years been justice of the peace, notary public and commissioner of deeds. He has been a frequent contributor to the Democratic press and historical publications, and it is said but few persons have a more extensive or accurate knowledge of the political and general history of the country than he.
vi.   Harriet Proctor, b. 17 Jan., 1829; m. 16 July, 1850, Hon. John M. Goodwin, counsellor at law, Biddeford, Me. He was b. in Baldwin, 3 Sep., 1822; A. B., Bowdoin College, 1845; was a member of the State Senate, 1856, and of the House of Representatives, 1863 and 1864; has been president of the York County Savings Bank since its incorporation in 1860.

Children: 1. Francis Jones, b. 12 Jan., 1852, of Malden, Mass., A. B., Amherst College, 1873, m. 1875, Emily B. Milliken, of Brantford, Ontario; 2. George Brown, b. 4 Mch., 1855, of Boston, Mass., sometime editor of the Bangor (Me.) Daily Commercial, and one of the editorial staff of the Boston Post, and now U. S. Consul at Annaburg, Germany; m. 1881, Grace L. Webster, of Orono, Me.; 3. Mary Isabella, b. 22 Feb., 1857, m. 1885, Frederick Gold Lyman, of Montreal, Canada; 4. Henry Herrick, b. 29 Nov., 1859, Vice Consul at Annaburg, Germany, m. 1887, Jennie Marie Murray, of Cincinnati, O.; 5. William Burton, b. 11 Jan., 1864, graduated at Yale, 1886.

394. Nancy Merrill[7] (*John, Nathaniel, Daniel, John, Lot, Roger*), b. 27 Dec., 1796, in Alfred; d. in Portland, Me., Nov., 1865. She m. 10 Dec., 1818, in Alfred, David, son of Dr. Abiel and Mary (Farnum) Hall, of Alfred. He was a merchant, doing business in company with his brother-in-law, Alvah Conant, at Alfred and Portland. He was b. 8 Oct., 1791; d. 22 Apr., 1863.

Children of DAVID and NANCY M. (CONANT) HALL:—

i. Augustus, d. y.
ii. Lucy Maria, d. y.
iii. Marianna, d. y.
iv. Charles Conant, b. 5 Aug., 1822, in Alfred, Me.; m. 7 June, 1848, Catherine, dr. of George Warren, of Portland. He was a merchant, of Portland. He d. 19 May, 1881. Children: 1. Frederick Sumner; 2. S. Washburn, d. 1854; 3. George Warren; 4. Caroline Bradford, d. 1875; 5. Walter David, d. 1861; 6. Annie Conant.
v. Lydia Augusta, b. 21 Jan., 1828; d. 13 Dec., 1885; m. 31 Oct., 1849, Jude Snow, of Boston, Mass., b. in Chesterfield, N. H., 23 Sep., 1820; d. in Portland, Me., 6 June, 1867. He was a merchant, of Boston, Mass., and Portland, Me. Children: 1. David William, b. 10 Nov., 1851, in Boston, Mass.; entered Bowdoin College in the class of 1873, but did not graduate on account of ill health; he is now a lawyer, of Portland, Me.; he m. 12 June, 1885, Martha H., dr. of William H. and Caroline (Vinton) Hemenway, b. in Atkinson, N. H., 9 Jan., 1855; 2. Lucien Burton, b. 21 Oct., 1854, m. 9 Feb., 1882, Nellie W., dr. of Hon. Samuel E. and Zilpah W. (Barker) Spring, of Portland, b. 29 Aug., 1861; has Lucien, b. 4 Dec., 1885; 3. Edward Hall, b. 28 Oct., 1859, m. 10 Sep., 1884, Alice G., dr. of William Trott and Henrietta (Baker) King; 4. Ella Post, b. 7 Jan., 1867.

395. **Alvah**[7] (*John, Nathaniel, Daniel, John, Lot, Roger*), b. 17 (or 19*) Dec., 1800, in Kennebunk, Me.; moved to Alfred, with his parents. He attended the common schools of Alfred, and Wakefield, N. H., and Fryeburg, Me., Academies. He then engaged as a clerk with George and Ivory Lord, at Kennebunk, but soon returned to Alfred and went into business with his father; this was as early as 1826. His father retired from business soon after, and Mr. Conant formed a partnership with his brother-in-law, David Hall, and later with his brother, George. In the autumn of 1838 he moved to Portland, Me., and engaged in the wholesale grocery business with Mr. Hall, under the firm name of Hall & Conant. In 1849 his son, Richard O., was admitted to the firm, the style of which was then changed to Hall, Conant & Company. Their store was at first on the north-east corner of Fore and Central streets, but when Commercial street was built, in 1851, they moved to the store since occupied by the firm. In 1856 Mr. Conant's son, Richard O., bought out Mr. Hall, and has continued the business to the present time. When he first moved to Portland he lived with his father-in-law, Richard Odell, on India street, but soon moved to State street, thence to Gray street, in 1845, where he resided till his death.

Mr. Conant never sought public office, but in the old militia days was commissioned captain in the second brigade of state militia, by Gov. Parris, in 1822; in 1843 and 1844 was a member of the common council of Portland, and in 1849 and 1850 was a member of the board of aldermen from the sixth ward. In 1859 he retired from business and devoted his time to the management of his private affairs. He was a director of the Cumberland National Bank for many years, and its president at the time of his death. He was also one of the first board of directors of the York and Cumberland Railroad. He bore a character of strict integrity, was a consistent christian and a member of the State Street Congregational Church. In person he was of about the medium height, rather sparely built, and very erect. He d. 2 Apr., 1876, at his residence on Gray street, in Portland.

---

*This is the date given in the family Bible, recorded sometime afterward, but Mr. Conant always celebrated the 17th as his birthday.

Alvah Conant

He m. (1) in Conway, N. H., 30 Oct., 1826, Almira, dr. of
Hon. Richard and Molly (Eastman) Odell, of Conway, b. in
Conway, 8 Sep., 1803, and d. in Portland, 23 Jan., 1841. Hon.
Richard Odell was frequently representative from Conway to
the N. H. legislature, and a member of the Governor's council.
He moved to Portland, Me., in 1837, where he d. 1850. He
was son of Joseph and Sarah (Ingalls) Odell; g. s. of William
and Martha (Collins) Odell, of Andover, Mass.; g. g. s. of
Reginald and Priscilla Odell (also written Wodell and Wod-
hull), of Boston. Molly Eastman was dr. of Richard and
Hannah (Merrill) Eastman; g. dr. of John and Martha (Fitts)
Eastman; g. g. dr. of John and Huldah (Kingsbury) Eastman;
g. g. g. dr. of John and Mary (Boynton) Eastman; g. g. g. g.
dr. of Roger and Sarah Eastman, of Salisbury, Mass. Mr.
Conant m. (2) 27 Apr., 1843, Judith, dr. of Joseph Osborn, of
Danvers, Mass., b. 21 Oct., 1804, d. 3 Feb., 1857; m. (3) in
Portland, Me., 8 July, 1858, Rebecca P., dr. of Samuel Cook,
of Taunton, Mass., b. 29 Feb., 1815, d. 17 Jan., 1863; and he
m. (4) in Manchester, Conn., 5 Sep., 1866, Mary (Sumner)
Woodbridge, who survived him, and d. in Portland; she was
dr. of Reuben Sumner, of Hebron, Conn., b. 20 Sep., 1816, d.
20 Mch., 1883.

Children of ALVAH and ALMIRA (ODELL) CONANT:—

644. Richard Odell, b. 1 Apr., 1828, in Alfred, Me.
645. Emma Dow, b. 4 Apr., 1830, in Alfred, Me.

396. Cyrus King[7] (*John, Nathaniel, Daniel, John, Lot,
Roger*), b. 1 Jan., 1803, in Alfred, Me. He was appointed to
a cadetship in the U. S. Military Academy at West Point, in
1819, but resigned 30 Nov., 1821. He then studied medicine
with Dr. Abiel Hall, in Alfred, and with Dr. Usher Parsons, in
Providence, R. I. He practiced in Alfred, Waterboro' and
Harrison, Me. In 1861 he retired from active practice and removed to Watertown, Mass., where he d. 10 Apr., 1871. He
m. in Alfred, 27 Dec., 1825, Abigail, dr. of Thomas and Joanna (Smith) Gile, of Alfred, b. 14 Jan., 1803; she d. in
Watertown, Mass., 21 May, 1887, at the residence of her son
John H. Conant.

Children of Cyrus K. and Abigail (Gile) Conant:—

Adeline Bedell, b. 1 May, 1828; d. y.
John H., b. 25 Feb., 1830; d. y.
Francis Adeline, b. 4 Mch., 1833; d. 1 Mch., 1842.
Caroline Sumner, b. 5 Apr., 1835; she lives, unmarried, with
her brother, John H. Conant.
646. John Henry, b. 10 Dec., 1836.
647. Alvah, b. 4 Nov., 1838.
648. Cyrus Gile, b. 4 Oct., 1845.

397. **Caroline**[7] (*John, Nathaniel, Daniel, John, Lot, Roger*), b. 16 Apr., 1809, in Alfred, Me.; m. in Alfred, 22 Sep., 1830, Hiram Frederick Sumner, of Hartford, Conn., b. 14 Feb., 1800, in Hebron, Conn. He was a book publisher, of Hartford, where he d. 3 Mch., 1874. She d. in Brooklyn, N. Y., 28 Feb., 1883.

Children of Hiram F. and Caroline (Conant) Sumner:—

i.   Frederick Conant, b. 25 July, 1835.
ii. George Alfred, b. 21 June, 1837; m. in Hartford, 13 Oct., 1869, Elizabeth D., dr. of William W. House. Children: William Alfred, b. 8 July, 1874, and George Alfred, b. 15 Oct., 1875. He is a commission merchant, doing business in New York; residence, Haledon, near Paterson, N. J.
iii. Albert Eugene, b. 28 Nov., 1840; d. 1882. He received his literary and classical education at Trinity College, and his degree of Doctor of Medicine from the University of New York. "If life is measured by deeds rather than years Dr. Sumner, although dying at the age of forty-two, still lived to a ripe old age, accomplishing a life's work in his score of professional years. The kindly nature, the warm sympathy ever roused at the sight of suffering and poverty, the great, noble, unselfish nature which made his friends' troubles his own, entering into their joys and sorrows, rejoicing when they rejoiced, and bringing to their aid, when the clouds of sorrow or adversity hung cold and dark over them, his skill as a physician, his advice as a friend, or his purse, when it would add to their comfort, was the magnetism which grappled his friends to him as with hooks of steel, and will keep his memory green in their hearts. Not only his genial nature, but his ready tact and quick wit, made him warm and fast friends, and carried him over many a difficult place, where those with less ample resources would have stumbled. This was illustrated in his application for a position as surgeon in the navy, in response to the call of the Government in 1861. He had passed his examination successfully, when he was asked if he was a homœopath. He

replied that he denied their right to ask that question in connection with his examination, and when an answer was positively demanded, he said: 'I positively refuse to answer your question, and if I am rejected on this ground, I shall appeal to the Secretary of the Navy,' who was an old family friend. The appeal was unnecessary, and the young surgeon found when assigned to the Corwin for service that not only the captain but most of the officers were homœopaths. He remained in the service eighteen months and then established himself in Brooklyn, shortly after entering into a partnership with Dr. A. Cook Hull. He was one of the lecturers in the New York Homœopathic Medical College, on diseases of the skin. At about the same time he was appointed medical director of a little dispensary in Atlantic street, which at the time of his death had expanded, under his fostering care, to the Cumberland Street Hospital and Dispensary, one of the best appointed hospitals in the country. The Brooklyn Maternity and Training School for Nurses also owes its existence to his energy and effective work. What prouder monument could any physician desire than institutions like these great fountains of healing, from which we trust will flow in living streams the blessings of our art through generations yet to come. Dr. Sumner had remained on his farm nearly all summer and enjoyed unusually good health. While getting out of his carriage in the city he reeled and would have fallen but for his coachman. He was taken to the house of his friend, Dr. Keep, and died in half an hour, from apoplexy" (New York Medical Times). He m. Louisa, dr. of George Beers, Esq., of New York. They had five children, two of whom d. y.

398. Lucy Maria[7] (*John, Nathaniel, Daniel, John, Lot, Roger*), b. 7 Dec., 1812, in Alfred, Me.; d. 4 June, 1883. She m. in Boston, Mass., 17 Dec., 1844, Daniel, son of Col. Daniel and Abigail (Parsons) Lewis. He was a merchant, of Boston, doing business with his brother-in-law, E. C. Drew. He was b. in Alfred, 3 Mch., 1803, and d. in Boston, 26 Jan., 1868.

Children of DANIEL and LUCY M. (CONANT) LEWIS:—

i.   Charles Hall, d. y,
ii.   Anna Hale, b. 5 Aug., 1847, in Boston, Mass.
iii. Charles Ward, b. 9 Nov., 1850, in Boston; graduated at Williams College, 1874, and from the Medical Department of Columbia College, 1876. He d. 15 May, 1879.
iv.   Alvah Conant, b. 26 Oct., 1854, in Boston; graduated from Williams College, 1876, and from the Medical Department of Columbia College, 1877. He is a practicing physician, of

Brooklyn, N. Y. He m. 12 Jan., 1887, Katherine L. Gate-house.

399. Lydia Haynes[7] (*John, Nathaniel, Daniel, John, Lot, Roger*), b. 25 Apr., 1816, in Alfred, Me.; d. 18 Oct., 1854. She m. 20 Oct., 1841, Elijah Chesley Drew, who was a merchant, of Boston, Mass.

Child of ELIJAH C. and LYDIA H. (CONANT) DREW:—

Emma Conant, b. 5 May, 1846; d. 24 Nov., 1886; m. 24 Aug., 1870, Charles C. Barton, a lawyer, of Boston; resides in Newton Centre. He was b. in Salisbury, Conn., 14 Sep., 1844. Children: 1. Charles Clarence, b. 21 July, 1871; 2. Chesley Drew, b. 26 Nov., 1873; 3. Kittie Louise, b. 18 Jan., 1877; 4. Philip Lockwood, b. 15 Nov., 1880; 5. Elizabeth Conant, b. 4 Nov., 1884.

400. Lucinda[7] (*Andrew, Nathaniel, Daniel, John, Lot, Roger*), b. 9 Feb., 1806, in Alfred, Me.; d. 1861, in Dexter, Me.; m. Simon Foss, of Somers; published 19 Jan., 1826.

Children of SIMON and LUCINDA (CONANT) FOSS:—

i.   Sarah, b. 1828; d. 1876; m. William Copeland. They had five children, three of whom are now (1885) living in Leadville, Col.
ii.   Mary, b. ——; m. Hon. Josiah Crosby, of Dexter, Me. They have eight children.
iii.   Lucinda, who m. J. Merrill.
iv.   Andrew Conant, b. 1832; d. 1863; was in the U. S. army. He m. Abigail Jones, and had an only child.
v.   Simon H., d. y.
vi.   Isabella, d. y.
vii.   Ann E., who m. (1) B. Weston; m. (2) J. A. Sewall, and is at present living in Boulder City, Col.
viii. Ellen H., b. 1842; d. 1862.
ix.   Simon H., m. Susie Bullock; lives in Denver, Col.; has two children.
x.   Samuel M., d. 1881, in Denver, Col.

401. Sarah P.[7] (*Andrew, Nathaniel, Daniel, John, Lot, Roger*), b. July, 1811; m. Calvin Copeland; residence, Tonica, Ill.

Children of CALVIN and SARAH P. (CONANT) COPELAND:—

i.   Sarah Francis, b. 1843; m. J. A. Wilson, of Tonica.
ii.   Willis E., b. 1845; m. (1) Edwina Lincoln; m. (2) Fannie Stearns; is of Halstead, Kas.
iii. Clara A., b. 1851; d. 1855.

402. **Andrew Emerson**[7] (*Andrew, Nathaniel, Daniel, John, Lot, Roger*), b. 7 Dec., 1815, in Alfred, Me.; moved to Dexter, Me., with his parents, and thence to Plainfield, Ill., where he now lives. He m. (1) Addie Smith; m. (2) Lizzie Philbrook.

Children of ANDREW E. and ——— (———) CONANT:—

> Addie, d. 1881, aged 23.
> Joseph E., b.-1860.
> Hattie, b. 1862; d. 1865.
> Lewis P., b. 1865.
> Otis K., b. 1868.

403. **Hosea**[7] (*Rufus, Josiah, Daniel, John, Lot, Roger*), b. 2 Mch., 1793, in Dudley, Mass., where he lived. He d. 11 Sep., 1843. He m. (1) 11 June, 1818, Lucy King, who d. 25 Apr., 1834, aged 40; m. (2) 2 May, 1839, Polly King.

Children of HOSEA and LUCY (KING) CONANT:—

> Daniel King, b. 19 May, 1819.
> Mary Lucy, b. 26 May, 1822; d. 20 Mch., 1826.
> Caroline Elizabeth, b. 2 Oct., 1824.
> Rufus Leander, b. 20 Sep., 1828.

404. **Rufus**[7] (*Rufus, Josiah, Daniel, John, Lot, Roger*), b. 16 Mch., 1805, in Dudley, Mass.; settled in Charlton, Mass.; a farmer. He d. in Southbridge, Mass., 25 Aug., 1877. He m. (1) in Dudley, 14 Mch., 1830, Clarissa, dr. of John and Lucretia (Putnam) Nichols, who d. 1836, in Charlton; m. (2) 3 Apr., 1838, Rumahah G. Johnson.

Children of RUFUS and CLARISSA (NICHOLS) CONANT:—

> Lucy Ann, b. 9 Jan., 1831.
> 649. Charles Rufus, b. 5 Dec., 1833.
> Julius Augustus, b. 18 May, 1836; d. unm., 1863.

Children of RUFUS and RUMAHAH G. (JOHNSON) CONANT:—

> Nancy Merriam, b. 29 June, 1839; m. (1) 4 July, 1860, Van Buren McKinstry; m. (2) 7 Mch., 1875, William Vinton.
> Albert Henry, b. 28 May, 1843.
> Ellen Amelia, b. 22 July, 1844; d. unm., 1864.
> 650. Harrison Johnson, b. 3 May, 1848.
> Herbert Butler, b. 29 Oct., 1850; m. 4 May, 1871, Hattie Chaffee; has no children.
> Arthur Gibbs, b. 6 Sep., 1853.

24

405. **Hervey**[7] (*Josiah, Josiah, Daniel, John, Lot, Roger*),
b. 3 June, 1796, in Dudley, Mass. He succeeded to his father's
farm and mills at the age of seventeen years, managing very
successfully till about the year 1823, when he sold out, and engaged in the manufacture of woolen cloth with Aaron Tufts
and others, under the name of the Tufts Manufacturing Company.
They built quite a village in addition to their manufacturing
plant, which was embraced in one large building of stone and
several smaller buildings, some of stone and some of wood,
which were equipped with what was then the best improved
machinery. Mr. Tufts was president and treasurer, John Jewett was superintendent and Mr. Conant secretary and book-
keeper of the company.

For some unaccountable reason Mr. Conant withdrew from
his position as book-keeper, and opened a general store, after
less than five years in that position. He succeeded fairly in
business, and at one time had a partner, the firm name being
then Conant & Fitts. Later this store was destroyed by fire,
inflicting a severe loss. It was immediately rebuilt, however,
and the business continued with unflagging energy for several
years. The memory of the fire was slowly fading from peoples' minds when a second fire destroyed the establishment,
inflicting a second and more disastrous loss. He, nevertheless,
erected another building, and stocked it, purposing to continue
the same business, but having a favorable offer sold out and
for several years tried hotel keeping in East Webster, Mass.,
but not prospering at that to his satisfaction, returned to Dudley, and settling on his wife's father's estate followed farming
for a number of years. About 1847 he removed to Worcester,
where one of his sons had settled. His residence in Worcester covered a space of nearly twenty years, but he died in
West Boylston, Mass., on a small estate which he had rented
and occupied with his son, Josiah, who was a practicing homœopathic physician in that place. He was a quiet, christian
gentleman, of an even, genial disposition, much beloved and
respected by all who knew him. Although of more than aver-
age abilities, and well qualified by education, he did not seek
public office. He was of a modest, retiring habit, but always

Henrey Conon t

ready to do a kind action. Throughout his adult life he was a consistent member of the Congregational church. He d. 21 May, 1868. He m. (1) 13 May, 1819, Dolly, dr. of Maj. Lemuel and Dolly (Corbin) Healy, b. 15 Dec., 1796; d. 22 May, 1845; Maj. Healy was a farmer, of Dudley, a soldier in the Revolutionary War, and later major of militia. He m. (2) Susan Stone, of Grantham, N. H., who d. 1869.

Children of HERVEY and DOLLY (HEALY) CONANT:—

Lucy Foskett, b. 24 May, 1820; m. 5 May, 1845, Nelson Bennett, of Sturbridge. She d. May, 1846, leaving one child.
Dolly Healy, b. 13 Dec., 1821; m. 2 Mch., 1843, Ralph U. Davidson, of Brooklyn, Conn.
Samuel Hervey, b. 29 July, 1825; d. 11 Oct., 1850.
651. Hezekiah, b. 28 July, 1827.
Sylvia, b. 9 Nov., 1829.
Josiah, b. 2 June, 1832. He attended the public schools of Dudley until his twelfth year, when, his family moving to Worcester, he became a pupil in the High School of that city. After leaving school he learned the trade of a machinist. In 1851 he went West, where he remained until 1859, when he began the study of medicine with Dr. Green, of Boston. During nine months of the war he assisted in taking care of the sick and wounded soldiers in the hospitals at Washington. He then attended a medical college in Philadelphia, graduating in 1865. After practicing a short time in Boston he settled in West Boylston, Mass., where he remained till the death of his father, when he removed to Great Falls, N. H., where he gained a large and successful practice. In the spring of 1881 he was obliged to go South for his health, but received no benefit from the trip, and on his return was obliged to give up his practice; in July of the same year he entirely lost the use of his lower limbs, from paralysis, and has since been confined to his bed and rolling chair. He m. 1878, Lucy C. Pratt, of So. Berwick, Me. They have no children. He d. 1887.
Elizabeth, b. 6 Aug., 1834; m. George W. Adams, of Boston, Mass. They now live in Thonotolassa, near Tampa, Fla.

406. Josiah[7] (*Josiah, Josiah, Daniel, John, Lot, Roger*), b. 7 Dec., 1804, in Dudley, Mass., where he lived. He inherited a small farm from his father; was a mill-wright by trade, and worked at that and farming. He was attacked by sudden and severe illness one day while at work in the hay-field, from which he d. 7 July, 1839. He m. Alice Chaffee.

Child of Josiah and Alice (Chaffee) Conant:—

Pitt Chaffee, b. 26 Nov., 1834; d. 1 Sep., 1844.

407. Sally[7] (*Ezra, Ezra, Benjamin, John, Lot, Roger*),
b. 15 May, 1777, in Warwick, Mass.; m. 15 Nov., 1801, Elias
Pratt, of Oxford, b. 4 Mch., 1773. He was a farmer, moved
to Sutton, thence to Worcester, Mass., where he d. 2 Sep., 1854.
Children of Elias and Sally (Conant) Pratt:—

i.   Sally, b. 4 July, 1802; d. 13 Sep., 1804.
ii.   Ezra, b. 6 Oct., 1804; d. 1 Oct., 1805.
iii. Serena, b. 14 Aug., 1806; m. Charles King, of Sutton.
iv.   Sarah, b. 29 Jan., 1808; m. Joshua C. Lewis.
v.   Sumner, b. 30 Sep., 1809; a merchant, of Worcester; m. 19
      May, 1836, Serena, dr. of Caleb and Fanny (Harris) Chase.
      Children: 1. Frederick Sumner, b. 1845; 2. Emma Amanda,
      b. 1848. He m. (2) Abby C., dr. of Ebenezer and Sarah
      (Curtis) Read. Child: Edward R., b. 1851.
vi.   Emeline, b. 14 Dec., 1812; m. L. Woodbury.
vii. Amanda, b. 11 Aug., 1815; d. unm.

408. Samuel[7] (*Amos, Ezra, Benjamin, John, Lot, Roger*),
b. 8 Mch., 1781, in Claremont, N. H.; moved to Irasburg, Vt.,
with his parents; was a carpenter and farmer. Late in life he
moved to Janesville, Wis., where he d. 17 Feb., 1858. He m.
in Irasburg, Vt., 7 Jan., 1809, Sally Richardson, b. in Lancaster, N. H., 12 Apr., 1789; d. in Janesville, Wis., 4 Feb., 1874.
Children of Samuel and Sally (Richardson) Conant:—

         Clarissa, b. 16 Aug., 1808.
652.   Amos, b. 30 July, 1810.
653.   Ezra D., b. 3 Nov., 1812.
         Maria, b. 22 Apr., 1815.
         Almira, b. 28 Aug., 1817; m. Horace Knight, of Eureka, Cal.
654.   Samuel Davis, b. 27 Nov., 1820.
         John Richardson, b. 12 Apr., 1823; of Somerville, Mass. He
           is a merchant, doing business in Boston; the firm is Conant
           & Nowers.
         Horace Richardson, b. 24 Mch., 1826; d. before 1883.
         Solomon Jackson, b. 18 Sep., 1828; d. before 1883.
         Lovantia Ermina Luretta, b. 31 Mch., 1831; m. Frank Whit-
           tier. They live in Santa Rosa, Cal.

409. Ebenezer[7] (*Amos, Ezra, Benjamin, John, Lot, Roger*),
b. 20 May, 1785, in Claremont, N. H.; moved to Irasburg,
Vt., with his parents. He was a physician; settled in Plain-

field, Vt., where he d. 1852. He m. in Montpelier, Vt., Lucinda Ormsbee, b. 2 Feb., 1794, in Montpelier.

Children of EBENEZER and LUCINDA (ORMSBEE) CONANT:—

Mariette.
Clark C.
Albert G.
655. Charles Carroll, b. 29 Aug., 1820.
Mensil M., b. 14 July, 1822; moved to Janesville, Wis. He is now in business in Johnstown Centre, Wis.
Laurilla E.
Byron G.
Henry C.

410. Charles[7] (*Amos, Ezra, Benjamin, John, Lot, Roger*), b. 30 Sep., 1787, in Claremont, N. H.; moved to Irasburg, Vt., with his parents. He setttled in Troy, Vt.

Children of CHARLES and —— (——) CONANT:—

Curtis P., of Boston, Mass. Is the proprietor of the Province House. Has a son, Edgar A., who is an engraver, of Boston.
656. Charles Olin, b. 6 July, 1822.
A son.
A son.
A daughter, who m. —— Houghton.

411. Newell[7] (*John, Ezra, Benjamin, John, Lot, Roger*), b. 5 Nov., 1782, in Warwick, Mass.; moved, with his father, to Glover, Vt., and thence to Craftsburg; was a miller and farmer. He d. 29 Apr., 1844, in Craftsburg. He m. 11 Aug., 1810, Sarah Pierce, b. 14 Jan., 1789, d. 1 July, 1849.

Children of NEWELL and SARAH (PIERCE) CONANT:—

657. Horace Hamilton, b. 13 Oct., 1812, in Craftsburg.
Eliza Ann, b. 1 Sep., 1814; d. 30 Oct., 1835, of consumption.
658. William Augustus, b. 9 Nov., 1816.
Franklin Pierce, b. 8 Jan., 1822, in Craftsburg, Vt.; d. 22 July, 1852. He m. 20 Jan., 1844, Mary Jane Russell, and had a daughter, Augusta, who now resides in New York.
Mary Hamilton, b. 20 Mch., 1825; d. 25 Sep., 1826.

412. Ezra[7] (*John, Ezra, Benjamin, John, Lot, Roger*), b. 1 Feb., 1788, in Warwick, Mass.; moved to Glover, Vt., with his parents; settled in Bennington, Vt. He moved to Silver Lake, Pa., and thence to Lockport, N. Y., where he was killed in a railroad accident, 1863. He was a farmer. He m. 28 Jan.,

1816, Achsah Doty, who d. in Lockport, N. Y., 7 Nov., 1847.
Children of EZRA and ACHSAH (DOTY) CONANT:—

659.   Edward, b. 26 Feb., 1825.
       Anna.
       Lucy.

413.   Benjamin[7] (*Benjamin, Ezra, Benjamin, John, Lot,
Roger*), b. 28 Mch., 1785, in Warwick, Mass. He settled in
Waterbury, Vt., where he d. He m. (1) 9 Mch., 1809, Philena,
dr. of (180) Josiah and Olive (Gale) Conant; m. (2) ———.
   Children of BENJAMIN and PHILENA (CONANT) CONANT:—

       James, d. y.
       Maria, d. 25 Oct., 1862, aged 51.

   Child of BENJAMIN and ——— (———) CONANT:—
       Benjamin, said to be a physician, of Stowe, Vt.

414.   Dean[7] (*Clark, Ezra, Benjamin, John, Lot, Roger*),
b. 1800. He settled in Charlestown, N. H., as clerk in his uncle Aaron Dean's store, and succeeded him in business. He
d. 13 May, 1835. He m. Oct., 1825, Almira, dr. of West Bonney, b. 9 Sep., 1807. The Evangelical Church of Charlestown
was organized in her house. After the marriage of her daughter to Dr. E. C. Worcester, she lived with her in Thetford, Vt.
   Children of DEAN and ALMIRA (BONNEY) CONANT:—

660.   Ellen Hunt, b. 20 Sep., 1826.
       Lewis, b. 1829; d. y.
       Catherine Dean, b. 1 May, 1832; m. 19 Sep., 1865, James Har-
          vey Lewis, b. 6 Sep., 1834. Children: 1. Eleanor Bonney,
          b. 10 Nov., 1870; 2. Arthur, b. 7 Aug., 1873.

415.   Samuel[7] (*Benjamin, Benjamin, Benjamin, John,
Lot, Roger*), b. 20 June, 1808, in Warwick, Mass. He moved
to Hartland, Vt. He was a farmer and surveyor; was also a
justice of the peace. He d. in Hartland, 20 Apr., 1883. He
m. in Warwick, 6 July, 1831, Lucy A., dr. of A. and Patience
(Smith) Corrall, b. in Brookfield, Mass., 22 Oct., 1808.
   Child of SAMUEL and LUCY A. (CORRALL) CONANT:—
       Addie A., now living in Hartland.

416.   Harvey[7] (*Benjamin, Benjamin, Benjamin, John,*

Lot, Roger), b. 28 June, 1811, in Warwick; a farmer; d. 15 May, 1872. He m. 19 June, 1836, Hannah Cheney, dr. of Abijah and Beulah (Cheney) Eddy, b. 28 Sep., 1812.

Children of HARVEY and HANNAH C. (EDDY) CONANT:—

Henry Cheney, b. 22 Oct., 1837; d. 20 July, 1861.
Susan Elizabeth, b. 16 Nov., 1844; m. 16 Nov., 1863, George D. Porter; had Anna L., b. 9 Sep., 1865. She d. 28 Feb., 1867.
661. Horace Mann, b. 13 Jan., 1850, in Warwick.

417. Samuel H.[7] (*Samuel, Benjamin, Benjamin, John, Lot, Roger*), b. 14 July, 1822, in Troy, Pa.; moved to Cuba, N. Y., with his parents, where he d. 1874; was a farmer. He m. 17 Feb., 1844, Phebe Blowers.

Children of SAMUEL H. and PHEBE (BLOWERS) CONANT:—

Eugene F., b. 22 Nov., 1847, in Cuba, N. Y.; m. 6 Apr., 1875, Ella Eaton. He is now in the employ of the W. J. Kinsey Implement Company, at Denver, Col.
Francis J., b. 12 Apr., 1849, in Cuba, N. Y.
James H., b. 8 May, 1853, in Cuba, N. Y. He is living in Bradford, Pa.; has a son, Allen E.

418. Charles L.[7] (*Samuel, Benjamin, Benjamin, John, Lot, Roger*), b. 25 Aug., 1827, in Cuba, N. Y.; settled in Grand Rapids, Mich.

Children of CHARLES L. and ——— (———) CONANT:—

Anne.
Bell.
Lucy.

419. Sabrina[7] (*Asa, Asa, Benjamin, John, Lot, Roger*), b. 6 May, 1807, in Warwick, Mass.; now living in Winchester, N. H. She m. 9 July, 1825, in Warwick, Silas, son of Eli and Olive (Parker) Lewis, b. 7 Apr., 1799, in Granville, Vt.

Children of SILAS and SABRINA (CONANT) LEWIS:—

i. Zenas Cornelius, b. 4 June, 1825, in Granville, Vt.
ii. Clara Adaliza, b. 31 Dec., 1826, in Warwick, Mass.
iii. Devine Ann, b. 20 June, 1829, in Potsdam, N. Y.
iv. Asa Conant, b. 26 May, 1831, in Potsdam, N. Y.
v. Olive Sabrina, b. 20 Feb., 1837, in Granville, Vt.
vi. Silas Hopkins, b. 27 Nov., 1839, in Winchester, N. H.
vii. Freeman Amherst, b. 4 Sep., 1841, in Winchester, N. H.; was

killed, 1862, in the War of the Rebellion.
viii.   Marvin Delamont, b. 15 Jan., 1846, in Winchester.

420. Asa Hopkins[7] (*Asa, Asa, Benjamin, John, Lot, Roger*), b. 23 May, 1811, in Warwick, Mass., where he d. 10 Oct., 1872. He m. (1) 3 Nov., 1835, Semira Fuller, who d. 23 Aug., 1839; m. (2) Anna Goddard, who d. 25 Aug., 1853; m. (3) ——— Fay.

   Children of Asa H. and Semira (Fuller) Conant:—

   Henry H., b. 7 Sep., 1836; d. 3 June, 1837.
   Hannah A., b. 17 Sep., 1837; d. 17 Aug., 1838.

421. Israel Elliot[7] (*Jonathan, Jonathan, Jonathan, Lot, Lot, Roger*), b. 6 Oct., 1789, in Mt. Vernon, N. H. He moved to Antrim, N. H., with his parents, in 1811, and in 1816 to New Haven, Vt. He d. in Vergennes, Vt., 1857. He m. 1815, Eliza Holt, of Antrim.

   Children of Israel E. and Eliza (Holt) Conant:—

   Albert, b. 3 Oct., 1815.
662. William, b. 25 Nov., 1816.
   Elbridge, b. 18 July, 1818; of Hudson, Mich.
   Edwin, b. 2 Nov., 1820.
   Susan, b. 14 Apr., 1822; m. Newman Hunt, of New Haven, Vt.
   John B., b. 10 Aug., 1824; of New Haven, Vt.
   Nancy M., b. 22 Dec., 1826; m. 20 Oct., 1852, Andrew J., son of John and Nancy (Noble) Merithew, of Gouverneur, N. Y. They live in De Kalb, N. Y.

422. William[7] (*Jonathan, Jonathan, Jonathan, Lot, Lot, Roger*), b. 31 Oct., 1802, in Mt. Vernon, N. H. (then Amherst), where he was living in 1885. He was a deacon of the Congregational church. He m. Hannah Forniss, of Beverly.

   Children of William and Hannah (Forniss) Conant:—

663. William Henry, b. 5 June, 1829.
664. Albert, b. 19 Oct., 1830.
665. Charles Edwin, b. 30 June, 1833.
666. Walter Scott, b. 8 June, 1834.
   John, b. 1 Mch., 1836.
667. Harlan Page, b. 3 Mch., 1837.
   Martha Ellen, b. 30 Nov., 1842; d. at Somerville, Mass., 18 May, 1884.
   Fanny Lovett, b. 1 Apr., 1844.
   Marcella Elisa, b. 31 Dec., 1845.

423. Daniel Lunt[7] (*Joseph, Bartholomew, Joseph, Lot, Lot, Roger*), b. 25 Sep., 1807, in Topsham, Me. He settled in Peru, Me., before 1840. He m. 1840, in Peru, Mary A. French.

Child of Daniel L. and Mary A. (French) Conant:—

William H., who now lives in Peru; a trader.

424. Thomas[7] (*Joseph, Bartholomew, Joseph, Lot, Lot, Roger*), b. 30 Mch., 1809, in Topsham, Me. He was a tinsmith and stove manufacturer. He settled in Augusta, Me. He m. Nov., 1851, Rosetta, dr. of Ephraim and Hannah (Brainard) Leighton, b. in Parkman, Me., 30 Dec., 1830.

Child of Thomas and Rosetta (Leighton) Conant:—

668. William Henry, b. in Wayne, Me., 7 Sep., 1855.

425. George[7] (*Bartholomew, Joseph, Joseph, Lot, Lot, Roger*), b. 13 Dec., 1804, in Portland, Me. He is now living in Freeport, Me. He m. (1) Eliza Ann, dr. of Benjamin and Sarah Thomes; m. (2) in Portland, 12 Mch., 1854, Sarah W. Smith.

Children of George and Eliza A. (Thomes) Conant:—

669. George, b. 29 Oct., 1828, in Portland.
Catherine, b. 21 Dec., 1830; m. William H. H. Stackpole, and lives in Boston, Mass.
670. Washington, b. 22 Feb., 1832.
Harriet Ann, b. 16 Mch., 1834; d. 13 Aug., 1836.
Octavia, b. 16 Oct., 1835; d. 9 Jan., 1836.
John Wilbur, b. 16 Oct., 1836; m. Helen Abbot, who d. 1885, and had George, Lewis and Lena. He is of Boston.
Harriet I., b. 4 Sep., 1838; m. (1) 9 July, 1856, Edward H. Seely, of Rockland, Me.; m. (2) —— Braeunlich, and lives in Brooklyn, N. Y.
Mary C., b. 29 May, 1840; m. 16 Mch., 1860, Daniel W. Loveitt, of Portland, Me. Children: 1. Hattie E., b. 6 Mch., 1861; 2. Ella G., b. 6 Mch., 1862; 3. Grace H., b. 6 Sep., 1863; 4. Maggie, b. 28 Mch., 1868; 5. Joshua D., b. 10 Mch., 1873.
Almira, b. 1 Sep., 1842; m. William E. Timmons, of Portland, and has Edward H., William F. and Frederick G.
Hannah Ann, b. 29 July, 1844.
Louisa, b. 16 Jan., 1846; m. Edgar Orr, of Portland, and has Frank E. and George Clifford.
Benjamin F., b. 21 Dec., 1847; now of Freeport, Me.; m. Ada Woodman, and has William Gore.

Eliza Ann, b. 26 Mch., 1850; m. Charles H. Pepper, b. in England, and lives in New York; has Gertrude.

Child of GEORGE and SARAH W. (SMITH) CONANT:—

Charles Edward, b. 17 Jan., 1855, in Portland; graduated from Colby Univ., 1879; studied law, and is now an attorney and counsellor at law, practicing in Minneapolis, Minn. He m. in Portland, 12 Aug., 1880, Edith W. Stinchfield, of Portland.

426.   Oliver[7] (*Thomas, Joseph, Joseph, Lot, Lot, Roger*), b. 20 Feb., 1796, in Lisbon or Topsham, Me. He was a soldier in the War of 1812, at the age of seventeen. Settled in Topsham; m. Abigail Field.

Children of OLIVER and ABIGAIL (FIELD) CONANT:—

Sarah W., b. 9 Sep., 1820; m. William Bridge, of Mechanic Falls, Me.

Lot C., b. 25 Oct., 1822; m. Priscilla Harmon. Children: Hattie, who m. Frank Hall, of Brunswick, Me., and Emma.

671.   Mark P., b. 9 Oct., 1824.
672.   Samuel Field, b. 5 Oct., 1827.
673.   James McKeen, b. 25 Feb., 1829.

Philena F., b. 10 Aug., 1832; d. 20 Jan., 1833.

Anna M., b. 3 July, 1834; m. Henry Penny.

674.   Francis A., b. 7 Apr., 1837.
675.   Charles Bean, b. 15 Oct., 1839.

Hannah R., b. 3 May, 1842; m. George Stevens.

Mary E., b. 8 Jan., 1846; d. 2 Mch., 1875.

427.   Lot[7] (*Thomas, Joseph, Joseph, Lot, Lot, Roger*), b. 1798; moved to Topsham and Lisbon, with his parents; m. Delia Porter. He d. about 1856, and his widow m. (2) in Lewiston, Me., George Boubier, or Bubar. She d. 1863.

Child of LOT and DELIA (PORTER) CONANT:—

Thomas. After his father's death he was adopted by a family named Douglass, then living at Lisbon Falls. When he became of age he took the name Douglass.

428.   Ann[7] (*Thomas, Joseph, Joseph, Lot, Lot, Roger*), b. 1800, in Topsham or Lisbon, Me. She m. Abraham Whitney.

Children of ABRAHAM and ANN (CONANT) WHITNEY:—

i.   Rachael, m. William Gerrish.
ii.   Mehitable A., b. 7 Apr., 1822; d. 9 Oct., 1875; m. James Strout, b. 28 July, 1822; d. 10 Aug., 1874. Children: Revillo M., b. 1843; Onanna L., b. 1845; Melville C., b. 1847;

Orville D., b. 1849; Francella, b. 1852; Elalie, b. 1854; Idella, b. 1856.

iii. Aphia, m. —— Lambert.
iv. William, of Salem, Mass.
v. Louisa, m. Emery S. Warren.

429. Lydia[7] (*Thomas, Joseph, Joseph, Lot, Lot, Roger*), b. about 1803; m. Eliphalet Bryant.

Children of ELIPHALET and LYDIA (CONANT) BRYANT:—

i. George, d. 1852.
ii. Frances.
iii. Elizabeth.
iv. Henry.
v. Abel.

430. Daniel[7] (*Thomas, Joseph, Joseph, Lot, Lot, Roger*), b. Oct., 1806, in Lisbon, Me.; settled in Topsham, where he engaged in the lumber business; removed to Lewiston in 1849, where he d. about Dec., 1853. He m. Abigail Bishop, dr. of William and Elizabeth Getchell, b. 3 July, 1810, and now (1886) living in Providence, R. I.

Children of DANIEL and ABIGAIL B. (GETCHELL) CONANT:—

676. William Thomas, b. 7 May, 1834, in Topsham, Me.
677. Alfred Perkins, b. 3 Feb., 1836.
Elizabeth Bishop, b. Jan., 1838; d. 13 Feb., 1865; m. 1862, Arthur G. Larrabee, and had Jennie F., b. 1864, d. 1866, and William A., b. 20 Aug., 1866.
Clement P., b. 1840; d. in infancy.
Jane Walker, b. 1842; d. 1866; m. 1864, John Emerson, and had Daniel.
Daniel Jackson, b. 1844. He enlisted at Lewiston, in Co. C, 17th U. S. Infantry; was transferred to Co. B, and was killed 17 Jan., 1861, at the battle of Gaines' Mill.
Abigail Rachael, b. 29 Apr., 1846, in Topsham.
Vesta Burbank, b. 23 Sep., 1849, in Lewiston, Me.; m. (1) 1868, George Boomer, and had Perley, b. 18 Dec., 1874; was divorced, and m. (2) 1878, Eugene J. Boutelle, and had Lillian May, b. 16 Oct., 1879, d. 10 Mch., 1883.
Annie Melissa, b. 15 Mch., 1852; lives in Providence, R. I., with her mother.

431. Elizabeth C.[7] (*Thomas, Joseph, Joseph, Lot, Lot, Roger*), b. 13 Feb., 1814; d. 21 Jan., 1853. She m. William B. Osgood, of Auburn, Me. He d. 22 Apr., 1881.

Children of WILLIAM B. and ELIZABETH C. (CONANT) OS-
GOOD :—

i.   William B.
ii.   Thomas C., d. in infancy.
iii.   Clarissa C., m. Clarence L. Marston, of Portland, Me., and
       d. 1871.

432. Henry[7] (*Nathaniel, Joshua, Joshua, Lot, Lot, Roger*),
b. 17 Dec., 1797, in Londonderry, N. H.; settled in Roxbury, Mass., where he d. 23 Aug., 1846. He m. in Roxbury,
4 Jan., 1824, Cynthia Scott.
Children of HENRY and CYNTHIA (SCOTT) CONANT:—

> Eliza C., b. 1823; d. 13 Nov., 1830.
> Henry, b. 1825; d. 3 Nov., 1830.
> Cynthia, b. Sep., 1829; d. 9 Dec., 1830.
> Helen M., b. 1835; d. 9 Sep., 1839.
> Charles E., b. May, 1838; d. 18 Jan., 1839.
> Alfred M., b. June, 1839; d. 3 Aug., 1839.
> Henry, b. ——; m. 11 June, 1856, in Londonderry, N. H.,
>   Mary Frances Hovey.

433. William Heath[7] (*Nathaniel, Joshua, Joshua, Lot,
Lot, Roger*), b. 29 Dec., 1807, in Londonderry, N. H., where
he lived. He d. 16 Dec., 1881. He m. in Manchester, N. H.,
June, 1835, Rachael Watts Garvin, of Manchester, who d. 17
Nov., 1877.
Children of WILLIAM H. and RACHAEL W. (GARVIN) Co-
NANT:—

678.   Annie, b. 22 Mch., 1837, in Londonderry.
679.   Antoinette Rebecca, b. Dec., 1838, in Londonderry.
680.   Lyman Augustus, b. 1 May, 1840, in Lowell, Mass.
681.   Charles Edwin, b. 25 Nov., 1843, in Londonderry.
       Julia Maria, b. 3 Nov., 1845; m. 18 June, 1884, William Pecker,
       of Salem, N. H., where they now live.
682.   Sarah Ann, b. 24 Aug., 1848.
       Clara Frances, b. 17 Sep., 1850; m. in Boston, Mass., 10 July,
       1878, Ezra Thomas Corbett Stephenson, of Hingham, Mass.;
       has Gertrude, b. 18 May, 1879, in Boston.
       Selwyn Frank, b. 25 Apr., 1853; m. in Springfield, Mass.,
       Dec., 1877, Sarah Heilborn, of Boston. He is a conductor
       on the Boston and Albany R. R. Lives in Cambridge.
       Grace Eva, b. 29 Oct., 1855.

434. Joshua[7] (*Joshua, Joshua, Joshua, Lot, Lot, Roger*),

b. 11 Mch., 1798, in Londonderry, N. H.; settled in Antrim, N. H., in 1860. He m. (1) 1824, Rebecca, dr. of Samuel Preston, b. in Stoddard, N. H., 18 Feb., 1799, d. 28 June, 1848; m. (2) 25 July, 1852, Eliza A. Read, of Stoddard.

Children of Joshua and Rebecca (Preston) Conant:—

683. Ruel K., b. 2 Sep., 1825.

Hiram P., b. 18 Sep., 1830; settled in Pittsburg, Pa., in 1853; m. · —— Kelley.

Freeman C., b. 3 Aug., 1837. He settled in Cavendish, Vt.; was a currier by trade. On the breaking out of the Rebellion he enlisted, May 2, 1861, in Co. E, 1st Regt., and served through the entire war. He then settled in Wilton, Iowa, where he now lives. He m. Alice C. Stryker.

And several children who died young.

Children of Joshua and Eliza A. (Read) Conant:—

Abilene, b. 17 Apr., 1855, in Stoddard, m. 1 Oct., 1873, Willard A. Paige, of Munsonville.

Augusta, d. y.

435. **Nathaniel**[7] (*Joshua, Joshua, Joshua, Lot, Lot, Roger*), b. 11 Apr., 1802, in Londonderry, N. H. He moved to Charlotte, Me.; was a lumberman and farmer. He d. 13 July, 1878, in Meddybemps. He was sheriff of Aroostook co. at one time. He m. in Charlotte, Me., 29 Mch., 1827, Rachael R., dr. of John and Anne (Hitchings) Bridges, b. 1804.

Children of Nathaniel and Rachael (Bridges) Conant:—

684. Nathaniel Putnam, b. 13 Apr., 1829.

Rachael Jane, m. Allen Nesbitt, and had John and Minnie.

Mary Elizabeth, m. Abner Leland, and had Gertrude, Susan, Charles, Alice, Munroe, Annie and Simeon.

Annie Livingston, m. Loring Gardner, and had William and Lucinda; she d. 1865.

Isabella, b. about 1836, in Charlotte, Me.; m. Allen McDougal, and had Isaac, Mary, Oscar, Nathaniel and Herbert.

Margaretta, m. Thomas Leland, and had Edgar, Alice, Lettie and Addie.

Almira R., m. William McDonald, and had Helen, Millard, Gertrude, Grace and Burt.

Isaac B. He served during the late war in Co. C, First Me. Cavalry, and d. at Ship Island.

Lucena Eleanor.

Alice, m. George Bailey, and had Lillian and George.

436. **Martha**[7] (*Joshua, Joshua, Joshua, Lot, Lot, Roger*),

b. ———, in Londonderry, N. H.; d. in Chicago, Ill., 15 Dec., 1884; m. (1) Ezra Smith; m. (2) 1831, Ira Cogswell, b. 11 Oct., 1793, as his 2nd wife.

Child of Ezra and Martha (Conant) Smith:—

> Laura Jane, who m. William E. Polhamus, and now lives in Minneapolis, Minn.

Children of Ira and Martha (Conant) Cogswell:—

> Ira.
> Susan, d. y.
> Thankful Geraldine.

437. William[7] (*Joshua, Joshua, Joshua, Lot, Lot, Roger*), b. 27 Dec., 1810, in Londonderry, N. H.; moved to Plymouth, Me., where he still lives. He m. in Plymouth, 5 Sep., 1837, Rebecca, dr. of Joseph and Alice (Grafam) Taylor, b. in Unity, Me., 8 Jan., 1817.

Children of William and Rebecca (Taylor) Conant:—

> William Harrison, b. 16 July, 1839, in Plymouth, Me.; a farmer. He served in the War of the Rebellion from 1862 to the close of the war; was in Co. K, 11th Regt., Me. Vols., and was wounded at the battle of Drury's Bluff. He m. (1) 19 Nov., 1869, Sophia B., dr. of Sewell and Mary (Stevens) Hopkins, who d. 26 Sep., 1875; m. (2) 25 Dec., 1876, Cordelia, dr. of George and Louisa (Twitchell) Morse, b. 6 Jan., 1843, in Dixmont, Me. No children.
>
> 685. Roxanna, b. 2 Mch., 1841.
> 686. Joshua Randall, b. 27 Nov., 1843.
> Laminda Jane, b. 24 Aug., 1845; d. aged 4.
> Elizabeth Alice, b. 20 Feb., 1849; m. in Carmel, Me., 17 Jan., 1872, Albert, son of George and Clarissa (Bassford) Maloon, and had Olive, b. 1872; Ada M., b. 1 May, 1874; Ora J., b. Nov., 1880. Lives in Detroit, Me.
> Orlando Waldence, b. 21 Aug., 1851; now of Minneapolis, Minn.
> 687. Alphonso Bence, b. 8 Aug., 1854.

438. Enoch[7] (*Joshua, Joshua, Joshua, Lot, Lot, Roger*), b. ———, in Londonderry, N. H.; moved to Orono, Me.; is a millwright. He m. Emeline, dr. of Elisha Sleeper.

Children of Enoch and Emeline (Sleeper) Conant:—

> Frank, d. y.
> Howard Enoch.

439. William Foster[7] (*William, William, William, Lot, Lot, Roger*), b. 17 July, 1802, in Ipswich, Mass., where he lived. He m. (1) 1828, Martha Potter; m. (2) 21 Aug., 1832, Martha Perley.

Child of WILLIAM F. and MARTHA (POTTER) CONANT:—

William Potter, b. ——; d. 17 Jan., 1830.

Children of WILLIAM F. and MARTHA (PERLEY) CONANT:—

Martha Mary, b. 18 Oct., 1833.
Cyrus William, b. 16 July, 1837.
Charles Augustus, b. 7 Jan., 1841.
Jacob Coggin, b. 4 Feb., 1845.
Abba Lizzie, b. ——.

440. Gilbert[7] (*William, William, William, Lot, Lot, Roger*), b. 1 Aug., 1804, in Ipswich, where he lived. He published "Poems on the Celebration of the 250th Birthday of Ipswich." (Essex: Burnham's Job Print, 1884. 18 mo., pp. 12.) He was greatly interested in the family history, and rendered the compiler valuable assistance. He d. 21 Mch., 1885. He m. 26 Oct., 1831, Lavinia Foster.

Children of GILBERT and LAVINIA (FOSTER) CONANT:—

Gilbert Roger, b. 19 Aug., 1832; m. Apr., 1859, Mary Abigail, dr. of Daniel Proctor Pingree, and had a son, Roger Gilbert, b. 7 Jan., 1860, who d. y. He d. in Linebrook Parish, Ipswich, 19 Oct., 1859. After his death she m. 1865, Allen Perley, of Rowley.
Caroline Lavinia, b. 9 Nov., 1834; now living in Ipswich.

441. Daniel[7] (*William, William, William, Lot, Lot, Roger*), b. 11 Mch., 1806, in Ipswich, Mass., where he lived. He m. (1) 22 Apr., 1830, Irene Foster, b. 18 Apr., 1809, d. 28 Feb., 1838; m. (2) 1838, Hannah Conant.

Child of DANIEL and IRENE (FOSTER) CONANT:—

Lucy Elizabeth, b. 31 July, 1835.

Children of DANIEL and HANNAH (CONANT) CONANT:—

Eliza M., b. 13 Nov., 1841.
Alicia Octavia, b. 23 Feb., 1844.
Mary Jane.
Delia Augusta, b. ——; m. Lewis Anson, son of Amos S. and Eliza A. (Perkins) Chapman, b. 23 July, 1848.

442. John[7] (*John, William, William, Lot, Lot, Roger*), b.
about 1800, in Topsfield, Mass., where he lived; d. 16 Dec.,
1853. On June 2, 1818, John Conant, of Topsfield, yeoman,
sells land in Bridgton, Me., to Elias Berry, of Denmark (Cumberland Deeds, Vol. 79, p. 400). He m. 5 Dec., 1820, Ann
Maria Brown.

Children of John and Ann M. (Brown) Conant:—

 Mary R.
 John B.
 William.
 Elizabeth C.
 Daniel A.

443. Joseph Perkins[7] (*Joseph, William, William, Lot,
Lot, Roger*), b. 10 Mch., 1823, in Ipswich, Mass. He is now
living in Woburn; a farmer. He m. in Rowley, 3 Oct., 1852,
Ruth Ann Cressey.

Children of Joseph P. and Ruth A. (Cressey) Conant:—

 Annie Josephine, b. 16 Mch., 1856, in Wrentham.
 Osmyn Perkins, b. 20 Feb., 1858. He is (1884) superintendent
  of schools at South Framingham, Mass.
 Lizzie Ruth, b. 12 Mch., 1860; d. in Franklin, 13 Aug., 1865.

444. Daniel Webster[7] (*Joseph, William, William, Lot,
Lot, Roger*), b. 23 Aug., 1831, in Ipswich, Mass. Settled in
Boxford, where he now lives; a farmer. He m. in Boxford,
30 Nov., 1854, Matilda Annie, dr. of John Hale, b. 12 Apr.,
1836.

Children of Daniel W. and Matilda A. (Hale) Conant:—

 Annie May, b. 21 Sep., 1855; d. 28 Sep., 1856.
 Carrie May, b. 13 Nov., 1857.
 William Roger, b. 3 Nov., 1859.
 Elmer Ellsworth, b. 7 Dec., 1861; he is now a clerk, in Boston.
 Hattie Emma, b. 3 June, 1864.
 Annie Lillian, b. 4 May, 1866.
 Daniel Austin, b. 4 Sep., 1870.
 Nellie Hale, b. 15 Nov., 1878.

445. Samuel Dorman[7] (*Samuel, Aaron, William, Lot,
Lot, Roger*), b. 14 Aug., 1819, in Topsfield, Mass.; is a boot
and shoe maker; now living in Champaign, Ill. He m. (1) in
Georgetown, Mass., 17 Apr., 1845, Mahala Ann Flanders, who

d. 18 Apr., 1848; m. (2) in Springfield, Ill., 2 Jan., 1851, Mary Elizabeth Stratton.

Children of SAMUEL D. and MARY E. (STRATTON) CONANT:—

Joanna Electa, b. 4 Sep., 1852, in Winchester, Ill.
Samuel William, b. 12 Mch., 1856, in Selbyville, Ill.

446. Eunice[7] (*Samuel, Aaron, William, Lot, Lot, Roger*), b. 3 Aug., 1821, in Lynnfield, Mass.; m. 1854, David Knowles, of Hampton, N. H. They lived in Hampton some years, thence removed to Newburyport, Mass., where he died.

Children of DAVID and EUNICE (CONANT) KNOWLES:—

i. Roger William, d. y.
ii. Charles Walter, of Salisbury, Mass.
iii. Frank Austin.

447. Lydia Ann[7] (*Samuel, Aaron, William, Lot, Lot, Roger*), b. 2 Dec., 1838, in Wenham, Mass.; m. 17 Oct., 1859, Calvin B. Dodge, of Wenham. They now live in Beverly.

Children of CALVIN B. and LYDIA A. (CONANT) DODGE:—

i. Susie Curtis, b. 11 June, 1861.
ii. Arthur Herbert, b. 4 Aug., 1863.
iii. Anne Louisa, b. 17 Dec., 1866.
iv. Freddie Austin, b. 19 May, 1872; d. 2 Aug., 1872.
v. Benjamin Conant, b. 12 June, 1873.

448. Nathaniel Peabody[7] (*Aaron, Aaron, William, Lot, Lot, Roger*), b. 10 Nov., 1819, in Topsfield, Mass.; moved to Portsmouth, N. H., with his parents, thence to Danvers and Lowell, Mass. He is a watchmaker and jeweler, at present living in Council Bluffs, Iowa. He m. in Newburyport, Mass., 26 Nov., 1844, Sophronia Thompson, dr. of Samuel and Mary (French) Hartford, b. 8 Aug., 1825.

Children of NATHANIEL P. and SOPHRONIA T. (HARTFORD) CONANT:—

Emma Frances, b. 29 Apr., 1846, in Topsfield.
Eliza Osborne, b. 16 Mch., 1848, in Danvers.

449. William[7] (*Elias, David, David, William, Lot, Roger*), b. about 1780, in Bridgewater, Mass.; moved to Lyme, N. H.; was a carpenter. He m. 1803, Martha Forbes. After his

25

death she m. David Sloan, and moved to Palmyra, N. Y.

Children of WILLIAM and MARTHA (FORBES) CONANT:—

Huldah.
Lewis.
Betsey.

450. Martin[7] (*Elias, David, David, William, Lot, Roger*),
b. 26 Aug., 1787, in Bridgewater, Mass.; moved to Lyme, N.
H.; was a shoemaker and farmer; d. 8 Apr., 1877. He m. in
Bridgewater, 1805, Lucy McHurin, b. 9 July, 1785, in Bridgewater; d. in Lyme, 1 June, 1873.

Children of MARTIN and LUCY (McHURIN) CONANT:—

688. Marcus, b. 12 Sep., 1806.
 Asa, b. 26 Dec., 1807, in Lyme; was a farmer.
 Calvin, b. 25 May, 1809; m. Olive Meerson. He settled in
  West Dennis, Mass., and d. 4 Aug., 1883. No children.
 William, b. 1 Dec., 1810; d. 8 Aug., 1811.
 Sarah, b. 29 Mch., 1812; d. 15 Apr., 1876; m. Harrison Bow-
  man, of Sandwich, Mass. He d. 12 Apr., 1877.
 Phebe, b. 2 Jan., 1814; d. 16 July, 1836, in Bridgewater; m.
  Pyam Whitman.
689. Martin Allen, b. 21 Oct., 1815.
 Seth P., b. 11 Aug., 1817; m. Eliz. Ball.
 Lucy Jane, b. 18 Mch., 1821; d. Sep., 1851; m. John Alvin
  Powers, of Milford, N. H.
 Hannah, b. 21 Jan., 1824.
 Joanna, b. 18 Apr., 1826; d. 13 May, 1851; m. Erastus Chilton
  Hayward, of Bridgewater.
690. William Henry, b. 7 Mch., 1828.
 Susan, b. 24 Sep., 1830; d. 24 Mch., 1885.

451. Ezra[7] (*Rufus, David, David, William, Lot, Roger*),
b. about 1784, in Bridgewater or Lyme. He moved to N. Y.
state.

Children of EZRA and —— (——) CONANT:—

Harrison Gilbert.
Lydia.
Celia.
Ezra.
Mary.
Thomas Lothrop.
Clarissa.
Rufus.
Betsey.
Wallace.

452. George[7] (*Rufus, David, David, William, Lot, Roger*),
b. 28 Apr., 1789, in Lyme, N. H.; was a trader; settled in
North Marshfield, Mass. He d. 6 Aug., 1830. He m. in No.
Marshfield, 22 Dec., 1817, Bithiah Hatch, b. 6 Sep., 1783; d.
20 Apr., 1875.

Children of GEORGE and BITHIAH (HATCH) CONANT:—

Laura Ann, b. 22 Apr., 1818, in No. Marshfield.
George, b. 12 June, 1819. He is said to be a professor in a
seminary at Alexander, N. Y., and to have m. a g. g. g. dr.
of John and Martha (Conant) Friend.
Celia Hatch, b. 14 Mch., 1821.
Rufus Leonard, b. 16 July, 1823.
Mary Thankful, b. 6 July, 1826, in No. Marshfield, where she
now lives.

453. Rufus[7] (*Rufus, David, David, William, Lot, Roger*),
b. 21 Aug., 1794, in Lyme, N. H.; settled in Sandwich, Mass.;
a merchant; d. 28 Apr., 1868. He m. in Provincetown, 1
Apr., 1820, Mary Fuller.

Children of RUFUS and MARY (FULLER) CONANT:—

Benjamin Fuller, b. 7 Mch., 1821, in Provincetown.
Abbie Freeman, b. 4 Nov., 1822, in Provincetown.
Cassandra, b. 10 June, 1825.
George, b. 8 May, 1827.
Rufus, b. 27 Apr., 1829. (Perhaps m. in Providence, R. I., 4
Apr., 1855, Anne W. Flint.)
Joseph Fuller, b. 16 Mch., 1831, in Sandwich. (Was perhaps
of Providence, R. I., where his son, Harry W., d. 5 Oct.,
1868, aged 2 years.)
Mary, b. 8 Sep., 1834, in Provincetown.

454. Leonard[7] (*Rufus, David, David, William, Lot,
Roger*), b. about 1800, in Lyme, N. H.; was a farmer of Lyme;
m. Sabrina Chatman.

Children of LEONARD and SABRINA (CHATMAN) CONANT:—

Walsten V.
691. Leonard, b. 7 Apr., 1826.
Mary.
Cassandra.
John.
Samuel.

455. David[7] (*David, David, David, William, Lot, Roger*),

b. 10 Mch., 1787, in Lyme, N. H., where he lived; was a mechanic; d. 28 Apr., 1862. He m. Estella Forbes, of Lyme.

Children of DAVID and ESTELLA (FORBES) CONANT:—

> John Adams, b. 11 Mch., 1809.
> Jane, b. 17 Jan., 1813; m. Ralph Perkins, and settled in New York.
> Elizabeth.
> 692. Bela Forbes, b. 22 Sep., 1822.
> And perhaps others.

456. Jonathan[7] (*Josiah, Jonathan, David, William, Lot, Roger*), b. 15 June, 1793, in Lyme, N. H.; moved, with his parents, to Orange, Vt., but after his father's death returned to Lyme. He was a carpenter, a soldier in the War of 1812, and a colonel of militia. He d. 2 Oct., 1863. He m. 9 Nov., 1820, Clarissa Dimmick, one of a family of twenty-one children; she d. 1842.

Children of JONATHAN and CLARISSA (DIMMICK) CONANT:—

> Lucy U., b. 18 Sep., 1821; d. 13 Oct., 1840.
> 693. Jonathan Josiah, b. 6 June, 1823.
> 694. David Sloan, b. 21 Jan., 1825.
> Samuel Dimmick, b. 3 Jan., 1827; d. 20 Apr., 1844.
> Clarissa O., b. 4 Aug., 1829; m. Jacob T. Calkins; is a widow, living in Brooklyn, N. H., with her daughter, Clara.
> 695. Chester Cook, b. 4 Sep., 1831.
> Frederick Dodge, b. 22 July, 1833; now of Colerain, Mass. He is m. and has Clara E., b. 1861, and Frederick Wells, b. 1867.
> Abel Blood, b. 5 Jan., 1837. Was surgeon of the 14th Regt., Kentucky Vols., for three years during the Rebellion. He d. in New York, 22 Dec., 1864.

457. Cynthia[7] (*John, Ebenezer, Ebenezer, Roger, Lot, Roger*), b. 2 June, 1795, in Ashburnham, Mass.; moved to Brandon, Vt., with her parents; she d. 1 June, 1877. She m. 23 June, 1817, Dr. Isaac Foster, son of David and Phebe (Foster) Merriam, b. in Brandon, 27 July, 1790; d. 30 Sep., 1856. He was town clerk of Brandon many years.

Children of ISAAC F. and CYNTHIA (CONANT) MERRIAM:—

> John Conant, b. 9 Jan., 1819; m. in Minerva, Ky., 3 July, 1845, Aurora Nancy, dr. of Leonard and Nancy (Caryl) Holton, b. in Chester, Vt., 5 Sep., 1822. He now resides in Logansport, Ind.; was a dealer in general merchan-

dise for forty years; has now retired from business. Children: Caryl Conant, b. 1849; Julia Leonora, b. 1853; Minnie Caroline, b. 1857; John A., b. 1860.

Maria Louisa, b. 6 Aug., 1820; m. Morton Smith, of Dexter, Mich.

Julia Chara, b. 8 Aug., 1822; d. 7 Dec., 1873; m. 19 Sep., 1848, Sidney Keith, b. in Winslow, Me., 2 Mch., 1818. He is a lawyer, of Rochester, Ind.; has been county clerk and judge of circuit court. Children: Annie Cynthia, d. y., John Conant, and Julia Alice.

Samuel Judson, b. 22 Mch., 1824; d. 18 Apr., 1868.

James Foster, b. 24 June, 1828.

Delia Augusta, b. 15 Jan., 1831; d. 16 Apr., 1863.

Sidney, b. 13 Aug., 1833; d. 27 Mch., 1852.

Charles M., b. 28 Jan., 1836; d. 16 Apr., 1883.

458. Samuel Stillman[7] (*John, Ebenezer, Ebenezer, Roger, Lot, Roger*), b. 26 Mch., 1797, in Ashburnham, Mass.; moved to Brandon, Vt., with his parents. He moved to New York, N. Y.; was a merchant, later an editor. He d. in Brandon, Vt., 5 Nov., 1830. He m. in West Hartford, Conn., 6 Feb., 1817, Elizabeth Trumbull, dr. of Rev. Samuel Mills, of Chester, Conn. She d. in Montclair, N. J., at the residence of her son, William C., 26 Oct., 1884, aged 91 years.

Children of SAMUEL S. and ELIZABETH T. (MILLS) CONANT:—

696. Claudius Buchanan, b. 8 May, 1819.

Samuel Mills, b. 22 Nov., 1820, in Brandon, Vt. He graduated at Middletown College, 1844; lived at Caldwell, N.Y.; occupation unknown.

John Howard, b. 19 Oct., 1822, in Brandon, Vt.

Thomas Tucker, b. 19 Mch., 1824, in N. Y. city.

697. William Cooper, b. 7 Oct., 1825, " "

Elizabeth Mills, b. 3 Feb., 1828; m. E. D. Selden, of Brandon. They moved to Saratoga, N. Y.

459. Chauncey Washington[7] (*John, Ebenezer, Ebenezer, Roger, Lot, Roger*), b. 11 Jan., 1799, in Brandon, Vt. He was associated with his father and brother, John A. Conant, in the extensive and varied industries carried on by them. He d. 19 Sep., 1872, in Brandon. He m. 30 May, 1821, Rachael Fuller, b. in Clarendon, 2 Aug., 1803; d. 30 Aug., 1882.

Children of CHAUNCEY W. and RACHAEL (FULLER) CONANT:—

Eugene Sidney, b. 20 Nov., 1825. He d. at the residence of

Claudius B. Conant, in N. Y. city, 9 Feb., 1873, of progressive paralysis.

Caroline, b. 29 Nov., 1827.

Caro D., b. 27 Aug., 1834.

Cornelia, b. ———; m. Col. Thomas Halsey, U. S. A. She d. in Brooklyn, N. Y., 18 Feb., 1876; was buried in Brandon, Vt.

And four children who died young.

460. Thomas Jefferson[7] (*John, Ebenezer, Ebenezer, Roger, Lot, Roger*), b. 13 Dec., 1802, in Brandon, Vt. He graduated from Middlebury College, 1823, and for the next two years pursued philosophical studies under the personal supervision of Prof. R. B. Patton, in New York. After teaching a short time in Columbia College, at Washington, D. C., he accepted the professorship of languages in Waterville College (now Colby University), Me. He became deeply interested in Oriental philology, and resigned his professorship at Waterville in 1833, and took up his residence near Boston, Mass., where he could better prosecute his studies in the Hebrew, Chaldee, Syriac and Arabic languages. He had become convinced of the necessity of a new translation of the Scriptures, which should be an adequate representation of the original text, and has since devoted his time principally to this object. In 1835 he was made Professor of Biblical Literature and Criticism in the Baptist Theological Seminary at Hamilton, N. Y., which he held till 1850. While at Hamilton he spent two years abroad in the universities of Halle and Berlin, to perfect his scholarship. In 1839, while at Hamilton, he translated the Hebrew Grammar of Gesenius, with the additions of Rödiger, a work which he subsequently enlarged. It has now become the standard text book in America and Great Britain. In 1847 he published a "*Defense of the Hebrew Grammar of Gesenius against Prof. Stubbs' Translation.*" In 1850 he became Professor of Biblical Literature in the University of Rochester, N. Y., but resigned in 1857 and removed to Brooklyn, to devote himself exclusively to the labor of Biblical revision, in the service of the American Bible Union. His first published work on the Bible was the revision of "*The Book of Job,*" with explanatory notes, which appeared in 1857. It opens that wonderful poem to the reader in a way that the old versions could not, so that he may see and admire its beauties and truths. In 1860 the "*Gospel of Matthew*" appeared; the same year he published "*Baptisein: its Meaning and Use philologically and historically investigated;*" "*The Book of Genesis*" (1868); "*The Book of Psalms*" (1868, and in the American edition of *Lange's* "*Commentary*" in 1872); "*The Book of Proverbs*" (1872) followed. "He has thrown great light on many obscure texts of the common version. It is admitted that he stands in the front rank of Oriental scholars" (*Baptist Encyclopædia*). For some years he has been a member of the Old Testament Company of the American Committee, coöperating with the Committee of the Convocation of Canterbury, England, in the revision of the authorized English version of the Bible. He also compiled, with the assistance of his daughter, Blandina, "*A General and Analytical Index to the American Cyclopædia*" (New York: D. Appleton & Co. 1880).

He m. 12 July, 1830, Hannah, dr. of Rev. Jeremiah Chaplin, D. D., the first president of Colby University, b. in Danvers, Mass., 5 Sep., 1809; d. in Brooklyn, 18 Feb., 1865. She was a frequent contributor to literary and religious periodicals, and a great help to her husband in his literary work. In 1838 she became editor of the *Mother's Journal*, a monthly periodical, which she edited for years. In 1844 she translated "*Lea, or, the Baptism in Jordan*," from the German of Strauss, the court preacher of Berlin. In 1850-2 she translated the commentaries of Neander on the Epistle of Paul to the Philippians, on the Epistle of James, and on the first Epistle of John. In 1855 she wrote a biographical sketch of Dr. Judson, the missionary, entitled, "*The Earnest Man*," and in 1857 translated from the German of Ullen, "*The New England Theocracy*," a sketch of the early ecclesiastical history of New England. Her most important work is "*The History of the English Bible*," a history of the translation of the Scriptures into the English language. This was published 1856.

Children of THOMAS J. and HANNAH (CHAPLIN) CONANT:—

698. Samuel Stillman, b. 11 Dec., 1831.

Roger, b. 15 July, 1833; a lawyer; m. Helen ——. He is living in California.

Caroline, b. 12 Feb., 1835.

Blandina, b. 12 Jan., 1837.

699. Thomas Oakes, b. 15 Oct., 1838.

Marcia H., b. 12 June, 1840.

Susan H., b. 29 May, 1842; m. Gotlieb Cramer, of Vienna, Austria.

Chara B., b. 9 Jan., 1844.

Mary C., b. 28 Nov., 1846.

John, b. 8 May, 1853; d. 1862.

461. Sophronia[7] (*John, Ebenezer, Ebenezer, Roger, Lot, Roger*), b. 14 May, 1805, in Brandon, Vt.; m. 27 Jan., 1827, Hon. Samuel Hoard, b. 20 May, 1800, with whom she celebrated her golden wedding in 1877. They settled in Chicago, Ill., when it was a small settlement. In 1840 he took the first census of Cook county, then containing only about 5000 inhabitants. He was a judge of the municipal court, a deacon of the Baptist church, and a prominent and liberal citizen for nearly half a century. When the first brick Baptist church in Chicago was built, he mortgaged his house to aid in building it, and was prominent in the organization and sustaining of the Orphan Asylum and other charities. He d. 25 Nov., 1881. She is still living.

Adopted child of SAMUEL and SOPHRONIA (CONANT) HOARD:—

Genevieve, who m. Oscar W. Barrett, and has a family.

462. Caroline Cerusa[7] (*John, Ebenezer, Ebenezer, Roger, Lot, Roger*), b. 8 Mch., 1807, in Brandon, Vt.; d. in Hyde Park, Ill., 5 Feb., 1873. She m. 22 Sep., 1829, James Long, b. in Washington, D. C., 24 Mch., 1805. They were very early settlers in Cook co., Ill., and well known to most of the old residents of Chicago. He was a real estate agent; was alderman of the first ward at one time, and school agent. He d. in Paris, France, 10 Apr., 1876.

Children of JAMES and CAROLINE C. (CONANT) LONG:—

Frances Maria, b. 27 July, 1830, in Brandon; m. in Chicago, 28 Nov., 1850, Joseph A. Barker, a lawyer, of Chicago.

Emma Conant, b. 15 Mch., 1833; d. 1852.

Eugene Conant, b. 31 Oct., 1834; now of Chicago, Ill. He m. 10 Oct., 1858, Hattie E. A. Higgins.

John Conant, b. 26 Oct., 1836, in Des Plaines, Ill.; m. (1) 1 June, 1859, Catherine C. Banks, who d. 1875; m. (2) 29 Oct., 1885, Marion H., dr. of George A. Warren. He has no children. He was commissioned 2nd lieut. Co. A, 19th Ill. Vols., in 1861; appointed acting assistant adjutant general of 4th div., Army of the Tennesee, in 1862; brevetted captain, 1865, for meritorious services. He received special mention in Gen'l Hurlbut's report of the battle of Pittsburg Landing, for bravery. (Putnam's *Record of the Rebellion.*)

Chara Conant, b. 26 Jan., 1839; m. 7 May, 1860, Horatio L. Wait. He was a paymaster in the navy during the war; is now master in chancery of Cook co. They live in Hyde Park, Ill.

Andrew, b. 29 Sep., 1840; d. 1843.

Alice, b. 8 May, 1842; d. 1843.

James Henry, b. 5 Mch., 1844, in Chicago, Ill.; m. June, 1865, Belle Johnson. He served in Battery A, 1st Regt., Ill. Light Artillery during the war, from 1862 to 1865; was at Pittsburg Landing, Corinth and in all the battles of Sherman's army, from Vicksburg to Savannah, Ga.

Samuel Hoard, b. 4 Mch., 1848; d. 1851.

463. Chara Emily[7] (*John, Ebenezer, Ebenezer, Roger, Lot, Roger*), b. 21 May, 1809, in Brandon, Vt.; is still living, in Tarrytown, N. Y. She m. in Brandon, 13 May, 1828, Rev. Pharcellus Church, D. D., b. 11 Sep., 1801, near Geneva, N. Y. He studied for the ministry at Hamilton, N. Y., and was first settled as pastor at Poultney, Vt., in 1825. In 1828 he became pastor of what is now the Central Baptist Church, of Providence, R. I. In 1848 he accepted the pastorate of the Bowdoin Square Baptist Church, of Boston, Mass., but was obliged to resign on account of sickness. In 1855 he became editor of the New York *Chronicle*, and continued ten years. Since 1865 he has spent considerable time abroad, studying the scriptures in the original, and writing for the press. He has written and published many works of a theological nature, and for reviews and periodicals. He is a man of great intellect, fine culture, and great vigor as a writer.

Children of PHARCELLUS and CHARA E. (CONANT) CHURCH:—

Clara O'Brien, b. 23 Feb., 1829, in Providence, R. I.

Emma Conant, b. 20 May, 1831,   "   "

Pharcellus Conant, b. 1 Apr., 1834, in Providence, R. I.

William Conant, b. 11 Aug., 1836, in Rochester, N. Y. He is now a resident of New York, and editor of the Army and Navy Journal.

Frank Pharcellus, b. 22 Feb., 1839.

Sarah Jane, b. 13 Jan., 1841.

John Adams, b. 5 Apr., 1843. He is (1884) superintendent of the Tombstone Mill and Mining Co., Tombstone, Arizona Territory.

464. **Augustus Hammond**[7] (*Eben, Ebenezer, Ebenezer, Roger, Lot, Roger*), b. 16 Oct., 1811, in Brandon, Vt. The Rev. Robert Collyer has written his life, entitled, "*A Man in Earnest: Life of A. H. Conant*," which was published (1875) by Lee & Shepard, from which the following particulars have been gathered. His early education was very limited; during his fourth year he went to school and learned to read easily; after this his only schooling was when he could be spared from his father's farm. As he grew up he began to wish for a liberal education and a profession, but his father thought there were too many professional men already, and it was settled that he should become a farmer. When he was about twenty-one years old he determined to go West, and started in September, 1832. During the journey he kept a journal. At Schenectady he saw, for the first time, a railroad; the "train" consisted of two cars, drawn by one horse. From Buffalo he went to Detroit, by water, and at Cleveland himself counted *no less than twelve schooners*, and remarked on its greatness as a place of business. On leaving Detroit he determined to walk, and "came that evening to Saline, footsore and very weary." At Niles he stopped three days, built a chimney and taught a class of four young men stenography. The fifteenth day from Detroit he arrived at Chicago. At Keokuk he found "a sink of depravity, by far the most wicked place I have ever seen." He went down the river on a steamboat and was disgusted by the sight of slaves and the open gambling carried on all day and all night long. He then went up the Ohio, and took the stage from Pittsburg to Erie, and thence home. About 1835 the whole family moved to Illinois, and settled at Des Plaines, about twenty miles from Chicago. Here, amid

the struggles and trials of the wilderness, he found time for self-improvement, as is to be seen by the following laconic entries from his diary:

"1836, Jan. 1. Attended to the survey of my claim. 5. Went to Chicago with a load of potatoes. Read Mason on Self-Knowledge. Read Latin Grammar. Brought in a deer. Made and bottomed chairs. May 10. Mrs. Hoard and Betsy Kelsey arrived. 11. Planted corn and prepared for the wedding. 12 Married Betsy Kelsey. Weather fine and clear. June 4. Wife eighteen to-day. Read Paley's 'Natural Theology.' Meeting at my house. Sep. 28. Heard big wolves howling. Hunted deer. ˙ Dressed pig and calves torn by wolves. Killed a badger. 1837, May 4. Wrote a temperance address. Read Croly's British Poets, Dick's Philosophy of a Future State; studied Algebra. Hunted a panther. 1838, Feb. 18. Meeting at my house; I read a sermon. 1839, May 12. Read Bancroft's Sermons. June 29. Agreed to deliver an oration. July 4. Delivered my oration. Oct. 20. Wrote a sermon from Matt. VI., 9, 27. 1840, Feb. 9. Preached at Geneva. 25. Read Norton on Trinity. Made soap. Wrote a sermon on the Aim of Life. May 25. Started for New England to attend the Divinity School in Cambridge."

And so it happened he became a minister. The extracts need no comment—they speak for themselves. It is said that the Fourth of July oration was a denunciation of slavery such as few at that time dared to deliver. Mr. Conant was denounced, insulted, and invited to eat his words. He thereupon went to Chicago and had the oration printed at his own expense, and distributed it widely. At about this time he made the acquaintance of the mother of Rev. James Freeman Clarke, who says of him:

"He came into my son's store to make some purchases, and while standing at the counter took up the 'Western Messenger;' was so interested in it that he forgot everything besides until he had read it through. After this, when Dr. Hosmer came from Buffalo to preach for us, Mr. Conant came in to hear him. I introduced him to the preacher after meeting, and the result was that Dr. Hosmer advised him to go East and study for the ministry; offered to write to Dr. Ware about receiving him, and to the Unitarian Association to help him. 'No,' said the young man, 'I thank you, but I had rather not begin by begging. I will sell my crops and take orders for payment in Vermont, and then take my wife and two children to live with their folks while I am studying at Cambridge.'"

In the spring he sold his crops and went to Vermont, only to find that he could not get his checks cashed. In despair he almost determined to give up his studies, but finally decided to visit Dr. Ware and lay the matter before him. On his arrival at Cambridge he told the Doctor that it was impossible for him to go to school, but found that some friend had sent a letter to Dr. Ware for him containing fifty dollars, which enabled him to begin his studies. He remained at Cambridge about a year, being obliged to work all his spare time to support himself. While at Cambridge President Quincy, Dr. Ware, and others, assisted and opened their homes to him, and he also had the opportunity of hearing the best preachers. He says of Beecher: "I have been to hear Dr. Beecher; there must have been a thousand people present. I could heartily agree with most he said. He is a rather hard featured old fellow, 'awful powerful' as the Hoosiers say, and I thought if his pulpit cushions are not well stuffed I should not like to lend him my fists to preach with." He was ordained as an Evangelist at Bullfinch Street Church, Boston, 27 June, 1841. On Aug. 1, 1841, he began to preach in Geneva, Ill., under the auspices of the American Unitarian Association, but in June, 1842, a new society was organized, as the First Christian Society of Geneva. Mr. Conant was chosen pastor, Samuel Clarke and Scott Clarke, assistants. He continued there sixteen years. Making Geneva a center, he worked in all the surrounding country incessantly. Aug. 1, 1842, he says: "One year since I returned from Cambridge. During the year I find I have travelled as a missionary 1844 miles, distributed 150 volumes and 1000 tracts." The field of his labors extended through Illinois, Wisconsin, and even into Iowa and Missouri. In 1850 he was preaching regularly in Geneva and Elgin, and besides that at a school house midway between those places, beside his missionary labors. In 1852 he went to Cincinnati, to help organize the Western Unitarian Conference. In 1857 he received a call to become pastor of the Unitarian Church in Rockford, Ill., which he accepted, and continued there till July, 1861, when he resigned his charge and went to Chicago, proposing to go out as a chaplain in the army. He became chaplain in the 19th Illinois regiment, under command of Col. Turchin. The story of his life in the army would be interesting, but a few extracts from his letters must be sufficient:

"1861, Sep. 26. If the rebels should suffer a thorough defeat in the vicinity of Washington, it would probably hasten their expulsion from Kentucky and Missouri; or, if the government should send a naval force South, acting aggressively instead of defensively, we may expect a retreat of the traitors from this neighborhood. But the miserable temporizing of the government in relation to slavery, and the apparent fear of offending slave-holders, and the manœuvring to keep clear of interference with the infernal institution which is at the bottom of all treason, so encourages the rebels that it would in be no matter of surprise if they should defeat us half a dozen times, and until we are ready to strike at the heart of their treason. Huntsville, Aug. 19, 1862. A scene. Two ladies in a carriage, with a negro driver, have been to head-quarters slave hunting. Had heard that one named Andrew was here. Inquired for the chaplain's tent, and proposed to search that. Chaplain closed the tent and told them that it belonged to him and they could not enter it. Ladies held out a paper which they said was General Rosseau's permit of search. Chaplain told them neither they nor the general could enter his tent for such a purpose. Ladies left to bring the general in person to catch the negro. After the ladies were gone Andy took a walk; I did not notice which way he went. Aug. 22. The women came again, reinforced by an escort of three cavalry, with orders to take Andy dead or alive. Andy was not in camp. Seeing my tent shut up, they suspected Andy was there; so one of the escort came intending to look in. I bade him stand back, told him he could not enter. He presented General Rosseau's order. I told him the order was to search the camp, not my tent; he might go the length of his order, but in such an infamous business not an hair's breadth further. Jan. 2, 1863. We have been fighting three days nearly on the same ground, and the battle is not yet decided. I write to say I am yet unharmed, and that I saw our dear son, Neray, after the severest of the fight, in which his regiment was engaged, about noon, and that he was unhurt also, though, as Col. Marsh said, 'he had fought like a tiger.' I worked all night, till four o'clock in the morning, night before last, bringing in the wounded from the battle-field. While so employed I was made a prisoner, and my ambulance and assistants were also captured; but we told them what we were doing, so after some parley they let us go."

In Jan., 1863, while engaged in this hospital duty near Murfreesborough, Tenn., he was taken sick, and died 8 Feb., 1863. He m. 12 May, 1836, Betsey Merriam Kelsey (his cousin).

Children of AUGUSTUS H. and BETSEY M. (KELSEY) CoNANT:—

700. Neray, b. 2 Dec., 1837, in Cook co., Ill.

John, b. 9 Feb., 1839. He lives in Rockford, Ill.; has a dr.,
Lulu.
Coretta, b. 11 Feb., 1843, in Geneva.
Augustus Turchin, b. 10 Mch., 1862, in Geneva.

465. Charles Rich⁷ (*Calvin, Ebenezer, Ebenezer, Roger,
Lot, Roger*), b. 5 Dec., 1807, in Pittsford, Vt.; moved to Putnam, O., with his parents, and thence, about 1830, to California; in 1833 he went to Mexico, and settled at Santa Jesus
Maria, province of Chihuahua. He d. some years ago. He
m. 11 May, 1840, Simona Maldinado.

Children of CHARLES R. and SIMONA (MALDINADO) Co-
NANT:—

701. Charles F., b. 20 Jan., 1842, in Guaymas, Sonora, Mexico.
Thomas, b. 20 Dec., 1844.
Francis James, b. 29 Jan., 1846.
702. Mary Malinda, b. 12 Oct., 1847.
Simona Frances, b. 2 Dec., 1849, in Guaymas, Mexico.
Joseph Benjamin, b. 17 May, 1852, in French Camp, Cal.; of
Bancari, Sonora, Mexico.

466. Lorenzo⁷ (*Calvin, Ebenezer, Ebenezer, Roger, Lot,
Roger*), b. 22 Sep., 1812, in Sheldon, Vt.; a carpenter and
millwright; moved to Ohio with his parents. He settled in
Bertrand, Mich., 1835, where he worked at his trade. In 1849
moved to Buchanan, Mich., and engaged in the milling business with a Mr. Dutton, until 1852, when he settled on a farm.
In 1854 he bought a saw mill, near Galena, Mich., in company
with James Wilson; while there he lost the fingers of his left
hand, and returned to the farm. In 1857 he went back to Buchanan, kept store for a while, and then took charge of a grist
mill for Messrs. Bainton and Pears, in whose employ he continued till his death, 19 Feb., 1864. He m. 1848, in Bertrand,
Elizabeth Jane, dr. of Elijah and Ruth (Harry) Egbert, b. 14
Apr., 1829.

Children of LORENZO and ELIZABETH J. (EGBERT) Co-
NANT:—

Ruth, b. 4 Aug., 1849, in Buchanan, Mich.; m. 4 July, 1872,
Robert M., son of David M. and Mehitable Rundell; has
Lottie May, b. 21 Apr., 1873.
John Calvin, b. 8 Nov., 1852; d. 4 July, 1859.

HARRY CONANT, M. D.

Annie R., b. 29 Jan., 1855, in Galena Township.

Esther, b. 17 Sep., 1857, in Buchanan; m. William Redding, of Ottumwa, Iowa, and has Ethel A., b. 1882.

Mary, b. 15 Sep., 1859; m. Joseph Wachs, and has Arula, Bertha and Ann Louise.

467. William[7] (*Luther, Ebenezer, Ebenezer, Roger, Lot, Roger*), b. 13 Mch., 1819, in Brandon, Vt.; moved to Geneva, Ill., where he now lives. He m. 9 Sep., 1840, Melissa White, b. in Salisbury, Vt., 23 Mch., 1821; d. in Geneva, Ill., 3 Apr., 1884.

Children of WILLIAM and MELISSA (WHITE) CONANT:—

Ellen Amanda, b. 31 Aug., 1841, in Brandon; m. —— Akers, of Iona, Ks.

703. Luther, b. 29 May, 1844, in Brandon.

Jessie, b. ——.

468. Polly[7] (*Samuel, Samuel, Roger, Roger, Lot, Roger*), b. 17 July, 1785, in Boston, or Charlestown, Mass.; m. 19 Nov., 1813, Dr. Andrew, son of Bossenger and—— (Craigie) Foster, b. 7 Sep., 1780. In 1814 Samuel Conant and Polly, wife of Andrew Foster, of Dedham, sell land in Charlestown to E. Cook. Bossenger Foster was son of Thomas Foster, jr., and m. two sisters of Andrew Craigie, of Cambridge, who was the apothecary general of the Revolutionary army, and owner of the famous Craigie house at Cambridge. This house was Washington's head-quarters during the siege of Boston, and has since become famous as the home of Longfellow. Andrew Craigie d. without children, and the house passed to his sisters. Dr. Andrew Foster graduated at Harvard University, 1800, and d. 17 May, 1831.

Children of ANDREW and POLLY (CONANT) FOSTER:—

i. Andrew, a lawyer.

ii. Samuel Conant, a physician. Among his children are Conant, Mary Conant, and J. Reginald, now of New York city.

iii. James, an officer in the U. S. navy.

iv. Mary Conant, d. y.

v. George, b. 5 Oct., 1820, in Roxbury, Mass.; m. in New York, 30 Nov., 1848, Louisa Adeline, dr. of George Miller and Mary D. (Billings) Gibbons. He was Col. of the First Regt., Long Island Vols., in the Rebellion. Children: 1. Edith,

b. 1849; 2. George Craigie, b. 1850; 3. Samuel Conant, b. 1852; 4. Fitz-Gibbons, b. 1860. He d. in Brooklyn, N. Y., 1866.

vi.   Mary Conant, d. y.

469. John Washington[7] (*John, Israel, Israel, Roger, Lot, Roger*), b. 11 June, 1805, in Merrimack, N. H.; m. in Dunstable, N. H., 20 Nov., 1833, Caroline Fowler. He resided in Manchester, N. H.; d. there 13 Oct., 1884.

Children of JOHN W. and CAROLINE (FOWLER) CONANT:—

John F., b. 4 May, 1835, in Merrimack, N. H.
Mary Jane, b. 26 Sep., 1840, in Weare, N. H.
Laura, d. y.

470. Benjamin Israel[7] (*John, Israel, Israel, Roger, Lot, Roger*), b. 24 Apr., 1808, in Merrimack, N. H.; settled in Milford, N. H., about 1830. He was a mill owner and lumber dealer. He was one of the selectmen of Milford several years, and deputy sheriff of Hillsborough co. for one or more terms. He d. in Brookline, N. H., 12 June, 1865. He m. (1) Louisa Hammond Gutterson, b. in Milford, N. H., 27 Feb., 1813, d. 7 July, 1846; m. (2) Lucy Maria Crosby, of Amherst, N. H., b. 16 June, 1814, d. 8 Nov., 1883.

Children of BENJAMIN I. and LOUISA H. (GUTTERSON) CONANT:—

704.   Charles Francis, b. 22 Apr., 1835.
Ann Louisa, b. 11 Sep., 1836; d. 3 Aug., 1859.
Sarah Catherine, b. 14 Aug., 1839; d. 8 Jan., 1872.
Clara Farley, b. 13 Jan., 1842; d. 30 Apr., 1860.

Children of BENJAMIN I. and LUCY M. (CROSBY) CONANT:—

Frederick Fitch, b. 8 June, 1843; d. 24 Mch., 1873.
George Alvaro, b. 19 Nov., 1849; m. 14 Nov., 1882, Ida M. Parcher, of Livermore, Me.

471. Mary Joanna[7] (*John, Israel, Israel, Roger, Lot, Roger*), b. 25 Aug., 1809; d. in Nashua, N. H., 9 Nov., 1834; m. 5 Sep., 1833, Gilman, son of Zebediah and Elizabeth (Martin) Shattuck, of Nashua, N. H., b. in Hillsborough, N. H., 2 Dec., 1802. He was a prominent citizen of Nashua, N. H., holding at different times the offices of town treasurer, assessor and selectman. He was well known in business circles, having been a merchant and bank director for many years. He m. (2) 1847, Emeline B. Dutton, and had other children. He d. 17 July, 1860.

Child of GILMAN and MARY J. (CONANT) SHATTUCK:—

> Gilman Conant, b. 23 Oct., 1834, in Nashua, where he still resides. He has recently retired from mercantile business, in which he was engaged for thirty years. He has served his city as councilman, alderman and member of the board of education, and has also been for many years a trustee of the Nashua Savings Bank. He has been a member of the Pilgrim Congregational Church since its organization, two years superintendent of its Sunday school, and twice elected deacon for a term of three years. He m. (1) in Hillsborough Centre, N. H., 25 Oct., 1855, Caroline Weed, dr. of Samuel G. and Betsey (Dutton) Barnes, b. 3 June, 1833; d. 22 Oct., 1868. Children: 1. Fred Curtis, b. 19 Aug., 1856, d. 9 Aug., 1872; 2. Fannie Adaline, b. 25 Sep., 1858, d. 27 Apr., 1861; 3. Estelle Caroline, b. 15 Dec., 1861, who is a teacher in the public schools of Nashua; 4. George Gilman, b. 25 Feb., 1864, d. 2 Aug., 1864. He m. (2) in Cambridge, Mass., 22 Oct., 1868, Estelle Maria, dr. of John and Sarah Ann (Locke) Barnes. Children: 5. Arthur Gilman, b. 9 July, 1870; 6. Fanny Conant, b. 22 June, 1872; 7. Harold Bemis, b. 17 Nov., 1873; 8. Helen Barnes, b. 14 Apr., 1878; 9. Roger Conant, b. 3 July, 1884.

472. Jotham Shepard[7] (*John, Israel, Israel, Roger, Lot, Roger*), b. 18 Aug., 1816, in Merrimack, N. H. He learned the trade of an engraver on steel rolls, for printing designs on cloth, in Lowell, Mass.; but owing to declining health he abandoned his trade and removed to New York city, where he engaged in the business of constructing and repairing machinery. Later he removed to Newark, N. J., where he was engaged in business for several years. His health again failing, he removed to Lowell, Mass., where he d. 12 May, 1879. He m. 11 May, 1848, Catherine Paul, b. 11 May, 1828.

Child of JOTHAM S. and CATHERINE (PAUL) CONANT:—

> Kate Shepard, b. 4 May, 1851; d. 23 Sep., 1853.

473. Stephen Kendrick[7] (*John, Israel, Israel, Roger, Lot, Roger*), b. 10 Feb., 1821, in Merrimack, N. H. He resides in Boston, Mass. He m. 3 Sep., 1865, Mary A. Claflin, of Boston.

Children of STEPHEN K. and MARY A. (CLAFLIN) CONANT:—

Fannie M., b. 2 Aug., 1868, in Newport, R. I.
Stephen Shepard, b. 21 June, 1879, in Boston, Mass.

474. **Frederick Josiah**[7] (*Josiah, Josiah, Josiah, Roger, Lot, Roger*), b. 19 Feb., 1799, in Hollis, N. H. When fourteen years of age he went from Hollis to Boston, Mass., and entered the employ of his uncle, Ralph Jewett; but after remaining with his uncle about five years, being anxious to progress more rapidly, went to South America and engaged in business for himself, spending the most of his time in Caraccas, Venezuela. Not content with the activity of business life in South America, he returned to the United States, and settled in New York city. Here he engaged in the wholesale clothing business—his store being one of the first in that branch of business in New York—and continued in active business for over fifty years. When he retired from business he removed to Elizabeth, N. J., where he d. 7 Mch., 1883. He was a regular attendant and member of the Presbyterian church. He m. in New York city, 1835, Amanda C., dr. of James Young, of New York.

Children of FREDERICK J. and AMANDA C. (YOUNG) CONANT:—

Georgiana Amanda, m. G. Soulé Davis; no children.
Augusta Frances, m. William W. Gilbert; has five children.
Louisa Matilda, unm.; lives in Elizabeth, N. J.
Julia Ann, m. Rev. J. W. Buckmaster, and has four children.
Mary Frederica, unm.; of Elizabeth, N. J.

475. **William**[7] (*Josiah, Josiah, Josiah, Roger, Lot, Roger*), b. 1 June, 1801, in Hollis, N. H.; a cabinet maker. He moved to Walpole, N. H., thence to Bellows Falls, Vt. He m. (1) 15 Nov., 1827, Sarah Holden Hale; she d. in Walpole, N. H., 8 Mch., 1830; m. (2) 23 Apr., 1843, Laurinda Huntingdon.

Child of WILLIAM and SARAH H. (HALE) CONANT:—

Sarah Elizabeth, b. 19 Oct., 1828, in Walpole, N. H.; m. in

F. S. Conant

Bellows Falls, Vt., 18 Oct., 1854, Hon. Jabez Delano Bridgman. No children. He d. 7 Apr., 1887.

Child of WILLIAM and LAURINDA (HUNTINGDON) CONANT:—

William Jewett, b. 28 Feb., 1843. He lives in Bellows Falls, Vt.; has children.

476. Addison Lorenzo[7] (*Josiah, Josiah, Josiah, Roger, Lot, Roger*), b. 26 May, 1808, in Hollis, N. H. Was a cabinet maker. Settled in Cincinnati, Ohio, after death of his first wife; removed from there to California, where he died. He m. (1) about 1834, ——— ———. He m. (2) in Cincinnati, 24 Nov., 1840, Eliza, dr. of John and Eliza (Wilson) Martin, who was born in Jonesboro', Tenn. After the death of Mr. Conant she m., 1862, Thomas Gilmore, who d. 5 Feb., 1884. She is still living.

Child of ADDISON L. and ——— (———) CONANT:—

Mary, b. 1836.

Children of ADDISON L. and ELIZA (MARTIN) CONANT:—

Carrie, b. 19 Aug., 1844, in Cincinnati. She m. in Cincinnati, 12 Oct., 1871, Charles, son of Thomas and Ellen Maguire, a native of Sligo, Ireland. They reside in Indianapolis, Ind. Children: William Gilmore, b. 19 July, 1872, in Indianapolis; Albert Martin, b. 5 Apr., 1874, in Indianapolis.
705. John Addison, b. 22 Nov., 1846.

477. Clarissa[7] (*Josiah, Josiah, Josiah, Roger, Lot, Roger*), b. 1 May, 1814, in Hollis, N. H.; d. 3 July, 1873, in Mt. Vernon, N. H. She m. in West Cambridge, Mass., 17 Dec., 1846, Dr. Sylvanus Bunton, b. in Allenstown, N. H., 8 Mch., 1812. He graduated at Dartmouth College, 1840; studied medicine in Baltimore, Md.; settled in Manchester, N. H., where he lived till June, 1864. He was then appointed assistant surgeon in the 7th N. H. Regt., and in Aug., 1864, promoted to surgeon; was mustered out 20 July, 1865. He settled then in Hollis, where he remained three years, then removed to Mt. Vernon, N. H., where he d. 13 Aug., 1884.

Children of SYLVANUS and CLARISSA (CONANT) BUNTON:—
i. Henry S., b. 6 Apr., 1848, in Manchester, N. H.; m. in Winthrop, Mass., 9 Nov., 1880, Mary Greenwood Giles. He is

treasurer of the Hyde Park (Mass.) Savings Bank.
ii.   Leonard Jewett, b. 28 Dec., 1858; d. 1859.

478. Ebenezer Tolman[7] (*William, Josiah, Josiah, Roger, Lot, Roger*), b. 13 July, 1813, in Greensboro', Vt. He was a farmer, a member of the Congregational church and superintendent of the Sunday school. He m. in Bedford, N. H., 5 Feb., 1850, Mary Jane, dr. of Ebenezer and Jane (Orr) Fisher, b. in Londonderry, N. H., 10 Aug., 1820.

Children of EBENEZER T. and MARY J. (FISHER) CONANT:—

> Jane E., b. 3 Jan., 1851.
> Harriet B., b. 10 June, 1852.
> Henrietta H., b. 10 June, 1852.
> Helen M., b. 30 Mch., 1854.
> Ann Orr, b. 20 Feb., 1856.
> William F., b. 14 Feb., 1858.
> Charles Sumner, b. 2 July, 1860; m. 22 Jan., 1884, Martha Phebe Burnham, b. 28 Sep., 1858, in St. Johnsbury. He is a music teacher, of St. Johnsbury, Vt.
> Alice T., b. 29 July, 1862.

479. James Edwin[7] (*Abel, Abel, Josiah, Roger, Lot, Roger*), b. 3 Feb., 1831, in Pepperell, Mass. When he was about two years of age his parents removed to Lowell, Mass.; at the age of eighteen he was given a position in the Interior Department at Washington, D. C., by President Pierce. While in Washington he formed a friendship with Senator Yulee, of Florida, and through his influence went to Florida where he gained his first experience in railway matters on the Florida railroads. On the breaking out of the war, his sympathy with the North being well known, he returned to Washington where he obtained a position in the War Department. His wife died soon after, and he removed to New York, where he was engaged in business till his death. Mr. Conant was well known in railroad and commercial circles, in New York and in the West, having been connected with the construction of a number of railroads. During the last years of his life he was associated with Col. J. Condit Smith in the construction of the Chicago & Atlantic railway. In 1867 Mr. Conant moved his family to Elizabeth, N. J., where he afterwards resided. He died 1 Oct., 1886, at the residence of his brother-in-law, William H. Lyman, in Lowell, Mass. He m. (1) in Washington, D. C., 9 Feb., 1854, Susan Amelia Rutherford. He m. (2) Sallie Lee, of Cincinnati, Ohio.

Children of JAMES E. and SUSAN A. (RUTHERFORD) CO-NANT :—

> Edward Rutherford, b. 13 Nov., 1854, in Lowell, Mass.
> Leonard Hubbard, b. 25 Apr., 1856, in Washington, D. C.
> Susie Hattie, b. 5 Dec., 1857, in Washington, D. C.

480. James Augustus[7] (*James, Abel, Josiah, Roger, Lot, Roger*), b. 8 June, 1809, in Hollis, N. H.; m. ——— Carter, of Hardwick, Vt.

Children of JAMES A. and ——— (CARTER) CONANT :—

> Daniel.
> David.

481. Joseph Fletcher[7] (*James, Abel, Josiah, Roger, Lot, Roger*), b. 16 Nov., 1811, in Hollis, N. H.; moved to Hardwick, Vt. (and thence to Lowell, Mass.?); m. Mary Maine.

Children of JOSEPH F. and MARY (MAINE) CONANT :—

> Miltimore.
> Lyman.
> Solon A.
> Eliza.
> Mary, m. Dr. Lavigne, of Lowell, Mass.
> Marion.
> Myra.

482. Abel E.[7] (*James, Abel, Josiah, Roger, Lot, Roger*), b. 20 Sep., 1817, in Hollis, N. H. He m. Frances, dr. of Archibald and Susan (Young) Sloan, of Andover, Mass.

Children of ABEL E. and FRANCES (SLOAN) CONANT :—

> George W., b. 1846; of Lowell, Mass.
> Charles F., b. 1848; 	"		"
> Gilbert B., b. 1850; 	"		"
> Elizabeth T., b. 1857; 	"		"
> Susan M., b. 1868; m. Edwin Whitcomb, of Reading, Mass.;
> 	resides in Wakefield, Mass.

483. John[7] (*Samuel, John, John, Joshua, Joshua, Roger*), b. 24 Aug., 1793, in Provincetown, Mass. He m. Eliza Bowley.

Children of JOHN and ELIZA (BOWLEY) CONANT :—

706.   Oliver B.
       Eliza.
       Frank, now of Charlestown, Mass.
       John,   "   "   "
       Lucy,   "   Gloucester,   "

484. **Betsey**[7] (*Samuel, John, John, Joshua, Joshua, Roger*), b. 10 June, 1807, in Provincetown, Mass.   She m. 23 Nov., 1824, Thomas Long.

Children of THOMAS and BETSEY (CONANT) LONG:—

i.   Mary Abigail, b. 17 Aug., 1828; m. 5 Dec., 1849, William Poore, and has: 1. William, b. 17 Sep., 1863; 2. Nellie N., b. 17 Oct., 1865; 3. A. Thomas, b. 25 Oct., 1867.
ii. Samuel T., b. 10 Nov., 1830; m. 25 Nov., 1852, Melissa V. Smith; no children.
iii. Charles F., b. 15 Aug., 1833; m. 8 Dec., 1859, Sylva C. Atwood, and has Elsie, b. June, 1866.
iv. Betsey C., b. 7 Dec., 1837.

485. **Sarah Jane**[7] (*Simeon, John, John, Joshua, Joshua, Roger*), b. 29 Jan., 1819, in Provincetown, Mass.; d. 11 Jan., 1849; m. 5 Jan., 1845, John Smith, b. 26 Dec., 1804, in Barnstable.   He was a merchant, of Provincetown; was deputy collector of customs.   He d. 14 Mch., 1873.

Children of JOHN and SARAH J. (CONANT) SMITH:—

i.   Simeon Conant, b. 10 Aug., 1845; m. 17 Sep., 1871, Emily F., dr. of Joshua and Rebecca (Whorf) Atkins, b. 21 June, 1849. Children: 1. Sarah Jane, b. 13 Apr., 1872; 2. Simeon Conant, b. 29 June, 1874; 3. Sarah Whorf, b. 30 Nov., 1878.   He is a dealer in boots and shoes, in Provincetown.
ii. Stephen Henry, b. 23 Dec., 1847.

486. **Austin Benezette**[7] (*Horatio, Eleazer, Shubael, Josiah, Exercise, Roger*), b. 7 Mch., 1838, in South Toledo, O. He was a resident of McMinnville, Tenn., in 1884.   He m. in Perrysburg, O., 24 Dec., 1868, Mary Jane Charles.

Children of AUSTIN B. and MARY J. (CHARLES) CONANT:—

Horatio, b. 13 Jan., 1870, in So. Toledo.
Charles, b. 14 Nov., 1871,   "   "
Harry Austin, b. 10 Jan., 1874; d. 1878.
Helen Eunice, b. 10 Jan., 1874.
Samuel Storrs, b. 22 Oct., 1878.
Mary Angeline, b. 22 Oct., 1878.

487.   Martha Ann[7] (*Harry, Eleazer, Shubael, Josiah, Exercise, Roger*), b. 3 Dec., 1825, in Monroe, Mich.; m. in Monroe, 30 May, 1850, James W. Tillman, of Detroit.   After the death of Mr. Tillman, she m. (2) 16 Sep., 1873, in Detroit, Maj. General Alpheus Starkey Williams.   Gen. Williams was b. at Saybrooke, Conn., 20 Sep., 1810; graduated at Yale College in 1831, and studied in the Yale Law School in 1832-3. After travelling in Europe two years he settled in Michigan in 1836.   From 1840 to 1844 he was judge of probate for Wayne co.; in 1843 was alderman of Detroit, and in 1844 was recorder of the city.   During the Mexican War he ·served as lieut. colonel of the 1st Mich. Vols., and from 1849 to 1853 served as postmaster of Detroit.   On the breaking out of the civil war he was appointed by the President (Aug., 1861) brigadier general of volunteers.   He commanded the 12th army corps in the battles of South Mountain, Antietam and Gettysburg, and the 20th corps during the siege of Atlanta and in Sherman's march to the sea.   He was mustered out in Jan., 1866, and in Aug. was appointed by the President to adjust military claims in Missouri.   From 1866 to 1869 he was minister resident to the republic of San Salvador.   He was elected to the 44th Congress to represent the 1st district of Mich., in 1876, on the democratic ticket, and was re-elected in 1878.   He died in Washington, D. C., before the close of his second term.   Mrs. Williams still resides in Detroit.

Children of JAMES W. and MARTHA A. (CONANT) TILLMAN :—

i.   Harry Conant, b. 9 Mch., 1851. He graduated as a civil engineer at the Pennsylvania Military Academy, at Chester, Pa. He m. in Chicago, Ill., 23 Nov., 1880, Amanda McCormick Shields.   They reside in Detroit.
ii.   Kate Whitelsey, b. 30 Sep., 1856; m. in Santa Barbara, Cal., 5 Mch., 1878, Lieut. James Henry Bull, U. S. A.   Resides in Santa Barbara, Cal.
iii.   James Stuart, b. 9 Dec., 1858; d. 12 July, 1860.
iv.   Louie Stuart, b. 19 June, 1861; m. in Detroit, 26 Feb., 1880, Samuel Carson, of San Francisco.   Resides in San Francisco, Cal.

488.   Sarah[7] (*Harry, Eleazer, Shubael, Josiah, Exercise,*

Roger), b. 3 Feb., 1832. She m. in Monroe, Mich., 29 Nov., 1864, Hon. John P. Hogarth, as his second wife. "Mr. Hogarth was born in Geneva, N. Y., 7 Apr., 1820, and died in the 67th year of his age. He was educated at the old Geneva Academy, and was a merchant and banker in Geneva, a merchant in San Francisco in 1851, and later in mercantile business in Detroit for many years. He was appointed bank examiner by Gen. Grant, during his first term, which position he has since held. He was one of the most methodical and scrupulously exact of men in his business affairs and labors. He was a man of extensive reading, rare culture and intelligence, broad and liberal views and unusual high mindedness." (Monroe Commercial, Sep. 24, 1886.) Mr. Hogarth left several children by his first wife, among them Mr. William Hogarth, of Cleveland, and a daughter, the wife of W. H. Elliott, of Detroit. He d. 18 Sep., 1886, in Monroe, Mich.

Child of JOHN P. and SARAH (CONANT) HOGARTH:—

Maria Conant, b. 3 Apr., 1871; d. 17 Aug., 1872.

489. John Shubael[7] (*Harry, Eleazer, Shubael, Josiah, Exercise, Roger*), b. 27 May, 1841, in Monroe, Mich. He attended school in Monroe, and the State Normal School at Ypsilanti. He enlisted Sep. 11, 1862, in the 25th regt., Mich. Infantry, as commissary sergeant; was promoted through the different grades to captain; was discharged for disability, 23 Feb., 1864. He then engaged in the drug business in Muskegon, Mich., as a member of the firm of Wayne & Conant, but retired from business in 1871 on account of ill health. He then travelled in Europe for two years and returned to Detroit, but his health still being poor went to Santa Barbara, Cal., in 1876, where he remained two years and returned to Detroit. In 1883 he removed to Princeton, N. J. He m. Mary, dr. of Rev. John McLaren, D. D., of Alleghany City, Pa., and sister of Rt. Rev. Bishop McLaren, of Illinois.

Child of JOHN S. and MARY (MCLAREN) CONANT:—

William Shubael, b. Feb., 1868, who is attending Princeton College.

490. Harry Armitage[7] (*Harry, Eleazer, Shubael, Josiah,*

Exercise, Roger), b. 5 May, 1844, in Munroe, Mich., where he resides. He was prepared for college in the schools of Monroe, and entered Michigan University, at Ann Arbor, in the class of 1865. After leaving college he engaged in mercantile and manufacturing pursuits for some years. His present occupation is that of an attorney at law, having been admitted to the bar in 1878. In politics he has always been a "stalwart" Republican, and possesses the confidence of his party to a remarkable degree, having received at different times, without solicitation on his part, the nominations for mayor, alderman, supervisor and state senator. He was elected to the three latter offices in a strong Democratic section. In 1880 he received the appointment of consul at Naples, Italy, which he resigned after a residence abroad of seven months. In 1882 he was elected secretary of state of Michigan, and re-elected in 1884. He m. in Pontiac, Mich., 27 May, 1868, Mary Morris Thurber.

Children of HARRY A. and MARY M. (THURBER) CONANT:—

Helen Armitage, b. 16 Apr., 1869, in Monroe; d. 8 Aug., 1869.
Horace Thurber, b. 4 Oct., 1871.
Marguerite Stewart, b. 15 June, 1874.

491. Erasmus Darwin[7] (*Seth, Seth, Malachi, Caleb, Exercise, Roger*), b. 30 Aug., 1803, in Mansfield, Conn.; moved to New York state, with his parents. He was a deacon, elder and Sunday school superintendent of the Presbyterian church, and at the time of his death a member of the Throop Avenue Presbyterian Church, of Brooklyn, New York. He d. in Brooklyn, N. Y., 30 Nov., 1880. He m. 31 Jan., 1828, Elizabeth Arkills, of Fishkill, N. Y., with whom he celebrated his golden wedding in 1878.

Children of ERASMUS D. and ELIZABETH (ARKILLS) CONANT:—

A daughter, d. in infancy.
707. William E., b. 9 Nov., 1828.
708. Charles F., b. 3 Nov., 1835.
709. George H., b. 11 Dec., 1840.

492. Nelson[7] (*Sylvanus, Sylvanus, Malachi, Caleb, Exercise, Roger*), b. 5 Sep., 1808, in Mansfield, Conn. He was a farmer and a member of the Congregational church. He m. Sally, dr. of Ethan Burrows.

Children of NELSON and SALLY (BURROWS) CONANT:—

Elizabeth Ann, b. 23 May, 1838; m. but no children.
Edward D., b. 3 Nov., 1839; m. Abba, dr. of E. B. Smith, Esq., of Mansfield, Conn. They have no children. He served during the war in the 21st regt., Conn. Vols.

493. Albert A.[7] (*James, Sylvanus, Malachi, Caleb, Exercise, Roger*), b. 11 Sep., 1821, in Mansfield, Conn. He m. 25 May, 1848, Amanda Crittenden.

Children of ALBERT A. and AMANDA (CRITTENDEN) CONANT:—

Ella, d. y.
George Albert, b. 27 June, 1856; he graduated from Amherst College, and is now a lawyer, of Willimantic, Conn.

494. Theodore Delos[7] (*Chester, Sylvanus, Malachi, Caleb, Exercise, Roger*), b. 4 Feb., 1819, in Mansfield, Conn., where he lives. He is a member of the Methodist Episcopal church. He m. (1) 21 Nov., 1841, Louisa Wright; m. (2) Harriet (Conant), widow of Palmer Knowlton, of Ashford.

Child of THEODORE D. and LOUISA (WRIGHT) CONANT:—

710. Delos Wright, b. 14 Jan., 1843.

Children of THEODORE D. and HARRIET (CONANT) CONANT:—

Ellen M., b. 13 Jan., 1847; d. 28 Nov., 1856.
Mary Elizabeth, b. 31 May, 1849; d. 21 Feb., 1871.
Otis H., b. 4 Oct., 1852; m. 8 Oct., 1873, Lydia R. Jacobs.

495. Henry Washington[7] (*Chester, Sylvanus, Malachi, Caleb, Exercise, Roger*), b. 14 Jan., 1825, in Mansfield, Conn. He is a minister of the Methodist Episcopal church; is secretary of the R. I. State Temperance Union. He lives in Providence, R. I.

Children of HENRY W. and ——— (———) CONANT:—

Henry.
Carrie.
Saxton.

496. Rufus Fielder[7] (*Edmund, Sylvanus, Malachi, Ca-*

leb, Exercise, Roger), b. 27 May, 1827, in Mansfield, Conn., where he lived; he d. 1865. He m. ———, Minerva Balch.

Children of RUFUS F. and MINERVA (BALCH) CONANT:—

> Isadore, b. 12 Mch., 1849.
> Mary Ann Jeannette, b. 17 Aug., 1850.

497. Julius Edmund[7] (*Edmund, Sylvanus, Malachi, Caleb, Exercise, Roger*), b. 19 Sep., 1829, in Mansfield, Conn. He lived in Mansfield, Conn., Elmira, N. Y., and Lowell, Mass.; was an auctioneer, appraiser and stable keeper. He d. 7 Aug., 1878, in Gloucester, Mass. He m. in Lowell, Mass., 23 Feb., 1854, Laura Maria, dr. of Asa and Rachael (True) Batchelder, of Litchfield, Me., b. 12 Dec., 1828.

Children of JULIUS E. and SARAH M. (BATCHELDER) CO-NANT:—

> Edmund Batchelder, b. 1 Apr., 1856, in Elmira, N. Y.
> 711.   Frederick, b. 11 Sep., 1857, in Elmira, N. Y.
> Frank Hersey, b. 6 Apr., 1859, in Elmira, N. Y. Graduated from Lowell High School, 1877, then studied one year at Warren Academy, Woburn, Mass. In 1878 entered the U. S. Naval Academy as a cadet engineer, and graduated 1882. Has recently returned from a trip round the world in the U. S. S. Pensacola.
> George Washington, b. 22 Feb., 1862, in Lowell, Mass.
> Maud Baker, b. 12 Mch., 1864; d. 19 Dec., 1884.
> Augusta, b. 9 Dec., 1868, in Lowell, Mass.

498. Harriet Marilla[7] (*Lucius, Sylvanus, Malachi, Caleb, Exercise, Roger*), b. 30 June, 1823, in Mansfield, Conn.; m. 4 Oct., 1843, William H. Atwood, of Mansfield.

Children of WILLIAM H. and HARRIET M. (CONANT) AT-WOOD:—

> William Orlo.
> Arthur.
> Leon.

499. Lydia Amanda[7] (*Lucius, Sylvauus, Malachi, Caleb, Exercise, Roger*), b. 27 Feb., 1825, in Mansfield, Conn.; m. 16 Dec., 1845, John E. Atwood, who is engaged with his son, under the firm name of the Atwood Machine Company, in the manufacture of silk working and other machinery.

Child of JOHN H. and LYDIA A. (CONANT) ATWOOD:—

Eugene, b. 20 Sep., 1846.

500.   John A.[7] (*Lucius, Sylvanus, Malachi, Caleb, Exercise, Roger*), b. 16 Aug., 1829, in Mansfield, Conn. He has lived in Hartford and Waterbury, and is now a resident of Willimantic, Conn. When nine years old he went to live with his uncle, George Eaton, in Tolland, who was a strong advocate of temperance and the abolition of slavery. In 1843 Mr. Eaton was one of the organizers of a Weslyan Methodist church, which Mr. Conant joined, he being then fourteen years of age. On his removal to Hartford he joined the Fourth Congregational Church of that city, and has since continued a member of various Congregational churches until 1881, when he, with others, formed the First Berean Church of Willimantic. In theology their society is Calvinistic, they baptize by immersion, and admit no one to membership who uses alcohol or tobacco in any form, or who is an adhering member of any secret society. He has been a constant laborer in the cause of reform. He was from the beginning of the movement an abolitionist, and voted with the free-soil party until its development into the Republican party. In 1856 he, with Hon. Joseph R. Hawley and a few others, met one evening in Hartford to consider the best method of organizing against the system of slavery. This meeting resulted in the organization of the Republican party in Connecticut. He voted with that party till 1872, when he assisted in the formation of the Prohibition party in his state, with which he has continued to coöperate in part ever since. He noticed the growing influence of secret societies, and saw that they were endeavoring to control the prohibition movement; he therefore became a member of the American party, and in 1884 was its candidate for Vice-President, Ex-Senator Pomeroy, of Kansas, being the candidate for President.

At the age of fourteen Mr. Conant commenced to learn the silk business, and has during his life been engaged in that occupation. Since 1866 he has been connected with the Holland Manufacturing Company, at Willimantic, engaged in the

J. A. Conant

manufacture of twist and silk sewings. He m. (1) 11 May, 1852, Caroline Augusta, dr. of Deacon Simon C. Chapman, of Ellington; m. (2) 18 Nov., 1864, Marietta (French) Brown.

Child of JOHN A. and CAROLINE A. (CHAPMAN) CONANT:—

712. John Winslow, b. 30 Aug., 1854, in Hartford, Conn.

Children of JOHN A. and MARIETTA (FRENCH) CONANT:—

Henry W. D., b. 24 July, 1861; d. 14 May, 1862.
George Andrew, b. 21 Apr., 1866.
Julius Deliverance, b. 28 Oct., 1869.

501. David Philo[7] (*Lucius, Sylvanus, Malachi, Caleb, Exercise, Roger*), b. 29 Aug., 1833, in Mansfield, Conn. He removed to Canton, Mass., where he now lives. He m. 25 Sep., 1855, Sarah Jane Stillwell, of Morrisville, N. Y.

Child of DAVID P. and SARAH J. (STILLWELL) CONANT:—

Lucius W., b. 28 Feb., 1866.

502. Hiram Ellsworth[7] (*Lucius, Sylvanus, Malachi, Caleb, Exercise, Roger*), b. 13 Sep., 1839, in Mansfield, Conn.; m. 28 Nov., 1860, Lena Shattle, a native of Germany.

Children of HIRAM E. and LENA (SHATTLE) CONANT:—

Frank, b. 12 Aug., 1867.
Dwight, b. 21 Apr., 1872.

503. Susan Asenath[7] (*Elam Lucius, Edmund, Malachi, Caleb, Exercise, Roger*), b. 10 June, 1831, in East Farnham, Canada; m. in Peacham, Vt., 8 Dec., 1853, Daniel, son of Samuel and Hannah (Bailey) Aiken, b. 14 July, 1819, in Barnet, Vt. He is a farmer, of Barnet.

Children of DANIEL and SUSAN A. (CONANT) AIKEN:—

i. Viana Vandalia, b. 23 Mch., 1854; d. 11 Sep., 1876; m. 2 Sep., 1875, William L. Gilfillan, of Barnet.
ii. Charles Benjamin, b. 19 Apr., 1855; m. 19 Oct., 1881, Sarah Ann, dr. of John Bartlett, of Sunapee, N. H. Children: 1. Arthur Raymond, b. 1882; 2. Maud Viana, b. 1883; 3. A son, b. 1885, in Lawrence, Mass.
iii. Daniel Lucius, b. 24 Jan., 1857.
iv. Iantha Jane, b. 21 Feb., 1862; m. 23 Dec., 1884, Frank J., son of Andrew Lackie, of Barnet.
v. A daughter, b. and d. 8 Mch., 1865.
vi. William Albert, b. 16 Sep., 1869.

504. **Lucius Malachi Augustus**[7] (*Elam Lucius, Edmund, Malachi, Caleb, Exercise, Roger*), b. 21 Apr., 1833, in East Farnham, Canada. He removed to Peacham and thence to Walden, Vt., where he now lives; a farmer. He m. in Peacham, 1 Jan., 1862, Mary Jane, dr. of James S. and Mary L. (Wetherspoon) Smith, b. in Cabot, Vt., 19 Oct., 1839.

Children of LUCIUS M. A. and MARY J. (SMITH) CONANT:—

Almira Jane, b. 21 Oct., 1862.
James Elam, b. 8 July, 1869.
Alice Dorinda, b. 7 Apr., 1876.

505. **Rovilla Philura**[7] (*Elam Lucius, Edmund, Malachi, Caleb, Exercise, Roger*), b. 23 Oct., 1835; m. 20 Feb., 1858, Samuel M., son of Tucker and Lucy (Fuller) Tucker. He was b. 7 July, 1830, and is a farmer, of Corinth, Vt.

Children of SAMUEL M. and ROVILLA P. (CONANT) TUCKER:—

i.   Frank Estes, b. 27 Sep., 1859.
ii.   George McLellan, b. 2 Aug., 1869.

506. **Edmund**[7] (*Matthew Watson Marcy, Edmund, Malachi, Caleb, Exercise, Roger*), b. 27 Dec., 1829, in Broome, Canada. He is a farmer, of Chelsea, Vt. He m. (1) in Tunbridge, Vt., 27 May, 1857, Mary C. Bennett; she d. Sep., 1864; m. (2) 1 Apr., 1866, Sophronia A. Smith, of Cabot, Vt.

Children of EDMUND and MARY C. (BENNETT) CONANT:—

Frank W., b. 28 Sep., 1861, in Tunbridge, Vt.
Mary E., b. 23 Oct., 1863,   "   "   "

Children of EDMUND and SOPHRONIA A. (SMITH) CONANT:—

Minnie D., b. 5 Jan., 1867, in Peacham, Vt.
Amelia Maria, b. 17 Aug., 1868, in Peacham, Vt.
Edmund Estes, b. 1 May, 1870, in Tunbridge.
Carrie L., b. 3 Dec., 1871, in South Royalton, Vt.
Emma B., b. 17 Jan., 1873, in Tunbridge.
Henry Harrison, b. 20 Dec., 1875, in So. Royalton.

507. **Joseph Jacobs**[7] (*Matthew W. M., Edmund, Malachi, Caleb, Exercise, Roger*), b. 4 Apr., 1837, in Barre, Vt.; is now of Somerville, Mass. He m. 1856, Ann M. Tucker.

Children of JOSEPH J. and ANN M. (TUCKER) CONANT:—

Mary Elizabeth, d. y.

Martha H., b. 19 Sep., 1858; m. A. A. Bullen, of Cambridge, Mass., and has two children.

George Henry, b. ——; m. in Cambridge, Mass., Mary Hatch.

Herbert, d. y.

Joseph Ernest, now employed in office of Boston Globe; of Somerville, Mass.; is married.

Charles, d. y.

William, d. y.

Frank Austin Hobbs; is married; employed in office of Boston Globe.

Clarence Tucker.

Alvah Waite.

Sumner.

Josie.

508. Henry Harrison[7] (*Matthew W. M., Edmund, Malachi, Caleb, Exercise, Roger*), b. 11 Nov., 1840, in Grafton, Vt.; moved to Boston, Mass., with his parents. He enlisted in the First Regt., Mass. Vols., during the Rebellion, and was twice wounded. He was at the first battle of Bull Run, and at Seven Pines, where he was wounded. Since the war has been engaged in commercial pursuits. Has lived in New York, N. Y., Kennebunk and Portland, Me., and Boston, Mass. He m. (1) 9 Nov., 1862, in Boston, Sarah Merritt; m. (2) in New York city, 19 Mch., 1880, Mary J. Goodwin.

Children of HENRY H. and SARAH (MERRITT) CONANT:—

Mary Elizabeth, b. 24 Dec., 1863, in Boston.

George Hall, b. 5 Feb., 1866, in Boston.

Harry Watson, b. 17 Sep., 1867, in Boston.

Annie, b. 1 Apr., 1870; d. 6 Mch., 1876.

Alice Louise, b. 26 June, 1872.

Edward Stacy, b. 20 Feb., 1874.

Sadie, b. 10 Dec., 1875; d. 21 Aug., 1878.

Hattie, b. 3 July, 1877, in Cambridgeport; d. 17 Aug., 1878.

Children of HENRY H. and MARY J. (GOODWIN) CONANT:—

Gracie, b. 17 June, 1881, in New York city.

Harold, b. 1 May, 1884, in Boston, Mass.

Arthur, b. 21 May, 1886, in Portland, Me.

509. George Washington Smith[7] (*Matthew W. M., Edmund, Malachi, Caleb, Exercise, Roger*), b. 31 Jan., 1843, in Royalton, Vt.; is now in the employ of Houghton, Mifflin & Co., Boston; lives in Cambridge. He m. Georgiana Robart.

Children of GEORGE W. S. and GEORGIANA (ROBART) Co-
NANT:—

 Arthur Raynor, b. 18 Feb., 1874; d. y.
 Mabel.
 Effie.
 Ella.

510. William B.[7] (*Gideon, Nathaniel, Malachi, Caleb, Exercise, Roger*), b. 14 July, 1816, in Saratoga Springs, N. Y. He
was in the brokerage and real estate business in Albany, N. Y.,
for many years; is now in the real estate and insurance business
in St. Paul, Minn. He has been city assessor and alderman.
He m. in Schenectady, N. Y., 7 Dec., 1840, Sarah Wilkinson,
dr. of Daniel and Sarah (Wilkinson) Fuller, b. in Schenectady,
17 Jan., 1823.
 Children of WILLIAM B. and SARAH W. (FULLER) CONANT:—

 Isabella, d. y.
 William B., b. 29 Oct., 1855; d. y.
 Benjamin Franklin, b. 10 June, 1860, in Albany; d. Dec., 1864.

511. Daniel Marshall[7] (*Timothy, Caleb, Benajah, Caleb,
Exercise, Roger*), b. in Herkimer co., N. Y., 19 Feb., 1796.
He moved to Ohio, with his parents, about 1820. He was an
itinerant Methodist minister, belonging to the North Ohio Con-
ference, and an active preacher for nearly fifty-eight years.
He d. 17 Dec., 1873. He m. in Cayuga co., N. Y., 17 Sep.,
1816, Zimena, dr. of Isaac and Bithiah (Chase) Wardwell, b.
13 Sep., 1800. She is now living (1887) in San Francisco, Cal.
 Children of DANIEL M. and ZIMENA (WARDWELL) Co-
NANT:—

 Caroline, b. 18 May, 1818, in Cayuga co., N. Y.; m. ——
  Hotchkiss; lives in Creston, Union co., Iowa.
 Phebe, b. 7 Feb., 1821, in Richfield, Ohio; m. (1) —— High;
  m. (2) —— DeWitt; lives in Mt. Gilead, Morrow co., Ohio.
 Charles W., b. 12 Nov., 1823, in Richfield, Ohio; d. unm.
713. William M., b. 16 Sep., 1825, in Aurora, O.
 Maria, b. 14 Sep., 1828, in Hinckley, O.; m. —— Clark; lives
  in Wooster, Wayne co., Ohio.
 Aurelia, b. 19 Apr., 1832, in Hinckley, O.; m. —— Griffith;
  lives in San Francisco, Cal.
714. Russell B., b. 5 Feb., 1841, in Brooklyn, O.

512. Timothy B.[7] (*Timothy, Caleb, Benajah, Caleb, Exercise, Roger*), b. 22 Sep., 1798, in Warren, Herkimer co., N. Y.; removed to Hinckley, Medina co., Ohio, where he is still (1886) living; a farmer. He m. 11 Oct., 1820, Abigail Buck.

Children of TIMOTHY B. and ABIGAIL (BUCK) CONANT:—

Alice, b. 6 July, 1821.
Pamelia, b. 7 Mch., 1823; d. before 1886.
715. Lewis, b. 19 Jan., 1825.
Plimpton, b. 12 Jan., 1827.
Timothy, b. 26 Nov., 1828; of San José, Cal.
Melissa, b. 16 Mch., 1831; d. before 1886.
Nancy, b. 14 Apr., 1833; d. before 1886.
Amanda, b. 23 Aug., 1835.
Sanford, b. 5 Apr., 1840; d. before 1886.
Olive, b. 10 Jan., 1842.
Darius, b. 12 Feb., 1844.
Isaiah, b. 9 June, 1845.

513. Aaron[7] (*Timothy, Caleb, Benajah, Caleb, Exercise, Roger*), b. ———; of Hinckley, O.; carpenter and farmer. At 65 was youngest of seven children, all alive and well. He d. Mch., 1886.

Children of AARON and ——— (———) CONANT:—

Hiram; was in Union army, and d. during the war.
Emeline.
Daniel.
Alvira.
Ethan.

514. Sarah Ann Willis[7] (*Samuel W., Jonathan, Benajah, Caleb, Exercise, Roger*), b. 2 Sep., 1819; d. 24 Apr., 1865. She m. 7 Dec., 1845, John Brown, jr., of Baltimore, Md., where they lived.

Children of JOHN and SARAH A. W. (CONANT) BROWN:—

i.   Laura Jane, b. 25 Dec., 1846; m. William D. Reddish, jr.
ii. Robert, b. 14 Sep., 1848; d. 14 Oct., 1848.
iii. Albert Stewart, b. 3 Nov., 1849; m. Nettie Wayson.
iv. Mary Taylor, b. 19 Nov., 1850; m. Wm. Miller.
v.   Samuel Conant, b. 15 Mch., 1854; d. 15 Jan., 1855.
vi. Charles Louis, b. 10 Nov., 1856; m. Mary Elizabeth Watts.
vii. Samuel Edwin Conant, b. 2 Apr., 1859; m. Mamie Miller.
viii. Sarah Elizabeth, b. 1 Jan., 1864; d. 29 June, 1865.

515. Catherine Mary[7] (*Samuel W., Jonathan, Benajah,*

Caleb, Exercise, Roger), b. 22 Dec., 1823, in Boston, Mass.; moved to Baltimore, Md., with her parents, where she m. 22 May, 1844, Robert Hamill.

Children of ROBERT and CATHERINE M. (CONANT) HAMILL:—

i.   Charles Webb, b. 2 Mch., 1845. He is a manufacturer of silver plated ware, in Baltimore, Md. He m. 2 Apr., 1873, Elizabeth F. Wellener. Children: 1. Grace Wellener, b. 7 Dec., 1873; 2. Harry Winslow, b. 27 June, 1875; 3. Frank Wesley, b. 20 Nov., 1876; 4. George Wade, b. 27 June, 1878; 5. Carl Webb, b. 13 Oct., 1879; 6. Hattie Winslow, b. 1 Mch., 1881.

ii. Robert Henry, b. 31 Mch., 1847; m. 3 Sep., 1866, Margaret V. Nickum. Children: 1. Samuel Nickum, b. 22 Sep., 1869, d. 1869; 2. John Stout, b. 22 Nov., 1870, d. 1870.

iii. William Holland, b. 29 Jan., 1849;. m. 24 Dec., 1878, Mary Orr.

iv. Albert Conant, b. 24 July, 1850.

v.   Kate Winslow, b. 1 Apr., 1852; m. 7 May, 1873, Basil S. Wellener, jr. Children: 1. George Hamill, b. 14 Mch., 1874, d. 1874; 2. Charles Edwin, b. 16 Feb., 1876; 3. Robert Hamill, b. 3 Apr., 1878, d. 1879; 4. Basil Smith, b. 7 Feb., 1880; 5. Lillian, b. 8 July, 1883; 6. Mary Halbert, b. 18 Mch., 1885.

vi. Clara Melvina, b. Dec., 1854; d. 6 Apr., 1855.

vii. Harry Edgar, b. 8 Aug., 1856; d. y.

viii. George Ash, b. 19 Dec., 1858; d. y.

516. Samuel Williams[7] (*Samuel W., Jonathan, Benajah, Caleb, Exercise, Roger*), b. 12 Sep., 1832, in Baltimore, Md.; a shoemaker. He served in the First Md. Infantry during the war. He d. 7 Feb., 1885. He m. 11 Mch., 1861, Martha Sands, dr. of James Hussey.

Children of SAMUEL W. and MARTHA S. (HUSSEY) CONANT:—

Hannah Sally Columbia, b. 8 Aug., 1866.
Florence May, b. 18 May, 1869.
Georgiana Sophia, b. 1871.
Edith Cornelia, b. 19 June, 1874.
Samuel James, b. 2 June, 1879.

517. John Harvey[7] (*Caleb, Jonathan, Benajah, Caleb, Exercise, Roger*), b. 2 Oct., 1818, in Chelsea, Vt. He removed to North Lawrence, N. Y., and thence to Michigan. He now lives in Detroit, Mich. He is a member of the First Congregational Church, of which he is sexton. He m. in Manchester, Vt., 12 Aug., 1849, Louisa Maria Farnsworth.

Children of JOHN H. and LOUISA M. (FARNSWORTH) CO-
NANT :—

William F., b. 16 June, 1849, in Troy, N. Y. He is engrossing
clerk in the office of the city clerk of Detroit. He m. in
Detroit, 17 Apr., 1880, Elizabeth Edith Cummings.
Franklin Henry, b. 3 Oct., 1863, in Grand Rapids, Mich.

518. **Alban Jasper**[7] (*Caleb, Jonathan, Benajah, Caleb,
Exercise, Roger*), b. 24 Sep., 1821, in Chelsea, Vt. He moved
to North Lawrence, N. Y., and in 1857 to St. Louis, Mo. He
was prepared for college at fifteen, but did not take a regular
course at the University. He went to New York and received
lessons in portrait painting, and soon became favorably known
in St. Louis as an artist. He visited Washington and painted
portraits of Attorney General Bates, Hon. E. M. Stanton, Secretary of War, and others. His best portraits are of President
Lincoln, the Garrison family, and some in possession of J. B.
Eads, Esq. He has devoted much time to archæological studies, and his " Footprints of Vanished Races," a work on the
mounds and mound builders of the West, is highly commended
for originality and research. He is a curator of the University
of Missouri, and has lectured acceptably before it. He was a
member of the Second Baptist Church, of St. Louis. He now
resides in New York city. He m. (1) in St. Louis, Sarah M.,
dr. of Charles and Lydia (Barnes) Howes; she d. 30 Sep., 1867,
and he m. (2) 27 July, 1869, Brionia Constance, dr. of Nicholas
Bryan, who d. 7 Mch., 1875.

Children of ALBAN J. and SARAH M. (HOWES) CONANT :—

716. Fanny Emily, b. 21 Oct., 1847, in Troy, N. Y.
George R. Davis, b. 22 Sep., 1849; d. 12 Nov., 1851.
Charles Alban, b. 31 Aug., 1852; d. 2 June, 1853.
Caroline Steele, b. 20 Aug., 1855; m. Amos Woodruff Smith,
of New York; they have a son Roger.
Edward William, b. 4 July, 1858, in St. Louis, Mo.; d. in
Washington, D. C., 24 Feb., 1862.
Alban Jasper, b. 17 Nov., 1860, in St. Louis; d. in Washing-
ton, 14 Jan., 1862.
Mary Alice, b. 17 Mch., 1863, in Buffalo, N. Y.; d. 8 Jan., 1870.
Helen Blanche, b. 17 Nov., 1865; she is attending Wellesley
College.

Child of ALBAN J. and BRIONIA C. (BRYAN) CONANT:—

Alban Jasper, b. 23 Oct., 1870, in St. Louis.

519. Henry Albert[7] (*Caleb, Jonathan, Benajah, Caleb, Exercise, Roger*), b. 7 Aug., 1828, in Chelsea, Vt.; moved to Troy, N. Y., where he is engaged in business. He m. 2 Jan., 1854, in Troy, Anna Eliza Mackie.

Children of HENRY A. and ANNA E. (MACKIE) CONANT:—

Lillie Sherwood, b. 14 Aug., 1854, in Troy.
Florence, b. 1 Feb., 1859, in Troy.
Fred Sherwood, b. 20 Jan., 1861, in Troy.

EIGHTH GENERATION.

520. Cyrus Whitman[8] (*Gaius, Ezra, Thomas, Nathaniel, Nathaniel, Lot, Roger*), b. 27 Nov., 1803, in Bridgewater, Mass. He graduated from Union College, 1824; studied for the ministry. He preached for some time in Savannah, Ga., and afterwards removed to Scoffold Prairie, Greene county, Indiana, where he d. 24 Nov., 1883. He m. 25 Sep., 1831, at Scaffold Prairie, Nancy Dayhoff.

Children of CYRUS W. and NANCY (DAYHOFF) CONANT:—

Fred. Dayhoff, b. 24 Jan., 1833, in Owen co., Ind.
Gaius, b. 1 Dec., 1834, in Scaffold Prairie.
Mary Ann, b. 11 Jan., 1837.
Cassandra, b. 16 Oct., 1839.
Marcia R., b. 1 Jan., 1842.
Susan, b. 5 Jan., 1844.
Sarah Catherine, b. 15 Apr., 1846.
Benjamin, b. 20 Oct., 1849; m. 6 Jan., 1884, Josie Noble. He is a farmer of Scaffold Prairie.

521. Ezra Styles[8] (*Gaius, Ezra, Thomas, Nathaniel, Nathaniel, Lot, Roger*), b. 9 Nov., 1805. He settled in Randolph, Mass., where he was engaged in the lumber business for forty years. He was president of the Randolph Savings Bank, a member of the general court of Massachusetts and a delegate to the Cincinnati convention which nominated Buchanan.

He was president of the Mass. Temperance Alliance, and at one time candidate of the temperance party for lieutenant governor of Massachusetts. He m. 3 July, 1825, Elvira Beals, b. 28 Feb., 1806.

Children of EZRA S. and ELVIRA (BEALS) CONANT:—

717. Ezra Beals, b. 8 May, 1826.
  Elvira Ann, b. 10 Aug., 1828; m. 7 Mch., 1872, John Clapp, of Scituate, Mass.
718. Cyrus C., b. 16 Feb., 1834.
719. Royal Benjamin, b. 7 Nov., 1836.

522. Benjamin Kilbourn[8] (*Gaius, Ezra, Thomas, Nathaniel, Nathaniel, Lot, Roger*), b. 20 Nov., 1807, in Bridgewater, Mass. He was of Boylston and Worcester, Mass.; a mason and builder. He d. 15 Dec., 1860, in Boylston. He m. 17 Apr., 1833, Elizabeth, dr. of Aaron and Mary White, of Boylston; she d. in Framingham, 4 Apr., 1877.

Children of BENJAMIN K. and ELIZABETH (WHITE) CONANT:—

  Myron, b. 12 Mch., 1834; d. 10 Aug., 1856, in Worcester.
  Benjamin Whitman, b. 29 Dec., 1835; d. 2 Aug., 1881.
  Francis Adams, b. 28 Feb., 1838; d. 13 June, 1865.
  Mary White, b. 13 Oct., 1840.
  Charles Blanchard, b. 3 Aug., 1843; d. 19 Apr., 1846.
720. Edward Davis, b. 25 May, 1846.
  William Albert, b. 26 Aug., 1850; d. 19 Aug., 1852.

523. Mary Angeline[8] (*Gaius, Ezra, Thomas, Nathaniel, Nathaniel, Lot, Roger*), b. 24 Nov., 1809, in Paxton, Mass.; m. 20 May, 1829, Deacon Silas Newton Grosvenor, b. 20 May, 1808. He was a carpenter and builder. He d. in Worthington, Ind., 30 Sep., 1865. She is still (1884) living.

Children of SILAS N. and MARY A. (CONANT) GROSVENOR:—

i. Eliza Cassandra, b. 30 May, 1830, in Paxton.
ii. Lemuel Conant, b. 22 Mch., 1832, in Paxton. He is a physician and surgeon, practicing in Chicago, Ill. He m. (1) in Dorchester, Mass., 27 Feb., 1865, Ellen M. Prouty. Children: Nettie C., b. 1868, Lorenzo N., b. 1868, Wallace F. and Ellen E., b. 1873. He m. (2) in Taunton, Mass., 25 June, 1877, Naomi Josephine Barrett. Children: Gertrude N., b. 1879, David B., b. 1881, and Lucy E., b. 1882.
iii. David Gaius, b. 26 Feb., 1834.

iv. Jane Tracey, b. 13 Feb., 1837, in Petersham, Mass.
v. Silas Nelson, b. 23 June, 1840, in Paxton.
vi. Lucy Leonard, b. 10 Apr., 1843, in Paxton,

524. William[8] (*Gaius, Ezra, Thomas, Nathaniel, Nathaniel, Lot, Roger*), b. 11 June, 1816, in Paxton, Mass.; a farmer; m. in Fairlee, Vt., 27 Mch., 1838, Clarissa Palmer. He d. in Paxton, 28 July, 1864.

Children of WILLIAM and CLARISSA (PALMER) CONANT:—

  Edward E., b. 17 Apr., 1840, in Paxton; d. y.
721. Everett William, b. 28 July, 1843, in Paxton.
  Clara P., b. 22 Sep., 1847, in Paxton; m. —— Morgan, of Worcester, Mass.

525. Chauncey[8] (*Robert, Daniel, Jeremiah, Nathaniel, Nathaniel, Lot, Roger*), b. 24 May, 1800, in Fairfield, N. Y.; a farmer, of Fowler, N. Y.; m. Cordelia, dr. of Timothy Sheldon.

Children of CHAUNCEY and CORDELIA (SHELDON) CONANT:—

722. Rodney T., b. 5 Oct., 1829, in Fowler.
  Emily.
  Charles H., who was killed at the battle of South Mountain during the war.
  Nancy B.

526. Jeremiah[8] (*Jeremiah, Daniel, Jeremiah, Nathaniel, Nathaniel, Lot, Roger*), b. about 1810, in Herkimer co., N. Y.; moved to Athens co., Ohio, with his father, about 1822. He now lives in Big Run, O. He m. 1830, Mary, dr. of Francis and Sarah (Mickenham) Muns, b. 1811.

Children of JEREMIAH and MARY (MUNS) CONANT:—

  Alfred, b. 1831; d. aged 5.
723. Sanford, b. 18 Mch., 1833.
724. Ambrose, b. 1835.
  Amanda, b. 1841; m. George Jarvis.

527. Roger[8] (*Abel, Roger, Jeremiah, Nathaniel, Nathaniel, Lot, Roger*), b. 15 Oct., 1805, in Darlington, Canada; moved to Scarborough, about ten miles east of Toronto, with his parents. He is now living in Capac, Mich. He remembers many incidents of adventures—with the Indians and dur-

Roger Conant

ing the Revolutionary War—related to him by his grand-father, Roger Conant, who moved from Massachusetts to Canada. He was engaged in farming and lumbering occupations until prevented by age. He now resides with his daughter, Mrs. A. J. West. He m. in Toronto Township, Can., 20 June, 1842, Margaret, dr. of Peter and Nancy (Ayreheart) Van Valkenburg, b. in Nelson Township, Can., 3 Dec., 1825.

Children of ROGER and MARGARET (VAN VALKENBURG) CONANT:—

725. Eliphalet, b. 17 June, 1843, in Pickering, Ontario.
726. Elizabeth Jane, b. 25 Apr., 1845, in Pickering, Ontario.
Margaret Ann, b. 1 Aug., 1847; m. William Thompson.
Cornelius, b. 19 Nov., 1848, in Chippewa, Can.; moved to Michigan, with his parents; m. in Unionville, Apr., 1884, Charlotte Barrenger, and has Ella.
Delilah, b. 1 May, 1854, in Port Huron, Mich.; m. 29 Nov., 1883, Charles Cady.
727. Rhoda Matilda, b. 18 Mch., 1856, in Port Huron, Mich.
Eliza Ellen, b. 17 June, 1857, in Port Huron, Mich.; m. 10 Oct., 1880, Max Ritze.
Charles Frederick, b. 26 Feb., 1860, in Port Huron, Mich.; m. in St. Clair, 28 Feb., 1881, Margaret Lee. Children: Florence and William.
Ida May, b. 1 May, 1863, in China, Mich.; m. in Port Huron, 25 June, 1883, Rudolph Ritze, and has Claude, b. 1884.

528. Daniel[8] (*Thomas, Roger, Jeremiah, Nathaniel, Nathaniel, Lot, Roger*), b. 4 July, 1818, in Darlington, Canada. He was a resident of Oshawa, and a large land owner; also owned vessels on the lakes. He was a school trustee and church warden. He d. 26 Jan., 1879, in Oshawa. He m. in Oshawa, 12 Jan., 1841, Mary Eliza, dr. of Caleb and Louisa (Curtis) Shipman, b. in Clarenceville, Quebec, Canada, 27 Apr., 1818.

Children of DANIEL and MARY E. (SHIPMAN) CONANT:—

728. Thomas, b. 15 Apr., 1842, in Oshawa.
Louisa, b. 17 Dec., 1845; m. in Toronto, Canada, 12 Jan., 1868, Myron V. Curtis, b. 18 Feb., 1843, in Clarenceville, Quebec, where they reside. He is son of Enoch and Lucretia (Colton) Curtis. Children: 1. Earl Conant, b. 23 Apr., 1869; 2. Hermon, b. 19 July, 1870; 3. Gordon Burnaby, b. 2 July, 1885.
William Henry, b. 12 Jan., 1850.

Electa Eliza, b. 24 Oct., 1852; m. 11 Jan. 1872, George, son of Sanford and Fatima (Ellsworth) Martin, b. 24 Oct., 1852. Children: 1. Walter Conant, b. 5 May, 1873; 2. Sanford Frederick, b. 23 Aug., 1874; 3. Frank Ellsworth, b. 26 Sep., 1876; 4. Mailland Warner, b. 8 June, 1883.
Edna Mary, b. 4 July, 1856.
Ethel Amelia, b. 3 Mch., 1860.

529. David Fales[8] (*Marlborough, John, John, Nathaniel, Nathaniel, Lot, Roger*), b. 3 Oct., 1802, in Thomaston (now Rockland), Me. He was a lime manufacturer; d. 13 Dec., 1872. He m. 20 Oct., 1824, Sabra Rankin, d. 5 Oct., 1859.

Children of DAVID F. and SABRA (RANKIN) CONANT:—

729.   Oliver Jackson, b. 14 Dec., 1825.
Melissa D., b. 9 Feb., 1830; m. 20 Nov., 1851, James Kelly.
Charles H., b. 7 Sep., 1834; m. Carrie Thomas. He served as 2nd and 1st lieutenant of Co. C, 4th Me. Infantry, and captain of Co.'s C and F of the same regiment, during the war (see Maine Adj. Gen. Report, 1862, Appendix E, p. 14).
Joseph R., b. 8 Oct., 1837. He was 1st lieutenant Co. C, 4th Me. Infantry, and died of wounds received in battle.
Hannah H., b. 12 Apr., 1840; d. 24 Feb., 1854.
William Eugene, b. 31 Aug., 1843.

530. Ebenezer Benson[8] (*Martin, John, John, Nathaniel, Nathaniel, Lot, Roger*), b. 16 Oct., 1811, in Bridgewater, Mass.; moved to Canton, Me., with his parents; a farmer. He m. in Jay, Me., 30 Nov., 1836, Sarah Parker Haines.

Children of EBENEZER B. and SARAH P. (HAINES) CONANT:—

Rosanna Rowell, b. 23 Oct., 1837, in Canton; m. in Peru, 14 Mch., 1861, Albert Dunn; had Floyd Alvaro, b. 1864, d. 1884.
Rose Luella, b. 8 July, 1842.
Abbie Barbour, b. 25 Feb., 1846.

531. John Martin[8] (*Martin, John, John, Nathaniel, Nathaniel, Lot, Roger*), b. 9 Nov., 1815, in Canton, Me.; a farmer, of Weld, Me. He m. 2 Jan., 1836, Leonora H. Ireland.

Children of JOHN M. and LEONORA H. (IRELAND) CONANT:—

Oscar F., b. 29 Jan., 1840; m. Oct., 1865, Jane E. Masterman.
Ronelo A., b. 13 Oct., 1846; m. 11 Sep., 1871, in New Sharon, Me., Jennie M. Jones. He is now a dry goods merchant, of Pittsfield.

Augustus H., b. 25 Jan., 1850, in Dixfield. He m. ———,
and lives in Norridgewock, Me.
Augusta A., b. 25 Jan., 1850; d. y.

532. Seth Wilder[8] (*Seth, John, John, Nathaniel, Nathaniel, Lot, Roger*), b. 15 Mch., 1822, in Bridgewater, Mass.
He enlisted 22 Sep., 1862, in Co. K, 3rd Mass. Vols., for nine
months; re-enlisted 1 Mch., 1864, Co. D, 58th Mass. Vols., and
was taken prisoner at Burnside's Mine, 30 July, 1864, and in-
stantly shot. He m. 23 Nov., 1845, Eliza, dr. of Martin and
Ruth (Sturdivant) Wentworth (see *Wentworth Genealogy*).

Children of SETH W. and ELIZA (WENTWORTH) CONANT:—

730. Alvin, b. 17 Sep., 1846, in Bridgewater.
Louisa, b. 15 Nov., 1847.
Lucius, b. 15 Nov., 1847. He enlisted 1 Mch., 1864, in Co. D,
58th Mass. Vols., and was killed in the battle of Spottsyl-
vania, 12 May, 1864. His father was one of the party de-
tailed to take up the wounded, and his son was the first
dead that he found.
Marshall, b. 13 Aug., 1849.
Sarah Jane, b. 30 Mch., 1852.
Ida Frances, b. 27 Dec., 1854.
John Martin, b. 16 Mch., 1856.
Annie Meserve, b. 5 June, 1858.
William Sumner, b. 19 Dec., 1860.

533. Azro B.[8] (*Leonard, Jeremiah, John, Nathaniel, Nathaniel, Lot, Roger*), b. 31 July, 1821, in Malone, N. Y.; a
farmer. He m. Dec., 1843, Fanny Wood.

Child of AZRO B. and FANNY (WOOD) CONANT:—

Frederick Ophir, b. 12 Sep., 1844; m. Addie Sampson, of
Malone.

534. Marshall[8] (*Leonard, Jeremiah, John, Nathaniel,
Nathaniel, Lot, Roger*), b. 9 Nov., 1822, in Malone, N. Y. He
went West as a land agent for a railroad company, and is now
a real estate agent at La Crosse, Wis. He m. in West Constable, N. Y., 6 June, 1849, Caroline F. Man.

Children of MARSHALL and CAROLINE F. (MAN) CONANT:—

Eben L., b. 12 Feb., 1851, in Malone.
May C., b. 22 May, 1866.

535. Chauncey[8] (*John, Jeremiah, John, Nathaniel, Na-

thaniel, Lot, Roger), b. 18 Aug., 1814, in Pomfret, Vt.; a merchant. He now resides in South Boston, Mass. He m. (1) in No. Bridgewater, 30 Sep., 1839, Harriet Jane Wales; m. (2) in Barnstable, Mass., 18 May, 1862, Mary Sturgis Crocker.

Child of CHAUNCEY and HARRIET J. (WALES) CONANT:—

A son, b. 27 July, 1845; d. 29 July, 1847, in No. Bridgewater.

Child of CHAUNCEY and MARY S. (CROCKER) CONANT:—

Albert Francis, b. 11 Mch., 1863, in Barnstable. He received a musical education at Petersilea Academy, Boston; is now a pianist, of Boston.

536. Albert[8] (*John, Jeremiah, John, Nathaniel, Nathaniel, Lot, Roger*), b. 6 July, 1821, in Pomfret, Vt.; an artist; resides in Boston. He m. in Brooklyn, Conn., 27 Dec., 1848, Catherine, dr. of Philip and Deidamia (Prince) Scarborough, b. in Brooklyn, 6 Sep., 1823.

Children of ALBERT and CATHERINE (SCARBOROUGH) CONANT:—

Theodore Scarborough, b. 9 July, 1850; m. 18 Jan., 1883, Lucy Elizabeth, dr. of Alanson and Anne Rebecca (Bangs) Bigelow. He is a book-keeper, with Hilton, Weston & Co., Boston, Mass.
Frederick Prince, b. 10 Sep., 1860; d. 4 Sep., 1861.
Lucy Scarborough, b. 10 Mch., 1867.

537. Edward[8] (*Seth, Jeremiah, John, Nathaniel, Nathaniel, Lot, Roger*), b. 10 May, 1829, in Pomfret, Vt. He is principal of the State Normal School, at Johnston, Vt., and is the author of several educational publications. He m. in Woodstock, Vt., 10 May, 1858, Cynthia H. Taggart.

Children of EDWARD and CYNTHIA H. (TAGGART) CONANT:—

Frank Herbert, b. 17 June, 1859, in Pomfret.
Seth Edward, b. 12 Sep., 1864, in Randolph, Vt.
Nell Florence, b. 24 Apr., 1869,   "   "
Grace Lucia, b. 3 Aug., 1872,   "   "

538. Thomas[8] (*Thomas, Jeremiah, John, Nathaniel, Nathaniel, Lot, Roger*), b. 10 July, 1841, in East Bridgewater, Mass. He served three years in the late war, as sergeant and 2nd lieutenant, in the 29th Regt. Mass. Vols. He is now a physician, of Gloucester,Mass. He m. 1867, Mary S., dr. of Francis Worcester.

Children of THOMAS ad MARY S. (WORCESTER) CONANT:—

> Roger Winthrop, b.———, 1869.
> Genevieve, d. y.
> Edward, d. y.
> Robert, d. y.
> Harold Sargent, b. 879.

539. **James Scott**[8] *Thomas, Jeremiah, John, Nathaniel, Nathaniel, Lot, Roger*, b. 4 Jan., 1844, in East Bridgewater, Mass. He enlisted in May, 1861, in Co. C, 29th Mass. Vols.; was sent home ill after the seven days' retreat before Richmond. After his recovery he entered the navy as master-at-arms, and served about a year. He is now proprietor of a large wood engraving establishment in Boston. He m. in Wollaston, Mass., 16 Oct., 1880, Jennet Orr, dr. of Seth and Jane (Breed) Bryant, b. 28 Dec., 1851.

Child of JAMES S. and JENNET O. (BRYANT) CONANT:—

> Esther, b. 13 Feb., 1882.

540. **Rufus**[8] (*Thomas, Thomas, John, Nathaniel, Nathaniel, Lot, Roger*), b. about 1824, in Westford, Vt.; moved to Dorset, Ohio, with his parents, and thence to Castle Rock, Douglass co., Colorado, where he now lives.

Children of RUFUS and ——— (———) CONANT:—

> Thomas.
> Henry.
> Charles.
> Lottie.
> Alwilda.
> Lillian.

541. **Sidney**[8] (*Thomas, Thomas, John, Nathaniel, Nathaniel, Lot, Roger*), b. 17 Sep., 1831, in Westford, Vt. He is now a farmer, of Arcadia, Wisconsin. He m. in Wattsburg, Erie co., Pa., 4 Nov., 1851, Elizabeth, dr. of David and Philinda (Evans) Lillibridge, b. 5 Feb., 1835.

Children of SIDNEY and ELIZABETH (LILLIBRIDGE) CONANT:—

Ella Henrietta, b. 24 May, 1853, in Vattsburg, Pa.
Alvin Cassius, b. 30 Aug., 1855, " "
Lucy Emma, b. 7 Oct., 1860, " "
Lewis Gardner, b. 1 Dec., 1866, in Arcadia, Wis.
Clinton Sidney, b. 4 July, 1876, " "

542. Everett Quincy[8] (*Sylvanus, Silvanus, Gershom, Lot, Nathaniel, Lot, Roger*), b. 2 Apr., 1809, in Turner, Me.; a farmer; d. 27 Dec., 1868, in Turner. He m. 6 Jan., 1839, Lurania, dr. of Bradish and Abigail (Bailey) Turner, b. 25 Jan., 1813, in Livermore.

Children of EVERETT Q. and LURANIA. (TURNER) CONANT:—

Sylvia Ann, b. 2 Nov., 1839, in Turner; d. May, 1870; m. Thomas H. King, and had two sons. He lives in Lynn, Mass.

731. Howard Turner, b. 26 Oct., 1840.

Martha Jane, b. 19 Dec., 1841; lives in New York, N. Y.; m. John August Wollmer.

732. Everett Sanford, b. 12 Feb., 1843.
733. Hiram Augustus, b. 21 Feb., 1845.

Mary, b. 14 Nov., 1847; d. Oct., 1879; m. John McLeod, and had one son.

Sarah, b. 21 July, 1849; d. y.
Ed........ ...., 1849; d. y.
..... W., b. 2 Apr., 1851; now of Winton Place, Ohio; m. Florence Crawford.

Sarah Louisa, b. 8 Dec., 1852; d. Jan., 1870.
Albert Anson, b. 17 July, 1855; d. y.

543. Alonzo[8] (*Benjamin, Benjamin, Lot, Lot, Nathaniel, Lot, Roger*), b. 1817, in Turner, Me. He settled in Van Wert, Ohio; is president of the First National Bank of Van Wert. He m. 1 Nov., 1849, Esther A. Clark, in Ohio.

Children of ALONZO and ESTHER A. (CLARK) CONANT:—

Mary E., b. 1850.
Myrtle A., b. 1856, in Van Wert.
Ione E., b. 1854.
Lida E., b. 1861.

544. Leonard[8] (*Benjamin, Benjamin, Lot, Lot, Nathaniel, Lot, Roger*), b. 1818, in Turner, Me.; moved to Charlestown, Mass.; was a commission merchant, doing business in Fanueil Hall Market, Boston. He d. 6 Aug., 1877, in Charlestown. He m. (1) in Somerville, Mass., 10 Dec., 1846, Lavinia, dr. of Thomas and Martha (Collins) Woodbury, b. 28 July, 1823; m. (2) Harriet M. Berry.

Children of LEONARD and LAVINIA (WOODBURY) CONANT:—

Emma Lavinia, b. 4 Apr., 1848.
Almeda Ellethea, b. 7 May, 1850, in Somerville.
Martha Clarinda, b. 15 May, 1853, in Charlestown.
Leonard, b. 3 June, 1856.
Ida May, b. 6 Sep., 1859.

Child of LEONARD and HARRIET M. (BERRY) CONANT:—

Frank Clark, b. 3 July, 1865.

545. Benjamin[8] (*Benjamin, Benjamin, Lot, Lot, Nathaniel, Lot, Roger*), b. 5 Sep., 1825, in Turner, Me. He settled in Auburn, Me., and in 1850 formed a partnership with Mr. Lewis Bradford for the manufacture of veneered looking-glass frames. About 1852 the firm added the manufacture of furniture, and in 1858 opened a store in Lewiston, on Main street, and in 1883 moved to Lisbon street. Mr. Conant was a man of rare social and business qualities, and much respected in his community. He d. 11 Jan., 1885.

Children of BENJAMIN and ——— (———) CONANT:—

Eva, b. May, 1853; d. 3 Aug., 1853.
Frank R., b. 14 Aug., 1854.
William L., b. 1 Aug., 1855; d. Feb., 1856.
Carrie A., b. 16 Mch., 1859.
Edith S., b. 15 Aug., 1862.
Lizzie E., b. 18 Sep., 1865.
Albert H., b. 6 Jan., 1868.
Charles R., b. 19 Feb., 1870.

546. Calvin[8] (*Hooper, Benjamin, Lot, Lot, Nathaniel, Lot, Roger*), b. 15 June, 1817, in Turner, Me., where he now lives; a farmer. He m. 7 Oct., 1841, Celia L. Staples.

Children of CALVIN and CELIA L. (STAPLES) CONANT:—

Winslow, b. 3 Oct., 1842; m. 9 May, 1868, Sarah E. Emerson, of Auburn; a farmer.
Charles S., b. 1 Nov., 1843; m. 2 Dec., 1874, Mary E. Palmer. He is a lawyer, of Lewiston.
Phebe A., b. 19 Dec., 1844; d. 3 June, 1875; m. James W. Talbot, of Turner.
James A., b. 1 Dec., 1846. He is married and lives in Cherokee, Iowa.

Olivia C., b. 22 July, 1848; m. 18 Mrch., 1868, William R. Dill, of Auburn.

George C., b. 1 Apr., 1850. He is a grain dealer, of Cherokee, Iowa. He m. 1872, Mary E. Batterson.

Lizzie E., b. 15 Sep., 1851; m. 15 Nov., 1873, Clarence C. Young, of Turner.

Albion L., b. 14 Aug., 1853; d. 20 Sep., 1854.

Lois D., b. 13 Nov., 1854; m. 19 Feb., 1878, Frederick P. Talbot, of Turner.

Henry F., b. 13 Oct., 1856; m. 30 May, 1879, Rose S. Hodsdon, of Turner. He is a grocer.

Hannah A., b. 28 Feb., 1858; d. 9 Mch., 1862.

Frederick L., b. 24 Aug., 1860.

Alonzo J., b. 25 Dec., 1861.

547. Anna Briggs[8] (*Hooper, Benjamin, Lot, Lot, Nathaniel, Lot, Roger*), b. 31 Aug., 1818; m. 1 Jan., 1839, Isaac Haskell, of Auburn, Me.

Children of Isaac and Anna B. (Conant) Haskell:—

i. Ellen M., b. 4 Apr., 1840, in Auburn; m. 4 Apr., 1864, S. P. Merrill, of Auburn. Child: Kate H., b. 1868.

ii. Kate F., b. 10 Jan., 1843; m. 29 Nov., 1871, W. E. Holmes, of Auburn; had Perley H., b. 1878, d. y.

iii. Lizzie H., b. 11 Aug., 1846; m. 19 Sep., 1864, A. M. Peables, M. D., of Auburn. Children: Virginia O., b. 1866; Lizzie M., b. 1868; Margie A., b. 1880.

iv. Frank A., b. 30 Sep., 1850; m. 27 Nov., 1873, Eva A. Eaton. He is a grocer, of Auburn.

v. Annie C., b. 2 Sep., 1854.

vi. J. Newton, b. 15 Apr., 1856; m. 28 Nov., 1877, Fannie Rowe White, of Readfield; m. (2) Minnie A. Packard, of Auburn. He is a grocer.

vii. F. Nelson, b. 15 Apr., 1856; d. 25 Sep., 1856.

viii. Charles S., b. 30 Mch., 1858; m. 22 Aug., 1882, Dellie L. Coburn, of Lewiston. He is a teacher.

548. Lot[8] (*Hooper, Benjamin, Lot, Lot, Nathaniel, Lot, Roger*), b. 15 Feb., 1820, in Turner, Me., where he lives; a farmer. He m. 17 Nov., 1853, Roxa Staples, b. 24 Dec., 1829.

Children of Lot and Roxa (Staples) Conant:—

Hezekiah H., b. 19 July, 1855; d. 8 Jan., 1856.

Frank, b. 30 Jan., 1857; d. 26 Oct., 1863.

Joseph H., b. 8 Mch., 1859.

Charles H., b. 9 Mch., 1862.

Annie M., b. 12 June, 1866.

Wilfred L., b. 9 Sep., 1870.

The last will and testament of Lot Conant
dated the 24 of ye 7th month 1674

I Lot Conant aged about fiftie yeares, bei
sicke and weake, yet of perfect understanding
doe hereby declare my last will and testamen
wherein in the first place, I doe bequeth my soul
unto god that gaue it, and my body to the groun
in hope of a blessed resurrection; and for my
outward estate and goods, I doe bequeth and giue
unto my fiue sonns to eary of them fifty pound
and unto my sonn nathaniell the boy and tooll o
caluer the rest, and unto my fiue daughters
twenty pounds to eary of them; and this estate I leaue
to lye would undevided till they come to full age or to
marriage estate, and in the mean time, to be would to
rest in the hands of my wife, and for the bringing
up of the children, and furthermore my will is that
my wife be executrix, and that the land be not still
disposed of from the children, and that my wife
haue the dwelling house and orchard for her lifetime
as also that my kinswoman mari Leere haue a cow
or heifer at her being married or going from my wife
And for giuing unto my wife in this matter I to inde[...]
and desire mr John Hale, captaine Lathrop, and my
brother George Conant to be assisting heer unto
I haue herehunto set my hand this 24 of the 7 month
1674

Witness
Roger Conant
Exercise Conant

Lot Conant

Roger Conant ye 24 this testament sworne in court at salem the
7:7 that this was his act as his last will and testament, as he
heard the above written ye his last will published ; there
be [...]

549. Winslow[8] (*Hooper, Benjamin, Lot, Lot, Nathaniel, Lot, Roger*), b. 28 May, 1822, in Turner, Me.; he lived in Auburn; d. 13 July, 1863. He m. 27 Nov., 1850, Mary Ann Gore.

Children of WINSLOW and MARY A. (GORE) CONANT:—

Mary Ella, b. 11 Sep., 1853; d. 24 Nov., 1853.
Walter W., b. 15 Oct., 1855; d. 26 Mch., 1874.
Calvin H., b. 20 Jan., 1857; d. 27 July, 1857.
Herbert C., b. 16 Apr., 1859.

550. Lucitty K.[8] (*Hooper, Benjamin, Lot, Lot, Nathaniel, Lot, Roger*), b. 23 Dec., 1823, in Turner, Me.; m. Thomas Merrow, b. in Minot, Me., 31 Aug., 1818.

Children of THOMAS and LUCITTY K. (CONANT) MERROW:—

i. Lucretia V. T., b. 22 Sep., 1850; m. George Marston, of Lewiston.
ii. Eunice A., b. 18 Feb., 1852, in Auburn; m. Charles Cole.
iii. Emma F., b. 17 Aug., 1854, in Auburn.
iv. Sarah W., b. 29 June, 1856; m. John McCarthy.
v. Lucetta, b. 5 Oct., 1858; m. William H. Whitten. She d. 15 June, 1879.
vi. Hiram H., b. 7 Dec., 1860.
vii. Thomas, b. 15 Sep., 1862.
viii. Horace, b. 21 Aug., 1864.
ix. Ellen K., b. 8 Sep., 1866.

551. Hannah Allen[8] (*Galen, Phinehas, Phinehas, Lot, Nathaniel, Lot, Roger*), b. 17 Aug., 1814, in Bridgewater, Mass.; d. Mch., 1864. She m. ———, Ariston Miltimore, son of Eliab and Celia (Leach) Hayward, b. 13 Nov., 1812, in Bridgewater, where they lived.

Children of ARISTON M. and HANNAH A. (CONANT) HAYWARD:—

i. Mary Antoinette, b. 30 Aug., 1838.
ii. Celia Leach, b. 16 Dec., 1840; d. 16 Mch., 1879; m. 29 Nov., 1866, Deacon Wales Hayward, b. 19 Nov., 1841. He is now of North Middleboro', Mass.
iii. Ariston Ebenezer, b. 8 Oct., 1848.
iv. Hannah Conant, b. 16 Dec., 1852.

552. Ira M.[8] (*Ira, Phinehas, Phinehas, Lot, Nathaniel, Lot, Roger*), b. 3 Jan., 1827, in Bridgewater, Mass. He is engaged in the rubber business in Boston, with his brother, under the style of the Gossamer Rubber Clothing Company. He is treasurer of the recently organized Gossamer Manufacturers' Association. He m. Mary F. Bassett.

Children of IRA M. and MARY F. (BASSETT) CONANT:—

734. George Mitchell, b. 18 Dec., 1853.
735. William M.
       Mary, d. y.
736. Herbert I.

553. William Henry[8] (*Ira, Phinehas, Phinehas, Lot, Nathaniel, Lot, Roger*), b. 13 Mch., 1834. He lives in Boston; is engaged in the rubber business, under the firm name of the Gossamer Rubber Co. He is a director of the Boston Base Ball Club. He m. Dora Shepardson.

Children of WILLIAM H. and DORA (SHEPARDSON) CONANT:—

William A.
Charles.

554. Robert Taft[8] (*Elijah, James, Timothy, Lot, Nathaniel, Lot, Roger*), b. 1 Sep., 1810, in Barre, Mass. He graduated at Amherst College, 1836, and at Auburn Theological Seminary. Was a Congregational clergyman, pastor at Moira, Oswegatshie, Morristown, Evans Mills, Antwerp and Henvelton, N. Y. Was obliged to give up preaching on account of a throat trouble, and for last twelve years a teacher of the classics. He d. in Ogdensburg, N. Y., 28 Jan., 1879. He m. 14 Oct., 1841, Caroline E. Weston.

Children of ROBERT T. and CAROLINE E. (WESTON) CONANT:—

Augusta M., b. 13 Aug., 1842; m. David J. Riley; now lives at Detroit, Mich.
Frederick Weston, b. 14 Feb., 1845. He lived at Buffalo, N. Y.; was m. but had no children; d. 24 July, 1885.
Cynthia A., b. 20 Mch., 1847; d. 20 Sep., 1862.
Robert Taft, b. 12 Aug., 1854; d. 27 Dec., 1877.
Edwin M., b. 21 Dec., 1860; d. 19 Nov., 1879.

555. Luke[8] (*Lot, James, Timothy, Lot, Nathaniel, Lot, Roger*), b. 4 June, 1817, in Barre, Mass.; moved to Brooke co., West Virginia, with his father. He m. 13 May, 1856, Elizabeth, dr. of Thomas McCord.

Children of LUKE and ELIZABETH (McCORD) CONANT:—

Annie, b. 5 Dec., 1857.
Ida May, b. 22 June, 1859.

556. Mary H.[8] (*Lot, James, Timothy, Lot, Nathaniel, Lot, Roger*), b. 8 July, 1825, in Barre, Mass.; moved to West Virginia, with her parents; m. 15 May, 1849, Charles G. Eaton, M. D., of Clyde, Ohio, where they reside. He was a colonel in the war of the Rebellion.

Children of CHARLES G. and MARY H. (CONANT) EATON:—

i.   Charles H., b. 15 Mch., 1849.
ii.   Mary J., b. 31 Oct., 1851.

557. Abigail S.[8] (*Lot, James, Timothy, Lot, Nathaniel, Lot, Roger*), b. 22 Jan., 1828, in Barre, Mass.; moved to West Virginia, with her parents; m. 23 Feb., 1858, Joseph L., son of Abraham and Margaret (Deavers) Bedilion. They live in Wheeling, West Va.

Children of JOSEPH L. and ABIGAIL S. (CONANT) BE-DILION:—

i.   Mary E., b. 12 Jan., 1859.
ii.   Margaret L., b. 23 Feb., 1861.
iii.   Abigail J., b. 20 Sep., 1863.
iv.   Julia E., b. 2 June, 1867.

558. Sarah Jane[8] (*Lot, James, Timothy, Lot, Nathaniel, Lot, Roger*), b. 22 June, 1834, in Ohio co., West Va.; m. 30 July, 1857, William Clow, b. 16 June, 1819.

Children of WILLIAM and SARAH J. (CONANT) CLOW:—

i.   William L., b. 13 May, 1858.
ii.   George H., b. 6 Feb., 1860.
iii.   David H., b. 29 July, 1862.

559. George W.[8] (*Lot, James, Timothy, Lot, Nathaniel, Lot, Roger*), b. 20 June, 1837, in West Virginia. He is a steamboat pilot on the Ohio river, and resides in Beaver, Pa. He m. in Pittsburg, Pa., 21 May, 1867, Hannah E. Brown, b. 3 Sep., 1848.

Children of GEORGE W. and HANNAH E. (BROWN) CO-
NANT:—

>   George W., b. 20 June, 1868.
>   Emma Wilson, b. 27 May, 1870.
>   George Nelson, b. 11 Nov., 1873; d. 18 Feb., 1875.
>   Eva May, b. 18 Aug., 1875; d. 5 Mch., 1878.
>   Pearl, b. 8 Nov., 1878.
>   Lot, b. 10 Feb., 1880.
>   Carlton Cable, b. 10 May, 1882.
>   Carrie, b. 10 May, 1882.
>   Fred Odell, } twins, b. ——.
>   A daughter, }

560.   **George F.**[8] (*James, James, Timothy, Lot, Nathaniel, Lot, Roger*), b. 10 Apr., 1819, in New Braintree, Mass.
He is a merchant, of Oakham, Mass.   He m. in Ludlow, Mass.,
29 Apr., 1851, Mary Rumrill.

>   Child of GEORGE F. and MARY (RUMRILL) CONANT:—

>   Frank S., b. 7 Apr., 1856, in East Brookfield; is a jeweler of
>   Oakham; m. 13 Sep., 1883, Lilian E. Crawford, and has
>   Roger, b. 16 Sep., 1884.

561.   **John**[8] (*James, James, Timothy, Lot, Nathaniel, Lot,
Roger*), b. 21 Feb., 1823, in Oakham, Mass.; lived in East
Brookfield.   He m. Elizabeth Sennet.

>   Child of JOHN and ELIZABETH (SENNET) CONANT:—

>   John Herbert, b. 1855.

562.   **Albert S.**[8] (*James, James, Timothy, Lot, Nathaniel,
Lot, Roger*), b. 18 Apr., 1835, in Oakham, Mass.; m. 29 Nov.,
1860, Susan A. Whipple.

>   Child of ALBERT S. and SUSAN A. (WHIPPLE) CONANT:—

>   Nellie, b. 12 Mch., 1868.

563.   **Abigail A.**[8] (*Sullivan, Luther, Timothy, Lot, Nathaniel, Lot, Roger*), b. 5 July, 1823, in Shutesbury, Mass.;
moved to Springfield, Ill., with her parents.   She m. William
W. Lee, who was b. 20 Aug., 1822, in Delaware, and d. 12
July, 1870.

>   Children of WILLIAM W. and ABIGAIL A. (CONANT) LEE:—

i.   Laura A., b. 15 Oct., 1844; m. 7 May, 1867, John T. Capps,

b. 1841, in Clarke co., Ky. Children: Olive and William
L. Mr. Capps was a student in Illinois College when the
Rebellion broke out. He enlisted Aug., 1861, in Co. B, 10th
Ill. Infantry, for three years, and re-enlisted for one year,
Jan., 1864. After the war he entered Eastman's Business
College, at Poughkeepsie, N. Y., and graduated 6 Feb.,
1866. He is now one of the firm of Dickerman & Co., en-
gaged in the manufacture of woolens, at Springfield.

ii.   Lydia E., b. 23 Mch., 1847; m. 21 Dec., 1869, S. O. Stockwell,
b. in Auburn, N. Y.; has Clara L. They reside in Columbus, O.

iii.   Thomas S., b. 9 Jan., 1849, in Bloomington, Ill.; m. in Springfield, 29 May, 1872, Mary J. Eaton, and has Addie. He
is engaged in the grain business at Edinburg, Ill.

iv.   Edward W., b. 9 Mch., 1853, in Taylorville; m. in Springfield,
6 Oct., 1875, Lou H. Pasfield, and resides in Edinburg, Ill.

564. William S.[8] (*Sullivan, Luther, Timothy, Lot, Nathaniel, Lot, Roger*), b. 27 Feb., 1825, in Shutesbury, Mass.;
moved to Springfield, Ill., with his parents. He was engaged
in 1874 in the furniture business in Petersburg, Ill. He m. (1)
in Springfield, Ill., Mary Sykes, who d. 12 Feb., 1864; m. (2)
Eliza Kinkead.

Children of WILLIAM S. and MARY (SYKES) CONANT:—

James, b. in Petersburg, Ill. He is in business with his father.
Katie.

565. Susan E.[8] (*Sullivan, Luther, Timothy, Lot, Nathaniel, Lot, Roger*), b. 10 Mch., 1827, in Shutesbury, Mass.;
moved to Springfield, Ill., with her parents. She m. (1) 27
Jan., 1845, George R. Connelly, b. 18 Jan., 1822, in the District
of Columbia; she m. (2) Charles Dougherty, b. 10 Oct., 1822,
in Wheeling, W. Va., as his second wife, and resides in Daw-
son, Ill.

Children of GEORGE R. and SUSAN E. (CONANT) CON-
NELLY:—

i.   John L., who is a physician, of Harristown, Ill. He has a
family.

ii.   George S., of Springfield, Ill.

iii. Lillie E.

Children of CHARLES and SUSAN E. (CONANT) DOUGHERTY:—

i.   Omar.

ii.   Allen.

iii. Lydia J.

566. Levi J.[8] (*Sullivan, Luther, Timothy, Lot, Nathaniel, Lot, Roger*), b. 25 Oct., 1831, in Shutesbury, Mass.; moved to Springfield, Ill., with his parents. He is a grocer, of Springfield. He m. (1) 28 July, 1858, Elizabeth Brodie, who d. 14 Feb., 1865; m. (2) in Vincennes, Ill., 1 Mch., 1875, Mrs. Sarah A. (Hargraves) Baker, b. 24 Apr., 1841, in Manchester, England.
Children of LEVI J. and ELIZABETH (BRODIE) CONANT :—

> John B.
> William S.

567. Phineas H.[8] (*Sullivan, Luther, Timothy, Lot, Nathaniel, Lot, Roger*), b. 12 Apr., 1837, in Springfield, Ill. He enlisted for three years in Co. H, 124th Ill. Infantry, and was mustered in as corporal. He was honorably discharged, for disability, 6 Feb., 1864. In 1866 he was appointed deputy city marshal of Springfield, and served about three years. He has also served as deputy sheriff and deputy U. S. collector. He is now a commercial traveller. He lives in Springfield. He m. 4 Jan., 1857, Sarah J. Hobbs, b. 1 Dec., 1838, in Jacksonville, Illinois.
Children of PHINEAS H. and SARAH J. (HOBBS) CONANT :—

> Julia E.
> Minnie L.
> Pearl R.

568. Amos[8] (*Silas, Samuel, Robert, Lot, John, Lot, Roger*), b. 20 Oct., 1771, in (Stow?) Mass.; moved to Sudbury, with his parents; was a farmer. He d. 3 Apr., 1831. He m. ———, Sarah Stone, b. 12 Aug., 1778, in Wayland, Mass.; d. 1 Oct., 1832, in Sudbury.
Children of AMOS and SARAH (STONE) CONANT :—

737.   Emory, b. 23 Nov., 1797.
       Dexter, b. 23 Nov., 1797; d. 14 Dec., 1820.
738.   Silas, b. 2 Feb., 1801.
739.   Amos, b. 23 Apr., 1805.

569. Levi[8] (*Silas, Samuel, Robert, Lot, John, Lot, Roger*), b. 24 May, 1775, in (Stow?) Mass.; moved to Sutton and thence to Hubbardston. He d. 4 Dec., 1825. He m. ———, Sarah Foster, b. 11 Feb., 1776; d. 22 Sep., 1849.

Children of LEVI and SARAH (FOSTER) CONANT:—

740. Levi, b. 25 May, 1802.
Benjamin, b. ———.

570. Abraham[8] (*Oliver, Samuel, Robert, Lot, John, Lot, Roger*), b. 2 Sep., 1778, in Weston, Mass. He moved to Frankfort, now Winterport, Me., about 1804; was a farmer; d. 1849. He m. 1803, Thankful Lombard, of Truro, Mass., who d. about 1860.

Children of ABRAHAM and THANKFUL (LOMBARD) CONANT:—

Lydia, b. 1 Dec., 1804; m. Terrel White; had Lydia.
741. Isaac, b. 13 June, 1807.
742. Amasa S., b. 12 Feb., 1809.
Jacob, b. 4 Feb., 1811; m. but had no children.
743. Charles, b. 24 Dec., 1812.
Sarah, b. 23 May, 1815; d. Mch., 1816.
Sarah Snow, b. 20 Apr., 1817.
Abraham, b. 8 Jan., 1822.
Thankful L., b. 1 Apr., 1824; m. Elihu Hoxie, and had Walter, Artemus H. and Alice.
Artemus Henry, b. 24 Apr., 1826, in Frankfort, Me. Is m. and has Caroline, Mary T., Artemus H. and J. Bradbury.

571. Isaac[8] (*Oliver, Samuel, Robert, Lot, John, Lot, Roger*), b. 13 Nov., 1779, in Weston; settled in Cambridge, Mass., where he died.

Children of ISAAC and ——— (———) CONANT:—

Sarah, b. ———; m. B. F. Nourse, of Chicago, Ill.
Hannah, b. ———; m. I. A. Bassett, of Boston.
Mary Lydia, b. ———; m. ——— Streeter, of Manchester, N. H.
744. Thatcher M.

572. Asa W.[8] (*Oliver, Samuel, Robert, Lot, John, Lot, Roger*), b. 1787, in Weston, Mass.; settled in Barre, Mass.; moved to Worcester, where he d. 1859. He was a carriage manufacturer and miller. He m. in Barre, Nov., 1814, Mary Kendall, who is still (1884) living.

Children of ASA W. and MARY (KENDALL) CONANT:—

745. George W., b. 6 Apr., 1816, in Athol.
Charles, b. 4 Feb., 1818, in Barre.

573. Josiah[8] (*Oliver, Samuel, Robert, Lot, John, Lot,*

Roger), b. about 1789, in Weston, Mass.; settled in Monson, Mass.

Children of JOSIAH and —— (——) CONANT:—

—— Frederick Augustus, who moved to New Orleans, La., about 1845, where he still lives.

Seneca F., of Monson.

Andrew W.; lives in Palmer, Mass.; has several children, among them Frederick J., of Palmer.

Harriet Caroline, b. ——; m. Calvin Perry.

Maria L., d. 1870.

Clorinda A.; unm.; of Monson.

574. Nathan[8] (*Samuel, Samuel, Robert, Lot, John, Lot, Roger*), b. 1777, in Stow, Mass.; settled in Sumner, Me. He was a farmer; was deputy sheriff and justice of the peace. He d. in Leeds, Me. He m. (1) 1800, Pamela Wright; m. (2) Hannah Briggs, of Sumner, Me.

Children of NATHAN and PAMELA (WRIGHT) CONANT:—

Maria, b. 1801; m. (1) Samuel, son of Asa Dunham; had Henry, Sarah L., John M., Pamela and Eliza; m. (2) Jonas Baker.

Sarah, b. 1804; m. Timothy Ludden, of Turner. He was judge of probate for Oxford co. Child: Virginia White.

Calista, b. 1806; m. Ephraim Farris, and had Calista, who m. Lemuel Gurney.

746. John, b. 1808.

Louisa, b. 1811; d. unm.

Polly, b. 1813; m. Hiram Barrows, and had Hiram, Samuel, Louisa, Lucinda, Nathan D. and George.

Samuel, b. 1815; now of Wakefield, Mass.; a stone mason. He m. (1) July, 1844, in Salem, Mass., Sarah W. Gerrish, of Salem; m. (2) July, 1852, in South Reading, now Wakefield, Mass., Harriet H. Knight, of Woburn, Mass. He had two children, who d. in infancy.

575. Jacob[8] (*Samuel, Samuel, Robert, Lot, John, Lot, Roger*), b. 13 Jan., 1783, in Sudbury, Mass.; settled in Sterling, Mass.; was a farmer, and also engaged in various commercial pursuits. He held one or more of the principal town offices for the last thirty years of his life; was a justice of the peace, and also represented the town in the General Court. He d. 4 Sep., 1839. He m. (1) in Sterling, 26 Apr., 1810, Relief Burpee, b. May, 1790, d. 26 Dec., 1814; m. (2) 31 Jan., 1816, Betsey Pope.

Children of JACOB and RELIEF (BURPEE) CONANT :—

747. Edwin, b. 20 Aug., 1810, in Sterling.
Elizabeth, b. 14 Dec., 1813; d. 27 Dec., 1816.

Child of JACOB and BETSEY (POPE) CONANT :—

Nancy, b. 31 Dec., 1828; m. Harrison Gray Otis, son of Hon.
Francis and Eliza A. (Chandler) Blake, b. 10 Apr., 1816. He
graduated at Harvard College, 1835, and was a clergyman,
of Worcester, Mass. (see *Chandler Family*, p. 829). She d.
16 Apr., 1872.

576. **Sally**[8] (*Samuel, Samuel, Robert, Lot, John, Lot,
Roger*), b. about 1786; m. Benjamin Willard, of Lancaster,
Mass.

Children of BENJAMIN and SALLY (CONANT) WILLARD :—

i. Frederick; he graduated at Brown University; was a Baptist
minister, of Worcester, Mass.
ii. A son, who d. while attending Brown University.
iii. George, a Baptist minister. He d. in Westerly, R. I., about
1882.
iv. Horace; he graduated at Brown University; is of Lancaster,
Mass.

577. **Joel**[8] (*John, Samuel, Robert, Lot, John, Lot, Roger*),
b. 1 Feb., 1788, in
Stow, Mass.; settled
in Acton, where he
d. 16 July, 1843.
(1824.)
He m. (1) Hannah Hayward, who d. 30 Sep., 1828; m. (2) B.
Spaulding, who d. 1838; m. (3) Charlotte Jewell.

Children of JOEL and HANNAH (HAYWARD) CONANT:—

748. Joel Hobart, b. 15 June, 1813.
William Lee, b. 13 Oct., d. 16 Dec., 1814.
749. William Hayward, b. 22 Oct., 1815.
Mary, b. 19 Jan., 1817.
Hannah E., b. 15 May, 1818; m. 18 June, 1840, James W. Hay-
ward.
750. John, b. 17 Nov., 1821.
Caroline, b. 6 July, d. 11 Nov., 1825.
Francis, b. 6 Nov., 1826; d. 11 Nov., 1834.
Jane Stewart, b. 1828; d. 25 June, 1829.

Children of JOEL and CHARLOTTE (JEWELL) CONANT:—

Ophelia Augusta, b. 21 Apr., 1840.
Evelina, b. 30 Mch., 1843.

578. John[8] (*John, Samuel, Robert, Lot, John, Lot, Roger*), b. 12 Jan., 1790, in Stow, Mass. He was one of a family of sixteen children. At the age of eighteen his father gave him a mortgage of $1500 on a farm in Acton, which soon came into his possession. It is said that when twenty-one years of age he could hardly read intelligibly, or write his own name; but having married a wife of considerable culture, by her aid, added to an ardent desire for self-improvement, he was soon enabled to acquire a good fund of knowledge, such as to qualify him to discharge well the active duties of life. About 1816 he sold his farm in Acton and purchased the Thorndike farm, so called, in the town of Jaffrey, N. H. Here, by the means of a well directed industry, and the practice of a wise and strict economy, he amassed a large estate and became one of the most honored and respected citizens of his state. He was a model farmer; few with like opportunities have been able to show so successful results from their labor. With good business talents he united strict integrity of character, and an extensive knowledge of the affairs of his state and the Nation. He was a member of the N. H. legislature in 1834, '35 and '36. "While serving in the House of Representatives in this state," says Hon. G. W. Nesmith, of Franklin, who served two years with him, " we found him one of our most able debaters, especially upon subjects pertaining to financial matters." On the organization of the Monadnoc Bank, in 1850, he was made its first president. In disposing of his estate, which was large, he manifested good judgment and sound discretion. During his life he gave a valuable farm to the Cheshire County Agricultural Society, and made a generous donation to the N. H. Insane Asylum, of which institution he had been a trustee some years prior to his death. He also contributed some twenty-five thousand dollars towards the purchase of the Experimental Farm and Conant Hall, for the use of the New Hampshire College of Mechanical Arts, located at Hanover. In his will he made a generous bequest to the town of Jaffrey, gave $12,000 to New London Academy, and left $40,000 more to the college to found scholarships to aid poor and indigent young men of Cheshire county, or, if not to be found in that

county, then to the same class of young men elsewhere, to obtain a good theoretical and practical knowledge of the science of agriculture. His great aim was to raise the standard of learning among the agricultural class, and to provide means and encouragement to such as needed assistance. He d. 6 Apr., 1877. (See *Hist. of Jaffrey*, in which a lithograph of Mr. Conant may be found.) He m. (1) 12 Mch., 1814, Pamela Houghton, who d. 1 Mch., 1815; m. (2) Mary Prescott Hosmer, of Concord, who d. 9 Aug., 1858, aged 74; m. (3) 12 Nov., 1859, Mrs. Sally (Livermore) Kittredge, of Nelson.

Children of JOHN and MARY P. (HOSMER) CONANT:—

John, d. y.
Mary Hosmer, d. y.

579. Anna[8] (*Benjamin, Josiah, Robert, Lot, John, Lot, Roger*), b. about 1780, in Amherst or Milford, N. H.; d. 20 Oct., 1843; m. Joseph, son of Josiah and Elizabeth (Littlehale) Crosby, b. 19 Oct., 1774; d. 23 May, 1838.

Children of JOSEPH and ANNA (CONANT) CROSBY:—

i. Nancy, b. 27 Sep., 1801; m. Asa Burns, of Milford, and had: 1. Asa Putnam, b. 1824; went to Kansas; 2. Nancy Orinda, b. 1832, m. Ezra C. Towne, of Milford; 3. Harriet, b. 1838, m. F. W. Sargent, of Milford; 4. Joseph Crosby; 5. Charles Gray, b. 1840, lives in Wisconsin; 6. John Bradford, b. 1843, m. Lizzie Stetson, of Indianapolis, Ind., and lives there; he served during the late war in the 3rd N. H. Regt.
ii. Harriet, b. 20 Oct., 1802; m. Freeman, son of William Crosby.
iii. Lucy E., b. 29 Aug., 1804; m. Jabez Bills, of Amherst, N. H., and had Jabez F., Freeman C., Lucy A. M., Betsey J. and George H.
iv. Joseph, b. 3 Mch., 1806; m. Isabel Moore.
v. Benjamin, b. 7 Oct., 1807; m. Pamelia Lovejoy, of Milford.
vi. Josiah Dixey, b. 12 Nov., 1810; m. Almira Lovejoy. He was in the 16th N. H. Regt. during the war; d. at Brashear City, La., 10 May, 1863.
vii. Betsey, b. 26 Feb., 1812; m. Abraham Fifield, of Lowell, Mass.
viii. Rachael Orinda, b. 2 Aug., 1813; m. in Charlestown, Md., 1837, Rev. Samuel K. Snead, of New Albany, Ind.
ix. Abel Conant, b. 28 Nov., 1815; m. Joanna S. Trufant, of Winthrop, Me. He was of Milford,
x. Mary, b. 12 Oct., 1817; m. John L. Minot, of Milford; removed to Louisville, Ky.
xi. Deborah Gutterson, b. 8 Dec., 1819; d. 1866; m. Joseph Lund, of Merrimack, N. H.

580. Josiah Franklin[8] (*Shebuel, Josiah, Robert, Lot, John, Lot, Roger*), b. Apr., 1806, in Pepperell, Mass.; a merchant, of Boston, where he d. 1869.

Child of JOSIAH and NANCY L. (———) CONANT:—

Alonzo G., b. ———; he is a commission merchant and fruit broker, doing business in New York city.

581. Asa[8] (*Ephraim, Peter, Robert, Lot, John, Lot, Roger*), b. about 1778, in (Temple?) N. H. He moved to Temple, Me., with his parents, and thence to Camden, Me., where he d. 1824; a farmer. He m. 5 May, 1800, Deborah, dr. of Ansel Norton, b. in Martha's Vineyard, Mass.

Children of ASA and DEBORAH (NORTON) CONANT:—

Deborah Norton, b. 1806, in Industry, Me.; d. 20 Aug., 1887; m. 1 Sep., 1833, Coburn Johnson Tyler, of Camden, Me. During the war of 1812 he served in Capt. Peter Chadwick's company of the 34th Regt. U. S. Infantry. Children: Scion Conant, b. 1836, Hannah Wright and Ada Anna.
751. Ansel.
Almira, b. in Industry, Me.; m. in Northport, Prince Rogers, of Eastport, where they lived. Children: William, of New York, N. Y., and Adelia.
752. Simeon.
753. Nathan Warren, b. 10 Dec., 1812.
754. Isaiah Sewell, b. 3 Mch., 1814.
755. Sophia Ann, b. 23 Oct., 1817.

582. Ephraim[8] (*Ephraim, Peter, Robert, Lot, John, Lot, Roger*), b. 7 Feb., 1781, in Stow, Mass., or Temple, N. H.; moved to Temple, Me., about 1803. He learned the shoemaker's trade, at which he worked till 1810, then kept a general store till 1820, when he settled on a farm. He removed to Phillips, Me., in 1834, where he remained till a few weeks before his death. He was a justice of the peace. He d. in Strong, Me., 24 Feb., 1865. He m. (1) Elizabeth, dr. of Gideon and Susan Staples, b. in Kittery, Me., d. 14 Jan., 1849, in Phillips; m. (2) ——— ———.

Children of EPHRAIM and ELIZABETH (STAPLES) CONANT:—

Joanna King, b. 1803; m. Hugh K. Staples. Children: 1. Mary; 2. Shuah; 3. Tryphena; 4. Ephraim; 5. Hugh; 6. Elizabeth; 7. Samuel; 8. William; 9. Anna; 10. Hiram.
756. Rebecca, b. 1804.

Eliza, b. 14 Feb., 1806; 'm. Thomas Russell. Children: 1. Lovina; 2. Violetta; 3. Isaac J.

Mary, b. Feb., 1808; m. Ira Verrill.

757. Ephraim, b. 17 Dec., 1809, in Temple.

758. Susan, b. 7 Feb., 1812.

John, b. ——; d. in infancy.

759. Sarah, b. ——.

Abigail, b. ——; m. William B. Toothaker, of Phillips. Children: 1. Morrill; 2. Louisa; 3. Laforest; 4. Abigail.

Emilia, b. ——; m. Noah C. Davenport. Child: Noah Thaxter.

760. John Gideon, b. 9 Nov., 1821.

Nancy W., b. 27 Feb., 1827; m. (1) ——; m. (2) Isaac Holt, and had Eva N. and Edgar.

James Simeon, b. 24 Mch., 1829; m. Mrs. Sarah Montgomery, and had Ada.

583. Joseph[8] (*Ephraim, Peter, Robert, Lot, John, Lot, Roger*), b. 25 Jan., 1783, in Temple, N. H.; moved to Temple, Me., about 1803; was a farmer; held various town offices; was a captain of militia. He d. 26 July, 1845. He m. in Temple, Me., 9 June, 1809, Betsey Drury, b. June, 1790, d. Dec., 1875.

Children of JOSEPH and BETSEY (DRURY) CONANT:—

761. Joseph Hayward, b. 30 June, 1810.

Betsey Drury, b. 6 May, 1812; m. 7 Apr., 1834, —— Mitchell, of Temple Mills.

762. John, b. 14 Sep., 1814.

William, b. 26 Nov., 1816; d. y.

Mary, b. 6 Mch., 1818; m. —— Sampson, and had Leroy and John, of Minneapolis, Minn.

Lucy Ann, b. 8 July, 1820.

Sarah, b. 10 Oct., 1822; m. Ammi Colcord, of Bunker Hill, Ill.; had James and George.

Martha, b. 12 May, 1825.

763. Daniel Alexander, b. 3 Dec., 1827.

Alice Hillman, b. 25 Jan., 1829.

Myra Abigail, b. 6 Sep., 1831; m. Daniel Dunham, of Le Grange, Me.; had Edward, of Boston, Mass.

764. Charles Albion, b. 28 July, 1833.

584. Abraham[8] (*Ephraim, Peter, Robert, Lot, John, Lot, Roger*), b. 7 Mch., 1789, in Temple, N. H. He moved to Temple, Me., and thence to Hope, Me., where he died. He m. 21 Oct., 1813, Emily, dr. of Enoch and Azubah (Bradford) Wentworth (see *Wentworth Genealogy*, Vol. 1, p. 616), b. 12 Oct., 1792; d. 4 July, 1865.

Children of ABRAHAM and EMILY (WENTWORTH) CONANT:—

765. Enoch Wentworth, b. Oct., 1815, in Hope.
766. Isaac, b. 19 Feb., 1817, in Friendship.
767. Azubah B., b. (20 Feb., ?) 1819, in Hope.
768. Marcus G., b. 7 Aug., 1820,   "   "
769. Emily, b. 17 July, 1822,   "   "
     Nancy, b. 1824,   "   "
770. Sylvanus, b. 13 Mch., 1826,   "   "
     Julia, b. ——,   "   "
     Silas, b. 14 July, 1830; m. 8 Jan., 1858, Victoria McIntyre. He d. 28 July, 1860.
     Abram, b. 18 Aug., 1833, in Hope; m. 14 Feb., 1864, Hannah Jameson, b. Mch., 1835, and had Benjamin D., b. 23 Oct., 1865, and Eddie C., b. 6 Aug., 1869.
     John H., b. 11 Dec., 1836; d. 21 Aug., 1867.

585. Isaac[8] (*Ephraim, Peter, Robert, Lot, John, Lot, Roger*), b. 18 Jan., 1793, in Temple, N. H.; moved to Maine, with his parents; settled in Hope, afterwards lived in Appleton; d. 18 Dec., 1863. He m. Nov., 1814, Nancy Wentworth (see *Wentworth Genealogy*, Vol. 1, p. 618), b. in Cushing, Me., 29 Dec., 1794, d. in Hope, 14 Dec., 1838.

Children of ISAAC and NANCY (WENTWORTH) CONANT:—

     Rebecca, b. 31 July, 1815; d. 11 Feb., 1829.
     William Bradford, b. 11 Aug., 1817. He is a merchant, of Belfast, Me.; is m. but has no children of his own. He has an adopted daughter. He has been a member of the Maine legislature.
     Albert, b. 20 May, 1820, in Hope, Me.; of Belfast. Is m. and has a dr., Elva, b. 1859.
     Benjamin Wentworth, b. 20 Jan., 1823; a merchant, of Belfast. Has an adopted daughter.
771. Elisha Harding, b. 22 Jan., 1826.
     Andrew J., b. 15 Dec., 1828; d. in infancy.
772. Joseph Augustus, b. 5 Jan., 1830.
     Nancy, b. 22 Dec., 1832; m. and had a family.
     Rebecca, b. 15 May, 1835; m. and had a family.

586. Phineas[8] (*Peter, Peter, Robert, Lot, John, Lot, Roger*), b. about 1783, in Stow, Mass., where he lived till 1827; was selectman and postmaster several years. In 1827 he went to Maine and worked at his trade as a mill-wright till

1836, when he settled in Constantia, N. Y. He d. 18 July, 1842. He m. in Harvard, Mass., 1807, Susan, dr. of Isaac and Lucy (Mead) Whitney, b. 26 Mch., 1791.

Children of PHINEAS and SUSAN (WHITNEY) CONANT:—

Daniel Gates, b. 17 Jan., 1808, in Stow; d. y.
773. Jonathan Newell, b. 13 Aug., 1810.
Charles, b. 5 July, 1812; d. y.
774. Andrew, b. 18 May, 1814.

587. Francis[8] (*Peter, Peter, Robert, Lot, John, Lot, Roger*), b. 12 Sep., 1789, in Stow, Mass.; was a farmer and merchant; d. 19 Sep., 1856. He m. in Stow, 20 Apr., 1813, Mary, dr. of Abraham Gates; she d. 31 July, 1850.

Children of FRANCIS and MARY (GATES) CONANT:—

775. Francis Henry, b. 19 Sep., 1815, in Albany, N. Y.
Mary Anna, b. 20 July, 1817.
Charles W., b. 29 Nov., 1818, in Stow, Mass. Is m. and has: 1. Edward; 2. Arthur, of Watertown, Mass.; 3. Albert F., of New York, N. Y.
George I., b. 29 July, 1822, in Stow, Mass.
Mary Louise, b. 13 Feb., 1830; m. —— Hayward, of Stow.

588. Winthrop Faulkner[8] (*Abraham, Daniel, Robert, Lot, John, Lot, Roger*), b. 11 June, 1814, in Acton, Mass., where he lived. He m. 29 Dec., 1842, Sophia Wetherbee.

Children of WINTHROP F. and SOPHIA (WETHERBEE) CO-NANT:—

Sophia Augusta, b. 13 Oct., 1843.
Abbie, now living unm. in Acton.
Arthur.
Edward.
Ellen.

589. Francis[8] (*Benjamin, Daniel, Robert, Lot, John, Lot, Roger*), b. 15 Nov., 1814, in Stow; a farmer; lived in Acton, Boxboro' and Littleton. He d. 2 July, 1878, in Littleton, Mass. He m. in Littleton, 21 Dec., 1841, Sophia Goldsmith.

Children of FRANCIS and SOPHIA (GOLDSMITH) CONANT:—

776. Albert Francis, b. 8 June, 1843, in Acton.
777. Charles Henry, b. 28 Sep., 1844, " "
778. Nelson Brainard, b. 6 Dec., 1845, " "
Julia Sophia, b. 5 Apr., 1847, " "

John Goldsmith, b. 1 Feb., 1849, in Acton.
Edwin Herbert, b. 1 Feb., 1851, in Boxboro'.
George Ellery, b. 1 July, 1852.
Waldo Emery, b. 1 Feb., 1855.
Amelia Maria, b. 16 July, 1857.
Sarah Elizabeth, b. 1 July, 1860.

590. **Mary**[8] (*Benjamin, Daniel, Robert, Lot, John, Lot, Roger*), b. 3 June, 1822, in Stow; m. 29 May, 1849, Daniel P. Houghton. She d. 8 Jan., 1853.

Child of DANIEL P. and MARY (CONANT) HOUGHTON :—

Mary Elizabeth, d. 19 Jan., 1854, aged 3 years.

591. **Martha**[8] (*Benjamin, Daniel, Robert, Lot, John, Lot, Roger*), b. 3 June, 1822, in Stow; m. 19 Jan., 1848, William Kendall. She d. 5 Sep., 1853.

Children of WILLIAM and MARTHA (CONANT) KENDALL :—

i. Georgiana, b. 27 Aug., 1849; m. Geo. H. Averill, of Arlington Heights.
ii. Henry Hubert, b. 23 Nov., 1850; m. Louisa A. Lander.
iii. Mary Elizabeth, d. 28 Aug., 1853, aged 1 mo. 10 days.

592.- **Martha Maria**[8] (*Simeon, Daniel, Robert, Lot, John, Lot, Roger*), b. 23 May, 1818, in Stow; m. 28 Sep., 1839, Obil, son of Micah and Elizabeth (Caswell) Shattuck. She d. 15 June, 1852. He d. of cholera in Louisville, Ky., 5 July, 1849.

Children of OBIL and MARTHA M. (CONANT) SHATTUCK :—

i. Oramel, b. 11 Jan., 1841; d. 10 July, 1865.
ii. Elizabeth C., b. 11 Mch., d. 13 Mch., 1843.
iii. Minerva, b. 15 Oct., 1845; d. 3 Apr., 1879.
iv. Corinna, b. 21 Apr., 1848; she is a missionary of the A. B. C. F. M., stationed at Merach, Turkey.

593. **Betsey H.**[8] (*Simeon, Daniel, Robert, Lot, John, Lot, Roger*), b. 23 Feb., 1828, in Stow; m. Luther Piper. She d. 30 June, 1857.

Children of LUTHER and BETSEY H. (CONANT) PIPER :—

i. Lizzie S., b. 30 Sep., 1852.
ii. Anson G., b. 18 Jan., 1855.

594. **Joseph**[8] (*Zebulon, Andrew, Andrew, Lot, John, Lot, Roger*), b. 31 Mch., 1781, in Concord; moved to New Ipswich,

N. H., with his parents. He settled in Bolton, but soon removed to Leominster, Mass., where he began the manufacture of shoes as early as 1810, which he continued for twenty years. He d. 26 June, 1859. He m. (1) 18 Sep., 1806, Patience Sawyer, of Bolton, b. 10 May, 1782, d. 20 May, 1845; m. (2) 25 Dec., 1845, Nancy (Symonds) Puffer.

Children of JOSEPH and PATIENCE (SAWYER) CONANT:—

Joseph Lysander, b. 11 June, 1807.
779. Peter Horace, b. 24 May, 1809.
780. Nestor Wright, b. 4 Jan., 1811.
Joshua Sawyer, b. 23 Jan., d. 29 Feb., 1813.
Andrew Pearson, b. 21 Apr., 1816; was of West Newton, Mass.; d. in Boston, 29 Nov., 1879.
Elizabeth Whitcomb, b. 26 Mch., 1818; d. 28 Jan., 1846; m. in St. Louis, Mo., —— Nichols.
Charles, b. 17 Dec., 1820; d. 11 Nov., 1860, in Keokuk, Ia.
Mary, b. 30 Dec., 1825; m. —— Farrington.

595. **Andrew**[8] (*Zebulon, Andrew, Andrew, Lot, John, Lot, Roger*), b. 12 Feb., 1796, in New Ipswich, N. H., where he lived till about 1840, then moved to Lunenburg, Mass.; was a farmer. He m. Emily Farnsworth, b. July, 1799, in Stoddard, N. H.

Children of ANDREW and EMILY (FARNSWORTH) CONANT:—

Lovander Wright, b. 1820, in New Ipswich.
781. Charles Farnsworth, b. 1821.
782. Andrew Philander, b. 8 May, 1823.
Samuel Stillman, b. Mch., 1825.
Susan E., b. 1827; m. —— Crossman, of Boston, Mass.
Lucy Hale, b. 1829; m. —— Kingsbury, of Lunenburg, Mass.
783. Adoniram Judson, b. 30 Apr., 1831.
Emily Hazelton, b. 1833; m. —— Searles, of Leominster, Mass.
784. James Quincy, b. 13 Apr., 1835.
Mary Ann, b. 1837; m. —— Marshall, of Leominster.
George Washington, b. 1839; of Lunenburg.
Ellen Elizabeth, b. 1843; d. y.

596. **Nathan**[8] (*Samuel Potter, Silas, Andrew, Lot, John, Lot, Roger*), b. 30 Oct., 1791, in Littleton, Mass. He is now (1884, Mch. 6) living in Guilford, Vt.; a cooper by trade. He m. in Acton, 26 Sep., 1816, Susan Davis, b. 1793, d. 1860.

Children of NATHAN and SUSAN (DAVIS) CONANT:—

Lucius, b. 19 Aug., 1818, in Guilford, Vt.
Susan, b. 31 Mch., 1821, "   "   "
Caroline, b. 7 Aug., 1823; m. —— Penniman.
Maria B., b. 22 Aug., 1831.

597. Paul[8] (*Samuel Potter, Silas, Andrew, Lot, John, Lot, Roger*), b. 23 Jan., 1793, in Acton, Mass., where he lived; a farmer. He d. 7 July, 1843, and the family removed to Nashua, N. H. He m. in Acton, 8 Apr., 1817, Matilda Jewett, of Boxboro', who d. in Nashua, 8 July, 1874.

Children of PAUL and MATILDA (JEWETT) CONANT:—

Samuel, b. 11 Apr., 1818; d. 11 Apr., 1839.
Emeline, b. 4 June, 1820; m. 23 Apr., 1839, William H. Conant.
Sophia, b. 27 Jan., 1822; d. 30 Dec., 1847; m. 5 May, 1842,
    Phineas Harrington.
John, b. 11 Oct., 1824; d. 16 Aug., 1828.
Francis, b. 3 Sep., 1827; is of South Acton. He m. (1) 10 May,
    1849, Martha Ann Jones; m. (2) 14 Apr., 1880, Mrs. Ellen J.
    Marshall; no children.
Maria, b. 14 Oct., 1830; d. 6 Sep., 1845.
785. Henry S., b. 27 May, 1835.

598. Silas[8] (*Samuel Potter, Silas, Andrew, Lot, John, Lot, Roger*), b. 4 May, 1803, in Acton, Mass.; m. in Acton, Mass., 22 Feb., 1825, Elizabeth Wheeler.

Children of SILAS and ELIZABETH (WHEELER) CONANT:—

Silas, b. 15 Oct., 1825.
Nathan, b. 16 Sep., 1827.
Eliza, b. 10 Sep., 1829; m. 31 Jan., 1849, George Lawrence, of
    Lincoln.
Susan Chaffin, b. 28 July, 1832.
George, b. 28 Apr., 1835; m. 27 Apr., 1856, Maria Dorney.
Simon Tuttle, b. 15 Dec., 1837.
Elbridge, b. 22 Jan., 1841. He was in the army, and d. in Suf-
    folk, Va., 9 Feb., 1863.
Charlotte Augusta, b. 3 Nov., 1843; m. 2 Jan., 1864, Nelson
    Holman, of Fitchburg.
Henrietta, b. 16 July, 1846; m. 10 Oct., 1863, George M. Ken-
    dall, of Acton.

599. Nahum[8] (*Samuel Potter, Silas, Andrew, Lot, John, Lot, Roger*), b. 2 Oct., 1810, in Acton, Mass. He lived in Cambridge. He m. 21 Jan., 1832, Eliza A. Gibson, b. 2 Feb., 1809.

Children of NAHUM and ELIZA A. (GIBSON) CONANT:—

Nahum, b. 23 Aug., 1833, in Cambridge, Mass.; was a cooper; removed to Philadelphia, Pa. He m. (1) 1857, in Philadelphia, Elmira Webb Dougherty, who d. 1860, and had Laura Louise, b. 5 June, 1858, who lives in Philadelphia. He m. a second time.

Eliza A., b. 28 Dec., 1835.

Amelia, b. 20 Sep., 1838.

Marcus, b. 24 Oct., 1842.

William, b. 24 Oct., 1842.

Susanna C., b. 26 June, 1845. ⎱ · Their names were changed 3
Robert C., b. 26 June, 1845. ⎰ Jan., 1860, to Susannah Conant Chaffin and Robert Conant Chaffin. (See List of Persons whose names have been changed in Massachusetts, p. 156.)

600. Silas[8] (*Silas, Silas, Andrew, Lot, John, Lot, Roger*), b. 24 Dec., 1798, in Acton, Mass.; a farmer; d. 4 Sep., 1865. He m. 1 Apr., 1824, Sarah Hayward.

Children of SILAS and SARAH (HAYWARD) CONANT:—

786. Cyrus Hayward, b. 30 July, 1825.

Sarah Pierce, b. 17 June, 1827; m. 9 Dec., 1852, Charles M. Barrett. She d. 26 Nov., 1858. Child: Mary.

George Henry, b. 30 July, 1829; m. 1855, Emma F. Hanscom. Children: Dwight Henry, b. 28 May, 1857, d. 18 Oct., 1866; Charles, b. 10 Nov., 1860; and a child, b. 1 June, 1870, d. y.

Ellen Ruth, b. June, 1833; m. 1856, Dwight L. Dimmock. She d. 18 Jan., 1864. Child: Dwight Hersey.

Mary N., b. 13 Oct., 1835; d. 13 Feb., 1854.

Silas, b. Aug., 1839; m. 2 Sep., 1860, Angeronia S. Tarbell, and has Nellie Frances, b. 21 July, 1861. He is a shoe manufacturer, of Danvers, Mass. The firm is J. E. Farrar & Co.

Andrew, b. June, 1841; unm.

601. Joshua L.[8] (*Silas, Silas, Andrew, Lot, John, Lot, Roger*), b. 3 Oct., 1801, in Concord. He moved to Lowell and thence to Boston. He m. 29 Apr., 1828, Adeline A. Merriam.

Children of JOSHUA and ADELINE A. (MERRIAM) CONANT:—

Adeline.

William A., of New York city.

Martha.

John Merriam, b. 7 June, 1844, in Lowell. He is now engaged in the manufacture of piano forte hardware in New York.

602. James Franklin[8] (*James, Silas, Andrew, Lot, John, Lot, Roger*), b. 23 Nov., 1814, in Acton, Mass.; moved to New

29

Ipswich, N. H., with his parents. Was a member of the New Ipswich Rifle Rangers at the time of the "Madawaska" war. He was by trade a shoemaker. Settled in Stoneham, Mass., where he d. 16 July, 1880. He m. in Nelson, N. H., 5 Nov., 1839, Lucy, dr. of Isaac and Susanna (Cobb) Follett, b. 23 Nov., 1804; d. 13 July, 1872, in Stoneham.

Children of JAMES F. and LUCY (FOLLETT) CONANT:—

787. Calvin Harrison, b. 29 Aug., 1841.
    Lucy Ann Seba, b. 27 Nov., 1845, in Stoneham. She m. ——
    Jaquith, and lives in Reading, Mass.

603. **Andrew**[8] (*James, Silas, Andrew, Lot, John, Lot, Roger*), b. 13 Nov., 1822, in Acton, Mass. He moved to New Ipswich, with his parents; settled in Nashua, N. H.; is a cigar manufacturer. He m. in Brattleboro', Vt., 3 July, 1846, Margaret Annie, dr. of Edward A. and Martha Chadwell, b. 12 Mch., 1831.

Children of ANDREW and MARGARET A. (CHADWELL) CONANT:—

    Edward Andrew, b. 31 July, 1851, in New Ipswich, N. H.
    Nellie Frances, b. 30 Aug., 1861, in Nashua, N. H.; d. 22 June, 1863.

604. **John**[8] (*John Gardiner, Eli, Andrew, Lot, John, Lot, Roger*), b. about 1792, in Pawlet, Vt. In the *History of Pawlet* he is called Capt. John. He m. Martha, dr. of Findley McNaughton.

Children of JOHN and MARTHA (McNAUGHTON) CONANT:—

    Daniel, of Little Falls, N. Y.
    Orlando.
    Charlotte, m. H. Pratt, of White Creek, N. Y. .
    Maria.

605. **Wesley**[8] (*John Gardiner, Eli, Andrew, Lot, John, Lot, Roger*), b. May, 1806, in Pawlet, Vt.; removed to Ida, Monroe county, Mich., about 1840. He was township clerk at Ida for ten years, and also supervisor. He d. 27 Mch., 1848, in Ida, Mich. He m. in Pawlet, Vt., 28 Feb., 1833, Ann Eliza, dr. of Joel and Mary (Cunningham) Norton, b. in Granville, N. Y., 30 Mch., 1812. After his death she m. (2) F. L. Wells, and now lives in Trenton, Mo.

Children of WESLEY and ANN E. (NORTON) CONANT:—

788. Joel N., b. 15 Mch., 1834.
Elizabeth A., b. 18 May, 1840; m. Mch., 1856, M. D. Smith.
Cornelia R., b. 18 Dec., 1842; m. Oct., 1865, S. D. Burrill, of
Trenton, Mo.
Helen, b. 8 Dec., 1844; m. Feb., 1863, E. L. Burrill.

606. **Alpheus**[8] (*George, Eli, Andrew, Lot, John, Lot,
Roger*), b. 17 Mch., 1810, in Enfield, N. H., where he lived.
He d. 19 Apr., 1867. He m. Mary A. Currier, b. 19 Mch., 1810.
Children of ALPHEUS and MARY A. (CURRIER) CONANT:—

Ellen M., b. 1835; d. 26 Sep., 1857.
789. Washington Irving, b. 6 Sep., 1841.
Lilian, b. 1850; m. —— Whitney, and has Maud Lilian, b.
3 Feb., 1882.

607. **George W.**[8] (*George, Eli, Andrew, Lot, John, Lot,
Roger*), b. 2 July, 1812, in Enfield, N. H. He m. Louisa Ann
Merrill, of Enfield.
Children of GEORGE W. and LOUISA A. (MERRILL) CO-
NANT:—

Thomas Merrill, b. 1850; of Boston, Mass.
A daughter, who m. B. F. Dutton, of the firm of Houghton
& Dutton, of Boston, Mass.

608. **George Franklin**[8] (*Abel, Abel, Andrew, Lot, John,
Lot, Roger*), b. 13 Sep., 1805, in Concord, Mass. He is now
(1885) living in Somerville, Mass.
Children of GEORGE F. and —— (——) CONANT:—

George H., b. 1830; of Somerville, Mass.
John F., b. 1832; of Cincinnati, Ohio.

609. **Emery**[8] (*Simeon, William, William, Lot, John, Lot,
Roger*), b. 20 Jan., 1791, in (Harvard?) Mass.; removed to
Grafton, Vt., with his parents, and thence to Vestal, Broome
co., N. Y. He d. 7 May, 1867, in Oswego, N. Y. He m. Rox-
anna Severance, who d. Oct., 1841.
Children of EMERY and ROXANNA (SEVERANCE) CONANT:—

Nancy.
Emery.
790. Luther, b. 7 Oct., 1822, in Vestal, N. Y.

Clarinda.
Alphonso.
Simeon.
Benjamin.
Diantha.
Mary.
Roxanna.

610. Luther[8] (*Simeon, William, William, Lot, John, Lot, Roger*), b. 19 Sep., 1793, in Massachusetts; moved to Grafton, Vt., with his parents; d. 29 May, 1878. He m. Mary Hill.

Children of LUTHER and MARY (HILL) CONANT:—

    Mary C., b. 17 Nov., 1818; m. ——, Samuel S. Bailey, of Grafton. Children: Marcia C., Ossian F., Rosetta F., Etta C.

791. Simeon Dexter, b. 3 Nov., 1820; of Grafton.

611. Elizabeth[8] (*Simeon, William, William, Lot, John, Lot, Roger*), b. 7 Nov., 1796, in Massachusetts; m. in Grafton, Vt., 27 Nov., 1817, Stephen White, who d. 16 May, 1870. She d. 24 Mch., 1873.

Children of STEPHEN and ELIZABETH (CONANT) WHITE:—

i. Eliza, b. 16 May, 1819; m. in Rockingham, Vt., Henry Ober. Children: Eugene, of Nashua, N. H., Harriet, Ellen, Edwin, of Grafton, Vt.

ii. Lewis, b. 10 Apr., 1821; m. in Dorset, Vt., Harriet Hanley. He is of Windham.

iii. Willard, b. 23 Feb., 1823; m. in Walpole, N. H., 1847, Elizabeth Ross. Children: Elbridge, of Castile, N. Y., Willis, of Greenville, N. H., William, of Chester, Vt., and Stella.

iv. George, b. 15 Feb., 1825; m. in Keene, N. H., Sylvina Estey. Children: Charles, of Marlboro', N. H., Emma, Eva, Elmer and Ella.

v. William, b. 9 July, 1827; m. in Walpole, N. H., Mary Ware. Children: Carrie, Sarah, Edwin, of Westmoreland, N. H., William and Lewis.

vi. Henry, b. 24 Dec., 1829; m. in Athol, Mass., Harriet Moore. Children: George, of Chester, Vt., Fred and Lizzie.

vii. Martha, b. 19 Jan., 1832; m. in Wilmington, Vt., Cornelius Barnard. Children: Jennie, Bessie, Charles, Edward, William and Mattie.

viii. Charles, b. 1 May, 1834; m. in Brookline, Vt., Carrie Merrifield. Children: Minnie, Mattie, Albert, of Grafton, Vt., and Arthur, of Grafton.

ix. Mary Ann, b. 25 May, 1836; m. in Grafton, Prescott Lawrence. Children: William and Elinor.

x.   Lauretta, b. 10 Jan., 1839; m. Lucius Edson. Children: Annie, Lillie and Bertie.

612. Ruxby[8] (*Simeon, William, William, Lot, John, Lot, Roger*), b. 23 Mch., 1803; m. 21 Apr., 1825, in Grafton, Vt., Mark Batchelder.

Children of MARK and RUXBY (CONANT) BATCHELDER:—

i.   Nancy, b. 21 Oct., 1827.
ii.   Martha M., b. 5 July, 1830.
iii. John L., b. 29 Apr., 1833; of Detroit, Mich.
iv. Mahala R., b. 9 Nov., 1837.

613. Benjamin[8] (*Levi, William, William, Lot, John, Lot, Roger*), b. 13 July, 1795, in Harvard, Mass.; m. ——— Davis.

Children of BENJAMIN and ——— (DAVIS) CONANT:—

    Abigail Davis, b. 1833; m. William A. Norris, of Hyannis, Mass., and is now of Springfield.
    Rebecca, who lived in Springfield, Mass.

614. Rebecca[8] (*Levi, William, William, Lot, John, Lot, Roger*), b. 23 Jan., 1797, in Harvard, Mass.; d. 1 Aug., 1873. She m. in Hopkinton, 1820, Robert G. Wilson, b. 1792, d. 8 May, 1858. He was a farmer.

Children of ROBERT G. and REBECCA (CONANT) WILSON:—

i.   John Orerin, b. 31 May, 1821. He is a shoe manufacturer at Natick, Mass. He m. 25 Nov., 1843, Mary Morse. Children: 1. Edward H., b. 10 Oct., 1845, d. 1882; m. Ella M. Coolidge, and had Helen H. and John E.; 2. John Howard, b. 9 Mch., 1847; 3. Mary Lizzie, b. 12 May, 1851; m. Frederick H. Ripley, and has Helen L., Grace W. and Frederick; 4. Nellie F.
ii.   Mary Ann Bigelow, b. 10 Aug., 1822; m. 24 Oct., 1849, Edwin Coolidge Morse, of Natick. He was b. in West Natick, 1817, and in early life was a school teacher. About 1850 he engaged in the manufacture of boots and shoes, but at the breaking out of the war he gave up business to become paymaster in the army, with the rank of major. After the war he spent some years in the South, but returned to Natick, and in 1877 bought a part interest in the Natick Citizen, of which he was editor four years. At the time of his death (1886) he was judge of the Natick Police Court. Children: 1. Eugene E., b. 1850, d. 1851; 2. Edwin Wilson, b. 29 Mch., 1855; graduated at Exeter and Harvard; is a ~journalist in New York city; m. Florence Stone; 3. Charles Wilson, b. 11 Aug., 1860, d. 1861.

iii.   Robert Gardner, b. 4 Mch., 1824.
iv.   Joseph Warren, b. 4 Jan., 1826. He is an attorney and coun-
        sellor at law, of Norwalk, Conn. He m. 9 Feb., 1859, Julia
        Virginia Phelps. Children: 1. Eugene Phelps, b. 12 Nov.,
        1859; 2. Joseph Warren, b. 26 June, 1861; 3. Robert Gard-
        ner, b. 18 Mch., 1866; 4. Henry Hamilton, b. 26 Feb., 1868.
v.   Rebecca Frances, b. 1 Nov., 1832; d. 1883.
vi.   Charles Oscar, b. 1839; d. 1883.

615. Lucinda[8] (*Levi, William, William, Lot, John, Lot,
Roger*), b. 26 Apr., 1804, in Harvard, Mass.; d. 13 Mch., 1844,
in Boxboro'. She m. 4 Oct., 1827, Samuel Mead, b. 4 Mch.,
1795, in Boxboro', where they lived. He was a farmer. He
d. 16 Nov., 1856, in Lunenburg.
      Children of SAMUEL and LUCINDA (CONANT) MEAD:—

i.   Lucinda, b. 22 July, 1828; m. L. Howe, of Natick.
ii.   Albert, b. 23 Apr., 1830; of Natick.
iii.   Alfred, b. 10 Feb., 1832; m. 21 Feb., 1854, in Stow, Hannah
        Maria Miles. Children: 1. Albert Arthur, b. 2 Mch., 1856,
        d. 1874; 2. Annie Louise, b. 13 Apr., 1861; m. Frank M.
        Forbush.
iv.   Abba Conant, b. 2 Apr., 1834.
v.   Anna Rebecca, b. 2 Jan., 1836; d. 26 Apr., 1860.
vi.   Mary Stevens, b. 20 June, 1840; d. 22 Dec., 1846.

616. George W.[8] (*Levi, William, William, Lot, John,
Lot, Roger*), b. 10 Apr., 1805, in Harvard, Mass.; m. 1829,
Anna, dr. of William and Anna (Mead) Stevens, of Boxboro'.
      Children of GEORGE W. and ANNA (STEVENS) CONANT:—

Abbie A., b. 1830; m. George G., son of Daniel Winch, of
      Pepperell.
George, b. 1832; d. 1834.
Sarah S., b. 1833.
Mary I., b. 1835.
Francis S., b. 1838; d. 1844.
Susan S., b. 1841; d. 1865.
Harriet M., b. 1848.

617. Levi[8] (*Levi, William, William, Lot, John, Lot,
Roger*), b. 6 Feb., 1810, in Harvard, Mass. He settled in Littleton, where he is still living. He is a farmer. He m. in
Littleton, 4 May, 1836, Anna Whitney, dr. of Abraham Mead,
who d. 15 Feb., 1873.

Children of Levi and Anna W. (Mead) Conant:—

792. Benjamin, b. 28 July, 1837, in Dublin, N. H.
793. Sherman, b. 13 Dec., 1839, "   "   "
      Henry, b. 18 Dec., 1842; d. 1847.
794. Nellie Sherman, b. 19 July, 1846, in Littleton, Mass.
795. Anna Jane, b. 16 Nov., 1848,   "   "   "
      Amelia Breck, b. 11 July, 1851, in Littleton, Mass.; m. 1875,
      Thomas H., son of Thomas L. and Jane Wakefield, of Ded-
      ham. He is a lawyer, of Boston. Child: Harold H., b. 1881.
      George Arthur, b. 31 May, 1854; he d. 26 Oct., 1883, in Abe-
      line, Texas, where he owned a large sheep ranch.
      Levi Leonard, b. 3 Mch., 1857; he m. 1884, Laura D. Chamber-
      lain, of Southboro', Mass. He is a teacher; lives in Rapid
      City, Dakota Ter.
      Elmer Kimball, b. 30 June, 1862. He is engaged in business
      in New York city.

618. Henry[8] (*Levi, William, William, Lot, John, Lot,
Roger*), b. 18 Sep., 1815, in Harvard, Mass.; moved to Fitchburg and then to Pepperell; a farmer. He m. in Pepperell, 18
Sep., 1838, Harriet Ann, dr. of Jonathan Blood, b. in Groton,
21 Apr., 1817.

Child of Henry and Harriet A. (Blood) Conant:—

      Susie Jane, b. 11 Apr., 1840, in Pepperell. She m. (1) 26 Oct.,
      1867, Alfred Dana, son of Milo and Betsey (Ames) Wright.
      He d. 25 Feb., 1876, and she m. (2) 11 Apr., 1882, in Hudson,
      Mass., Caleb, son of Henry and Charlotte (Batchelder)
      Richardson, b. 30 Nov., 1824, in Corinth, Vt. He is an in-
      surance agent, in Nashua, N. H. *Page 515. 516*

619. Nathaniel[8] (*Nathan, Nathaniel, John, Lot, John,
Lot, Roger*), b. 1805, in West Townsend, Mass.; moved to
Boston, Mass.; d. 9 June, 1876. He m. 1825, in Boston, Clar-
issa Burnham Kimball, b. in Buxton, Me., 24 Mch., 1803.

      Children of Nathan and Clarissa B. (Kimball) Co- *Page 515. 51*
NANT:—

      Josephine, d. y.
      Charles, d. y.
796. Charles Nathan, b. 26 May, 1833.
797. Edgar Alonzo, b. 5 Aug., 1837.
      George Washington, b. 27 Oct., 1841; m. 19 Aug., 1878, in
      Brooklyn, N. Y., Augusta Marianna Halstrick. He is a
      deputy collector in the Boston ~~custom house~~. *City Hall*
      Albert M. b. 8 Nov., 1843; m. 24 May, 1870, Catherine H.
      Closson.

620. John[8] (*Nathan, Nathaniel, John, Lot, John, Lot, Roger*), b. 15 Apr., 1807, in West Townsend, Mass. He m. 17 Dec., 1834, Susan Rice, b. 1811.

Children of JOHN and SUSAN (RICE) CONANT:—

> Mary E., b. 17 Nov., 1835; m. 17 Feb., 1856, —— Farman; has Harvey J.
> John E., b. 8 Nov., 1838; n. m.
> 798.   James S., b. 8 Nov., 1838.

621. David[8] (*Levi, Nathaniel, John, Lot, John, Lot, Roger*), b. 8 Apr., 1809, in Ludlow, Vt.; a farmer. He lived in Chester, Vt., where he d. 6 Dec., 1876. He m. in Mount Holly, Vt., 18 Apr., 1837, Julia Anna, dr. of Marvel and Julia Anna (Mason) Johnson, b. in Mount Holly, 4 Aug., 1814; d. in Chester, 3 Mch., 1853.

Children of DAVID and JULIA ANNA (JOHNSON) CONANT:—

> Julia A. M., b. 9 Apr., 1839, in Mt. Holly; m. in Chester, Vt., 4 June, 1861, Charles T., son of Thomas H. and Emeline (Cobb) Whitman, b. 24 June, 1835. They live in Mt. Holly, Vt.
> 799.   Marvel J., b. 7 July, 1843, in Mt. Holly.
> Ella M., b. 3 Jan., 1849,   "   "   "

622. Noah[8] (*Noah Farrar, John, John, Lot, John, Lot, Roger*), b. 11 Aug., 1812, in Townsend, Mass. He is now a grocer, of Lowell, Mass. He m. in Rockport, Mass., 10 June, 1837, Esther Tarr Clark.

Child of NOAH and ESTHER T. (CLARK) CONANT:—

> Esther Maria, b. 4 Sep., 1838, in Lowell.

623. Joseph Stearns[8] (*Noah Farrar, John, John, Lot, John, Lot, Roger*), b. 16 Feb., 1817, in Lowell, Vt. He is now a farmer, of Dracut, Mass. He m. in Lowell, Vt., 25 Dec., 1839, Lydia Margaret French.

Children of JOSEPH S. and LYDIA M. (FRENCH) CONANT:—

> Francina, b. 1842; d. in infancy.
> Edwin, b. 1844; d. 1846.
> Romanus E., b. 10 Oct., 1843, in Dracut (now Lowell).
> Charles Perkins, b. 29 Apr., 1852; m. 13 Aug., 1878, Mary Ranger. He is a contractor and builder, of Lowell, Mass.
> F—— W——, b. 29 May, 1854.

624. Isabella Eliza[8] (*Lot, Lot, Ezra, Lot, John, Lot, Roger*), b. 30 Dec., 1819, in Reading, Vt.; d. 3 Jan., 1853; m. 26 Dec., 1837, William W. Estabrook.

Children of WILLIAM W. and ISABELLA E. (CONANT) ESTABROOK:—

> Frances M., b. 24 Dec., 1838.
> Harriet A., b. 13 Mch., 1840; d. 18 Jan., 1850.
> Oscar A., b. 18 Nov., 1842.
> Edgar A., b. 30 July, 1844.
> Jasper L., b. 21 Oct., 1845. He was in the army during the war of the Rebellion, and d. 26 Nov., 1862.
> George F., b. 18 Jan., 1852; d. 7 Mch., 1864.

625. Thaddeus Elisha[8] (*Lot, Lot, Ezra, Lot, John, Lot, Roger*), b. 23 June, 1835, in Reading, Vt.; m. 22 Jan., 1858, Rosella, dr. of Salmon and Lois C. (Robinson) Hildreth. He is a furniture manufacturer.

Children of THADDEUS E. and ROSELLA (HILDRETH) CONANT:—

> Charles Thaddeus, b. 28 Dec., 1861.
> Lyndon Ferdinand, b. 20 Oct., 1864; d. 28 Mch., 1866.

626. James Henry[8] (*Thaddeus, Lot, Ezra, Lot, John, Lot, Roger*), b. 13 July, 1823, in Boston, Mass. He is a merchant, of New York city. He m. (1) in Charlestown, Mass., 12 Jan., 1854, Jane Maria Whipple, dr. of Edward and Harriet (Howard) Adams, b. 5 May, 1825; m. (2) in Brooklyn, N. Y., 16 June, 1881, Matilda Amelia Lyons.

Children of JAMES H. and JANE M. W. (ADAMS) CONANT:—

> Henry Hubbel, b. 15 Dec., 1854.
> Ella Frances, d. y.
> Etta Jane, b. 15 June, 1858.
> Francis, b. 21 Aug., 1859.

Child of JAMES H. and MATILDA A. (LYONS) CONANT:—

> A child, b. 1884.

627. William Henry[8] (*Elisha Lockwood, Lot, Ezra, Lot, John, Lot, Roger*), b. 24 Dec., 1834, in Cincinnati, Ohio; removed to Evansville, Ind., with his parents, where he now lives. He is a steamboat agent. He m. 1 June, 1859, in Evansville, Ann Elizabeth Cunningham.

Children of WILLIAM H. and ANN E. (CUNNINGHAM) CO-
NANT:—

> George Hurdus, b. 19 Jan., 1864, in Caseyville, Ky.; is a clerk
> in his father's office.
>
> Marie Hurdus, b. 31 Sep., 1869; d. 10 July, 1877.

628. John[8] (*John, John, John, John, John, Lot, Roger*),
b. 5 Oct., 1793, in Topsfield, Mass.; was a shoemaker and
farmer. He m. in Topsfield, 5 Oct., 1816, Ruth, dr. of Wells
and Ruth (Baker) Standley, b. 18 Feb., 1798.

Children of JOHN and RUTH (STANDLEY) CONANT:—

800. John, b. 17 Jan., 1818.
801. Ruth, b. 2 Feb., 1822; m. Moses Cheever, of Brimfield.
802. Irene, b. 14 July, 1825.
> Benjamin, b. 26 Apr., 1828; d. 24 May, 1829.
> Wells Standley, b. 22 June, 1833; m. Jane Spencer. He is a
> baker; lives in McGregor, Iowa.
> Sarah, b. 7 Sep., 1830.
803. Benjamin, b. 29 Dec., 1835.
> Henry, b. 16 Oct., 1841; m. 4 Oct., 1864, Hannah W., dr. of
> Enoch Cressy, of Danvers, b. 25 Aug., 1845. He is a stair
> builder, of Salem, Mass.

629. Sarah[8] (*John, John, John, John, John, Lot, Roger*),
b. 5 Oct., 1796, in Topsfield, Mass.; d. 19 Feb., 1883. She m.
James Giles, son of David and Hannah (Giles) Raymond, of
Beverly. He d. 14 Mch., 1854, aged 71 years.

Children of JAMES and SARAH (CONANT) RAYMOND:—

i.   George W., b. 17 Oct., 1818; d. 1851; m. Harriet Wood.
ii.   James M., b. 15 Oct., 1820; d. 1878; m. Mary Ann Adams.
iii.   Charles F., b. 11 Nov., 1822; d. in St. Louis; m. Jane Fielding.
iv.   Benjamin Conant, b. 13 Jan., 1825; m. Sarah Woodbury; had
       Sarah, George, Frank, Nellie, Charles and Henry.
v.   John W., b. 25 Sep., 1827; m. (1) Sarah Trow; m. (2) Mary
       Ann Caldwell. Children: Jennie Frances, Jesse Free-
       mont, John William and James. He served through the
       war of the Rebellion; rose from the rank of lieutenant to
       colonel. At the close of the war he bought a plantation in
       Florida, but afterwards returned to Massachusetts. He
       now lives on Balch street, North Beverly; is county com-
       missioner.
vi.   Joshua Augustus Lovett, b. 20 Oct., 1833; d. 1851.
vii.   Edwin Stone, b. 25 Apr., 1836; he is a shoe manufacturer, of
       Beverly. He m. (1) Sarah A. Webber; m. (2) Abby (Grant)
       Ober.

630. Harriet[8] (*John, John, John, John, John, Lot, Roger*),
b. June, 1799, in Topsfield, Mass.; m. Benjamin Kent.

Children of BENJAMIN and HARRIET (CONANT) KENT:—

i. Sarah, b. 1820; m. Henry Norton. Children: 1. Cyrus Hill, of Peabody; 2. William Henry, of Salem; 3. George, of Peabody; 4. Mary; 5. Benjamin, of Peabody.
ii. Irene, b. Sep., 1822, in Beverly; m. Frank Gould; now of Humboldt, Cal.
iii. Harriet, b. 1826; resides, unm., in Greene, Ia.
iv. Emma.
v. Benjamin Franklin, b. 1834, in Danvers; m. in De Sota, Wis., Mary Kendall. He removed to Greene, Ia. Children: Charles and Mary.

631. Joseph[8] (*Ezra, John, John, John, John, Lot, Roger*),
b. 6 May, 1816, in Beverly. He is a cabinet maker, of Mt. Vernon, N. H. He m. 19 Sep., 1844, Abigail, dr. of John and Mary Elliot, b. in Mt. Vernon, 9 Feb., 1826.

Children of JOSEPH and ABIGAIL (ELLIOT) CONANT:—

Abigail J., b. 31 Jan., 1847; m. Stephen F. Hathaway, of Beverly.
Mary E., b. 23 Dec., 1848.
Alethea, b. 29 May, 1850; m. John W. Bell, of Beverly.
Joseph F., b. 11 May, 1856; is in business in Boston, Mass.
Charles E., b. 23 Dec., 1858.
Josephine, b. 6 May, d. 4 Sep., 1861.
Willie E., b. 21 Mch., 1866.

632. John[8] (*Ezra, John, John, John, John, Lot, Roger*),
b. 20 Sep., 1818, in Beverly. He was a mason. He d. in Wenham, 19 June, 1849. He m. Anna, dr. of Benjamin Edwards.

Children of JOHN and ANNA (EDWARDS) CONANT:—

Eveline, b. 1 Feb., 1846; m. Charles Dodge, of Providence, R. I.
John Parker, b. 23 Oct., 1849; a carpenter, of Wenham.

633. Ezra[8] (*Ezra, John, John, John, John, Lot, Roger*),
b. 14 Sep., 1820, in Beverly, Mass.; lived in Beverly and Wenham. He m. Sarah E., dr. of Stephen and Sarah Dodge.

Children of EZRA and SARAH E. (DODGE) CONANT:—

Helen, b. Dec., 1850.
Elizabeth, b. 11 Aug., 1854; m. Charles Elliot.

634. Herbert Thorndike[8] (*Ezra, John, John, John, John, Lot, Roger*), b. 4 Mch., 1823, in Beverly, Mass. He moved from Beverly to Salem in 1844. He is a mason. He m. 7 May, 1857, Jane Saunders, b. in Devonshire, England.

Children of HERBERT T. and JANE (SAUNDERS) CONANT:—

Mary J., b. 28 Apr., d. 19 Sep., 1859.
Henry T., b. 1 Oct., 1861.

635. James A.[8] (*Gardner, Josiah, Daniel, Daniel, John, Lot, Roger*), b. 31 Mch., 1827, in Warwick, Mass., where he lives. He m. Mary E. Adams.

Child of JAMES A. and MARY E. (ADAMS) CONANT:—

Eva L., b. 16 Nov., 1854; m. Arthur E. Albee.

636. Samuel D.[8] (*Gardner, Josiah, Daniel, Daniel, John, Lot, Roger*), b. 8 Apr., 1835, in Warwick, Mass., where he lived. He m. Flora M. Campbell.

Children of SAMUEL D. and FLORA M. (CAMPBELL) CONANT:—

Melinda M., b. 19 Dec., 1875.
Henry G., b. Feb., d. Apr., 1878.
Bessie H., b. 29 July, 1882; d. 6 Mch., 1883.

637. Josiah[8] (*Gardner, Josiah, Daniel, Daniel, John, Lot, Roger*), b. 17 Jan., 1840, in Warwick, Mass., where he lived. He m. Ellen M. Fisher.

Children of JOSIAH and ELLEN M. (FISHER) CONANT:—

Maud L., b. 27 Mch., 1877.
Mertie, d. y.

638. Edward Everett[8] (*Hiram, Josiah, Daniel, Daniel, John, Lot, Roger*), b. 9 Mch., 1837, in Holden, Mass. He is a physician, residing in Boston. He m. in Boston, 22 July, 1863, Ella F. Brown.

Children of EDWARD E. and ELLA F. (BROWN) CONANT:—

Carrie Louise, b. 9 Feb., 1866, in North Attleboro'.
Hiram Edward, b. 1 June, 1871, in Miller's Falls.
Alice Maud, b. 19 Aug., 1873,   "   "   "

639. Ransom Merritt[8] (*Hiram, Josiah, Daniel, Daniel,*

Nathan D. Conant

John, Lot, Roger), b. 20 Aug., 1852, in Richmond, Vt., where he lives. He is a dealer in country produce. He m. 15 Apr., 1872, Dora E. Flagg.

Children of RANSOM M. and DORA E. (FLAGG) CONANT:—

> Willard S., b. 26 Apr., 1875.
> Sadie M., b. 15 May, 1876.
> Fay Wyman, b. 6 Apr., 1884.

640. Hiram Solomon[8] (*Hiram, Josiah, Daniel, Daniel, John, Lot, Roger*), b. 20 Apr., 1854, in Richmond, Vt. He m. 20 Oct., 1880, Cynthia Kenyon.

Child of HIRAM S. and CYNTHIA (KENYON) CONANT:—

> Roby Edwin, b. 5 Apr., 1884.

641. Nathan Dodge[8] (*Nathaniel, Joshua, Nathaniel, Daniel, John, Lot, Roger*), b. 1 Apr., 1825, in Shapleigh, Me. In 1846 he went to Boston, Mass., and entered the employ of Nahum Ward, and in time became one of the firm of N. Ward & Co., successors to N. Ward. In 1869 he was a member of the city council of Boston. He d. 5 May, 1873. He m. 7 Oct., 1849, Elizabeth C. Simpson, of Brunswick, Me., who d. 30 Mch., 1880.

Children of NATHAN D. and ELIZABETH C. (SIMPSON) CONANT:—

> Lewis S., b. 11 July, 1851. He is director of the N. Ward Company, of Boston. He lives in Roxbury.
> Emma A., b. 17 Mch., 1853.
> Ella E., b. ——; m. James Hurst, of Fall River, Mass.; has family.
> Helen A., b. Nov., 1855.
> Mary F., b. 30 Oct., 1856; d. 6 Apr., 1871.

642. Nathaniel[8] (*Joshua, Joshua, Nathaniel, Daniel, John, Lot, Roger*), b. 26 Mch., 1837, in Alfred, Me. He lives in Brookline, Mass. He m. 28 Oct., 1868, Susan J. Came, of Alfred, Me.

Children of NATHANIEL and SUSAN J. (CAME) CONANT:—

> Susan M., b. 11 June, 1870.
> Lizzie, b. 6 Aug., d. 28 Aug., 1871.
> Rosa, b. 20 Feb., d. 13 Mch., 1875.

643. William Henry[8] (*William Green, Joshua, Nathan-*

iel, Daniel, John, Lot, Roger), b. 20 May, 1830, in Alfred, Me.
He is treasurer of Portland & Rochester railroad, and lives
in Portland. He m. in Middletown, Conn., 12 Dec., 1856,
Mary E. Davis.

Children of WILLIAM H. and MARY E. (DAVIS) CONANT :—

Emma L., b. 14 Aug., 1862, in Alfred.
William G., b. 6 Nov., 1866; d. 8 Aug., 1880, in Portland.
Ellen M., b. 19 Apr., 1869, in Alfred.

644.   Richard Odell[8] (*Alvah, John, Nathaniel, Daniel,
John, Lot, Roger*), b. 1 Apr., 1828, in Alfred, Me.; removed
to Portland, with his parents, in 1839, and has since resided in
Portland and Cumberland. He was educated in the public
schools and at North Yarmouth Academy. When sixteen
years of age he entered his father's store as a clerk, and in
1849 was admitted to the firm of Hall & Conant, then doing
the largest grocery business in Portland. In.1856 he bought out
Mr. Hall, and in 1859 his father retired from business. In
1862 he admitted Mr. Sumner C. Rand to partnership, under
the firm name of R. O. Conant & Co.; in 1866 the style was
changed to Conant & Rand. The business was conducted by
them till 1882, when Mr. Rand retired, and Mr. Conant admitted his son, Frederick O., and Mr. Daniel H. Patrick to the
firm, under the style of Conant, Patrick & Co. Mr. Conant
was a member of the common council of Portland, in 1869 and
1870, which is the only public office he has ever held. He was
a director of the Ocean Insurance Co. for ten years, and its
secretary three years; was a director of the Portland & Rochester Railroad two years. He has been a director of the National Traders Bank for twenty years, and its vice-president
eight years; and has been director and trustee of several other
commercial corporations. He has taken a great interest in
agricultural matters, and has been director and president of
the Cumberland County Agricultural Society and the Maine
Poultry Association. He m. in Cumberland, Me., 8 Jan., 1857,
Mrs. Emma (Loring) Manly, b. 6 May, 1829, widow of Charles
Manly and dr. of Capt. Solomon and Alethea (Drinkwater)
Loring. Capt. Solomon Loring was son of Solomon and Han-

nah (Davis) Loring, g. s. of Solomon and Alice (Cushing) Loring, g. g. s. of John Loring, who was son of John, son of Thomas Loring, who came from Axminster, Devon, England, to Hingham, Mass., about 1630. Hannah Davis was dr. of Timothy and Margaret (Davis) Davis, of Amesbury, Mass., and Biddeford and No. Yarmouth, Me. Timothy Davis was son of Thomas and Deborah (Martin) Davis. Deborah Martin was g. dr. of George Martin, an early and prominent settler of Amesbury, whose widow, Susanna (North), was hung at Salem, July 19, 1692, as a witch. (For a full report of the trial, and absurd testimony upon which she was convicted, see Merrill's *Hist. of Amesbury*, pp. 125-136.) Alethea Drinkwater was dr. of Sylvanus and Rachael (Sweetser) Drinkwater, g. dr. of Joseph and Jane (Latham) Drinkwater, g. g. dr. of Thomas and Elizabeth (Haskell) Drinkwater. Elizabeth Haskell was dr. of John Haskell, whose wife, Patience Soule, was dr. of George Soule, who came in the Mayflower, 1620. Jane Latham was dr. of Thomas and Deborah (Harden) Latham, g. dr. of James Latham, g. g. dr. of Robert Latham, whose wife, Susanna, was dr. of John Winslow (brother of Governor Edward Winslow) and Mary (Chilton), his wife, said to have been the first woman to land from the Mayflower. (For genealogies of the Drinkwater and Sweetser families, see *Old Times in North Yarmouth*, pp. 386, 1138 and 1142.)

Child of RICHARD O. and EMMA (LORING) CONANT:—

804. Frederick Odell, b. 1 Oct., 1857, in Portland.

645. Emma Dow[8] (*Alvah, John, Nathaniel, Daniel, John, Lot, Roger*), b. 4 Apr., 1830, in Alfred, Me.; moved to Portland, with her parents. She m. 12 Oct., 1854, Henry Martin, son of Rev. Edward Payson, D. D. He is a banker and broker, of Portland.

Children of HENRY M. and EMMA D. (CONANT) PAYSON:—

i. Franklin Conant, b. 4 Sep., 1856; graduated at Bowdoin College, 1876; studied law with Hon. William L. Putnam, and is now a member of the law firm of Holmes & Payson. He m. 4 Oct., 1883, Grace Wheaton, dr. of Eliphalet and Margaret F. (Webb) Merrill, b. 12 Feb., 1858. Child: Robert, b. 30 Aug., 1884.

ii. George Shipman, b. 14 Feb., 1858; graduated at Bowdoin Col-
lege, 1880; is now in business with his father. He m. 12
Oct., 1882, Louise Godfrey, dr. of Sidney and Sophronia
(Chase) Thaxter, b. in Bangor, Me., 16 Sep., 1859. Children:
Edith, who d. in infancy, and Harold Conant, b. 17 Dec.,
1886.

iii. Henry Storer, b. 4 Mch., 1860; graduated at Bowdoin College, 1881. He studied law with Hon. W. L. Putnam, and
is now an attorney and counsellor at law.

iv. Horace Gilman, b. 12 May, d. 10 Oct., 1866.

v. Marion, b. 28 Aug., 1869; d. 7 Mch., 1870.

vi. Richard Conant, 5 Nov., 1870.

646. John Henry[8] (*Cyrus King, John, Nathaniel, Daniel,
John, Lot, Roger*), b. 10 Dec., 1836, in Alfred, Me.; moved to
Watertown, Mass., with his parents. He was for many years
a member of the firm of Kilham & Loud, doing a ship brokerage business in Boston. He now carries on the business under
the firm name of J. H. Conant & Company. He m. 12 Dec.,
1864, Caroline, dr. of Asa and Caroline (Heald) Melvin, b. in
Concord, Mass., 16 Jan., 1836.

Children of JOHN H. and CAROLINE (MELVIN) CONANT:—

Henry John, b. 17 Mch., 1866. He is a graduate of the Insti-
tute of Technology in Boston.
Abbie Buxton, b. 9 Jan., 1868.
Francis Melvin, b. 6 Nov., 1874.

647. Alvah[8] (*Cyrus King, John, Nathaniel, Daniel, John,
Lot, Roger*), b. 4 Nov., 1838, in Alfred, Me. He is now a
manufacturer of wood pulp, in Bath, N. H. He m. in Quebec,
Canada, 29 Oct., 1867, Laura, dr. of Holland and Sylvia
(Wakefield) Plimpton, of Wardsboro', Vt., b. 5 Apr., 1839.

Children of ALVAH and LAURA (PLIMPTON) CONANT:—

Myrtie P., b. 27 Sep., 1868.
Carrie E., b. 1 July, 1870.
Mabel S., b. 26 Apr., 1872.
Fannie A., b. 14 Feb., 1874; d. 16 Mch., 1880.
Winnie L., b. 19 Oct., 1878.
Alvah Lewis, b. 14 July, 1882.

648. Cyrus Gile[8] (*Cyrus King, John, Nathaniel, Daniel,
John, Lot, Roger*), b. 4 Oct., 1845, in Alfred, Me.; moved to
Watertown, with his parents. He now lives in East Boston,

and is engaged in business with his brother, John H. He m.
in E. Boston, 27 Nov., 1878, Florence, dr. of William T. and
Sarah F. (Bunker) Hight, of East Boston.

Children of CYRUS G. and FLORENCE (HIGHT) CONANT:—

> Charles Hight, b. 15 Sep., 1879.
> Cyrus Fred., b. 27 Sep., 1881.
> Roger William, b. 2 Aug., 1887.

649. **Charles Rufus**[8] (*Rufus, Rufus, Josiah, Daniel,
John, Lot, Roger*), b. 5 Dec., 1833, in Charlton, Mass. He d.
in Stanton, Va, 27 June, 1864. He m. in East Woodstock,
Conn., 19 Nov., 1854, Ann Frances Ross.

Children of CHARLES R. and ANN F. (ROSS) CONANT:—

> Victor Augustine, b. 20 Dec., 1855, in Dudley, Mass.; now of
> Webster; m. 1879, Alice Isabel Bates, and has Charles
> Francis, b. Oct., 1880, and Harold Augustine, b. 1882.
> Ernest Lee, b. 11 Sep., 1857, in Dudley, Mass. He graduated
> at Harvard College, 1883, and is now teaching in Baltimore,
> Maryland. *Married Blanche Allen of Cincinnati*
> Charles Francis, b. 1863. *died at 2 years.*

650. **Harrison Johnson**[8] (*Rufus, Rufus, Josiah, Daniel,
John, Lot, Roger*), b. 3 May, 1848, in Charlton, Mass. He is
now a dealer in hardware, in Southbridge, Mass. He m. in
Sturbridge, Mass., 3 Jan., 1872, Ellen Lucy Bennett.

Children of HARRISON J. and ELLEN L. (BENNETT) CO-
NANT:—

> Frederick Rufus, b. 24 July, 1875, in Southbridge.
> Lucy Flora, b. 11 Nov., 1878.
> Harrison Josiah, b. June, 1881.

651. **Hezekiah**[8] (*Hervey, Josiah, Josiah, Daniel, John,
Lot, Roger*), b. 28 July, 1827, in Dudley, Mass. He received
an academical education at Nichols Academy, in Dudley, obtained mostly during the winter months, being employed on
his father's farm during the summer. When seventeen years
of age he left home and became an apprentice with the firm of
Estey & Evans, printers, and at that time publishers of the
Worcester County Gazette, an anti-slavery weekly newspaper;
about two years later the firm failed, and he then obtained employment in the National Aegis establishment. After a year's

30

service there he went to work in a machine shop, where he had
less night work, giving him an opportunity for self-improvement. After two years in the shop he was enabled, by his
savings, to give himself a year's schooling at Nichols Academy.
He then returned to the machine shop and applied himself to
his work, improving his leisure time and evenings in learning
mechanical draughting and studying works on mechanical en-
gineering. About 1852, at the suggestion of some shoe making friend, he invented a novel pair of "lasting pincers," and
obtained a patent for them, but it did not prove a financial
success. Soon after this he went from Worcester to Boston,
where he worked a while in the "Union Works," then back
to Worcester, working for Samuel Flagg & Co. and Woodburn,
Light & Co.; thence he went to Hartford, Conn., and soon entered Colt's firearms manufactory, where he remained some
time. At Hartford he made the acquaintance of Mr. Christian
Sharp, the inventor of the celebrated "Sharp's rifle," and was
employed by him to make drawings of, and assist him in getting up, some machines for making projectiles for his rifle. In
1856 he invented and patented an improvement in the "Sharp's
rifle," known as the "gas check," which was considered so important that the United States and British governments immediately ordered its application to all arms manufactured by the
Sharp's Rifle Co. for them. In the same year (1856) he was
applied to by Samuel Slater & Sons, of Webster, Mass., to
construct a machine for sewing the selvage on the woolen
cloths manufactured by them and known as "doeskins." He
constructed a machine which was entirely successful and has
been in use over twenty-five years. No patent was ever sought
for this machine, as it was for a special purpose, and Mr. Conant thought the number that would find employment would
be very limited. The construction of a machine for dressing
sewing thread next engaged his attention, and at the same time
he commenced drawings for an automatic machine for winding
spool cotton. After completing the dressing machine he built
a model of the "winder," and made application for a patent.
The Willimantic Linen Co., hearing of this new machine, sent
for Mr. Conant to go to Willimantic and exhibit his machine,

H. Conant.

which he did at their stockholders' annual meeting, in Jan., 1859. They were so well pleased with the machine that they purchased one-half of the patent right, and made arrangements with him to enter their service as a mechanical expert, giving his entire time to them for three years. He entered upon this engagement Feb. 1, 1859; this contract was twice renewed, increasing his salary the last term to double what it was at first. During the first term he invented and constructed a machine for affixing the labels on spools of thread, which is known as the "ticketing machine." This machine cuts out the labels, gums them, and applies them simultaneously to each end of the spool, at the rate of one hundred spools per minute. The last three years of his stay at Willimantic, Mr. Conant was superintendent of the works. In 1864 he went to Europe, to visit the manufacturing districts of England and Scotland, in the interest and at the expense of the Willimantic Linen Co. He was successful in gaining admission to some twenty or thirty of the best spinning establishments, and also the spool thread establishments of J. & P. Coats and the Messrs. Clark, in Scotland, and also visited London and Paris. At the expiration of his last contract in Willimantic, he tendered his resignation, which was accepted, thus terminating nine years of service, during which the company had more than doubled its capital and also its production.

In 1868 he removed to Pawtucket, R. I., and in the latter part of that year engaged in the formation of a new thread company, with a capital of $100,000, to be called the Conant Thread Company, with himself as treasurer and manager. A charter was procured from the legislature, and a wooden building 50 feet wide by 100 feet long was erected. Twisting and winding machinery was at once put in motion, while the supplies of yarn were imported from England. Soon after this small manufactory was opened circumstances induced him to open negotiations with the firm of J. & P. Coats, of Paisley, Scotland, for the manufacture of their goods in this country. He made his second trip to England in May, 1869, and returned in June with contracts to manufacture their celebrated goods, and power to enlarge the capital and increase the plant to an extent not dreamed of when the first building was erected. A new mill, 70 feet wide, 300 feet long and four stories high, was at once commenced, and finished the following April. The following season a bleachery was erected and the machinery and operatives of this mill were imported from Scotland. The business was successful, and the demand for the goods increased as fast as it was convenient to arrange to increase the supply. A change in the tariff laws, increasing the duties on yarns, made it desirable to produce the yarns in this country, and a large spinning mill was added to the plant of the company in 1873, known as No. 3. This mill was of brick, 375 feet long by 100 feet wide, three stories high, and was equipped with 500 horse power Corliss engines and boilers, and the best English machinery throughout. In 1876 mill No. 4 was started with 1000 horse power engines, built by Corliss; this mill was equipped with twisting and spinning machinery of the best English and American manufacture. In 1877 a dyehouse was added, and in 1881 mill No. 5, with engines of 1400 horse power and a floor area nearly equal to No. 3 and No. 4 mills together. The plant is now one of the largest in the United States, and represents an investment of over $4,000,000, and without doubt is the best arranged, best equipped and best organized manufacturing establishment of its kind in the world, giving constant employment to about 2000 hands. Mr. Conant is still the treasurer and manager of this large corporation, and devotes his whole time to its interests, declining all inducements to accept public offices or any duties that would interfere with his efficiency as the head of this model establishment. Nevertheless, the financial transactions are on such a large scale that he has been invited to sit at the board of direction of the banks in Pawtucket, of which there are three, and also to accept the position of president of the Pawtucket Institution for Savings. His inventions and manufacturing interests have prospered and been successful beyond his expectations, and a kind Providence has always seemed to attend his plans and reward his efforts. Under such circumstances he has felt it to be a privilege as well as a duty to use some of his means to benefit his fellow men, and acting under this prompting he has attempted to resuscitate the old and dilapidated academy buildings in his native town of Dudley, and has erected new school and dormitory buildings of ample proportions, and besides has erected an observatory equipped with two good telescopes and a full set of meteorological instruments from the celebrated house of Cassella & Co., of London, England. Combined with this is a fine library and reading room for the use of the students of Nichols Academy. The library has over 2000 volumes of the latest and best literary and scientific works, and the reading room has all the standard periodicals, both literary and scientific, as well as the local newspapers. Beside all this, Mr. Conant has 'contributed in various ways to the welfare and adornment of the town of Dudley, where he and his family spend the summer months.

He m. (1) 4 Oct., 1853, Sarah Williams, dr. of Col. Morris and Elizabeth (Eaton) Learned, b. 8 Dec., 1829, d. 17 July, 1855; m. (2) Nov., 1859, Harriet Knight Learned (sister of above), b. 10 May, 1828, d. 6 July, 1864; m. (3) 5 Dec., 1865, Mary Eaton, dr. of Dr. Samuel P. and Harriet (Eaton) Knight, b. 19 Jan., 1834.

Children of HEZEKIAH and HARRIET K. (LEARNED) CO-NANT :—

> Samuel, b. 9 Dec., 1861.
> Edith A., b. 19 Sep., 1863.

652. Amos[8] (*Samuel, Amos, Ezra, Benjamin, John, Lot, Roger*), b. 30 July, 1810, in Irasburg, Vt. He settled in Nashua, N. H.; is a shuttle manufacturer. He m. (1) in Nashua, 27 Dec., 1855, Mary Jane French; m. (2) in Hudson, N. Y., 6 July, 1858, Elizabeth Amanda Hedges.

Children of AMOS and MARY J. (FRENCH) CONANT :—

> Helen Lovantia, b. 29 Apr., 1839, in Nashua, N. H.
> Laura Frances, b. 12 Nov., 1843, " " "
> Mary Jane, b. 30 June, 1846, " " "
> Harriet Maria, b. 28 Aug., 1848, " " "
> Cyrus Baldwin, b. 7 Nov., 1850, " " "
> Laura Ann, b. 27 Nov., 1853, " " "

Children of AMOS and ELIZABETH A. (HEDGES) CONANT :—

> Edwin William, b. 31 May, 1859, in Nashua, N. H.

Bertine, b. 5 Sep., 1862, in Hudson, N. Y.
Emma, b. 30 Jan., 1866,   "   "   "
Antoinette, b. 12 Jan., 1869, in Hudson, N. Y.
Grace, b. 26 Feb., 1871,   "   "   "

653. Ezra D.[8] (*Samuel, Amos, Ezra, Benjamin, John, Lot, Roger*), b. 3 Nov., 1812, in Irasburg, Vt. He resided in Somerville, Mass.; was a wholesale grocer, doing business with his son in Boston. He was a member of Franklin Street Orthodox Church. He d. 10 Sep., 1887. He m. Feb., 1841, B. L. Skeele, of Danville, Vt.

Children of EZRA D. and B. L. (SKEELE) CONANT:—

Edwin S., b. 25 Feb., 1843, in Glover, Vt.
Martha F., b. 19 May, 1847; m. S. H. O. Hadley; has Henry K. and Arthur D. They live in Somerville.
Carrie E., b. 15 Dec., 1855, in Somerville, Mass. She m. Rufus H., son of Rufus B. Stickney, of the firm of Stickney & Poor, Boston, Mass. He d. 1886.

654. Samuel Davis[8] (*Samuel, Amos, Ezra, Benjamin, John, Lot, Roger*), b. 27 Nov., 1820, in Irasburg, Vt. He is now a merchant, of Janesville, Wis. He m. in Irasburg, Vt., 1848, Louisa Ann Pearson.

Children of SAMUEL D. and LOUISA A. (PEARSON) CONANT:—

Theodore P., b. 1850, in Irasburg. He lives in St. Louis, Mo.; is married and has a son, George K., b. 1881.
Harriet A., b. 1852; m. —— Faville, of Oshkosh, Wis.; has Harold C. and Theodore.

655. Charles Carroll[8] (*Ebenezer, Amos, Ezra, Benjamin, John, Lot, Roger*), b. 29 Aug., 1820, in Plainfield, Vt. He is now a farmer, of Crasburg, Vt. He m. in Manchester, N. H., 11 Oct., 1846, Frances Jane, dr. of Benjamin and Nancy (Durgin) Sherburne, b. in Norwood, N. H., 26 Aug., 1825.

Children of CHARLES C. and FRANCES J. (SHERBURNE) CONANT:—

Ellen Jane, b. 22 Dec., 1847, in Plainfield, Vt.
Mary Edna, b. 2 May, 1849,   "   "   "
Sarah Frances, b. 22 May, 1851, in Concord, N. H.
Charles Carroll, b. 19 Sep., 1864, in Craftsburg, Vt.

656. Charles Olin[8] (*Charles, Amos, Ezra, Benjamin,*

John, Lot, Roger), b. 6 July, 1822, in Troy, Vt. He was a soldier in the Mexican war and in the war of the Rebellion. He d. in Boston, Mass., 2 Jan., 1872.

Children of CHARLES O. and ——— (———) CONANT:—

> Charles C., who was clerk of U. S. Court, in Boston.
> George C., who lives in Boston.

657. Horace Hamilton[8] (*Newell, John, Ezra, Benjamin, John, Lot, Roger*), b. 13 Oct., 1812, in Craftsburg, Vt. He is now a harness manufacturer, of Orford, N. H., where he removed in 1845. He is a justice of the peace and has been deputy sheriff of the county. He m. 8 Apr., 1841, Susan, dr. of Seba and Philabe (Allen) Stimson.

Children of HORACE H. and SUSAN (STIMSON) CONANT:—

> Augustus Franklin, b. 12 Mch., 1846. He now resides in Burlington, Vt.; is superintendent of a steamboat line on lake Champlain. He is married but has no children.
> 805. Hamilton Stimson, b. 22 May, 1851.
> William Rawson, b. 16 Aug., 1856. He graduated at Dartmouth College, 1883; is a teacher, at Meriden, N. H.

658. William Augustus[8] (*Newell, John, Ezra, Benjamin, John, Lot, Roger*), b. 9 Nov., 1816, in Craftsburg, Vt. He now (1885) resides in Colorado Springs, Col., and is in the employ of the Atlantic and Pacific Railroad Company. He m. in New York city, 8 Mch., 1837, Maria Louisa Weed (see *Whitney Family Genealogy*).

Children of WILLIAM A. and MARIA L. (WEED) CONANT:—

> William L., b. 30 May, 1841, in New York.
> 806. Frederick Herbert, b. 1 Jan., 1847, in New York.
> Florence C., b. 13 Apr., 1849, in New York.

659. Edward[8] (*Ezra, John, Ezra, Benjamin, John, Lot, Roger*), b. 26 Feb., 1825, in Silver Lake, Susquehanna co., Pa.; moved to Lockport, N. Y., with his parents, and in 1847 he removed to Horicon, Wis. In 1851 he went to Chicago, Ill., and was employed by the Galena & Chicago Union R. R., as conductor. He was afterwards captain of a steamer running between Fulton, Ill., and Clinton, Iowa, in which employment he continued four years. In 1861 he engaged in the milling business, in Clinton, Iowa, and in 1867 built the Farmers' Mill on First street. Upon its completion Messrs. Buck and Bishop were taken in by him as partners, and the mill was operated by the firm of E. Conant & Co. till 1878, when Mr. Conant retired from business. He served as alderman of Clinton five years, as poor director two years and as street commissioner. " The deceased has been noted for years as one of the most industrious, hard working men in the city. His memory will ever be revered as an honest, kindhearted man, always willing to extend a helping hand to the destitute or afflicted, and at all times ready to assist in the upbuilding of his adopted city" (Obituary in Clinton Daily News). He d. 28 Dec., 1885. He m. 22 Apr., 1845, in Lockport, N. Y., Elizabeth Harriet, dr. of Philemon and Eunice (Anderson) Webb, b. ———.

Children of EDWARD and ELIZABETH H. (WEBB) CONANT:—

Achsah Lodema, b. 26 Apr., d. 28 Aug., 1847.
Edna Lodema, b. ———, in Horicon, Wis.; m. (1) 14 Apr., 1870, John H. Tierney, and had Edna May, b. 1 May, 1872. They were divorced 1877, and she m. (2) 3 May, 1881, George E. Correll. Child: George E., b. 25 Sep., 1882, d. 17 July, 1884.

Adopted child of EDWARD CONANT:—

Edward Webster, b. 25 Oct., 1861; was adopted Feb., 1863, and bears the name Edward Conant.

660. **Ellen Hunt**[8] (*Dean, Clark, Ezra, Benjamin, John, Lot, Roger*), b. 20 Sep., 1826, in Charlestown, N. H.; m. 23 Aug., 1843, Dr. E. C. Worcester, of Thetford, Vt., where they reside.

Children of E. C. and ELLEN H. (CONANT) WORCESTER:—

i.   William Leonard, b. 21 Apr., 1845.
ii.   Catherine Ellen, b. 23 Nov., 1847.
iii. George Steele, b. 24 Sep., 1849.
iv.   Alice Elizabeth, b. 5 June, 1856.
v.   Jane Shedd, b. 13 Apr., 1858.
vi.   Henry Everts, b. 15 Nov., 1859.
vii. Dean Conant, b. 1 Oct., 1866.
viii. Eleanor Bonney, b. 7 Feb., 1869.

661. **Horace Mann**[8] (*Harvey, Benjamin, Benjamin, Benjamin, John, Lot, Roger*), b. 13 Jan., 1850, in Warwick,

Mass. He removed to Winchester, N. H., where he now lives; a farmer. He m. in Winchendon, 8 Oct., 1873, Abbie Ann, dr. of Robert W. and Ruby (Moody) Pratt, b. in Winchester, N. H., 23 May, 1851. *died Nov. 5, 1889. She d. Sept. 1891*

Children of HORACE M. and ABBIE A. (PRATT) CONANT:—

Effie Winfred, b. 3 Apr., 1874, in Warwick. *m. Bert E. Hawkes*
Harvey Clifford, b. 20 June, 1878, in Keene, N. H.
Margie Blanche, b. 12 June, 1880, " " "
Ruby Florence, b. 12 Oct., 1881, in Winchester. *Mr. Glum*
Robert Pratt, b. 1 May, 1883.

662. William[8] (*Israel Elliot, Jonathan, Jonathan, Jonathan, Lot, Lot, Roger*), b. 25 Nov., 1816, in New Haven, Vt. He removed to Canton, St. Lawrence co., N. Y.; was a farmer. He d. 2 Jan., 1862. He m. Eliza Kelly, who d. 6 Jan., 1862.

Children of WILLIAM and ELIZA (KELLY) CONANT:—

807. Edson Alvinza, b. 7 Feb., 1848, in Canton, N. Y.
Mary E., b. 12 Sep., 1851; m. Luman Bailey, of Canton, and has two children.

663. William Henry[8] (*William, Jonathan, Jonathan, Jonathan, Lot, Lot, Roger*), b. 5 June, 1829, in Mt. Vernon, N. H. He is a prominent citizen of Mt. Vernon; is a deacon of the Congregational church. He m. Sarah Emeline Cloutman.

Children of WILLIAM H. and SARAH E. (CLOUTMAN) CONANT:—

Ellen Frances, b. 18 Dec., 1857.
Ada Emeline, b. 6 Sep., 1859; m. 17 Jan., 1884, Francis C., son of Dexter Greenwood. He is of New York city.
Willie, d. 3 May, 1861, aged 4 mo.
Cecil Franklin, d. 18 Apr., 1873, aged 10 years.
Mary Grace, b. 23 Mch., 1865.
Albert Forness, b. 6 May, 1869.
Freddie, d. 16 Aug., 1873, aged 8 mo.
Ruth Stevens, b. 26 Nov., 1876.

664. Albert[8] (*William, Jonathan, Jonathan, Jonathan, Lot, Lot, Roger*), b. 19 Oct., 1830, in Mt. Vernon, N. H. He resides in Charlestown, Mass.; is a dealer in looking glasses and mirror plates. He m. (1) Eliza Ann Beard; m. (2) Susan

Frances Bancroft, who d. 30 Jan., 1885, in Charlestown, Mass., aged 49.

Children of ALBERT and ELIZA A. (BEARD) CONANT:—

Isabel Eliza, b. 23 May, 1859.
Carrie Frances, b. 22, d. 27 Dec., 1860.

Children of ALBERT and SUSAN F. (BANCROFT) CONANT:—

Alice Bancroft, b. 19 Oct., 1868, in Charlestown, Mass.
Annie Sanborne, b. 10 Feb., 1871.
Harry Winthrop, b. 5 Feb., 1875.
John Bancroft, b. 17 Apr., 1878.

665. Charles Edwin[8] (*William, Jonathan, Jonathan, Jonathan, Lot, Lot, Roger*), b. 30 June, 1833, in Mt. Vernon, N. H. He lives in Winchester, Mass.; is in business with his brothers, Albert and Harlan P., in Boston. He m. Marion Crawford Wallace.

Children of CHARLES E. and MARION C. (WALLACE) CO-NANT:—

Charles Arthur, b. 3 July, 1861; is a reporter for the Boston Daily Advertiser.
Grace Wallace, b. 4 Sep., 1864.

666. Walter Scott[8] (*William, Jonathan, Jonathan, Jonathan, Lot, Lot, Roger*), b. 8 June, 1834, in Mt. Vernon, N. H. He resides in Jersey City, N. J., and is a manufacturer of wood, plush and leather boxes, and writing desks. He m. Mary Larkin Lewis.

Children of WALTER S. and MARY L. (LEWIS) CONANT:—

Mabel Frances, b. 1 June, 1867, in Charlestown, Mass.
Roger Lewis, b. 1 Apr., 1873, in Jersey City, N. J.

667. Harlan Page[8] (*William, Jonathan, Jonathan, Jonathan, Lot, Lot, Roger*), b. 3 Mch., 1837, in Mt. Vernon, N. H. He resides in Somerville, Mass.; is in business with his brothers, Albert and Charles E., in Boston. He m. 16 Feb., 1864, Sarah P. Chase, b. 31 Mch., 1835.

Children of HARLAN P. and SARAH P. (CHASE) CONANT:—

Bertha Adams, b. 3 Feb., 1867, in Charlestown.
William Chase, b. 4 Oct., 1868, "   "
Helen Pearson, b. 11 Nov., 1870, "   "
Sarah Florence, b. 14 Aug., 1876, in Somerville.

668. William Henry[8] (*Thomas, Joseph, Bartholomew, Joseph, Lot, Lot, Roger*), b. 7 Sep., 1855, in Wayne, Me. He is a manufacturer of stoves and tin ware, of Augusta, Me. He m. in Wayne, 9 June, 1882, Kate, dr. of Laughlin and Effie McKinnon, b. 3 Sep., 1861, in New Canada, N. S.

Child of WILLIAM H. and KATE (McKINNON) CONANT:—

Thomas Hoyt, b. 22 July, 1883.

669. George[8] (*George, Bartholomew, Joseph, Joseph, Lot, Lot, Roger*), b. 29 Oct., 1828, in Portland, Me. He removed to Minneapolis, Minn., where he d. 1885. He was a merchant. He m. 1 Mch., 1855, in Portland, Mary E. A. Gray.

Children of GEORGE and MARY E. A. (GRAY) CONANT:—

Arthur Gray, b. 26 Apr., 1859.
Roger, b. ———.
Edward.

670. Washington[8] (*George, Bartholomew, Joseph, Joseph, Lot, Lot, Roger*), b. 22 Feb., 1832, in Portland, Me. He lived in Portland; was a soldier in the war of the Rebellion. He m. 29 Aug., 1854, Celia Verrill, who m. (2) 16 Oct., 1873, Eugene C. Tyler.

Children of WASHINGTON and CELIA (VERRILL) CONANT:—

Walter A., b. 29 Oct., 1859; d. 15 Jan., 1863.
Louis Abbott, b. 3 July, 1862; m. 5 Sep. 1883, Flora Lunt, of Falmouth; has George and Agnes. He lives in Portland, Me.

671. Mark P.[8] (*Oliver, Thomas, Joseph, Joseph, Lot, Lot, Roger*), b. 9 Oct., 1824, in Topsham, Me., where he d. 13 Mch., 1860. He m. Martha A. Harmon.

Children of MARK P. and MARTHA A. (HARMON) CONANT:—

William Curtis, of Brunswick, Me.
Charles Bean, of Mechanic Falls, Me.
Albertina.
Mary C.

672. Samuel Fields[8] (*Oliver, Thomas, Joseph, Joseph, Lot, Lot, Roger*), b. 5 Oct., 1827, in Topsham, Me. He is a photographer, of Skowhegan, Me., and inventor of a vapor bath which he manufactures. He m. Nov., 1853, in Vienna, Me., Ann Jane, dr. of James and Nancy (Ladd) Gilman.

Children of SAMUEL F. and ANN J. (GILMAN) CONANT:—

Abbie Ella.
Fred Lewis.

673.   James McKeen[8] (*Oliver, Thomas, Joseph, Joseph, Lot, Lot, Roger*), b. 25 Feb., 1829, in Topsham, Me.   He resides in Mattapan, Mass.; is a baker, of Boston.   He m. in Newburyport, Mass., 14 Nov., 1851, Mary Elizabeth, dr. of David and Athelia (Foote) Smilie, b. in Brunswick, Me., 14 Feb., 1832.

Children of JAMES McK. and MARY E. (SMILIE) CONANT:—

Edgar Sumner, b. 7 Nov., 1852, in Newburyport, Mass.
Ada Mabel, b. 10 Jan., 1859, in Charlestown, Mass.
William Everett, b. 6 Jan., 1869, in Skowhegan, Me.

674.   Francis A.[8] (*Oliver, Thomas, Joseph, Joseph, Lot, Lot, Roger*), b. 7 Apr., 1837, in Topsham, Me.   He is an insurance agent, of Lewiston, Me.   He served during the war in Co. A, 23rd Me. Regt.; was mustered in Sep. 29, 1862 (see Maine Adjutant General's Report, 1862).

Children of FRANCIS A. and ——— (———) CONANT:—

Edgar F., b. 26 Jan., 1867.
Alice B., b. 18 Feb., 1878.

675.   Charles Bean[8] (*Oliver, Thomas, Joseph, Joseph, Lot, Lot, Roger*), b. 15 Oct., 1839, in Topsham, Me.   He is a photographer.   He m. 5 Mch., 1862, Eleanor Frazier McIntosh.

Children of CHARLES B. and ELEANOR F. (McINTOSH) CONANT:—

Charles Milton, b. 14 Dec., 1866.
Harry Weston, b. 12 July, 1869; of Portland, Me.
Grace Lilian, b. 27 Jan., 1872.
Francis Elmer, b. 16 Nov., 1878.
Louise Foster, b. 27 Jan., 1881.

676.   William Thomas[8] (*Daniel, Thomas, Joseph, Joseph, Lot, Lot, Roger*), b. 7 May, 1834, in Topsham, Me.   He was for some years a surveyor of lumber, in Philadelphia, Pa., and afterwards an insurance agent.   He now resides in Boston, Mass.   He m. (1) in Lewiston, Me., Oct., 1873, Minnie B., dr. of William D. and Sarah Reed, of Newfield, Me., widow of Royal B. Snell; she d. 10 June, 1876. He m. (2) in Lawrence, Mass., 18 Aug., 1881, Jennie K. D., dr. of John and Martha Ann Dunse or Dunn; she was b. 23 July, 1854, in Bothwell parish, Lanarkshire, Scotland.

Child of WILLIAM T. and MINNIE B. (REED) CONANT:—

Florence Jane, b. Dec., 1875, in Poland, Me.; d. Aug., 1876.

Children of WILLIAM T. and JENNIE K. D. (DUNN) CONANT:—

Joseph Knapp, b. 4 July, 1882, in Somerville, Mass.
William E., b. 19 Mch., 1886, in Boston, Mass.

677. **Alfred Perkins**[8] (*Daniel, Thomas, Joseph, Joseph, Lot, Lot, Roger*), b. 3 Feb., 1836, in Topsham, Me.; removed to Lewiston, with his parents. He is a grocer, of Lewiston, Me. He m. in Lewiston, 20 Oct., 1861, Hannah Jane, dr. of Cyrus and Sarah (Allen) Smith, b. in Plymouth, 21 June, 1835.

Child of ALFRED P. and HANNAH J. (SMITH) CONANT:—

Helen Alfreda, b. 21 Feb., 1863.

678. **Annie**[8] (*William Heath, Nathaniel, Joshua, Joshua, Lot, Lot, Roger*), b. 22 Mch., 1837, in Londonderry, N. H.; m. in Londonderry, 2 May, 1861, Lemuel Foster Morse, of Roxbury, Mass. He is an auctioneer and real estate agent.

Children of L. FOSTER and ANNIE (CONANT) MORSE:—

i.   Grace Eliza, b. 21 Feb., 1863.
ii. Annie Conant, b. 4 Sep., 1869.
iii. Gertrude Frances, b. 16 Jan., 1872; d. 14 Jan., 1874.

679. **Antoinette Rebecca**[8] (*William Heath, Nathaniel, Joshua, Joshua, Lot, Lot, Roger*), b. Dec., 1838, in Londonderry, N. H.; d. 9 Sep., 1880. She m. (1) 11 Nov., 1854, Edward Payson Moore, of Londonderry. He was a soldier in the 4th N. H. Regt., and d. 15 Aug., 1864, in Beverly, N. J., from wounds received in battle. She m. (2) Edward Brown.

Children of EDWARD P. and ANTOINETTE R. (CONANT) MOORE:—

i.   Lina Antoinette, b. 17 June, 1858; d. Sep., 1864.
ii. Carrie A., b. 6 Dec., 1860; m. Thomas Riley.
iii. Lyman Edward, b. 14 Mch., 1862.

Children of EDWARD and ANTOINETTE R. (CONANT)
BROWN:—

iv.   Eva.
v.   Edward.

680. Lyman Augustus[8] (*William Heath,* *Nathaniel,*
Joshua, Joshua, Lot, Lot, Roger), b. 1 May, 1840, in Lowell,
Mass. He was in business in Tilton, N. H., and Manchester,
Iowa, but is now a coal dealer, of Needham, Mass. He m. (1)
15 June, 1865, in Haverhill, Mass., Mary Ann, dr. of Josiah P.
Brown, b. 19 Aug., 1841, in Wentworth, N. H.; she d. 29
Mch., 1870, in Tilton, N. H. He m. (2) in Canterbury, N. H.,
8 Nov., 1876, Mary Sargent.
    Children of LYMAN A. and MARY A. (BROWN) CONANT:—

Maud Webster, b. 30 June, 1866, in Haverhill.
Vance Darwood, b. 23 Feb., 1869, in Tilton, N. H.

    Child of LYMAN A. and MARY (SARGENT) CONANT:—
Samuel.

681. Charles Edwin[8] (*William Heath, Nathaniel, Joshua,*
Joshua, Lot, Lot, Roger), b. 25 Nov., 1843, in Londonderry,
N. H. He was a soldier in Co. F. 8th N. H. Regt., during the
war, and was wounded at Port Hudson. He was mustered in
20 Dec., 1861, for three years' service; promoted to corporal
14 Jan., 1863; wounded 14 June, 1863; discharged on account
of wounds 11 Apr., 1864 (see N. H. Adj. Gen.'s Report, 1866,
p. 290). He is now a shoe manufacturer, of Ayer's Village,
Mass. He m. 21 Oct., 1866, Georgiana F. Spinney.
    Children of CHARLES E. and GEORGIANA F. (SPINNEY)
CONANT:—

A child, b. 3 Jan., 1872; d. same day.
Forrest Edwin, b. 20 Feb., 1882, in Ayer's Village, Mass.; d.
    17 Aug., 1883.

682. Sarah Ann[8] (*William Heath, Nathaniel, Joshua,*
Joshua, Lot, Lot, Roger), b. 24 Aug., 1848, in Londonderry,
N. H. She m. in Manchester, N. H., 5 July, 1865, Benjamin
L. Willey, of Londonderry. He d. 19 Sep., 1871. She is liv-
ing in Roxbury, Mass.

Children of BENJAMIN L. and SARAH A. (CONANT) WIL-LEY:—

i.   Edith Augusta, b. 29 July, 1867.
ii. Julia Conant, b. 5 Apr., 1869.

683.   Ruel K.[8] (*Joshua, Joshua, Joshua, Joshua, Lot, Lot, Roger*), b. 2 Sep., 1825, in (Londonderry?) N. H.   He settled in Springfield, Mass., in 1848, where he now resides.   He is a passenger conductor on the railroad between Springfield and New Haven, Conn.   He m. 6 Oct., 1851, Julia A., dr. of Levi Curtis.

Children of RUEL K. and JULIA A. (CURTIS) CONANT:—

Ella R.
George W.
Mary L.

684.   Nathaniel Putnam[8] (*Nathaniel, Joshua, Joshua, Joshua, Lot, Lot, Roger*), b. 13 Apr., 1829, in Charlotte, Me. He enlisted in 1862, in Co. H, 14th Mass. Vols., and served nine months as corporal.   In 1865 served again in the 14th Me. Regt.   He is now a farmer and lumberman, of Meddybemps, Me.   He m. in Meddybemps, 29 Mch., 1861, Mary Ellen, dr. of Capt. John and Mary Elizabeth (Prescott) Bridge, b. 2 May, 1835.

Children of NATHANIEL P. and MARY E. (BRIDGE) CO-NANT:—

Angelina Ellen, b. 21 Aug., 1862.
Clarence Fuller, b. 19 Jan., 1865.
Florence Capitola, b. 28 July, 1868.
Frank Grey, b. 3 May, 1871.
Mary Lulu, b. 15 Oct., 1874; d. y.
Burt Clare, b. 23 Aug., 1877.

685.   Roxanna[8] (*William, Joshua, Joshua, Joshua, Lot, Lot, Roger*), b. 21 Mch., 1841, in Plymouth, Me.; moved to Lewiston, Me., where she m. 17 Oct., 1860, Jackson Davis.

Children of JACKSON and ROXANNA (CONANT) DAVIS:—

i.   William Ernest, b. 17 July, 1863.
ii.   Laminda Ella, b. 5 Mch., 1865.
iii. Charles Coolidge, b. 18 Aug., 1867.
iv.   Ernest Lincoln, b. 20 Dec., 1872.

v. Walter Irvin, b. 29 Nov., 1875; d. aged 1 year.
vi. Alice Gertrude, b. 13 Aug., 1877.

686. Joshua Randall[8] (*William, Joshua, Joshua, Joshua, Lot, Lot, Roger*), b. 27 Nov., 1843, in Plymouth, Me. He removed to Carmel, Me., and thence to Colorado, where he d. 15 Dec., 1879. He m. Eunice, dr. of George and Clarissa Maloon, of Detroit, Me., who d. in Carmel, 23 Aug., 1878.

Children of JOSHUA R. and EUNICE (MALOON) CONANT:—

Addie Florence, b. 1866, in Carmel; an adopted daughter.
Clara Alice, b. 3 May, 1868, in Carmel.
Maud Eunice, b. 25 Mch., 1874, in Carmel.

687. Alphonso Bence[8] (*William, Joshua, Joshua, Joshua, Lot, Lot, Roger*), b. 8 Aug., 1854, in Plymouth, Me., where he lives. He m. in Carmel, 17 Apr., 1879, Ella J., dr. of Thompson and Abby (Whiley) Eldridge, b. 20 Dec., 1858, in Etna, Me.

Children of ALPHONSO B. and ELLA J. (ELDRIDGE) CONANT:—

William Alphonso, b. 12 Dec., 1879, in Plymouth.
Viola E., b. 18 Oct., 1881, in Plymouth.
Edith E., b. 17 July, 1884; d. 13 June, 1885.

688. Marcus[8] (*Martin, Elias, David, David, William, Lot, Roger*), b. 12 Sep., 1806, in Lyme, N. H. He was a wheelwright; removed from Lyme to Bridgewater, Mass., where he now (1885) lives. He m. 17 May, 1835, Hannah Keith, dr. of Hosea and Hannah (Keith) Leach, b. in Rochester, Mass., 29 Jan., 1813.

Children of MARCUS and HANNAH K. (LEACH) CONANT:—

Phebe, b. 21 Sep., 1836, in Bridgewater; m. 29 Apr., 1860, James Cushing, son of Alpheus Leach, b. 11 June, 1831. He is a wealthy and prominent citizen of Bridgewater. Children: 1. Harriet Allen, b. 5 Jan., d. 7 Aug., 1863; 2. Jason, b. 25 July, d. 26 Aug., 1865; 3. Albert Marcus, b. 18 Nov., 1871, d. 24 Aug., 1872.
Joanna Maria, b. 25 Apr., 1840; m. Alfred Hall, of Raynham, Mass.

689. Martin Allen[8] (*Martin, Elias, David, David, William, Lot, Roger*), b. 21 Oct., 1815, in Lyme, N. H. He removed to Natick, Mass.; a shoemaker. He m. in Natick, 28 Nov., 1847, Maria Antoinette, dr. of Daniel R. and Nancy (Baker) Mills, of Wayland, b. 27 Aug., 1826.

Children of MARTIN ALLEN and MARIA A. (MILLS)· CONANT:—

808. Herbert Eugene, b. 1 Aug., 1848, in Natick.
  Ella Josephine, b. 22 Jan., 1851, " "
  Lucy M. A., b. 2 May, 1855, " "
  Martin, b. 13 Mch., 1858,   " "
  Harrison Bowman, b. 15 Aug., 1862, " "
  Ida Rosabelle, b. 6 May, 1868, " "
  Florence Matella, b. 28 May, 1870.

690. **William Henry**[8] (*Martin, Elias, David, David, William, Lot, Roger*), b. 7 Mch., 1828, in Lyme, N. H., where he now lives; a farmer. He m. in Lyme, 7 June, 1877, Rhoda J., dr. of John F. Clough, of Canaan, N. H.; she d. 29 Oct., 1880, aged 29.

Child of WILLIAM H. and RHODA J. (CLOUGH) CONANT:—

  Lucy Martin, b. 6 Sep., 1879, in Lyme.

691. **Leonard**[8] (*Leonard, Rufus, David, David, William, Lot, Roger*), b. 7 Apr., 1826, in Lyme, N. H. He now lives in Tilton, N. H.; is a builder and contractor. He enlisted in Co. D, 12th N. H. Regt., 5 Sep., 1862, and was mustered out 18 June, 1865. He m. 8 Feb., 1848, in Manchester, N. H., Dorothy A. Jacobs.

Children of LEONARD and DOROTHY A. (JACOBS) CONANT:—

  Charles L., b. 30 Dec., 1849, in Lowell, Mass.
  Clara A., b. 8 Sep., 1851, in Concord, N. H.
  Cassandra H., b. 23 Sep., 1853, in Tilton, N. H.
  Cyrus A., b. 2 Apr., 1855, " " "
  Clinton R., b. 3 Mch., 1858, " " "

692. **Bela Forbes**[8] (*David, David, David, David, William, Lot, Roger*), b. 22 Sep., 1822, in Lyme, N. H.; removed to Laconia, N. H. He was a cabinet maker. He d. 5 May, 1882. He m. 17 Oct., 1842, Mary Ann, dr. of Joseph and Nancy (Cook) Ham, b. in Dorchester, N. H., 14 Mch., 1826.

Children of BELA F. and MARY A. (HAM) CONANT:—

31

Henry Adams, b. 29 May, 1846; m. Feb., 1869, in Laconia,
Sabra Foster Ford, and lives in Concord, N. H.
Mary Jane, b. 8 Nov., 1852.
809.   David Perkins, b. 19 Mch., 1854.
. Ella Estella, b. ————.
George Adams.
John Adams, b. 9 June, 1863.
Laura May.

693. Jonathan Josiah[8] (*Jonathan, Josiah, Jonathan, David, William, Lot, Roger*), b. 6 June, 1823, in Lyme, N. H.
He is now a farmer, of North Thetford, Vt.   He m. (1) Octavia Howard, who d. 1 Apr., 1853; m. (2) Martha P. Howard.
Children of JONATHAN J. and OCTAVIA (HOWARD) CONANT:—

810.   Samuel Dimick, b. 9 Jan., 1850.
Octavia, b. 17 Mch., 1853; m. ———— Jones, of Hastings, Neb.

Children of JONATHAN J. and MARTHA P. (HOWARD) CONANT:—

Sarah Howard, b. 18 Feb., 1864.
David Sloan, b. 7 Dec., 1865.
Mary Chilton, b. 5 July, 1873.

694. David Sloan[8] (*Jonathan, Josiah, Jonathan, David, William, Lot, Roger*), b. 21 Jan., 1825, in Lyme, N. H.   He graduated from the Medical Department of Bowdoin College, 1851, and became professor of anatomy and physiology there in 1857.   In 1863 he was made professor of surgery in the New York Medical College.   He d. from blood poisoning, 8 Oct., 1865.
Children of DAVID S. and ———— (————) CONANT:—

Granville S., d. y.
Lucy Larrabee, b. 1864; is living in Brunswick, Me.

695. Chester Cook[8] (*Jonathan, Josiah, Jonathan, David, William, Lot, Roger*), b. 4 Sep., 1831, in Lyme, N. H.   He graduated at Dartmouth College, 1857, studied law, and now resides in Greenfield, Mass.   He has been Judge of Probate and Insolvency for Franklin county since 1870.   He m. in Portland, Me., 14 June, 1860, Sarah B., dr. of Rev. Roger S. Howard, D. D.

Children of CHESTER C. and SARAH B. (HOWARD) CONANT:—

Charlotte Howard, b. 3 Feb., 1862; she graduated from Wellesley College, 1884.
Martha Pike, b. 25 Nov., 1868.

696. Claudius Buchanan[8] (*Samuel Stillman, John, Ebenezer, Ebenezer, Roger, Lot, Roger*), b. 8 May, 1819, in New York, N. Y. He was a merchant, of New York, and d. in Madison, N. Y., 7 Nov., 1877. He m. in New York, 28 Oct., 1836, Eliza Ann Ayers.

Children of CLAUDIUS B. and ELIZA A. (AYERS) CONANT:—

Elizabeth Anne, b. 26 July, 1837, in New York.
Thomas Nelson, b. 25 Dec., 1839, in Andover, Ill.
Claudius William, b. 16 Feb., 1842, in New York; of Chicago, Illinois.
Eveline, b. 1 Jan., 1843.
Emily Ida, b. 17 Feb., 1845, in New York.
Sarah Payson, b. 28 Nov., 1846, in Williamsburg, N. Y.
Clarence Mortimer, d. in infancy.
811. Clarence Mortimer, b. 26 Mch., 1851, in Brooklyn, N. Y.
Samuel Mills, b. 28 Aug., 1858, at Lake George, N. Y.
Charles Edward, b. 22 July, 1861, at Lake George, N. Y.

697. William Cooper[8] (*Samuel Stillman, John, Ebenezer, Ebenezer, Roger, Lot, Roger*), b. 7 Oct., 1825, in New York, N. Y. His residence is Montclair, N. J. He is a frequent contributor to magazines, on literary and religious subjects, and the publisher of "*The Sanitary Era.*" He has published, among other works, "*Narratives of Remarkable Conversions; an Account of the Great Awakening*, 1857-8" (New York, 1858), and an account of the building of the Brooklyn Bridge. He m. in Brandon, Vt., 3 Feb., 1851, Marion, dr. of David Warren.

Child of WILLIAM C. and MARION (WARREN) CONANT:—

Robert Warren, b. 28 July, 1852, in Brooklyn, N. Y. He is a physician, of Chicago, Ill. He m. in Chicago, Mary L. Holmes, 2 Nov., 1882. (He graduated at Yale College, 1873?)

698. Samuel Stillman[8] (*Thomas Jefferson, John, Ebenezer, Ebenezer, Roger, Lot, Roger*), b. 11 Dec., 1831, in Waterville, Me.; removed to Brooklyn, N. Y., with his parents. He received a liberal education in this country, graduating at

Hamilton College, and afterwards studying in Germany and France. On his return from Europe, in 1862, he was given a position as reporter for the New York *Times;* in course of time he became night editor, and later on, managing editor, under Henry J. Raymond, by whom he was highly esteemed. After the death of Mr. Raymond, he became business editor of Harper's Weekly, a position he held till Jan., 1885, when he disappeared mysteriously and has never been heard from since. He was an occasional writer of verses, and the author of "*The Biography of Henry J. Raymond,*" published in 1871. He m. Helen Stevens. She has contributed poetry and many short sketches to periodical literature, and has published "*The Butterfly Hunters*" (Boston, 1868). She has recently been acting as editor of Harper's Bazar.

Child of SAMUEL S. and HELEN (STEVENS) CONANT :—

Thomas Peters, of Brooklyn, N. Y.

699. **Thomas Oakes**[8] (*Thomas Jefferson, John, Ebenezer, Ebenezer, Roger, Lot, Roger*), b. 15 Oct., 1838. He resides in Orange, N. J., and is employed in the U. S. Assay Office, in New York. He m. Martha Willson.

Children of THOMAS O. and MARTHA (WILLSON) CONANT :—

Henry D.
Susia.
Isabel.

700. **Neray**[8] (*Augustus Hammond, Eben, Ebenezer, Ebenezer, Roger, Lot, Roger*), b. 2 Dec., 1837, in Cook co., Ill. He is a dairyman, of Rockford, Ill. He was a soldier in the war of the Rebellion. He m. in Geneva, Ill., 16 June, 1870, Melissa W. Rich.

Children of NERAY and MELISSA W. (RICH) CONANT :—

Frank Augustus, b. 18 Mch., 1871.
Arthur Turchin, b. 27 Jan., 1873.
Anna Bell, b. 5 Sep., 1875.
Bert Neray, b. 26 June, 1876.

701. **Charles F.**[8] (*Charles Rich, Calvin, Ebenezer, Ebenezer, Roger, Lot, Roger*), b. 20 Jan., 1842, in the province of Chihuahua, Mexico. He is manager and part owner of the

Julianna Silver Mine, at Santa Jesus Maria, Chihuahua, Mexico. He has been twice married.

Children of CHARLES F. and SUSAN (———) CONANT:—

Charlotta.
Malinda.
Susan.

702. **Mary Melinda**[8] (*Charles Rich, Calvin, Ebenezer, Ebenezer, Roger, Lot, Roger*), b. in Guyamas, Sonora, Mexico, 12 Oct., 1847. She m. in Alamos, Sonora, Mexico, 25 July, 1868, Frederic, son of Philip and Mary (Messing) Planque, b. 2 Nov., 1843, in Cold Spring, Putnam co., N. Y. He is a physician, of San Francisco, Cal., where they reside.

Children of FREDERIC and MARY M. (CONANT) PLANQUE:—

i.   Amelia Augusta, b. 28 Aug., 1870, in Alamos, Mexico.
ii.   Frederic Philip, b. 28 Feb., 1876,   "   "   "
iii. Melinda Adela, b. 8 Aug., 1877,   "   "   "
iv.   William Charles, b. 7 Feb., 1881, " Bancari,   "
v.   Francis James, b. 21 Oct., 1884, in San Francisco, Cal.
vi.   Charles Richard, b. 22 June, 1886,   "   "   "

703. **Luther**[8] (*William, Luther, Ebenezer, Ebenezer, Roger, Lot, Roger*), b. 29 May, 1844, in Brandon, Vt. He removed to Geneva, Ill., with his parents, thence to Oak Park, Ill. He is secretary of the Subscription News Company, of which his father is president, doing business in Chicago. He m. ———, Emilia Cole.

Child of LUTHER and EMILIA (COLE) CONANT:—

William, b. 9 Oct., 1870, in Geneva, Ill.

704. **Charles Francis**[8] (*Benjamin Israel, John, Israel, Israel, Roger, Lot, Roger*), b. 22 Apr., 1835, in Milford, N. H. He acquired his education in the public schools and Milford Academy. He then entered his father's store, as clerk and book-keeper, and later succeeded him in business, but continued in it only a short time. Upon the first call for volunteers at the breaking out of the Rebellion, he enlisted and aided in raising a company. After his term of three months expired he helped raise a company for three years' service, but owing to severe illness was obliged to remain at home. In

1863 he was appointed to a clerkship in the office of the Secretary of War, which he retained till the closing of the war, in 1865, when he was offered, and accepted, a position in the Treasury Department. After several promotions he was appointed, Apr. 30, 1870, chief of the Division of Estimates, Warrants and Appropriations. In this position he had charge of the preparation and publication of the monthly "Debt Statement of the United States," a sheet familiar to all bankers and newspaper writers on financial matters. He also prepared the "Book of Estimates," of one of which Hon. Wm. A. Richardson, Secretary of the Treasury, said in his report to Congress, Dec. 1, 1873: "The Book of Estimates, now ready to be laid before Congress, thoroughly prepared under the immediate supervision of Mr. C. F. Conant, Chief of the Warrant Division of the Secretary's Office, whose watchful care, industry and judgment have made it a work of great accuracy, will prove to be of the utmost convenience to committees and members." On July 1, 1874, he was appointed, by President Grant, Assistant Secretary of the Treasury, and is, with perhaps a single exception, the only person who has risen from the lowest grade of clerkship to the second position in the Treasury Department. He continued in this position, at times acting as Secretary, until March, 1877, when he was appointed by Secretary Sherman funding agent of the Treasury Department, and directed to assume the general management and supervision of all business in London, England, arising from the refunding of the National debt. In this responsible and trying position he was very successful, and remained in charge of the London agency till Nov., 1879, when the refunding operations were completed. His correspondence with the Secretary during this period was transmitted to the House of Representatives, and published in a volume entitled, " *Specie Resumption and Refunding of the National Debt* " (Washington, 1880). On his return to the United States, Mr. Conant retired to private life, and took up his residence in Cambridge, Mass., seeking needed rest and relief from the cares of official position. He prepared a number of articles on financial matters, which were widely published, among

them a series of articles on the First National Bank, or Bank of North America, chartered by Congress in 1781, which appeared in "*The Republic*," of New York. In religious matters he was allied with the Episcopal church, and was a vestryman of St. James Parish, Cambridge, and several times served as delegate to the Diocesan Convention. He was a past master of Benevolent Lodge, A. F. and A. Masons, of Milford, N. H., a member of Meriden R. A. Chapter, of Nashua, N. H., and of Columbia Commandery, Washington, D. C., and an honorary member of the London (England) Statistical Society. Mr. Conant was widely and favorably known among public men, and was a personal friend of President Garfield. Had he chosen to continue in public life he could undoubtedly have secured an honorable and lucrative position. His courtesy and kindness to his subordinates were proverbial, though he could say "no" when occasion required. He had a happy faculty of making friends and retaining them. He was deeply interested in genealogical subjects, and a member of the New England Historic Genealogical Society. His kindly advice and assistance have been a great help to the compiler in the preparation of this Genealogy. He d. in Cambridge, 26 July, 1886, and was buried in Milford, N. H. He m. 19 Jan., 1860, Harriet Lincoln Shaw, of Canton, Mass., b. in Milford, N. H., 2 Dec., 1836.

Children of CHARLES F. and HARRIET L. (SHAW) CONANT:—

Clara Louisa, b. 2 July, 1868, in Canton, Mass.
Charles Edward, b. 7 Aug., 1872, in Washington, D. C.
Arthur Straiton, b. 1 Aug., 1879, in Brighton, England.

705. John Addison[8] (*Addison Lorenzo, Josiah, Josiah, Josiah, Roger, Lot, Roger*), b. 22 Nov., 1846, in Cincinnati, Ohio. Settled in Madisonville, O. He is an accountant, employed by the C., W. & B. Railroad. He m. in Madisonville, O., 14 Aug., 1872, Clara Frances, dr. of Leonidas and Amanda (Ward) Bailey, b. 4 Mch., 1855, in Madisonville.

Children of JOHN A. and CLARA F. (BAILEY) CONANT:—

Raymond Gilmore, b. 28 May, 1876, in Madisonville.
Frank Marvin, b. 7 Jan., 1882, in Madisonville.

706. **Oliver B.**[8] (*John, Samuel, John, John, Joshua, Joshua, Roger*), b. ———, in Provincetown, Mass. He m. ———, Bertha N. Atkins.

Children of OLIVER B. and BERTHA N. (ATKINS) CONANT:—

> George, who now lives in New Bedford, Mass.
> Eliza, living in Boston.
> Arthur, who lives in Newark, N. J.

707. **William E.**[8] (*Erasmus Darwin, Seth, Seth, Malachi, Caleb, Exercise, Roger*), b. 9 Nov., 1828. He resides in Brooklyn, N. Y. He m. 16 Oct., 1865, Euphemia Spence.

Children of WILLIAM E. and EUPHEMIA (SPENCE) CONANT:—

> Lilly, b. 1866; d. 6 Nov., 1874.
> George M., b. 1869; d. 9 Nov., 1874.
> Effie, b. Oct., 1877.
> Stella, b. Sep., 1881.

708. **Charles F.**[8] (*Erasmus Darwin, Seth, Seth, Malachi, Caleb, Exercise, Roger*), b. 3 Nov., 1835. He resides in Westfield, N. J.; is an agent for James Pyle & Son, of New York. He m. 11 Jan., 1857, Delia Morse.

Child of CHARLES F. and DELIA (MORSE) CONANT:—

> Foster E., b. 22 Oct., 1857.

709. **George H.**[8] (*Erasmus Darwin, Seth, Seth, Malachi, Caleb, Exercise, Roger*), b. 11 Dec., 1840. He resides in Brooklyn, N. Y.; is agent for the sale of Jesse Oakley & Co.'s soaps in New York city. He m. (1) 26 Sep., 1864, Sarah A. Washburn, who d. 6 Apr., 1878; m. (2) 16 Oct., 1879, Lillie J. Smith.

Child of GEORGE H. and SARAH A. (WASHBURN) CONANT:—

> Charles H., b. 19 June, 1867.

710. **Delos Wright**[8] (*Theodore Delos, Chester, Sylvanus, Malachi, Caleb, Exercise, Roger*), b. 14 Jan., 1843, in Mansfield, Conn. He m. 8 Oct., 1866, Evelina L. Bicknell, of Madison, N. Y.

Child of DELOS W. and EVELINA L. (BICKNELL) CONANT:—

> Emily.

711. **Frederick**[8] (*Julius Edmund, Edmund, Sylvanus, Malachi, Caleb, Exercise, Roger*), b. 11 Sep., 1857, in Elmira, N. Y. Moved to Lowell, Mass., with his parents, where he now lives. He m. 19 Dec., 1883, Josephine Frances Reed, of Lowell.

Child of FREDERICK and JÓSEPHINE F. (REED) CONANT:—

Maude Whitney, b. 12 Oct., 1884.

712. **John Winslow**[8] (*John A., Lucius, Sylvanus, Malachi, Caleb, Exercise, Roger*), b. 30 Aug., 1854, in Hartford, Conn. He is superintendent of the factory of the Eureka Silk Manufacturing Company, in East Hampton, Conn. He m. 7 Oct., 1879, in Brooklyn, Conn., Alice, dr. of Samuel James and Judith (Hyde) Burlingame, of Canterbury, Conn.

Children of JOHN W. and ALICE (BURLINGAME) CONANT:—

Carrie Augusta, b. 5 Sep., 1880, in E. Hampton.
Julia Abigail, b. 31 Mch., 1882.

713. **William M.**[8] (*Daniel Marshall, Timothy, Caleb, Benajah, Caleb, Exercise, Roger*), b. 16 Sep., 1825, in Aurora, Ohio; was a Methodist minister; d. 18 Dec., 1872. He m. Catherine, dr. of Judge Cretur, of Newcomerstown, O. After his death she m. (2) —— Patrick, and lives in Los Angeles, Cal.

Children of WILLIAM M. and CATHERINE (CRETUR) CONANT:—

Marshall M.; a physician; d. recently (1887) in Los Angeles.
William W.
Frank Wardwell.

714. **Russel B.**[8] (*Daniel Marshall, Timothy, Caleb, Benajah, Caleb, Exercise, Roger*), b. 5 Feb., 1841, in Brooklyn, O.; now of Columbus, O. He served during the Rebellion in an Ohio regiment; was prisoner of war fourteen months, during ten of which he was confined in Andersonville. He m. Naomi Mathers, of Chesterville, O.

Children of RUSSEL B. and NAOMI (MATHERS) CONANT:—

Orie, b. 1867.
Emma, b. 1869.

Ida, b. 1871.
Gertrude, b. 1875.
Charles, b. 1877.
Beulah, b. 1882.

715.   Lewis[8] (*Timothy B., Timothy, Caleb, Benajah, Caleb, Exercise, Roger*), b. 19 Jan., 1825, in Richfield, Summit co., Ohio.   He is a farmer, of Hinckley, Medina co., O.   He m. in Richfield, 25 Sep., 1848, Catherine Dunn.

Children of LEWIS and CATHERINE (DUNN) CONANT:—

812.   Charles Wesley, b. 28 Mch., 1850, in Hinckley, O.
Phebe.
Effie.
813.   Ward Lewis, b. 5 Mch., 1858.
Hattie.
Emma.
Jesse.

716.   Fanny Emily[8] (*Alban Jasper, Caleb, Jonathan, Benajah, Caleb, Exercise, Roger*), b. 21 Oct., 1847, in Troy, N. Y., where she m. 24 June, 1869, William D., son of Jacob V. R. and Euphemia M. (Dixon) Van Blarcom, b. in Paterson, N. J., 28 Nov., 1845.   He resides in Upper Alton, Ill.

Children of WILLIAM D. and FANNY E. (CONANT) VAN BLARCOM:—

i.   William Alban, b. 4 Apr., 1870, in St. Louis, Mo.
ii.   Howell, b. 1 Sep., 1872,   "   "   "
iii.   Blanche, b. 19 Mch., 1875,   "   "   "
iv.   Carrie G., b. 12 June, 1879, in Upper Alton, Ill.
v.   Dixon, b. 23 Nov., 1881,   "   "   "   "
vi.   Conant, b. 8 Feb., 1885,   "   "   "   "

NINTH GENERATION.

717.   Ezra Beals[9] (*Ezra Styles, Gaius, Ezra, Thomas, Nathaniel, Nathaniel, Lot, Roger*), b. 8 May, 1826, in Randolph, Mass.; m. 12 June, 1851, S. A. M. Jones, who d. 25 Dec., 1875.   He d. 25 Dec., 1860.

Edward D. Conant

Children of EZRA B. and S. A. M. (JONES) CONANT:—
Mary.
Annie.

718. **Cyrus C.**[9] (*Ezra Styles, Gaius, Ezra, Thomas, Nathaniel, Nathaniel, Lot, Roger*), b. 16 Feb., 1834, in Randolph, Mass., where he lives. He is a dealer in corn and lumber. He m. 25 Oct., 1859, Eunice Kendrick.

Children of CYRUS C. and EUNICE (KENDRICK) CONANT:—
Emma.
Edward.
Ruth Butler.
Ezra Styles.
Oliver Smith.

719. **Royal Benjamin**[9] (*Ezra Styles, Gaius, Ezra, Thomas, Nathaniel, Nathaniel, Lot, Roger*), b. 7 Nov., 1836, in Randolph, Mass. He was the first principal of the Stetson High School; a trustee of the Home Savings Bank, of Boston; cashier of the Elliot National Bank, of Boston. He is now general manager of Nelson's Banking, Steamship and Railroad Office, in Boston. He m. 4 Jan., 1858, Hannah W. dr. of Charles and Ann (Howard) Littlefield, of East Stoughton.

Children of ROYAL B. and HANNAH W. (LITTLEFIELD) CONANT:—
Frank Whitman, b. 14 Nov., 1858; d. 24 Mch., 1859.
Walter Whitman, b. 29 July, 1860.
Clarence Howard, b. 26 Nov., 1863; d. 30 July, 1865.
Florence Louise, b. 14 Nov., 1869.

720. **Edward Davis**[9] (*Benjamin Kilbourn, Gaius, Ezra, Thomas, Nathaniel, Nathaniel, Lot, Roger*), b. 25 May, 1846, in Worcester, Mass. He is a banker, of Worcester, Mass. He m. in Worcester, 9 Oct., 1872, Annetta Maria Chaplin.

Children of EDWARD D. and ANNETTA M. (CHAPLIN) CONANT:—
Edward Francis, b. 20 May, 1875.
Mabel Elizabeth, b. 14 Feb., 1877.
Elsie Davis, b. 7 Aug., 1879.
Amy Louise, b. 28 Feb., 1884.

721. **Everett William**[9] (*William, Gaius, Ezra, Thomas,*

Nathaniel, Nathaniel, Lot, Roger), b. 28 July, 1843, in Paxton. He is postmaster at Cherry Valley, Mass., and keeps a general store. He m. 14 Jan., 1872, in Zumbrota, Minn., Abbie Sarah Dam.

Children of EVERETT W. and ABBIE S. (DAM) CONANT:—

Virgie A., b. 4 Jan., 1876.
Herbert W., b. 15 Apr., 1878.
Della A., b. 17 June, 1880.

722. **Rodney Teal**[9] (*Chauncey, Robert, Daniel, Jeremiah, Nathaniel, Nathaniel, Lot, Roger*), b. 5 Oct., 1829, in Fowler, N. Y. He is now a dairyman, of De Kalb, N. Y. During the late war he served three years in the 11th Regt., N. Y. Cavalry, as commissary. He m. in Gouverneur, N. Y., 2 Feb., 1850, Lovina, dr. of John and Ruth (Goldthwaite) Kenney, of Gouverneur, b. 28 Sep., 1832.

Children of RODNEY T. and LOVINA (KENNEY) CONANT:—

Elizabeth S., b. 14 Sep., 1851; m. Dr. Eben E. Fisher, of Canton, now of Morristown, N. Y.
Merton C., b. 4 Mch., 1852; a lawyer, formerly of Stillwater and Minneapolis, Minn., now of Diana, Dakota Ter. He m. in Minneapolis, 28 May, 1882, Metta M., dr. of Nelson and Martha (Carpenter) Bigelow.
Grover T. C., b. 8 June, 1856.
Charles R., b. 14 Oct., 1865.

723. **Sanford**[9] (*Jeremiah, Jeremiah, Daniel, Jeremiah, Nathaniel, Nathaniel, Lot, Roger*), b. 18 Mch., 1833, in Athens co., Ohio. He served nearly three years in Co. G, 92nd Regt., Ohio Infantry, in the war of the Rebellion. He is now a druggist, of Salt Sick Bridge, West Virginia; is postmaster; has also been an itinerant preacher. He m. in Washington co., Ohio, Sarah Catherine, dr. of Thomas and Jane (Shrader) Featherstone.

Children of SANFORD and SARAH C. (FEATHERSTONE) CONANT:—

Mary Jane, b. 25 Aug., 1851, in Ohio.
Almeda, b. 14 Sep., 1852,   "   "
Sanford B., b. 16 Oct., 1854, "   "
Susan, b. 1 Aug., 1857,   "   "
Elizabeth A., b. 17 Jan., 1859, "   "

Sarah M., b. 26 Oct., 1862, in Ohio.
Herter F., b. 16 June, 1866, "   "
Flora T., b. 1 May, 1868,   "   "
John T., b. 14 Nov., 1870,   "   "
Millia, b. 20 Feb., 1872, in West Virginia.
William Henry, b. 22 July, 1874, in West Va.
Bertha, b. 7 Dec., 1876, in West Va.

724. **Ambrose**[9] (*Jeremiah, Jeremiah, Daniel, Jeremiah,
Nathaniel, Nathaniel, Lot, Roger*), b. 1835, in Athens co., O.
He m. Mahala Morris.

Children of AMBROSE and MAHALA (MORRIS) CONANT :—

Jeremiah.
Benajah, m. Arvilla Snittin.
William.
Samuel, d. 1866.
George E.
Ida Ann.
Harvey P.
Joseph.
Mary A.
Artemus.
Warden W.

725. **Eliphalet**[9] (*Roger, Abel, Roger, Jeremiah, Nathaniel, Nathaniel, Lot, Roger*), b. 17 June, 1843, in Pickering,
Ont., Can.; moved to Michigan, with his parents. He volun-
teered as a soldier during the Rebellion, but was not accepted
on account of poor health. During the last year of the war
he was employed in the construction corps, as a bridge builder.
He is now a farmer and mechanic, of Atlanta, Mich. He m.
in Marietta, Georgia, Julia Dabbs, b. 25 Apr., 1846.

Children of ELIPHALET and JULIA (DABBS) CONANT:—

Elizabeth Jane, b. 23 Oct., 1866.
Roger William, b. 4 Aug., 1870.

726. **Elizabeth Jane**[9] (*Roger, Abel, Roger, Jeremiah,
Nathaniel, Nathaniel, Lot, Roger*), b. 25 Apr., 1845, in Pick-
ering, Canada; moved to Michigan, with her parents. She m.
in Armada, Mich., 18 Sep., 1865, Alfred J., son of Josiah and
Sabrina (Jones) West, b. in Castle Creek, N. Y., 18 Sep., 1842.
He served through the late war; is now a real estate dealer, in
Capac, Mich.

Children of ALFRED J. and ELIZABETH J. (CONANT) WEST:—

i. Bina May, b. 18 May, 1867, in Columbus, Mich. She is a school and music teacher, at Capac.
ii. Alfred J., b. 14 Feb., 1870, in Columbus.
iii. Edward Frederick, b. 8 Nov., 1871, in Capac.
iv. Mabel Grace, b. 9 Apr., 1878, " "
v. Elbert Clair, b. 27 Nov., 1880, " "

727. **Rhoda Matilda**[9] (*Roger, Abel, Roger, Jeremiah, Nathaniel, Nathaniel, Lot, Roger*), b. 18 Mch., 1856, in Port Huron, Mich.; m. in St. Clair, 13 July, 1872, Edward Matteson, of Almont, Mich. He is a farmer, of Capac, Mich.

Children of EDWARD and RHODA M. (CONANT) MATTESON:—

i. Edward Charles, b. 18 Apr., 1874.
ii. William Franklin, b. 11 Aug., 1876.
iii. James R., b. 15 July, 1884.

728. **Thomas**[9] (*Daniel, Thomas, Roger, Jeremiah, Nathaniel, Nathaniel, Lot, Roger*), b. 15 Apr., 1842, in Oshawa, Ontario, Canada. He is a banker and broker. He is the only male representative, so far as known, of the descendants of Roger Conant who went to Canada after the Revolution and received large grants of land from the British Crown, in what was then Upper Canada, now Ontario. Several of the deeds, which are on parchment and bearing a large royal seal, as well as the lands conveyed, are still in possession of Thomas Conant. Mr. Conant has been often solicited to accept public office, but being of a studious turn of mind has always refused. He has travelled extensively in America, and in Europe as far as Russia. He has contributed largely to the Canadian press on political and agricultural topics. The portion of Ontario in which he resides (about thirty miles from Toronto) is extremely fertile, having a mild climate, is thickly settled and progressive. He has a commission in the Queen's Bench, and is a school trustee. He m. in Toronto, 12 Dec., 1866, Margaret, dr. of Lyman and Hannah (Pickel) Gifford, b. in East Whitby, Can., 19 Feb., 1844.

Children of THOMAS and MARGARET (GIFFORD) CONANT:—

Alberta Gertrude, b. 3 Apr., 1870.
Edith Julia, b. 25 Feb., 1872.

Alice May, b. 1 Sep., 1874.
Edna Mabel, b. 4 Nov., 1876; d. y.
Edna Louisa, b. 28 Nov., 1879.
Horace Thomas, b. 15 May, 1882.

729. **Oliver Jackson**[9] (*David Fales, Marlborough, John, John, Nathaniel, Nathaniel, Lot, Roger*), b. 14 Dec., 1825, in Rockland, Me. During the late war he was captain of Co. C, 4th Me. Regt. He is employed in the money order department of the Rockland post office. He m. (1) 20 Dec., 1847, in Rockland, Nancy P. Ames, who d. 29 Feb., 1866; m. (2) Martha Allen, who d. 3 Jan., 1876; m. (3) 1884, ———.
Children of OLIVER J. and NANCY P. (AMES) CONANT:—

Etta Oliver, b. 28 Jan., 1857; m. 15 Sep., 1881, Nathan D. Clark, of Boston, Mass., and has Frederick Conant, b. 26 June, 1882. They reside in Allston, Mass.
Anne Olive, b. 4 June, 1860.

730. **Alvin**[9] (*Seth Wilder, Seth, John, John, Nathaniel, Nathaniel, Lot, Roger*), b. 17 Sep., 1846, in Bridgewater, Mass. He enlisted 11 Aug., 1862, in Co. E, 38th Mass. Vols., and served till 8 June, 1865. He m. Ellen Besse, of Bridgewater, b. 1 May, 1847.
Child of ALVIN and ELLEN (BESSE) CONANT:—

Lilian Augusta, b. 10 Feb., 1867.

731. **Howard Turner**[9] (*Everett Quincy, Sylvanus, Silvanus, Gershom, Lot, Nathaniel, Lot, Roger*), b. 26 Oct., 1840, in Turner, Me., where he resides; a farmer. During the Rebellion he served nine months in Co. D, 23rd Regt., Me. Vols.; mustered in 29 Sep., 1862 (Maine Adjt. Gen.'s Report, 1863, p. 731). He m. 5 Dec., 1863, Lucinda Phillips, dr. of Martin Mason and Abigail Haskell (Phillips) Adkins, b. 13 Oct., 1845, in Turner.
Children of HOWARD T. and LUCINDA P. (ADKINS) CONANT:—

Anna Abigail, b. 19 Nov., 1864, in Turner; m. in Minot, 20 May, 1884, Clifton Winfield Davis, and has Sylvia Blanche, b. 11 June, 1885.
Charles Albert, b. 12 Dec., 1865, in Turner.
Ella Frances, b. 17 July, 1867, " "

Hattie Maria, b. 21 Dec., 1868, in Buckfield.
Alice Isabel, b. 12 May, 1873, in Turner.
Etta Lucinda, b. 31 Dec., 1874,   "
Frank Howard, b. 10 Mch., 1879.
Josephine Evelina, b. 5 Aug., 1886.

732. Everett Sanford[9] (*Everett Quincy, Sylvanus, Silvanus, Gershom, Lot, Nathaniel, Lot, Roger*), b. 12 Feb., 1843, in Turner, Me.; resides in Buckfield; a farmer. He enlisted 10 Sep., 1862, in Co. D, 23rd Regt., Me. Vols., and served nine months; enlisted again 1 Mch., 1865, to serve one year, and was discharged 14 June, 1865, on account of sickness (Maine Adj. Gen.'s Report, 1863, p. 731). He m. 7 Mch., 1867, Faustina, dr. of Lewis and Phebe (Spaulding) Record, b. in Buckfield, 13 Feb., 1846.

Children of EVERETT S. and FAUSTINA (RECORD) CONANT:—

Stanley Ellwood, b. 21 Dec., 1868, in Buckfield.
Mary Louisa, b. 6 Nov., 1870,   "   "
Fred Wilbur, b. 12 Mch., 1879,   "   "

733. Hiram Augustus[9] (*Everett Quincy, Sylvanus, Silvanus, Gershom, Lot, Nathaniel, Lot, Roger*), b. 21 Feb., 1845, in Turner, Me.; a farmer, of Buckfield. He served as a corporal for eighteen months in Co. D, 32nd Regt., Me. Vols.; was wounded 30 Sep., 1864, at one of the battles near Petersburg, Va. He m. 9 Feb., 1866, in Turner, Flora A., dr. of Martin M. and Abigail H. (Phillips) Adkins.

Children of HIRAM A. and FLORA A. (ADKINS) CONANT:—

Albert Augustus, b. 9 Sep., 1866, in Turner.
Edward Everett, b. 24 Oct., 1867,   "   "
Ellen Augusta, b. 14 Aug., 1869,   "   "
Hiram Wilson, b. 5 May, 1871,   "   "
Walter Grant, b. 5 Oct., 1872,   "   "
John Wollmer, b. 21 July, 1874,   "   "
George Isaiah, b. 29 Jan., 1876,   "   "
Sylvia Lilian, b. 6 Dec., 1878,   "   "
Henry Lowell, b. 11 Jan., 1880,   "   "
Ida May, b. 12 June, 1881,   " Buckfield.
Charles Bridgham, b. 9 Sep., 1883,   "   "
Sarah Louisa, b. 21 Jan., 1886,   "   "

734. George Mitchell[9] (*Ira M., Ira, Phinehas, Phinehas, Lot, Nathaniel, Lot, Roger*), b. 18 Dec., 1853. He is engaged with his brother, Herbert I., in the rubber business in Boston, under the firm name of the Conant Rubber Company. He m. (1) Ellen L. Hill; m. (2) Lydia, dr. of Augustine S. Bemis.

Children of GEORGE M. and LYDIA (BEMIS) CONANT:—

George W.
A child, not named.

735. **William M.**[9] (*Ira M., Ira, Phinehas, Phinehas, Lot, Nathaniel, Lot, Roger*), b. ———. He graduated at Harvard, 1879, and studied medicine. He is now a practicing physician, of Boston. He m. Mary A., dr. of Judge Edmund H. Bennett. Judge Bennett is Dean of the Boston Law School.

Child of WILLIAM M. and MARY A. (BENNETT) CONANT:—

Ruth.

736. **Herbert I.**[9] (*Ira M., Ira, Phinehas, Phinehas, Lot, Nathaniel, Lot, Roger*), b. ———. He is in business with his brother, George M., in Boston. He m. Alleda Pierce.

Children of HERBERT I. and ALLEDA (PIERCE) CONANT:—

Mary.
Beatrice.

737. **Emory**[9] (*Amos, Silas, Samuel, Robert, Lot, John, Lot, Roger*), b. 23 Nov., 1797, in Sudbury, Mass., where he lived. He d. 3 June, 1859. He m. Sarah Binney, b. 6 Nov., 1804, d. 18 Sep., 1886, at Sudbury Centre. She was a member of the Baptist church of Weston, fifty-eight years.

Children of EMORY and SARAH (BINNEY) CONANT:—

Sarah A., b. 17 Jan., 1830; d. 30 Oct., 1852.
John E., b. 9 July, 1833; d. 12 Apr., 1838.
Emily, b. 8 Mch., 1835; d. 13 Oct., 1856.
Celinda S., b. 16 Mch., 1839; d. 14 Aug., 1841.
Luman E., b. 23 May, 1840. He was a member of the firm of Chas. H. North & Co., Boston, but has retired from business, and lives in Sudbury.
Eveline J., b. 3 July, 1844; d. 13 Jan., 1869.

738. **Silas**[9] (*Amos, Silas, Samuel, Robert, Lot, John, Lot, Roger*), b. 2 Feb., 1801, in Sudbury, Mass., where he lived; d. 8 Nov., 1875. He m. 30 Mch., 1826, Caroline Stone, b. 19 Nov., 1801.

Children of SILAS and CAROLINE (STONE) CONANT:—

Caroline H., b. 30 Apr., 1827; m. 9 Oct., 1872, Abner Hill.
Dexter S., b. 22 Sep., 1828.
James H., b. 19 Dec., 1829; m. 12 May, 1852, Martha M.
Upham. •
Sarah D., b. 15 Jan., 1831; d. 5 Aug., 1867; m. Lyman Fisher,
who d. 13 Oct., 1878.
Israel F., b. 24 Aug., 1837.
Amos F., b. 27 Oct., 1843; m. 12 May, 1869, Jennie Farrington.

739. Amos[9] (*Amos, Silas, Samuel, Robert, Lot, John,
Lot, Roger*), b. 23 Apr., 1805, in Sudbury, Mass., where he
lived; a farmer. He d. 2 Oct., 1853. He m. in Guilford, Vt.,
12 June, 1826, Elizabeth Ballard, dr. of Mathew and Eliza
(Ballard) Stone, b. 30 May, 1805; d. 30 Oct., 1862.

Children of AMOS and ELIZABETH B. (STONE) CONANT:—

Edwin Augustus, b. 15 May, 1830; m. in Rockford, Ill., 19
Aug., 1858, Mary, dr. of Ezra and Catherine (Van Volkin-
burg) Troope, b. in German Flats, N. Y. No children. He
now lives in North Sudbury.
Eliza Ann, b. 8 Feb., 1833.
Nancy Barber, b. 21 May, 1835; m. 28 Sep., 1857, Oliver M.
Richards, and has a family.
814.   John Mathew, b. 19 Aug., 1838.   •

740. Levi[9] (*Levi, Silas, Samuel, Robert, Lot, John, Lot,
Roger*), b. 25 May, 1802, in Hubbardston, Mass., where he
lived. He d. 1 Dec., 1878. He m. 20 Feb., 1827, Eliza Savage.

Children of LEVI and ELIZA (SAVAGE) CONANT:—

Levi W., b. 3 Oct., 1827; m. Mary S. Parkhurst.
Mary Elizabeth, b. 1 Aug., 1830; m. (1) A. Damon; m. (2) J.
B. Flynn.
815.   Benjamin P., b. 7 May, 1832.
Frances Ann, b. 13 Dec., 1837; m. Dumont Mareau.

741. Isaac[9] (*Abraham, Oliver, Samuel, Robert, Lot, John,
Lot, Roger*), b. 13 June, 1807, in Frankfort, now Winterport,
Me.; a farmer; d. 8 Mch., 1869. He m. in Winterport, 3 Nov.,
1836, Jane Weston.

Children of ISAAC and JANE (WESTON) CONANT:—

816.   Edward W., b. 24 June, 1837.
Dameris, b. 15 July, 1839.
Charles H., b. 19 Aug., 1841; is of Bangor.

Albert, b. 3 Sep., 1843.
Augusta A., b. 14 Feb., 1846.
Sarah J., b. 29 July, 1848.
Mercy W., b. 9 Oct., 1850.
Maria E., b. 19 Nov., 1853.

742. **Amasa S.**[9] (*Abraham, Oliver, Samuel, Robert, Lot, John, Lot, Roger*), b. 12 Feb., 1809, in Frankfort, Me.; m. 12 Oct., 1831, Betsey, dr. of Joshua and Betsey (Woodman) Wentworth, of Frankfort, b. 11 Mch., 1805; she d. 15 Oct., 1866 (see *Wentworth Genealogy*). He lived in Orrington, Me.

Children of AMASA S. and BETSEY (WENTWORTH) CO-NANT:—

817. George Wentworth, b. 20 Apr., 1832.
Lorenzo Dow, b. 8 Oct., 1834; m. 29 Apr., 1866, Maria Antoinette, dr. of Charles R. Trask, of Orrington, Me.; no ch.
Edna Alice, b. 20 Sep., 1836; d. 30 Nov., 1873; m. 28 Dec., 1857, Charles Moore, son of John Wentworth, b. 20 Jan., 1831 (see *Wentworth Genealogy*). He enlisted Feb., 1863, in Baker's D. C. Cavalry, and served till 1865. They lived in Orrington, Me. Child: Alice Bernice, b. 14 Apr., 1870.
Sarah C., b. 2 Oct., 1838; d. 15 Sep., 1839.
Amasa Lumbert, b. 1 Dec., 1842; d. 13 Dec., 1843.
Amasa Lumbert, b. 31 Jan., 1844; m. 1 Jan., 1871, Abby M., dr. of Thomas Barstow, of Orrington. They lived in Bucksport. He served during the Rebellion in 22nd Regt., Me. Vols.
Mary Thankful, b. 24 Nov., 1846.
Walter, b. 4 Dec., 1848; d. 10 Nov., 1877.

743. **Charles**[9] (*Abraham, Oliver, Samuel, Robert, Lot, John, Lot, Roger*), b. 24 Dec., 1812, in Frankfort, Me., where he lived. He m. Hannah Weston.

Children of CHARLES and HANNAH (WESTON) CONANT:—

Frederick Augustus.
Lydia W.
Artemus Henry, b. 5 Dec., 1842; of Monroe, Me.; m. and had a son, Fred P., b. 1874, d. 1879.
Charles M.
Weatha.
Clara D.
Ellen.

744. **Thatcher M.**[9] (*Isaac, Oliver, Samuel, Robert, Lot, John, Lot, Roger*), b. ———, in Cambridge, Mass.; removed

to Manchester, N. H., and thence to New York, N. Y., where he now lives. He m. Olive J. Streeter.

Child of THATCHER M. and OLIVE J. (STREETER) CONANT:—

Thomas B., b. 5 Sep., 1855.

745. George W.[9] (*Asa W., Oliver, Samuel, Robert, Lot, John, Lot, Roger*), b. 6 Apr., 1816, in Athol, Mass.; a carpenter; moved to Barre; d. 13 Dec., 1860. He m. in Barre, 1840, Laura Cheney, b. 1819, d. 27 Oct., 1849.

Children of GEORGE W. and LAURA (CHENEY) CONANT:—

Mary J., b. 6 Dec., 1841, in Barre; m. Willard Clark, who d. 1886; had Charles Eaton.
Henry E., b. 24 May, 1843, in Barre; m. in Manchester, N. H., 1 May, 1878, Josephine E. Huntley. They live in Concord, N. H. He served during the Rebellion, from July, 1861, to July, 1865, in Co. K, 21st Regt., Mass. Vols.

746. John[9] (*Nathan, Samuel, Samuel, Robert, Lot, John, Lot, Roger*), b. 1808. He settled in Abington, Mass.; m. Alice Bosworth.

Children of JOHN and ALICE (BOSWORTH) CONANT:—

Lydia Ann, m. Alonzo Chase, of Abington.
818. John Greenleaf, b. 1837.
Albion.
Augusta, m. Algernon S. Robinson, of Sumner, Me.
Pamela.
Charles.

747. Edwin[9] (*Jacob, Samuel, Samuel, Robert, Lot, John, Lot, Roger*), b. 20 Aug., 1810, in Sterling, Mass. He graduated at Harvard, 1829; studied law at the Harvard Law School, and also with Rejoice Newton and William Lincoln. He practiced in Sterling till 1833, when he removed to Worcester, Mass., where he now resides, having retired from the practice of law some years ago. He has given a fine library building to Sterling, his native town. He m. (1) 8 Oct., 1833, Maria Estabrook; m. (2) Elizabeth S. Wheeler.

Children of EDWIN and MARIA (ESTABROOK) CONANT:—

Elizabeth Anne, b. 21 June, 1835; d. 4 Dec., 1883.
Helen Maria, b. 19 May, 1837.

748. Joel Hobart[9] (*Joel, John, Samuel, Robert, Lot, John,*

F. T. Stuart, Boston.

Edwin Conent

Lot, Roger), b. 15 June, 1813, in Acton, Mass. He moved to Nashua, N. H., and engaged in trade; then back to Acton, where he now resides. He m. Apr., 1840, Rachael Cunningham.

Children of JOEL H. and RACHAEL (CUNNINGHAM) CONANT:—

John Hobart, b. 13 July, 1842.
James Amory, b. 7 Nov., 1843.
Ellen Newman, b. 30 Jan., 1845.
Frank Newman, b. 27 Aug., 1851.

749. William Hayward[9] (*Joel, John, Samuel, Robert, Lot, John, Lot, Roger*), b. 22 Oct., 1815, in Acton, Mass.; a farmer; removed to Nashua, N. H., and thence to Woburn, Mass., where he now lives. He m. 23 Apr., 1839, Emeline, dr. of (597) Paul Conant, of Acton.

Children of WILLIAM H. and EMELINE (CONANT) CONANT:—

Lucien William, b. 29 Mch., 1840, in Acton.
Clara Frances, b. 30 July, 1844; d. 1846.
Anna Sophia, b. 14 June, 1848.
Emma Augusta, b. 26 July, 1852, in Nashua.

750. John[9] (*Joel, John, Samuel, Robert, Lot, John, Lot, Roger*), b. 17 Nov., 1821, in Acton, Mass.; removed to Jaffrey, N. H. He m. Nov., 1846, L. Robertson.

Children of JOHN and L——— (ROBERTSON) CONANT:—

Joel, b. 17 Nov., 1847.
Julia E., b. 13 Jan., 1849.
Mary E., b. 7 Jan., 1851.

751. Ansel[9] (*Asa, Ephraim, Peter, Robert, Lot, John, Lot, Roger*), b. in (Industry?) Me.; moved to Camden, Me. He was a sailor, and was lost at sea 8 Nov., 1845. He m. 6 Sep., 1835, in Camden, Maria, dr. of Isaac Bartlett, b. 8 Aug., 1818.

Children of ANSEL and MARIA (BARTLETT) CONANT:—

Charles William, b. 15 Mch., 1838; now of Patten, Me.
Isaac Adelbert, b. 9 Jan., 1844.

752. Simeon[9] (*Asa, Ephraim, Peter, Robert, Lot, John, Lot, Roger*), b. in Farmington, Me.; moved to Camden, with his parents, and thence to Vinalhaven. He was a sea captain; d. 1864. He m. ———, Lydia, dr. of Elisha Burgess.

Children of Simeon and Lydia (Burgess) Conant:—

> Mary Ann.
> Maria.
> Hannah.
> Sewell.
> Charlotte.
> Joseph A., of Vinalhaven.
> Harvey, d. y.

753. Nathan Warren[9] (*Asa, Ephraim, Peter, Robert, Lot, John, Lot, Roger*), b. 10 Dec., 1812, in Temple, Me.; moved to Camden, Me., with his parents; settled in Lincolnville; was a sea captain; d. 22 Mch., 1877. He m. in Lincolnville, 4 Oct., 1835, Mary J., dr. of Joseph and Mary (Holt) Thomas, b. 6 Aug., 1807.

Children of Nathan W. and Mary J. (Thomas) Conant:—

819. Joseph Tyler, b. 13 Mch., 1841, in Lincolnville.
820. Sumner Tyler, b. 9 Jan., 1843, "   "
821. Frank Warren, b. 14 May, 1851, in Camden.

754. Isaiah Sewell[9] (*Asa, Ephraim, Peter, Robert, Lot, John, Lot, Roger*), b. 3 Mch., 1814, in Farmington, Me.; removed to Camden, with his parents; d. 8 Apr., 1873. He m. in Lincolnville, 18 Oct., 1836, Mary, dr. of Charles and Thankful (Mariner) Thomas.

Children of Isaiah S. and Mary (Thomas) Conant:—

> Mary Augusta, b. 10 Mch., 1841; d. 4 Mch., 1842.
> Charles Sewell, b. 10 Jan., 1843.
> Abbie Anna, b. 3 Feb., 1845.
> Nelson Pendleton, b. 14 Nov., 1847; d. 20 Aug., 1848.
> George Henry, b. 7 Feb., d. 3 Aug., 1851.
> Frederick Leslie, b. 7 Feb., 1853; d. 28 Aug., 1861.
> Addie, b. 3 Aug., d. 17 Aug., 1855.
> Benjamin Wentworth, b. 1 May, 1858.

755. Sophia Ann[9] (*Asa, Ephraim, Peter, Robert, Lot, John, Lot, Roger*), b. 23 Oct., 1817; m. 10 Nov., 1839, Rufus Benson, b. 23 May, 1815, d. 6 Oct., 1860, at Savannah, Ga., of yellow fever. He was a sea captain. She d. 6 Oct., 1876.

Children of Rufus and Sophia A. (Conant) Benson:—

i.   William Wilson, b. 18 Aug., 1840.
ii. Silas Clark, b. 29 Nov., 1842.

iii.   Hiram Perry, b. 10 Dec., 1845.
iv.   Ellen Adelia, b. 21 June, 1847.
v.   Rufus Sherman, b. 23 July, 1850.
vi.   Warren Conant, b. 21 Apr., 1853.

756. Rebecca[9] (*Ephraim, Ephraim, Peter, Robert, Lot, John, Lot, Roger*), b. 1804, in Phillips, Me.; m. Samuel Doyen.
Children of SAMUEL and REBECCA (CONANT) DOYEN:—

i.   Ephraim Albert.
ii.   Warren.
iii.   Christiana.
iv.   Erasmus P., of Portland, Me.
v.   Wesley.
vi.   Abbie Maria, b. 26 Jan., 1843; m. 1865, Samuel Welch, b. 1837, in Sullivan, Pa. They lived in Morris Run, Pa., in 1875.

757. Ephraim[9] (*Ephraim, Ephraim, Peter, Robert, Lot, John, Lot, Roger*), b. 17 Dec., 1809, in Temple, Me.; moved to Strong, Me.; a farmer; d. 24 Jan., 1884. He m. Dec., 1834, in Salem, Me., Eliza S. Doble.
Children of EPHRAIM and ELIZA S. (DOBLE) CONANT:—

822.   Ephraim Franklin, b. 25 Sep., 1835.
      Israel Henry, b. 27 June, 1838.
823.   John Wesley, b. 16 Feb., 1840.
824.   James Harvey, b. 4 June, 1842.
      Charles Clinton, b. 7 Oct., 1844; d. 1 Jan., 1846.
      Eliza Ella, b. 15 Aug., 1846.
825.   Charles Barker, b. 19 Oct., 1848.
826.   Sylvanus Gideon, b. 6 Aug., 1850.
      Willie Scales, b. 13 Aug., 1854; d. 7 Dec., 1860.

758. Susan[9] (*Ephraim, Ephraim, Peter, Robert, Lot, John, Lot, Roger*), b. 7 Feb., 1812, in Temple, Me.; m. Nathaniel K. Staples.
Children of NATHANIEL K. and SUSAN (CONANT) STAPLES:—

i.   Susan Jane.
ii.   Fanny.
iii.   Lovina.
iv.   Sylvester.
v.   Abbie.
vi.   Olive.
vii.   Lizzie.
viii.   Gustavus B.
ix.   Rachael.
x.   David.
xi.   Esther.

759. **Sarah⁹** (*Ephraim, Ephraim, Peter, Robert, Lot, John, Lot, Roger*), b. in Temple, Me.; m. Brackett Wyman. Children of BRACKETT and SARAH (CONANT) WYMAN:—

i.   Allen.
ii.   Abram.
iii. Corydon.
iv.   Andrew.
v.   Sarah.
vi.   Elmira.
vii. Fidelia.
viii. Eliza.
ix.   Calvin.
x.   Jane.

760. **John Gideon⁹** (*Ephraim, Ephraim, Peter, Robert, Lot, John, Lot, Roger*), b. 9 Nov., 1821, in Temple, Me. He is now a millman and farmer, of Madrid, Me. He has been town clerk twelve years; selectman twelve years; is a justice of the peace and has been representative to the State legislature. He m. in Madrid, 19 May, 1852, Mary Wells, dr. of John and Hannah (Dunham) Sargent, b. 2 Dec., 1832.

Children of JOHN G. and MARY W. (SARGENT) CONANT:—

Lizzie H., b. 22 Dec., 1853; m. Warren H. Young, of West Farmington, Me.
Ella J., b. 17 Jan., 1857.
Ida M., b. 7 Mch., 1862.

761. **Joseph Hayward⁹** (*Joseph, Ephraim, Peter, Robert, Lot, John, Lot, Roger*), b. 30 June, 1810, in Temple, Me. He studied theology at Bangor Theological Seminary, where he graduated 1839. He preached at Thorndike, Me., for three years, then went to Chesterville, where he was ordained July, 1842, then to Monmouth, in 1857, then to Freedom and Richmond, in Maine, and thence to Nashua, N. H., where he d. 23 Nov., 1864. He m. 1839, in Wilton, Me., Dorcas Temperance Pease, who d. 16 Sep., 1871, in Concord, N. H.

Child of JOSEPH H. and DORCAS T. (PEASE) CONANT:—

827. Hermon, b. 5 Sep., 1840, in Thorndike, Me.

762. **John⁹** (*Joseph, Ephraim, Peter, Robert, Lot, John, Lot, Roger*), b. 14 Sep., 1814, in Temple, Me. In Nov., 1835,

he moved to Bangor, fitted for college and taught school in
Kenduskeag and Etna. In 1840 he went to Aroostook county
and bought a farm of 500 acres, where he remained till 1850.
He returned to Bangor in 1850, and engaged in the dry goods
business, where he remained until 1861, when he enlisted in
Co. F, 8th Regt., Me. Vols.; was promoted to captain of Co.
K, 8th Me. Regt., but resigned on account of ill health, and
returned home. He went South again, as a missionary and
teacher to the Freedmen, and bought a confiscated plantation
at Beaufort, S. C., where he still lives. He held a commission
as justice of the peace, in Maine, and has been U. S. marshal
and chairman of the Board of Registration, in S. C. He m.
21 July, 1842, in Crystal Plantation, Me., Elvira, dr. of Elisha
and Mary (Butler) Bradford, b. 14 Jan., 1820, in Farmington, Me.

Children of JOHN and ELVIRA (BRADFORD) CONANT:—

> Augustus Eugene, b. 7 Sep., 1843, in Crystal, Me. He en-
> listed 7 Sep., 1861, in Co. K, 8th Me. Regt.; was wounded
> May, 1864, at Bermuda Hundreds, and d. at Point Lookout,
> 28 May, 1864.
> Lucy Ann, b. 13 Nov., 1845; m. 12 Dec., 1870, James N., son
> of Jeremiah and Lydia Ann (Roberts) Emmons, b. 26 Oct.,
> 1845. He is a merchant, of Beaufort. Children: 1. John
> Conant, b. 3 Mch., 1874; 2. Catherine Wooding, b. 28 Aug.,
> 1875; 3. Erwin Augustus, b. 20 Aug., 1877; 4. Lydia, b. 20
> Aug., 1879; 5. George, b. 15 Aug., 1881; 6. Lutie, b. 12 Jan.,
> 1883; 7. Marion, b. 16 July, 1884.

763. **Daniel Alexander**[9] (*Joseph, Ephraim, Peter, Robert, Lot, John, Lot, Roger*), b. 3 Dec., 1827, in Temple, Me.
He was a soldier in the Army of the Potomac during the Rebellion. He is now a farmer, of Milford, Mass. He m. in
Brighton, Mass., 25 Nov., 1850, Abbie Drury Sampson.

Children of DANIEL A. and ABBIE D. (SAMPSON) CONANT:—

> 　　Alice Elizabeth, b. 2 Dec., 1851, in Temple.
> 828.　Edward Joseph, b. 3 July, 1855, in Norridgewock.
> 　　John Walter, b. 9 May, 1858,　　"　　　"

764. **Charles Albion**[9] (*Joseph, Ephraim, Peter, Robert,
Lot, John, Lot, Roger*), b. 28 July, 1833, in Temple, Me. He
graduated at Union College, 1859, then studied theology at
Bangor Theological Seminary. He settled at Alden, N. Y.,

then at Five Corners, N. Y., then Auburn, Mass. In 1876 he removed to Duluth, Minn.; is now a Congregationalist minister at St. Paul, Minn. He m. in Amsterdam, N. Y., Harriet L. Bunn.

Children of CHARLES A. and HARRIET L. (BUNN) CONANT:—

Elizabeth, b. 4 Jan., 1864, in Moravia, N. Y.
Mary Alice, b. 6 Apr., 1866, in Geneva, N. Y.
Howard, b. 11 Oct., 1868,   "   "   "
James Bronson, b. 31 Mch., 1870, "   "
Harriet, b. 25 Dec., 1871, in Pike, N. Y.

765. Enoch Wentworth[9] (*Abraham, Ephraim, Peter, Robert, Lot, John, Lot, Roger*), b. Oct., 1815, in Hope, Me. He is a farmer, of Appleton, Me. He m. Emily Bartlett, who d. 21 Apr., 1866.

Children of ENOCH W. and EMILY (BARTLETT) CONANT:—

Nathan Bartlett, b. 4 Apr., 1843.
Seth Bartlett, b. 18 Oct., 1844.
John Nason, b. 10 Nov., 1846; of Appleton, Me.; m. 12 June, 1870, Emily J., dr. of Thomas L. Wentworth (see *Wentworth Genealogy*).
Mary Amelia, b. 12 Dec., 1848; m. 30 Apr., 1871, Nelson L. Wentworth, b. 21 Nov., 1847 (see *Wentworth Genealogy*).
Sophronia Emily, b. 12 Apr., 1850.
Elizabeth V., b. 10 June, 1859.
Flora A., b. 27 Feb., 1865.

766. Isaac[9] (*Abraham, Ephraim, Peter, Robert, Lot, John, Lot, Roger*), b. 19 Feb., 1817, in Friendship, Me.; m. 31 Dec., 1839, Sarah Wellman.

Children of ISAAC and SARAH (WELLMAN) CONANT:—

A child, d. in infancy.
Nancy Silvinia, b. 31 Dec., 1840; m. 10 Oct., 1862, George W. Burgess, and removed to California.
Lucena, b. 11 Nov., 1844; m. 21 Nov., 1863, David S. Hall, b. 13 Dec., 1843. They live in Searsmont, Me. Children: 1. Leonard F., b. 23 Aug., 1865; 2. Willard E., b. 28 Dec., 1867; 3. George A., b. 28 Nov., 1869.
Francis Plympton, b. 23 Apr., 1846.
Celestia M., b. 11 Aug., 1848.

767. Azubah B.[9] (*Abraham, Ephraim, Peter, Robert, Lot, John, Lot, Roger*), b. (20 Feb.?) 1819, in Hope, Me.; m.

14 May, 1839, William Moody, b. 29 Aug., 1815; she d. 19
June, 1869.

Children of WILLIAM and AZUBAH B. (CONANT) MOODY:—

i.   Sarah M., b. 28 Aug., 1840; m. 7 Aug., 1859, Andrew J. Hoffses, and had: William M., b. 1 May, 1861; Sarah A., b. 11
Mch., 1863; Ernest H., b. 5 Jan., 1868.

ii.   Emily C., b. 16 Jan., 1842; d. 20 Feb., 1860.

iii.   Francelia, b. 11 Jan., 1844; m. 14 Feb., 1864, Judson Hoffses,
and had: Emily, b. 4 Apr., 1865; Lucy A., b. 9 Sep., 1867;
Lilla Maud, b. 11 Apr., 1870.

iv.   Robert F., b. 15 Jan., 1849.

768. **Marcus G.**[9] (*Abraham, Ephraim, Peter, Robert,
Lot, John, Lot, Roger*), b. 7 Aug., 1820, in Hope, Me.; m. 12
Feb., 1846, Lucena Wellman, b. 14 Feb., 1824.

Children of MARCUS G. and LUCENA (WELLMAN) CONANT:—

        Eliza E., b. 3 Dec., 1846.
829.   Deforest, b. 10 Feb., 1850.
        Martha A., b. 16 Nov., 1852.
        Charles M., b. 3 Mch., 1855.
        William, b. 13 Jan., 1856.
        Celia E., b. 6 Dec., 1858.
        Abram, b. 26 Jan., 1861.
        Medora E., b. 16 June, 1863.
        Julia F., b. 21 May, 1866.

769. **Emily**[9] (*Abraham, Ephraim, Peter, Robert, Lot,
John, Lot, Roger*), b. 17 July, 1822, in Hope, Me.; m. 22 Sep.,
1841, Andrew J. Clark, b. 24 July, 1819.

Children of ANDREW J. and EMILY (CONANT) CLARK:—

i.   Sarah A., b. 7 Nov., 1842; m. 1 July, 1860, Oliver P. Davis,
and had: Loyier M., b. 3 Mch., 1861; Lauretta H., b. 21
Jan., 1862; Emily V., b. 27 Mch., 1864; Sarah M., b. 22 Sep.,
1865; Julia C., b. 11 Aug., 1867.

ii.   Marcus C., b. 20 Nov., 1843; m. 31 Dec., 1868, Margaret A.
Killeran.

iii.   Julia R., b. 8 Dec., 1848; m. 28 June, 1868, Levi C. Robinson.

iv.   Lydia F., b. 17 Aug., 1850; m. 2 Aug., 1868, Isaac S. Jameson.

v.   Enoch C., b. 8 Sep., 1853.

vi.   Andrew C., b. 24 Sep., 1863.

vii.   Emily, b. 24 May, 1867.

770. **Sylvanus**[9] (*Abraham, Ephraim, Peter, Robert, Lot,
John, Lot, Roger*), b. 13 Mch., 1826; m. Oct., 1854, Catherine
Brazier, b. 1 Sep., 1832.

Children of SYLVANUS and CATHERINE (BRAZIER) CONANT:—

William V., b. 22 Feb., 1855.
George O., b. 19 Dec., 1857.
Imogene, b. ——.
A child, d. y.

771. **Elisha Harding**[9] (*Isaac, Ephraim, Peter, Robert, Lot, John, Lot, Roger*), b. 22 Jan., 1826, in Hope, Me. He is a merchant, of Belfast.
Children of ELISHA H. and —— (——) CONANT:—

Georgiana, b. 1853.
Ella, b. 1855.
Bancroft H., b. 1857.
Frank A., b. 1859.
Bertha J., b. 1861.
Eva, b. 1868.

772. **Joseph Augustus**[9] (*Isaac, Ephraim, Peter, Robert, Lot, John, Lot, Roger*), b. 5 Jan., 1830, in Hope, Me. He removed to Fort Fairfield, Aroostook county, Me., about 1845, where he now lives. He served one year in Co. G, 22nd Regt., Me. Vols., during the Rebellion. He m. 1848, ——.
Children of JOSEPH A. and —— (——) CONANT:—

Benjamin W., b. 25 Apr., 1849.
Nancy Abigail, b. 14 Jan., 1851.
Stephen R., b. 22 Dec., 1851.
Edward, b. 25 May, 1853.
William B., b. 6 Aug., 1854.
Lyman, b. 25 Nov., 1855.
Dudley, b. 13 Aug., 1857.
Oddellar, b. 12 July, 1859.
Joseph A., b. 11 Feb., 1862.
Abraham Lincoln, b. 1 Oct., 1864.
Isaac, b. 14 June, 1867.

773. **Jonathan Newell**[9] (*Phineas, Peter, Peter, Robert, Lot, John, Lot, Roger*), b. 13 Aug., 1810, in Stow, Mass. He removed to Maine, with his father, in 1827, and worked at mill building in Camden, Hope, Union, Stillwater, Great Works and Oldtown. In 1835 he removed to New York, and worked at his trade till 1850, when he settled on a farm in West Vienna, N. Y. He was postmaster there 16 years; has been a justice of the peace 22 years, county supervisor of the

poor for six years and railroad commissioner for six years. He
m. in West Vienna, 17 Feb., 1840, Sarah, dr. of Silas and
Sarah (Walcott) Jewell, b. 15 May, 1815, in Stow, Mass.

Children of JONATHAN N. and SARAH (JEWELL) CONANT:—

> Ellen Susan, b. 31 Dec., 1840; d. y.
> George Newell, b. 11 Mch., 1842; m. and has Charles Newell.
> Charles Waldo, b. 14 July, 1849.
> Mary W., b. 25 July, 1850; d. in infancy.

774. Andrew⁹ (*Phineas, Peter, Peter, Robert, Lot, John,
Lot, Roger*), b. 18 May, 1814, in Stow, Mass. He removed to
Cherokee, Iowa, and thence to Rock Island, Ill., where he is
now living. He m. Ann Bloomfield Jewell, b. 24 May, 1820,
in Oneida, N. Y.

Children of ANDREW and ANN B. (JEWELL) CONANT:—

> Anna J., b. 28 July, 1849, in New York.
> Carrie S., b. 25 June, 1853, in Oshkosh, Wis.
> 830. Homer Whitney, b. 29 Sep., 1857, in Rock Island, Ill.

775. Francis Henry⁹ (*Francis, Peter, Peter, Robert,
Lot, John, Lot, Roger*), b. 19 Sep., 1815, in Albany, N. Y.
He lived in Vienna and Camden, N. Y., where he was postmaster from 1848 to 1851. He removed to Toledo, Ohio, and
thence to Coldwater, Mich., where he still lives. He is a retired merchant and manufacturer. He m. (1) in Stow, Mass.,
25 Oct., 1836, Mary Eliza, dr. of Elisha and Mary (Conant)
Gates, b. 29 Jan., 1817, d. in Toledo, Ohio, 25 June, 1882; m.
(2) in Coldwater, Mich., 25 July, 1883, Sarah E. Buck.

Children of FRANCIS H. and MARY E. (GATES) CONANT:—

> Francis N., b. 12 May, 1840, in Vienna, N. Y.; d. 28 Aug., 1841.
> Francis E., b. 16 Jan., 1843, in Vienna, N. Y. He was adju-
> tant of the 108th N. Y. Regt., and killed at the battle of
> Antietam, 17 Sep., 1862.
> Walter N., b. 12 June, 1845, in Vienna. He is a manufacturer
> of and dealer in furniture, at Toledo, Ohio.
> 831. Eugene Henry, b. 12 June, 1847, in Vienna, N. Y.
> John A., b. 17 Jan., 1853, in Camden, N. Y. He is in business
> with his brother, at Toledo, Ohio.
> George F., b. 29 Sep., 1855, in Camden, N. Y., where he is in
> business with his brother, Eugene H.

776. Albert Francis⁹ (*Francis, Benjamin, Daniel, Rob-*

ert, Lot, John, Lot, Roger), b. 8 June, 1843, in Acton, Mass. He is a merchant, of Littleton, Mass. He m. in Westford, Mass., 18 Nov., 1859, Sarah Jane Patten.

Children of ALBERT F. and SARAH J. (PATTEN) CONANT:—

Grace Patten, b. in Littleton.
Goldsmith Hall, b. in Littleton.   ᛁ
William Francis, b. "   "

777.   Charles Henry[9] (*Francis, Benjamin, Daniel, Robert, Lot, John, Lot, Roger*), b. 28 Sep., 1844, in Acton, Mass. He resides in Lowell, Mass.; is a counsellor and attorney at law, of the firm of Conant & Carmichael. He m. in Lowell, 1 June, 1875, Alice Victoria Manning Wheeler.

Children of CHARLES H. and ALICE V. M. (WHEELER) CONANT:—

Harriet Wheeler, b. 9 Dec., 1876, in Lowell.
Helen Louisa, b. 3 Jan., 1879,   "   "
Charles Henry, b. 17 Jan., 1881,   "   "

778.   Nelson Brainard[9] (*Francis, Benjamin, Daniel, Robert, Lot, John, Lot, Roger*), b. 6 Dec., 1845, in Acton, Mass. He is a merchant, of Littleton, Mass., where he has held important town offices. He m. (1) 29 Apr., 1874, in Littleton, Frances U. Tuttle; m. (2) in East Hardwick, Vt., 1 Oct., 1885, Harriet W. Adgate.

Child of NELSON ·B. and FRANCES U. (TUTTLE) CONANT:—

Wallace B., b. 24 Mch., 1876, in Littleton.

779.   Peter Horace[9] (*Joseph, Zebulon, Andrew, Andrew, Lot, John, Lot, Roger*), b. 24 May, 1809, in Leominster, Mass. He removed to Madison, Ind., Louisville, Ky., and thence to Smithland, Ky., where he now resides. He is a miller. He m. (1) 9 Feb., 1832, Mary Ann Bowers, of Leominster, b. 9 Feb., 1813, who d. 18 Feb., 1876; m. (2) 29 Nov., 1877, Sarah Maria Bowers, b. 15 July, 1828.

Children of PETER H. and MARY A. (BOWERS) CONANT:—

832. Horace Artemus, b. 7 Feb., 1833.
George Henry, b. 8 Sep., 1834, in Louisville, Ky.; d. 22 Sep., 1855, in Smithland.
Ann Maria, b. 14 Feb., d. Sep., 1836.

Sarah Elizabeth, b. 11 Feb., 1838; d. 19 Mch., 1843.
Mary Sawyer, b. 28 Dec., 1840; d. in infancy.
833. John Heywood, b. 4 May, 1842.
Abbie Maria, b. 6 June, 1845; m. 17 May, 1871, Abram D.
Daugherty, of Coldwater, Mich. Child: Charles, b. 17
Feb., 1872.
834. Peter Andrew, b. 27 Aug., 1847.
Charles Withington, b. 27 Jan., 1852; m. in Smithland, 15
Feb., 1881, Cora Cade, b. 17 Sep., 1854.
835. Edward Taylor, b. 29 Mch., 1854.

780. **Nestor Wright**[9] (*Joseph, Zebulon, Andrew, Andrew, Lot, John, Lot, Roger*), b. 4 Jan., 1811, in Leominster, Mass. He is now a merchant, of Louisville, Ky., a member of the firm of N. W. Warren & Company. He m. 1844, in Madison, Ind., Maria Houghton Whitney.

Children of NESTOR W. and MARIA H. (WHITNEY) CO-NANT:—

Carrie E., b. 30 Dec., 1846, in Louisville, Ky.
Nelson Whitney, b. 11 Feb., 1848. He has dropped the name Nelson. Is now (1885) auditor of the Montreal and European Short Line Railroad, with head-quarters at New Glasgow, N. S. He graduated at the Mass. Institute of Technology, 1868.
Rolena Eliza, b. 1856; d. y.
Nelson F., d. in infancy.
Ruth M., b. 10 Mch., 1865.

781. **Charles Farnsworth**[9] (*Andrew, Zebulon, Andrew, Andrew, Lot, John, Lot, Roger*), b. 1821, in New Ipswich, N. H.; removed to Leominster, Mass. He m. Ora Burt, dr. of Lyman Bruce.

Children of CHARLES F. and ORA B. (BRUCE) CONANT:—

836. Charles Edward, b. 27 Mch., 1849, in Sturbridge.
Henry Lyman, b. 10 Aug., 1852, in Lunenburg.

782. **Andrew Philander**[9] (*Andrew, Zebulon, Andrew, Andrew, Lot, John, Lot, Roger*), b. 8 May, 1823, in New Ipswich, N. H. He is now the proprietor of a mineral spring at Terre Haute, Ind. He m. (2) in Lawrence, Mass., 14 Aug., 1854, Elizabeth Adelina, dr. of John and Mary (Littlefield) Cromwell, b. in Norridgewock, Me., 11 July, 1833.

Children of ANDREW P. and ——— (———) CONANT:—

Austin.
Ella.
Martha Ella Cobleigh.

Children of ANDREW P. and ELIZABETH A. (CROMWELL) CONANT:—

Ollie Adelina, b. 29 May, 1857, in Leominster, Mass.
Ossian Aconda Cromwell, b. 14 Dec., 1862, who is proprietor
    of a flouring mill at Terre Haute.
Ariel Hugo, b. 29 Dec., 1864; d. y.

783. **Adoniram Judson**[9] (*Andrew, Zebulon, Andrew, Andrew, Lot, John, Lot, Roger*), b. 30 Apr., 1831, in New Ipswich, N. H. He removed to Leominster, Mass., with his parents, and thence to Kentucky. He is now a miller, of Kuttawa, Ky. He m. in Leominster, 11 Feb., 1864, Roxana, dr. of John Cromwell, of Norridgewock, Me.

Child of ADONIRAM J. and ROXANA (CROMWELL) CONANT:—

Ada, b. 2 June, 1869, in Kuttawa, Ky.

784. **James Quincy**[9] (*Andrew, Zebulon, Andrew, Andrew, Lot, John, Lot, Roger*), b. 13 Apr., 1835, in New Ipswich, N. H.; removed to Leominster, Mass., where he now lives; a merchant. He m. 30 Apr., 1861, Clara Ann, dr. of Oliver and Clarissa Davenport (Stone) Hall, b. in Worcester, 31 Mch., 1841.

Children of JAMES Q. and CLARA A. (HALL) CONANT:—

Minnie Barbara, b. 17 Nov., 1862, in Mason Village, N. H.
Alice Cornelia, b. 31 Oct., 1864, in Leominster, Mass.
Gertrude Clara, b. 22 Feb., 1871, in Greenville, N. H.
Lillian Adeline, b. 12 Sep., 1873, "   "   "

785. **Henry S.**[9] (*Paul, Samuel Potter, Silas, Andrew, Lot, John, Lot, Roger*), b. 27 May, 1835, in Acton, Mass. He is a tailor. Lives in Nashua, N. H. He m. in Nashua, 26 Oct., 1854, Hannah F. Tolles.

Children of HENRY S. and HANNAH F. (TOLLES) CONANT:—

Flora May, b. 8 Dec., 1874; d. 27 Dec., 1876.
Effie Edna, b. 24 Mch., 1878.

786. **Cyrus Haywood**[9] (*Silas, Silas, Silas, Andrew, Lot, John, Lot, Roger*), b. 30 July, 1825, in Acton, Mass.; m. 26 Mch., 1851, Lovena Frances Dunlap, b. 1834, d. 15 Mch., 1855.

Child of CYRUS H. and LOVENA F. (DUNLAP) CONANT:—

Frances H., b. 6 July, 1853.

787. **Calvin Harrison**[9] (*James Franklin, James, Silas, Andrew, Lot, John, Lot, Roger*), b. 29 Aug., 1841, in Stoneham, Mass., where he has always resided; he is a mechanic. He enlisted 29 June, 1861, in the 13th Mass. Regt.; was corporal of Co. G, and mustered out 1 Aug., 1864. He took part in nineteen engagements with the enemy, but was never wounded. He was taken prisoner twice, first at Bull Run, second at Gettysburg, but was paroled, exchanged, and returned to duty each time. He m. (1) Lucinda A. Sprague, b. 24 Sep., 1845; m. (2) Susie L., dr. of Nelson and Mary Ann (Follett) Yardley, b. 8 Sep., 1845, in Nelson, N. H.

Child of CALVIN H. and LUCINDA A. (SPRAGUE) CONANT:—

Jennie Mabel, b. 3 Aug., 1868, in Stoneham.

Child of CALVIN H. and SUSIE L. (YARDLEY) CONANT:—

Nellie Etta, b. 3 Aug., 1874, in Stoneham.

788. **Joel N.**[9] (*Wesley, John Gardiner, Eli, Andrew, Lot, John, Lot, Roger*), b. 15 Mch., 1834, in Pawlet, Vt.; moved to Ida, Mich., with his parents. He is now a locomotive engineer on the Hannibal and St. Joseph R. R., living in Cameron, Mo. He m. in Indianapolis, Ind., 29 Oct., 1864, Anna, dr. of John and Ellen (Park) Lamb, b. in Fifeshire, Scotland, 15 Mch., 1843.

Children of JOEL N. and ANNA (LAMB) CONANT:—

Alice M., b. 27 May, 1870, in Cameron, Mo.
Anna B., b. 18 Dec., 1872, " " "
George, b. 8 Sep., 1874, " " "
Joel W., b. 28 Aug., 1876, " " "
Charles E., b. 24 Dec., 1879, " " "
Robert Franklin, b. 27 May, 1882, " "

789. **Washington Irving**[9] (*Alpheus, George, Eli, Andrew, Lot, John, Lot, Roger*), b. 6 Sep., 1841, in Enfield, N.

H., where he lives. He m. Ann F. Skinner, b. 27 May, 1847, in Plainfield, Vt.

Children of WASHINGTON I. and ANN F. (SKINNER) CO-NANT:—

> Mary Alice, b. 14 Nov., 1866; m. 9 June, 1885, Harry R. Love-joy, of West Lebanon, N. H.
> Ernest B., b. 21 May, 1870.

790. Luther[9] (*Emery, Simeon, William, William, Lot, John, Lot, Roger*), b. 7 Oct., 1822, in Vestal, Broome county, N. Y. He is a boot and shoe dealer, of Nichols, N. Y. He m. 10 Aug., 1853, in Nichols, N. Y., Emogene Jones.

Children of LUTHER and EMOGENE (JONES) CONANT:—

> Edward H., b. Aug., 1855, in Nichols.
> Mattie I., b. 1 Jan., 1860, "   "
> Etta May, b. 15 June, 1863, "   "

791. Simeon Dexter[9] (*Luther, Simeon, William, William, Lot, John, Lot, Roger*), b. 3 Nov., 1820, in Grafton, Vt., where he lives. He m. Wealthy W. Whitcomb.

Children of SIMEON D. and WEALTHY W. (WHITCOMB) CONANT:—

> Ellen M.
> Marcia E.
> Marion A.
> Myra E.

792. Benjamin[9] (*Levi, Levi, William, William, Lot, John, Lot, Roger*), b. 28 July, 1837, in Dublin, N. H.; moved to Littleton, Mass., when a child, with his parents. He lives in Cambridgeport, and is a printer, of the firm of Conant & Newhall, of Boston. He m. in Wakefield, Mass., 7 Jan., 1861, Clara M., dr. of Reuben and Emily Newhall, of So. Reading.

Children of BENJAMIN and CLARA M. (NEWHALL) CONANT:—

> Flora Maria, b. 10 Nov., 1863; d. 29 Apr., 1871, in Cambridge-port.
> Daisy Adelle, b. 31 May, 1872.
> Emily Kimball, b. 6 Oct., d. 4 Dec., 1874.

793. Sherman[9] (*Levi, Levi, William, William, Lot, John, Lot, Roger*), b. 13 Dec., 1839, in Dublin, N. H.; removed to

Littleton, Mass., with his parents. He enlisted in the 39th
Mass. Regt., in which he remained about one year; was promoted to a captaincy in the 3rd Regt., U. S. Colored Troops, and
stationed on Morris Island, where he remained till the first expedition to Florida, which he accompanied; was promoted to
the rank of major before the close of the war. After the war
settled in Jacksonville, Fla., and took an active part in reor-
ganizing the State government. He has been U. S. marshal
of that district, and is now general manager of the Florida
Southern Railroad. He m. 1867, Frances, dr. of Frederick
and Hannah (Pratt) Dewey, of Boston, Mass.

Children of SHERMAN and FRANCES (DEWEY) CONANT:—

> Annie Whitney, b. 1867; d. 1881.
> John Sherman, b. 1876.

794. Nellie Sherman[9] (*Levi, Levi, William, William,
Lot, John, Lot, Roger*), b. 19 July, 1846, in Littleton, Mass.;
m. 1870, Francis E., son of Francis G. and Abbie (Gibbs) Ballard, of Jamaica Plain. He is a farmer, of Lexington.

Children of FRANCIS E. and NELLIE S. (CONANT) BALLARD:—

i.   Alice Gibbs, b. 1872.
ii.   John Francis, b. 1873.
iii. Edith, b. 1875; d. 1876.
iv.   William Henry, b. 1879.
v.   Walter Clark, b. 1881.

795. Anna Jane[9] (*Levi, Levi, William, William, Lot,
John, Lot, Roger*), b. 16 Nov., 1848, in Littleton, Mass.; m.
1871, John H., son of John and Hannah (Farley) Hardy, of
Hollis, N. H. He resides in Arlington, and is a lawyer, of
Boston, Mass.

Children of JOHN H. and ANNA J. (CONANT) HARDY:—

i.   Harry Ballard, b. 1871; d. 1873.
ii.   John H., b. 1874.
iii. Horace D., b. 1877.

796. Charles Nathan[9] (*Nathaniel, Nathan, Nathaniel,
John, Lot, John, Lot, Roger*), b. 26 May, 1833, in Boston,
Mass., where he lives. He is employed in the National City
Bank. He m. 25 Nov., 1858, Hattie E. Greene, of Pittsfield,
N. H., b. 27 Apr., 1836.

Children of CHARLES N. and HATTIE E. (GREENE) Co-
NANT:—

Nathan Fletcher

Harry Greene, b. 2 Aug., d. 8 Sep., 1865.
Charles Harry, b. 3 Dec., 1868, in Dorchester.

797. Edgar Alonzo[9] (*Nathan N., Nathan, Nathaniel,
John, Lot, John, Lot, Roger*), b. 5 Aug., 1837, in Boston, Mass.,
where he lives. He is employed in the National Security Bank.
He m. 26 Aug., 1873, Hannah L. Sleeper, of Meriden, N. H.

Child of EDGAR A. and HANNAH L. (SLEEPER) CONANT:—

Clifford Sleeper, b. 22 June, 1879.   *Page 455*

798. James S.[9] (*John, Nathan, Nathaniel, John, Lot,
John, Lot, Roger*), b. 8 Nov., 1838, in (West Townsend?)
Mass.; m. 29 Oct., 1863, Sophronia Hitchcock.

Children of JAMES S. and SOPHRONIA (HITCHCOCK) Co-
NANT:—

Ella, b. 30 June, 1867; d. 8 Apr., 1882.
Anna, b. 5 June, 1870.

799. Marvel J.[9] (*David, Levi, Nathaniel, John, Lot,
John, Lot, Roger*), b. 7 July, 1843, in Mt. Holly, Vt. He
lives in Watertown, Mass.; is a produce dealer, in Boston.
He m. in Pepperell, Mass., 22 Feb., 1872, Nellie B. Ames.

Child of MARVEL J. and NELLIE B. (AMES) CONANT:—

Marjorie J., b. 19 Dec., 1882, in Watertown.

800. John[9] (*John, John, John, John, John, John, Lot,
Roger*), b. 17 Jan., 1818, in Topsfield, Mass.; was a mason, of
Salem, Mass. He d. 11 May, 1881. He m. in Salem, 1855,
Mary Boyington, of Mercer, Me.

Child of JOHN and MARY (BOYINGTON) CONANT:—

837.   Frank Roger, b. 27 Mch., 1857, in Salem.

801. Ruth[9] (*John, John, John, John, John, John, Lot,
Roger*), b. 2 Feb., 1822, in Topsfield, Mass.; m. Moses Cheever,
of Brimfield.

Children of MOSES and RUTH (CONANT) CHEEVER:—

i.   Sarah Augusta, b. Mch., 1848; d. in infancy.

ii. George, b. Sep., 1849; of North Brookfield.
iii. Helen Ayer, b. 2 Feb., 1853, in Spencer; of Brimfield.
iv. Edward Winthrop, b. Sep., 1855; a farmer, of Brimfield.

802. Irene[9] (*John, John, John, John, John, John, Lot, Roger*), b. 14 July, 1825, in Topsfield, Mass.; m. 13 Apr., 1847, Eben Hobson, son of Capt. John and Mary (Bailey) Moulton, b. in Wenham, 19 Feb., 1818. Capt. John Moulton was son of Jonathan and Mary (Tarbox) Moulton, of Wenham (see p. 164). They live in Beverly, on the land granted to Roger Conant in 1635, "at Bass River side," and very near the site of his house, as has been already mentioned. Mr. Moulton has rendered valuable assistance in the compilation of this Genealogy, and is himself a descendant of Roger Conant.

Children of EBEN H. and IRENE (CONANT) MOULTON:—

i. Lorenzo Gordon, b. 7 Feb., 1848; m. 1 Jan., 1874, Mrs. Maria (Jones) Palmer, of Taunton, Mass., and has Lillie Belle, b. in Hyde Park, 5 Mch., 1876. He lives in Boston.
ii. Mary Ellen, b. 23 Apr., 1849.
iii. Charles Standley, b. 17 Feb., 1851; d. 16 Aug., 1853.
iv. Sarah Frances, b. 5 Mch., 1853; m. 4 Feb., 1884, George Peabody, son of Dean Stiles.
v. Walter Standley, b. 21 Aug., 1861; of Lynn.
vi. Arthur Augustus, b. 3 Aug., 1863; of Lynn.
vii. Roger Conant, b. 7 Aug., d. 12 Aug., 1867.

803. Benjamin[9] (*John, John, John, John, John, John, Lot, Roger*), b. 29 Dec., 1835, in Topsfield, Mass., where he lives; is a farmer. He m. (1) 1857, Josephine B. Willson; m. (2) Margaret Sand.

Children of BENJAMIN and JOSEPHINE B. (WILLSON) CONANT:—

Frederick Wells, b. Jan., 1859, in Topsfield. He m. June, 1883, Virginia Garrett. He is a grain dealer, of Ipswich.
Arthur Henry, b. June, 1862; a milk dealer, of Salem; unm.
Clarence Leslie, b. Feb., 1864; a farmer, of Topsfield.
Albert Standley, b. Aug., 1867; of Topsfield.
Josephine Bonaparte, b. 23 July, 1871.

Children of BENJAMIN and MARGARET (SAND) CONANT:—

Frank Stanwood, b. Sep., 1873.
Ruth Cheever, b. Nov., 1874.
Clara N., b. Jan., 1876.
Benjamin, b. June, 1880.

804.   Frederick Odell[9] (*Richard Odell, Alvah, John, Na-thaniel, Daniel, John, Lot, Roger*), b. 1 Oct., 1857, in Port-land, Me.   He was prepared for college in the public schools of Portland, and graduated at Bowdoin College; B. S. 1880, and M. A. 1883.   In 1874 he went to California, by way of Panama, stopping in Kingston, Jamaica, and various Mexican and Central American ports, and returning overland from San Francisco.   In 1879 he went to Cuba, visited the important cities, and returned home by way of Key West, Cedar Keys, Jacksonville, Fla., Savannah, Ga., Charleston, S. C., and Washington, D. C.   In 1880 he entered his father's store as a clerk, and was admitted to partnership Jan. 1, 1882.   He is a member of Casco Lodge, No. 36, A. F. and A. M., and of Cum-berland Chapter, No. 35, of Yarmouth, Me.   He is the com-piler of this Genealogy.   He m. in Yarmouth, Me., 31 Oct., 1883, Eva, dr. of Capt. Reuben and Hannah Elizabeth (Blan-chard) Merrill, of Yarmouth.   Reuben Merrill was son of William and Lydia (Sturdivant) Merrill, grand–son of Ad-ams and Elizabeth (Titcomb) Merrill, g. g. s. of James and Mary (Adams) Merrill, who were early settlers of Falmouth, Me.   James Merrill was son of Abel, who was son of Nathan-iel Merrill, of Newbury, Mass., the immigrant.   Hannah Eliz-abeth Blanchard was dr. of Capt. Reuben and Christiana (Loring) Blanchard, g. dr. of Beza and Prudence (Rideout) Blanchard, g. g. dr. of Nathaniel and Bithiah (Mitchell) Blan-chard.   Nathaniel Blanchard was fifth in descent from Thomas Blanchard, the immigrant; his wife, Bithiah Mitchell, was dr. of Seth Mitchell, son of Jacob and Rebecca (Cushman) Mitch-ell.   Jacob Mitchell was g. s. of Experience Mitchell, one of the Leyden Pilgrims, whose wife, Jane, was dr. of Francis Cook, who came in the Mayflower.   Rebecca (Cushman) Mitchell was dr. of Rev. Isaac Cushman, son of Thomas and Mary (Allerton) Cushman, g. s. of Robert Cushman.   Robert Cushman was one of the most active promoters of the migra-tion from Holland, in 1620, and came over on the Fortune, the second vessel; his son, Thomas, married Mary, dr. of Isaac Allerton; she d. 1699, the last survivor of the Mayflower's passengers.   [See *Old Times in North Yarmouth*, p. 247

Frederick Odell Conant

(Mitchell); *Old Times*, p. 1089 (Blanchard); *History of New-bury*, p. 309, and *Maine Hist. and Gen. Recorder*, Vol. iii., p. 178 (Merrill); Savage's *Genealogical Dict.*, Vol. i., pp. 38 and 492 (Allerton and Cushman).]

Children of FREDERICK O. and EVA (MERRILL) CONANT:—

Elizabeth Merrill, b. 11 Jan., 1886.
Persis Loring, b. 29 May, 1887.

805. Hamilton Stimson[9] (*Horace Hamilton, Newell, John, Ezra, Benjamin, John, Lot, Roger*), b. 22 May, 1851, in Orford, N. H. He lived in Brooklyn, N. Y., and was superintendent of a large manufacturing establishment. He now lives in Providence, R. I.; is general secretary of the Y. M. C. A., and a deacon of the Reformed church. He m. in Brooklyn, N. Y., 29 Nov., 1871, Hannah Louise, dr. of Eli and Josephine Louise Ferguson, of Jersey City, N. J.

Children of HAMILTON S. and HANNAH (FERGUSON) CONANT:—

Franklin Norton, b. 4 Aug., 1873.
Mary Estell Stimson, b. 28 Sep., 1877, in Brooklyn, N. Y.
William Horace Robinson, b. 21 July, 1881, in Brooklyn, N.Y.

806. Frederick Herbert[9] (*William Augustus, Newell, John, Ezra, Benjamin, John, Lot, Roger*), b. 1 Jan., 1847, in New York city. He is engaged in the mining business in Leadville, Col., a member of the firm of DeLan & Conant. He m. in Huntington, L. I., 25 Oct., 1866, Mary Ella Crozier.

Children of FREDERICK H. and MARY E. (CROZIER) CONANT:—

Charles Platt, b. 24 Sep., 1867, in Black Hawk, Col.
Francis Slasen, b. 22 Sep., 1869, "   "   "
Frederick William, b. 6 Jan., 1871,   "   "   "
Alice Hill, b. 8 Nov., 1873,   "   "   "
Jennie Brown, b. 4 Aug., 1876, in Brooklyn, N. Y.
Edward Ketchum, b. 26 Dec., 1881, in Leadville, Col.

807. Edson Alvinza[9] (*William, Israel Elliot, Jonathan, Jonathan, Jonathan, Lot, Lot, Roger*), b. 7 Feb., 1848, in Canton, N. Y.; is a merchant, of Hermon, N. Y. He m. 30 Mch., 1876, in Hermon, Ellen Knox.

Children of EDSON A. and ELLEN (KNOX) CONANT:—

Daniel Franklin, b. 2 July, 1877.
Eva Eliza, b. 23 Sep., 1880.

808. **Herbert Eugene**[9] (*Martin Allen, Martin, Elias, David, David, William, Lot, Roger*), b. 1 Aug., 1848, in Natick, Mass., where he lives. He m. (1) Anna Littlefield; m. (2) 1879, Octavia Gould, of Baring, Me.

Children of HERBERT E. and ANNA (LITTLEFIELD) CONANT:—

Lucy, b. 1874.
Herbert E., d. aged 4 years.

Children of HERBERT E. and OCTAVIA (GOULD) CONANT:—

Ora Alean, b. 1880.
Ernest, b. 1883.

809. **David Perkins**[9] (*Bela Forbes, David, David, David, David, William, Lot, Roger*), b. 19 Mch., 1854, in Lyme, N. H.; moved to Laconia, N. H., with his parents; is a mechanic. He m. in Laconia, 17 Feb., 1877, Abbie Jane, dr. of John O. and Mary Jane (Aldrich) Stevens, b. in Gilmanton, N. H., 14 July, 1853.

Child of DAVID P. and ABBIE JANE (STEVENS) CONANT:—

Ida May, b. 13 Apr., 1878.

810. **Samuel Dimick**[9] (*Jonathan Josiah, Jonathan, Josiah, Jonathan, David, William, Lot, Roger*), b. 9 Jan., 1851, in Lyme, N. H.; moved to North Thetford, Vt., with his parents. He is now an attorney at law, in company with his uncle, Judge Chester C. Conant, and lives in Greenfield, Mass. He m. in Barre, Vt., 18 Apr., 1876, Mary Isabella, dr. of Loren and Martha (Cook) Ketchum.

Children of SAMUEL D. and MARY I. (KETCHUM) CONANT:—

Octavia Mildred, b. 23 Jan., 1882, in Greenfield, Mass.
William Chester, b. 1 Feb., 1884.

811. **Clarence Mortimer**[9] (*Claudius Buchanan, Samuel Stillman, John, Ebenezer, Ebenezer, Roger, Lot, Roger*), b. 26 Mch., 1851, in Brooklyn, N. Y. He is a homœopathic phy-

sician and surgeon, of Orange, N. J.; was formerly of Middletown, N. Y. He m. in Goshen, N. Y., 6 Oct., 1874, Charlotte Gedney Ostrom.

Children of CLARENCE M. and CHARLOTTE G. (OSTROM) CONANT:—

Roger Ostrom, b. 10 Sep., 1875, in Middletown.
Stuart Mortimer, b. 15 July, 1879, in Middletown.

812. Charles Wesley[9] (*Lewis, Timothy B., Timothy, Caleb, Benajah, Caleb, Exercise, Roger*), b. 28 Mch., 1850, in Hinckley, Ohio. He is now a teamster, at Cleveland, O. He m. in Granger, O., 26 Mch., 1868, Ida E. Albertson.

Children of CHARLES W. and IDA E. (ALBERTSON) CONANT:—

Albert, b. 21 Mch., 1869, in Hinckley.
Maggie, b. 1 Feb., 1871, "	"
Merton, b. 17 Feb., 1873.

813. Ward Lewis[9] (*Lewis, Timothy B., Timothy, Caleb, Benajah, Caleb, Exercise, Roger*), b. 5 Mch., 1858, in Hinckley, O. He now lives in Cleveland, O. He m. in Cleveland, 19 Nov., 1878, Sarah Annie, dr. of John and Annie Pryor (Hopkins) Indoe, who was b. 1858, at Keinton, Mandeville, Somersetshire, England.

Children of WARD L. and SARAH A. (INDOE) CONANT:—

Ward Henry, b. 9 Dec., 1879, in Granger, O.
Eva Annie, b. 11 Aug., 1881, in Cleveland, O.
John Lewis, b. 9 Aug., 1883, "	"	"

TENTH GENERATION.

814. John M.[10] (*Amos, Amos, Silas, Samuel, Robert, Lot, John, Lot, Roger*), b. 19 Aug., 1838, in Sudbury, Mass., where he lives. He has held various town offices. He m. Lucretia Richards.

Children of JOHN M. and LUCRETIA (RICHARDS) CONANT:—

Clara J., b. 1861.
Lilian.
Louisa.
Edwin A., b. 1871.

815.   Benjamin P.[10] (*Levi, Levi, Silas, Samuel, Robert, Lot, John, Lot, Roger*), b. 7 May, 1832, in Hubbardston, Mass.; m. 10 Aug., 1854, Harriet Morse, who d. 30 May, 1880. He d. 22 Nov., 1879.

Children of BENJAMIN P. and HARRIET (MORSE) CONANT:—

Etta D., b. 26 May, 1855; m. E. Wheeler.
Fred. Arthur, b. 27 June, 1864; d. 1864.

816.   Edward W.[10] (*Isaac, Abraham, Oliver, Samuel, Robert, Lot, John, Lot, Roger*), b. 24 June, 1837, in Winterport, Me. He is a lumber manufacturer; lives in Oldtown, Me. He was grand master of the Grand Lodge, I. O. O. F., of Maine, for 1884 and 1885. He m. (1) in Oldtown, Me., 2 Sep., 1860, Carrie E. Bailey, of Milford, who d. 24 Dec., 1874; m. (2) 30 Aug., 1881, Mary L. McFarlan, of Oldtown, who d. 16 Mch., 1882; m. (3) 10 Aug., 1885, Caro E. Smith.

Child of EDWARD W. and CARRIE E. (BAILEY) CONANT:—

Edward Allen, b. 28 Apr., 1867.

817.   George Wentworth[10] (*Amasa S., Abraham, Oliver, Samuel, Robert, Lot, John, Lot, Roger*), b. 20 Apr., 1832, in (Frankfort?) Me.; was of Orrington, Me. He d. 25 June, 1858, in Cuba, W. I. He m. 1 July, 1854, Martha Dow, of Deer Isle.

Children of GEORGE W. and MARTHA (DOW) CONANT:—

George Wentworth, b. July, 1857.
Lorenzo Dow, b. Feb., 1859.

818.   John Greenleaf[10] (*John, Nathan, Samuel, Samuel, Robert, Lot, John, Lot, Roger*), b. 1837, in Sumner, Me.; was a machinist, of Abington, Mass.; d. 26 Nov., 1885. He m. in Rockland, 2 Aug., 1861, Betsey Tirrell, dr. of Albert and Susan Loud (Tirrell) Whitmarsh, b. in Abington, 2 Jan., 1841.

Children of JOHN G. and BETSEY T. (WHITMARSH) CO-
NANT:—

> Willie Greenleaf, b. 22 Jan., 1863.
> Bessie Whitmarsh, b. 22 Apr., 1868.

819. Joseph Tyler[10] (*Nathan Warren, Asa, Ephraim,
Peter, Robert, Lot, John, Lot, Roger*), b. 13 Mch., 1841, in
Lincolnville, Me. He lives in Camden, Me.; was for a few
years a member of the firm of Dixon & Co., of Glasgow and
Greenock, Scotland. He managed the Greenock branch. He
is now a sea captain, engaged in the East India trade. He m.
in Camden, 7 May, 1863, Rebecca H., dr. of Isaac and Nancy
(Wentworth) Conant, of Appleton, Me.
Children of JOSEPH T. and REBECCA H. (CONANT) CO-
NANT:—

> Mabel W., b. 4 May, 1867.
> Josie M., b. 30 Sep., 1872.

820. Sumner Tyler[10] (*Nathan Warren, Asa, Ephraim,
Peter, Robert, Lot, John, Lot, Roger*), b. 9 Jan., 1843, in Lin-
colnville, Me.; is of Camden; a mechanic. During the late
war he served in Co. F, 26th Regt., Me. Vols., and also in the
33rd Regt., N. J. Vols. He m. (1) ——; m. (2) in Buxton,
Me., 28 Nov., 1875, Sarah Lizzie, dr. of Ansel and Amelia
Merrill, b. in Saco, Me., 3 May, 1848.
Children of SUMNER T. and —— (——) CONANT:—

> Mary Adella, b. 19 Jan., 1863.
> Walter, b. 10 Nov., 1867.

821. Frank Warren[10] (*Nathan Warren, Asa, Ephraim,
Peter, Robert, Lot, John, Lot, Roger*), b. 14 May, 1851, in
Camden, Me., where he now lives. He m. 25 Dec., 1873, in
North Haven, Sarah Margaret, dr. of George Arnold and Mary
Ann (Conant) Hall, b. in Belfast, Me., 23 Oct., 1856.
Children of FRANK W. and SARAH M. (HALL) CONANT:—

> Mary Thomas, b. 1 Nov., 1874.
> Lizzie Merrill, b. 29 Mch., 1877.
> George Hall, b. 15 Dec., 1878.

822. Ephraim Franklin[10] (*Ephraim, Ephraim, Ephraim,*

Peter, Robert, Lot, John, Lot, Roger), b. 25 Sep., 1835, in Temple, Me., where he lives. He is sheriff of Franklin county. He m. in Strong, 14 Oct., 1860, Eliza Ann Mitchell.

Child of EPHRAIM F. and ELIZA A. (MITCHELL) CONANT:—

Maud Capitola, b. 13 June, 1863.

823. **John Wesley**[10] (*Ephraim, Ephraim, Ephraim, Peter, Robert, Lot, John, Lot, Roger*), b. 16 Feb., 1840, in Temple, Me. He is a carpenter; lives in Cumberland Mills, Me. He m. in Strong, 5 May, 1866, Almira S. Cottle, who d. 5 Dec., 1880, in New Portland; m. (2) 1 July, 1882, in Saccarappa, Lizzie Murch, b. 10 Oct., 1852.

Children of JOHN W. and ALMIRA S. (COTTLE) CONANT:—

George W., b. 12 May, 1868, in Strong, Me.
Arthur L., b. 29 Oct., 1869,   "   "   "
Eugene W., b. 26 Jan., 1874, in Lisbon, Me.
Grace M., b. 17 May, 1876,   "   "   "
Ernest L., b. 26 Sep., 1878,   "   "   "

Child of JOHN W. and LIZZIE (MURCH) CONANT:—

Guy, b. 16 May, d. 8 Aug., 1883, in Cumberland Mills.

824. **James Harvey**[10] (*Ephraim, Ephraim, Ephraim, Peter, Robert, Lot, John, Lot, Roger*), b. 4 June, 1842, in Temple, Me.; is a farmer, of Strong, Me. He m. in Windsor, Vt., 5 Dec., 1863, Evelina Belcher Hunter.

Children of JAMES H. and EVELINA B. (HUNTER) CONANT:—

William Harvey, b. 20 Oct., 1864, in Windsor, Vt.
Albert Stoddard, b. 8 June, 1869, in Strong, Me.
Archibald Ephraim, b. 30 Oct., 1872, in Strong, Me.
Lydia Evelina, b. 20 Sep., 1878,   "   "   "
Sarah Hunter, b. 29 May, 1883,   "   "   "

825. **Charles Barker**[10] (*Ephraim, Ephraim, Ephraim, Peter, Robert, Lot, John, Lot, Roger*), b. 19 Oct., 1848; a farmer, of Strong, Me.; m. in Boston, Mass., 29 June, 1873, Tryphena S. Staples.

Child of CHARLES B. and TRYPHENA S. (STAPLES) CONANT:—

Ella M., b. 1 Aug., 1875, in Phillips, Me.

826. **Sylvanus Gideon**[10] (*Ephraim, Ephraim, Ephraim,*

Peter, Robert, Lot, John, Lot, Roger), b. 6 Aug., 1850, in (Strong?) Me.; m. in Lisbon, Me., 28 May, 1876, Jennie M. Brown. He died in Cumberland Mills (Westbrook), Me., 4 Feb., 1886.

Children of SYLVANUS G. and JENNIE M. (BROWN) CO-NANT:—

Herbert E., b. 5 Dec., 1877, in Lisbon.
Algier M., b. 15 Nov., 1879, in Cumberland Mills.

827. Hermon[10] (*Joseph Haywood, Joseph, Ephraim, Peter, Robert, Lot, John, Lot, Roger*), b. 5 Sep., 1840, in Thorndike, Me. He lives in Brooklyn; is in business in New York city. He m. in Brooklyn, N. Y., 16 Sep., 1868, Jennie Brown.

Children of HERMON and JENNIE (BROWN) CONANT:—

Harold Beecher, b. 17 Mch., 1871, in New York city.
William Haywood, b. 6 Mch., 1874, in Brooklyn.

828. Edward Joseph[10] (*Daniel Alexander, Joseph, Ephraim, Peter, Robert, Lot, John, Lot, Roger*), b. 3 July, 1855, in Norridgewock, Me.; m. in Charleston, S. C., 9 Dec., 1879, Courtney Woling.

Children of EDWARD J. and COURTNEY (WOLING) CONANT:—

Ella, b. 24 Nov., 1880, in Charleston, S. C.
Nellie, b. 3 June, 1882," " "

829. Deforest[10] (*Marcus G., Abraham, Ephraim, Peter, Robert, Lot, John, Lot, Roger*), b. 10 Feb., 1850, in Hope, Me.; m. 5 June, 1868, Laura J. Newbit, b. 20 Mch., 1846.

Child of DEFOREST and LAURA J. (NEWBIT) CONANT:—

Percie R., b. 23 Sep., 1870.

830. Homer Whitney[10] (*Andrew, Phineas, Peter, Peter, Robert, Lot, John, Lot, Roger*), b. 29 Sep., 1857, in Rock Island, Ill. He is now a grocer, of Sheldon, Iowa. He has been a member of the city council of Sheldon, and chief of the fire department. He m. in Newell, Iowa, 10 Oct., 1883, Florence E., dr. of James and Amelia Coleman, b. in Richmond, Ill., 25 June, 1859.

Child of HOMER W. and FLORENCE E. (COLEMAN) CONANT:—

Florence Jewell, b. 3 Sep., 1884, in Sheldon.

831.   Eugene Henry[10] (*Francis Henry, Francis, Peter, Peter, Robert, Lot, John, Lot, Roger*), b. 12 June, 1847, in Vienna, N. Y.   He is a chair manufacturer, of Camden, N. Y. He m. ———.

Children of EUGENE H. and ——— (———) CONANT:—

> Harold T., b. 1877.
> Alice Pauline, b. ———.
> Mary Eliza.

832.   Horace Artemus[10] (*Peter Horace, Joseph, Zebulon, Andrew, Andrew, Lot, John, Lot, Roger*), b. 7 Feb., 1833; moved to Louisville, Ky., with his parents.   He was of St. Louis, Mo.   During the first year of the war he was aide-de-camp of Gen. N. Lyons, with the rank of captain.   He d. in Washington, D. C., 5 Oct., 1862.   He m. in Louisville, Ky., 18 Dec., 1856, Lydia Augusta Sisson.   After the death of her husband she removed to Burlington, N. J., and in 1867 to Wilmington, Del.

Child of HORACE A. and LYDIA A. (SISSON) CONANT:—

> Heywood, b. 25 Dec., 1857, in St. Louis, Mo.   He entered Cornell University, 1874, graduating B. S. 1878, and since that time has been engaged in journalism.   He is now on the editorial staff of the Wilmington "Every Evening" newspaper.

833.   John Heywood[10] (*Peter Horace, Joseph, Zebulon, Andrew, Andrew, Lot, John, Lot, Roger*), b. 4 May, 1842, in Louisville, Ky.; m. (1) in St. Louis, Mo., 29 Sep., 1864, Eliza Buck, b. 2 Apr., 1843, d. 17 June, 1865; m. (2) in Washington, D. C., 29 Jan., 1870, Rosetta Melissa Squires, b. 10 Oct., 1847.

Child of JOHN H. and ELIZA (BUCK) CONANT:—

> Lilian, b. 17 June, 1865; d. 9 Sep., 1865.

Children of JOHN H. and ROSETTA M. (SQUIRES) CONANT:—

> Sarah, b. 20 Mch., 1871; d. y.
> Gordon Paine, b. 18 Dec., 1872.
> Lyda, b. 24 Oct., 1874.
> Edith, b. 31 Jan., 1877.
> Grace, b. 6 Apr., 1879.
> Thaddeus, b. 30 Apr., 1881.

834.   Peter Andrew[10] (*Peter Horace, Joseph, Zebulon,*

Andrew, Andrew, Lot, John, Lot, Roger), b. 27 Aug., 1847, in Louisville, Ky.; m. 12 Jan., 1867, in Smithland, Ky., Isabella Weston, b. 12 Jan., 1848.

Children of PETER A. and ISABELLA (WESTON) CONANT:—

Julia Ann, b. 22 Nov., 1868.
Mary Elizabeth, b. 27 June, 1871; d. 11 July, 1871.
Katie, b. 5 July, 1872; d. in infancy.
Addie Belle, b. 19 May, 1874; d. 21 May, 1874.
Richard Horace.

835. **Edward Taylor**[10] (*Peter Horace, Joseph, Zebulon, Andrew, Andrew, Lot, John, Lot, Roger*), b. 29 Mch., 1854, in Smithland, Ky.; m. 13 Sep., 1874, Mary Ann Clark, b. 12 Nov., 1855.

Children of EDWARD F. and MARY A. (CLARK) CONANT:—

Henry, b. 24 Apr., 1876; d. 8 Jan., 1881.
Abbie, b. 12 Jan., 1879.
Horace, b. 18 Nov., 1880.
Dollie, b. 19 Dec., 1882.

836. **Charles Edward**[10] (*Charles Farnsworth, Andrew, Zebulon, Andrew, Andrew, Lot, John, Lot, Roger*), b. 27 Mch., 1849, in Sturbridge, Mass. He resides in Dedham; is a member of the firm of Wheeler, Conant & Blodgett, doing business in Boston. He m. in Dedham, 1 Oct., 1874, Caroline Elizabeth, dr. of Lewis Hall and Eunice (Haven) Kingsbury, b. 10 May, 1855.

Children of CHARLES E. and CAROLINE E. (KINGSBURY) CONANT:—

Harry V., b. 21 Nov., 1875, in Dedham.
Lewis K., b. 23 Nov., 1877, "   "
Edith J., b. 19 Sep., 1879,   "   "
Roger B., b. 16 Sep., 1883,   "   "

837. **Frank Roger**[10] (*John, John, John, John, John, John, John, Lot, Roger*), b. 27 Mch., 1857, in Salem, Mass. He is a market gardener, of Danvers, Mass. He m. in Salem, 31 Jan., 1878, Sarah E., dr. of Alfred and Sarah Tyler.

Children of FRANK R. and SARAH E. (TYLER) CONANT:—

Frank J., b. 5 Mch., 1879.
Roger W., b. 17 Apr., 1880.
Mary E., b. 9 Apr., 1881.
Addie, b. 17 Apr., 1883.

DESCENDANTS OF GEORGE CONANT.

FIRST GENERATION.

I. **George Conant,** who came to Plymouth, Mass., from Exeter, England, about 1716, was perhaps son of George Conant, of Dunsford, a small parish of Devon, seven or eight miles west of Exeter. "George, the son of George Conant, was baptized Sep. 9, 1682" (see p. 17), at Dunsford. He is said to have been a haberdasher, of Exeter, and of considerable property, but the vessel in which he came being wrecked at Scituate, he lost all. He settled in Plymouth, and married there about 1718, Mary,* dr. of Joseph and Elizabeth (Southworth) Howland, b. about 1690. Joseph Howland was son of John Howland, who came in the Mayflower, and Elizabeth, dr. of John Tilley. Elizabeth Southworth was dr. of Thomas Southworth, the immigrant, who came in 1628, and Elizabeth, dr. of John Reyner. Mr. Conant while in Plymouth was a sailor and fisherman, and was preparing to visit England when he was, by accident, thrown out of a fishing boat and drowned, in 1731, in Plymouth harbor. His family continued to reside in Plymouth for a few years, and then removed to Barnstable, on Cape Cod. The widow married second, William Green, of Barnstable, and after a few years was again left a widow, after which she resided with her son, George, until her death, 23 Oct., 1756, in the 63rd year of her age.

Children of GEORGE and MARY (HOWLAND) CONANT:—

II.   Charles, b. June, 1720.
III.   George, b. 13 Jan., 1723.
       Elizabeth, b. ———; d. in infancy.

---

* This is as given by Davis in "*Ancient Landmarks of Plymouth*," and differs from the family tradition. A letter written in 1811 by George, grandson of the first George, to his nephew, George Erskine Conant, and now in his possession, states that George Conant, the immigrant, married Mary Southworth, whose mother was a Howland. The matter is still further complicated by the fact that the Barnstable Patriot, of 24 Mch., 1863, in an article on the early settlers of Barnstable, says that *Sarah*, wife of George Conant, is buried at West Barnstable, and that she died 16 Nov., 1736, in her 37th year. This probably refers to the second wife of George Conant, jr., who died 1756, aged 36.

SECOND GENERATION.

II. **Charles**[2] (*George*), b. June, 1720, in Plymouth, Mass.;
moved to Barnstable, with his mother. On the 26th June,
1776, he signed a petition to the General Court, protesting
against the action of the majority of the citizens of Barnstable
as unpatriotic, and affirming that if independence should be
declared the petitioners would support the measure; and
though he did not join the Revolutionary army, four of his
sons were almost continually in the service. He d. 23 Dec.,
1803. He m. 1743, Joanna, dr. of Jabez and Hannah Bursley,
b. 1719, of Barnstable, who d. 11 Jan., 1801.

Children of CHARLES and JOANNA (BURSLEY) CONANT :—

iv. Asa, b. 6 Feb., 1744-5.
   Mary, b. 18 Mch., 1745-6; m. Barnabas Crocker. Children:
      Anna, Hannah, Lemuel and Barnabas.
   Charity, b. 14 May, 1747.
   John, b. 17 Aug., 1748.
   Benjamin, b. 22 Oct., 1749.
   Barnabas, b. 2 Mch., 1750-1. In 1775 he was a private in Cap-
      tain Hamlen's company of Col. Freeman's regiment of the
      Revolutionary army (Mass. Archives, Muster Rolls, Vol. 36,
      p. 60); in 1776 he was sergeant in Grannis' company, sta-
      tioned on the Elizabeth Islands (Vol. 36, pp. 80, 81, 82); and
      in 1777 and 1778 was in Greenwood's company of Gerrish's
      regiment (Vol. 19, pp. 119 and 152).
   Thomas, b. 8 Apr., 1752. In 1776 he was corporal of Grannis'
      company, at the Elizabeth Islands (Mass. Archives, Muster
      Rolls, Vol. 36, pp. 80, 81, 82); in 1778 was in Micah Ham-
      len's company of Freeman's regiment (Vol. 36, p. 216); in
      1779 was in the same company (Vol. 36, pp. 32, 34).
   Elizabeth, b. 14 Apr., 1753; m. Edmund Crocker. Children:
      Charles, Mary, Olive, Asenath, Thomas, Sarah, Elizabeth,
      Edmund and Lucretia.
   Sarah, b. 7 June, 1754.
   Hannah, b. 20 Oct., 1755; m. Seth Casley.
   Lemuel, b. 28 Jan., 1757. He was in Hamlen's company of
      Freeman's regiment, in the Revolutionary army, in 1775
      (Muster Rolls, Vol. 36, p. 60); in 1776 was in Grannis' com-
      pany, at the Elizabeth Islands (Vol. 36, p. 80) and on the
      brig Rising Empire (Vol. 40, p. 35); in 1778 was sergeant of
      Griffin's company of Jacob's regiment (Vol. 19, p. 137); in
      1779 was in Baker's company of Freeman's regiment (Vol.
      35, p. 81); in 1780 was in the 7th division of 6 months' men,
      under Captain Dix; is described as "of Amherst, age 23,
      height 5 ft. 8 in., freckled complexion" (Vol. 35, p. 188);

and in 1781 was in Smith's company of Col. Rufus Putnam's regiment (Mass. Archives, Worcester Rolls).

Olive, b. 11 Sep., 1758; m. Zachariah Jenkins, and had Barnabas.·

Martha, b. 19 Aug., 1761; m. James Holley. Children: Lemuel, Mary, Asenath and Sarah.

III. **George²** (*George*), b. 13 Jan., 1723, in Plymouth, Mass.; moved to Barnstable, with his mother. In 1776 he was in Jenkins' company, stationed at Dartmouth (Mass. Arch., Muster Rolls, Vol. 36, p. 129); and in 1777 in Baker's company of Freeman's regiment, for a short time (Vol. 1, p. 66); and also in Minot's company of Whitney's regiment (Vol. 2, p. 213). He was a merchant tailor, of Barnstable, till 1779, when being afraid his sons would become sailors, he removed to Becket, in Berkshire county, where he became one of the most respected citizens. Both he and his wife were members of the Congregational Church of Becket. He d. 3 Mch., 1792, and was buried in the church yard near the First Congregational Church. He m. (1) 20 June, 1753, Sarah, dr. of Roger Goodspeed, who d. 16 Mch., 1754, aged 26 years. Roger Goodspeed was son of Benjamin and Mary (Davis), g. s. of Roger and Alice (Layton) Goodspeed.

Child of George and Sarah (Goodspeed) Conant:—

George, b. 15 Feb., 1754; d. in infancy.

He m. (2) 30 Jan., 1755, Susanna, dr. of Ebenezer and Hannah (Hall) Crocker, b. 20 Oct., 1720, d. 1756. Ebenezer Crocker was son of Josiah and Melatiah (Hinckley) Crocker, g. s. of William Crocker. Melatiah Hinckley was dr. of Governor Thomas Hinckley.

Child of George and Susanna (Crocker) Conant:—

George, b. 1756; d. aged 18 months.

He m. (3) 1757, Elizabeth, dr. of Thomas and Mehitable (Dimick) Crocker, who d. 17 Sep., 1759. Thomas Crocker was son of Thomas and Elizabeth (Lothrop) Crocker, and g. s. of Deacon Job and Mary (Wally) Crocker.

Child of George and Elizabeth (Crocker) Conant:—

Crocker, b. 23 June, 1759; d. aged 16 years.

He m. (4) 1761, Lydia, dr. of Thatcher and Anna (Gray) Freeman, b. 1733, d. 16 Jan., 1808. Thatcher Freeman was son of Joseph Freeman and Lydia, dr. of Joseph Thatcher. He m. Anna, dr. of John and Susanna (Clark) Gray.

Children of GEORGE and LYDIA (FREEMAN) CONANT:—

v.   George, b. 27 July, 1762.
       Thatcher, b. 13 Aug., 1763; d. 18 Nov., 1763.
vi.   Thatcher, b. 2 Mch., 1767.

THIRD GENERATION.

IV.   **Asa**[3] (*Charles, George*), b. 6 Feb., 1744-5, in Barnstable, Mass., where he lived. In 1776 he was a sailor on the brig "Rising Empire," under Captain Richard Wheeler (Mass. Arch., Muster Rolls, Vol. 40, p. 35), and also in Nye's company, at the Elizabeth Islands (Vol. 36, p. 143); in 1778-9 he was in Hamlen's company of Freeman's regiment, in the Revolutionary army (Vol. 36, pp. 34, 216). He m. (1) the widow Sarah (Percival) Atwood. He m. (2) Mehitable Braman, who d. 3 Aug., 1807.

Children of ASA and MEHITABLE (BRAMAN) CONANT:—

Charles.
Sarah.
Asa.

He m. (3) 24 Dec., 1807, Anna Smith.

Children of ASA and ANNA (SMITH) CONANT:—

Mehitable, b. 16 Sep., 1808.
John, b. 25 Nov., 1810. He is said to have settled in New York State.

V.   **George**[3] (*George, George*), b. 27 July, 1762, in Barnstable, Mass.; moved to Becket, Mass., with his parents; was a tailor. He was one of the most respected and prominent citizens of Becket, and was honored with almost every office within the gift of the town. He was a member of the Congregational Church, and clerk of the society for many years. He was a

justice of the peace for twenty-five years, was often town
clerk, and seventeen times elected to represent the town in
the General Court of Massachusetts. He d. 22 Feb., 1831, in
Becket. He m. 19 Sep., 1784, Hannah, dr. of Deacon Ebenezer Walden, and sister of Judge Ebenezer Walden, of Buffalo,
N. Y. She d. in Avon, Ohio, 7 Feb., 1843.

Children of George and Hannah (Walden) Conant:—

> Anna Gray, b. 16 July, 1785, in Becket, Mass.; d. 26 Aug.,
> 1856; m. in Windham, O., Mch., 1821, Franklin Snow, b. 27
> Jan., 1779, as his second wife. He was a farmer, of Mantua,
> Portage co., O., and d. 24 Nov., 1863. Child: Hannah, b.
> 9 Sep., 1824; m. 31 Mch., 1859, in Avon, O., Harris Lewis,
> b. in Narborough, England, 1 Apr., 1822. They lived in
> Oberlin, O.

VII. George Crocker, b. 24 Feb., 1787.

> Lydia, b. 12 Oct., 1788.

VIII. John, b. 17 Feb., 1790.

> Elizabeth, b. 19 Sep., 1792; m. —— Russell, and had a dr.,
> who m. Dr. A. D. Lord. Mrs. Lord was matron of the
> State Asylum for the Blind, at Columbus, Ohio, for over
> twenty years.
>
> Sarah Maria, b. 11 Aug., 1795.
>
> Hannah Augusta, b. 18 Apr., 1797.

IX. Charles Walden, b. 13 Oct., 1802.

> Abigail Harriet, b. 23 Jan., 1804; m. in Becket, Mass., 22 Sep.,
> 1831, Stephen Wadsworth Snow. They lived in Becket.
> Children: 1. Sarah Corlinda, b. 29 June, 1832; 2. Harriet
> Cerelia, b. 13 May, 1839.
>
> Lucretia Urania, b. 15 July, 1806.

VI. **Thatcher**[3] (*George, George*), b. 2 Mch., 1767, in
Barnstable, Mass.; removed to Becket, with his parents, in
June, 1779. He was one of the organizers of a colony of
about ninety who, in June and July, 1811, removed from
Becket and vicinity to Windham, Portage county, Ohio. Their
household goods were removed on ox carts. Their first labor
was to build a log house, which was completed on the Saturday
after their arrival, and on the Sabbath religious services were
held in it. He d. 19 June, 1840. He m. 5 Mch., 1789, Elizabeth, dr. of Asa and Chloe Manley, b. 9 Feb., 1769, in Coventry, Conn., and moved to Becket in 1788, with her parents.
She d. 1 Oct., 1845.

. Children of THATCHER and ELIZABETH (MANLEY) CONANT:—

Susanna, b. 25 Nov., 1789; m. 22 Oct., 1812, in Poland, Trumbull co., Ohio, James Robb.

x. Thatcher Freeman, b. 20 Aug., 1791.

Mehitable, b. 24 July, 1793; m. 17 Aug., 1813, Artemus Baker.

Elizabeth Edna, b. 8 Oct., 1795; m. 6 Apr., 1814, Leroy Alford.

Rebecca, b. 14 Feb., 1798; d. 12 Mch., 1828; m. 1822, Leander Sackett (see p. 247).

xi. Asa Manley, b. 16 Mch., 1800.

Chloe Bridgman, b. 3 Oct., 1802; d. 22 Feb., 1846; m. 1823, Horatio N. Bearce.

xii. George Erskine, b. 28 May, 1805.

Lydia Mary, b. 23 Feb., 1808; d. 20 June, 1853; m. 1830, Robert M. Higley.

Angelina Gray, b. 20 Oct., 1810; d. 13 Nov., 1864; m. 1839, Alexander Bearce.

FOURTH GENERATION.

VII. **George Crocker**[4] (*George, George, George*), b. 24 Feb., 1787, in Becket, Mass. He settled in Lisbon, near Ogdensburg, N. Y. He was a lawyer and also an active business man, carrying on a large farm during the latter part of his life. He d. in Ogdensburg, N. Y., July, 1854. He m. Sarah M. (Tibbetts) Perkins, widow of Matthew Perkins, who d. in Lisbon.

Child of GEORGE C. and SARAH M. (TIBBETTS) CONANT:—

xiii. George, b. 19 Aug., 1820.

VIII. **John**[4] (*George, George, George*), b. 17 Feb., 1790, in Becket, Mass.; removed from Becket to Ohio in the fall of 1831, and settled on Tract No. 5, now Rochester, Lorain county, and thence to Dwight, Ill. He was a man of high moral character and marked ability. He held various town and county offices. He d. in Dwight, Ill., 4 Feb., 1860. He m. in Blandford, Mass., 27 Nov., 1811, Orpha Johnson, b. in Blandford, 27 Nov., 1791. She is a sister to the late Hon. Thomas A. Johnson, who was judge of the Supreme Court for the 7th Judicial District of New York for twenty-five years. On Apr. 22, 1884, when nearly ninety-three years of age, she wrote a long letter to the compiler which is full of information about her husband's branch of the family.

Children of JOHN and ORPHA (JOHNSON) CONANT:—

XIV. Sarah Elizabeth, b. 24 Aug., 1813.
XV. Hannah Maria, b. 25 Dec., 1815.
Mary C., b. 24 Dec., 1825; d. in Circleville, O., 11 Mch., 1865; m. Hon. John Lynch, who now resides in Benicia, Cal. Child: John Conant, a lawyer, of Benicia.
John Francis, b. 4 Apr., 1828; d. unm., in El Dorado county, Cal., 10 Sep., 1854.
XVI. George Thatcher, b. 13 May, 1831.
Henry Franklin, b. 28 June, 1834; d. unm., in Dwight, Ill., 25 Sep., 1858.

IX. **Charles Walden**[4] (*George, George, George*), b. 13 Oct., 1802, in Becket, Mass.; removed to Ohio, with his parents, in 1831, thence to Piercetown, Ind., and finally to Big Rapids, Mich. He was a dairy farmer. He d. in Big Rapids, 20 Dec., 1877. He m. Eliza Babcock, who d. 10 Feb., 1878.

Child of CHARLES W. and ELIZA (BABCOCK) CONANT:—

XVII. Watson Charles, b. 1829.

X. **Thatcher Freeman**[4] (*Thatcher, George, George*), b. 20 Aug., 1791, in Becket, Mass.; moved to Ohio, with his parents, in 1811; was a farmer; lived in Windham, O. He m. in Nelson, O., 1818, Irene, dr. of Eber Maxfield, b. in Cornwall, Conn.

Children of THATCHER F. and IRENE (MAXFIELD) CONANT:—

XVIII. Eber Maxfield, b. 10 Aug., 1819.
XIX. Leander Tanner, b. 17 Dec., 1820.
XX. Mary Jane, b. 10 July, 1822.
Sylvester Freeman, b. 4 Mch., 1826. He removed to Jamestown, N. Y., where he now resides; is a grocer and produce dealer. He m. at Massilon, O., 17 Dec., 1853, Sarah Ellen, dr. of James Jacoby; no children.
XXI. Rebecca Angeline, b. 22 Mch., 1829.
George Thatcher, b. 15 Aug., 1834.

XI. **Asa Manley**[4] (*Thatcher, George, George*), b. 16 Mch., 1800, in Becket, Mass.; removed to Ohio, with his par-

ents, and settled in Windham, O. He d. 22 Feb., 1846. He
m. 24 Sep., 1824, in Windham, Eunice Hunt, dr. of Philo
Bearce, b. in Cornwall, Conn., 22 Jan., 1801; d. 7 May, 1878,
in Windham, O.

Children of Asa M. and Eunice H. (Bearce) Conant:—

George Bushrod, b. 12 Oct., 1825.
XXII.   Philo Bearce, b. 3 Aug., 1827.
XXIII.   Thatcher Gray, b. 29 Dec., 1829.
XXIV.   Horatio Nelson Bearce, b. 30 Aug., 1831.
Frederick, b. 31 July, 1833.
Amanda, b. 11 July, 1835.
Lucy, b. 2 Feb., 1837.
Henry, b. 2 Sep., 1838. He is now a merchant, of Kelton,
    Utah Ter. He m. in Boise City, Idaho Ter., 15 May,
    1871, Jennie Harr; no children.
XXV.   Edward, b. 23 Dec., 1840.

XII. George Erskine[4] (*Thatcher, George, George*), b.
28 May, 1805, in Becket, Mass.; moved to Ohio, with his parents. He settled in Lawrence, Kansas, as a physician and
surgeon, where he now resides. He m. (1) in Nelson, O., 1
Oct., 1829, Charity Foot; m. (2) in Nelson, 10 Apr., 1845,
Abigail L. Paine.

Children of George E. and Charity (Foot) Conant:—

XXVI.   Abigail Josephine, b. 13 Sep., 1830, in Windham, O.
George Francis, b. 10 June, 1832, in Windham, O.; d. y.
Alvan Hyde, b. 4 July, 1836, in Huntington, O.
XXVII.   George Francis, b. 3 Sep., 1839,   "   "
John Quincy Adams, b. 7 July, 1843, "   "

Children of George E. and Abigail L. (Paine) Conant:—

XXVIII. Lucretia, b. 7 July, 1846, in Windham, O.
XXIX.   Alvan Paine, b. 7 Sep., 1849, in Oconowoc, Wis.
Hannah J., b. 3 Apr., 1853, in Nelson, O.; removed to
    Kansas, with her parents; m. Samuel Johnson, a phy-
    sician, of Oskaloosa, Ks. Child: Allen Conant, b. 17
    Jan., 1883.

FIFTH GENERATION.

XIII. George[5] (*George Crocker, George, George, George*),

b. 19 Aug., 1820, in Lisbon, N. Y. He was a merchant, of
New York city, but has retired from active business owing to
ill health. He m. Sophia Seymour.

Child of GEORGE and SOPHIA (SEYMOUR) CONANT:—

> George Seymour, b. 10 Oct., 1853. He is a physician, of New
> York city.

XIV. Sarah Elizabeth[5] (*John, George, George, George*),
b. 24 Aug., 1813, in Becket, Mass.; moved to Ohio, with her
parents; d. in Covington, Ky., 29 Mch., 1876. She m. in Rochester, Ohio, 7 Dec., 1836, Eber Earl, b. in Newtown, O., 24
Sep., 1811; d. in Covington, Ky., 1 Mch., 1876.

Children of EBER and SARAH E. (CONANT) EARL:—

> Francis Eber, b. 12 Oct., 1838, in Windham, O. He is a com-
> mission merchant, of Cincinnati, O. He m. Virginia Doug-
> lass Lyon. Children: Kate E., b. 1864; Alice K., b. 1867;
> Virginia D., b. 1871.
> Charles Howard, b. 4 Apr., 1841, in Windham.

XV. Hannah Maria[5] (*John, George, George, George*),
b. 25 Dec., 1815, in Becket, Mass.; moved to Ohio, with her
parents. She is a physician and lecturer, and resides in Cob-
den, Ill. She is well known also as a correspondent of the
" Woman's Journal;" was matron of the Asylum for the Deaf
and Dumb at Columbus, O.; was sent to England as correspondent of the "Columbus State Journal" during the first
World's Exposition. During the late war she was president
of the Illinois Aid Society. She m. (1) in Rochester, O., John
Martin Tracy, who d. Sep., 1844. He was a Universalist clergyman. She m. (2) Samuel Cutler, of Brookfield, Mass., a
nephew of Pliny Cutler, of Boston.

Children of JOHN M. and HANNAH M. (CONANT) TRACY:—

> Melaine, b. 12 Jan., 1836; m. —— Earle.
> Mary, b. 17 Nov., 1841, in Sandusky, O.; m. —— Mott.
> John Martin, b. 21 Dec., 1844. He lives in Greenwich, Conn.,
> and is well known as a painter of animals. He m. in Paris,
> France, 23 May, 1874, Melanie Guillemin. Children: Mar-
> guerite, b. in Paris, France, 1875; Jaques Hubert, b. in
> Greenwich, Conn., 1882.

XVI. George Thatcher[5] (*John, George, George, George*),

b. 13 May, 1831, in Becket, Mass.; moved to Ohio, with his
parents. He is a farmer and carpenter, of Dwight, Ill. He
m. in Lowell, Wis., 3 July, 1856, Harriet Newell Blair.

Child of GEORGE T. and HARRIET N. (BLAIR) CONANT:—

Ella Melissa, b. 20 Sep., 1866, in Beaver Dam, Wis.

XVII. **Watson Charles**[5] (*Charles   Walden,   George,
George, George*), b. 1829. He settled in Piercetown, Ind.;
removed thence to Big Rapids, Mich., where he carried on a
large lumber business. He d. 30 July, 1880, in Dwight, Ill.
He m. Margaret Fenner, who now resides in Piercetown, Ind.

Children of WATSON C. and MARGARET (FENNER) CONANT:—

Francis T.
And two daughters.

XVIII. **Eber Maxfield**[5] (*Thatcher Freeman, Thatcher,
George, George*), b. 10 Aug., 1819, in Windham, O.; removed
to Adrian, Mich. He is a shoemaker. He m. in Braceville,
O., Apr., 1843, ———.

Children of EBER M. and ——— (———) CONANT:—

Mary Elizabeth, b. 26 Mch., 1844.
Julia Cornelia, b. 5 Apr., 1845.
Rebecca Angeline, b. 13 Apr., 1847.
Thatcher Freeman, b. 31 Mch., 1849.
George Washington, b. 2 Oct., 1851.
Sarah Virginia, b. 29 June, 1854.
And three who d. in infancy.

XIX. **Leander Tanner**[5] (*Thatcher Freeman, Thatcher,
George, George*), b. 17 Dec., 1820, in Windham, Ohio; settled
in East Liverpool, O. He is a wholesale and retail grocer.
He has held various town offices. He m. in Columbiana, O.,
25 Dec., 1855, Carrie Elizabeth, dr. of Thomas Perry and
Phebe (Jolley) Smith, b. in Madison, O., 10 Feb., 1836.

Children of LEANDER T. and CARRIE E. (SMITH) CONANT:—

Oella Rosalind, b. 30 May, 1857; m. Thomas H. Cope, and has
two children.
Leander Bonaparte, b. 25 July, 1858.

XX. **Mary Jane**[5] (*Thatcher Freeman, Thatcher, George,
George*), b. 10 July, 1822, in Windham, O.; d. 18 Aug., 1849.

She m. 30 Jan., 1844, James Oliver Herrick, b. in Worthington, Mass., 9 Nov., 1820; d. 28 Sep., 1849. They lived in Twinsburg, Summit county, O.

Children of JAMES O. and MARY J. (CONANT) HERRICK:—

> Mary Irene, b. 14 Mch., 1845; m. 25 Dec., 1866, Albert G. Smith, of Kankakee, Ill. Children: 1. Ernest Freeman, b. 26 Jan., 1869; 2. Alfred William Thomas, b. 17 Apr., 1871; 3. Walter Earl, b. 27 Sep., 1873; 4. Lucy Bertha, b. 12 Mch., 1878; 5. Asthes Garfield, b. 21 Aug., 1880; 6. Leslie Carlton, b. 6 June, 1883.
>
> Zipporah Jane, b. 14 Dec., 1846; m. 17 Mch., 1870, William T. Pottenger, b. 17 Apr., 1848, of Denver, Col. They live near Kankakee, Ill. Children: 1. Mary Bell, b. 16 July, 1874; 2. James H., b. 7 Feb., 1876; 3. Nellie Zipporah, b. 23 June, 1878; 4. William Albert, b. 25 Jan., 1881; 5. Avery K., b. 22 May, 1884.
>
> James F., b. 8 Feb., 1849; d. 1849.

XXI.   **Rebecca Angeline**[5] (*Thatcher Freeman, Thatcher, George, George*), b. 22 Mch., 1829, in Windham, O.; m. Daniel Pardee, and resides in Garrettville, O.

Children of DANIEL and REBECCA A. (CONANT) PARDEE:—

> Dwight Mason, b. 16 May, 1849, in Windham, O.
> Cassius Adelbert, b. 20 Nov., 1850, in Windham, O.
> Clarence Daniel, b. 19 July, 1852, in Windham, O.
> Rollin Dillazon, b. 11 July, 1858, in Nelson, O.
> Ann Irene, b. 9 Sep., 1862, in Nelson, O.

XXII.   **Philo Bearce**[5] (*Asa Manley, Thatcher, George, George*), b. 3 Aug., 1827, in Windham, O.; removed to Ravenna, O. He is an attorney at law and judge of the Municipal Court of Ravenna. He m. in Ravenna, 1 May, 1861, Alice Selby Whittlesey.

Children of PHILO B. and ALICE S. (WHITTLESEY) CONANT:—

> Paul, b. 2 Feb., 1862.
> Edward Mason, b. 17 June, 1863.
> Ellen Whittlesey, b. 24 Oct., 1866.
> Ruth Julia, b. 15 July, 1869.
> Alice, b. 9 Nov., 1873.
> Philo Bearce, b. 14 Jan., 1877.

XXIII.   **Thatcher Gray**[5] (*Asa Manley, Thatcher, George,*

George), b. 29 Dec., 1829, in Windham, O. He is now a merchant, of St. Louis, Mo. He m. ———.

Child of THATCHER G. and ——— (———) CONANT:—

Lewis Gray, b. 1862.

XXIV. **Horatio Nelson Bearce**[5] (*Asa Manley, Thatcher, George, George*), b. 30 Aug., 1831, in Windham, O., where he lives; a farmer. He m. Apr., 1857, Rebecca, dr. of Elisha and Patience (Comstock) Arnold, b. 1828, in Hopewell, N. Y.

Children of H. NELSON B. and. REBECCA (ARNOLD) CONANT:—

Addie E., b. 10 July, 1858; m. 5 May, 1881, ——— Andrews. They live in Cleveland, O.
Clarence Arnold, b. 7 Feb., 1864.

XXV. **Edward**[5] (*Asa Manley, Thatcher, George, George*), b. 23 Dec., 1841, in Windham, O. He is now a merchant, of Conant, Cassia county, Idaho Ter. He m. in Boise City, Idaho Ter., 19 Feb., 1878, Edella Frances, dr. of Nelson Reed and Mary (Miles) Basil, b. in Keokuk co., Iowa, 1 Nov., 1858.

Children of EDWARD and EDELLA F. (BASIL) CONANT:—

Edward Basil, b. 15 Mch., 1879; d. 13 Aug., 1884.
Leonie, b. 16 Sep., 1880.

XXVI. **Abigail Josephine**[5] (*George Erskine, Thatcher, George, George*), b. 13 Sep., 1830, in Windham, O.; m. Roland Moffat. He is a Methodist Episcopal minister, and resides in Washburn, Mo.

Children of ROLAND and ABIGAIL J. (CONANT) MOFFAT:—

George Roland, b. 11 May, 1855.
John Wesley, b. 29 Apr., 1857.
Emily Asintha, b. 7 Oct., 1862.
Pliny Roland, b. 25 Aug., 1868.
Abigail Amanda, b. 10 Sep., 1873.

XXVII. **George Francis**[5] (*George Erskine, Thatcher, George, George*), b. 3 Sep., 1839, in Huntington, Ohio. He settled in Nashville, Tenn., where he d. from an injury received in a railroad accident. He m. ———.

Children of GEORGE F. and ——— (———) CONANT:—

Ada E., b. 25 Dec., 1865.

Cora C., b. 2 Feb., 1868.
Francis, b. 24 Nov., 1871.

XXVIII. Lucretia[5] (*George Erskine, Thatcher, George, George*), b. 7 July, 1846, in Windham, O.; m. Ambrose Bigsby, of Lawrence, Kansas.
Children of AMBROSE and LUCRETIA (CONANT) BIGSBY:—

George William, b. 11 Apr., 1865.
Guy Ambrose, b. 14 Feb., 1870.
Laura Belle, b. 7 July, 1872.
Abigail Sarah, b. 13 Aug., 1877.

XXIX. Alvan Paine[5] (*George Erskine, Thatcher, George, George*), b. 7 Sep., 1849, in Oconowoc, Wis.; moved to Lawrence, Kansas, with his parents, where he now resides. He m. Alice Coleman.
Children of ALVAN P. and ALICE (COLEMAN) CONANT:—

Annie, b. 25 Mch., 1874.
George Alvan, b. 12 Dec., 1878.

CONANTS WHOSE ORIGIN IS UNTRACED.

i. **Amos Conant,** b. 28 Jan., 1737, in Concord, Mass.; said to have been a son of Lot Conant, of Concord; but as Lot's eleventh child was born 1732, it seems more likely that he may have been a son of (53) Israel, who had two or three children whose names have not been ascertained. The dates and facts as to his family were furnished by Reuben Conant Fosbury, of West Bainbridge, N. Y., a grandson, now nearly eighty years of age. The ancient family record is in his possession. He lived in Concord and Westminster, Mass., Halifax, Vt., and Bainbridge, N. Y. About the year 1800 he moved from Vermont to Jerico, now Bainbridge, N. Y., with his wife and children, Israel, William, James, Abel, Reuben, Betsey and Leafia; an older son, Levi, remained in Vermont. He d. 8 Dec., 1817, in Bainbridge, N. Y. He m. 4 Dec., 1763, Mary

Bowers, b. 13 Sep., 1743, in Lancaster, Mass. Her mother was a Jocelin. She d. 22 Feb., 1824, in Bainbridge.

Children of AMOS and MARY (BOWERS) CONANT:—

Sally, b. 15 Jan., 1766, d. 30 Jan., 1769, in Westminster, Mass.
ii.   Levi, b. 7 May, 1768, in Westminster.
Sally, b. 25 May, 1770, in Westminster; d. 28 July, 1785, in Halifax, Vt.
Israel, b. 6 Mch., 1772, in Westminster, Mass. He is said to have been a college graduate. He m. but had no children. He d. 24 Sep., 1807, in New York, N. Y.
Polly, b. 2 Mch., 1775, in Westminster. She d. in Halifax, Vt., 1817. She m. James Henry; had a son, James, who removed to Illinois.
William, b. 2 Dec., 1777, in Westminster; d. 10 Oct., 1805, in Jerico, N. Y.
James, b. 4 Mch., 1780; place of birth not mentioned; d. 21 June, 1807, in Jerico, N. Y.
iii.   Abel, b. 1 Mch., 1782; place of birth not mentioned.
Reuben, b. 3 Nov., 1784, in Halifax, Vt.; d. 13 Mch., 1809, in Jerico, N. Y.
iv.   Betsey, b. 25 May, 1788; place of birth not mentioned.
Leafia, b. 9 Oct., 1791; was married but died soon after.

ii. **Levi** (*Amos*), b. 7 May, 1768, in Westminster, Mass.; a farmer and wheelwright. He is said, by family tradition, to have moved from Coleraine, Mass., to Tinmouth, Vt., and thence to Moreau, Saratoga co., N. Y., where he d. 17 Feb., 1847. Wife's name unknown.

Children of LEVI and ——— (———) CONANT:—

Born in (Coleraine, Mass.?) and Tinmouth, Vt., in the following order, dates unknown.

Israel; never married; moved from Moreau, N. Y., to Illinois, with his brother, Elihu, and there died.
v.   Levi.
vi.   Elihu.
Betsey; m. Edward Woodruff, of Tinmouth, Vt., where they lived. Children: Franklin, Hannibal, Delia and Elizabeth.
Martha; never married; d. in Rutland, Vt., about 1866.
Mary; married Samuel Wood, and had five children; believed to be still (1886) living. Residence unknown.
Sophia; unmarried; moved to Illinois, with her brother, Elihu, and there died.

iii. **Abel** (*Amos*), b. 1 Mch., 1782; removed from Vermont to Jerico, now Bainbridge, N. Y., with his parents. An old family record is said to be in possession of his family. He d. 5 Sep., 1840, in Bainbridge. He m. Asenath ———. She is said to have married a second husband, and to be still living in Illinois.

Children of ABEL and ASENATH (———) CONANT:—

Franklin; lives near Joliet, Ill.
A daughter; m. Stephen Pettys, of Winsor, N. Y.
Caroline; m. —— Ferris.
Adelia; never married.
Mary; was married and had a family.
Phebe A., b. 29 Nov., 1823; d. 3 Apr., 1855. She m. 13 Apr., 1844, Albert Mudge, as his second wife, b. 17 Aug., 1815, in Sherburne, N. Y. He was a farmer, of Bainbridge; removed to New Lenox, Ill. (1844), and thence to Cool Spring, Ind., in 1855. Children: 1. Emily Estelle, b. 18 Dec., 1846, m. Lawson Hamlin, of Belvidere, Ill.; 2. Abraham L., b. 28 Aug., 1850.

iv.   Betsey (*Amos*), b. 25 May, 1788; m. 1805, in Bainbridge, N. Y., Stephen Fosbury, b. 15 Nov., 1783, in Scobarrie, N. Y. He settled in Bainbridge in 1802, and died there 15 Nov., 1850. She d. 15 May, 1847.

Children of STEPHEN and BETSEY (CONANT) FOSBURY:—

Reuben Conant, b. 17 Aug., 1807. He is a farmer, of West Bainbridge; has been assessor and justice of the peace for 25 years. He m. 17 Nov., 1832, Frances E., dr. of Seth and Mary (Hough) Johnson, b. in Connecticut, 8 Feb., 1809. Children: 1. Ellen C., b. 20 Mch., 1834; 2. Jane E., b. 28 July, 1835, m. —— Lyon; 3. Mary A., b. 15 Nov., 1837, m. —— Lane; 4. Emma, b. 9 Feb., 1839, m. —— Hopkins; 5. Rubiet, b. 1 Feb., 1841, m. —— Aylesworth; 6. Abel Conant, b. 23 Sep., 1842; served three years during the Rebellion in the 114th N. Y. Regt.; 7. Franklin, b. 11 Mch., 1844; 8. Seth, b. 11 Mch., 1844; dead; 9. Delos R., b. 29 Mch., 1850.
James C., b. 30 July, 1809; d. in Iowa City, 1871, leaving a family of five sons and four daughters.

v.   Levi (*Levi, Amos*), b. in (Coleraine?) Mass., about 1788; a mechanic and farmer; moved to Tinmouth, Vt., with his parents, and thence to Salisbury, Vt., about 1815. He d. in Salisbury, about 1855. He m. about 1815, Hephzibah Waterhouse, of Enosburg, Vt. She d. in Salisbury, 27 Jan., 1879, aged 89.

Children of LEVI and HEPHZIBAH (WATERHOUSE) CONANT:—

vii.   Alonzo, b. in Salisbury, Vt., 4 Sep., 1816.

Lorenzo, b. 1819, in Salisbury, Vt., where he lives; m. Harriet Nichols, who d. 1867. Children: 1. Charles, b. 1855, m. and has William, Charles and Minnie; 2. Emily, b. 1857.

Harriet, b. 1820; m. Paul Champlin, of Middlebury, Vt., by whom she had a family. She d. in Melrose, Wis., 1880.

William, b. 1822, in Salisbury, Vt.; m. Maria Oliver, and has Edward, Lottie and Ada.

Julia, b. about 1823; m. Joseph Bliss, about 1850, and moved to Oskaloosa, Kansas, in 1857. Has a family.

Alphonso, b. about 1833; unmarried; was an architect; d. 1877, in Atchison, Kansas.

vi.   **Elihu** (*Levi, Amos*), b. about 1790; moved from Tinmouth, Vt., to Moreau, N. Y., with his parents. He was a farmer. About 1845 moved from Moreau to Paw Paw Grove, Illinois, where he d. about 1876. He m. Jeannette Johnson, of Chenango, N. Y.

Child of ELIHU and JEANNETTE (JOHNSON) CONANT:—

William Elihu, b. about 1836; a farmer, living near Paw Paw Grove, Ill.

vii.   **Alonzo** (*Levi, Levi, Amos*), b. 4 Sep., 1816, in Salisbury, Vt.; a farmer. He moved from Salisbury to Middle Granville, N. Y., in 1840, and still lives there. He m. (1) 4 Aug., 1837, Elizabeth, dr. of Thomas and Sarah (Rockwell) Gwyer, of Shoreham, Vt. She was b. 22 Aug., 1818; d. 10 Oct., 1870. He m. (2) 14 July, 1874, Mrs. Mary Cary.

Children of ALONZO and ELIZABETH (GWYER) CONANT:—

Martha Helena, b. 28 Mch., 1841, in Middle Granville; m. 11 Dec., 1872, Aden B. Rogers, a merchant, of Middle Granville. She d. 10 Oct., 1880. Child: Henry Hosford, b. Dec., 1874.

Duane, b. 7 Oct., 1843. He graduated at Hamilton College, Clinton, N. Y., 1867, and from Columbia College Law School (LL. B.), 1869. He was unmarried; practiced law in Jersey City, N. J., where he d. 10 Aug., 1876.

Allen Gwyer, b. 8 Oct., 1850. He graduated at Middlebury College (B. A.), 1874; was admitted attorney at law, 1877; counsellor of Supreme Court, 1879. He is unmarried, and since 1875 has resided in Salem, N. Y. He is the editor of the 10th Vol. of Edmonds' Edition of the General Laws of New York.

a. Timothy Conant, b. 1752; lived in Rehoboth, Norton and Brimfield, Mass. He served in Dyer's company of Carpenter's regiment, in the Revolutionary army, in 1776, and in Nathaniel Carpenter's company of Thomas Carpenter's regiment, in 1777 (Mass. Arch., Muster Rolls, Vol. 1, pp. 160 and 191). He d. 5 Mch., 1826, in Norton or Brimfield. His wife was Sarah ——, who d. 23 Feb., 1826, aged 74.

Children of Timothy and Sarah (——) Conant:—

Polly, b. 1775; d. 12 May, 1836.
Nancy, b. ——; m. 30 Oct., 1817, John Lazell, and had children: Nancy, b. 28 May, 1821, Charles, b. 28 Dec., 1823, and Daniel, b. 5 June, 1826.
Leonard, b. 1781; m. 10 Mch., 1803, —— ——, and d. 19 Aug., 1811. Children: 1. Ichabod Perry, b. 23 June, 1804; 2. Peter Edson, b. 23 Sep., 1806; 3. Leonard Hathaway, b. 27 Sep., 1808; 4. Gaius Bradford, b. 13 May, 1811.
b. Timothy, b. 17 June, 1784.
Roxana, b. ——.
c. William, b. 1795.

b. Timothy (*Timothy*), b. 17 June, 1784, in Norton, Mass. He settled in Rehoboth, Mass.; was a shoemaker; removed to Woodstock, Conn., where he d. 28 July, 1850. He m. 19 Apr., 1812, in Rehoboth, Nancy Warren, b. in Upton, Mass., 28 July, 1791.

Children of Timothy and Nancy (Warren) Conant:—

Timothy William, b. 17 Feb., 1813; d. 17 Oct., 1817.
Charlotte Perry, b. 25 July, 1815; d. 26 Mch., 1816.
Timothy Warren, b. 28 Jan., 1817.
Abner George, b. 11 June, 1819; of Norwich, Conn.
Charlotte Hannah, b. 20 Jan., 1822.
Jesse Eddy, b. 20 Oct., 1824.
d. Thomas Alvin, b. 9 Nov., 1826.
Lucy Perry, b. 10 Aug., 1829.
Daniel Metcalf, b. 21 Nov., 1832.
e. Sylvanus Augustus, b. 28 Aug., 1836.

c. William (*Timothy*), b. 1795; d. 17 July, 1823; m. 16 Feb., 1817, Achsah Eliza, dr. of Isaac Perry, of Attleboro'.

Children of William and Achsah E. (Perry) Conant:—

Lydia Almeda, b. 1818.
Vashta, b. 1820.
f. Prelet Drake, b. 20 Sep., 1822.
Mary Jane, b. 1824.

d. Thomas Alvin (*Timothy, Timothy*), b. 9 Nov., 1826, in (Northbridge?) Mass.; removed to Norwich, Conn.; was a physician. He d. some years ago. He m. (1) ———; m. (2) in Dudley, Mass., 23 May, 1862, Mary S. Lane.

Children of Thomas A. and ——— (———) Conant:—

Emma, b. 1849.
Frank V., b. 1852, in Millville, Mass.; m. in Norwich, Conn., Emily Burchard, and has two children, a son, b. 1879, and a daughter, b. 1881.
Jerome F., b. ———; m. ———; a cigar manufacturer, of Norwich, Conn.

e. Sylvanus Augustus (*Timothy, Timothy*), b. 28 Aug., 1836, in Northbridge, Mass., where he lives; a watchmaker. He m. 17 June, 1861, in Providence, R. I., Harriet E., dr. of John and Elizabeth Gill, b. in Duckenfield, England, 15 Apr., 1843.

Children of Sylvanus A. and Harriet (Gill) Conant:—

Harriet M., b. 1863.
Lucy E., b. 16 May, 1865.
Augustus Sylvanus, b. 7 June, 1872.

f. Prelet Drake (*William, Timothy*), b. 20 Sep., 1822, in Attleboro', Mass. He resides in Fall River, Mass.; is a dealer in hardware, paints, etc. He m. in Rehoboth, Aug., 1843, Irene Munroe Rounds.

Children of Prelet D. and Irene M. (Rounds) Conant:—

Mary Jane, b. 31 Aug., 1844.
Thomas Leprelet, d. y.
Minnie Ida, d. y.

A. William Conant, of Wareham, Mass.; was in Capt. Eddy's company in the Revolutionary army, in 1779 (Mass. Archives, Muster Rolls, Vol. 27, p. 140), and was sergeant in Gibbs' company of Jacobs' regiment, in 1780 (Vol. 2, p. 58), He was, perhaps, brother of Timothy Conant (p. 544), of Rehoboth, and may have been son of that William Connett, of Plymouth, who was published to Martha Wicket, of Sandwich, in 1740 (see *Ancient Landmarks of Plymouth*).

Children of WILLIAM and ——— (———) CONANT:—

Mary, m. in Wareham, 7 Nov., 1794, Asa David, of Rochester.
Betsey, m. 24 Oct., 1799, David Besse, jr. (William H. Besse, of New Bedford, is a grandson.)

B.   Lothrop, b. about 1788.

B. Lothrop (*William*), b. about 1788, in Wareham; m. in Plymouth, 1812, Sarah, dr. of Rufus Albertson. He lived in Plymouth a while, then moved to Portland, Me., and later to Brooklyn, N. Y., where he d. about 1864.

Children of LOTHROP and SARAH (ALBERTSON) CONANT:—

Lothrop, b. 1814, in Plymouth; was of Providence, Mass., where he had Elizabeth T., d. 20 Feb., 1864, aged 25; Lothrop, d. 6 Jan., 1868, aged 25; and perhaps others.

C.   Albert Augustus, b. 1816, in Plymouth.

C. Albert Augustus (*Lothrop, William*), b. 1816, in Plymouth, Mass. He lived in Winnegance, near Bath, Me. He d. in Phipsburg, 23 Apr., 1886, aged 70 years 3 mos. He m. in Taunton, Mass., 3 Feb., 1837, Sarah Maria, dr. of Jabez Carver, b. 9 Feb., 1819, in Calais, Vt.

Children of ALBERT A. and SARAH M. (CARVER) CONANT:—

Henry A., b. 12 May, 1838, in Taunton, Mass.
Charles L., b. June, 1846, in New London, Conn.

D.   Frederick Carver, b. 8 Aug., 1849, in New London, Conn.
Edward J., b. 1851, in New London, Conn.
William A., b. 1854.
Julius, b. 1857.

D. Frederick Carver (*Albert Augustus, Lothrop, William*), b. 8 Aug., 1849, in New London, Conn.; removed to Bath, Me., with his parents. He now lives in East Boston, Mass.; a machinist. He m. in Bath, Me., 24 Dec., 1874, Mary Elizabeth Clark.

Child of FREDERICK C. and MARY E. (CLARK) CONANT:—

John Franklin, b. 27 Sep., 1877, in Bath, Me.

———————

a. **Benjamin Conant** is said, by family tradition, to have come from Scotland, and settled in Westmoreland, N. H., about 1780. He must have been born about 1760. The names of his sons, Josiah, Shubael and Origen, indicate a descent from Roger Conant through the Connecticut branch of the family. He removed from Westmoreland to Alleghany county, N. Y. His wife, Ruth ———, is said to have come from Ireland.

Children of BENJAMIN and RUTH (———) CONANT:—

Josiah, d. unm., in Alleghany co., N. Y.
Shubael, who m. and had a family.
b.   Origen, b. ———.
Olive, m. and lived in Alleghany co., N. Y.
Electa, m. Jonathan Barnard, and moved West. Children:
    Truman, George, Darius, and two daughters.
Clarissa, m. and lived in New England.
Sally, m. and lived in New England.

b. **Origen** (*Benjamin*), b. about 1786; m. Mary Butler; removed to New York; a farmer.

Children of ORIGEN and MARY (BUTLER) CONANT:—

i.   Harriet, b. 19 Jan., 1812; d. 1883; m. Jeremiah Wicks, of McLane, Erie co., Pa. Children: 1. Samantha; 2. Clarinda; 3. Martha; 4. Delphy; 5. Belle; 6. Monroe; 7. Freeman.
ii.   Arial, b. 15 Mch., 1813; m. Ruhama Johnson, of McKean, Pa. Children: 1. Anson; 2. William.
iii.   Clarissa, b. 15 Dec., 1814; m. John Butler, of McLane, Pa. Children: 1. Almira; 2. Hersey; 3. Louisa; 4. Hannah; 5. Caroline.
iv.   John, b. 20 Sep., 1816; m. and had children: 1. Mary; 2. Albert.
v.   Lewis, b. 19 Feb., 1818. Lived in Bennington, Darien and Alexander, N. Y., and in Girard, Pa., where he d. 15 Feb., 1884. He m. in Bennington, N. Y., 10 June, 1841, Huldah Ann, dr. of Orson and Hannah (Harris) Watson, b. 11 Apr., 1821, in Ridgeway, N. Y. Children: 1. Orson H., b. 29 May, 1842, in Bennington; 2. Clarissa M., b. 14 Nov., 1844, in Bennington; 3. Hannah P., b. 21 May, 1847, in Bennington; 4. Oliver G., b. 11 Dec., 1851, in Darien; 5. Origen L., b. 21 Jan., 1854, in Darien; 6. Eugene J., b. 15 May, 1856, in Darien; 7. Emegene J., b. 15 May, 1856, in Darien; 8. Oel Frank, b. 12 Dec., 1860, in Alexander, who now lives in Rochester, N. Y.
vi.   Laura, b. 28 Jan., 1820; m. Elijah Holt, of Edinboro', Pa. Children: 1. Elijah; 2. Eli; 3. Melissa.
vii.   Lovisa, b. 12 May, 1821; m. Andrew Makin, of Hart, Mich. Children: 1. Mathias; 2. Amanda; 3. Austin; 4. Flora; 5. Frank; 6. Harriet.
viii.   Anson, b. 19 Dec., 1822; m. Helen Osborne, and moved West. Children: 1. Clara; 2. Anna; 3. William.

ix. Maria, b. 2 Sep., 1823; m. Daniel C. Gibson, of Edinboro', Pa. Children: 1. Mary; 2. Vincent; 3. Martha; 4. Reed; 5. Emmet, of Erie, Pa., who has given the information about this family; 6. Esther; 7. Elizabeth; 8. Perry.

x. Jane, b. 5 July, 1824; m. (1) Emmons; (2) Middleton; (3) Cook; (4) Brower. She is of Springfield, Pa. Children: 1. Elizabeth; 2. Anna; 3. Caroline; 4. Eva; 5. Josie; 6. Jay; 7. Frank; 8. Lewis.

xi. Chestina, b. 25 Nov., 1826; m. Seth Holt, brother of Elijah, above. They live in Stetson, Mich. Children: 1. Arthur; 2. Josephine; 3. George; 4. Noble; 5. Julius; ¦6. Mary; 7. Hattie; 8. Richard.

A. **Timothy Conant**, b. 16 Mch., 1775, in Connecticut; removed to Eaton, Madison co., N. Y. He was a farmer and blacksmith, and a deacon of the Baptist church. He d. in Lebanon, Madison co., N. Y., 7 Apr., 1829. He m. in New Lebanon, Columbia co., N. Y., 27 Apr., 1797, Mary, dr. of Nathan and ——— (Kidder) Herrick; she was b. 16 May, 1780, and d. in Georgetown, N. Y., 1 Feb., 1866.

Children of TIMOTHY and MARY (HERRICK) CONANT:—

Alexa, b. 15 Feb., 1798; m. Sep., 1824, Alvin Mosely; she d. 1831.

Eunice, b. 6 Aug., 1799; d. 1800.

John Wesley, b. 2 Mch., 1801; went to Orleans co., N. Y., in 1818, where he married and had two sons and two daughters. In 1833 removed to Michigan. His children now live in Van Buren, Wayne co., Mich.

B. Mary, b. 15 June, 1805.

Roxa, b. 21 June, 1807.

Dorcas, b. 10 May, 1809; m. Mason Lazell.

C. William Stoughton, b. 7 Apr., 1814.

D. Jane M., b. 17 Apr., 1816.

Susan, b. 18 Mch., 1818; m. E. Whitmore.

Clarissa, b. 21 Apr., 1822; m. 1849, Harvey Campbell, of Hamilton, N. Y., and went to Burmah, as a missionary. Mr. Campbell d. in Burmah, and she returned to the United States, where she m. (2) Rev. Samuel Gorman, and is now in New Mexico.

B. **Mary** (*Timothy*), b. 15 June, 1805; d. 28 Mch., 1870, in Georgetown, N. Y. She m. in Lebanon, N. Y., 21 Sep., 1821, Zinah Josiah, son of Eben and Sarah Mosely, b. 5 Oct., 1803, in Hoosick, Rensselaer co., N. Y. He was a farmer, hotel keeper and merchant, and held the office of justice of the peace. He d. 27 Dec., 1881, in Georgetown.

Children of ZINAH J. and MARY (CONANT) MOSELY:—

Roxa Eusebia, b. 20 Jan., 1824, in Lebanon, N. Y.
Orrin E., b. 13 Apr., 1833, in Lebanon.
Mary O., b. 6 June, 1838, in Georgetown, N. Y.
Mary S., b. 16 July, 1842; m. in Georgetown, 19 Sep., 1866, Milton S. Allen, b. in Stockbridge, N. Y., 2 Feb., 1837. Children: Arthur Mosely, b. 22 Aug., 1867, and Mary Lena, b. 2 Jan., 1870.

C. **William Stoughton** (*Timothy*), b. 7 Apr., 1814, in New York state. He was a merchant in New York city, where he d. 6 Oct., 1869. His family live in Flushing. He m. Cornelia D. Whitmore, and had several children.

Child of WILLIAM S. and CORNELIA D. (WHITMORE) CONANT:—

Frederick.

D. **Jane M.** (*Timothy*), b. 17 Apr., 1816; m. 10 Nov., 1840, Russell Whitmore, of Georgetown, N. Y.

Children of RUSSELL and JANE M. (CONANT) WHITMORE:—

Cornelia, b. 11 Nov., 1843; m. 28 Mch., 1868, Edwin Smith, of Ohio. He was a school teacher and artist. She d. 1 Jan., 1877.
Otis H., b. 29 Jan., 1848; is a farmer, of Georgetown; has been a justice of the peace nine years (1886) and superintendent of Sabbath school for fifteen years. He m. 4 Dec., 1878, Nellie Tillotson.
Francis E., b. 2 Sep., 1850; m. 17 Oct., 1880, Carrie H. Thompson. They are both graduates of the Oswego Normal School.
Mary J., b. 27 Dec., 1852; d. 26 Apr., 1872.
Martha, b. 28 Nov., 1855; unmarried.
Hamlin, b. 3 Mch., 1861, who lives on the homestead at Georgetown.

---

1. **John Conant**; was a shoemaker, of Boston, Mass.; was in the War of 1812; moved to New York, and thence to Ohio, about 1830, where he died. He was twice married, the second time to a widow Babb.

Children of JOHN CONANT:—

Richard, said to have settled in Virginia.

Sarah, m. John Battles, and had Alfred and William, and two daughters. Battles d. in Pennsylvania.

Anna, m. Ruel Stevens.

2.   Caleb, b. 20 July, 1809.

2. Caleb (*John*), b. 20 July, 1809, in New York state; removed to Geauga county, Ohio, with his father, and removed thence to Lambertville, Mich., about 1845, where he d. 20 Sep., 1849. He m. in Ohio, Margaret Lane, b. 3 May, 1813.

Children of CALEB and MARGARET (LANE) CONANT:—

3.   Lyman Allen, b. 2 Sep., 1831.
4.   Andrew M., b. 3 Apr., 1833.
    Phineas, of Albion, Mich.
5.   Ruth Amelia, b. 15 May, 1842.
    Mary Ann, d. y.
    Loyal T., d. y.
    Jane, d. y.
    Henrietta.
    Henry, of Attica, N. Y.

3. Lyman Allen (*Caleb, John*), b. 2 Sep., 1831, in Geauga county, O.; removed to Lambertville, Mich., with his parents, where he now resides. He is a farmer and local preacher of the M. E. church. He furnished the information about this family. He m. in Bedford, Mich., 7 Nov., 1852, Emily, dr. of Samuel P. and Maria (Blair) Prather, b. 4 Jan., 1836, in Maryland.

Children of LYMAN A. and EMILY (PRATHER) CONANT:—

Frank Allen, b. 21 Feb., 1860, in Bedford, Mich.
Mary Ida, b. 12 Jan., 1862,   "   "   "
Ruth, b. 16 Aug., 1864; d. 15 Oct., 1865.
Richard Arthur, b. 16 Jan., 1867; d. 17 June, 1868.
Clara Louise, b. 6 Feb., 1869, in Whiteford, Mich.
Charles Alfred, b. 10 Mch., 1871, in Bedford.

4. Andrew M. (*Caleb, John*), b. 3 Apr., 1833; m. 18 Aug., 1861, Mary Jane Spriggs.

Children of ANDREW M. and MARY J. (SPRIGGS) CONANT:—

Leona D., b. 23 May, 1862; m. 3 May, 1883, Byron McKenzie.
Almeda, b. 7 Dec., 1863.

5. Ruth Amelia (*Caleb, John*), b. 15 May, 1842; m. 1 Jan., 1861, Henry Coy.

Children of HENRY and RUTH A. (CONANT) COY:—

Jennie, b. 2 Feb., 1864; m. 15 Sep., 1882, Charles Curson, and
has Clarence, b. 21 June, 1883.
Addie M., b. 7 June, 1866.
Ernest E., b. 7 Mch., 1872.

A. **Chesley Conant,** said to have been born in South
Carolina, about 1790, and d. in Mississippi, about 1844; a far-
mer. He m. (1) ——; m. (2) in Williamsburg, Ky., 1832,
Elizabeth, dr. of Thomas and Eliza Cox, who d. in Ky., 1842.
Children of CHESLEY and —— (——) CONANT:—

James Hardee, settled in Alabama.
Alexander Hamilton, settled in Alabama.
Charlotte.
Pamelia.

Child of CHESLEY and ELIZABETH (COX) CONANT:—

B.   Milton Allen, b. 10 Mch., 1833.

B. **Milton Allen** (*Chesley*), b. 10 Mch., 1833, in Williams-
burg, Ky. He is a harness manufacturer, of Somerset, Ky.
He m. in Somerset, 1854, Amanda Jane, dr. of Haven and
Mary (Withers) McBeath, b. in Somerset, 3 Oct., 1835.
Children of MILTON A. and AMANDA J. (McBEATH) Co-
NANT:—

C.   John Milton, b. 5 Jan., 1856.
William Scuyler, b. in Somerset, Ky.
Mary, b. in Somerset, Ky.; d. in infancy.
Laura Alice, b. in Somerset, Ky.
Charles McBeath, b. in Somerset, Ky.
Harriet Perkins, b. in Somerset, Ky.

C. **John Milton** (*Milton Allen, Chesley*), b. 5 Jan., 1856,
in Somerset, Ky.; is a farmer, of Pineville, Ky. He and his
father have furnished information of this branch of the family.
He m. 30 Aug., 1877, in Conant, Ky., Lydia Reid, dr. of Edward Ray and Lucinda (Toulmin) Gibson, of Manchester, Ky.
Children of JOHN M. and LYDIA R. (GIBSON) CONANT:—

Edward G., b. 12 Aug., 1879, in Conant, Ky.
Laura Toulmin, b. 28 Mch., 1883, in Conant, Ky.

Otis Conant, b. in (Athol?) Mass., about 1830; d. aged 42; was superintendent of the Bay State Shoe and Leather Co., of Worcester. He d. in Warwick, Mass. He m. Martha H., dr. of Eben and Abby (Simonds) Pierce, of Royalston.

Children of OTIS and MARTHA H. (PIERCE) CONANT:—

> Edwin, d. in infancy.
> Arthur F. P., b. 10 July, 1850, in Worcester, Mass. He now lives in Orange, Mass. He m. in Warwick, Mass., 23 Mch., 1884, Jennie E. Bass.
> Emma L., d. y.
> Abbie R., b. 22 July, 1865.

Mary Conant, of Salem, Mass.; m. 1740, Rufus Herrick, of Cherry Hill, Beverly, Mass. He removed to Pomfret, Conn., after 1761, and d. in Sheffield, Mass., 1814, aged 93 (see *Herrick Genealogy*).

Children of RUFUS and MARY (CONANT) HERRICK:—

> Rufus, b. 20 Dec., 1742.
> Benjamin, b. 24 Sep., 1744.
> Martyn, b. 7 May, 1747.
> Mary, b. 17 Aug., 1749.
> Ephraim, b. 2 Mch., 1752; d. 1753.
> Ephraim, b. 17 Aug., 1754; d. 1814, in Poultney, N. Y.
> Sarah, b. 6 Dec., 1756; m. Zebulon Stevens.
> Ann, b. 6 Feb., 1759; m. Joseph Goodrich.
> Martha, b. 5 June, 1761; m. Jonathan Goodrich.

Andrew Conant moved from Pawlet, Vt., to Ohio, about 1830; was a clothier. He d. in Chagrin Falls, O., 1854. He m. Elizabeth, dr. of Beriah and Elizabeth (Smith) Green, who d. 1877 in Bedford, O. They had twelve children, of whom three survive in 1887. Some members of his branch of the family live in Michigan.

Children of ANDREW and ELIZABETH (GREEN) CONANT:—

> Henry, b. in Vermont; one of the elder children; lives in Bedford, O.
> Charles Preston, b. 30 Dec., 1836, in Twinsburg, Summit co., O.; was one of the youngest children. He served during the Rebellion in the 23rd Regiment, Ohio Volunteers, from May 1, 1861, to Aug. 5, 1865; was first lieutenant; was

wounded at Winchester, Va., July 24, 1864, and at the battle of Fisher's Hill, Sep. 22, 1864. He is now agent for the Prudential Insurance Co., and lives at 925 Pearl street, Cleveland, O. He m. in Bedford, O., 1 Oct., 1866, Arvilla, dr. of Timothy and Lyda (Edwards) Davis, b. in Bedford, 1847. Child: Eva, b. 24 July, 1867; d. Mch., 1872.

Rufus P. Conant (perhaps son of (350) John Gardiner) moved from Enfield, N. H., to Pawlet, Vt., in 1811; m. (1) Fanny Lathe, who d. 1829, aged 41; m. (2) Nancy Goodrich, and removed to Wisconsin (see *Hist. of Pawlet, Vt.*).

James W. Conant, of 115 Smithfield street, Pittsburg, Pa., writes that his father's name was Adoniram B. and his great grandfather's name was Peter, who was born and raised in Plymouth (Bridgewater?), Mass. Repeated letters fail to elicit further information.

John Conant, of Plymouth, Mass., by wife, Phebe, had Cynthia, b. 1814, Maria, 1818, and William R., 1829 (Davis' *Ancient Landmarks of Plymouth*).

William Conant was taxed at Billerica, Mass., 1776 to 1779. Betsey, daughter of William, baptized there Aug., 1795 (*Hist. of Billerica*).

Caroline Louisa Conant, b. in Charlestown, Mass., 31 Aug., 1840; was dr. of Oliver J. and Elizabeth A. (Berry) Conant; she m. George W. Calef, who was b. in Keene, N. H. He was killed in the army, at Gettysburg. She resides in Chelsea, Mass. Child: Kate Agnes, b. 2 Feb., 1858, in Exeter, N. H.

George Conant, of Somerville, Mass. (perhaps son of (608) George F., of Somerville); m. 25 Dec., 1856, Abbie, dr. of Nathaniel and Abigail (Wellington) Pierce, b. 15 Nov., 1835 (*Hist. of Lexington*, p. 185).

Samuel Conant witnessed a deed from Nathaniel Conant, of Bridgewater, Mass., to his brother, John Conant, of Beverly, dated 7 Jan., 1691-2 (Essex Deeds, Vol. 21, p. 226).

Samuel Conant

(1691-2.)

There was no Samuel Conant living in New England at this time, so far as known. Compare this signature with that on p. 67.

MARRIAGES.

Esther Conant, of Stow, and Ebenezer Davis, of Acton, m. 14 Jan., 1748-9, in Acton, Mass.

Mary Conant, of Provincetown, m. 17 Nov., 1755, Naomi Holbrook, of Eastham, Mass. (perhaps dr. of (57) John).

Mrs. Conant m. Henry, son of Archibald McNeil, and went to London during the Revolutionary war (Wyman's *Gen. and Estates of Charlestown*, p. 644).

Silas Conant, of Stow, m. Adelia Emmons, dr. of Richard Johonnot, who was b. 14 Apr., 1775.

Sarah Conant m. David K., son of Israel Hoyt, b. 1799. They lived in Boston (*Hoyt Genealogy*).

R. M. Conant m. Terza Ann, dr. of Gilbert Hoyt, of Deerfield, Mass., and Buffalo, N. Y. Gilbert Hoyt was b. 1789 (*Hoyt Genealogy*).

Harriet L. Conant m. Samuel Jenkins, jr., 30 Mch., 1820 (*Hist. of Townsend, Mass.*, p. 415).

Rebekah Conant m. Capt. Samuel Scripture, of Nelson, N. H., 31 May, 1826 (*Hist. of Townsend*, p. 419).

Timothy Conant, m. 1858, in Dayton, Minn., Martha D. Davis, b. 11 Nov., 1828, in Bangor, Me. (*Jordan Genealogy*).

Mary Conant m. 27 Mch., 1839, Horace L., son of Perley and Sally (Fitts) Enos, of Leicester, Vt. He was b. 29 Sep., 1814; they moved to Lawrence, Ks. (*Fitts Genealogy*).

Mary Conant, of Acton, m. 11 May, 1837, Charles H. Spaulding, of Cambridge (Acton, Mass., Records).

Mary J. Conant m. 31 July, 1863, Joseph O'Neil (Providence, R. I., Records).

Ida M. Conant m. 12 Aug., 1869, Samuel C. Thomas (colored) (Providence, R. I., Records).

Ada M. Conant m. Jan. 1, 1885, Albert Parrott (Boston).

Albert A. Conant m. Sep. 3, 1887, Nellie M. Alden, of East Livermore, Me. (East Hebron, Me.).

Benjamin W. Conant m. 29 Nov., 1885, Lydia J. Dickey, in Northport, Me.

Della Conant m. 4 Apr., 1887, Frank O. Clark, in Camden, Me.

Rebecca Conant, of Concord, m. 14 Apr., 1743, William Baker, of Concord (Concord Records).

Elizabeth Conant m. 24 Mch., 1784, Jacob French (Concord, Mass., Records).

Lydia Conant, of Concord, m. 6 June, 1797, Josiah Haynes, of Sudbury (Concord, Mass., Records).

Lois P. Conant, of Concord, m. 27 Nov., 1828, Joseph Haynes, of Lowell (Concord, Mass., Records).

Bithiah Conant m. 28 Mch., 1830, Joseph Leonard (Concord, Mass., Records).

Mary A. Conant m. 15 June, 1837, Jesse Hosmer (Concord, Mass., Records).

Benjamin Conant m. Louisa, dr. of Peter Noble, b. 9 Apr., 1777, in Tinmouth, Vt.; see d. in Schenectady, N. Y.

Mrs. Clara A. Conant m. 6 Nov. (1886?), Charles A. Bean, both of Portland, Me. (Portland Records).

Lucy Conant m. in Waterford, Me., Leander Jewett (see pp. 262 and 342).

DEATHS.

Mrs. Conant d. 1 Mch., 1781, aged 34 (Concord, Mass., Records).

Miss Conant d. 16 June, 1790, aged 16 (Concord, Mass., Records).

Mary Conant, widow, d. 5 Mch., 1783 (Lincoln, Mass., Records).

Sarah White Conant, d. 1807, aged 77 (Copp's Hill Burying Ground, Boston).

Abigail Conant, widow, d. 10 Jan., 1840 (Acton Mass., Records).

Roxanna Conant, widow, d. 17 June, 1863, aged 75 (Providence, R. I., Records).

Cardinal C. Conant d. 12 Dec., 1854, aged 48 (Forest Hills Cemetery Register, Boston).

Annie Conant d. 30 Nov., 1844, aged 64 years 8 mo. 26 d. (Forest Hills Cemetery Register, Boston).

Abigail Conant d. 5 Feb., 1861, aged 73 (Forest Hills Cemetery Register, Boston).

John H. Conant, of Taunton, Mass., d. 29 Dec., 1876, aged 51 (Forest Hills Cemetery Register).

Benjamin W. Conant d. 2 Aug., 1881, aged 45 years 7 mo. 3 d. (Forest Hills Cemetery Register).

Fanny A. Conant d. 4 Aug., 1875, aged 43 years 3 mo. 8 d. (Forest Hills Cemetery Register).

Mary F. Conant d. 6 Apr., 1871, aged 14 years 5 mo. 6 d. (Forest Hills Cemetery Register).

Addie Conant d. 20 Nov., 1864, aged 3 years 10 mo. 18 d. (Forest Hills Cemetery Register).

Nellie, wife of J. F. Conant, dr. of Allen Dodge, of Lowell, Mass., d. 15 Aug., 188–, aged 26.

Ethan Conant, aged about 21, living about 15 miles from Parlin Pond, Somerset co., Me., committed suicide, 1883. He came from Massachusetts.

COLLEGE GRADUATES.

Shubael, Yale, 1732.
Sylvanus, Harvard, 1740.
Shubael, Yale, 1756.
Roger, Yale, 1765.
William, Yale, 1770; LL. D., Dartmouth, 1780.
Eleazer, Yale, 1776.

Jacob, Harvard, 1777.
Ezra, Harvard, 1784.
Gaius, Brown, 1800.
Horatio, Middlebury, 1810.
Harry, Middlebury, 1813.
Abel, Dartmouth, 1815.
Liba, Brown, 1819; LL. D., Dartmouth, 1837.
Thomas Jefferson, D. D.; Middlebury, 1823.
Cyrus Whitman, Union, 1824.
Edwin, Harvard, 1829.
Robert Taft, Amherst, 1836.
Marshall, LL. D., Dartmouth, 1839.
Samuel Mills, Middlebury, 1844; Union Theo., 1847.
David Sloan, M. D., Bowdoin, 1851.
Chester Cook, Dartmouth, 1857.
Abel Blood, M. D., Columbia, 1862.
Edward Card, Bowdoin, 1858; M. D., Harvard, 1865.
(Samuel Stillman, Hamilton?)
Edward, Middlebury, 1866.
Duane, Hamilton, 1867; LL. B., Columbia, 1869.
Thomas, Harvard, 1868.
Robert Warren, Yale, 1873.
Allen Gwyer, Middlebury, 1874.
George Abbott, Amherst, 1878.
Heywood, Cornell, 1878.
William Merritt, Harvard, 1879.
Charles Edward, Colby, 1879.
Frederick Odell, Sc. B., Bowdoin, 1880, A. M., 1883.
Ernest Lee, Harvard, 1883.
William Rawson, Dartmouth, 1883.
Charlotte Howard, Wellesley, 1884.
Helen Blanche, Wellesley, 1887.

LISTS OF SOLDIERS.

KING PHILIP'S WAR (1675).

Daniel (Connit), of Connecticut, *vide postea*.
John, of Beverly, Mass., p. 147.
Lot, of Beverly, p. 151.

FIRST FRENCH WAR (1690).

Exercise, of Beverly, p. 138.

SECOND FRENCH WAR (1702-1712).

Caleb (Cunnit), p. 194.

SEVEN YEARS' WAR, OR FRENCH AND INDIAN WAR (1755-1763).

Nathaniel, of Beverly, p. 217.
Nathaniel, of Bridgewater, p. 250.

REVOLUTIONARY WAR.

Aaron, of Ipswich, Mass., p. 234.
Abel, of Hollis, N. H., p. 242.
Amos, of Claremont, N. H., p. 278.
Asa, of Barnstable, Mass., p. 531.
Barnabas, of Barnstable, p. 529.
Bartholomew, of Falmouth, Me., p. 230.
Benjamin, of Bridgewater, p. 257.
Benjamin, of Beverly, p. 270.
Caleb, of Bridgewater, Mass., p. 319.
Daniel, of Stow, p. 262.
Daniel, of Townsend, p. 266.
David, of Bridgewater, p. 295.
Ebenezer, of Ashburnham, p. 236.
Eleazer, of Mansfield, p. 246.
Eli, of Concord, p. 264.
Elias, of Bridgewater, p. 294.
Ephraim, of Stow, p. 341.
Ezra, of Bridgewater, p. 251.
Ezra, of Concord, p. 212.
Fortune, of Billerica. (Served three years in the Continental army
   (Mass. Arch., Continental Army Rolls). Not identified.)
George, of Barnstable, p. 530.
Isaac, of Stow, p. 262.
Israel, of Palmer; was in Walker's company of Danielson's regi-
   ment (Mass. Arch., Worcester Coat Rolls).
Israel, of Wilbraham, p. 240.
James, of Oakham, p. 259.
Jeremiah, of Bridgewater, p. 255.
John, of Bridgewater, p. 254.
John, of Beverly, p. 268.
John, of Stow, p. 339.
John, of Townsend, p. 267.
John, of Warwick, p. 280.
Jonathan, of Beverly, p. 228.
Jonathan, jr., of Beverly, p. 283.
Jonathan, of Orange, Vt., p. 235.
Jonathan, of Lebanon, N. H., p. 249.
Jonathan, of Shirley, p. 240.
Joseph, of Sandwich (colored), aged 16 in 1780 (Vol. 35, p. 201).
Joshua, of Londonderry, N. H., p. 231.
Josiah, of Hollis, N. H., p. 241.
Josiah, of Westminster, p. 243.
Josiah, of Barnstable (Mass. Arch., Muster Rolls, Vol. 25, p. 203).
Lemuel, of Barnstable, p. 529.
Lemuel (deserter from British army: R. I. Col. Records, Vol. viii.,
   p. 105).
Lot, of Ipswich, p. 231.
Lot, of Beverly, p. 214.

Luther, of Hardwick, p. 259.
Malachi, of Mansfield, Conn., p. 198.
Moses, of Ipswich, p. 234.
Nathan, of Townsend, p. 265.
Nathaniel, of Bridgewater, p. 252.
Oliver, of Sudbury, p. 338.
Peter, of Bridgewater, p. 258.
Peter, of Stow, p. 261.
Phinehas, of Bridgewater, p. 258.
Reuben, of Harvard, p. 348.
Roger, of Easton, p. 252.
Roger, of Mansfield, p. 245.
Rufus, of Bridgewater, p. 294.
Samuel, of Beverly, p. 269.
Samuel, of Mansfield, Conn., p. 198.
Shebuel, of Pepperell, p. 341.
Shubael, of Mansfield, p. 196.
Simeon, of Harvard, p. 349.
Solomon, of Bridgewater, p, 294.
Solomon, of Eastham, p. 195.
Stephen, of Warwick, p. 224.
Silvanus, of Bridgewater, p. 256.
Sylvanus, of Middleboro', p. 203.
Thomas, of Barnstable, p. 529.
Timothy, of Rehoboth, p. 544.
Timothy, of Oakham, p. 205.
William, of Falmouth, Me., p. 232.
William, of Wareham, p. 545.
William, of Charlestown, p. 238.
William; was in Reed's co., Baldwin's regiment, at White Plains,
   N. Y., 28 Oct., 1776 (N. H. State Papers, Vol. 14, p. 419). Perhaps
   William of Lyme, N. H., p. 189.
Zebulon, of Winchendon, p. 344.
Zenas, of Bridgewater, p. 202.

WAR OF 1812.

Artemus (Sen. Docs., No. 465, 28th Cong., 1st Ses., Vol. 19, p. 264.)
Jeremiah, of Athens co., Ohio, p. 325.
James, of Oakham, p. 336.
James, of Acton, p. 346.
Jonas, of Warwick, p. 282.
Jonathan, of Lyme, N. H., p. 388.
Lot, of Oakham, Mass., p. 335.
Oliver, of Lisbon, Me., p. 378.
Sylvanus, of Turner, Me., p. 332.
Thomas, of Oakham, p. 256.

MEXICAN WAR.

Charles Olin, of Troy, Vt., p. 471. (Lieut.)

WAR OF THE REBELLION.

Abel Blood, of Lyme, N. H., p. 388.

Albert Samuel, of South Lyndeboro', N. H., *vide postea.*

Alvin, of Bridgewater, p. 495.

Amasa Lumbert, of Orrington, Me., p. 499.

Andrew (Connett), of Flemington, N. J., *vide postea.*

Andrew H., of Nashua, N. H., enlisted 20 Sep., 1862, Co. I, 13th N. H. Regt.; discharged for disability, 20 Sep., 1863; re-enlisted 4 Jan., 1864; transferred to Co. A, Veteran Battalion, 8th N. H. Regt., 1 Jan., 1865 (N. H. Adj. Gen.'s Report, 1866, p. 290).

Andrew H. (of Hollis, N. H.?); enlisted at Manchester, N. H., 20 Dec., 1861, for three years; mustered in 23 Dec., 1861; went to Ship Island; promoted to corporal 14 Feb., 1863; re-enlisted 4 Jan., 1864; d. at Natchez, Miss., 10 Oct., 1865 (*Hist. of Hollis, N. H.*, p. 224).

Augustus Eugene, of Bangor, Me., p. 505.

Augustus Hammond, of Geneva, Ill., p. 396.

Calvin Harrison, of Stoneham, Mass., p. 513.

Calvin L., in navy, from New York (not identified).

Charles Edwin, of Londonderry, N. H., p. 478.

Charles Francis, of Milford, N. H., p. 585.

Charles H., of Thomaston, Me., p. 424.

Charles Olin, of Troy, Vt., p. 471.

Charles Preston, of Cleveland, O., p. 552.

Charles William, of Patten, Me., p. 501.

Daniel Alexander, of Milford, Mass. (or Temple, Me.), p. 505.

Daniel J., of Lewiston, Me., p. 379.

Edmund, of Chelsea, Vt., p. 414.

Edward D., of Mansfield, Conn., p. 410.

Elbridge, of Acton, Mass., p. 448.

Estes, of Chelsea, Vt., p. 315.

Everett Sanford, of Turner, Me., p. 496.

Ezra W., of Vermont; enlisted 14 July, 1862, Co. B, 10th Vt. Regt.; transferred to Veteran Reserve Corps, 9 July, 1864; not identified. (Vt. Adjt. Gen.'s Report.)

Francis A., of Lewiston, Me., p. 476.

Francis E., of Vienna, N. Y., p. 509.

Freeman C., of Cavendish, Vt., p. 381.

George (Conet), of Manchester, N. H., ward 4; mustered in Sep., 1864; promoted to corporal 26 Feb., 1865; mustered out 15 June, 1865; Co. C, 1st Regt., Heavy Artillery (N. H. Adj. Gen.'s Rept.).

George H., was captain in 31st Regt., Mass. Vols.; bearer of dispatches from Gen. Butler to Admiral Farragut (Rebellion Records).

Henry E., of Barre, Mass., p. 500.

~~Henry Thompson, of~~ Boston, p. 415. *G. W. S.*

Hiram Augustus, of Turner, Me., p. 496.

Hiram, of Hinckley, O., p. 417.

Horace Artemus, of St. Louis, Mo., p. 526.

Howard Turner, of Turner, Me., p. 495.

Isaac B., of Charlotte, Me., p. 381.

James M., of Portland, Me.; enlisted 1 Dec., 1861, Troop B, 2nd R. I. Cavalry; transferred 24 Aug., 1863, to 1st La. Cavalry; transferred 14 Jan., 1864, to Troop H, 3rd R. I. Cavalry; taken prisoner; parolled; mustered out 1 Aug., 1865 (R. I. Adj. Gen.'s Report, 1865). (Perhaps (673) James McKeen, p. 476.)

James Scott, of Bridgewater, Mass., p. 427.

John, of Bridgewater, Mass., p. 330.

John, of Bangor, Me., p. 504.

John A., of Vermont, aged 23; enlisted 28 Aug., 1861, Co. II, 4th Vt. Infantry; died 21 Oct., 1862 (Vt. Adjt. Gen.'s Report). (Perhaps of Lyme, N. H.)

John H.; was lieutenant in Battery H, 1st Mo. Light Artillery (Rebellion Records).

John Shubael, of Monroe, Mich., p. 408.

John W., of Vermont, aged 23; enlisted 18 Dec., 1863, Co. A, 8th Vt. Regt.; 31 Aug., 1864, was sick in general hospital (Vt. Adj. Gen.'s Report).

Joseph Augustus, of Fort Fairfield, Me., p. 508.

Joseph B., of Vermont, aged 21; enlisted 22 Sep., 1862, Co. C, 15th Regt., Vt. Vols.; died 12 Apr., 1863 (Vt. Adj. Gen.'s Report, 1864, p. 433, Appendix D).

Joseph R., of Thomaston, Me., p. 424.

Leonard, of Tilton, N. H., p. 481.

Lorenzo, died in army; was in Co. D, 7th Me. Regt., Infantry (Me. Adj. Gen.'s Report, 1863, Appendix 1, p. 6).

Lucius, of Bridgewater, Mass., p. 425.

Luther, of Acton, Mass., p. 348.

Marcus, of Massachusetts; mustered 24 Aug., 1863, in 3rd Mass. Heavy Artillery; served till 18 Sep., 1865 (*Hist. of Westford, Mass.*, p. 195). (Perhaps son of (599) Nahum, p. 449.)

Mahlon H. (Connett), of Bedford, Iowa.

Neray, of Rockfort, Ill., p. 484.

Oliver J., of Rockland, Me., p. 495.

Oscar, of Connecticut; enlisted 2 Sep., 1864, 14th Regt., Conn. Vols.; transferred 31 May, 1865, to 2nd Artillery (Norwich, Conn., Memorial). Not identified.

Phineas H., of Springfield, Ill., p. 436.

Rodney T., of DeKalb, N. Y., p. 492.

Russel B., of Columbus, O., p. 489.

Samuel, of Townsend, Mass., p. 350.

Samuel G., of Vermont, aged 23; enlisted 30 Aug., mustered 15 Sep., 1862, Co. A, 2nd Vt. Regt. (Vt. Adj. Gen.'s Report, 1864). Not identified.

Samuel P., of Richmond, Vt., p. 359 (Vt. Adj. Gen.'s Report, 1864, p. 517).

Samuel Williams, of Baltimore, Md., p. 418.

Sanford, of Athens, O., p. 492.

Seth Wilder, of Bridgewater, Mass., p. 425.

Sumner Tyler, of Camden, Me., p. 523.

Thomas, of Gloucester, Mass., p. 426.

Washington, of Portland, Me., p. 475.

William E., of Maine; died in army; Co. D, 2nd U. S. Inf. (Me. Adj. Gen.'s Report, 1863, Appendix 1, p. 6).

William D., of Vermont, aged 39; enlisted 26 Aug., 1862, Co. A, 16th Regt., Vt. Vols. (Vt. Adj. Gen.'s Report, 1864, p. 449).

William H., of Plymouth, Me., p. 382.

William J., of Vermont, aged 18; enlisted 17 May, 1861, in Co. K, 2nd Vt. Regt.; discharged 8 June, 1862 (Vt. Adj. Gen.'s Report, 1864, Appendix D, p. 50). Perhaps William Jewett, of Bellows Falls, Vt., p. 403.

A son of Abraham, of Sycamore, Ill., p. 342.

Two sons of Chester, of Michigan, p. 316.

NAMES FROM VARIOUS DIRECTORIES.

Surnames Conant unless otherwise stated.

A., tailor, Portland, Oregon, 1872.

A. F., 326 Westminster st., Providence, R. I., 1887.

A. P., Eddysville, Ky., 1872.

Mrs. A. R., Gardiner, Me., 1886.

Albert Forbes, 31 Hildrop Road, Camden Road, London, N., England, 1883.

Alexander B., West Auburn, Me., 1886.

Allen, carpenter, 393 Elk st., Buffalo, N. Y., 1870.

Andrew, farmer, Forest st., Bridgewater, Mass., 1872 (see p. 324).

Mrs. Anna A., 20 Prospect st., Albany, N. Y. (widow of Gideon, who d. 13 Apr., 1886?).

Mrs. Anna B., Lewiston, Me., 1887.

Arthur, Cass st., Providence, R. I., 1887.

Arthur J., clerk, 65 Elm st., New Bedford, Mass., 1883 (son of (706) Oliver B.?).

Bertha, domestic, Antisdel House, Detroit, Mich., 1886.

C. P., printer, Albany, N. Y., 1887.

Charles C., printer, 5 Cannon st., Troy, N. Y.; lives West Troy.

Charles L., electrician, 130 North st., Providence, R. I., 1887.

Charles T., Gold st., Meriden, Conn., 1886.

Chauncey, Barnstable, Mass., 1885.

Clarence, Phillips, Me., 1884.

Dewey, miller, Buffalo, N. Y., 1885.

Dow L., deck hand, 71 Eutaw st., Boston, 1886.

Earl G., 20 Prospect st., Albany, N. Y. (son of Gideon?).

Edgar F., son of Mrs. Anna B., Lewiston, Me., 1887.

Edward, Auburn, Me., 1887.

Edward P., 36 McLean st., Boston, 1886.

Eliza, widow of Asa, lived in Grand st., N. Y., 1863.

Elmer G., plumber, 52 Messer st., Providence, R. I., 1887.

F. A., 326 Westminster st., Providence, R. I., 1887.

Frank W., 19 Polk st., Boston, Mass., 1886.

Franklin, insurance agent, 364 23rd st., Detroit, Mich., 1886.

George, Ionia, Mich., 1886.

George, was quartermaster on the yacht Volunteer in race for the America cup, 1887.

George A., Boston or Medford, 1886.

George H., expert, Fairbanks, Morse & Co., 1914 Clinton Ave., Minneapolis, Minn.

George M., 107 Elm st., New Bedford, Mass. (son of (706) Oliver B.?).

George P., Geneva Lake, Wis., 1882.

George W., bridge builder, 17 Arnold st., Boston, Mass., 1886.

Hannah, widow of Daniel, Haverhill, Mass.

Henry, Attica, N. Y.

Ira E., miller, 378 Coghlan st., Detroit, Mich., 1886.

J. F., mail messenger, Dubuque, Iowa, 1884.

Jacob, tailor, 15 Chapman Place, Boston; house in Lynn.

John, driver, 19 Polk st., Boston, Mass., 1886.

Dr. John, Prairie du Chien, Wis., 1885.

John H., hackman, 58 Chambers st., Boston, 1886.

Lewis W., 64 Pearl st., Providence, R. I.

Louis, clothing, Sycamore, Ill., 1872 (see p. 342).

Mary, nurse, 171 E. Adams st., Syracuse, N. Y., 1886.

Melnot, 89 Cambridge st., Boston, Mass., 1886.

Mrs. Priscilla, Everett st., Brunswick, Me., 1887.

Mrs. Rossie, Auburn, Me., 1887.

Sherman, confectioner, 18 Oxford st., Boston, 1886.

Thomas B., 16 Lyndon st., Concord, N. H., 1883.

Thomas N., in Railway Mail Service between Centralia and Chicago, Ill., 1884.

Walter, Taft st., Fitchburg, Mass., 1881.

Washington J., 3 Linden st., Fitchburg, Mass., 1881.

William D., 46 Buena Vista st., Detroit, Mich., 1884.

William F., box maker, Haverhill, Mass., 1884.

William F., 36 Temple Place, Provident Institution for Savings, Boston, Mass., 1886; house at Melrose.

William H., 506 E. 18th st., Minneapolis, Minn., 1887.

William R., 61 Fort Avenue, Boston, Mass., 1886.

Winslow, trader, Marshfield, Mass., 1885.

Virgil Van., South st., Bridgewater, 1872.

Conat, Abram, laborer, Detroit, Mich., 1886.

Conat, Wilmot, Detroit, Mich., 1886.

Connant, William, grocer, Saulsbury, Tenn., 1872.

NAMES CHANGED.

Nathaniel Conant, 2nd, of Danvers, Mass., to Nathaniel P. Conant, Mch. 24, 1849.

Nancy M. Conant, of Stow, Mass., to Annie M. Conant, June 9, 1863.

Arthur W. Conant, of Gardner, Mass., to Arthur Warren Conant Loverwell, May, 3, 1864.

Mary A. Reynolds (adopted), of Lowell, Mass., to Mary Eva Conant, Dec. 26, 1871.

Mary Eva Conant, of Lowell, Mass., to Ethel Blanche Aldrich, Jan. 7, 1873.

Herbert Eugene Conant and Lucy Perry Conant, of Natick, Mass., to Herbert Eugene Pebbles and Lucy Perry Pebbles, May 28, 1876 (see under No. 808).

Evelina Comeau (adopted), of Gloucester, Mass., to Evelina Conant, July 2, 1880.

(See List of Persons whose names have been changed in Massachusetts, 1780-1883, pp. 124, 164, 168, 196, 204, 218 and 238.)

TOWNS NAMED CONANT.

Conant, Perry county, Illinois, on the Wabash, Chester and Western Railroad.

Conant, Allen county, Ohio, on the Eastern Division of the Chicago and Atlantic Railroad.

Conant, Bell county, Kentucky, nearest railroad station Woodbine, on the Knoxville and Nashville Railroad (named for John Milton Conant, p. 551).   .

Conant, Sumter county, Florida, on the Florida Southern Railroad (named for Maj. Sherman Conant, p. 514).

Conant, Cassia county, Idaho Territory, nearest railroad station Kelton, Utah Territory, on the Central Pacific Railroad (named for Edward Conant, p. 539).

CONNET, CONNETT AND CONNIT FAMILIES.

1. Henry Connet and **Samuel Connet** were living in the borough of Elizabeth, eastern province of New Jersey, 1741. Henry Connet died 10 July, 1761, aged 63; his widow died 31 Aug., 1771; both in New Providence or Elizabeth. Children (see Littell's *Passaic Valley Genealogies*):

2. i.   William.
3. ii.   John.
   iii.   Daniel, m. 26 Nov., 1769, Eleanor Woodruff.
   iv.   Hannah, d. unmarried, 14 May, 1764.

2. William (*Henry*), lived opposite the Franklin mill, and was deacon and elder of the Presbyterian Church in New

Providence. He m. (1) 18 Dec., 1766, Sarah Rogers; m. (2) 24 May, 1790, Mary, widow of Aaron Decamp. By his first wife he had children:

   i.   William, m. 25 Apr., 1791, Charity Bowers.
   ii.   Jemima, bapt. 21 Apr., 1771; m. 10 Apr., 1793, Daniel Bowers.
   iii. Sarah, m. 14 Nov., 1793, Phineas Bowers.
4. iv.   Henry.

   3. **John** (*Henry*), a carpenter; lived near Mendham, N. J. He d. about 1820. He m. 13 Dec., 1767, Rachel Allen, and had children:

   i.   Luther.
   ii.   Abner.
5. iii. Samuel, b. 6 Mch., 1773.
   iv. Allen, b. 7 May, 1776.
   v.   John, b. 28 July, 1779.
   vi. William, b. 12 Feb., 1782.
   vii. Sarah.
   viii. Lydia.

   4. **Henry** (*William, Henry*), married and lived on Water street, near Mendham, N. J. Children:

   i.   Lockey, m. Mr. Lindley, and went to Mount Auburn, Ill.
   ii.   Mary, m. Charles Marsh, and lived at Morristown, N. J.
   iii. Sarah.
   iv. William, m. a Wilson; moved to Ohio, and d. there.
6. v.   Ira.

   5. **Samuel** (*John, Henry*), b. 6 Mch., 1773, in Brookside, Morris co., N. J.; d. 22 Sep., 1837. He m. Elizabeth Earle, b. in Springfield, N. J., 25 Mch., 1771; d. 19 Feb., 1843. Children:

   i.   Rachel, b. 30 Mch., 1794.
   ii.   Sarah, b. 8 Aug., 1795.
   iii. Betsy, b. 6 Oct., 1797.
   iv. Lydia, b. 23 Oct., 1799; d. 8 Oct., 1800.
   v.   Ebenezer Allen, b. 28 Nov., 1801; lives at White House, N. J. (1886).
7. vi. Stephen Earle, b. 31 Mch., 1805.
   vii. Lyda, b. 25 Aug., 1807; d. 27 Sep., 1813.
8. viii. Samuel, b. 4 Sep., 1811.

   6. **Ira** (*Henry, William, Henry*), a miller; lived on the

homestead, near Mendham, N. J.; m. Phebe Runnels (or Reynolds), and had children:

i.   George Minturn.
ii.   Sarah Wilson.
iii. Mary Elizabeth.
iv.   Henry, d. unmarried.
v.   Samuel Runnels.
vi.   Caroline.
vii. Louisa.
viii. Henrietta.
ix.   Florentine.

7. **Stephen Earle** (*Samuel, John, Henry*), b. 31 Mch., 1805, in Brookside, N. J.; owned a saw mill and farm; d. 9 Feb., 1877. He m. 14 July, 1825, Belinda, dr. of Jonathan Dean, b. 14 July, 1807, and had children:

i.   Earle F., b. 24 Aug., 1826.
ii.   Julia Ann, b. 31 June, 1829.
iii. Harriet B., b. 13 Aug., 1834.
iv.   Madison M., b. 10 May, 1843.
v.   Manning F., b. 10 May, 1843; m. in Newark, N. J., 9 Aug., 1871, Rebecca H., dr. of Enos Harvey and Almira (Hunt) Bunting, b. 8 June, 1850, in Sussex co., N. J. Children: 1. Arthur Mitchell, b. 1 July, 1875; 2. Samuel Earle, b. 21 Nov., 1878. He is a dealer in dry goods, in Newark.

8. **Samuel** (*Samuel, John, Henry*), b. 4 Sep., 1811, in Brookside, N. J.; a stone mason by trade, but now a farmer, of Readington, N. J. He m. in Readington, 10 Jan., 1835, Hannah, dr. of Andrew and Susanna (Lane) Thompson, b. 29 Mch., 1817, in Pleasant Run, N. J. Children:

i.   Stephen, b. 28 June, 1836; d. 21 Jan., 1839.
ii.   Susan Elizabeth, b. 9 Oct., 1838; d. 14 Jan., 1839.
iii. Ellenor Ann, b. 24 Oct., 1839.
iv.   Andrew Thompson, b. 4 Feb., 1842; was a private in Co. H, 3rd N. J. Infantry, 1861, and lieutenant in Co. D, 31st N. J. Vols.; served about one year; has been commander of G. A. R. Post. He is now keeping a general store in Flemington, N. J. He m. in Stanton, N. J., 22 May, 1866, Joanna S., dr. of Abraham D. and Mary K. (Shurts) Nevins, b. 14 Jan., 1844, in Hunterdon co., N. J. Children: 1. Frederick Nevins, b. 16 Oct., 1867, now (1886) a student at Stevens Institute, Hoboken, N. J.; 2. Joanna Nevins, b. 14 Nov., 1870, d. 12 Nov., 1882; 3. Earle Thompson, b. 1 Oct., 1872; 4. Hugh Irving, b. 16 Feb., 1881.

v.   Peter Elmer, b. 5 Mch., 1844.
vi. William, b. 25 Apr., 1846.
vii. John Lane, b. 10 Oct., 1848; graduated at Rutgers College;
       is practicing law in Flemington.
viii. Sarah Louisa, b. 13 Nov., 1851.
ix. Charles Ellis, b. 25 Sep., 1855; is a printer and stationer, of
       Readington, N. J.

---

1. James Connet, b. about 1730, probably in New Jersey; lived at Bound Brook; settled in Washington co., Pa., where he d. He was twice married; the second wife was Amy Kelly.

Children by first wife:

i.   Moses.
ii.   William.
iii. John, who was murdered by a man named McDaniel, who
        was executed.
iv.   Sarah.
v.   Mary.

Children by second wife:

2. i.   James, b. 14 April, 1764, at Bound Brook, Somerset co., N. J.
   ii. Spencer.

2. James (*James*), b. 14 Apr., 1764, at Bound Brook, N. J.; was a weaver; removed to Prosperity, Washington co., Pa., about 1801, with his parents, and d. there 25 June, 1845. He m. at Bound Brook, 21 Oct., 1793, Jane, dr. of Joseph and Elizabeth Powell, b. 17 Dec., 1776; d. 2 Sep., 1846. Children:

   i.   Sarah, b. 8 Oct., 1794, at Bound Brook, N. J.
3. ii.   James, b. 16 Jan., 1797, "   "   "   "
   iii. Elizabeth, b. 31 Dec., 1798, "   "   "
   iv.   Joseph, b. 17 Jan., 1801,   "   "   "
   v.   Mary, b. 25 Jan., 1803, at Prosperity, Pa.
4. vi.   Isaac, b. 13 Mch., 1805,   "   "   "
   vii. Priscilla, b. 16 June, 1807,   "   "
   viii. Lydia, b. 17 July, 1809,   "   "
   ix.   Jane, b. 23 May, 1813,   "   "
   x.   Melissa, b. 11 Feb., 1816,   "   "
   xi.   Edward, b. ——; d. Oct., 1824, "   "
   xii. John, b. 11 Aug., 1818,   "   "
   xiii. Spencer, b. 13 Sep., 1820,   "   "

3. James (*James, James*), b. 16 Jan., 1797, at Bound

Brook, N. J.; a farmer; removed to Prosperity, Pa., with his parents, where he d. 31 May, 1882. He m. in Prosperity, 16 June, 1821, Rebecca P., dr. of Henry and Sarah (Day) Cary, b. 16 Jan., 1804, in Morristown, N. J.; d. 22 Sep., 1875, in Prosperity. They had children:

    i.   Henry, b. 25 Feb., 1822.
5. ii.   Isaac Newton, b. 18 Mch., 1826.
    iii.   Oliver C., b. 20 Sep., 1830.

4. Isaac (*James, James*), b. 13 Mch., 1805, in Prosperity, Pa.; a farmer and miller; removed to Noble co., O., Salisbury, Ind., and Champaign, Ill. He d. near Champaign, Ill., 21 Feb., 1865. He m. 7 Sep., 1826, in Pennsylvania, Abigail, dr. of Aaron and Ruth (Coe) French, b. 23 Dec., 1799. Children:

    i.   Amanda, b. 11 Feb., 1828.
    ii.   Nelson, b. 23 June, 1830, in Green co., Pa.; now of Stanford, Ind.
    iii.   Madison, b. 23 Oct., 1832; of Champaign, Ill.
6. iv.   Alfred, b. 17 Oct., 1834.
    v.   Silas, b. 9 May, 1837; now of Ozark, Mo.
    vi.   Minerva, b. 20 Sep., 1839; m. a Thompson, of Cawker City, Kansas.
    vii.   Milton, b. 2 Oct., 1841.
    viii.   Rachel, b. 15 Sep., 1844.

He m. (2) ———, and had children:

    i.   Dickey, b. 21 July, 1856, in Salisbury, Ind.
    ii.   Oscar, b. 29 Nov., 1858, " " "
    iii.   Oliver, b. 8 Oct., 1860; of Champaign, Ill.
    iv.   Ella, b. 2 Apr., 1863.

5. Isaac Newton (*James, James, James*), b. 18 Mch., 1826, in Prosperity, Pa.; a farmer. He m. in Prosperity, 23 Sep., 1847, Lucinda, dr. of Lewis and Bethany (Day) Lindley, b. 24 Jan., 1828. He spells his name *Connett*. Children:

    i.   Flora C., b. 21 May, 1849, in Prosperity.
    ii.   Hannah R., b. 10 Apr., 1851, "
    iii.   Sadie C., b. 10 Aug., 1857, "
    iv.   Clara B., b. 17 Nov., 1861, "

6. Alfred (*Isaac, James, James*), b. 17 Oct., 1834, near the line between Washington and Green counties, Pa. He is principal of the Bethany High School, and pastor of the First and Second Congregational churches at McLeansville, N. C. He is preparing a genealogy of the Connet family. He m. near Owensville, Ind., 17 Oct., 1861, Anna Electa Pollard, dr. of Rev. Levin and Henrietta (McReynolds) Wilson, b. 12 Oct., 1841. Children:

   i.   Levin, b. 5 Aug., 1862, in Oberlin, O.
   ii. Minette, b. 24 Oct., 1863, in Cynthiana, Ind.
  iii. Myrie Henrietta, b. 21 Sep., 1865, in Cynthiana, Ind.
  iv. Orthy, b. 7 Mch., 1868, in Bone Gap, Ind.
   v. Adelaide, b. 20 Feb., 1871, in St. Mary's, Ks.
  vi. Roy, b. 14 Nov., 1875, in Salisbury, Ind.
 vii. Agele, b. 6 Mch., 1878, "   "   "
viii. Photos, b. 18 Nov., 1881, in McLeansville, N. C.

Sarah Connet, m. in New York, N. Y., 21 Aug., 1772, John Blank, jr.

John Connet. In a list of prisoners confined in Dorchester goal for complicity in Monmouth's Rebellion (1685), the name of John Connett appears. In a list of convicted rebels put on board the Betty, of London, at the port of Weymouth, in the county of Dorset, James May, commander, and bound for the island of Barbadoes, the name of John Connet appears. And in a "List of rebels, by his Majesty's mercy granted to Gerome Nepho to be transported to this island, received by Charles Thomas and John Penne," the name of John Connett appears, as sold to William Merchant. (Hotten's *Lists of Emigrants*, pp. 318, 319 and 424.)

Mary Connet, was buried in St. Michael's Parish, Barbadoes, 7 Aug., 1678 (Hotten's Lists, p. 428).

----

   1. William Connett, b. 30 May, 1774, in Woodbridge, Middlesex co., N. J.; a farmer. In 1750 Catherine Connett, widow, and Jonathan Connett, administrators of the estate of Benjamin Connett, yeoman, of Woodbridge, deceased, sell his home plantation, it being land he bought of his brother, Jonathan (the same above administrator). As the papers relating to this transfer are now in possession of William Connett's grandson, it is probable that the parties to it were his ancestors.

There is a tradition in this branch of the family that their ancestors went from New England to New Jersey. William Connett, d. 10 Jan., 1851. He m. 10 Dec., 1804, Sarah Force, who d. 23 Feb., 1867. Their children were:

2. i. Daniel B., b. 5 June, 1807.
   ii. Susan E., b. ———; m. Wm. B. Morton.
   iii. Mary J., b. ———; m. Simeon D. Brown.

2. Daniel B. (*William*), b. 5 June, 1807; m. 29 Dec., 18—, Mary B. Clarkson. They lived in South Orange, N. J. Children :

   i. Isaac S., b. 29 Oct., 18—, in Woodbridge, N. J.
3. ii. Eugene V., b. ———, in Norfolk, Va.
   iii. Jonathan T., b. ———, in Woodbridge, N. J.

3. Eugene V. (*Daniel B., William*), b. in Norfolk, Va. He is a hat manufacturer, of New York city; residence South Orange, N. J. He m. in Newark, N. J., Sophia Rutan, and has children :

   i. Albert N.
   ii. Eugene V.
   iii. Ernest.
   iv. Lyndon.

George Connett, b. 20 Dec., 1811; son of Abner and Elizabeth Connett; a farmer and cloth dresser, of Wolf's Plains, O.; m. 24 Nov., 1836, Lydia Dow, b. 1 Jan., 1814, and had children :

   i. Eliza Jane, b. 3 Jan., 1838; m. 16 Sep., 1857, Rev. Elias Nichols.
   ii. George Wallace, b. 17 Mch., 1840; d. 1852.
   iii. Andrew, b. 5 Aug., 1842.
   iv. Lydia, b. 27 Apr., 1845.
   v. Eliza, b. 5 July, 1848.
   vi. Lewis William, b. 23 Aug., 1851.
   vii. Loring Snelling, b. 23 Aug., 1851.

Gardner Connett was a settler in Westfield, Union co., N. J., at the time of the first allotment of land, 1726 or 1728.

William Connett, an Indian. "Thomas Hinckley, senior, and Joseph Laythorp, Agents for the Purchasers of the

Lands of Sepecan, vs. William Connett, Indian, sometimes resident at Yantick. This was an action of trespass; amount claimed £100. The jury find for the defendant; verdict set aside by the court, Mch. 6, 1682-3. Suit entered Oct. 31, 1683, but not pleaded; parties came to an agreement" (Plymouth Colony Records, Vol. VII., p. 258).

William Connett, published to Martha Wicket, of Sandwich, 1740. John Connett, m. Bathsheba Valentine, 1811. William Connett, published to Harrison Joseph, 1817. (Davis' *Annals of Plymouth, Mass.*)

Nancy Connett, m. 13 Jan., 1823, Lewis Condit. She is still living, with her daughter, Mrs. Mary Pierson, in Grinell, Iowa. He was b. in Mendham, N. J.; moved West about 1836, and d. 8 Nov., 1848. (*Condit Genealogy.*)

Mahlon Coleman Connett, lives in Bedford, Iowa; is a physician. He is son of William and ——— (Coleman) Connett, g. s. of William Connett, whose father was born in New Jersey. During the Rebellion he was a captain in the 6th Indiana Infantry.

Woodruff Connett, of Chauncy, O., m. 1858, Lucy Dow, b. 11 May, 1809, in Athens, O.

Jerusha Conet, b. 14 Mch., 1743; d. 29 Mch., 1819; m. Zebulon, son of Ebenezer and Martha (Nicholson) Marcy, b. in Dover, Duchess co., N. Y., 28 May, 1744. He was an early settler in the Wyoming Valley (see Record of the Marcy Family, p. 7), and they were sufferers from the famous Wyoming Massacre. In the flight from the Indians she carried an infant six weeks old in her arms, at the same time leading a child two years old; the latter died in the wilderness (see Peck's *Hist. of Wyoming*, pp. 220-226, and Miner's *Hist. of Wyoming*, p. 59). Their children were:

   i.   Zebulon, b. 9 Oct., 1767; d. 19 Jan., 1770.
   ii. John, b. 9 June, 1769; d. 5 May, 1840.
  iii. Lydia, b. 3 Jan., 1772; d. 18 June, 1817.
  iv. Nicholson, b. 3 Nov., 1773; d. 30 Jan., 1827; was of Tunk-

hannock, Pa.; m. Hannah, dr. of Col. Hutchinson, of
Danvers, Mass. Children: 1. William N.; 2. Zebulon
Conant; 3. Susan; 4. Albert Nicholson; 5. Israel H.; 6.
Oliver H. Perry, who was proprietor of the Tunkhannock
Republican; 7. Harriet N.; 8. Eunice H.; 9. Porter; 10.
Martha Curtis.

  v.   Sarah, b. 9 Aug., 1776; d. on Pocono Mountain, in the flight
       from the "Massacre."
  vi.   Sarah, b. 24 June, 1778; d. 14 Oct., 1854.
  vii. Zebulon, b. 10 July, 1780; d. 9 Nov., 1834; was of Scranton,
       Pa.
  viii. Abel, b. 24 Apr., 1782; m. Eunice Spencer.
  ix.   Jerusha, b. 8 Nov., 1783.

Lizzie L. Connitt, of Portland, Me., is a daughter of
George W. Connitt (b. in Elysia, O., 20 Sep., 1823), of Hart-
ford, Conn. His brother, Henry E. Connit, is a lawyer, of
Fond du Lac, Wis. They are sons of John and Phebe (Par-
ker) Connit, who were married about 1817, in Gorham, or
Bloomfield, N. Y. John Connit was b. in New Jersey and
moved to Westmoreland, N. Y.; his mother's name was
Mary Furguson.

Daniel Connit was one of the grantees of Voluntown,
Conn., granted for service in the Narragansett war. His
name appears in a list made July 1, 1701, at Stonington
(*Narragansett Hist. Reg.,* Vol. I., p. 145).

Martin V. Connett is a blacksmith at Fort Wayne, Ind., 1883.

John Connett lives at Fort Wayne, Ind., 1883.

Mealion J. Connett is a carpenter at Fort Wayne, Ind., 1883.

Zenas Connett lives at Newark, N. J.

Luther Connett lives at Jersey City, N. J.

Henry Connett lives at Brooklyn, N. Y.

Connet Bros. are in business in St. Joseph, Mo.

Isaac and Edward Connet live at Fort Wayne, Ind.: said to
be descended from a Daniel Connet, b. about 1740.

Picket Connet is a physician at New Hebron, Ill.

Mrs. Myra F. (Connet) Bingham lives at (Abronia?) Mich.

ADDITIONS AND CORRECTIONS.

p. 6, note line 8, for Endes read Eudes.

p. 9, line 9, for Henrias read Henricus; line 5, from bottom, for Passener read Passemer.

p. 10, line 5, for Cornet read Connet; line 6, for Gittisham read Giddisham; line 8, for alis Giddisham read alias Giddesham; line 13, for Margaret read Margret.

p. 11, line 13, for Josup, the soone of Thomas Counnet, read Joseph, ye sonne of Thom: Conant; line 14, for Margaret read Margret.

p. 12, line 4, from bottom, for Connett read Counnett in both instances.

p. 16, line 11, for Alphington read Affington; line 10, from bottom, for (Melony?) read Melony.

p. 17, line 2, for Melonge read Melony.

p. 22, line 4, for Lytchett Matravers, Somerset, read Lytchett Matravers, Dorset.

p. 24, line 8, for 1719 read 1619.

Under head of Extracts from Parochial Registers, add: Colby, Norfolk. 1612—Ellena, daughter of William Connant, baptized 21 Jan., and was buried 3 Feb. 1613—Thomas, son of William Connant, baptized 20 Dec., and was buried 31 Dec. 1616—Richard, son of William Connant, baptized 9 Feb.

p. 28, line 7, from bottom, for Colyton, Ranlegh read Colyton Rawlegh.

p. 29, line 3, insert (missing) at end of line; line 20, for Briston read Bickton; line 26, for Grenica read Gracia.

p. 30, line 5, from bottom, for Conant read Connaunte; line 2, from bottom, for Jane read Johan.

p. 31, line 5, for Brodheare read Brodbeare.

p. 32, line 2, for Tees read Tees; line 7, for 1653 read 1663; line 7, from bottom, for Bridsford read Bridford.

p. 33, line 18, for 1606 read 1706.

p. 34, under head of Abstracts of Wills, add:

Robert Connante, of Knighton, Hennock, Devon; dated 4 Dec., 1616, proved 28 Mch., 1617. To poor of Hennock, £5. To poor of Bovitracie, 40 sh. To wife, all the goods that were her first husband, Thomas Morey's, £10 in money and all horses and kine left after the heriots are paid. To my only daughter, Susan Hoare, £40. To my son in law George Hore, her husband, £10. To their daughter Mary, £10 at age of fifteen. To my son Zachary, £10. To my son Joseph, 100 marks at age of twenty-four. To my son Benjamin, 100 marks at age of twenty-four. To my wife's son Thomas Morey, £40, in lieu of such bequests as may be due unto him by the will of his father, Thomas Morey. To my sister Elizabeth Hill, £5. To my sister Clapp, 10 sh., and each of her children 10 sh. To my sister Jane Burde, 10 sh., and to each of her children 10 sh. To my sister Mary Wheaton's children, 13 sh. 4 d. each. To my three brothers, Thomas, Robert and Edward, and their children, each 10 sh. To my nephew William Webber, 20 nobles. To my servant Joan Collings, £5. To my man servant John Potter, 40 sh. To Mary Hooper, 20 sh. To Mary Hobbs, 10 sh. To John Hooper, my hose and doublet. Residue to my son John Connante, whom I make executor. My cozen Radford Maverick, vicar of Ilsington, and friend John Burchill, vicar of Bovitracie, overseers and witnesses. Inventory, £360 13s. 4d.

Joseph Cunnant, of Awliscombe. Adm'on granted to Edward Cunnant, his son, and John Hutchins. Inventory dated 1 Sep., 1680; total, £20.

John Connant, of Sidmouth. Adm'on granted to Joanna Connant, widow, John Kerslake, of Farway, Gent., and Joseph Potter, of Exeter, haberdasher, July, 1704.

George Connett, of Dunsford, Devon, yeoman; dated 15 Feb., 1708-9; inventory dated 18 Jan., 1709-10; estate, £400 9s. 6d. To poor of Dunsford, 10 sh. To my son George, 5 sh. To my son Nicholas, 5 sh., and to Robert, son of said Nicholas, £5 when he is twenty. To my son John, my estate of Townsend and Higher Walcheycombe, Larchabrooke meadow and Smabriges down, To Magery, my wife, £12 yearly, to be paid by my son John. To my son Robert, all my right in a cottage in Britten street, all my estate in Easter Broadmeadow and certain fields called Furspke. To my son Richard, the estate of Britton. To my son Thomas, a cottage on the eastern side of Dunsford Church, at age of eighteen, and also Wester [Western] broadmeadow. To my son Jeremiah, all remainder of my estate in [Brunhages?] cottage in Britton street. Witnesses, Sarah Shilston and Robert Shilston.

Jonathan Cunnett, of Exeter. Adm'on granted to Margery Hamblyn, his daughter, wife of John Hamblyn, barber, Oct., 1722.

p. 43, before "Miscellaneous Records" insert: Letter from Edward, Viscount Conway, to Foulke Reed, 6 Dec., 1631. Conant has importuned the writer for a horse. Reed is to give him the worst that is fit for him. Under date Ragley, 18 Dec., 1631, Reed writes: "Conant shall have Bedlam delivered to him; none is left so bad as he" (State Papers, Domestic, 1631). Also Petition of Edmund Fortesque and Benjamin Connant to the King. The petitioners represent that in Devon and Cornwall smuggling is frequent, and pray for letters patent for 21 years authorizing them to take bonds from suspected parties, with power to seize smuggled goods (State Papers, Domestic, Charles I., 1637-8, p. 43).

p. 43, under "Miscellaneous Records" insert: In a list of the villains of the parish of Swaffham Purbeck, Cambridgeshire, 7. Edward I. (1278-9), the name Sarra Connet is found (*Rotuli Hundredorum*, Vol. I., p. 495).

p. 47, line 4, for Halsted's read Hasted's.

p. 47, before "Graduates of English Colleges" insert: Robert Conant was one of the church-wardens of the parish of Ashburton, co Devon, in 1522-3, and the next year Robert Conan, probably the same person, filled the office ("*The Parish Accounts of Ashburton*," published anonymously, 1870).

p. 56, line 29. Jane, dr. of Richard and Agnes Conant, wife of Philip Wotton, was living at East Budleigh as late as Mch. 14, 1664-5 (Letter of Dr. John Conant, D. D., to Samuel Conant, in Hutchins' *Hist. of Dorset*, Vol. iii., p. 335).

p. 68, line 4. Perhaps the Samuel Conant, rector of Holy Trinity, Dorchester, was Samuel, son of (K) Malachi (p. 91), whose M. I. is given below.

p. 68, line 18, add: The will of Samuel Conant, of Lytchett, is at Blandford, Dorset; the date of probate is not given, nor the court in which it was proved. It is dated Apr. 3, 1717. The testator, aged about 88, gives to nephew Thomas Rowe, of the City of London, thirteen acres of land and other hereditaments at Huntspil, co. Somerset, and also certain hereditaments at Holton Heath. He mentions, also, nephews John and Samuel Rowe, of London, sister Sarah Rowe, of Huntspil, and kinswoman Sarah Wren. Thomas Rowe, executor. There is a fine armorial seal, "Gules, 10 billets, or, 4, 3, 2, 1."

p. 68, line 21. Timothy Sacheverell and wife were living at Tarrant Hinton, Dorset, 23 Feb., 1662-3 (Letter of Dr. John Conant, D. D., to Samuel Conant, rector of Lytchett Matravers, quoted in Hutchins' *Dorset*, iii., p. 334). Hutchins has confounded the two John Conants, and quite likely the two Samuels. He states that the letters he quotes were written by John Conant, LL. D. (son of John Conant, D. D.), who at this time was only nine years old, and evidently not the writer of the letters as the writer mentions *his wife*. The letters relate mainly to a proposed removal (on invitation of Samuel Conant, of Lytchett Matravers) of John Conant, D. D., from Oxford to Lytchett Matravers. Dr. John Conant had been ejected from the rectorship of Exeter College the preceding September. He did not avail himself of the invitation, but remained some time at Oxford and then settled at Northampton.

p. 71. The children of Hilliard and Mary (Conant) Veren were baptized as follows: Mary and Deliverance, 29: 1: 1647; Hilliard, 27: 3: 1649; Dorcas, 7: 1: 1652; Sarah, 22: 8: 1654; Abigail, 21: 8: 1655. Hilliard Veren, senior, had brothers, Nathaniel, Philip and Joshua. (See Genealogical Dict. of Rhode Island.)

p. 86, line 4, from bottom, for Aug. 25, 1725, read Aug. 23, 1723, and erase, "The date is evidently a mistake for 1723." The inscription is correct; Broderick misquotes. The M. I. to John Conant is still to be seen in Kidlington Church, but is rapidly wearing away. A rubbing is in possession of the compiler.

p. 91, line 14, from bottom. Mary, daughter of Malachi and Jane Conant, was buried in the parish church of Wimborne Minster, co. Dorset, where on a slab of Purbeck marble in the floor at the east corner of the north aisle of the choir, the following inscription remains: Here lyeth the Body | of Mary Conant | Daughter

of Malachi | Conant S T B former | Vicar of Beeding in | Svs-
sex who died the | 24th Day of Feb Anno Dom | 1686 Ætatis
Svae 14.

p. 91, line 8, from bottom. The inscription to Samuel Conant, in
Holy Trinity Church, is as follows: M. S. | Sam^lis Conant, A. M.
et Collegij | D. M. Magdalenae apud Oxonienses Socij | Cujus exi-
mia eruditio morumq sanctitas | Ad Regimen Ecclesiae de Dor-
cestria apud Durotriges | eum summo applausu provexerunt | At
quam subitae rerum vices | Vix munus attigerat atq in gravem
Pthisim incidit | Victusq malo in otia Collegij suj recessit | (No-
luit enim vir bonus ultra sustinere | quod Exequi non potuit.) |
Verum illic quoq proh dolor: | Insecuta est illum molesta Comes
| Quam cum nulla arte neq equitando posset excutere | Gymnas-
tica defatigatus Medicina | hic loci occubuit XVIII. die Maij | An
Do. 1706, Ætat suae tricesimo. | *Accipe fortuitum Hunc Hospitem.
Alma Mater | Eumq qui Literis intabuit in bonarum Artium Sedi-
bus | Inter Vestros Academicos | Honesta dignator Loco.* The
tablet is well carved and well preserved; the arms are at the top.

p. 92, line 15. (M) John Conant was instituted in the living of
Morden, co. Dorset, 11 July, 1695; patron, Thomas Earle, Esq.
(Hutchins' *Dorset*, iii., p. 514).

p. 94, *Conant Arms.* The only grant of arms to the name Conant
recorded in the Herald's College, in London, is that quoted in
full on p. 94. Two other coats have been used by the family.
First: "Gules, ten billets, or," borne by descendants of Richard
Conant, of East Budleigh (see p. 48). Papworth (*Ordinary of
British Armorials*, London, 1874, p. 293) assigns these arms to
Caudrey, Caundrey, Cawdrey, Peres de Coudrai, *Conant*, Sir
Thomas Cowdray and Cowdrey of co. Berks and co. Hants, and
quotes Glover's Ordinary, Cotton MSS., Tiberius, D. 10, as au-
thority. On reference to Glover's Ordinary it was found that he
did not mention the name Conant, but on fol. 123 (or p. 406) as-
signs the arms "Argent, 10 roundles, 4, 3, 2, 1, gules," to the name
Convnter. In the part devoted to billets the nearest approach to
"Gules, ten billets, or," is this: William de Colevill, tempus
Edward I., "Or, ten billets, gules" (Glover's Ordinary, Cotton
MSS., p. 614 or fol. 226). A Radulph de Colevill was connected with
Colevill, co. Devon, in the third year of Edward I., and it seems
likely that the Conants assumed the arms of Colevill, simply re-
versing the tinctures. Second: "Paley of six, on a chief an eagle
displayed," borne by John Conant, of Sidmouth (see p. 18).
Papworth assigns these arms to the families of Court, of co.
Somerset, and Covert, of co. Sussex.

p. 125, line 5, from bottom. The name Holyroad is not mentioned
by Savage. The compiler hazards the conjecture that the tran-
scriber of the church records mistook Holgrave for Holyroad,
and that it was Love Holgrave who m. John Stevens. John Holgrave was an early settler of Salem, and one of the representatives to the first General Court in 1634; his son, Joshua, had a

daughter Love, baptized 17 Apr., 1642 (Essex Inst. Hist. Coll., Vol. 6, p. 38). Joshua Holgrave is not mentioned in the records after this and perhaps died soon after. Roger Conant left a legacy to the daughters of his cousin, Jane Mason, deceased, including the children of Love Stevens. The only Jane Mason at Salem at this time, so far as the compiler has been able to discover, was Jane, wife of Elias, who d. 9: 9: 1661 (Essex Inst. Hist. Coll., Vol. 2, p. 297); their first child was baptized 23 May, 1647. It is possible that after the death of Joshua Holgrave, his widow, Jane, m. Elias Mason. Both the Jane Mason and Love Stevens mentioned in the will were dead at the time it was made, 1677, as has been shown were Jane wife of Elias Mason and Love wife of John Stevens.

p. 134, line 5, from bottom, for Apr. 42, 1738, read Apr. 24, 1738.

p. 142, line 14, from bottom. Exercise Conant was lieutenant of Capt. William Raymond's company, in the expedition to Canada under Sir William Phips, in 1690. The town of Raymond (Cumberland county, Maine) was granted to the soldiers of this company, and William Moulton, his son-in-law, drew lot No. 30, as his representative, Apr. 7, 1735 (MS. Records of the Proprietors of Raymond).

p. 145, line 23, for 27 Nov., 1680, read 27 Nov., 1681.

p. 167, line 17, for 15 July, 1710, read 15 July, 1711.

p. 175, line 12, for Bean Manor read Beau Manor.

p. 181, line 10, for Francis read Frances.

p. 187, line 15, from bottom. Erase (Rebecca m. Jesse Patridge?). Rebecca, wife of Jesse Patridge, was dr. of John Bailey (Cumberland Deeds, Vol. 21, p. 207).

p. 195, line 5. Benjamin Green was of Truro, and was m. in Eastham.

p. 214. (86) Lot Conant was in Shaw's company at the time of the "Lexington Alarm" (Mass. Arch., Muster Rolls, Vol. 13, p. 128).

p. 232. (103) William Conant was fifer in Jesse Patridge's company, in Creighton's regiment, at White Plains, N. Y., 1778; enlisted for nine months (Mass. Arch., Muster Rolls, Vol. 23, p. 15).

p. 233, line 22. Ann Conant m. 8 Nov., 1808, Mark Babb (Maine Hist. and Gen. Recorder, Vol. iv., p. 168).

p. 234, line 10. Mary Wildes was dr. of Amos and Hannah (Perkins) Wildes, b. 7 Feb., 1752.

p. 240. (116) Israel Conant, "aged 38, height 5 ft. 6 in., brown complexion," was in King's company of Bliss' regiment, in the Revolutionary army, 1779 (Mass. Arch., Muster Rolls, Vol. 45, pp. 111 and 266, and Vol. 42, p. 136).

p. 243. (120) Josiah Conant was in the Revolutionary army, 1777 (Mass. Arch., Muster Rolls, Vol. 26, p. 419½).

p. 251. (136) Ezra Conant was in Allen's company of Cary's regiment, in the Revolutionary army, 1780 (Mass. Arch., Muster Rolls, Vol. 1, p. 15).

p. 262, line 4. Israel Conant, of Sudbury, "aged 18, 5 ft. 6 in. in height, light complexion," was in the Revolutionary army, 1778, and in Silas Taylor's company, under Gen. Gates, in 1777 (Mass. Arch., Muster Rolls, Vol. 23, p. 179).

p. 262, line 10. Eunice Conant, widow of Abraham Conant, late of Waterford, prays for administration, Mch. 15, 1796 (Eastern Herald, Mch. 24, 1796).

p. 267, lines 12 and 13, for Farrer read Farrar.

p. 269. (173) Samuel Conant's children were of Westford, Mass.

p. 270, line 6, for "Children" read "No children."

p. 270, line 14, erase "and had two children." and insert: was a wheelwright; d. of consumption in Antrim, N. H., 16 Feb., 1848. He m. in Greenfield, N. H., 2 Mch., 1837, Eliza Abigail, dr. of Nathaniel and Eliza (Marsh) Reynolds, b. in Greenfield, 21 July, 1819. After his death she m. (2) John B. Dolliver, and is still living, in So. Lyndeboro', N. H. Children of Samuel A. and Eliza A. (Reynolds) Conant: i. Albert Samuel, b. 21 July, 1840, in Antrim, N. H. He served three years during the Rebellion; was sergeant in the 8th regiment, N. H. volunteers; was wounded, and a prisoner in Libby prison. He is now a carpenter and builder, of Lyndeboro', N. H. He m. (1) in Wilton, N. H., 12 Sep., 1868, Amanda J., dr. of Joseph and Arvilla (Kidder) Ford, b. 27 Sep., 1850. Child: Cora Jane, b. 7 Apr., 1870, in Fitchburg, Mass. He m. (2) in Lyndeboro', 11 Oct., 1879, Abbie J., dr. of John G. and Roxana (Hutchinson) Raymond, b. 29 Aug., 1850. Children: 1. John, b. 23 Nov., 1880, in Lyndeboro'; 2. Florence Jane, b. 15 Aug., 1882. ii. Charles William, b. 27 Nov., 1843, in Antrim, N. H.; of Leominster, Mass.

p. 270. (177) Benjamin Conant was in the Revolutionary army (Mass. Arch., Muster Rolls, Vol. 4, p. 50).

p. 274, line 7, from bottom. Erase "but d. 1842, without children," and insert, d. 1842, leaving Abigail, now of Alfred, and Hannah, who m. 25 Dec., 1855, Jeremiah Ricker.

p. 283. (206) Jonathan Conant was in Porter's company of Tupper's regiment, in the Revolutionary army, at West Point, in 1779 (*Hist. of Beverly*, p. 177).

p. 308, line 5, for Rebecca (Wright) read Lucy (Wright).

p. 315, line 2, from bottom. Estes Conant served during the Rebellion in 2nd Co., 6th Vt. Regt. (Vt. Adj. Gen.'s Report, 1864).

p. 321. (286) Gaius published "An Oration pronounced at Franklin on the Anniversary of the Independence of the United States of America" (Providence, 1863, 8vo.).

p. 327, line 12, from bottom, for 1833 read 1837.

p. 345, line 7, from bottom, for 1825 read 1805; line 5, from bottom, insert, he d. 24 Sep., 1835, aged 27, at Acton, Mass.

p. 351, last line. Fred Plummer Conant lives at 613 Tremont street, Boston; is a carpenter; has Edgar J., Edward M., George F. and perhaps other children.

p. 354, line 12, from bottom, for Helen Francis read Helen Frances.

p. 360, line 13, from bottom, insert, m. in Alfred, Me., 5 Aug., 1856, William Heath.

p. 361, line 9. Hannah Jones (Herrick) Conant d. in Portland, Me., 10 July, 1886, aged 81.

p. 366, line 4, for Francis Adeline read Frances Adeline.

p. 382, line 16, from bottom, for 2 Mch., 1841, read 21 Mch., 1841.

p. 387. Rufus Conant, son of (453) Rufus, lived in Boston, Mass., and d. there 17 Mch., 1880. His widow lives in Brookline with her son-in-law, C. H. Bacall. Joseph Fuller Conant, another son, d. in Falmouth, Mass., 21 May, 1886.

p. 414. (506) Edmund Conant served during the Rebellion in the 2nd company of the 6th Vt. Regt. (Vt. Adj. Gen.'s Report, 1864).

p. 420, line 16, for Scoffold read Scaffold.

p. 423, last line. William Henry Conant lives at South Bend, Ind. (1886).

p. 424, line 5, for Mailland read Maitland; line 6, insert, m. in Oshawa, 25 Sep., 1878, Joseph, son of Joseph and Caroline Maria (Gibbs) Caldwell, b. 1 Feb., 1852; he is a dentist, of Belleville, Canada. Child: Thomas Wilfrid, b. 27 July, 1879; line 7, insert, m. —— Thompson.

p. 437, line 2, from bottom, insert, m. a (Warren?), and had Carrie, Anne, Charles, Hamet and William. The sons were married. The family lived in Framingham.

p. 438, line 18. Samuel Dunham was b. 30 Apr., 1794; lived in Paris, Me. (*Hist. Woodstock, Me.*, p. 210).

p. 439, line 15, from bottom. Charlotte Jewell was widow of Ezra (see p. 343); she d. 1 Nov., 1886, at Wellesley Hills, Mass., aged 90 years 2 months.

p. 461, line 14, from bottom. Emma A. Conant d. at Poland Springs, Me., 6 Aug., 1886.

p. 473, line 13, from bottom. Ellen Frances Conant m. 30 Sep., 1885, Col. W. H. Stimson, of Dunbarton, N. H. Master of the N. H. State Grange.

p. 475, line 6, from bottom. To children of Mark P. Conant add, Jacob J., of Brunswick, Me.

p. 482, line 15, for 9 Jan., 1850, read 9 Jan., 1851.

p. 483. (698) Samuel Stillman Conant translated "*The Circassian Boy*," from the Russian, through the German, published 1875, 8vo. His wife translated "*The Ancient Cities of the New World*," from the French (New York, Harpers, 1887).

p. 495. (729) Oliver Jackson Conant m. (3) Mrs. Helen L. Rich.

p. 500. (747) Edwin Conant published a "Statement of facts concerning the sources of business of the intended railroad from Worcester, Mass., to Nashua, N. H." (1845, 8vo.).

p. 501, line 6, from bottom. Charles William Conant enlisted 10 Oct., 1862, in Co. E, 22nd Regt., Me. Vols. (Maine Adj. Gen.'s Report, 1863). He d. Jan., 1887, in Patten, Me., unmarried.

INDEXES.

INDEX OF CONANTS.

This index includes the name of every person born a Conant, or who has assumed the name otherwise than by marriage, mentioned in the book, except those who died under five years of age. The account of any person who became a Conant by marriage may be found by the surname in the second index, or by the name of the husband. The letter *a* prefixed to a date in left hand column indicates that the person was born about that year; *d*, died in that year; *l*, living that year; *m*, married that year. The reference is in all cases to pages.

—	1747	Abijah,	180	1833	Albert Austin,	293
	1855	Abilene,	381		Albert F.,[10]	445
a	1771	Abner [Connet],	564	l 1883	Albert Forbes,	561
a	1788	Abner [Connett],	569	1869	Albert Forness,	473
	1846	Abner,	200	1843	Albert Francis,	509
	1819	Abner George,	544	1863	Albert Francis,	426
	1842	Abner G.,	315		Albert G.,[8]	373
		Abraham,	262	1868	Albert H.,	429
	1778	Abraham,	437	1809	Albert Henry,	347
a	1780	Abraham,	343	1843	Albert Henry,	369
	1789	Abraham,	443	1843	Albert M.,	455
a	1791	Abraham,	342		Albert N. [Connett],	569
	1822	Abraham,	437	1835	Albert S.,	434
	1821	Abraham K.,	293	1867	Albert Standley,	517
	1864	Abraham Lincoln,	508	1869	Albert Stoddard,	524
	1833	Abram,	444	1870	Alberta Gertrude,	494
	1838	Abram,	333		Albertina,[9]	475
	1861	Abram,	507		Albion,[10]	500
		Abram [Conat],	562	1850	Alethea,	459
	1805	Achsah,	256	1798	Alexa,	548
	1847	Achsah,	472	l 1327	Alexander,	34
	1869	Ada,	512		Alexander,[8]	333
	1865	Ada E.,	539	l 1886	Alexander B.,	561
	1859	Ada Emeline,	473		Alexander Hamilton,	551
		Ada M.,	554	1834	Alfred [Connet],	567
	1859	Ada Mabel,	476	1836	Alfred Perkins,	477
	1805	Adaline,	351	1879	Algier M.,	525
	1858	Addie,	367	m 1613	Alice,	10
	1883	Addie,	527	m 1629	Alice,	25
		Addie A.,[8]	374	l 1653	Alice,	27
	1858	Addie E.,	539	1700	Alice,	93
	1866	Addie Florence,	480	1773	Alice,	235
	1808	Addison Lorenzo,	403	1821	Alice,	417
	1871	Adelaide [Connet],	568	1823	Alice,	309
		Adelia,	542		Alice,[8]	381
		Adeline,[9]	449	1873	Alice,	538
		Adoniram B.,	553	1878	Alice B.,	476
	1831	Adoniram Judson,	512	1868	Alice Bancroft,	474
	1878	Agele [Connet],	568	1864	Alice Cornelia,	512
d	1572	Agnes,	9	1876	Alice Dorinda,	414
		Agnes (Clarke),	{12, 13 52, 53}	1851	Alice Elizabeth,	505
				1873	Alice Hill,	519
b	1620	Agnes,	31	1829	Alice Hillman,	443
d	1741	Agnes,	19	1873	Alice Isabel,	496
a	1886	Agnes,[10]	475	1872	Alice Louise,	415
l	1332	Alan,	34	1870	Alice M.,	513
	1821	Alban Jasper,	419	1873	Alice Maud,	460
	1870	Alban Jasper,	420	1874	Alice May,	495
	1830	Alban Slaughter,	317	a 1879	Alice Pauline,	526
	1815	Albert,	376	1862	Alice T.,	404
	1820	Albert,	444	1844	Alicia Octavia,	383
	1821	Albert,	426	1776	Allen [Connet],	564
	1830	Albert,	473	l 1870	Allen,	561
		Albert,[8]	328		Allen E.,[9]	375
		Albert,[9]	339	1850	Allen Gwyer,	543
	1843	Albert,	499	1795	Alma,	247
	1869	Albert,	521	1834	Almeda,	333
		Albert,	547	1852	Almeda,	492
	1821	Albert A.,	410	1863	Almeda,	550
		Albert A.,	554	1850	Almeda Ellethea,	429
	1816	Albert Augustus,	546	1806	Almira,	282
	1866	Albert Augustus,	496	a 1809	Almira,	442

1817	Almira,	372		1814	Andrew,	509
1819	Almira,	290		1822	Andrew,	450
1842	Almira,	377		1841	Andrew,	449
1862	Almira Jane,	414		1842	Andrew [Connett],	509
	Almira R.,[8]	381			Andrew,	552
	Alonzo,[8]	325		1796	Andrew Buckley,	268
1816	Alonzo,	543		1828	Andrew Burnham,	357
1817	Alonzo,	428		1815	Andrew Emerson,	369
	Alonzo G.,	442		1795	Andrew G.,	347
1861	Alonzo J.,	430	l	1862	Andrew H.,	559
1810	Alpheus,	451		1833	Andrew M.,	550
	Alphonso,[9]	452		1816	Andrew Pearson,	447
1833	Alphonso,	543		1823	Andrew Philander,	511
1854	Alphonso Bence,	480		1842	Andrew T. [Connet],	565
1800	Alvah,	364			Andrew W.,[9]	438
1838	Alvah,	464		1810	Angelina Gray,	533
	Alvah,[8]	325		1862	Angelina Ellen,	479
1882	Alvah Lewis,	464		1816	Angeline,	311
	Alvah Waite,[8]	415			Anguinette,[9]	334
1849	Alvan Paine,	540	d	1775	Ann,	17
1846	Alvin,	495			Ann,	87
1855	Alvin Cassius,	428		1703	Ann,	92
	Alvin T.,[7]	288		1758	Ann,	20
	Alvira,[8]	417		1788	Ann,	233
	Alwilda,[9]	427	a	1800	Ann,	378
1809	Amanda,	302		1836	Ann Louise,	400
1809	Amanda,	359		1856	Ann Orr,	404
1828	Amanda [Connet],	567	d	1661	Anna,	34
1835	Amanda,	417		1728	Anna,	17
1835	Amanda,	535		1752	Anna,	199
1841	Amanda,	422		1763	Anna,	199
1844	Amasa Lumbert,	499		1771	Anna,	224
1809	Amasa S.,	499		1771	Anna,	264
1835	Ambrose,	493		1775	Anna,	264
1779	Amelia,	246	a	1780	Anna,	441
1812	Amelia,	302		1793	Anna,	280
1838	Amelia,	449		1799	Anna,	347
1851	Amelia Breck,	455		1803	Anna,	328
1828	Amelia Maria,	315		1811	Anna,	312
1857	Amelia Maria,	446		1870	Anna,	516
1868	Amelia Maria,	414			Anna,[7]	252
1737	Amos,	540			Anna,[8]	374
1753	Amos,	278			Anna,	550
1771	Amos,	436			Anna A.,	561
1780	Amos,	278		1864	Anna Abigail,	495
1805	Amos,	498			Anna B.,	561
1810	Amos,	469		1872	Anna B.,	513
1765	Amos B.,	249		1875	Anna Bell,	484
1843	Amos F.,	498		1818	Anna Briggs,	430
1633	Amy,	25		1821	Anna Eliza,	311
1675	Amy,	32		1785	Anna Gray,	532
1884	Amy Louise,	491			Anna J.,[8]	324
1600	Andrew,	38		1849	Anna J.,	509
1703	Andrew,	208		1848	Anna Jane,	515
1725	Andrew,	262		1843	Anna L.,	328
1773	Andrew,	275		1837	Anna Louise,	317
1773	Andrew,	345		1834	Anna M.,	378
1774	Andrew,	324, 561		1860	Anna Olive,	495
1782	Andrew,	263		1848	Anna Sophia,	501
1796	Andrew,	447	m	1562	Anne,	23
1808	Andrew,	324	l	1657	Anne,	27
1808	Andrew,	346	d	1675	Anne,	16

1709	Anne,	21, 93	1750	Asa,	225
1740	Anne,	203	1773	Asa,	282
1751	Anne,	20	*a* 1778	Asa,	442
a 1766	Anne,	231	1795	Asa,	352
	Anne,[8]	375	1800	Asa,	276
	Annette,[8]	330	1807	Asa,	386
	Annie,	555		Asa,	561
1837	Annie,	477	1811	Asa Hopkins,	376
a 1854	Annie,	491	1800	Asa Manley,	534
1857	Annie,	433	1816	Asa Warren,	534
1874	Annie,	540	1788	Asa Wildes,	201
1856	Annie Josephine,	384	1790	Asenath,	296
a 1815	Annie Leonard,	324	1792	Asenath,	248
1866	Annie Lillian, ·	384	1756	Augusta,	197
	Annie Livingston,[8]	381	1760	Augusta,	199
1866	Annie M.,	430	1868	Augusta,	411
1852	Annie Melissa,	379		Augusta,[8]	373
1858	Annie Meserve,	425		Augusta,[8]	381
1855	Annie R.,	399		Augusta,[10]	500
1871	Annie Sanborn,	474		Augusta Frances,[8]	402
1867	Annie Whitney,	515	1842	Augusta M.,	432
	Ansel,[9]	501	1828	Augustine,	348
1822	Anson,	547	1843	Augustus Eugene,	505
1869	Antoinette,	470	1846	Augustus Franklin,	471
1839	Antoinette Rebecca,	477	1850	Augustus H.,	425
1789	Antha,	248	1811	Augustus Hammond,	394
	Apollos,[8]	328	1872	Augustus Sylvanus,	545
	Arba,	248	1862	Augustus Turchin,	398
	Archibald,	252	1832	Aurelia,	416
1872	Archibald Ephraim,	524		Austin,[10]	512
1813	Arial,	547	1838	Austin Benezette,	406
1863	Ariel Hugo,	512	1821	Azro B.,	425
1812	Arnold William,	347	1739	Azubah,	201
	Arta,	248	1819	Azubah B.,	506
1779	Artemus,	264			
a 1787	Artemus,	342			
	Artemus,[10]	493		Bailey,[8]	342
	Artemus B.,[9]	342	1811	Ballard Smith,	304
	Artemus H.,[10]	437	1857	Bancroft H.,	508
1826	Artemus Henry,	437	1637	Barbara,	17, 32
1842	Artemus Henry,	499	*d* 1670	Barbara,	29, 32
1886	Arthur,	415	1751	Barnabas,	529
	Arthur,[9]	445	1761	Barnabas,	271
	Arthur,[9]	488		Barnabas,[7]	253
	Arthur,[10]	445	1803	Barnabas,	326
	Arthur,	561	1712	Bartholomew,	155
1850	Arthur F. P.,	552	*a* 1732	Bartholomew,	229
1853	Arthur Gibbs,	369	*a* 1768	Bartholomew,	287
1859	Arthur Gray,	475	*a* 1770	Bartholomew,	231
1862	Arthur Henry,	517		Bartholomew,[7]	287
l 1883	Arthur J.,	561		Barzillai,	204
1869	Arthur L.,	524		Beatrice,	497
1875	Arthur M. [Connet],	565	1748	Beersheba,	198
1879	Arthur Straiton,	487	1822	Bela Forbes,	481
1873	Arthur Turchin,	484		Bell,[8]	375
l 1864	Arthur W.,	563	1717	Benajah,	198
	Arvilla,[8]	325		Benajah,[10]	493
	Arvilla,[8]	331		Benedict,[8]	325
1735	Asa,	209	1600	Benjamin,	15, 28, 572, 573
1736	Asa,	180	1662	Benjamin,	11, 33
1745	Asa,	531	1698	Benjamin,	{ 148-151, 160 175, 179
1746	Asa,	224			

1797	Caroline,	260	1839	Celinda S.,		497
1798	Caroline,	247	1844	Chara B.,		302
1809	Caroline,	366	1809	Chara Emily,		393
1810	Caroline,	312	1747	Charity,		529
1818	Caroline,	416	1634	Charles,	16, 17,	32
1823	Caroline,	448	1720	Charles,		528
1827	Caroline,	390	*a* 1767	Charles,		531
1828	Caroline,	348	1769	Charles,		281
1835	Caroline,	392	1787	Charles,		373
	Caroline,[10]	437	1798	Charles,		259
	Caroline,	542	1803	Charles,		247
	Caroline [Connet],	565	1807	Charles,		334
1843	Caroline A.,	337	1812	Charles,		499
1807	Caroline Cerusa,	392	1818	Charles,	437,	578
1832	Caroline Dean,	374	1820	Charles,		447
	Caroline E.,[7]	293	1821	Charles,		359
1836	Caroline E.,	292	1860	Charles,		449
1824	Caroline Elizabeth,	369	1871	Charles,		406
1827	Caroline H.,	498	1877	Charles,		490
1810	Caroline Jane,	304		Charles,		98
1831	Caroline L.,	335		Charles,[8]		326
	Caroline Louisa,	553		Charles,[9]		427
1855	Caroline Steele,	419		Charles,[9]		432
1835	Caroline Sumner,	366		Charles,[10]		500
1844	Carrie,	403	1865	Charles Albert,		495
1882	Carrie,	434	1833	Charles Albion,		505
	Carrie,[8]	410	1871	Charles Alfred,		550
	Carrie,[10]	578	1861	Charles Arthur,	464 47	c
1859	Carrie A.,	429	1841	Charles Augustus,		383
1880	Carrie Augusta,	489	1848	Charles Baker,		524
1846	Carrie E.,	511	1839	Charles Bean,		476
1855	Carrie E.,	470		Charles Bean,[9]		475
1870	Carrie E.,	464	1828	Charles Bennett,		281
1860	Carrie Frances,	474	1883	Charles Bridgman,		496
1871	Carrie L.,	414	1837	Charles C.,		335
1866	Carrie Louise,	460	*l* 1886	Charles C.,		561
1857	Carrie May,	384		Charles C.,[9]		471
1853	Carrie S.,	509	1820	Charles Carroll,		470
	Cassandra,[7]	295	1864	Charles Carroll,		470
1825	Cassandra,	387	1844	Charles Clinton,		503
ι 1830	Cassandra,	387	1858	Charles E.,		459
1839	Cassandra,	420	1879	Charles E.,		513
1853	Cassandra H.,	481	1849	Charles Edward,		527
1812	Cassandra Whitman,	321	1855	Charles Edward,		378
1625	Catherine,	11, 32	1861	Charles Edward,		483
1753	Catherine,	194	1872	Charles Edward,		487
1773	Catherine,	241	1833	Charles Edwin,		474
1784	Catherine,	353	1843	Charles Edwin,		478
1784	Catherine,	267	1855	Charles E. [Connet],		566
1822	Catherine,	97	1835	Charles F.,		488
1830	Catherine,	377	1842	Charles F.,		484
	Catherine [Connett],	568	1848	Charles F.,		405
1787	Catherine E.,	243	1821	Charles Farnsworth,		511
1823	Catherine Mary,	417	1835	Charles Francis,		485
1812	Catherine Ruggles,	311	1863	Charles Francis,		465
ι 1855	Cecelia Eva,	97	1880	Charles Francis,		465
1873	Cecil Franklin,	473	1860	Charles Frederick,		423
1848	Celestina M.,	506	1826	Charles G.,		357
	Celia,[7]	295	1834	Charles H.,		424
	Celia,[8]	386	1841	Charles H.,		498
1858	Celia E.,	507	1862	Charles H.,		430
1821	Celia Hatch,	387	1867	Charles H.,		488

	Charles H.,[9]	422		1561	Christine,	13
1868	Charles Harry,	516		1588	Christopher, { 13, 24, 41	
1844	Charles Henry,	510			{ 46, 56, 99	
1881	Charles Henry,	510		1614	Christopher,	9, 10
1879	Charles Hight,	465	d	1641	Christopher,	23
1827	Charles L.,	375		1641	Christopher,	17, 32
1846	Charles L.,	546	l	1672	Christopher,	23
1849	Charles L.,	481		1675	Christopher,	23
1887	Charles L.,	561		1753	Christopher,	20
1844	Charles M.,	499		1788	Clara,	247
1855	Charles M.,	507			Clara A.;	555
	Charles McBeath,	551		1851	Clara A.,	481
1827	Charles Merriam,	282		1868	Clara Alice,	480
1866	Charles Milton,	476		1861	Clara B. [Connett],	567
1833	Charles Nathan,	515			Clara D.,[10]	499
	Charles Newell,[11]	509		1861	Clara E.,	388
1822	Charles Olin,	470		1842	Clara Farley,	400
1852	Charles Perkins,	456		1850	Clara Frances,	380
1867	Charles Platt,	519		1861	Clara J.,	522
1865	Charles R.,	492		1868	Clara Louise,	487
1870	Charles R.,	429		1869	Clara Louise,	550
1807	Charles Rich,	398		1876	Clara N.,	517
1833	Charles Rufus,	465		1847	Clara P.,	422
1836	Charles Preston,	552	l	1884	Clarence,	561
1843	Charles S.,	429		1864	Clarence Arnold,	539
1843	Charles Sewell,	502		1865	Clarence Fuller,	479
1860	Charles Sumner,	404		1863	Clarence Howard,	491
1886	Charles T.,	561		1864	Clarence Leslie,	517
1861	Charles Thaddeus,	457		1851	Clarence Mortimer,	520
1818	Charles W.,	445			Clarence Tucker,[8]	415
1823	Charles W.,	416	a	1824	Clarinda,	452
1833	Charles W.,	308		1775	Clarissa,	246
1802	Charles Walden,	534		1791	Clarissa,	276
1849	Charles Waldo,	509		1808	Clarissa,	372
1850	Charles Wesley,	521		1812	Clarissa,	312
1838	Charles William, 501,	578		1814	Clarissa,	403
1843	Charles William,	577		1814	Clarissa,	547
1852	Charles Withington,	511		1822	Clarissa,	548
1772	Charlotte,	263			Clarissa,[8]	333
1801	Charlotte,	284			Clarissa,[8]	386
1820	Charlotte,	343			Clarissa,	547
	Charlotte,	551		1844	Clarissa M.,	547
	Charlotte,[8]	325		1830	Clarissa Maria,	357
	Charlotte,[9]	450		1829	Clarissa O.,	388
	Charlotte,[9]	485		1773	Clark,	280
	Charlotte,[10]	502			Clark C.,[8]	373
1843	Charlotte Augusta,	448		1819	Claudius Buchanan,	483
1822	Charlotte Hannah,	544		1842	Claudius William,	483
1862	Charlotte Howard,	483			Clement P.,[8]	379
1815	Charlotte Warren,	352		1879	Clifford Sleeper,	516
1800	Chauncey,	422		1858	Clinton R.,	481
1814	Chauncey,	425		1876	Clinton Sidney,	428
1885	Chauncey,	561			Clorinda A.,[9]	438
1799	Chauncey W.	389		1868	Cora E.,	540
1790	Chesley,	551		1870	Cora Jane,	577
1790	Chester,	312		1830	Cordelia Ann,	307
	Chester,[7]	316		1843	Coretta,	398
1831	Chester Cook,	482	a	1836	Cornelia,	390
1826	Chestina,	548		1842	Cornelia R.,	451
1755	Chloe,	201	a	1776	Cornelius,	325
1795	Chloe,	255			Cornelius,[8]	325
1802	Chloe Bridgman,	533			Cornelius,[9]	342

1843	Duane,	543	1841	Edward,		539
1857	Dudley,	508	1853	Edward,		508
1809	Dwight,	256		Edward,		98
1872	Dwight,	413		Edward,[6]		232
1857	Dwight Henry,	449		Edward,[9]		445
			a 1860	Edward,[9]		475
	-		*a* 1863	Edward,[10]		491
1807	Eana,	281		Edward,		445
	Earl G.,	561	*l* 1887	Edward,		561
1826	Earle F.,	565	1867	Edward Allen,		522
1872	Earle Thompson,	565	1851	Edward Andrew,		450
1777	Eben,	301	1835	Edward Card,		360
1851	Eben L.,	425	1839	Edward D.,		410
1698	Ebenezer, 134, 160,	190	1846	Edward Davis,		491
1731	Ebenezer,	180	1837	Edward Everett,		460
1743	Ebenezer,	236	1867	Edward Everett,		496
1756	Ebenezer,	224	1875	Edward Francis,		491
1762	Ebenezer,	249	1879	Edward G.,		551
t 1762	Ebenezer,	342	1855	Edward H.,		514
1779	Ebenezer,	281	1847	Edward Henry,		97
t 1780	Ebenezer,	348	1851	Edward J.,		546
1785	Ebenezer,	372	1855	Edward Joseph,		525
	Ebenezer,[8]	342	1881	Edward Ketchum,		519
1823	Ebenezer,	281		Edward M.,[9]		577
1801	Ebenezer Allen,	564	1863	Edward Mason,		538
1811	Ebenezer Benson,	424	1820	Edward Nathaniel,		97
1813	Ebenezer Tolman,	404	*l* 1886	Edward P.,		561
1819	Eber Maxfield,	537	1854	Edward Rutherford,	405
	Ede,	31	1874	Edward Stacy,		415
1869	Eddie C.,	444	1854	Edward Taylor,		527
	Edgar A.,[9]	373	1837	Edward W.,		522
1837	Edgar Alonzo,	516	*d* 1664	Edwin,		17
	Edgar F.,	561	1810	Edwin,	500,	578
1867	Edgar F.,	476	1820	Edwin,		376
	Edgar J.,[9]	577	1871	Edwin A.,		522
1852	Edgar Sumner,	476	1811	Edwin Anthony,		332
l 1621	Edith,	29	1830	Edwin Augustus,		498
1877	Edith,	526	1851	Edwin Herbert,		446
1863	Edith A.,	469	1835	Edwin Lysander,		313
1874	Edith Cornelia,	418	1860	Edwin M.,		432
1879	Edith J.,	527	1840	Edwin Ruthven,		317
1872	Edith Julia,	494	1843	Edwin S.,		470
1862	Edith S.,	429	1851	Edwin W.,		428
1759	Edmund,	248	1859	Edwin William,		469
1787	Edmund,	247	*a* 1854	Effie,		490
1796	Edmund,	313	1877	Effie,		488
1829	Edmund, 414,	578	*a* 1878	Effie,		416
1856	Edmund Batchelder,	411	1878	Effie Edna,		512
1870	Edmund Estes,	414	1874	Effie Winfred,		473
1836	Edna Alice,	499	1798	Elam Lucius,		314
t 1849	Edna Lodema,	472	1818	Elbridge,		376
1879	Edna Louisa,	495	1841	Elbridge,		448
1856	Edna Mary, 424,	578	1829	Elbridge F.,		293
1790	Edson,	331	1748	Eleanor,		216
1848	Edson Alvinza,	519	*a* 1820	Eleanor,[7]		290
1589	Edward,	40	1827	Eleanor Elizabeth,	311
1617	Edward, 27,	572	1751	Eleazer,		246
l 1646	Edward,	27		Electa,		547
1669	Edward, 85, 86,	87	1837	Electa Ann,		354
1752	Edward,	198	1852	Electa Eliza,		424
1825	Edward,	471	1742	Eli,		263
1829	Edward,	426	1749	Elias,		293

1750	Elias,	94	a 1705	Elizabeth,		93
1892	Elias,	306	1715	Elizabeth,	153,	155
1834	Elias Cornelius,	291	1715	Elizabeth,		174
1790	Elihu,	543	d 1720	Elizabeth,		20
1783	Elijah,	335	1723	Elizabeth,		176
a 1786	Elijah,	339	1724	Elizabeth,		209
a 1774	Eliphalet,	326	1726	Elizabeth,		195
1843	Eliphalet,	493	1727	Elizabeth,		202
1823	Elisha Ferdinand,	354	1733	Elizabeth,		228
1826	Elisha Harding,	508	1735	Elizabeth,		178
1801	Elisha Lockwood,	354	1745	Elizabeth,		20
1779	Eliza,	95	1745	Elizabeth,		214
1798	Eliza,	276	1745	Elizabeth,		232
1801	Eliza,	349	1753	Elizabeth,		529
1803	Eliza,	284	1755	Elizabeth,		191
1806	Eliza,	443	1761	Elizabeth,		213
1807	Eliza,	351	1768	Elizabeth,		244
1819	Eliza,	352	d 1769	Elizabeth,		19
1829	Eliza,	448	1771	Elizabeth,		241
1848	Eliza [Connett],	569	d 1773	Elizabeth,		19
	Eliza,[5]	288	1775	Elizabeth,		300
	Eliza,[7]	289	d 1776	Elizabeth,		30
	Eliza,[7]	316	d 1779	Elizabeth,		19
	Eliza,[8]	405	d 1786	Elizabeth,		17
	Eliza,[8]	406	1789	Elizabeth,		259
	Eliza,[9]	488	1791	Elizabeth,		271
1831	Eliza A.,	337	1791	Elizabeth,		289
1835	Eliza A.,	449	1792	Elizabeth,		532
1814	Eliza Ann,	573	1796	Elizabeth,		452
1822	Eliza Ann,	348	1798	Elizabeth [Connet],		566
1833	Eliza Ann,	498	1799	Elizabeth,		247
1850	Eliza Ann,	378	1800	Elizabeth,		306
1846	Eliza E.,	507	1803	Elizabeth,		248
1846	Eliza Ella,	503	a 1807	Elizabeth,		248
1857	Eliza Ellen,	423	1807	Elizabeth,		347
1838	Eliza Jane [Connett],	569	1811	Elizabeth,		291
1841	Eliza M.,	383	1811	Elizabeth,		305
1848	Eliza Osborne,	385	1834	Elizabeth,		371
	Elizabeth (see also		1854	Elizabeth,		459
	under Bessie, Bet-		1864	Elizabeth,		506
	ty and Betsey).			Elizabeth,[3]		188
d 1576	Elizabeth,	9		Elizabeth,[7]		296
1586	Elizabeth,	10		Elizabeth,[8]		388
d 1591	Elizabeth,	28		Elizabeth,[9]		342
d 1597	Elizabeth,	9		Elizabeth,		554
1612	Elizabeth,	9, 10	1840	Elizabeth A.,		451
m 1613	Elizabeth,	10	1859	Elizabeth A.,		492
a 1634	Elizabeth,	124, 128	1849	Elizabeth Alice,		382
1635	Elizabeth,	16	1808	Elizabeth Amelia,		268
d 1657	Elizabeth,	27	1838	Elizabeth Ann,		410
d 1658	Elizabeth,	14, 88	1835	Elizabeth Anne,		500
1658	Elizabeth,	87	1837	Elizabeth Anne,		483
1660	Elizabeth,	73	1838	Elizabeth Bishop,		379
1660	Elizabeth,	131		Elizabeth C.,[8]		384
1676	Elizabeth,	17	1814	Elizabeth C.,		379
1677	Elizabeth,	165	1795	Elizabeth Edna,		533
1679	Elizabeth,	15, 88	1821	Elizabeth Jane,		334
m 1682	Elizabeth,	10	1845	Elizabeth Jane,		493
1682	Elizabeth,	174	1866	Elizabeth Jane,		493
1683	Elizabeth,	17	1886	Elizabeth Merrill,		519
1700	Elizabeth,	11	1828	Elizabeth Mills,		389
1702	Elizabeth,	190	1851	Elizabeth S.,		492

	1839	Elizabeth T.,	546		Emily,[9]	422
	1857	Elizabeth T.,	405		Emily,[9]	488
	1859	Elizabeth V.,	506	a 1849	Emily Agnes,	97
	1818	Elizabeth Whitcomb,	447	1833	Emily Hazelton,.	447
	1826	Elizabeth Wyman,	307	1845	Emily Ida,	483
	1855	Ella,	508	1821	Emily Maria,	354
	1863	Ella [Connet],	567	1823	Emily Mary,	318
	1867	Ella,	516	1830	Emily Susanna,	354
	1880	Ella,	525	1776	Emma,	356
u	1880	Ella,	416	1849	Emma,	545
		Ella,[10]	423	a 1861	Emma,[10]	491
		Ella,[10]	512	a 1862	Emma,[9]	490
u	1854	Ella E.,	461	1866	Emma,	470
u	1856	Ella Estella,	482	1869	Emma,	489
	1867	Ella Frances,	495		Emma,[9]	378
	1853	Ella Henrietta,	428	1853	Emma A.,	461
	1857	Ella J.,	504	1852	Emma Augusta,	501
	1851	Ella Josephine,	481	1873	Emma B.,	414
	1849	Ella M.,	456	1830	Emma Dow,	463
	1875	Ella M.,	524	1849	Emma Elizabeth,	355
	1866	Ella Melissa,	537	1846	Emma Frances,	385
		Ella R.,[9]	479	1862	Emma L.,	462
d	1583	Ellen,	30	1848	Emma Lavina,	429
		Ellen,[8]	361	1830	Emma T.,	357
		Ellen,[9]	445	1870	Emma Wilson,	434
		Ellen,[10]	499	1797	Emory,	497
	1841	Ellen Amanda,	399	1592	Enfanor,	15
	1844	Ellen Amelia,	369	1803	Enoch,	329
	1869	Ellen Augusta,	496		Enoch,[7]	382
	1857	Ellen Frances,	473	1815	Enoch Wentworth,	506
	1826	Ellen Hunt,	472	1757	Ephraim,	341
	1847	Ellen Jane,	470	1781	Ephraim,	442
	1840	Ellen Louisa,	354	1809	Ephraim,	503
	1835	Ellen M.,	451		Ephraim,[7]	289
	1869	Ellen M.,	462	1835	Ephraim Franklin,	523
		Ellen M.,[10]	514	1803	Erasmus Darwin,	409
	1833	Ellen McAllister,	334		Erastus,[8]	324
	1845	Ellen Newman,	501		Erick,	98
	1831	Ellen Olive,	359		Ernest [Connett],	569
	1833	Ellen Ruth,	449	1883	Ernest,	520
	1840	Ellen Susan,	509	1870	Ernest B.,	514
	1866	Ellen Whittlesey,	538	1878	Ernest L.,	524
	1839	Ellenor A. [Connet],	565	1857	Ernest Lee,	465
d	1619	Ellery,	29, 33	1852	Ernest William P.,	97
	1861	Elmer Ellsworth,	384	1800	Estes,	315
l	1887	Elmer G.,	561	1833	Estes,	315, 577
	1862	Elmer Kimball,	455	a 1728	Esther,	208
	1841	Elsie,	358	l 1748	Esther,	554
	1879	Elsie Davis,	491	1758	Esther,	216
	1859	Elva,	444	1787	Esther,	269
	1828	Elvira Ann,	421	1857	Esther,	399
	1856	Emegene J.,	547	1838	Esther Maria,	456
	1820	Emeline,	448		Ethan,[8]	417
		Emeline,[8]	417		Ethan,	555
	1791	Emery,	451	1860	Ethel Amelia,	424
u	1820	Emery,	451	1855	Etta D.,	522
u	1819	Emilia,	443	1858	Etta Jane,	457
	1800	Emily,	328	1874	Etta Lucinda,	496
	1801	Emily,	243	1863	Etta May,	514
	1822	Emily,	507	1857	Etta Oliver,	495
	1824	Emily,	348	1847	Eugene F.,	375
	1835	Emily,	497	1847	Eugene Henry,	526

1856	Eugene J.,	547
1825	Eugene Sidney,	389
	Eugene V. [Connett],	569
1874	Eugene W.,	524
1736	Eunice,	244
1743	Eunice,	203
1745	Eunice,	190
a 1757	Eunice,	188
1763	Eunice,	285
1769	Eunice,	231
1780	Eunice,	234
1785	Eunice,	225
1786	Eunice,	233
1796	Eunice,	304
1802	Eunice,	350
1805	Eunice,	311
1807	Eunice,	357
1821	Eunice,	281
1821	Eunice,	385
1825	Eunice,	291
	Eunice,[6]	247
	Eunice,[7]	288
	Eunice,[8]	326
1867	Eva,	553
1868	Eva,	508
1881	Eva Annie,	521
1880	Eva Eliza,	520
1809	Evelina,	345
1843	Evelina,	439
l 1880	Evelina,	562
1843	Eveline,	483
1846	Eveline,	459
1844	Eveline J.,	497
1809	Everett Quincy,	428
1843	Everett Sanford,	496
1843	Everett William,	491
a 1637	Exercise,	68, 117, 122, 126, 129, 138, 162, 164, 576
	Experience,[7]	252
1724	Ezra,	223
1730	Ezra,	212
1750	Ezra,	251, 576
1751	Ezra,	277
1763	Ezra,	267
a 1775	Ezra,	251
1780	Ezra,	356
a 1784	Ezra,[7]	386
1788	Ezra,	373
1792	Ezra,	278
1812	Ezra,	355
1820	Ezra,	459
	Ezra,[8]	386
1826	Ezra Beals,	490
1812	Ezra D.,	470
1849	Ezra Russell,	355
1805	Ezra Styles,	420
a 1867	Ezra Styles,	491
	Ezra W.,	559
l 1887	F. A.,	562

1854	F. W.,	456
	Fanny,[7]	254
	Fanny,[7]	284
	Fanny,[9]	326
	Fanny A.,	555
1810	Fanny Amelia,	301
1847	Fanny Emily,	490
1844	Fanny Loveitt,	376
1868	Fanny M.,	402
1793	Farwell,	307
1884	Fay Wyman,	461
1760	Fidelia,	197
1779	Fidelia,	246
1802	Filinda,	304
l 1277	Filota,	2
1865	Flora A.,	506
1849	Flora C. [Connett],	567
	Flora E.,[9]	328
1874	Flora May,	512
1868	Flora T.,	493
1859	Florence,	420
	Florence,[10]	423
1849	Florence C.,	471
1868	Florence Capitola,	479
1875	Florence Jane,	477
1882	Florence Jane,	577
1884	Florence Jewell,	525
1869	Florence Louise,	491
1870	Florence Matilda,	481
1869	Florence May,	418
	Florentine [Connet],	565
1882	Forrest Edwin,	478
l 1780	Fortune,	557
1857	Foster E.,	488
. 1667	Frances,	85, 87
a 1710	Frances,	92
1780	Frances,	95
1837	Frances Ann,	498
a 1846	Frances Ann,	97
1853	Frances H.,	513
1812	Frances Maria,	300
d 1710	Francis,	30
1789	Francis,	445
1814	Francis,	445
1827	Francis,	448
1859	Francis,	457
1871	Francis,	540
1837	Francis A.,	476
1838	Francis Adams,	421
1843	Francis E.,	509
1878	Francis Elmer,	476
1815	Francis Henry,	509
1849	Francis J.,	375
1846	Francis James,	398
1874	Francis Melvin,	464
1846	Francis Plimpton,	506
1869	Francis Slasen,	519
	Francis T.,	537
1867	Frank,	413
	Frank,[7]	287
	Frank,[8]	382
	Frank,[8]	406

1853	Hannah J.,	535
1815	Hannah Maria,	536
1847	Hannah P.,	547
1842	Hannah R.,	378
1851	Hannah R. [Connett],	567
1866	Hannah S. Columbia,	418
1837	Harlan Page,	474
1884	Harold,	415
1882	Harold Augustine,	465
1871	Harold Beecher,	525
1879	Harold Sargent,	427
1799	Harriet,	459
1812	Harriet,	547
1818	Harriet,	290
1820	Harriet, ⁌ •	543
1871	Harriet,	506
1852	Harriet A.,	470
1850	Harriet Anna,	355
1834	Harriet B. [Connet],	565
1852	Harriet B.,	404
	Harriet Caroline,[9]	438
1831	Harriet Clementina,	354
1812	Harriet Elizabeth,	311
1821	Harriet Elizabeth,	346
1834	Harriet Elizabeth,	346
1838	Harriet I.,	377
	Harriet L.,	554
1823	Harriet M.,	334
1863	Harriet M.,	545
1825	Harriet Maria,	307
1848	Harriet Maria,	469
1823	Harriet Marilla,	411
1850	Harriet Melinda,	359
1815	Harriet Mercy,	301
	Harriet Perkins,	551
1822	Harriet Pierce,	310
1817	Harriet Stone,	336
1876	Harriet Wheeler,	510
1862	Harrison Bowman,	481
	Harrison Gilbert,[8]	386
1848	Harrison Johnson,	465
1881	Harrison Josiah,	465
d 1570	Harry,	9
a 1856	Harry,	98
1790	Harry,	309
1844	Harry Armitage,	408
1875	Harry V.,	527
	Harry W.,[9]	387
1867	Harry Watson,	415
1869	Harry Weston,	476
1875	Harry Winthrop,	474
1811	Harvey,	375
	Harvey,[10]	502
1878	Harvey Clifford,	473
	Harvey P.,[10]	493
d 1860	Hattie,	490
	Hattie,[9]	378
1864	Hattie Emma,	384
1863	Hattie L.,	289
1868	Hattie Maria,	496
1844	Helen,	451
1850	Helen,	459

1855	Helen A.,	461
1863	Helen Alfreda,	477
1865	Helen Blanche,	419
1874	Helen Eunice,	406
1828	Helen Frances,	354
1879	Helen Louisa,	510
1839	Helen Lovantia,	469
1854	Helen M.,	404
1828	Helen Maria,	310
1837	Helen Maria,	500
1870	Helen Pearson,	474
	Henrietta,[7]	316
1846	Henrietta,	448
	Henrietta,	550
	Henrietta [Connet],	565
1852	Henrietta A.,	404
l 1523	Henry,	35
l 1580	Henry (d. 1605),	9, 37
l 1610	Henry,	10, 32, 37
1627	Henry,	9, 11
1656	Henry,	11, 33
d 1664	Henry,	17
l 1669	Henry,	32
d 1684	Henry,	17, 18, 32
1689	Henry,	24
d 1699	Henry,	13
d 1713	Henry,	30
l 1741	Henry [Connet],	563
1754	Henry,	19, 20
1755	Henry,	18
a 1775	Henry [Connet],	564
1779	Henry,	20
1797	Henry,	380
1815	Henry,	455
1819	Henry,	336
1822	Henry [Connet],	567
1838	Henry,	535
1841	Henry,	458
a 1841	Henry,	380
l 1850	Henry,	18
l 1886	Henry [Connett],	571
	Henry,[6]	240
	Henry,[7]	316
	Henry,[8]	325
	Henry,[8]	410
	Henry,[9]	427
	Henry,	550
	Henry,	552
	Henry,	562
	Henry [Connet],	565
1838	Henry A.,	546
1846	Henry Adams,	482
1828	Henry Albert,	420
	Henry C.,[8]	373
1837	Henry Cheney,	375
1840	Henry Clay,	359
1825	Henry D.,	352
	Henry D.,[9]	484
1841	Henry E.,	500
	Henry E. [Connit],	571
1856	Henry F.,	430
1829	Henry Francis,	334

1834	Henry Franklin,	534		1831	Horatio N. Bearce,	539
1836	Henry H.,	376		1793	Hosea,	369
1840	Henry Harrison,	415		1868	Howard,	506
1875	Henry Harrison,	414			Howard Enoch,[8]	382
1854	Henry Hubbel,	457		1840	Howard Turner,	495
1866	Henry John,	464	l	1379	Hugh,	46
1841	Henry L.,	337		1881	Hugh I. [Connet],	565
1880	Henry Lowell,	499			Huldah,[7]	294
1852	Henry Lyman,	511			Huldah,[7]	295
1835	Henry S.,	512			Huldah,[8]	339
1861	Henry T.,	460			Huldah,[8]	386
1845	Henry Thaddeus,	317		1809	Huldah P.,	281
1825	Henry Washington,	410				
1729	Hephzibah,	178				
1760	Hephzibah,	221		1804	Ichabod Perry,	544
1767	Hephzibah,	222		1871	Ida,	490
1791	Hephzibah,	273			Ida Ann,[10]	493
1808	Hephzibah,	329		1854	Ida Frances,	425
1743	Herbert,	93		1862	Ida M.,	504
1774	Herbert,	269	m	1869	Ida M..	554
1850	Herbert Butler,	369		1859	Ida May,	429
1859	Herbert C.,	431		1859	Ida May,	433
1877	Herbert E.,	525		1863	Ida May,	423
1848	Herbert Eugene,	520		1878	Ida May,	520
	Herbert I.,[9]	497		1881	Ida May,	496
1823	Herbert Thorndike,	460		1868	Ida Rosabelle,	481
1878	Herbert W.,	492	a	1859	Imogene,	508
	Herman,[8]	325		1854	Ione E.,	428
1840	Hermon,	525	a	1792	Ira,	335
1866	Herter F.,	493			Ira,[8]	332
1773	Hervey,	271			Ira [Connet],	564
1796	Hervey,	370	l	1886	Ira E.,	562
1857	Heywood,	526		1827	Ira M.,	431
1795	Hezekiah,	333		1796	Irene,	250
1811	Hezekiah,	281		1808	Irene,	356
1827	Hezekiah,	333		1825	Irene,	517
1827	Hezekiah,	465		1835	Irene,	358
1799	Hiram,	358			Irene,[8]	328
	Hiram,[8]	417		1824	Irene Bennett,	317
1845	Hiram Augustus,	496	a	1760	Isaac,[7]	262
1871	Hiram Edward,	460		1779	Isaac,	437
1839	Hiram Ellsworth,	413	a	1781	Isaac,	342
1832	Hiram Malachi,	315		1789	Isaac,	266
1830	Hiram P.,	381		1792	Isaac,	296
1829	Hiram Reed,	359		1793	Isaac,	444
1854	Hiram Solomon,	461	a	1796	Isaac,	294
1871	Hiram Wilson,	496		1805	Isaac [Connet],	567
1857	Homer Whitney,	525		1807	Isaac,	498
1793	Hooper,	333		1817	Isaac,	506
1880	Horace,	527		1826	Isaac,	333
1883	Horace Artemus,	526		1867	Isaac,	508
1812	Horace Hamilton,	471			Isaac,[9]	342
1827	Horace J.,	307			Isaac [Connet],	571
1850	Horace Mann,	472		1844	Isaac Adelbert,	501
1826	Horace Richardson,	372			Isaac B.,[8]	381
1882	Horace Thomas,	495		1807	Isaac Kilbourn,	347
1871	Horace Thurber,	409		1826	Isaac N. [Connett],	567
1785	Horatio,	309			Isaac S. [Connett],	569
1870	Horatio,	406			Isabel,[9]	484
	Horatio,[8]	325		1859	Isabel Eliza,	474
1826	Horatio Gates,	332	a	1836	Isabella,	381
1820	Horatio Nelson,	305		1819	Isabella Eliza,	457

1849	Isadore,	411	1823	James Henry,	457
1845	Isaiah,	417	1797	James Jewett,	305
1814	Isaiah Sewell,	502		James M.,	560
1707	Israel,	160, 192	1829	James McKeen;	476
t 1738	Israel,	240, 576	1829	James P.,	282
1767	Israel,	284	1835	James Q.,	512
1768	Israel,	240	1838	James S.,	516
t 1772	Israel,	231	1844	James Scott,	427
1772	Israel,	541	1829	James Simeon,	443
1775	Israel,	241		James W.,	553
	Israel,	541	1584	Jane,	13, 56
	Israel,	557	1611	Jane,	14, 57
1789	Israel Elliot,	376	1643	Jane,	15
1837	Israel F.,	498	*a* 1674	Jane,	91
1838	Israel Henry,	503	*l* 1675	Jane,	32
1795	Ivory,	274	1675	Jane,	165
			1760	Jane,	235
			1809	Jane,	334
	J. Bradbury,[10]	437	1813	Jane,	388
l 1784	J. F.,	562	1813	Jane [Connet],	566
d 1690	Jacob,	29	1819	Jane,	288
1758	Jacob,	240	1820	Jane,	306
1768	Jacob,	205	1824	Jane,	548
1783	Jacob,	438		Jane,[7]	296
t 1788	Jacob,	334	1851	Jane E.,	404
1797	Jacob,	341	1816	Jane M.,	549
1811	Jacob,	437	1842	Jane Walker,	379
l 1886	Jacob,	562		Jason,[8]	325
1845	Jacob Coggin,	383	1752	Jedediah,	200
l 1543	James,	36	1809	Jefferson,	350
l 1562	James,	42	1737	Jehoaddan,	185
1604	James,	16	1701	Jemima,	181
1630	James,	16	1732	Jemima,	189
1666	James,	11, 33	1755	Jemima,	180
1730	James [Connet],	566	1760	Jemima,	224
1755	James,	259	1771	Jemima [Connet],	504
1760	James,	20	1778	Jemima,	225
1762	James,	20		Jemima,[8]	325
1764	James [Connet],	566	1876	Jennie Brown,	519
1780	James,	541	1868	Jennie Mabel,	513
1784	James,	312	*d* 1708	Jeremiah,	26
1786	James,	307	1720	Jeremiah,	200
1788	James,	346	1749	Jeremiah,	202
1793	James,	336	1758	Jeremiah,	254
1797	James,	566	*a* 1778	Jeremiah,	326
	James,[7]	288	*a* 1780	Jeremiah,	325
	James,[8]	374	1789	Jeremiah,	330
	James,[9]	435	1796	Jeremiah,	324
1827	James A.,	460	*d* 1797	Jeremiah,	30
1846	James A.,	429	*d* 1798	Jeremiah,	30
a 1814	James Allen,	321	*a* 1810	Jeremiah,	422
1843	James Amory,	501		Jeremiah,[8]	331
1809	James Augustus,	405		Jeremiah,[10]	493
1833	James Austin,	292		Jerome F.,	545
1870	James Bronson,	506	1702	Jerusha,	172
1831	James Edwin,	404	1743	Jerusha,	185
1869	James Elam,	414	1743	Jerusha [Conet],	570
1814	James Franklin,	449	1764	Jerusha,	255
1829	James H.,	498		Jerusha,[7]	270
1853	James H.,	375	*a* 1797	Jephthah,	339
	James Hardee,	551	*a* 1864	Jesse,	490
1842	James Harvey,	524	1818	Jesse Davis,	346

n 1771	John,		19	1805	John Avery,	256
1771	John,		274	1824	John B.,	376
1771	John,	146, 226,	355		John B.,[8]	384
1772	John,		352		John B.,[9]	436
1773	John,		297	1878	John Bancroft,	474
1773	John,		304	1819	John Batchelder,	291
1776	John,		290	1803	John Calvin,	243
l 1777	John,		30	1852	John Calvin,	398
1777	John,		266	1833	John E.,	497
1779	John,		564	1838	John E.,	456
1780	John,		20	1777	John Edward,	96
l 1785	John,		30	1832	John F.,	451
1786	John,		266	1835	John F.,	400
1787	John,		329	1828	John Francis,	534
1790	John,		440	1877	John Franklin,	546
1790	John,		553	1768	John Gardiner,	347
t 1792	John,		450	1821	John Gideon,	504
1793	John,		405	1849	John Goldsmith,	446
1793	John,		458	1837	John Greenleaf,	522
1795	John,		339	1823	John H.,	307
t 1800	John,		384	1825	John H.,	555
1801	John,		259	1836	John H.,	444
1807	John,		456		John H.,	560
1808	John,		500	l 1883	John H.,	571
1810	John,		531	l 1886	John H.,	562
1811	John,		570	1818	John Harvey,	418
1814	John,		352	1836	John Henry,	464
1814	John,		504	1855	John Herbert,	434
1816	John,		547	1842	John Heywood,	526
1818	John,		459	1842	John Hobart.	501
1818	John,		516	1822	John Howard,	389
1818	John,		566	1848	John Lane [Connet],	566
1821	John,		501	1883	John Lewis,	521
1823	John,		434	1838	John M.,	521
; 1832	John,		387	1815	John Martin,	424
1836	John,		376	1856	John Martin,	425
1837	John,		330	1844	John Merriam,	449
1839	John,		398	1817	John Milton,	313
1853	John,		392	1856	John Milton,	551
1880	John,		577	1846	John Nason,	506
	John,[7]		287	1823	John P.,	288
	John,[7]		289	1849	John Parker,	459
	John,[8]		325	1815	John Perley,	290
	John,[8]		361	1829	John R.,	308
	John,[8]		406	1823	John Richardson,	372
	John,[9]		342	1799	John Sherlock,	244
	John,		553	1876	John Sherman,	515
	John,		549	1841	John Shubael,	408
1850	John,		18	1870	John T.,	493
1886	John,		17	1803	John W.,	311
1886	John,		562	a 1840	John W.,	560
1885	John,		562	1858	John Walter,	505
	John A.,[7]		295	1805	John Washington,	400
	John A.,		560	1801	John Wesley,	548
1829	John A.,		412	1840	John Wesley,	524
1853	John A.,		509	1836	John Wilbur,	377
1800	John Adams,		299	1824	John William,	97, 98
	John Adams,[7]		295	1854	John Winslow,	489
1809	John Adams,		388	1874	John Wolmer,	496
1863	John Adams,		482	1775	Jonas,	282
1846	John Addison,		487	1791	Jonas,	267
1824	John Anson,		332	1808	Jonas Leonard,	282

l 1657	Jonathan,		33
d 1675	Jonathan,		32
l 1675	Jonathan,		32
1692	Jonathan,	134, 153,	181
m 1702	Jonathan,		10
d 1722	Jonathan,	30,	573
1733	Jonathan,		240
1734	Jonathan,		235
1737	Jonathan,	118, 176,	226
1746	Jonathan,		270
l 1750	Jonathan [Connet],		568
1756	Jonathan,		214
1760	Jonathan,	283,	577
1761	Jonathan,		249
1767	Jonathan,		304
1779	Jonathan,		271
1793	Jonathan,		388
1796	Jonathan,		250
	Jonathan,[7]		284
1823	Jonathan Josiah,		482
1810	Jonathan Newell,		508
	Jonathan T. [Connet]		569
1578	Jone,		10
l 1669	Jone,		32
l 1657	Joseph,		27
d 1663	Joseph,		29
1663	Joseph,		11
d 1680	Joseph,		573
1701	Joseph,	183,	187
1709	Joseph,		202
m 1713	Joseph,		23
d 1732	Joseph,		30
a 1738	Joseph,		230
d 1740	Joseph,		33
d 1753	Joseph,		19
1756	Joseph,		20
1756	Joseph,		20
m 1756	Joseph,		21
1766	Joseph,		228
1767	Joseph,		287
a 1780	Joseph,		288
1781	Joseph,		446
1782	Joseph,		290
1783	Joseph,		443
1791	Joseph,		241
1792	Joseph,		243
1792	Joseph,		313
1801	Joseph [Connet],		566
1816	Joseph,		459
1821	Joseph,		336
	Joseph,[7]		288
	Joseph,[7]		289
	Joseph,[10]		493
1862	Joseph A.,		508
	Joseph A.,[10]		502
1830	Joseph Augustus,		508
a 1841	Joseph B.,		560
1852	Joseph Benjamin,		398
1802	Joseph Chapman,		290
1860	Joseph E.,		369
	Joseph Ernest,[8]		415
1856	Joseph F.,		459

1811	Joseph Fletcher,		405
1831	Joseph Fuller,		387
1859	Joseph H.,		430
1810	Joseph Hayward,		504
1837	Joseph Jacobs,		414
1882	Joseph Knapp,		477
1807	Joseph Lysander,		447
1823	Joseph Perkins,		384
1837	Joseph R.,		424
1817	Joseph Stearns,		456
1841	Joseph Tyler,		523
1871	Josephine Bonaparte,		517
1886	Josephine Evelina,		496
a 1630	Joshua,		136
1657	Joshua,	124,	162
1678	Joshua,		163
1707	Joshua,	153,	185
1724	Joshua,	134,	194
1750	Joshua,		231
1764	Joshua,		273
1779	Joshua,		289
1796	Joshua,		360
1798	Joshua,		380
	Joshua,[7]		288
1801	Joshua L.,		449
1843	Joshua Randall,		480
1680	Josiah,	69, 70,	166
1681	Josiah,	144,	169
1711	Josiah,		192
1718	Josiah,		172
1724	Josiah,		198
a 1724	Josiah,		261
1732	Josiah,		222
1746	Josiah,		241
1750	Josiah,		340
1754	Josiah,		199
1758	Josiah,	243,	576
1763	Josiah,		271
a 1765	Josiah,		342
1768	Josiah,		295
1770	Josiah,		277
1770	Josiah,		304
1776	Josiah,		228
a 1789	Josiah,		437
1793	Josiah,		271
1796	Josiah,		358
1799	Josiah,		243
1804	Josiah,		371
1821	Josiah,		352
1832	Josiah,		371
1840	Josiah,		460
	Josiah,[8]		342
	Josiah,		547
1806	Josiah Franklin,		442
1845	Josiah Gardner,		359
	Josie,[8]		415
1872	Josie M.,		523
1816	Jotham Shepard,		401
1823	Julia,		543
1824	Julia,		312
a 1828	Julia,		444
	Julia,[7]		295

	Julia,[8]	288		Leonard Hubbard,	405
1839	Julia A. M.,	456	1862	Leona D.,	550
1882	Julia Abigail,	489	1880	Leonie,	539
1829	Julia Ann [Connet],	565	1767	Levi,	349
1868	Julia Ann,	527	1768	Levi,	541
	Julia Ann,[8]	402	1775	Levi,	436
1845	Julia Cornelia,	537	1779	Levi,	350
1849	Julia E.,	501	*a* 1788	Levi,	542
	Julia E.,[9]	436	1791	Levi,	244
1866	Julia F.,	507	1801	Levi,	350
1845	Julia Maria,	380	1802	Levi,	498
1847	Julia Sophia,	445	1810	Levi,	454
1807	Juliette,	328		Levi,[7]	261
1843	Juliette,	314		Levi,[8]	342
1857	Julius,	307	1831	Levi J.,	436
1836	Julius Augustus,	369	1857	Levi Leonard,	455
1869	Julius Deliverance,	413	1827	Levi W.,	498
1829	Julius Edmund,	411	1862	Levin [Connet],	568
1809	Justus,	337	1798	Lewis,	304
	Justus,[7]	337	1802	Lewis,	331
			1818	Lewis,	547
			1825	Lewis,	490
1851	Kate Shepard,	401	1829	Lewis,	374
1673	Katherine,	17	1830	Lewis,	333
	Katie,[9]	435		Lewis,[8]	325
1756	Keturah,	200		Lewis,[8]	331
1691	Kezia,	163		Lewis,[8]	386
1721	Kezia,	194	1866	Lewis Gardner,	428
1745	Kezia,	197	1862	Lewis Gray,	539
1769	Kezia,	263	1877	Lewis K.,	527
1788	Kezia,	248	1865	Lewis P.,	369
1789	Kezia,	345	1851	Lewis S.,	461
			l 1886	Lewis W.,	562
			1851	Lewis W. [Connett],	569
1845	Laminda Jane,	382	1793	Liba,	334
	Latham,[7]	294	1761	Lida E.,	428
1820	Laura,	547	1850	Lilian,	451
1823	Laura,	312		Lilian,[11]	522
	Laura,[8]	332	1867	Lilian Augusta,	495
	Laura Alice,	551		Lillian,[9]	427
1818	Laura Ann,	387	1873	Lillian Adeline,	512
1821	Laura Ann,	354	1854	Lillian Sherwood,	420
1853	Laura Ann,	469	1866	Lilly,	488
1844	Laura Jane,	355		Lizzie, see also Elizabeth.	
1858	Laura Louise,	449			
1833	Laura Lovett,	354	1851	Lizzie E.,	430
l 1865	Laura May,	482	1853	Lizzie H.,	504
1883	Laura Toulmin,	551		Lizzie L. [Connitt],	571
	Laurilla E.,[8]	373	1877	Lizzie Merrill,	523
1803	Lavina,	350	1860	Lizzie Ruth,	384
1809	Lawson,	243	1865	Lizzie S.,	429
1791	Leafia,	541		Lockey [Connet],	564
1820	Leander Tanner,	537	1762	Lodema,	222
1784	Learned,	278	1802	Lodema,	276
1757	Lemuel,	529	1738	Lois,	209
1781	Leonard,	544	1756	Lois,	250
1783	Leonard,	329	1774	Lois,	263
l 1800	Leonard,	387	1799	Lois,	248
1818	Leonard,	428	1810	Lois,	291
1826	Leonard,	481	1819	Lois,	291
1856	Leonard,	429		Lois,[6]	234
1808	Leonard Hathaway,	544		Lois,[7]	260

1854	Lois D.,	430		Lucia,[8]	330
1803	Lois P.,	346, 554	1840	Lucien William,	501
1812	Lorenzo,	398	1814	Lucina Amelia,	313
1819	Lorenzo,	543	1800	Lucinda,	350
	Lorenzo,	560	1804	Lucinda,	454
1834	Lorenzo Dow,	499	1806	Lucinda,	271
1859	Lorenzo Dow,	522	1806	Lucinda,	368
	Loring S. [Connett],	569		Lucinda,[7]	254
a 1624	Lot,	111, 117, 120 / 122, 128, 142	1823	Lucitty K.,	431
			1799	Lucius,	313
1658	Lot,	140, 151, 102	1818	Lucius,	448
1679	Lot,	134, 148, 173	1847	Lucius,	425
1689	Lot,	144, 173	1833	Lucius Malachi A.,	414
1718	Lot,	203	1866	Lucius W.,	413
1721	Lot,	182	1846	Lucretia,	540
1728	Lot,	184	1806	Lucretia Urania,	532
1735	Lot,	146, 214, 576	1718	Lucy,	215
1746	Lot,	231	1740	Lucy,	209
1754	Lot,	267	1753	Lucy,	254
1758	Lot,	199	1754	Lucy,	180
1764	Lot,	284	1757	Lucy,	213
1785	Lot,	335	1757	Lucy,	271
1792	Lot,	353	1758	Lucy,	222
1798	Lot,	378	1762	Lucy,	206
1820	Lot,	430	1775	Lucy,	295
1880	Lot,	434	1777	Lucy,	271
1822	Lot C.,	378	1786	Lucy,	259
1788	Lothrop,	546	1786	Lucy,	280
1814	Lothrop,	546	1787	Lucy,	243
1843	Lothrop,	546	1789	Lucy,	296
	Lottie,[9]	427	a 1790	Lucy,	319
l 1872	Louis,	562	1806	Lucy,	305
1862	Louis Abbott,	475	1811	Lucy,	329
a 1786	Louisa,	338	1815	Lucy,	282
1805	Louisa,	274	1837	Lucy,	535
1811	Louisa,	438	1874	Lucy,	520
1815	Louisa,	312		Lucy,[7]	254
1818	Louisa,	281		Lucy,[8]	349
1828	Louisa,	336		Lucy,[8]	374
1834	Louisa,	317		Lucy,[8]	375
1845	Louisa,	423		Lucy,[8]	406
1846	Louisa,	377		Lucy,[9]	348
1847	Louisa,	425		Lucy,	555
	Louisa,[7]	260	1816	Lucy Abigail,	346
	Louisa,[7]	265	1820	Lucy Ann,	443
	Louisa,[7]	287	1831	Lucy Ann,	360
	Louisa,[11]	522	1845	Lucy Ann,	505
	Louisa [Connet],	505	1845	Lucy Ann,	450
1792	Louisa Anna,	281	1865	Lucy E.,	545
1881	Louisa Foster,	476		Lucy Edson,[8]	331
1812	Louisa J.,	346	1835	Lucy Elizabeth,	383
1830	Louisa L.,	336	1860	Lucy Emma,	428
	Louisa Matilda,[8]	402	1878	Lucy Flora,	465
1820	Lovander Wright,	447	1820	Lucy Foskett,	371
1831	Lovantia Ermina L.,	372	1829	Lucy Hale,	447
1791	Lovia,	266	1821	Lucy Jane,	386
1821	Lovisa,	547	1864	Lucy Larrabee,	482
	Loyal T.,	550	1855	Lucy M. A.,	481
	Luana A.,[8]	358	1812	Lucy Maria,	367
1844	Lucena,	506	1824	Lucy Maria,	335
	Lucena Eleanor,[8]	381	1837	Lucy Maria,	308
1803	Lucia,	256	1879	Lucy Martin,	481

d	1791	Mary,	30	1812	Mary Ann,	346
	1794	Mary,	270	1813	Mary Ann,	332
	1796	Mary,	233	1816	Mary Ann,	282
	1797	Mary,	243	1817	Mary Ann,	291
	1799	Mary,	361	1817	Mary Ann,	445
	1803	Mary [Connet],	566	1823	Mary Ann,	308
	1804	Mary,	347	1837	Mary Ann,	420
	1804	Mary,	352	1837	Mary Ann,	447
a	1805	Mary,	248		Mary Ann,[9]	348
	1805	Mary,	548		Mary Ann,[10]	502
	1808	Mary,	443	1850	Mary Ann Jeanette,	411
	1815	Mary,	302	1818	Mary C.,	452
	1816	Mary,	290	1825	Mary C.,	534
	1817	Mary,	439	1840	Mary C.,	377
	1818	Mary,	443	1846	Mary C.,	392
	1820	Mary,	346	1866	Mary C.,	425
a	1821	Mary,[8]	357		Mary C.,[9]	475
	1821	Mary,	352	1873	Mary Chilton,	482
	1822	Mary,	446	1835	Mary E.,	456
	1824	Mary,	352	1837	Mary E.,	358
	1825	Mary,	447	1846	Mary E.,	378
a	1828	Mary,	387	1848	Mary E.,	459
	1834	Mary,	387	1850	Mary E.,	428
	1836	Mary,	403	1851	Mary E.,	473
	1847	Mary,	428	1851	Mary E.,	501
a	1852	Mary,[10]	491	1863	Mary E.,	414
	1859	Mary,	399	1881	Mary E.,	527
		Mary,[7]	284	1849	Mary Edna,	470
		Mary,[7]	288	a 1881	Mary Eliza,	526
		Mary,[7]	295	1811	Mary Elizabeth,	306
		Mary,[7]	316	1830	Mary Elizabeth,	498
		Mary,[7]	343	1844	Mary Elizabeth,	537
		Mary,[8]	333	1863	Mary Elizabeth,	415
		Mary,[8]	335		Mary Elizabeth,[8]	381
		Mary,[8]	342		Mary E. [Connet],	565
		Mary,[8]	349	1851	Mary Ellen,	289
		Mary,[8]	386	1877	Mary Estell Stimson,	519
		Mary,[9]	452		Mary Eva,	563
		Mary,[10]	497		Mary F.,	555
d	1883	Mary,	14		Mary Frederica,[8]	402
l	1886	Mary,	562	1865	Mary Grace,	473
		Mary,	541	1825	Mary H.,	433
		Mary,	542	1833	Mary H.,	360
		Mary,	546		Mary H.,	554
		Mary,	547	1862	Mary Ida,	550
		Mary,	554	a 1811	Mary J. [Connett],	569
		Mary,	555		Mary J.,	554
		Mary,	564	1822	Mary Jane,	537
	1828	Mary A.,	360	1824	Mary Jane,	544
	1833	Mary A.,	337	1826	Mary Jane,	311
		Mary A.,[10]	493	1827	Mary Jane,	313
		Mary A.,	555	1840	Mary Jane,	400
	1863	Mary Adella,	523	1841	Mary Jane,	500
	1863	Mary Alice,	419	1844	Mary Jane,	545
	1866	Mary Alice,	506	1846	Mary Jane,	469
	1866	Mary Alice,	514	1851	Mary Jane,	492
	1802	Mary Amanda,	347	1852	Mary Jane,	482
	1828	Mary Amelia,	354		Mary Jane,[8]	383
	1848	Mary Amelia,	506	1809	Mary Joanna,	400
	1809	Mary Angelina,	421	1839	Mary L.,	328
	1878	Mary Angelina,	406		Mary L.,[9]	479
	1810	Mary Ann,	345	1830	Mary Louise,	445

1870	Mary Louise,	496		Minerva,[8]	331
1874	Mary Lulu,	479	1839	Minerva [Connet],	567
	Mary Lydia,[9]	437	1863	Minette [Connet],	568
1847	Mary Malinda,	485	1862	Minnie Barbara,	512
1835	Mary N.,	449	1867	Minnie D.,	414
	Mary R.,[8]	384		Minnie Ida,	545
1809	Mary Sophronia,	312		Minnie L.,[9]	436
	Mary T.,[10]	437	1749	Miriam,	198
1826	Mary Thankful,	387	1792	Miriam,	225
1846	Mary Thankful,	499	a 1732	Molly,	212
1874	Mary Thomas,	523	1743	Molly,	209
1850	Mary W.,	509	1775	Molly,	271
1840	Mary White,	421	a 1749	Moses,	234
1807	Matilda,	276	a 1752	Moses [Connet],	566
1840	Matilda Ames,	355	a 1774	Moses,	231
1586	Matthew,	50	1801	Moses Thurston,	243
1659	Matthew,	11	1572	Mychael,	34
l 1706	Matthew,	33	1800	Myra,	250
1807	Matthew Watson M.,	315		Myra,[8]	405
1860	Mattie J.,	514	1831	Myra Abigail,	443
	Matty,[6]	234		Myra E.,[10]	514
1864	Maud Baker,	411	1865	Myrie H. [Connet],	568
1863	Maud Capitola,	524	1834	Myron,	421
1874	Maud Eunice,	480	1868	Myrtie P.,	464
1877	Maud L.,	460	1856	Myrtle A.,	428
1866	Maud Webster,	478			
1884	Maud Whitney,	480			
	Mealion J. [Connett],	571	1760	Nabby,	270
1863	Medora E.,	507	1810	Nahum,	448
1715	Mehitable,	161	1833	Nahum,	448
1758	Mehitable,	198	1789	Nancy,	243
1760	Mehitable,	249	1793	Nancy,	339
a 1778	Mehitable,	251	1793	Nancy,	345
1793	Mehitable,	533	1799	Nancy,	349
1808	Mehitable,	531	a 1805	Nancy,	319
	Mehitable,[7]	284	m 1823	Nancy [Connett],	570
1875	Melinda,	460	1824	Nancy,	444
1841	Melinda L.,	358	1828	Nancy,	439
1814	Melinda T.,	328	1832	Nancy,	444
1816	Melissa [Connet],	566	1833	Nancy,	344
1831	Melissa,	417	1833	Nancy,	417
1830	Melissa D.,	424		Nancy,[7]	295
l 1886	Melnot,	562		Nancy,[7]	284
1632	Melonge,	17		Nancy,[7]	357
d 1672	Melonge,	16		Nancy,[9]	451
1822	Mensil M.,	373		Nancy,	544
1792	Mercia,	270	1851	Nancy Abigail,	508
1726	Mercy,	182		Nancy B.,[9]	422
1771	Mercy,	224	1835	Nancy Barber,	498
1771	Mercy,	225	1826	Nancy M.,	376
1790	Mercy,	280	1839	Nancy Merriam,	369
1823	Mercy,[8]	357	1796	Nancy Merrill,	363
1850	Mercy W.,	499	1840	Nancy Silvinia,	506
1873	Merton,	521	1827	Nancy W.,	443
1852	Merton C.,	492	1706	Nathan,	169
1872	Millia,	493	1731	Nathan,	250
1754	Millicent,	224	1751	Nathan,	209
1781	Millicent,	280	1766	Nathan,	350
1782	Millicent,	266	1777	Nathan,	263
	Miltimore,[8]	405	1777	Nathan,	438
1841	Milton [Connet],	567	1788	Nathan,	345
1833	Milton Allen,	551	1790	Nathan,	244

	1593	Richard,	15	1833	Roger,	392
_l_	1616	Richard,	29	_a_ 1857	Roger,	475
	1616	Richard,	572	1884	Roger,	434
	1622	Richard,	13, 14, 53, 71	1883	Roger B.,	527
_i_	1622	Richard,	14, 87	1860	Roger Gilbert,	382
_i_	1629	Richard,	68, 125	1873	Roger Lewis,	474
_l_	1643	Richard,	9	1875	Roger Ostrom,	521
	1645	Richard,	88	1880	Roger W.,	527
	1663	Richard,	74	1870	Roger William,	493
_l_	1676	Richard,	34	1887	Roger William,	465
_i_	1700	Richard,	92	1869	Roger Winthrop,	427
	1772	Richard,	20	1843	Romanus E.,	456
		Richard,	549	1846	Ronelo A.,	424
_i_	1876	Richard Horace,	527		Rosalind,[7]	288
	1828	Richard Odell,	462	1837	Rosanna Rowell,	424
		Rispah,[6]	205	1842	Rose Luella,	424
_l_	1277	Robert,	2, 39	_l_ 1887	Rossie,	562
_l_	1281	Robert,	40	1835	Rovilla Philura,	414
_l_	1525	Robert,	35	1807	Roxa,	337
_i_	1565	Robert,	28, 572	1807	Roxa,	548
_i_	1570	Robert,	27, 572	1808	Roxa,	248
_i_	1582	Robert,	13, 37, 53, 54, 58	1841	Roxanna,	479
_l_	1603	Robert,	16, 31		Roxanna,[9]	452
_i_	1617	Robert,	27, 572		Roxanna,	544
	1620	Robert,	31		Roxanna,	555
	1624	Robert,	38	1820	Roxanna W.,	351
_i_	1640	Robert,	14, 88	1875	Roy [Connet],	568
_l_	1643	Robert,	29	1836	Royal Benjamin,	491
	1670	Robert,	85, 86, 91	1881	Ruby Florence,	473
_l_	1682	Robert,	29	1825	Ruel K.,	479
	1699	Robert,	206	1757	Rufus,	294
	1707	Robert,	92	1760	Rufus,	276
	1708	Robert,	17	_a_ 1781	Rufus,	264
_l_	1725	Robert,	30	1794	Rufus,	387
_l_	1747	Robert,	30	_a_ 1797	Rufus,[8]	347
	1752	Robert,	18, 25	1805	Rufus,	369
	1754	Robert,	261	1810	Rufus,	282
	1768	Robert,	324	_a_ 1824	Rufus,	427
	1781	Robert,	20	1829	Rufus,	387, 578
_m_	1806	Robert,	13		Rufus,[8]	386
		Robert,[8]	324	1827	Rufus Fielder,	410
	1845	Robert C.,	449	1828	Rufus Leander,	369
	1882	Robert Franklin,	513	1823	Rufus Leonard,	387
	1883	Robert Pratt,	473		Rufus P.,	553
	1810	Robert Taft,	432	1841	Russell B.,	489
	1854	Robert Taft,	432	1702	Ruth,	155
	1852	Robert Warren,	483	1711	Ruth,	160
	1884	Roby Edwin,	461	1720	Ruth,	167, 196
	1829	Rodney Teal,	492	1745	Ruth,	209
_l_	1524	Roger,	35	1749	Ruth,	246
_l_	1585	Roger,	31	1752	Ruth,	191
	1592	Roger,	14, 22, 41, 53 57, 99-129 137, 146, 162	1772	Ruth,	344
				1775	Ruth,	264
				1782	Ruth,	241
_m_	1596	Roger,	24, 29	_a_ 1782	Ruth,	258
	1626	Roger,	131	1787	Ruth,	359
	1669	Roger,	134, 143, 160, 192	_a_ 1793	Ruth,[7]	284
	1695	Roger,	155	1814	Ruth,	291
	1701	Roger,	160, 191	1822	Ruth,	516
	1744	Roger,	245	1849	Ruth,	398
	1748	Roger,	252		Ruth,[10]	497
	1805	Roger,	422	1842	Ruth Amelia,	550

a 1865	Ruth Butler,	491	
1874	Ruth Cheever,	517	
1869	Ruth Julia,	538	
1865	Ruth M.,	511	
1876	Ruth Stevens,	473	
1803	Ruxby,	453	
1846	S. Evelyn,	328	
1807	Sabrina,	375	
1857	Sadie C. [Connett],	567	
1876	Sadie M.,	461	
	Sally, see Sarah.		
1761	Sally,	235	
1765	Sally,	269	
1770	Sally,	541	
1777	Sally,	372	
a 1784	Sally,	338	
1786	Sally,	258	
a 1786	Sally,	439	
1787	Sally,	244	
1798	Sally,	270	
1798	Sally,	350	
1803	Sally,	350	
	Sally,[7]	262	
	Sally,[7]	289	
	Sally,[8]	326	
	Sally,	547	
1805	Sally F.,	346	
a 1812	Sally,	340	
· 1795	Salmon,	256	
1619	Salter,	9, 10, 32, 33	
1627	Samuel,	22, 67, 574	
1654	Samuel,	87	
d 1672	Samuel,	132	
a 1678	Samuel,	91, 574, 575	
l 1692	Samuel,	143, 553	
1717	Samuel,	186	
a 1722	Samuel,	261	
1730	Samuel,	146, 214	
1730	Samuel,	239	
l 1741	Samuel,	563	
1751	Samuel,	269	
1752	Samuel,	338	
1754	Samuel,	198	
1755	Samuel,	303	
1765	Samuel,	308	
1767	Samuel,	20	
1769	Samuel,	239	
1775	Samuel,	240	
1779	Samuel,	249	
1780	Samuel,	278	
1781	Samuel,	281	
1781	Samuel,	372	
a 1782	Samuel,	232	
1784	Samuel,	291	
1784	Samuel,	339	
a 1784	Samuel,	303	
1789	Samuel,	250	
1790	Samuel,	345	
1791	Samuel,	347	
1803	Samuel,	359	

1808	Samuel,	374	
1811	Samuel [Connet],	565	
1815	Samuel,	438	
1816	Samuel,	335	
1818	Samuel,	448	
a 1834	Samuel,	387	
1861	Samuel,	469	
	Samuel,[7]	288	
	Samuel,[8]	303	
	Samuel,[8]	347	
	Samuel,[8]	350	
	Samuel,[9]	478	
	Samuel,[10]	493	
	Samuel A.,	270, 577	
1820	Samuel Davis,	470	
1827	Samuel Dimmick,	388	
1851	Samuel Dimick,	520	
1819	Samuel Dorman,	384	
1878	Samuel E. [Connet],	565	
1827	Samuel Fields,	475	
l 1862	Samuel G.,	560	
1822	Samuel H.,	375	
1825	Samuel Hervey,	371	
1879	Samuel Jones,	418	
1810	Samuel M.,	288	
1805	Samuel Malachi A.,	315	
1856	Samuel Marshall,	315	
1820	Samuel Mills,	389	
1858	Samuel Mills,	483	
1848	Samuel Pierce,	359	
1767	Samuel Potter,	345	
	Samuel R. [Connet],	565	
1797	Samuel Stillman,	389	
1825	Samuel Stillman,	447	
1831	Samuel Stillman,	483, 578	
1878	Samuel Storrs,	406	
1789	Samuel Williams,	317	
1832	Samuel Williams,	418	
1856	Samuel William,	385	
1833	Sanford,	492	
1840	Sanford,	417	
· 1854	Sanford R.,	492	
l 1279	Sarah,	573	
1624	Sarah,	58	
1628	Sarah,	53, 124, 135	
a 1637	Sarah,	24, 67, 69	
l 1657	Sarah,	27	
1661	Sarah,	87	
1662	Sarah,	88	
1667	Sarah,	158	
1669	Sarah,	163	
1671	Sarah,	11	
1677	Sarah,	19	
1693	Sarah,	155	
1695	Sarah,	163	
1708	Sarah,	160	
l 1713	Sarah,	33	
1714	Sarah,	161	
1718	Sarah,	167	
1725	Sarah,	176	
a 1730	Sarah,	211	
1732	Sarah,	174	

1732	Sarah,	182		1825	Sarah Ann,	346
1733	Sarah,	184		1827	Sarah Ann,	334
1733	Sarah,	200		1848	Sarah Ann,	478
1743	Sarah,	198		1819	Sarah Ann Willis,	417
1743	Sarah,	203		1839	Sarah Catherine,	400
1752	Sarah,	205		1846	Sarah Catherine,	420
1752	Sarah,	214		1831	Sarah D.,	498
1753	Sarah,	198		1826	Sarah Davis,	281
1754	Sarah,	529		1813	Sarah Elizabeth,	536
1758	Sarah,	215		1828	Sarah Elizabeth,	402
1758	Sarah [Connet],	566		1860	Sarah Elizabeth,	446
1760	Sarah,	239		1876	Sarah Florence,	474
1761	Sarah,	230		1793	Sarah Foster,	268
1768	Sarah,	19, 20		1851	Sarah Frances,	470
1769	Sarah,	531		1784	Sarah Healy,	271
1770	Sarah,	228		1864	Sarah Howard,	482
1770	Sarah,	296		1883	Sarah Hunter,	524
1772	Sarah,	244		1829	Sarah Isabella,	307
1772	Sarah [Connett],	568		1846	Sarah J.,	499
1774	Sarah,	206		1819	Sarah Jane,	406
1774	Sarah,	264	a	1819	Sarah Jane,	357
1779	Sarah,	241		1834	Sarah Jane,	433
1779	Sarah,	280		1852	Sarah Jane,	425
1780	Sarah,	17		1851	Sarah L. [Connet],	566
1780	Sarah,	248		1852	Sarah Louisa,	428
1780	Sarah,	267		1886	Sarah Louisa,	496
1781	Sarah,	320		1862	Sarah M.,	493
1783	Sarah,	225		1795	Sarah Maria,	532
1783	Sarah,	295		1814	Sarah Maria,	313
1784	Sarah,	564		1800	Sarah McAllister,	288
1787	Sarah,	341		1811	Sarah P.,	276
1789	Sarah,	241		1846	Sarah Payson,	483
1789	Sarah,	349		1827	Sarah Pierce,	449
1793	Sarah,	564		1817	Sarah Snow,	437
1794	Sarah,	250		1838	Sarah Stacy,	316
1794	Sarah [Connet],	566		1854	Sarah Virginia,	537
1795	Sarah [Connet],	564		1820	Sarah W.,	378
1796	Sarah,	458		1730	Sarah White,	555
1804	Sarah,	290			Sarah W. [Connet],	565
1804	Sarah,	438			Saxton,[8]	410
1806	Sarah,	261			Seeth,	136
1812	Sarah,	386		1853	Selwyn Frank,	380
1813	Sarah,	307			Seneca F.,[9]	438
1813	Sarah,	312		1748	Seth,	247
1817	Sarah,	329		1782	Seth,	311
1818	Sarah,	305		1796	Seth,	330
1822	Sarah,	443	a	1779	Seth,	328
1832	Sarah,	407		1844	Seth Bartlett,	506
1833	Sarah,	344		1818	Seth Dill,	311
	Sarah,[6]	231		1864	Seth Edward,	426
	Sarah,[7]	254		1817	Seth P.,	386
	Sarah,[7]	343		1833	Seth Webb,	315
	Sarah,[8]	342		1822	Seth Wilder,	425
	Sarah,[9]	342		1798	Sewall,	349
	Sarah,[9]	437			Sewall,[10]	502
	Sarah,[9]	504		1756	Shebuel,	341
	Sarah,	549		1839	Sherman,	514
	Sarah,	554	l	1886	Sherman,	562
	Sarah [Connet],	564			Sherman,[9]	340
1819	Sarah A.,	307		1810	Sherman G.,	340
1830	Sarah A.,	497			Shoah,[6]	233
1807	Sarah Almira,	304		1711	Shubael,	195

1739	Shubael,	197
1783	Shubael,	247
	Shubael,	547
1831	Sidney,	427
1740	Silas,	263
1747	Silas,	338
a 1775	Silas,	554
1776	Silas,	345
1798	Silas,	449
1801	Silas,	497
1803	Silas,	448
1825	Silas,	448
1830	Silas,	444
1837	Silas [Connet],	567
1839	Silas,	449
1764	Silence,	239
1781	Silence,	252
1747	Silvanus,	256
1755	Silvia,	202
a 1780	Silvia,	258
	Silvia,[7]	257
1762	Simeon,	340
1779	Simeon,	341
1780	Simeon,	308
a 1784	Simeon,	344
1811	Simeon,	308
a 1827	Simeon,	452
	Simeon,[8]	345
	Simeon,[9]	501
1820	Simeon Dexter,	514
1837	Simon Tuttle,	448
1849	Simona Frances,	398
1733	Solomon,	195
1737	Solomon,	189
1756	Solomon,	204
1801	Solomon,	289
	Solomon,[7]	294
1828	Solomon Jackson,	372
	Solon A.,[8]	405
1796	Sophia,	241
1818	Sophia,	304
1822	Sophia,	448
	Sophia,	541
1807	Sophia Ann,	311
1817	Sophia Ann,	502
1843	Sophia Augusta,	445
1805	Sophronia,	392
1850	Sophronia Emily,	506
a 1766	Spencer [Connet],	566
1820	Spencer [Connet],	566
1868	Stanley Ellwood,	496
	Stedman,[8]	331
1881	Stella,	488
1762	Stephen,	224
1796	Stephen,	281
1805	Stephen E. [Connet],	565
1821	Stephen Kendrick,	401
1851	Stephen R.,	508
1879	Stephen Shepard,	402
1801	Sullivan,	337
1799	Sumner,	256
.	Sumner,[8]	415

1843	Sumner Tyler,	523
a 1598	Susan,	27
a 1600	Susan,	27
1608	Susan,	16, 31
1800	Susan,	328
a 1809	Susan,	260
1812	Susan,	503
1816	Susan,	344
1818	Susan,	548
1821	Susan,	448
1822	Susan,	376
1826	Susan,	336
1830	Susan,	386
1844	Susan,	420
1857	Susan,	492
	Susan,[8]	361
	Susan,[9]	485
1831	Susan Asenath,	413
1832	Susan Chaffin,	448
a 1809	Susan E. [Connett],	509
1827	Susan E.,	435
a 1827	Susan E.,	447
1844	Susan Elizabeth,	375
1842	Susan H.,	392
1868	Susan M.,	405
1870	Susan M.,	461
1632	Susanna,	16
1666	Susanna,	88
1711	Susanna,	172
a 1713	Susanna,	92
d 1727	Susanna,	30
1750	Susanna,	203
1760	Susanna,	206
1760	Susanna,	213
1764	Susanna,	20
1777	Susanna,	252
1783	Susanna,	282
1787	Susanna,	259
1789	Susanna,	533
1803	Susanna,	243
1805	Susanna,	308
1800	Susanna C.,	345
1845	Susanna C.,	449
1781	Susanna S.,	243
	Susia,[9]	484
1857	Susie Hattie,	405
1840	Susie Jane,	455
1720	Sylvanus,	203
1751	Sylvanus,	248
1773	Sylvanus,	200
1782	Sylvanus,	312
1787	Sylvanus,	332
1826	Sylvanus,	507
	Sylvanus,[8]	205
1836	Sylvanus Augustus,	545
1850	Sylvanus Gideon,	524
1850	Sylvanus Melville,	332
1810	Sylvester,	243
1826	Sylvester Freeman,	534
1798	Sylvia,	277
1829	Sylvia,	371
1839	Sylvia Ann,	428

NAMES OTHER THAN CONANT.

INDEX OF PLACES.

44

LIST OF SUBSCRIBERS.

Baker, Mrs. Juliaette Friend	Hudson, N. H.
Barton, Charles C.	Boston, Mass.
Beverly Public Library,	Beverly, Mass.
Boston Public Library,	Boston, Mass.
Brushfield, T. N.	Budleigh Salterton, Devon, Eng.
Bunton, Henry S.	Hyde Park, Mass.
Church, William C.	New York, N. Y.
Clarke, Robert & Co.,	Cincinnati, O.
Conant, A. & Co.,	Boston, Mass.
Conant, Allen G.	Salem, N. Y.
Conant, Alonzo	Middle Granville, N. Y.
Conant, Alvah	Bath, N. H.
Conant, Benjamin	Boston, Mass.
Conant, Calvin H.	Stoneham, Mass.
Conant, Charles	Ross Corner, Me.
Conant, Charles E.	Boston, Mass.
Conant, Charles F. (4)	Cambridge, Mass.
Conant, Charles H.	Lowell, Mass.
Conant, Charles W.	Gardner, Mass.
Conant, Chester C.	Greenfield, Mass.
Conant, David Philo	Canton, Mass.
Conant, Edmund B.	Lowell, Mass.
Conant, Edward	Conant, Idaho.
Conant, Edward D. (2)	Worcester, Mass.
Conant, Edward Nathaniel (5)	Lyndon, Oakham, Rutland, Eng.
Conant, Edward W.	Oldtown, Me.
Conant, Edwin (2)	Worcester, Mass.
Conant, Ernest Lee	Webster, Mass.
Conant, Eugene F. (2)	Denver, Col.
Conant, Ezra D.	Somerville Mass.
Conant, Ezra	Roxbury, Mass.
Conant, Frank Hersey	Lowell, Mass.
Conant, Frank S.	Oakham, Mass.
Conant, George	Ionia, Mich.
Conant, George Erskine	Lawrence, Ks.
Conant, George Seymour	New York, N. Y.
Conant, George W.	Lowell, Mass.
Conant, Harry Armitage (4)	Monroe, Mich.
Conant, Henry E.	Concord, N. H.
Conant, Henry Harrison	Portland, Me.
Conant, Hermon	New York, N. Y.
Conant, Heywood	Wilmington, Del.

Conant, Hezekiah (10)	Pawtucket, R. I.
Conant, Hiram S.	Richmond, Vt.
Conant, Horace H.	Orford, N. H.
Conant, Ira M.	Boston, Mass.
Conant, James H.	New York, N. Y.
Conant, John	Beaufort, S. C.
Conant, John A. (8)	Brandon, Vt.
Conant, John A.	Willimantic, Conn.
Conant, John R.	Somerville, Mass.
Conant, Josiah	Great Falls, N. H.
Conant, Leander T.	East Liverpool, O.
Conant, Lewis S. (2)	Roxbury, Mass.
Conant, Marshall	LaCrosse, Wis.
Conant, Mary F.	Elizabeth, N. J.
Conant, Merton C.	Diana, Dak.
Conant, Milton A.	Somerset, Ky.
Conant, Nathaniel (2)	Brookline, Mass.
Conant, Nathaniel P.	Charlotte, Me.
Conant, Richard Odell (10)	Cumberland, Me.
Conant, Rodney T.	DeKalb, N. Y.
Conant, Roger (4)	Capac, Mich.
Conant, Miss Sarah	Hyde Park, Mass.
Conant, Sherman	Palatka, Fla.
Conant, Silas	Danvers, Mass.
Conant, Sophia G.	Littleton, Mass.
Conant, Stephen K.	Boston, Mass.
Conant, Sumner Warren	Freeport, Me.
Conant, Thomas	Oshawa, Canada.
Conant, Walter N.	Toledo, O.
Conant, Washington I.	Enfield, N. H.
Conant, Whitney	New York, N. Y.
Conant, William Cooper	New York, N. Y.
Conant, William H.	Plymouth, Me.
Conant, William H.	Portland, Me.
Connet, Alfred	McLeansville, N. C.
Connett, Isaac N.	Prosperity, Pa.
Correll, Mrs. G. E.	Clinton, Iowa.
Dupee, Mrs. Rachael Conant	Westford, Mass.
Edwards, Mrs. J. W.	Gloversville, N. Y.
Estabrook, Elery	Westminster, Mass.
Giddings, Edward L.	Boston, Mass.
Gilbert, Mrs. W. W.	Elizabeth, N. J.
Harding, Mrs. Harriet C.	Medfield, Mass.
Herrick, Nathaniel Jones	Portland, Me.
James, Miss Frances B.	Rockbeare Manor, Exeter, Eng.
Lewis, Alvah (2)	Brooklyn, N. Y.
Lewis, Miss Anna	Brooklyn, N. Y.
Lewis, Mrs. O. J.	Boston, Mass.
Little, Edmund Conant,	East Hardwick, Vt.

Littlefield, George E. - - - - Boston, Mass.
Long, John Conant - - - - - Chicago, Ill.
Maguire, Mrs. Carrie E. - - - - Indianapolis, Ind.
Mansfield, Warren W. - - - - Portland, Me.
Merriam, John C. - - - - Logansport, Ind.
Meriam, R. N. - - - - Worcester, Mass.
Merrick, Mrs. J. L. - '- - Mechanicsville, N. Y.
Morse, L. Foster - - - - Roxbury, Mass.
Moulton, Eben H. - - - - Beverly, Mass.
Munsell's Sons, J. (3) - - - - - Albany, N. Y.
New Bedford Public Library, - - New Bedford, Mass.
New Hampshire State Library, - - - Concord, N. H.
Payson, Franklin Conant - - - Portland, Me.
Payson, George Shipman - - - Portland, Me.
Payson, Mrs. Henry M. - - - - Portland, Me.
Payson, Henry Storer - - - - Portland, Me.
Planque, Mrs. Mary Melinda Conant (4) - San Francisco, Cal.
Polhamus, William E. - - - Minneapolis, Minn.
Richardson, Mrs. Caleb - - - - Nashua, N. H.
Rockwood, W. J. - - - - Brookline, N. H.
Rundell, Mrs. Ruth C. - - - - Buchanan, Mich.
Shattuck, George C. - - - - - Nashua, N. H.
Smith, S. Conant - - - - Provincetown, Mass.
Snow, Mrs. A. H. - - - ' - - Becket, Mass.
Snow, D. William - - - - Portland, Me.
Snow, Lucien B. - - - - Portland, Me.
Storrs, Richard S., D. D., (2) - - - Brooklyn, N. Y.
Sumner, George A. - - - - New York, N. Y.
Thompson, Joseph P. - - - - Portland, Me.
Van Blarcom, Conant - - - Upper Alton, Ill.
Warren, Moses C. - - - - Boston, Mass.
West, Mrs. Albert J. (2) - - - - Capac, Mich.
Whitman, Charles S. - - - - Washington, D. C.
Whitmore, Mrs. Jane M. - - - Georgetown, N. Y.
Williams, Mrs. Alpheus S. - - - Detroit, Mich.

ADDITIONS AND CORRECTIONS.

p. 346, line 6: Lois P. Conant m. in Concord, Mass., 27 Nov., 1828, Joseph Haynes, of Lowell, Mass.

p. 371, last line: Alice (Chaffee), widow of Josiah Conant, m. (2) 26 Dec., 1866, John, son of Roger and Mary (Davis) Jewett. She d. 12 July, 1870, in Adrian, Mich.

p. 373, line 20: One of the sons of (410) Charles Conant was Ira, who served during the Rebellion in the 1st Mass. Regt.

p. 378, line 13: Sarah W., dr. of (426) Oliver Conant, m. 18 Aug., 1844, William Curtis Bridge, and had: i. William H., b. 22 Feb., 1845, d. 1848; ii. Franklin, b. 26 Feb., 1847, m. Ellen, dr. of Jason McNear; he served in Union army during the Rebellion; iii. Edward Lowe, b. 17 Dec., 1849, d. 1875; iv. Charlotte A., b. 6 Dec., 1851, m. Joseph W. Foster; v. Oliver C., b. 4 Dec., 1853, m. Hannah, dr. of Ephraim Gammon; vi. Andrew William, b. 26 Oct., 1856, m. Mary E., dr. of William Adams; vii. Charles A., b. 17 Oct., 1862. (See Bridge Genealogy.)

p. 457: (626) James H. Conant has ch. by Matilda A. (Lyons): i. Alvah Lyons, b. 11 Aug., 1884; ii. James Wattenburg, b. 14 July, 1886.

p. 496, line 1: Hattie Maud Conant m. 6 Nov., 1887, Eddie P. Davis, of Minot, Me.

p. 502: Mary, widow of (754) Isaiah S. Conant, d. 24 July, 1886, aged 73.

p. 556: To list of college graduates add John Lane Connet, Rutger's College.

p. 560, after line 1, insert: Ira Conant, of Boston, served in 1st Mass. Regt.; p. 373.

p. 586, second column, line 28, for 464 read 474.